WRITER'S CHOICE

GRAMMAR AND COMPOSITION

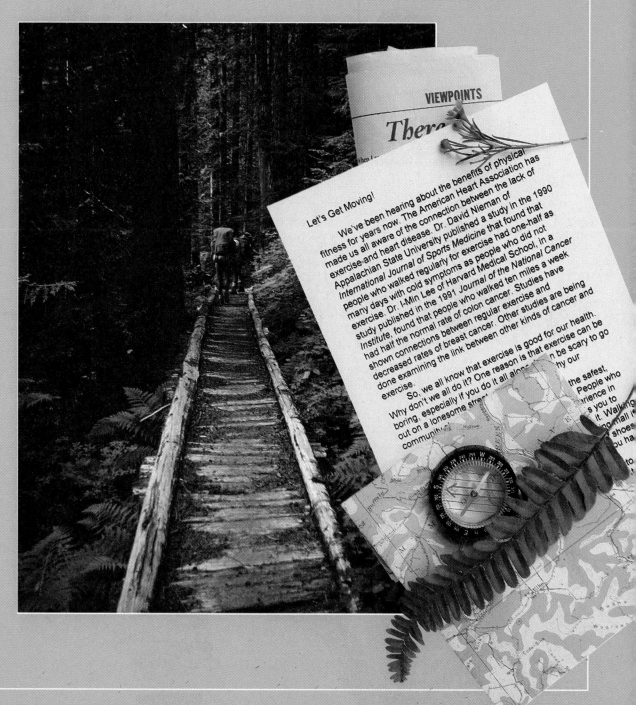

VIEWPOINTS

There

Let's Get Moving!

We've been hearing about the benefits of physical fitness for years now. The American Heart Association has made us all aware of the connection between the lack of exercise and heart disease. Dr. David Nieman of Appalachian State University published a study in the 1990 *International Journal of Sports Medicine* that found that people who walked regularly for exercise had one-half as many days with cold symptoms as people who did not exercise. Dr. I-Min Lee of Harvard Medical School, in a study published in the 1991 *Journal of the National Cancer Institute*, found that people who walked ten miles a week had half the normal rate of colon cancer. Studies have shown connections between regular exercise and decreased rates of breast cancer. Other studies are being done examining the link between other kinds of cancer and exercise.

So, we all know that exercise is good for our health. Why don't we all do it? One reason is that exercise can be boring, especially if you do it all along
out on a lonesome stree
communit

Student Advisory Board

Chris Fickes

Lucino Vences

Maritza Pagán

Rachel Hansen

Claire Monty

Torré Triplett

Yahna Awazu

WRITER'S CHOICE

GRAMMAR AND COMPOSITION

Edward Hopper, *Nighthawks*, 1942

Consulting Author for Composition
William Strong

Grammar Specialist
Mark Lester

Visual-Verbal Learning Specialists
Ligature, Inc.

GLENCOE
McGraw-Hill

New York, New York   Columbus, Ohio   Mission Hills, California   Peoria, Illinois

Printed in the United States of America.

Send all inquiries to:
Glencoe/McGraw-Hill
936 Eastwind Drive
Westerville, Ohio
43081

ISBN 0-02-635885-9
(Student Edition)
ISBN 0-02-635886-7
(Teacher's Wraparound Edition)

5 6 7 8 9 10   003   99 98 97

Consulting Author for Composition

William Strong is Professor of Secondary Education at Utah State University, Director of the Utah Writing Project, and a member of the National Writing Project Advisory Board. A nationally known authority in the teaching of composition, he is the author of many volumes, including, most recently, *Writing Incisively: Do-It-Yourself Prose Surgery* (McGraw-Hill, 1991).

As Consulting Author, Dr. Strong helped to develop the structure and content of Part 1: Composition. He reviewed and edited all Composition units. Dr. Strong also conceived and wrote Unit 8: Style Through Sentence Combining. He collaborated on Sentence Combining Blackline Masters, which accompanies *Writer's Choice*.

Grammar Specialist

Mark Lester is Professor of English at Eastern Washington University. He formerly served as Chair of the Department of English as a Second Language, University of Hawaii. He is the author of *Grammar in the Classroom* (Macmillan, 1990) and of numerous professional books and articles.

As Grammar Specialist, Dr. Lester reviewed student's edition material from Part 2: Grammar, Usage, and Mechanics. He collaborated on Grammar Reteaching Blackline Masters, which accompanies *Writer's Choice*.

Associate Consultant in Writing

Bonnie S. Sunstein is Associate Professor of English and Director of the Master of Arts in Teaching Program at Rivier College in Nashua, New Hampshire. Dr. Sunstein has taught extensively in New England in colleges and secondary schools, as well as in the New Hampshire Reading and Writing Program. She has published in the area of writing and teaching and is the coeditor of *Portfolio Portraits* (Heinemann, 1992) and the author of a forthcoming book about teachers and writing (Boynton/Cook).

As Associate Consultant in Writing, Dr. Sunstein established the theoretical framework for integrating writing portfolios into *Writer's Choice*.

Contributing Writers

Larry Beason is Assistant Professor of English at Eastern Washington University. Dr. Beason is the writer of Grammar Reteaching Blackline Masters, which accompanies *Writer's Choice*.

Willis L. Pitkin Jr. is Professor of English at Utah State University. Dr. Pitkin is the writer of *Sentence Combining Blackline Masters*, which accompanies *Writer's Choice*.

Visual-Verbal Learning Specialists

Ligature, Inc., is an educational research and development company with offices in Chicago and Boston. Ligature is committed to developing educational materials that bring visual-verbal learning to the tradition of the written word.

As visual-verbal and curriculum specialists, Ligature collaborated on conceiving and implementing the pedagogy of *Writer's Choice*.

Acknowledgments

Grateful acknowledgment is given authors, publishers, photographers, museums, and agents for permission to reprint the following copyrighted material. Every effort has been made to determine copyright owners. In the case of any omissions, the Publisher will be pleased to make suitable acknowledgments in future editions.

Continued on page 838

Composition Advisers

The advisers reviewed Composition lesson prototypes. Their contributions were instrumental in the development of the Writing Process in Action lessons.

Michael Angelotti
*Head of Division of Teacher
 Education
College of Education
University of Oklahoma*

Charles R. Duke
*Dean of the College of Education
 and Human Services
Clarion University*

Carol Booth Olson
*Director
University of California, Irvine,
Writing Project*

Judith Summerfield
*Associate Professor of English
Queens College, City University of
 New York*

Denny Wolfe
*Professor and Associate Dean
Darden College of Education
Old Dominion University
formerly Director, Tidewater Writing
 Project*

Educational Reviewers

The reviewers read and commented upon manuscripts during the writing process. They also critiqued early drafts of graphic organizers and page layouts.

Lenore Croudy
*Flint Community School
Flint, Michigan*

John A. Grant
*St. Louis Public Schools
St. Louis, Missouri*

Vicki Haker
*Mead Junior High School
Mead, Washington*

Frederick G. Johnson
*Georgia Department of Education
Atlanta, Georgia*

Sterling C. Jones Jr.
*Detroit Public Schools
Detroit, Michigan*

Barry Kincaid
*Raytown School District
Kansas City, Missouri*

Evelyn G. Lewis
*Newark Public Schools
Newark, New Jersey*

M. DeAnn Morris
*Crescenta Valley High School
La Crescenta, California*

Anita Moss
*University of North Carolina
Charlotte, North Carolina*

Ann S. O'Toole
*Chesterfield County Schools
Richmond, Virginia*

Suzanne Owens
*Glendale High School
Glendale, California*

Sally P. Pfeifer
*Lewis and Clark High School
Spokane, Washington*

Marie Rogers
*Independence High School
Charlotte, North Carolina*

Barbara Schubert
*Santa Clara County Office of
 Education
San Jose, California*

Ronnie Spilton
*Chattahoochee High School
Alpharetta, Georgia*

Robert Stolte
*Huntington Beach High School
Huntington Beach, California*

Student Advisory Board

The Student Advisory Board was formed in an effort to ensure student involvement in the development of *Writer's Choice*. The editors wish to thank members of the board for their enthusiasm and dedication to the project.

The editors also wish to thank the many student writers whose models appear in this book.

Thanks are also due to Miami University of Ohio for help in the selection of models from student portfolios and to *Merlyn's Pen* for cooperation in providing student models.

Contents

Part 1 Composition

Grammar Link

In general, avoid sentence fragments in your writing.

A *sentence fragment* is an error that occurs when an incomplete sentence is punctuated as if it were complete.

Revise the paragraph below to eliminate all sentence fragments.

[1] I really liked the book I just finished reading. [2] Because it was both funny and exciting. [3] I'd like to read more by that author. [4] One of his plays, maybe. [5] Although I think it's more difficult to read a play than a story. [6] Someday I would like to try writing a one-act play. [7] With a nice part for myself. [8] We could try it out

UNIT 3 Descriptive Writing

Grammar Link

Use prepositional phrases to show spatial relationships.

The literature models in this lesson used prepositional phrases, such as "in the middle of the floor," to establish spatial relationships.

Clarify position or location by adding at least one prepositional phrase to each sentence below.

1. A bookcase stood.
2. An overstuffed blue chair squatted.

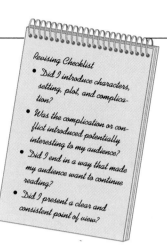

Revising Checklist
- *Did I introduce characters, setting, plot, and complication?*
- *Was the complication or conflict introduced potentially interesting to my audience?*
- *Did I end in a way that made my audience want to continue reading?*
- *Did I present a clear and consistent point of view?*

UNIT
4 Narrative Writing

Grammar Link

Use specific nouns and strong
modifiers.

Jennifer March uses precise language in
her argument on television commercials.

*Schools are **marketplaces** for ideas, not commercial turf.*

    Revise the sentences below, using spe-
cific nouns and adding strong modifiers.

1. Students in some towns should have
the same education opportunities as
students in others.
2. Some schools have a lot of things and
some don't.
3. School funds should come from many

UNIT 7 Research Paper Writing

Types of Research Papers

Summary	The writer explores a topic by summing up the opinions of other writers but does not express an opinion about it.
Evaluative	The writer states an opinion and backs it up with evidence found in primary and secondary sources.
Original	The writer does original research on a topic and reports on his or her findings.
Combination	The writer combines approaches, such as evaluating the research of others and then conducting original research.

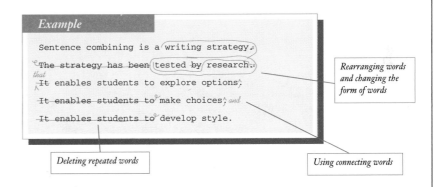

Example

Sentence combining is a writing strategy.
The strategy has been tested by research.
that It enables students to explore options.
It enables students to make choices; and
It enables students to develop style.

Rearranging words and changing the form of words

Deleting repeated words

Using connecting words

UNIT 9 Troubleshooter

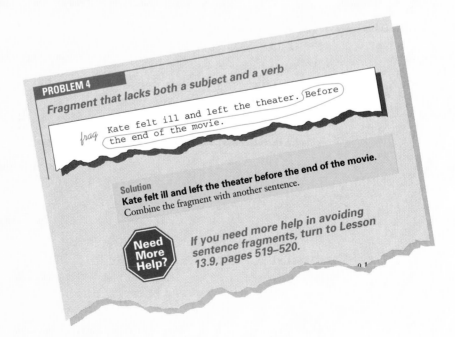

PROBLEM 4

Fragment that lacks both a subject and a verb

frag Kate felt ill and left the theater. Before the end of the movie.

Solution
Kate felt ill and left the theater before the end of the movie.
Combine the fragment with another sentence.

Need More Help? If you need more help in avoiding sentence fragments, turn to Lesson 13.9, pages 519–520.

Part 2 Grammar, Usage, and Mechanics

MAIN CLAUSE   MAIN CLAUSE

Stories entertain, and people listen.

SUBJECT   VERB   SUBJECT   VERB

Who will receive my letter?

To **whom** it may concern.

UNIT 17

Using Pronouns Correctly

UNIT 18

Using Modifiers Correctly

UNIT 19

Usage Glossary

Part 3 Resources and Skills

UNIT 22 ## History and Development of English

UNIT 23 ## Library Resources

UNIT 24 ## Using Dictionaries

Literature Models

Composition Models

Each literature selection is an extended example of the mode of writing taught in the unit.

William Least Heat-Moon, from *Blue Highways*
Alex Haley, from "My Furthest-Back Person—
    'The African' "
Gretel Ehrlich, from *The Solace of Open Spaces*
Rudolfo A. Anaya, from *Tortuga*
Sue Hubbell, from *A Book of Bees*
Mark Mathabane, "A Plague on Tennis"

Skill Models

Excerpts from outstanding works of fiction and non-fiction exemplify specific writing skills.

Sylvia Plath, from *The Journals of Sylvia Plath*
John Updike, from *Picked-Up Pieces*
Wayne Swanson, from "Exploring Proud Past
of Indians"
Lewis Mumford, from *Technics and Civilization*
Roy Blount Jr., from *About Three Bricks Shy of a
    Load*
William M. Mathers, from "*Nuestra Señora
    de la Concepción*"
Bette Bao Lord, from *Legacies: A Chinese Mosaic*
Robert D. Ballard, from "The *Bismarck* Found"
Stephen King, from *The Tommyknockers*
Sharon Oard Warner, from "A Simple Matter
    of Hunger"
Eugenia Collier, from "Marigolds"
Alice Munro, from "Boys and Girls"
Ameena Meer, from "The Only Living Boy
    in New York"
Virginia Woolf, from *To the Lighthouse*
McCandlish Phillips, from *City Notebook*
Edward Abbey, from "The Most Beautiful Place
    on Earth"
A. R. Ammons, from "Corsons Inlet"
Amber Coverdale Sumrall, from "Home Stretch"
Max Brand, from "Wine on the Desert"
T. Ernesto Bethancourt, from "User Friendly"
Mary Lavin, from "The Story of the
    Widow's Son"
Will Steger, from "Six Across Antarctica"

Mary Crow Dog and Richard Erdoes,
    from *Lakota Woman*
Betsy Armstrong and Knox Williams, from *The
    Avalanche Book*
Gretel Ehrlich, from *The Solace of Open Spaces*
David Lamb, from *The Africans*
James Wagenvoord, from *Hangin' Out: City Kids,
    City Games*
Frank Trippett, from "The Great American
    Cooling Machine"
Phil Sudo, from *Scholastic Update*
Wendell Berry, from "A Defense of the Family
    Farm"
Gina Lubrano, from "2 Condors to Fly Free
    Late in '91"
Rachel Carson, from *Silent Spring*
Newton Minow, from Address to the Broadcasting
    Industry
Tom Shales, from "MTV Has Shallow Look
    of Success"
George Varga, from "Is It MTV or Is It
    'Empty-V'?"
Jewelbox Advocates and Manufacturers, from "A Strong
    Case for a Strong Case"
Betty Berry, from "Debate"
Jennifer March, from "Debate"
Consumer Reports, from "In-Line Skates: They Aren't Just
    for Kids"
David Fricke, from "Sam Phillips and the Birth
    of Rock & Roll"

Language Models

Each Grammar Review uses excerpts to link grammar, usage, or mechanics to literature.

Yukio Mishima, from *The Sound of Waves*, translated from the Japanese by Meredith Weatherby

Naguib Mahfouz, from *Palace Walk*, translated from the Arabic by William Maynard Hutchins and Olive E. Kenny

Miguel Delibes, from *The Stuff of Heroes*, translated from the *Spanish* by Frances M. López-Morillas

Willa Cather, from *Death Comes for the Archbishop*

J. R. R. Tolkien, from *The Fellowship of the Ring*

Amos Oz, from *Elsewhere, Perhaps*, translated from the Hebrew by Nicholas de Lange

William Conton, from The African

Mark Helprin, from *A Soldier of the Great War*

Bruce Chatwin, from *In Patagonia*

Eudora Welty, from *One Writer's Beginnings*

Fine Art

Fine art—paintings, drawings, photos, and sculpture—is used to teach and stimulate ideas for writing.

Judith Leyster, *Self Portrait*
Carmen Lomas Garza, *Cumpleaños de Lala y Tudi*
Lenore Tawney, *Untitled*
Henri Rousseau, *The Sleeping Gypsy*
Maynard Dixon, *Earth Knower*
Jaune Quick-To-See Smith, *Osage Orange*
Suzanne Scheuer, *Newsgathering*
Edward Hopper, *Nighthawks*
Edna Jackson, *Kaaswoot*
Vincent van Gogh, *The Potato Eaters*
T. C. Cannon, *Turn of the Century Dandy*
David Hockney, *Paul Explaining Pictures to Mie Kakigahara*
Paul Sierra, *Arcadia*
Sofonisba Anguissola, *Three of the Artist's Sisters Playing Chess*
Howardena Pindell, *Autobiography: Water/Ancestors, Middle Passage/Family Ghosts*
Fredrick Prescott, *The New York Scene*
Beverly Buchanan, *Barnesville*
Blackbear Bosin, *Prairie Fire*
Childe Hassam, *Fifth Avenue*

John Marin, *Movement, Fifth Avenue*
Arthur Dove, *Sunrise*
Sonia Terk Delaunay, *Electric Prisms*
Allan Crite, *Shadow and Sunlight*
Frederic Remington, *The Fall of the Cowboy*
Ann Taylor, *Red Riding*
Faith Ringgold, *Tar Beach*
José Gamarra, *Five Centuries Later*
Richard Bosman, *Flight*
Gilberto Ruiz, *The Good News Call*
Edvard Munch, *The Scream*
Melissa Miller, *Salmon Run*
Rufino Tamayo, *Interior with Alarm Clock*
Joan Miró, *The Farm*
Zinaida Serebriakova, *Castle of Cards*
Jacob Lawrence, *Strike*
Maurits Cornelis Escher, *Day and Night*
Alma Thomas, *Iris, Tulips, Jonquils and Crocuses*
Ben Schonzeit, *Parrot Tulip*
Vincent van Gogh, *View of Arles*
Vincent van Gogh, *View of Arles with Irises*
Ernest Lawson, *Garden Landscape*
Judy Pfaff, *Wasco*
Jonathan Franklin, *Mad Hatters*
Mandy Martin, *Powerhouse*
Claude Monet, *Les Coquelicots (Wild Poppies)*
Charles March Gere, *The Tennis Party*
Jan Vermeer, *The Astronomer*
Chryssa, *Times Square Sky*
Andō Hiroshige, *Imagiri Promontory from Maizaka*
Henri Matisse, *The Casbah Gate*
Henri Cartier-Bresson, *Seville*
Georgia O'Keeffe, *Gate of Adobe Church*
Samuel Palmer, *Early Morning*
Elias Newman, *Wadi Musserara*
Clementine Hunter, Patchwork quilt
Albert Bierstadt, *Sunrise on the Matterhorn*
Louis Comfort Tiffany, *Autumn Landscape*
Winslow Homer, *Girl on a Garden Seat*

Case Studies:
Writers at Work

Each case study focuses on a real writer working on a real-life writing project. Come on backstage!

Thurston Clarke
Travel Writer
Travel Writing, *Clarke Follows the Equator*

Bobby Norfolk
Storyteller
Storytelling, *Norfolk Tells Tales*

Denise Chavez
Playwright, Poet, and Fiction Writer
Personal Journal Writing, *The Private Journals of Denise Chavez*

Mark Trahant
Investigative Reporter
Investigative Reporting, *Trahant Investigates Nuclear Transport*

Anastasia Toufexis
Health and Behavior Editor
Science Writing, *Behind the Science Feature*

Amy Krouse Rosenthal, Steven Wohlwender, and Marshall Ross
Advertising Executives
Ad Campaign, *Mitchiner, Ross and Kahn Asks, "What Will It Do To You?"*

Part 1

Composition

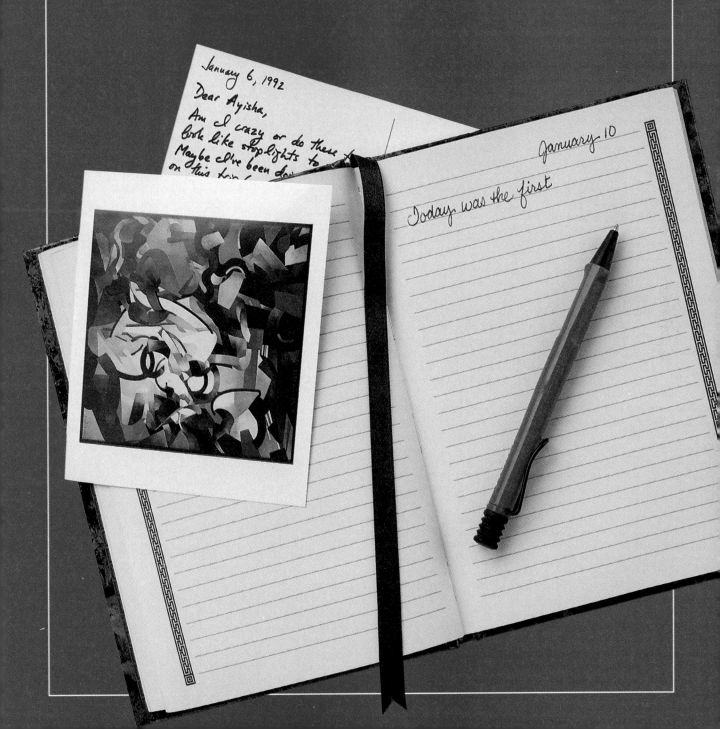

Part 1 Composition

Personal Writing in the Real World

The Private Journals of Denise Chavez

F O C U S: The process of journal writing is as unique as the individual who keeps the journal.

Denise Chavez has written and published plays, poems, novels, and short stories, including the award-winning collection *The Last of the Menu Girls*. In addition to these works, the author also completes two or three personal journals each year, which she keeps lined up on a shelf in her back room.

Chavez's journals help her look within herself and explore the world around her. They also serve as a vital testing ground for her professional writing.

"I've kept a journal for almost as long as I can remember," Chavez says. "I feel healthier and happier when I'm recording." The author received her first journal as a Christmas gift from her mother when she was about eight years old. She recalls, "I was a solitary child. My mother didn't like us to retreat to our rooms, so the journal was my way of closing

Author
Denise Chavez

> "My journal is a grab bag of my existence, a barometer of what's going on with me. Journal writing is like weeding. I clear the surface to get down to where the truth is."
>
> —Denise Chavez

the door. I'd write down poems I heard or things I liked. Eventually, I started writing my own things. In my journal I was able to process emotions that I couldn't put any place else."

Chavez writes her journals longhand. She says, "I like the physical feeling of moving the pen across the paper. I've always liked paper, the feel of it. I use artist's sketch pads, because I never write with lines. I think lines are very restrictive and don't allow for the organic, natural process. If I want to draw a picture or put in a newspaper clipping, I have room."

"Sometimes," she continues, "I write all the way around the page. That's when the writing is coming so fast, I can't stop. There's no time to flip the page. At other times, I may allow myself to put just one word on a page. I wrote 'yes' all by itself on a page once. I must have been happy and feeling good about myself."

Every time Chavez starts a new journal she gives it some kind of heading. She explains, "I may call it 'On the Road' or 'Becoming.' Each journal represents a chunk of time in which I'll be working on some personal goal, and the title gives me a point of focus. It's with great joy that I greet these new journals."

When Chavez forgets her journal and an idea hits her, she'll write on whatever is handy—whether a check stub or restaurant napkin.

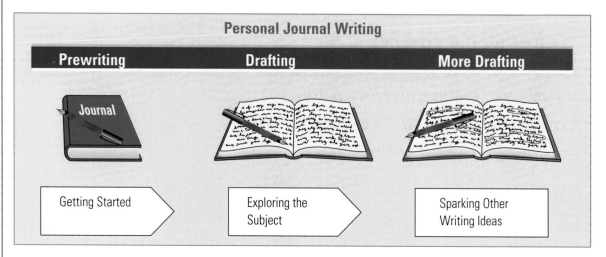

Personal Journal Writing

Prewriting	Drafting	More Drafting

Getting Started

Exploring the Subject

Sparking Other Writing Ideas

Prewriting

GETTING STARTED

A personal journal can be a record of your thoughts and memories. Whatever you choose to record, it's a place where you can try out your writing ideas in private.

For some journal writers, it is helpful to write daily entries. Chavez usually writes in her journal at night just before she goes to bed, but she tries to take her journal everywhere, just in case she gets the urge to jot something down.

Paying little attention to grammar, complete sentences, or spelling, Chavez feels completely free to write in her journals as she pleases. At this stage, the ideas are more important than syntax and spelling.

Drafting

EXPLORING THE SUBJECT

When Chavez writes in her journal, she can become immersed in a subject. She says, "When I write, I don't even think about the outside world because I'm the only audience for my journal. Without censoring me, my journal accepts everything I say. It's a private notebook of my growth as a human being."

Chavez continues, "Writing a journal helps me keep abreast of what's going on in my life. Looking back over my journal, I can see patterns of my own behavior and personality. I've learned a lot by what I've loved and by what I've chosen. Keeping a journal is something I do for mental health."

Chavez doesn't have to look far to find things to write about in her journal. She says, "I write more when I travel, but I don't have to go beyond my own house to find things to write about. We got a cat whom we named Pascualita. This brought to mind an aunt of my mother's and I found myself writing about Aunt Pascualita for several days."

Sometimes Chavez just writes about her favorite places. It seems that wherever she is writing, Chavez's next subject is nearby, waiting to be explored.

Years of journal keeping can result in a personal library of journals.

Denise Chavez's novel The Last of the Menu Girls *was also produced as a play.*

More Drafting

SPARKING OTHER WRITING IDEAS

Like many professional writers, Chavez finds that her journal entries frequently stimulate other writing projects. She says, "I have seen whole plays come out of my journal. Or I may use the journal to work out problems in my plays, such as biographical data about the characters or the setting."

Chavez began working on her short story "Evening in Paris" in her journal. She says, "I had a deadline to get this story in to a magazine. I just started writing about Christmas and putting together some of the smells. I

remembered that we always had a chicken for Christmas because we couldn't afford a turkey. I kept writing down things and I worked on it every day. Finally, I had pages of notes in my journal. When I began to write the story, I already had my guide, my road map, in the journal, so I was pretty sure of the road I'd be driving on as I wrote the story."

Chavez's journal writing exploration seems unlimited. She continues, "I never run out of things to write about. In fact, I'm booked for the rest of my life."

Responding to the Case Study

1. Discussion

Discuss these questions about Denise Chavez's journal writing.

- Why does Chavez feel that her journal is like a "barometer"?
- In what form does Chavez prefer to keep her journals? Why?
- What are some of the sources for Chavez's journal entries?
- Explain how Chavez's journal serves as a "road map" for other writing projects.

2. Personal Writing

Write a personal journal entry. Make a list of at least 10 phrases that could serve as prompts for writing in your journal—phrases such as "I saw," "I remember," or "I know." Select one phrase, and write it at the top of a piece of paper. Now write— without stopping—whatever comes to mind from that phrase for the next five minutes.

Grammar Link

Use adjective clauses to create variety in sentence structure.

An *adjective clause* is a subordinate clause that modifies a noun or a pronoun. For example, Denise Chavez writes:

*We got a cat **whom we named Pascualita**.*

An adjective clause that is not needed to make the meaning of a sentence clear is set off by commas.

Add an adjective clause to each sentence below, using correct punctuation.

1. My brother James keeps a journal.
2. He writes a lot about sports and about our dog.
3. Sometimes he also writes for the school paper.
4. James wrote a great story about the basketball team.
5. The coach wants him to do a feature story about sports injuries.

See Lesson 13.5, pages 511–512.

Personal Writing
Writing to Discover Your World

Recording ideas and feelings in a personal journal is a risk-free way to learn about yourself and your world.

Da Vinci, Renaissance artist, filled his note-books with detailed drawings and diagrams dealing with art, engineering, architecture, and other topics.

Plath, a modern American poet, wrote this entry when she was eighteen. What does this passage reveal about her reasons for keeping a journal?

Literature Model

S ome things are hard to write about. After something happens to you, you go to write it down, and either you overdramatize it or underplay it, exaggerate the wrong parts or ignore the important ones. At any rate, you never write it quite the way you want to. I've just got to put down what happened to me this afternoon. I can't tell Mother; not yet, anyway. She was in my room when I came home, fussing with clothes, and she didn't even sense that something had happened. She just kept scolding and chattering on and on. So I couldn't stop and tell her. No matter how it comes out, I have to write it.

Sylvia Plath, *The Journals of Sylvia Plath*

Start Your Own Personal Journal

A personal journal is a place where you can try out your writing ideas without risk. You can follow your thoughts wherever they lead, explore new ideas, and sort out feelings. Here are some tips for getting started with your own personal journal.

Tips for Journal Writing

1. Write whatever comes to mind. Write about thoughts and memories that have special significance for you.
2. Write on a regular basis, either every day or every other day.
3. Date each journal entry for future reference.

Try Out New Writing Ideas

A journal is the ideal place for exploring personal thoughts, and it is perfect for other kinds of writing, too. Some people experiment with poetry. Others try out ideas for stories and plays. You don't have to limit yourself to writing. You can include original cartoons, comic strips, even doodles. The following chart shows other kinds of items you can include in your journal.

Personal Journal Entries

Unsent Letters	Dear Gabby Letters	Tongue-in-Cheek Ads	Words and Music
to parents or friends dealing with problems that you would like to discuss face to face—but can't	about problems that bug you (you might want to play Gabby and write the replies, too)	about diet and exercise, mixing sound advice about nutrition and health with good-natured humor	for original songs —pop, country, or rock-and-roll (the choice is up to you)

Journal Writing

People choose a variety of formats for their personal journals—spiral notebooks, loose-leaf notebooks, even computer disks. Decide which format will work best for you, and start your own personal journal. In your first entry, write what you hope journal writing will do for you.

Don't Be Afraid to Experiment

You will want to experiment with different ways of recording information in your journal. Da Vinci, for example, filled his notebooks with drawings and diagrams, and he wrote backward. The following examples demonstrate different ways of exploring the same early childhood experiences.

Methods of Recording Information

Freewriting

I was born in the Texas Hill Country, and I remember spending most of my free time scrambling up and down the canyons that crisscross the landscape, chasing armadillos through the underbrush and flushing roadrunners out into the open. Rattlesnakes, too. I'll never forget the day I was edging down a cliff and found myself nose to nose with a diamondback! My happiest memory, though, is of fishing in the streams on my grandfather's ranch. There were always plenty of catfish and sunfish, but the bass were the best!

My family moved to Illinois when I was nine, and I didn't like it at first. The land was flat, so different from the wild canyons in Texas, but the fishing was just as good. Ice fishing in the wintertime—that was new to me, and I really enjoyed it.

One way of exploring early childhood memories is to write freely about each experience as it comes to mind.

Mapping

Another way is to create an experience map, with captions highlighting significant events.

I loved living in Texas (although I must admit I didn't really like those rattlesnakes).

My father took me ice fishing the first winter after we moved to Illinois, and I soon became an expert.

1.1 Writing Activities

Write a Journal Entry

The painting below shows an extended family at a birthday celebration. Examine the scene carefully. Then write your personal reactions in your journal.

- Explore feelings and memories of similar situations.
- Experiment with different ways of recording your ideas.

PURPOSE Self-discovery
AUDIENCE Yourself
LENGTH 2–3 paragraphs

Cooperative Learning

In a small group, assign each member a family role. Role-play for five minutes a family conversation—perhaps about an after-school activity. Each group member should write a journal entry about the conversation from the point of view of the role he or she played. Share journal entries and compare reactions.

Grammar Link

Avoid vague pronoun references.

Even your private writing should make sense when you reread it.

Revise each sentence below to make the pronoun reference clear.

1. Frank got maps for the Saturday hike to Nelson Park, which was a great idea.
2. That day they took along a picnic lunch, but it was cold.
3. Some folks climbed the firetower, which was a spectacular view.
4. The rangers had closed off one park trail, and that changed their plans.
5. The group wants to go on some longer hikes, and it will probably be during spring vacation.

See Lesson 17.6, pages 611–613.

Carmen Lomas Garza, *Cumpleaños de Lala y Tudi*, 1989

Personal Writing
Using a Learning Log

A learning log is a special kind of journal that can help you clarify your ideas about concepts covered in various classes. The example below shows a page from a learning log for biology, written after a class discussion of nutrition.

The log entry begins with the date and a brief summary of the discussion in class.

The entry includes a notation. It could also have indicated a point for further exploration. What other kinds of notations might you make?

The entry ends with the class assignment.

Biology   September 15, 1993

Finally began the study of nutrition.
Boy, was that an eye-opener!
I like burgers and fries—at
least I get enough protein.
But according to the
USDA food pyramid,
I'm not eating
nearly enough
fruit and
vegetables.
Four pieces
of fruit a
day! I never
knew that!
   I still don't understand how nutritionists
decide which foods are best. Why do they
recommend so much fish and poultry? And
why so few eggs? I'll have to remember to
ask about that tomorrow.

Homework Assignment: Read Chapter 3,
pp. 45–65 which discusses how regular
exercise relates to overall health.

FATS
OILS
SWEETS
USE SPARINGLY

MILK
YOGURT
AND
CHEESE
2-3 SERVINGS

MEAT
POULTRY, FISH
DRY BEANS,
EGGS AND
NUTS
2-3 SERVINGS

VEGETABLES
3-5 SERVINGS

FRUITS
2-4 SERVINGS

BREAD,
CEREAL
RICE
AND PASTAS
6-11 SERVINGS

Write on a Daily Basis

Learning logs work best when you use them on a day-to-day basis, with a separate section for each class. Here are a few tips for using a learning log to keep your studies on track.

Keeping a Learning Log			
Summarize the main ideas discussed in class. Did you learn anything new?	**Identify** difficult concepts you want to examine further. Where can you go for help?	**Discuss** a controversial idea that came up in class. Where do you stand on this issue?	**Evaluate** your progress on a weekly basis. How are you doing in this class?

Write to Learn

Writing can help you make sense out of new information in any subject area. You never fully know something until you can state it in your own words. The following chart shows some writing-to-learn techniques that you can use to clarify ideas and concepts. Remember that your goal is to make the information make sense to *you*.

A Variety of Writing Ideas	
Idea	**Example**
1. Try to summarize the significance of what you are studying in a single clear sentence.	1. "The study of nutrition teaches us how to select the best diet for better health and longer life."
2. Begin with a particular topic, start freewriting, and see where it leads.	2. "Diet and exercise, exercise and diet, that's all you hear about these days. . . ."
3. As you write, continue to ask why until you exhaust all questions.	3. "Why do we need so much fruit in our diet? For the vitamins, I know, but why are vitamins important?"
4. Set down your point of view, and then deliberately argue against it.	4. "I am dead set against junk food, but . . ."

Journal Writing

In your journal write at least two questions about today's class work in one of your school subjects. Note what you might do to answer your questions.

Make a Learning Log Work for You

Jenny King found the following passage in her biology textbook difficult to understand, so she used her learning log to help clarify the ideas. She began by creating a diagram to show how ideas in the passage relate. Then she rewrote the passage in her own words.

King made a diagram like this to show how the main ideas in the passage relate.

Muscle strength does not depend on the number of fibers, but rather on their thickness and on how many of them contract at one time. Thicker fibers are stronger and contribute to muscle mass. Exercise stresses muscles slightly; as a result, the fibers increase in size.

Regular exercise can result in overall body fitness and endurance that can affect muscle strength. Body fitness is related to the condition of the heart and the number of capillaries in body tissue. One component of physical fitness is the efficiency of the heart in pumping blood to the tissues. Increased physical fitness results in a greater number of capillaries in the muscle tissue. Endurance is a measure of how long you can continue to exercise and depends on how much fuel your muscles can store. A muscle that is continually exercised is stronger and can store more fuel.

```
              Exercise
            /          \
Greater muscle      Improved condition
    mass                of heart
     |                     |
Greater muscle       More efficient
  strength           blood supply
                           |
                      More endurance
```

Student Model

What evidence can you find that King used her diagram to rewrite the passage?

Muscle strength depends on the thickness of muscle fibers, how many of the fibers contract at one time, and the amount of fuel stored within the muscle tissue. Exercise relates to all three categories. Exercising the muscles causes slight stress. This stress causes the muscle fibers to increase in thickness and controls the fiber contractions. Exercise also improves the condition of the heart and increases the number of capillaries in body tissue, including muscle tissue. These increased capillaries increase the amount of energy stored within the muscle; therefore, muscle endurance is increased.

Jenny King, Henry Clay High School, Lexington, Kentucky

1.2 Writing Activities

Write a Learning Log

Start using your learning log today in your English, history, or math class, and keep it going for a week. At the end of the week, reread your log entries. Think about how they have helped you understand your class. Notice what different forms of record keeping you used. Then write a log entry evaluating your experience.

- Write on a regular basis; write for at least three to five minutes for each class session.
- Begin each entry with a brief summary of the class discussion.
- Make a note of any idea or concept that you find puzzling.
- End by describing the next assignment in your own words.

PURPOSE   To clarify concepts discussed in class
AUDIENCE Yourself
LENGTH   2–4 paragraphs

COMPUTER OPTION

If you have access to a personal computer, you may want to keep your learning log electronically. Set up separate files for your different classes. As you experiment with writing-to-learn techniques, save and date your entries. With your learning log on computer, you can easily return to concepts and pieces of writing you wish to explore further.

Grammar Link

Use commas to separate three or more words, phrases, or clauses in a series.

Muscle strength depends on the thickness of muscle fibers, how many of the fibers contract at one time, and the amount of fuel stored within the muscle tissue.

Add any needed comma or commas to each sentence below.

1. Our subway ride to the museum yesterday was long hot and crowded.
2. Over the weekend I had homework assignments for my science math history and English classes.
3. I can't decide whether to join the drama club the school debating team or a new after-school jazz club.
4. The jazz club will meet at our school at a neighboring school and at a professional jazz club downtown.
5. My music and German classes meet on Monday Wednesday and Friday.
6. We got to the museum at one stood in line for an hour and finally toured the exhibit with 35 fourth graders.
7. By Monday I have to memorize a poem finish a history paper plan my science project and make a poster.
8. I'm not sure whether the poem paper project or poster is the place to start.
9. My older brother says I am disorganized forgetful and hopeless.
10. Of course, he can't remember anyone's birthday our parents' anniversary or his own weekend plans.

See Lesson 21.6, page 705.

Personal Writing
Keeping a Commonplace Book

A commonplace book is a collection of items that have some special significance for you personally and that may eventually become a source of writing ideas that you can use for other writing. The model shows entries from a commonplace book assembled by poet Sheila P. Donohue.

Donohue collected several quotations that help her clarify her view of the world.

August 18, '86

"I arrived at the end of the tulips, the beginning of the rose; I left as the gladiolas began."

    Sharon, about Poland

Maybe the first sentence of a short story? - Idea of changes in the outside world representing emotional phases.

Late August

"Feed 'em, love 'em, and leave 'em alone."
    Dr. Spock on children

Hmm . . .

What do the annotations reveal about Donohue's reasons for keeping the quotations for future reference?

September 3, 1986

- Clam shells in piles decay, the stench of still water in their shiny throats.

- A quick eye for gulls dive-bombing the shells and leaving with a squawk and stiff flick of wings

from a 9/12/85 draft – the only interesting parts Maybe use in a new poem

(Good place names ↑)

Start Your Own Commonplace Book

You can collect whatever you want in your commonplace book—quotations, song lyrics, jokes, menus—anything that you find interesting or thought-provoking. The following display shows other kinds of items you might keep in your book.

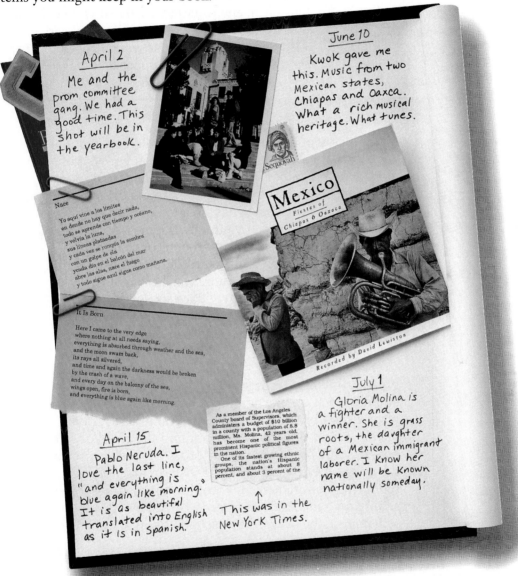

April 2
Me and the prom committee gang. We had a good time. This shot will be in the yearbook.

June 10
Kwok gave me this. Music from two Mexican states, Chiapas and Oaxca. What a rich musical heritage. What tunes.

Nace

Yo aquí vine a los límites,
en donde no hay que decir nada,
todo se aprende con tiempo y océano,
y volvía la luna,
sus líneas plateadas
y cada vez se rompía la sombra
con un golpe de ola
ycada día en el balcón del mar
abre las alas, nace el fuego
y todo sigue azul sigue como mañana.

It Is Born

Here I came to the very edge
where nothing at all needs saying,
everything is absorbed through weather and the sea,
and the moon swam back,
its rays all silvered,
and time and again the darkness would be broken
by the crash of a wave,
and every day on the balcony of the sea,
wings open, fire is born,
and everything is blue again like morning.

Mexico
Fiestas of
Chiapas & Oaxaca

Recorded by David Lewiston

As a member of the Los Angeles County board of Supervisors, which administers a budget of $10 billion in a county with a population of 8.8 million, Ms. Molina, 42 years old, has become one of the most prominent Hispanic political figures in the nation.
One of its fastest growing ethnic groups, the nation's Hispanic population stands at about 8 percent, and about 3 percent of the

April 15
Pablo Neruda. I love the last line, "and everything is blue again like morning." It is as beautiful translated into English as it is in Spanish.

↑ This was in the New York Times.

July 1
Gloria Molina is a fighter and a winner. She is grass roots, the daughter of a Mexican immigrant laborer. I know her name will be known nationally someday.

Journal Writing

Do some freewriting in your journal, assessing different kinds of items you might want to keep in your own commonplace book.

Explore Ideas for Writing

In her reading Nina Molumby ran across a quotation about responsibility. She wrote a note explaining why she thought the quotation worth saving, and she put the item in her commonplace book. Months later, Nina came across the item again, and it started her thinking. She decided to write a story about responsibility, but with a twist. She would show what could happen to a person who refused to take responsibility for her life.

Character—the willingness to accept responsibility for one's own life—is the source from which self-respect springs.

Joan Didion

Responsibility—that's a word you hear more and more these days:
"Take charge."
"Accept responsibility."
"Just say no."

Student Model

Sophie sat at her desk in her room, thinking about her life. Last year her mother had left, leaving Sophie alone with her father. Their family problems had intensified over the years with her father's drinking, her mother's irrational behavior, and Sophie's poor performance in school. Eventually, Sophie stopped seeing her friends, replacing busy afternoons of swimming practice and telephone calls with solitude. The only thing that seemed to matter any more was her orchids. She poured into them all her love, since she was unable to share it with anyone else. They served as a barrier, protecting Sophie from her family problems, her teachers' questions, and her own fear of being vulnerable.

Sophie broke out of her daze and drifted back into the present. A feeling of frustration swept over her. Was she another crack-up like her parents? How did other people resolve their problems? All that her family had tried usually failed. Still, there was nothing she could do. Her parents were the ones with the problem. They caused all the agony, leaving her only one place to hide—in her room with her orchids. How could she accept responsibility for a life that was already ruined by others? As for self-respect, the only pride she had was in her plants.

Nina Molumby, Evanston Township High School, Evanston, Illinois

Molumby's story revolves around a character named Sophie, whose life is on hold because of family troubles.

What echoes of Molumby's journal entry do you hear in these sentences?

When you leaf through your commonplace book looking for a writing idea, don't feel constrained by an annotation you might have written weeks or months before. The annotation is just a starting point. Open your mind, and let your thoughts flow freely. Follow your ideas wherever they lead. If one idea leads nowhere, choose another.

Write Commonplace Book Annotations

Set up your own commonplace book, and start collecting items that interest you. Look for things related to the themes of self-discovery and self-improvement. You can include such things as a cartoon, a photo, or lines from a song.

- Explain why each item is important.
- Write a brief note for it.

PURPOSE Self-discovery.
AUDIENCE Yourself
LENGTH 4 or more annotations

Lenore Tawney, *Untitled*, 1983

Grammar Link

A verb must agree with its subject, not with the predicate nominative that follows it.

In the student model, Nina Molumby correctly writes, *The only thing that seemed to matter . . . was her orchids.*

Complete each sentence to make the subject and verb agree.

1. In northern states, snowmobiles (is, are) a common form of winter transportation.
2. The puppies (is, are) an added expense for the family.
3. The first item on the agenda (was, were) the needs of the new tenants.
4. Baseball cards (is, are) his only topic of conversation.
5. The favorite dessert (was, were) strawberries with ice cream.

See Lesson 16.2, page 577.

Cooperative Learning

With a small group of classmates, create a "commonplace bulletin board" for the classroom. Choose a general theme for your collection. Have each group member contribute things he or she makes. Decide how to assemble the items for display, as Lenore Tawney arranged the paper scraps for her collage. You may wish to invite other classmates to contribute items as well.

Writing About Literature
Using a Reader-Response Journal

You can use a reader-response journal to record personal reactions to whatever you read. Notice how one student's reaction to the poem "The Eagle" changed when she read it a second time.

The Eagle

He clasps the crag with crooked hands;
Close to the sun in lonely lands,
Ringed with the azure world he stands.

The wrinkled sea beneath him crawls;
He watches from his mountain walls,
And like a thunderbolt he falls.

Alfred, Lord Tennyson

Student Model

How does Clare's response draw on particular lines from the poem?

When I first read "The Eagle," I wasn't too impressed, but reading it a second time made me change my mind. The poem is short and compact, but oh so powerful! There's just so much beauty and majestic feeling. Here we have an eagle, high above lonely lands, soaring through a sun-filled sky. Then, without warning, it drops from the sky and attacks! The image this poem conveys is so breathtaking it lingers in the mind like a fond memory.

Avilonia Clare, Kelvyn Park High School, Chicago, Illinois

Set Up the Journal

A reader-response journal gives you the opportunity to discover what you really think about the things that you read. You can set up a reader-response journal in a separate notebook or in a special section of your personal journal or learning log.

Once you set up your reader-response journal, start writing. Here are a number of creative ways of responding to works of fiction and nonfiction. What others can you think of?

Think of a story or novel that has a character you find appealing. Explain why you identify with the character.

Write a brief review of the book. Note its strengths and weaknesses as well as any suggestions you might have for making the book better.

Create a magazine ad that you think would help sell the book.

Rewrite an important scene from a different point of view.

Create a dust jacket with a new cover design and information about the author on the inside flap.

List questions you have about how the book is organized.

Journal Writing

Use the first page in your reader-response journal to begin exploring your reactions to what you read. Jot down an annotated list of some things you have read recently—perhaps the funniest, the saddest, the most interesting or surprising things, or something with which you strongly disagreed.

Unleash Your Imagination

Reading is a process of discovery, helping us gain insight into the world around us, the people we know, and ourselves. When student Dan Felten read John Steinbeck's novel *The Grapes of Wrath*, he was particularly struck by the courage with which ordinary people face adversity. He explored his reaction in his reader-response journal.

Student Model

Felten begins by discussing the undue pessimism he finds in some modern writers and intellectuals.

He then explains why he likes the boundless optimism he always finds in the works of Steinbeck.

I think that far too often writers and so-called intellectuals consider the human race to be basically hopeless. The problem with this kind of thinking is that it is usually based on personal assumptions about the human race as a whole. It rarely takes into account the personal hopes and triumphs of individuals.

John Steinbeck's novel *The Grapes of Wrath* does not neglect these hopes and triumphs. When I finished the book, I was left with the feeling that perhaps people aren't quite as hopeless as they sometimes seem. As always, Steinbeck is blunt in discussing various evils that people inflict upon one another, but he also helps us see how they strive to overcome these evils. This is Steinbeck's main point in *The Grapes of Wrath*, a point that I feel is often overlooked. Officials can be evil and do evil things, but they cannot stamp out the hopes and dreams of ordinary people. At the end of the novel, Steinbeck helps us understand that the hope that flames within the Joads will never be quenched.

Dan Felten, Evanston Township High School, Evanston, Illinois

Here is a list of questions to consider before you record your personal response to a piece of writing.

Questions to Consider

1. How did you feel when you finished reading? Happy? Sad? Inspired? Confused? Puzzled? Angry?
2. What did you like best about the piece? Is there anything you would change? What?
3. Did you agree with everything you read? Would you like to argue with the author? What would you say?
4. Did you learn anything that you didn't know before? What?

1.4 Writing Activities

Write a Reader-Response Journal Entry

Write a journal entry about a piece of literature that you have recently read and enjoyed. Use the following list to help you explore your feelings and reactions.

- Explain what you liked or disliked about the literature.
- Describe any self-discoveries that you made or insights into others that you had.
- Explain how you felt when you finished reading.

PURPOSE   To explore your response to literature
AUDIENCE   Yourself
LENGTH   4–6 paragraphs

Cross-Curricular: Journalism

The school paper has asked you to write a two-page review of a short story or book you have read recently. Look through your reader-response journal, and base your review on an entry you have made.

Outline your review carefully before writing. Use your journal entry to remind yourself of what you liked or didn't like. Write about what the literature might say—or not say— to your classmates and peers. Conclude by giving your fellow students your recommendation as to whether they should or should not read the literature.

Grammar Link

In general, avoid sentence fragments in your writing.

A *sentence fragment* is an error that occurs when an incomplete sentence is punctuated as if it were complete.

Revise the paragraph below to eliminate all sentence fragments.

¹I really liked the book I just finished reading. ²Because it was both funny and exciting. ³I'd like to read more by that author. ⁴One of his plays, maybe. ⁵Although I think it's more difficult to read a play than a story. ⁶Someday I would like to try writing a one-act play. ⁷With a nice juicy part for myself. ⁸We could try it out in English class. ⁹If I ever have the nerve to let anybody else read it! ¹⁰That is.

See Lesson 13.9, pages 519–520.

Writing About Literature
Responding to a Short Story

Novelist John Updike as a young man

Responding to a story in your reader-response journal can teach you something about yourself. Plot, theme, setting, and characters may evoke interesting opinions and connections. Notice how novelist John Updike responded to J. D. Salinger's stories.

Literature Models

*I*t's in Salinger that I first heard, as a college student in the early Fifties, the tone that spoke to my condition. I had a writing teacher . . . who read aloud to us some of Salinger's stories as they appeared in *The New Yorker*. They seemed to me to say something about the energies of people and the ways they encounter each other that I did not find in the short stories of Hemingway or John O'Hara or Dorothy Parker or any of that "wised-up" style of short-story writing. Salinger's stories were not wised up. They were very open to tender invasions.

John Updike, *Picked-Up Pieces*

How does Updike signal in the first sentence the effect that J. D. Salinger's stories had on him?

"*I* looked down at Charles, who was now resting the side of his face on his chair seat. When he saw that I was looking at him, he closed his eyes, sleepily, angelically, then stuck out his tongue—an appendage of startling length—and gave out what in *my* country would have been a glorious tribute to a myopic baseball umpire."

J. D. Salinger, "For Esmé—with Love and Squalor"

Updike found Salinger's stories especially meaningful because they contain characters with whom he could identify.

Get into the Spirit

The best way to find out how you really feel about a piece of literature is to write a personal response in your reader-response journal. As you explore your feelings about and reactions to a piece, you may even discover that you have an opinion different from the one you originally had. The following graphic lists a variety of ways you can respond to a short story.

Ways of Responding to a Short Story

Characters
The individuals in a story

- Pick one character you like and write a dialogue between the two of you.
- Write a letter to a character in the story, making connections with your life.

Setting
The time and place of the action

- Tell why the setting of the story has a special appeal for you.
- Create a drawing or painting depicting the setting of a major event.

Plot
The sequence of events

- Tell what you like or don't like about the ending of the story.
- Get a new perspective on the story by writing a different ending.

Theme
The underlying meaning

- Compare the story with another story that has the same general theme.
- Write about an experience of your own that had a similar meaning for you.

Journal Writing

What is the last short story you read? Did you like it? Why or why not? Which story element influenced your reaction the most? Spend a few minutes freewriting about your reaction in your reader-response journal.

Respond in Your Own Way

Most people like stories that have a character with whom they can identify, so they usually begin their personal response there. Don't overlook other elements of a short story. Speculating about setting, plot, and theme can be just as fruitful in discovering why a story has special appeal for you.

The following model shows how student Robin Borland responded to the short story "A Sunrise on the Veld" by Doris Lessing. The story tells how a fifteen-year-old boy in southern Africa, rejoicing in his own good health, suddenly comes face to face with the unpredictability of death. This theme touched Borland deeply because it reminded her of a time when she herself had come face to face with mortality.

Student Model

Borland begins by providing a brief summary of the story theme.

To feel helpless is just about the worst emotion a person can experience, especially to feel helpless for the first time. At the beginning of "A Sunrise on the Veld," the boy is brimming with enthusiasm for life. He is completely unprepared for the reality of death—in himself or in any other living creature. Then he stumbles upon a buck covered with ants, and he watches, powerless, as the shadows of death swarm over the dying animal. Had he not been there, the same thing would have happened, yet now he is left scarred with an image of mortality—an image he had no inkling of up until this time.

She then connects the story theme with something that happened in her own life.

I came face to face with this reality when a close friend of mine passed away this year. He was seventeen and had been fighting kidney disease for over three years. I continued to visit him during that time, holding fast to an inner belief that everything would be fine. I believed that life is great, that everything is eternal, that nothing goes wrong in this great place. There was no way that my friend was going to die. But then he died.

Notice how she uses her own experience to give her a deeper understanding of the story.

I know now that there was nothing I could have done. My visits weren't enough; the doctors weren't enough. I know how the boy in "Sunrise on the Veld" felt as he watched the ants swarm over the prey. The ants took away the boy's innocence. Death is unpredictable and unmerciful; it is not something that you can prepare for. It is the ultimate shock of feeling completely helpless.

Robin Borland, Evanston Township High School, Evanston, Illinois

1.5 Writing Activities

Write a Reader-Response Journal Entry

Reread a favorite short story. Then write a creative response in your journal.

- Use one of the suggestions in the chart on page 27.

PURPOSE To respond creatively to a short story
AUDIENCE Yourself
LENGTH 4–6 paragraphs

Cross-Curricular: Art

In your journal write your response to the painting below. Do you like it? Is the scene realistic? What do you imagine is happening, and what might happen next? Respond in prose or poetry.

Henri Rousseau, *The Sleeping Gypsy*, 1897

UNIT 1

WRITING PROCESS IN ACTION

PERSONAL WRITING

In preceding lessons you've learned about—and had the chance to practice—using personal writing to keep journals, learning logs, commonplace books, and reader-response journals. Now it's time to put together what you've learned. In this lesson you're invited to write a personal narrative about how you were changed as a result of something that happened to you—a turning point in your life.

• Assignment •

Context	Your new class journal, <u>Start Me Up</u>, is to serve as a source of models and inspiration for student writing. The class has chosen the issue of change and growth as the first topic for writing. Submission of articles for publication will be voluntary.
Purpose	To write a brief account of an incident or experience that caused you to change.
Audience	Yourself and maybe some of your peers
Length	1–2 pages

The following pages can help you plan and write your narrative. Read through them, and then refer to them when necessary, but don't feel limited by them. You are in charge of your own writing process.

Prewriting

First you need to select the right incident to write about—one that is clearly an experience that caused a change in you. If one does not immediately pop into your mind, you might get an idea by looking through your journal or commonplace book. Still stuck?

- Write the heads "People" and "Places," and list memories that come to mind in each category.
- Think back to earlier school years.
- Look at old photographs, or reminisce with your family or a close friend.

When you have selected one incident for your narrative, try to recall what happened as fully as possible. Make a list of specific details about the incident. The questions on the notepad may help you.

Prewriting Questions
- *Who was involved in this incident?*
- *What happened, and where?*
- *How did I feel while it was going on?*
- *What did I learn from this experience?*
- *What might others learn from my telling about it?*

Drafting

To begin drafting your narrative, simply tell what happened, step by step. Don't worry about how it sounds or the flow of the writing. Your goal in drafting is to set down your ideas without worrying about polishing them. A straight chronological retelling—writing in the order events took place—is often best, but you may want to experiment with other arrangements. You may want to take a humorous approach or use dialogue to make your narrative lively. Remember to tell why the event was important to you.

Since this is a personal narrative, it should include details that give readers a sense of who you are. Your narrative should sound like you, even if you are writing about something that happened to you a long time ago. You will also want to give the details that bring this particular incident to life. In the passage that follows, notice how William Least Heat-Moon provides specific information and sensory details that tell how he is feeling and allow the reader to picture the scene clearly.

Drafting Tip

For more information about starting to get your ideas down on paper, see Lesson 1.1, page 11.

Literature Model

I turned up the heater to blast level, went to the back, and wrapped a blanket around the sleeping bag. I undressed fast and got into a sweatsuit, two pairs of socks, my old Navy-issue watch cap, a pair of gloves. When I cut the engine, snow already had covered the windshield. Only a quarter tank of gas. While the warmth lasted, I hurried into the bag and pulled back the curtain to watch the fulminous [related to thunder and lightning] clouds blast the mountain. That sky was bent on having a storm, and I was in for a drubbing.

William Least Heat-Moon, *Blue Highways*

Revising

Revising Tip

To give your peer reviewers some ideas about questions they might consider when responding to your personal narrative, see Lesson 1.4, page 24.

To begin revising, read over your draft to make sure that what you've written fits your purpose and audience. Then have a **writing conference**. Read your draft to a partner or small group. Use your audience's reactions and the Revising Checklist below to help you evaluate your work.

Revising Checklist
- *Does my personal narrative tell my story clearly?*
- *Does it deal with my personal change or growth?*
- *Does it show why the incident was important to me?*
- *Does a sense of "me" come through?*

Editing

Once you are satisfied with the content and style of your narrative, **proofread** it carefully for errors in grammar, usage, mechanics, and spelling. Use the questions at the right as a guide.

In addition to proofreading, use the self-evaluation list below to make sure your narrative does all the things you want it to do. When you're satisfied, make a clean copy of your narrative and proofread it once more.

Editing Checklist
- *Have I avoided sentence fragments?*
- *Have I used commas correctly in a series?*
- *Have I avoided double negatives?*
- *Are my pronoun references clear?*
- *Have I checked spellings of any words I'm unsure of?*

Self-Evaluation
Make sure your personal narrative—

- focuses on a situation that caused you to change
- orients readers with a clear narration of what happened
- uses personal frames of reference to personalize the incident
- explains why the experience was important to you
- follows standard grammar, usage, mechanics, and spelling

Proofreading

For proofreading symbols, see page 88.

Presenting

You may wish to offer your narrative for inclusion in the class journal along with those of your classmates. If you feel your sketch is too personal to share with such a wide audience, keep it with your personal journal.

Journal Writing

Reflect on your writing process experience. Answer these questions in your journal: What do you like best about your personal narrative? What was the hardest part of writing it? What did you learn in your writing conference? What new things have you learned as a writer?

William Least Heat-Moon

FROM

A Journey into America

BLUE
HIGHWAYS

*William Least Heat-Moon is the pen name of writer William Trogdon, a Native
American of Sioux ancestry. In 1978 Trogdon packed his small truck and began a journey
across rural America—to discover both his country and himself. As you read this excerpt
from his book* Blue Highways: A Journey into America, *note what you think the
author discovered about himself during his travels. Then complete the activities in
Linking Writing and Literature on page 41.*

Somewhere out there was the Colorado River perfectly hidden
in the openness. The river wasn't more than a mile away, but I
couldn't make out the slightest indication of it in the desert

stretching level and unbroken for twenty or thirty miles west, although I was only fifty miles above where it enters Grand Canyon. This side of the Colorado gorge[1] was once an important Hopi[2] trail south, and, some say, the route Hopi guides took when they first led white men to the canyon. While the arid[3] path followed the river cleft,[4] water was an inaccessible four hundred feet down. Typically, the flexible Hopi solved the desert: women buried gourds of water at strategic points on the outward journey for use on the return.

The highway made an unexpected jog toward Navajo Bridge, a melding of silvery girders and rock cliffs. Suddenly, there it was, far below in the deep and scary canyon of sides so sheer they might have been cut with a stone saw, the naturally silted[5] water turned an unnatural green (*colorado* means "reddish") by the big settling basin a few miles upriver called Glen Canyon Dam. Navajo Bridge,

Maynard Dixon, *Earth Knower*, c. 1932

1 **gorge** a steep narrow pass between great heights
2 **Hopi** (hō′ pē) a Native American group from northeastern Arizona
3 **arid** (ar′ id) dry and barren
4 **cleft** An opening or crevice
5 **silted** filled or clogged with fine-grained sediment

built in 1929 when paved roads began opening the area, is the only crossing over the Colorado between Glen Canyon and Hoover Dam several hundred river miles downstream.

West of the gorge lay verdant[6] rangeland, much of it given to a buffalo herd maintained by the Arizona Game Commission; the great beasts lifted their heads to watch me pass, their dark, wet eyes catching the late sun. To the north rose the thousand-foot butt end of the Vermillion Cliffs; the cliffs weren't truly vermillion,[7] but contrasting with the green valley in the orange afternoon light, they seemed so.

In 1776, a few months after white-stockinged men in Philadelphia had declared independence, a Spanish expedition led by missionaries Francisco Silvestre Velez de Escalante and Francisco Atanasio Dominguez, returning from an unsuccessful search for a good northern route to the California missions, wandered dispiritedly along the Vermillion Cliffs as they tried to find in the maze of the Colorado a point to cross the river chasm.[8] They looked for ten days and were forced to eat boiled cactus and two of their horses before finding a place to ford; even then, they had to chop out steps to get down and back up the four-hundred-foot perpendicular walls. My crossing, accomplished sitting down, took twenty seconds. What I saw as a remarkable sight, the Spaniards saw as a terror that nearly did them in.

Escalante's struggles gave perspective to the easy passage I'd enjoyed across six thousand miles of America. Other than weather, some bad road, and a few zealous police, my difficulties had been only those of mind. In light of what was about to happen, my guilt over easy transit proved ironic.

I went up an enormous geologic upheaval called the Kaibab Plateau; with startling swiftness, the small desert bushes changed to immense conifers as the Kaibab forest deepened: ponderosa, fir, spruce. At six thousand feet, the temperature was sixty: a drop of thirty degrees in ten miles. On the north edge of the forest, the highway made a long gliding descent off the plateau into Utah. Here lay Kane and Garfield counties, a place of multicolored rock and baroque[9] stone columns and, under it all, the largest unexploited coalfield in the country. A land certain one day to be fought over.

At dusk I considered going into the Coral Sand Dunes for the night, but I'd had enough warmth and desert for a while, so I pushed north toward Cedar Breaks in the severe and beautiful Markagunt Plateau. The cool would refresh me. Sporadic splats of

---

6 **verdant** (vʉr′ d'nt) green
7 **vermilion** (vər mil′ yən) a bright red or scarlet
8 **chasm** (kaz′ 'm) a deep crack in the earth's surface
9 **baroque** (bə rōk′) irregular in shape

Jaune Quick-To-See Smith, *Osage Orange*, 1985

rain, not enough to pay attention to, hit the windshield. I turned
onto Utah 14, the cross-mountain road to Cedar City. In the dim light
of a mountainous sky, I could just make out a large sign:

ELEVATION 10,000 FEET
ROAD MAY BE IMPASSIBLE
DURING WINTER MONTHS.

So? It was nearly May. The rain popped, then stopped, popped and
stopped. The incline became steeper and light rain fell steadily,
rolling red desert dust off the roof; I hadn't hit showers since east
Texas. It was good. The pleasant cool turned to cold, and I switched
on the heater. The headlights glared off snowbanks edging closer to
the highway as it climbed, and the rain became sleet. That's when I
began thinking I might have made a little miscalculation. I looked
for a place to turn around, but there was only narrow, twisted road.
The sleet got heavier, and the headlights were cutting only thirty feet
into it. Maybe I could drive above and out of the storm. At eight
thousand feet, the wind came up—a rough, nasty wind that bullied

me about the slick road. Lear,[10] daring the storm to "strike flat the thick rotundity[11] of the world," cries, "Blow, winds, and crack your cheeks! Rage! Blow!" And that's just what they did.

A loud, sulphurous blast of thunder rattled the little truck, then another, and one more. Never had I seen lightning or heard thunder in a snowstorm. Although there were no signs, the map showed a campground near the summit. It would be suicide to stop, and maybe the same to go on. The wind pushed on Ghost Dancing[12] so, I was afraid of getting blown over the invisible edge. Had not the falling snow taken away my vision, I might have needed a blindfold like the ones medieval travelers wore to blunt their terror of crossing the Alps. A rule of the blue road: Be careful going in search of adventure—it's ridiculously easy to find.

Then I was on the top, ten thousand feet up. UP. The wind was horrendous. Utah 14 now cut through snowbanks higher than the truck. At the junction with route 143, a sign pointed north toward Cedar Breaks campground. I relaxed. I was going to live. I puffed up at having beaten the mountain.

Two hundred yards up 143, I couldn't believe what I saw. I got out and walked to it as the raving wind whipped my pantlegs and pulled my hair on end. I couldn't believe it. There it was, the striped centerline, glowing through the sleet, disappearing under a seven-foot snowbank. Blocked.

Back to the truck. My heart dropped like a stone through new snow. There had to be a mistake. I mean, this wasn't 1776. The days of Escalante were gone. But the only mistake was my judgment. I was stopped on state 143, and 143 lay under winter ice.

I turned up the heater to blast level, went to the back, and wrapped a blanket around the sleeping bag. I undressed fast and got into a sweatsuit, two pairs of socks, my old Navy-issue watch cap, a pair of gloves. When I cut the engine, snow already had covered the windshield. Only a quarter tank of gas. While the warmth lasted, I hurried into the bag and pulled back the curtain to watch the fulminous[13] clouds blast the mountain. That sky was bent on having a storm, and I was in for a drubbing.

At any particular moment in a man's life, he can say that everything he has done and not done, that has been done and not been done to him, has brought him to that moment. If he's being installed as Chieftain or receiving a Nobel Prize, that's a fulfilling notion. But

10 **Lear** a legendary British king and the central character of a tragedy by William Shakespeare

11 **rotundity** (rō tun′ di tē) roundness or fullness

12 **Ghost Dancing** the name that the author uses for his 1975 Econoline van

13 **fulminous** (fool′ mə nəs) of or related to thunder and lighting

Pawnee, Ceremonial drum, nineteenth century

if he's in a sleeping bag at ten thousand feet in a snowstorm, parked in the middle of a highway and waiting to freeze to death, the idea can make him feel calamitously stupid.

A loud racketing of hail fell on the steel box, and the wind seemed to have hands, it shook the Ghost so relentlessly. Lightning tried to outdo thunder in scaring me. So did those things scare me?

No. Not *those* things. It was something else. I was certain of a bear attack. That's what scared me.

Lightning strikes the earth about eight million times each day and kills a hundred and fifty Americans every year. I don't know how many die from exposure[14] and hypothermia,[15] but it must be at least a comparable number. As for bears eating people who sleep inside steel trucks, I haven't been able to find that figure. It made no sense to fear a bear coming out of hibernation in such weather to attack a truck. Yet I lay a long time, waiting for the beast, shaggy and immense, to claw through the metal, its hot breath on my head, to devour me like a gumdrop and roll the van over the edge.

Perhaps fatigue or strain prevented me from worrying about the real fear; perhaps some mechanism of mind hid the true and inescapable threat. Whatever it was, it finally came to me that I was crazy. Maybe I was already freezing to death. Maybe this was the way it happened. Black Elk prays for the Grandfather Spirit to help him face the winds and walk the good road to the day of quiet. Whitman too:

> *O to be self-balanced for contingencies,*
> *To confront night, storms, hunger, ridicule, accidents,*
> *rebuffs, as the trees and animals do.*

I wondered how long I might have to stay in the Breaks before I could drive down. The cold didn't worry me much: I had insulated the rig myself and slept in it once when the windchill was thirty-six below. I figured to survive if I didn't have to stay on top too long. Why hadn't I listened to friends who advised carrying a CB?[16] The headline showed darkly: FROZEN MAN FOUND IN AVALANCHE. The whole night I slept and woke, slept and woke, while the hail fell like iron shot, and thunder slammed around, and lightning seared the ice.

14 **exposure** (ik spō zhər) being overly exposed to extreme weather conditions
15 **hypothermia** (hī′ pə thʉr′ mēə) an extremely low body temperature
16 **CB** a citizens' band radio, sometimes used for communication among cars and trucks on highways

Linking Writing and Literature

Readers Respond to the Model

What makes William Least Heat-Moon's account of his journey both personal and memorable?

Explore William Least Heat-Moon's personal writing by answering these questions. Then read what other students liked about Heat-Moon's autobiographical account.

1. What are some of the most vivid personal details that the author includes in this personal account?

2. How does the author interweave information about past travelers with the story of his own journey? What impact does this have on the reader?

3. What is the effect of the author's precise description of the landscape through which he travels?

4. What do you think the author discovers about himself during this experience? Explain.

This selection was about a man caught in a severe snowstorm while on a dangerous mountain road. The part I remember most clearly was when the man had to stop his truck during the storm. The cliff-hanging description of how he lived through the night kept my attention. It created a feeling of waiting and suspense.

The narrator's point of view was first person. I believe Mr. Heat-Moon chose it to make the story very personal and believable. It helped bring the reality of his situation to life.

Rachel Hansen

In this selection from *Blue Highways,* William Least Heat-Moon created a suspenseful mood by detailing the possible danger that was awaiting him. This suspense kept me interested in the story; I wanted to read on and find out what happened next.

Claire Monty

Unit 1 Review

Reflecting on the Unit

Summarize what you learned in this unit by answering the following questions.

- What are the important functions of a personal journal in your development as an individual and as a writer?

- How can a learning log help you become actively involved in your school work?

- What is a commonplace book and what uses does it serve?

- How can a reader-response journal help in both your reading and your writing?

Adding to Your Portfolio

Choose a selection for your portfolio.
Look over the personal writing you have done in this unit. Select a completed piece of writing to put into your portfolio. The piece you choose should show one or both of the following:

- reactions to something you have seen, experienced, read, or studied
- your own personal thoughts and feelings

Reflect on your choice.
Attach a note to the piece you chose, explaining briefly why you chose it and what you learned from writing it.

Set goals.
How can you improve your writing? What skill will you focus on the next time you write?

Writing Across the Curriculum

Make a science connection.
Choose a science concept that interests you, and write a learning log entry about it. Summarize what you already know about the subject. Identify aspects of the concept that you want to examine further. Discuss any controversial ideas that relate to the concept. Make a list of questions you have that relate to the concept. Use pictures, charts, or diagrams as part of your entry.

The Writing Process

The Writing Process in the Real World

Trahant Investigates Nuclear Transport

FOCUS: Investigative reporters, like detectives, spend countless hours unearthing the truth. Then they use fair and accurate writing to present their findings.

Investigative reporter Mark Trahant

I t was late afternoon near Tucumcari, New Mexico, when investigative reporter Mark Trahant spotted the convoy barreling down I-40. Four white utility vehicles with darkened windows flanked a huge, unmarked eighteen-wheeler.

Trahant hit the accelerator, gradually pulled alongside the huge tractor trailer, and clocked it speeding at 72 miles per hour—well over the limit. In Trahant's opinion the truck was designed to carry missiles. "It might have been carrying a load of freight that could vaporize a good chunk of the surrounding land," he observed.

A few weeks earlier, Trahant, now editor of *Navaho Nation,* had persuaded his editor at the *Arizona Republic* to let him look into the transport of radioactive materials. The idea grew out of his interest in reporting on a New Mexico nuclear waste project—a plan to bury millions of cubic feet of plutonium waste in the desert near Carlsbad.

As Trahant checked the condition of roads leading to the waste site, he met townspeople who said they saw nuclear transport trucks all the time. That information made Trahant wonder just how many nuclear loads regularly traveled

America's interstates, and he called half a dozen sources to find out. The facts that emerged during his investigation surprised Trahant: *Almost 3 million loads of nuclear freight crisscross U.S. highways each year.*

At that point Trahant asked the Department of Energy (DOE) if he could ride in one of their SSTs—safe-secure trailers—designed to haul nuclear warheads, radioactive fuel rods, and other nuclear cargo. The DOE sidestepped his request.

The DOE's reluctance to cooperate and Trahant's well-focused idea—the safety of nuclear transport—hooked Trahant's editor on the story. Usually reporters have a harder sell. They have to summarize their story ideas and submit proposed budgets detailing the time and money needed to do their investigations. In this case, though, Trahant's editor agreed that everyone needed to learn about this situation, and he gave Trahant the go-ahead.

> *"I found out that in some parts of the country you could see nuclear transport trucks everywhere—that the truck parked next to you at [the fast food stop] might be carrying nuclear bombs. I figured people might not know that."*
>
> —Mark Trahant

Sleuthing for evidence— it's not a glamorous adventure but a demanding search for the facts.

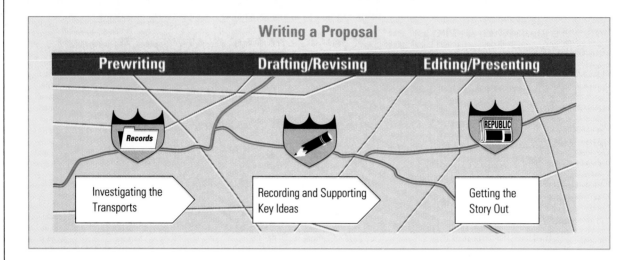

Writing a Proposal

Prewriting	Drafting/Revising	Editing/Presenting

Investigating the Transports

Recording and Supporting Key Ideas

Getting the Story Out

Prewriting

INVESTIGATING THE TRANSPORTS

Once Trahant got the go-ahead, he launched the "vacuum cleaner stage" in which he dug up everything he could find. "Successful investigative reporters are, above all, very good reporters," Trahant said. "They are curious. They want to see how a story affects people—the population of a city or county, as well as one person." They also have to remain impartial and doggedly seek out every side of the story. "Investigative reporters can't be seen as advocates of any side," he stressed.

For four weeks, ten to eighteen hours a day, Trahant traveled, talked, listened, and read. He scoured four years' worth of transportation records and safety complaints in Denver, El Paso, and Phoenix federal courts. He conducted more than fifty interviews with people on all sides of the issue—the DOE, experts on nuclear transport safety, scientists, peace activists, terrorism experts, people who live on the main routes. He tried, unsuccessfully, to talk to people in Texas at a major weapons manufacturing plant, which sends out twenty truck convoys a week.

After a month of research, Trahant had four reporter's notebooks full of notes and one-and-a-half file drawers of photocopied documents. At that point, he met with his editor, explained where the story was going, and asked for a full page of space in the paper—a tough thing to get. "You're in competition with other reporters and stories," Trahant explained. In this case, though, Trahant's editor thought the story warranted the full page and agreed to give Trahant 100 inches of copy space, enough for about 5,600 words.

Drafting/Revising

RECORDING AND SUPPORTING KEY IDEAS

Trahant approached the job of drafting the story with a reporter's strategy—write it fast the first time, then rewrite. "Journalism is literature in a hurry," he said.

To open the piece, Mark described the SST he clocked speeding at 72 miles an hour, an anecdote he had marked "lead" in his notebook. Then he drafted the body of the story, keeping in mind three or four key ideas that presented all sides of the story—and the need to interest readers. "Good writing is surprising [to the reader]," Trahant said. "It tells the reader something unusual, not expected. It's also concrete. It puts the reader there with examples of color, how something looked or sounded."

Trahant closed with a strong, positive quote, despite knowing that sometimes stories are cut from the end. "Most editors realize that a good story has a beginning, a middle, and an end," he said.

After getting the key ideas down, Trahant went back and inserted supporting details and quotations. Then he read the story aloud, checking for good rhythm.

Reporter Mark Trahant defines journalism as "literature in a hurry."

By the time a story reaches the morning breakfast table, an investigative reporter is following fresh leads for the next story and beginning the writing process again.

Editing/Presenting

GETTING THE STORY OUT

Before Trahant's story went to press, three editors reviewed it for good writing, complete and fair coverage, and correct style and grammar. Most papers ask an attorney to review very touchy stories before publication to be sure the paper won't be sued, but Trahant's piece went to press without legal review. "There was no real bad guy on this story," Trahant explained. His research pointed out two areas of public concern: The fact that about 20 percent of all SSTs were in poor mechanical condition and that the potential for accidents was growing as the number of trucks on the roads increased.

What happened as a result of Trahant's published article? "I always hope my work will result in improvements, but I know one story won't change much," he said. "My job is to dig up the information and present it in an interesting way. I leave change to the public."

Responding to the Case Study

1. Discussion

Discuss these questions about Mark Trahant's investigative writing.

- How did Trahant research the information for his investigative article?
- What was his purpose in writing the article?
- What reporter's strategies did Trahant use to draft his story?
- What happened to Trahant's article before it went to press?

2. Investigative Reporting

Write a review of an investigative report.

Watch an investigative report on a television program such as *60 Minutes* or *20/20.* Then write a review of the presentation. Tell the purpose of the report and the types of evidence and documentation the reporter(s) used to present the case. Evaluate the report's conclusions for their objectivity and fairness.

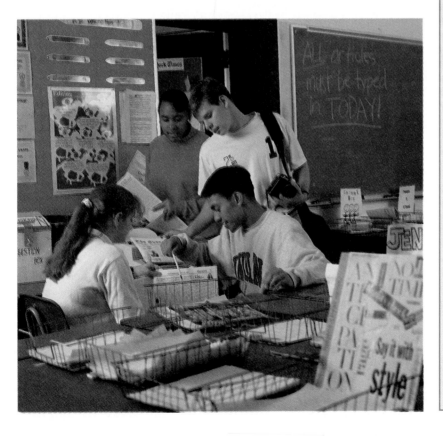

Grammar Link

Make verbs agree with nouns of amount.

The verb that follows a noun of amount is plural if that noun refers to many individual units: *Almost 3 million **loads** of nuclear freight **crisscross** U.S. highways each year.* The verb is singular if the noun refers to one single unit: *Three million **loads** is a lot.*

Complete each sentence below by writing the correct form of the verb in parentheses.

1. Three-fourths of Trahant's article (focuses, focus) on nuclear transports.
2. One-and-a-half file drawers (was, were) full of photocopied documents.
3. Four weeks (is, are) a long time to spend gathering evidence.
4. The 100 inches of copy space (was, were) more than most articles get.
5. Twenty percent of all SSTs (was, were) in poor mechanical condition.

See Lesson 16.4, pages 580–581.

The Writing Process
Stages of the Writing Process

The five stages of the writing process allow you to explore, investigate, and write about any topic. In the following pages you will follow the investigation and writing process of a high school student, Shella Calamba.

The Five Writing Process Stages

Writing is a process with different stages. Professional and student writers all follow processes made up of combinations of the stages shown below.

The Writing Process

Prewriting ⟷ Drafting ⟷ Revising ⟷ Editing → Presenting

Prewriting The first stage, called prewriting, is the idea stage. By probing your thoughts, you can discover a topic and a purpose for writing about it. This is the stage in which information or details are gathered and the paper is planned. Shella Calamba began investigating her family's history by using a prewriting technique called freewriting.

During the freewriting stage Calamba's ideas are random and free flowing, but they lead to a writing topic.

> *Exploring my family's history. Chinese and Spanish ancestors. Great-grandparents half Chinese. Great-grandfather Filipino. Great-grandmother very religious according to my mother. My mother was named after my great-grandmother, Josefa Parcarey. My great-grandfather was the mayor of the town. Both my grandparents were farmers. I could write about my mother's genealogy.*

Drafting Drafting is writing your ideas down in related sentences and paragraphs. The goal during drafting is to let your writing flow without worrying about grammar or mechanics. Notice how Calamba has combined related ideas in a paragraph.

> It is far from a coincidence that my mother was named after my great-grandmother, Josefa. My mother spent her early childhood years under my great-grandmother's watchful, firm eye. Later, she spent her teenage years in Manila, where she studied in high school and college.

How does Calamba give structure to her ideas in the drafting stage?

Revising Revision means reading your draft closely, reminding yourself of your purpose, and reworking and clarifying your ideas, as Calamba did here.

> My great-grandfather was the mayor of a Philippine province. My great-grandmother, Josefa, a religious woman, taught my mother Latin prayers. They ~~would~~ *used to* pray together *every afternoon at precisely five*.
>
> My grandparents raised eight children. Two aunts ~~were~~ *became* teachers, and one ~~has~~ *owns* a store. My mother is a pharmacist in Chicago. One uncle is ~~in business~~ *a restaurant owner*, and one is a nurse in Australia.

In revising this passage, what details has Calamba added? What effect do they have? What other changes did Calamba make?

Journal Writing

In your journal analyze your own writing process. Which of these first three stages do you find easy? What are your stumbling blocks? Do you always move straight forward, or do you sometimes return to a previous stage?

Editing Editing is the stage for looking closely at each paragraph, each sentence, and each word. Do your sentences flow smoothly? Are they grammatically correct? Are your spelling and punctuation correct? Notice how Calamba edited the paragraph below.

In editing this paragraph, Calamba corrected spelling and punctuation.

> My mother came here to the ~~U.S.~~ *United States* and became a pharmacist. All seven of her sisters and brothers have raised ~~familys~~ *families* of their own. For this reason, I have many cousins. I've never had to live in the ~~isalated~~ *isolated* world of the proverbial only child.

Presenting Sometimes presenting, or sharing your writing with a reader, simply means handing it in to your teacher. At other times you want your thoughts and ideas to go far beyond the teacher's desk. For example, Calamba might decide to submit her essay to her high school's prose and poetry magazine.

Move Among the Stages

Good writers move back and forth among stages in the writing process. For example, you might reach the revising stage and notice that one section needs more explanation. You could return to a prewriting task, such as freewriting, to explore those ideas in greater detail.

When you write, your mind is in a state of motion. This perpetual motion is absolutely necessary; after all, you are involved in an investigation to discover your thoughts.

Recursive Writing Process

Prewriting → Drafting → Revising → Editing → Presenting

Write a Personal Response

Follow the five stages of the writing process as you write about your response to the painting below. What does the painting, its mood, or the people remind you of?

- Freewrite to explore associations.
- Focus on a single aspect of your response as you begin to draft.
- Revise to clarify your ideas.
- Check grammar, spelling, and punctuation as you edit.
- Present your writing by reading it aloud to the class.

PURPOSE To use the stages of the writing process
AUDIENCE Your classmates
LENGTH 1-2 paragraphs

Cross-Curricular: Music

Use the writing process to draft a paragraph about a song, music video, or concert of your choice. Begin by identifying your topic and your purpose for writing about it.

Grammar Link

When you edit, correct run-on sentences.

Imagine that you are in the editing stage of the writing process. Rewrite the run-on sentences below.

1. Writing is a journey that is seldom smooth often it is an exploration of your thoughts and ideas.
2. There are five stages in the writing process prewriting is the first.
3. During the freewriting stage ideas are random but they can lead to a writing topic.
4. A good writer moves back and forth among stages for example while revising, a writer may choose to add details.
5. Presenting is the final stage you share your writing with a reader.

See Lesson 13.10, pages 521–523.

Edward Hopper, *Nighthawks*, 1942

The Writing Process
Prewriting: Finding a Writing Topic

Writers may use various techniques to zero in on a topic. When asked to write a feature story on Native Americans in southern California, journalist Wayne Swanson began by jotting down some ideas. Compare his freewriting with the first part of his article to see how he used his notes.

Sad truth, little left of Native American culture—time, conquest, conversion, development have buried. But long history, and if know where to look, possible to catch a glimpse of world before white people came.

So. I could focus on glimpses of their lost heritage, baskets and cemetery plots at missions, but also evidence of power that eradicated most of their history. Perhaps draw a picture of life along San Luis Rey valley. Where were their settlements? What did they do?

Through his freewriting, Swanson focused on a topic—glimpses of a lost Native American heritage.

How did the comments in the prewriting notes about drawing a picture lead to this introduction?

Literature Model

Imagine a time when the San Luis Rey River ran freely, even in dry years. Imagine irrigated fields of corn and grain thriving in its valleys. Imagine small, self-sufficient villages up along the valley slopes, scattered all the way from the ocean to Mt. Palomar and beyond.

In other words, imagine San Diego County before European adventurers claimed it for their own. As development moves relentlessly up the valley, the evidence of this earlier era becomes ever harder to find. Nevertheless, glimpses remain. They remain in the landscape and in the efforts of Native Americans and others to hold on to what is left.

Wayne Swanson, "Exploring Proud Past of Indians," *Los Angeles Times*

Discover Ideas

Like Wayne Swanson, you have countless ideas hidden in your mind, waiting to be uncovered. How can you get at them? There are several techniques you can use.

Freewriting Freewriting consists of writing nonstop for a set time, usually only five or ten minutes. The idea is to keep pace with your thoughts, getting them on paper before they vanish. Freewriting can start anywhere and go anywhere. Sometimes it begins with an assignment. Sometimes it grows out of a class discussion —for example, a biology class discussion on using animals in medical research. Read Shella Calamba's freewriting to see what ideas she uncovered as she thought about this topic.

Student Model

*T*he role of animals in medical research is an interesting topic. But what aspect? Which animals are used and why? Maybe pick one species and describe an experiment done on it. I can include safety precautions involved in using animals. I could write about rights and laws that protect animals. Controversy surrounding animals and research. I could investigate this. I could give my own opinions on the vital role of animals in research.

Shella Calamba, Lincoln Park High School, Chicago, Illinois

Freewriting Tips

1. Let your thoughts flow—ideas, memories, anything that comes to mind.
2. Don't edit or judge your thoughts; just write them down. You can evaluate them later.
3. Don't worry about spelling, punctuation, grammar, or even sense; just keep writing.
4. If you stop, rewrite your last sentence, or write "I'm stuck" until a new idea pops up.

Journal Writing

In your journal, spend five minutes freewriting about whatever comes to mind. Then make a list of the different ideas you came up with.

Brainstorming You freewrite on your own, but like the students shown below, you can brainstorm ideas with others. The student at the right is tossing out a question, and the others will answer it. These ideas will lead to new ideas as each student's comment starts the others thinking. The result of this interplay of ideas is a list like the one below. You should allow a set amount of time, ten to fifteen minutes, for each brainstorming session.

Brainstorming Tips
1. Choose someone to list ideas as they are called out.
2. Start with a topic (such as inventions) or a question.
3. Encourage everyone to join in freely.
4. Accept all ideas; do not evaluate them now.
5. Follow each idea as far as it goes.

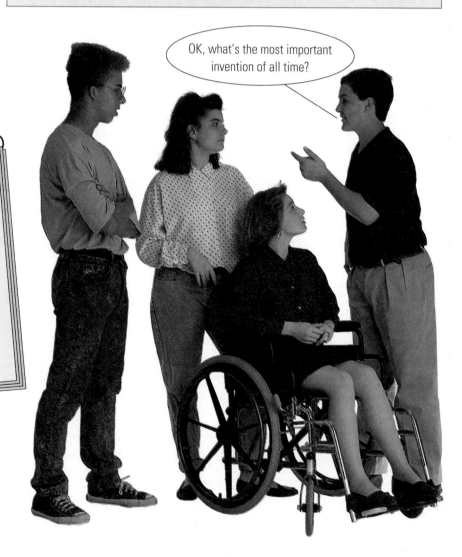

Inventions
1. Most important inventions:
   wheel, internal-combustion
   engine, movable type,
   electricity, penicillin,
   telephone
2. Unsuccessful inventions
3. How inventions happen
4. Inventions still needed

OK, what's the most important invention of all time?

Clustering Brainstorming is often a group activity, but you can also brainstorm by yourself. One way to focus your brainstorming is by clustering. Start by circling a word or phrase. Surround it with related ideas, and connect each of those ideas with others, creating groups, or clusters, of ideas. The following cluster started with one word, *inventions*.

Clustering Tips
1. Start with a key word or phrase circled in the center of your paper.
2. Brainstorm to discover related ideas; circle each one, and connect it to the central idea.
3. Branch out with new ideas that refine existing ideas by adding details.
4. Review your chart, looking for ideas or clusters of ideas that interest you.

Journal Writing

Some writers prefer to work alone, while others like working in groups. Write in your journal about the pros and cons of group activities like brainstorming and individual efforts like freewriting and clustering. Which approach do you think works better for you? Why?

Narrow Your Focus

Prewriting techniques—freewriting, brainstorming, clustering—help you discover your thoughts and ideas, but they have another value, too. They can help you narrow a topic so that you can use it for a short piece of writing, even a single paragraph.

Return to Freewriting Looping is one way to narrow your topic. Start by reading some of your freewriting, and choose one idea you touched upon that interests you. Freewrite about that idea for another five minutes. Review that freewriting, choose an idea from it, and try to focus it further in another freewriting session. Repeat the process two or three times. As shown below, your idea will be narrower and more focused with each "loop" until you discover a topic for writing.

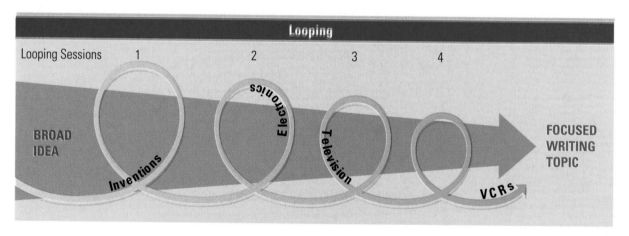

Return to Clustering Writing additional clusters is another way to narrow your topic. Look at the clustering you did to search for ideas, and choose an idea that seems promising—for example, "How inventions happen" from the cluster on page 57. Write it at the center of a new page, and start clustering again.

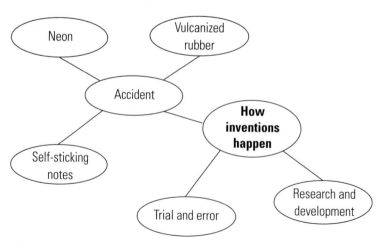

Write to Find a Topic

As you study this unit, you will be writing an investigative report about some subject that interests you. Use the prewriting methods discussed in this lesson to choose two or three possible topics for your report.

- Freewrite or use other sources to collect ideas.
- Cluster or brainstorm to generate related ideas.
- Use looping and clustering to narrow your focus.

PURPOSE To select writing topics
AUDIENCE Yourself
LENGTH 1–2 pages

Edna Jackson, *Kaaswoot*, 1983

Cooperative Learning

In a small group, study the self-portrait on this page. The artist is a Tlingit, a Native American of Alaska, whose mother's ancestors were Europeans. Brainstorm ideas about how the portrait reflects Jackson's dual heritage. Have each group member use the ideas generated by the group to write a paragraph about the painting. Compare and discuss the writings.

Grammar Link

Capitalize proper nouns.

In his news feature, Wayne Johnson capitalized the terms *Native Americans* and *San Luis Rey River* because they are proper nouns.

Rewrite the following sentences, adding or dropping capital letters as necessary.

1. The aztec built majestic Temples and Palaces in Central Mexico.
2. They constructed the great City of Tenochtitlán on a swampy Island in lake Texcoco.
3. By the the Fifteenth Century, this city was one of the largest in the World.
4. Only paris, Venice, naples, and milan had more people.
5. Aztec Culture is a popular theme in murals created by modern-day mexican artist diego rivera.

See Lesson 20.2, pages 677–683.

The Writing Process
Prewriting: Identifying Purpose and Audience

Knowing your purpose and audience will help determine your main idea, or what you want a piece of writing to say. Mike had different purposes and audiences in mind as he wrote the postcards below.

Decide on Your Purpose

Deciding on a purpose will determine what you include in your writing. To clarify your purpose, answer these questions:

1. Why do I want to write about this topic?
2. Is my purpose to describe? Inform? Narrate? Amuse? Persuade?
3. Will I have more than one purpose in this piece of writing?

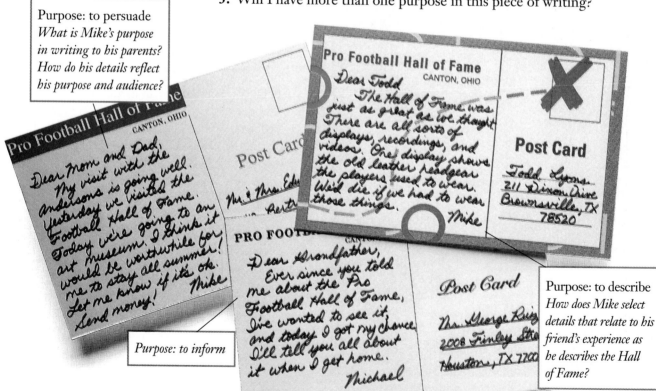

Purpose: to persuade
What is Mike's purpose in writing to his parents? How do his details reflect his purpose and audience?

Purpose: to inform

Purpose: to describe
How does Mike select details that relate to his friend's experience as he describes the Hall of Fame?

Identify Your Reader

Your audience is anyone who will be reading your writing. Sometimes you write just for yourself. Most often, however, you write to share information with others. The audience may include a few friends or family members, your classmates, or the population at large.

The writers of both excerpts below wrote with a similar purpose, to inform. Note that each had a different audience in mind.

Literature Model

[The sports hero] exhibits that complete skill to which the amateur vainly aspires. Instead of being looked upon as a servile and ignoble being, because of the very perfection of his physical efforts, as the Athenians in Socrates' time looked upon the professional athletes and dancers, this new hero represents the summit of the amateur's effort.

Lewis Mumford, *Technics and Civilization*

What words and details does Mumford use to appeal to his scholarly, academic audience?

Literature Model

Pro football players are adults who fly through the air in plastic hats and smash each other for a living. I now know a bunch of them, and I think they are good folks.

Roy Blount, Jr., *About Three Bricks Shy of a Load*

The writer's informal tone and choice of details appeal to a general-interest audience.

As you write, consider these questions about your audience:

1. Who will my audience be? What do I want to say to them?
2. What do my readers already know about my topic?
3. What types of information will interest my audience?

Journal Writing

Reread one sample of your recent writing and jot down your thoughts about these questions: How could I use the same ideas to write for a different purpose? How could I make this appeal to a different audience?

Write Your Main Idea Statement

With a topic, a purpose, and an audience in mind, you're almost ready to write. In the next step ask yourself, What's the big idea? Answer the question in one sentence. That sentence will be your main idea statement.

No matter how big or small your writing project is—a single paragraph or a twenty-page research paper—you should write a main idea statement. It will tell what you want your entire piece to say and will help you choose appropriate details for your topic. Later, as you draft your piece, it will keep your writing on track. As the chart below indicates, the main idea statement is central to any writing; all other ideas depend on it.

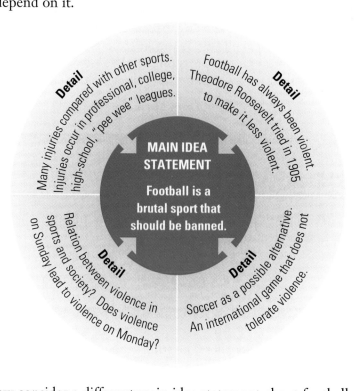

Now consider a different main idea statement about football: *Football is a game built on teamwork, discipline, and strategy.* To what audience might this topic appeal? What kinds of details could you use to develop the main idea?

Ask yourself the following questions as you develop your main idea statement for any piece of writing:

1. What point do I want to make?
2. Will my audience be interested in the idea?
3. Do I need to narrow my topic further?

2.3 Writing Activities

Identify Purpose and Audience

Before you make the final choice of topic for your investigative report, decide who you would like your audience to be and what your purpose will be. Look at your topic ideas. Ask yourself these questions.

- Will I write for my classmates, my family, a group or club, the school or town newspaper?
- What is my purpose—To point out a problem? Encourage people to take some action? Provide background information?

PURPOSE To identify audience and purpose; to select a topic

AUDIENCE Yourself

LENGTH 1–2 pages

Cooperative Learning

In groups of three or four, brainstorm ideas for presenting a suggestion for a change or improvement, and then choose one about which you could write. Discuss how your writing might vary with different audiences. For example, you would approach a good friend one way and the CEO of a major corporation another. Some possible audiences to consider in your discussion include the following: the principal, your parents, the mayor, the owner of a restaurant, the President of the United States, a boyfriend or girlfriend, or the manager of a large department store. Your group may also want to discuss other audiences. Work as a group to prepare two or three brief samples of how your writing would vary with the audience.

Grammar Link

Tailor your writing style to your audience.

For example, when you write for a young audience, you should use simple sentences and easy-to-understand vocabulary.

Rewrite the following sentences into simple sentences. Change wording as necessary.

1. Despite the fact that writing can be complex and time-consuming, it is frequently quite enjoyable.
2. Acquaintances who no longer live in the area savor receiving letters from me.
3. Now and again I take advantage of e-mail, which is extraordinarily fast, to communicate with my friends.
4. My older sibling has created a screen-play that is being filmed in San Antonio, Texas.
5. His script focuses mainly on Davy Crockett, who was an adventurer, a skilled rifleman, and a folk hero.

See Lesson 13.3, pages 507–508.

The Writing Process
Prewriting: Exploring a Topic

After you've identified a writing topic, you can explore it further by listing and organizing details, asking questions, and doing research.

Observe Closely

One good starting point for exploring a topic is simply to observe closely and list the details you see. What do you observe in this photo of 1960s students that reflects the social unrest of the time? What details can you list?

The next step is to arrange the items on your list into categories. For example, the details you listed about the photograph might fit into broad categories such as clothes, hairstyles, body language, and attitudes. The categories you choose depend on the details you observe and your writing goal. If you were going to describe a place—say, the campus where these students attended school—you might arrange your details according to the five senses, what you smell, hear, see, taste, and touch.

Ask Questions

Asking questions, another way of exploring a topic, is central to any investigation. Questions help you get at the facts of the matter. They also help you see your topic in new ways and probe its meaning for you. You may want to jot down questions about your topic in a notebook or journal. Notice the three kinds of questions listed below.

Questions for Exploring a Topic

Factual

1. What did 1960s young students wear? Did they all dress alike?
2. What music did they listen to? What books and magazines did they read?
3. What events and causes were important to them, and why?
4. How were they similar to kids today? How were they different?

Creative

1. How do today's styles in clothing and music reflect the 1960s?
2. Would I feel at home in the 1960s? Why or why not?
3. What if one of the kids in the photo were my parent?
4. What kind of conversation might I have with a student from the 1960s? What would we ask each other?

Personal

1. Why do I want to know about 1960s students?
2. What can I learn from them? Could they have learned from me?
3. What causes did 1960s kids support? Were their causes similar to mine?
4. What about their dreams?

Journal Writing

Observe something in the room around you, and record the details. Use one or more of the techniques explained in this lesson to find out as much as possible about the essential qualities of your subject.

Search Out Information

Outside sources of reliable information are important when you explore a topic. These sources include encyclopedias, books, articles, and a wide range of formal and informal sources. Are there photographs, filmstrips, records, videos, TV programs, interviews, field trips, or other resources that would give you information about your topic? The more creative you are in searching out information, the more likely you are to find full and satisfactory answers to the questions about your topic.

Create an Idea Tree

As you gather your information, you may begin to wonder how it all fits together. Creating an idea tree can help you analyze your topic visually. An idea tree like the one below can often make the relationships among the parts of your topic stand out and may even show you a plan for organizing your writing.

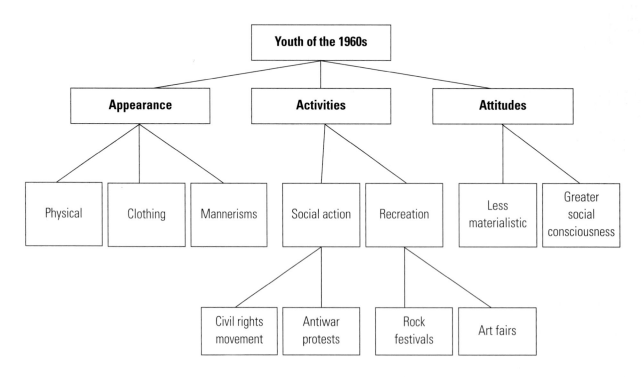

Make a Plan for Writing

Look at the topic you chose for your investigative report, and begin to plan your writing. No matter what kind of writing you do or who your audience is, you can follow these three steps.

- Identify your main idea.
- List your main points, questions, details, or incidents.
- Arrange them in an order that suits your purpose.

PURPOSE To plan your writing
AUDIENCE Yourself
LENGTH 1-2 pages

Cross-Curricular: Art

Study the painting on this page. What can you tell about the people pictured? How do you think the artist felt about these people? Write a list of questions you would like to answer by consulting an outside source for information about the artist, the place in which he lived, or the time period of the painting.

Vincent van Gogh, *The Potato Eaters*, 1885

The Writing Process
Prewriting: Interviewing

Interviewing someone is often the best way to get information on a topic. Successful interviews begin with carefully thought-out and organized questions.

Go Straight to the Source

An interview is a focused, structured encounter for which the interviewer has a topic and purpose firmly in mind. Interviewing is a vital part of prewriting for many writing projects, and the firsthand information you collect will add liveliness to your writing.

Journalist Wayne Swanson researched the Native American heritage of southern California for a newspaper feature story. His investigation took him to an archaeologist who is an expert on the subject. Here are some of the questions Swanson asked, along with their answers.

Q. How did you get involved in studying the Native Americans of southern California?

A. When I was in college, I went on an archaeological dig outside San Diego. When we discovered some artifacts, I felt an immediate link with the people. I wanted to learn more about them.

This question shows that Swanson has already done some research on his topic. But he wants to know more.

Q. Why has so little been written about them?

A. They did not fit the popular image of warriors on horseback. They had few confrontations with white people. Instead, they had a stable, self-sufficient culture.

Q. What is notable about these early Native Americans?

A. They are renowned for basketry and pottery making. They also had a remarkable knowledge of plants and pharmacology.

Ask Questions and Take Notes

As Swanson's interview shows, the success of an interview depends on asking good questions. Keep these points in mind when you prepare your interview questions:

1. Ask questions that require more than *yes* or *no* answers.
2. Ask questions that are clearly worded and easily understood.
3. Ask questions that relate directly to your topic and purpose.

Do Background Research Before an interview you should do preliminary research about the person and the topic. Informed questions will get you informative answers. What do the questions below tell you about the interviewer's preparation?

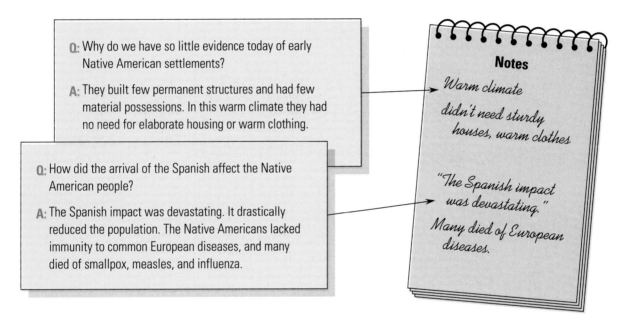

Q: Why do we have so little evidence today of early Native American settlements?

A: They built few permanent structures and had few material possessions. In this warm climate they had no need for elaborate housing or warm clothing.

Q: How did the arrival of the Spanish affect the Native American people?

A: The Spanish impact was devastating. It drastically reduced the population. The Native Americans lacked immunity to common European diseases, and many died of smallpox, measles, and influenza.

Notes

Warm climate didn't need sturdy houses, warm clothes

"The Spanish impact was devastating." Many died of European diseases.

Don't Write Every Word You want to capture your subject's ideas, but you don't have to become a human tape recorder. Listen carefully, and write down words and phrases that summarize the ideas. When the person makes a point in a way that stands out, write the exact words and enclose them in quotation marks. Even if you use a tape recorder, note taking can help you organize and summarize the information.

Journal Writing

Think about an interview you've read in a newspaper or magazine or watched on television. What questions helped to make the interview effective? List them.

Ask On-the-Spot Questions Some of the best questions can't be planned in advance. Listen closely to the subject's answers and be aware of opportunities to ask follow-up questions. Notice in the graphic below the insight that is lost when the interviewer plows ahead with a prepared question instead of considering a follow-up question.

Prepared question: What is the state of the Native American heritage today?

A. Native American language and customs are lost with each generation. But the culture is resilient.

 Not This

Next prepared question: How many Native Americans live in southern California now?

A. Many. Ten thousand in San Diego County alone.

 But This

 ?

Follow-up question: What do you mean by "resilient"?

A. The Native American culture never dies. It just reinvents itself.

 ?

Another follow-up question

Follow These Steps The following chart can help you plan and carry out an effective interview.

Set It Up
- Request an interview, explain your purpose, and make an appointment.
- Do background research about the person and the topic.
- Write a list of focused questions.
- Ask permission to tape the interview.

Listen More, Say Less
- Be polite, friendly, and businesslike.
- Listen well, and try not to interrupt. Let the person explain fully.
- Ask appropriate follow-up questions.
- In taking notes, summarize the main ideas, and quote well-stated remarks.

Get It All Down
- Listen to your tape. Review your notes. Then freewrite about your topic.
- If some information is unclear, check back with the person for clarification.
- Send the person a copy of your finished writing.

2.5 Writing Activities

Interview to Gather Information

Plan and conduct an interview to gather information for a written piece. If possible, interview someone who can tell you about the topic of your investigative report. If you cannot do that, plan a practice interview on some other topic of your choice. After the interview, summarize your findings.

- Set up an interview, explaining your purpose.
- Do background research about the person and topic.
- Use prepared and follow-up questions as appropriate.
- Accurately record main points and quotations.

PURPOSE   To plan and carry out an interview
AUDIENCE   Yourself
LENGTH   1–2 pages

COMPUTER OPTION

You might want to write up your interview as a script or prepare a dialogue for a mock interview to perform in front of the class. Use a word processing program to put your questions and answers in a script format—all the text indented after the name of the person speaking. You can make lines easy to distinguish by making one person's dialogue italic or bold or some other type style. Such visual distinctions make it easy to keep your place on the page.

Grammar Link

Enclose direct quotations in quotation marks.

When you take notes during an interview, enclose the subject's own exact words in quotation marks.

Rewrite any incorrect sentences below, adding quotation marks where they are needed.

1. In a recent interview, a telecommunications executive made this statement: The bottom line is that the information superhighway is going to change the way we live.
2. She added that the superhighway will dramatically affect the way we work and play.
3. The executive then went on to enumerate how the superhighway would transform the workplace.
4. What do you think will be the most significant change in the next five years? asked the interviewer.
5. In education, it will be long-distance learning, he answered, and in business, limitless opportunities for entrepreneurs.

See Lesson 21.9, pages 717–718.

The Writing Process
Drafting: Writing a Paragraph

In the drafting stage, you write down your ideas in sentences and paragraphs. Each paragraph should have a topic or main idea sentence that is supported by details.

A paragraph is a group of related sentences that work together to develop one main idea. Notice how William Mathers states the main idea in each paragraph in the model below.

Literature Model

The first sentence introduces the main idea: the author finds a small metal object. The supporting sentences describe it in detail.

The first sentence makes an observation about the nature of some items that were found. How do the following sentences support the first?

*A*nd then I catch a glimpse of metal—a small, luminous object poking from the sand. Probing carefully, I uncover a three-inch-wide fragment of hand-tooled gold plate. I am captivated by the image on the fragment: A woman in a swirling gown cradles a vase of flowers. Her left hand holds a cluster of roses. A small dog springs up at her feet. Floral designs embellish the fragment's border. . . .

Some items were touchingly personal. Along the edges of a small gold comb I made out "años 1618" inscribed in appliquéd gold dots. An abbreviated name, "doña catal d gusma" (short for Doña Catalina de Guzmán) was also visible. Later research revealed that she was a widow residing in Manila in 1634. Had she been aboard the stricken vessel? What was her ultimate fate? No one knows.

William M. Mathers, *"Nuestra Señora de la Concepción"*

The Topic Sentence

In many paragraphs the main idea is stated in a topic sentence, and then all the details in the paragraph develop that idea. The wheel illustrates the vital role of a topic sentence in controlling the paragraph. All the details must not only be on the same topic, but must also help support the idea in the topic sentence.

In the model paragraphs on the opposite page, the topic sentence comes at the beginning of each. Sometimes, though, the topic sentence comes at the end or in the middle. Wherever it is, it should tell two things: what your topic is and what your paragraph will say about it. Notice how Shella Calamba used a topic sentence to keep this paragraph on track.

Student Model

*I*n investigating my mother's family history, I think I've discovered the origin of many of my own traits. My grandfather, who enjoyed listening to music as loud as any teen-ager today, willed me his love of music. My grandmother taught me to be responsible and open-minded. Because two of my aunts were teachers, I learned to value education. I inherited my dark, sarcastic sense of humor from one of my uncles. He would play bizarre practical jokes, and of many I was the victim. My interest in history and politics came from my great-grandfather, once the mayor of a small Philippine province. Finally, I credit my mother with teaching me to be independent, strong-minded, and determined in going after whatever goals I set.

Shella Calamba, Lincoln Park High School, Chicago, Illinois

The topic sentence states the main idea, which Calamba has supported with details—in this case, specific examples.

Journal Writing

Take a piece of your recent writing, and examine some of your topic sentences. Experiment with ways you could make your topic sentences better.

Include Supporting Details

The details you include in your supporting sentences should prove, clarify, or expand on your main idea. The types of details that you decide to use will vary, but they will generally fall into the categories shown in the following chart.

Kinds of Supporting Details	
Concrete details	The *Mayflower*'s sails rustled, and the masts creaked in the breeze.
Examples	The heavy storm caused one more unhappy delay in the *Mayflower*'s departure.
Incidents	Five months after the Pilgrims landed, the *Mayflower* sailed for home.
Facts or statistics	A Common House served as a townhouse, arsenal, and meetinghouse.
Reasons	The Pilgrims looked for a land where they could live and worship freely.

In some paragraphs all the supporting details are the same type, as in the student model on page 73. More frequently, a paragraph will contain two or more types of details, all working to support the main idea. In a family memoir, Bette Bao Lord used concrete details and reasons to develop a paragraph about her grandfather's grave site in China. How do the two kinds of details work together to create a sense of the present and the forever, rather than a sense of the past and time?

Literature Model

Concrete details describe the grave site.

What kind of details explain why the grave site is important to the family?

Grandfather sleeps in the earth near Suzhou. He has mountains to shelter him from the wind, green farm lands to gaze upon, the shade of a bamboo grove, the vast tranquillity of Tai Hu Lake, and the singing mists just over the horizon. And he has a name. It is carved in stone. This man was born and lived and died. The stone will not be plowed under or smashed or abandoned or carted away. It will stand. It will endure. For my grandfather. For us. For my Chinese roots. So when one day the children of my children and their children, who won't speak Chinese, look Chinese or know China, visit this lone ancestor they will feel Chinese, as I did that afternoon at his grave.

Bette Bao Lord, *Legacies: A Chinese Mosaic*

2.6 Writing Activities

Write a Draft

You have planned for your investigative report. Now is the time to face that blank sheet of paper and begin your draft. Just write. Skip every other line to leave room for changes. Don't worry about correctness. At this stage, you are still exploring what you want to say.

- Use your prewriting notes.
- Get your ideas down on paper.

PURPOSE To create a draft
AUDIENCE Yourself
LENGTH 1–2 pages

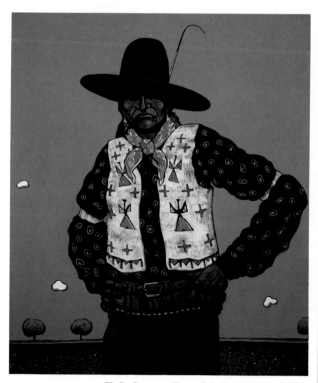

T. C. Cannon, *Turn of the Century Dandy*, 1976

Cooperative Learning

In a group discuss the painting on this page by a Native American artist. Notice the title. What idea does the painting express? How is this portrayal similar to other portrayals of Native Americans you have seen. How is it different? As a group compose a topic sentence based on your response to the painting, and write a paragraph using the supporting details you discussed.

Grammar Link

Use commas after introductory phrases and clauses.

Shella Calambra said: *Because two of my aunts were teachers, I learned to value education.*

Rewrite the sentences below, adding commas where they are needed.

1. Working with the latest underwater equipment the salvage team explored the ocean bottom.
2. Because they were seeking whatever remained of the Spanish ship's cargo they spent over two years in the Mariana Islands.
3. During the long search for the treasure many of the divers almost gave up hope.
4. By the time the project was completed the team had recovered almost 2,000 pieces of treasure.
5. Among the many items found a gold comb appliquéd with gold dots was the most interesting.

See Lesson 21.6, pages 709–710.

The Writing Process
Drafting: Organizing a Paragraph

Writers, like artists, put together pieces to create meaning. Just as the artist connected pieces of small snapshots to give his collage a meaning, a writer arranges and links details to express a main idea.

David Hockney, *Paul Explaining Pictures to Mie Kakigahara*, 1983

Order the Details

As you prepare to write, you accumulate many unconnected ideas and pieces of information. Your task, before you begin to write, is to sort your main ideas and the details that support them.

When you arrange details to express a main idea in writing, you can use one of several kinds of order.

Spatial Order One student, Mark Center, explored a department store on a busy day. Later, he described the store in spatial order, arranging the details according to their closeness to each other.

Student Model

*I*n the store's display window, two mannequins pose stiffly, showing off the season's newest styles. Inside, next to the window, an extravagant tropical tree reaches to the ceiling, its limbs spreading over racks of pastel plaid shorts and matching shirts. Behind the service counter, a salesman rings up a purchase for a distressed mother looking around for her child. The little girl is peering into a glass case filled with glittering jewelry. A few steps beyond, a thin, glamorous model tries to shower passing customers with Chanel No. 5. A frantic father drags his two small boys onto an escalator, while they fuss and cry. The store's rear entrance is jammed with exhausted shoppers leaving and enthusiastic shoppers entering.

Mark Center, Jefferson Davis High School, Montgomery, Alabama

Center begins with the display window in the front of the store and ends with the rear entrance.

What words does Center use to help his readers locate objects in this scene?

Other Kinds of Order Spatial order works well for descriptive writing, but when your primary purpose is to narrate, you will usually choose chronological order. Be aware of other types of order as well.

Four Kinds of Order			
Chronological	**Importance**	**Cause and Effect**	**Compare and Contrast**
To explain how a medical researcher went about her work, arrange the steps in time order.	To persuade people to donate money for cancer research, end with your strongest argument.	To convince someone that a certain drug is harmful, explain what happened to some of its users.	To explain a new and unfamiliar medical procedure, compare it with a familiar one.

Journal Writing

List possible topics that would be best described by each of the five kinds of order presented in this lesson.

Link the Details

Mark Center arranged his details about the department store in a logical order, but he also connected his ideas smoothly to each other and to the main idea. Mark used transition words and phrases as signposts to point his reader in the right direction. Notice how transitions help you follow the ideas in the paragraph below. It describes the discovery of a German battleship, the *Bismarck*, that sank in the North Atlantic in 1941.

> ### Literature Model
>
> We had been fooled by the debris from the clipper ship, but this time it would prove to be *Bismarck*. Following the trail northwestward, we soon encountered one of the battleship's four massive gun turrets. These had been held in place by the force of gravity, and they had fallen free when *Bismarck* capsized on her way to the bottom. Then at last on June 8 [1988] we came upon *Bismarck* herself, a great phantom shape resting in her grave three miles beneath the surface.
>
> Robert D. Ballard, "The *Bismarck* Found"

Transition words and phrases—"soon," "then," "at last"—clarify the order of the events and add coherence. The words "this" and "these" add coherence by referring to something mentioned earlier.

The transition words and phrases you choose will depend on your topic and purpose. The chart below shows some transitions you can use to connect ideas that are related in different ways. Not every sentence, however, needs a transition word or phrase. Too many transitions will make your writing sound awkward and artificial.

Transition Words and Phrases	
Time	first, when, until, next, before, later, finally, afterward, that night, meanwhile, then
Location	above, below, here, underneath, inside, next to, around the corner, in the distance
Importance	first, mainly, primarily, last, most important, secondly, next
Cause and Effect	as a result, because, consequently, for that reason, therefore, then
Compare	similarly, like, just as, also, in the same way
Contrast	but, even so, however, in contrast, on the other hand, unlike, on the contrary

Plan Ordered Paragraphs

Review the draft of your investigative report. Pick out two of the main ideas and plan an ordered paragraph for each.

- Decide what form of order best suits the content and purpose of the paragraphs.
- Arrange the supporting details in a suitable order.
- Use transitions to link the details.

PURPOSE To plan the structure of paragraphs
AUDIENCE Yourself
LENGTH 2 paragraphs

Cross-Curricular: History

Look through the table of contents or the historical atlas of your U.S. history textbook. Locate one or more maps showing the territorial growth of the country. Use the information in the map(s) to write a report describing the expansion of the United States from 1783 to 1853. You can write your report in chronological order, or you can organize your writing spatially, tracing expansion from east to west or north to south. If you are familiar with the events, you may want to present them in order of importance.

Grammar Link

Use a semicolon to separate main clauses joined by a conjunctive adverb (such as *however, therefore*) or by an expression (such as *for example* or *in fact*).

In such sentences the expression or adverb is also set off by a comma:

Divers finally located the sunken ship; however, it took more than 40 years.

This type of sentence structure is often useful when you write using transitions.

Rewrite the following sentences, using correct punctuation.

1. Each supporting detail in a paragraph is like a piece of a jigsaw puzzle that is it has little meaning by itself.
2. Spatial order works well for descriptive writing however it seldom works for narrative writing.
3. The relationship between sentences needs to be made clear for that reason transition words are often used to tie ideas together.
4. Transition words clarify the order of supporting details therefore they add coherence to your writing.
5. Not every sentence needs a transition furthermore too many transitions may make your writing awkward.

See Lesson 21.5, page 702, and Lesson 21.6, pages 708–710.

The Writing Process
Revising: Checking Unity and Coherence

When you revise your writing, work with a peer reviewer. Check unity; all sentences and details should help support the main idea. Also check for coherence, adding transitions to connect ideas.

All writers, even famous ones, keep trying to improve their writing. Here's how author E. B. White revised the conclusion of an essay about the day American astronauts first set foot on the moon.

still holds the key to madness

Kiss in every land

The moon stil belongs to lovers, and lovers are everywhere--not

just in America. What a pity we couldn't have planted some
          precisely   this unique, this incredible
emblem that ~~exactly~~ expressed the occasion, even if it were

nothing more than a white banner, with the legend: ~~xxxxxxxxx~~-y."
                                        that simply said I
"At last!"

handkerchief, symbol of the common ets.
which, like the moon, belongs to all
marking

This humorous ending adds unity by supporting the idea that the moon belongs to everyone, not just Americans.

Evaluate Your First Draft

Writers need to evaluate their first drafts objectively, at times ruthlessly. Often it helps to put your draft aside, returning to it a few days later. Then you can look at it objectively, asking yourself questions like the ones in the chart.

Your fellow writers are facing the same challenges, and you can help one another. A classmate can serve as a peer reviewer, who points out what works well in your draft and what does not. Here are three ways to work with a peer reviewer.

Questions to Consider
1. Is my writing interesting?
2. Is it easy to follow?
3. What do I like best about it?
4. How can I make it better?

Working with a Peer Reviewer

1. Read your first draft aloud; then discuss it with a peer reviewer.

2. Let your peer reviewer read your first draft silently, making comments right on the page.

3. Give your peer reviewer an evaluation form to fill out.

Journal Writing

How successful are you at evaluating your own work? List ways that a peer reviewer can help you. What other strategies might help you revise more successfully?

Use a Peer Reviewer's Comments

A peer reviewer can spot problems you may not be able to see. Notice how a peer reviewer's comments, shown in the margin, helped one writer.

I'd like to know when Bly was born.

I really like your introduction, but this detail about the name of the town doesn't seem to belong here.

How did the editor come up with that name?

> Nellie Bly, who was born ^in 1867^ in Cochran Mills, Pennsylvania, became the first celebrated woman investigative reporter in the United States. "Nellie Bly" was actually just her pen name. Her real name was Elizabeth Cochran. ~~I guess her family must have owned the town they lived in, because it had the same name.~~ Her pen name was suggested by the managing editor at The Pittsburgh Dispatch, where she was a reporter. *He took the name from a song by Stephen Foster.*

The paragraph below needed more extensive changes. Again, read the peer reviewer's suggestions in the margin. Which change corrected a problem in unity?

I don't think this sentence belongs here.

Shouldn't this sentence come after the first one?

What were the conditions like?

> In 1887, Nellie had joined the New York World. ^At the Dispatch, she had written about slum life and divorce.^ *Nellie* ~~She~~ pretended to be insane so that she could be admitted to Blackwell's Island, an insane asylum near New York. The World specialized in "muckraking," journalism that exposed corruption and scandal. She saw ~~the conditions~~ *the horrifying and inhumane treatment of the helpless inmates.* firsthand. Her story brought about reforms at Blackwell's Island.

Revise for Unity

In a unified paragraph, all sentences work together to support the main idea. When you revise, look at each paragraph to see whether every sentence relates to your main idea. Any sentences that introduce irrelevant ideas should be eliminated. The questions below will help you revise your paragraphs for unity.

Checking for Unity
1. Does my topic sentence accurately state what I want to say about my topic? Can it be more tightly focused?
2. Have I fully supported my topic sentence? Do I need to add details?
3. Do all supporting statements relate to the topic sentence? Should any be eliminated?

Examine the changes this writer made in response to her peer reviewer's comments. Which changes add unity to her writing? Which changes add detail to support her topic sentence?

Bly's ~~biggest~~ greatest triumph was her attempt to beat the record for traveling around the world set by Phileas Fogg in Jules Verne's novel <u>Around the World in Eighty Days</u>. ~~This popular book was made into an equally popular movie.~~ Bly sailed on November 14, 1889. [from New York] She rode ~~on many forms of~~ transportation [ships, trains, sampans, horses, and burros] as she circled the globe. She returned to New York 72 days, 6 hours, 11 minutes, and 14 seconds later. [She had beaten the record and given her readers a thrilling adventure to share.]

> *This is an interesting fact, but I don't think it relates to your topic sentence.*

> *I think your readers would like to know what kinds of transportation.*

Journal Writing

Look at a recent piece of writing and examine it for unity. In your journal experiment with ways you can change specific paragraphs to add unity to your writing.

Revise for Coherence

In a coherent paragraph, sentences are clearly and logically connected to each other. Look over your writing to see whether your paragraphs flow smoothly from one idea to the next. These questions can help you revise your paragraphs for coherence.

Checking for Coherence
1. Does each sentence follow in a logical order?
2. Would another means of organizing my ideas work better?
3. Do transition words and phrases clarify the relationships between ideas?

Notice how changes in the following paragraph reflect the peer reviewer's comments shown in the margin. How do the changes add coherence to the writing?

I think you're getting the story out of sequence here.

This belongs near the sentence where you mention the contest.

While Bly circled the globe, the editors at the World made her journey a national story. In fact, when she returned to San Francisco, a special train waited to carry her to New York. In addition to daily stories about Bly's exploits, the World, aiming to increase its circulation, held a contest. Whoever came closest to guessing the time of her journey would win a prize. The contest worked. The World received almost one million contest entries from readers who were following Bly's race around the world. Steaming across the country, the train was met at every stop by large crowds, brass bands, and fireworks. What's more, the contest winner would get a trip to Europe. Bly's triumph sparked the nation's imagination.

2.8 Writing Activities

Revise for Effective Paragraphs

Take another look at the draft of your investigative report. Work with a peer reviewer. Ask these questions about each of your paragraphs.

- Are all the sentences about one main idea?
- Does the paragraph need a topic sentence?
- Do I need to add transition words and phrases to link thoughts and show relationships?

Revise your paragraphs incorporating useful peer reviewer suggestions.

PURPOSE To revise for paragraph unity
AUDIENCE Yourself
LENGTH Changes on the draft

COMPUTER OPTION

If you have trouble making transitions, this might help: after you write your draft, convert all your transition words and phrases into boldface type. This way you can quickly identify trouble spots in the connections between your ideas, such as where a transition may be awkward or even missing. When you have finished revising, convert the entire file to plain text.

Grammar Link

When revising for clarity, look for misplaced or dangling modifiers.

In your sentences, place modifiers as close as possible to the words they modify so that your meaning is clear. For example, in the model on page 84 the writer states:

Steaming across the country, *the train was met at every stop by large crowds, brass bands, and fireworks.*

The reader understands that the modifier describes the train.

Rewrite the sentences below, correcting the misplaced or dangling modifier in each.

1. The main character in Jules Verne's novel *Around the World in Eighty Days*, reporter Nellie Bly wanted to break the travel record of Phileas Fogg.
2. She rode on horses and camels traveling around the world.
3. Beating Fogg's record, newspaper readers shared Bly's thrilling experience.
4. While circling the globe, the editors at the *World* made Bly's journey a front-page story.
5. Hoping to increase circulation, a contest was held by the newspaper.
6. A tempting prize, the winner would receive a trip to Europe.
7. A special train only was sent 72 days later to meet Bly in San Francisco.
8. Tired but exhilarated, the train carried Nellie Bly back home.

See Lesson 18.7, pages 636–641.

The Writing Process
Editing: Toward a Final Version

The fourth stage in the writing process is editing. Like the framers of the United States Constitution, shown below, you are now ready to correct your errors so that they do not distract the reader from your ideas.

"So, then . . . Would that be 'us the people' or 'we the people'?"

Edit to Correct Sentence Errors

Begin the editing stage by taking a careful look at your sentences. Make sure that each sentence expresses a complete thought in a way that is grammatically correct. Compare the edited draft below with the checklist. Which sentence-editing guidelines did the writer apply?

Sentence-Editing Checklist	
1. Have I avoided sentence fragments?	**4.** Are all verbs used correctly?
2. Have I avoided run-on sentences?	**5.** Have I avoided double negatives?
3. Are all pronouns used correctly?	**6.** Have I avoided wordiness?

Scientists ~~who are~~ searching for clues about what ~~it was that~~ caused the extinction of the dinosaurs *have* ~~has~~ debated various theories. One theory suggests that dinosaurs became extinct suddenly∧ ~~After~~ a gigantic comet or meteor collided with the earth. The impact spewed debris into the atmosphere. The sunlight was blocked for months. Temperatures dropped, *and* ∧ many species of plants and animals perished.

Journal Writing

Perhaps you have found yourself in this situation: a teacher likes the content of your paper but has marked your work down for errors. "But you know what I meant," you complain. "Why does it matter how I said it?" Write a response from your teacher's point of view.

Proofread for Spelling and Mechanics

Proofreading is the part of editing that focuses on spelling and on mechanics—capital letters and punctuation marks. Use the checklist below to identify errors and the proofreading symbols as a shorthand means to mark needed changes.

Proofreading		
Checklist		**Symbols**

Checklist:

1. Does each sentence have the right end punctuation?

2. Are commas and semicolons used as needed?

3. Are other punctuation marks used as needed?

4. Are all words spelled correctly?

5. Are possessives and contractions written correctly?

6. Are capital letters used as needed?

Symbols:

∧	Insert
ℰ	Remove
⌣	Exchange
¶	New paragraph
⊙	Add period
∧	Add comma
≡	Uppercase
/	Lowercase
◡	Close space

¶Until recently, many scientists theorized that the extinction of the dinosaur was a gradual process. One theory held that poisons slowly built up in earth's vegetation over the years, slowly killing the dinosaurs. Another theory was that mamals ate the dinosaur eggs still another theory was that dinosaurs could not adapt to gradual changes in earth's climate and plant life. Today, however most scientists think that a sudden and catastrophic event--perhaps caused by a crashing Meteor or colliding planet--caused the extinction of dinosaurs.

What change does each proof-reading symbol indicate?

Proofreading is the last part of the editing process. Your investigation of your subject, which may have started with just a glimpse of an idea, has resulted in a fully developed piece of writing. Now is the time to prepare your final version and present your writing to its audience.

2.9 Writing Activities

Edit Your Draft

When you are satisfied that your investigative report says what you want it to say in the best way you can express it, it is time to edit your writing.

- Use the chart on page 87 to edit your sentences.
- Use the proofreading checklist on page 88 to check your work.
- Proofread for one kind of error at a time.
- Use proofreading symbols.

PURPOSE To edit for correctness
AUDIENCE Yourself
LENGTH Changes on the draft

COMPUTER OPTION

Sharpen your keyboard skills as well as your proofreading skills by having a paragraph from this textbook read aloud to you while you sit at your computer. As you listen to the passage, type it as a document in your word-processing program. Later check for typographical errors you may have made, as well as errors in punctuation, spelling, and capitalization.

Grammar Link

Make sure subjects and verbs agree in person and number.

Check subject-verb agreement as you edit your work. Be especially careful with sentences in which phrases intervene between the subject and the verb. For example, look at the first sentence of the model on page 87. The subject, *scientists*, is plural. The writer changed the verb to its plural form to agree with the subject.

Rewrite the sentences below to make subjects and verbs agree.

1. Scientists from all over the world is studying the effects of climate changes.
2. This scientist, in addition to many of his colleagues, believe that severe climate changes caused the extinction of dinosaurs.
3. An ice age thousands of years ago probably were responsible for migrations of early people.
4. Perhaps the poisons slowly building up in the earth's vegetation was the cause of dinosaurs disappearing.
5. A definitive answer to this question, as well to the reason for migrations, continue to elude scientists.

See Lessons 16.1, page 576, and Lesson 16.6, pages 583–584.

The Writing Process
Presenting: Sharing Your Writing

Presenting your work—sharing it with others—is the final stage in the writing process. You may think your job is done when you hand your work in to your teacher, but other avenues are available to help you get the word out.

Shown below are just a few possible places where you could present your work. When you've spent the time and effort to put your thoughts on paper, you owe it to yourself—and your potential readers—to share your ideas.

Prewriting: "None of my friends are cooks. How can I interest them in salsa recipes?"

Drafting: "A description of REM's last concert will grab my readers' attention."

Revising: "My cousin doesn't use a computer. I'd better explain what a mouse is."

Editing: "Is it o-s-m-o-s-e-s or o-s-m-o-s-i-s? Mr. Dorn teaches science, so I'd better spell it right."

Presenting: "Hey, I think I've got it now. Got a minute to listen to this?"

Reach Your Audience

Whenever you write, you're writing for an audience. As the photos suggest, your audience should affect every stage of your writing process. Your audience can be yourself when you write in your journal or a friend when you scribble a note. It can be the large and far-flung audience you reach by publishing your work. Who might learn from your writing, be entertained or persuaded by it, or be interested in some other way by your work? Here are some ways to present what you write.

Places to Publish	
Publication	**Audience**
School publications: literary magazine, newspaper, yearbook	Your fellow students
General-interest newspapers and magazines	The general student and adult population
Special interest newsletters and magazines	People interested in a particular subject: hobby, sport, cause, career
Computer networks: on-line bulletin boards, special-interest networks	Computer users linked by common interests

Journal Writing

Choose a piece of writing from your journal. Write about the audience you'd like to present it to and how you'd prepare it.

Publish Together

Today it's easier than ever for writers to see their work in print. Desktop publishing allows anyone with access to a computer and a printer to produce high-quality graphic art and professional-looking layouts. Even without a computer, you can create interesting and effective publications—with just a typewriter and a copy machine.

What type of publication could your class produce? Would you like to produce a literary magazine that will be a forum for stories, poetry, and reviews? Or a general magazine covering topics of interest to your class? Or perhaps a series of special reports, each covering one topic or issue in depth? Look at the examples below for ideas your class might use to create its own publication.

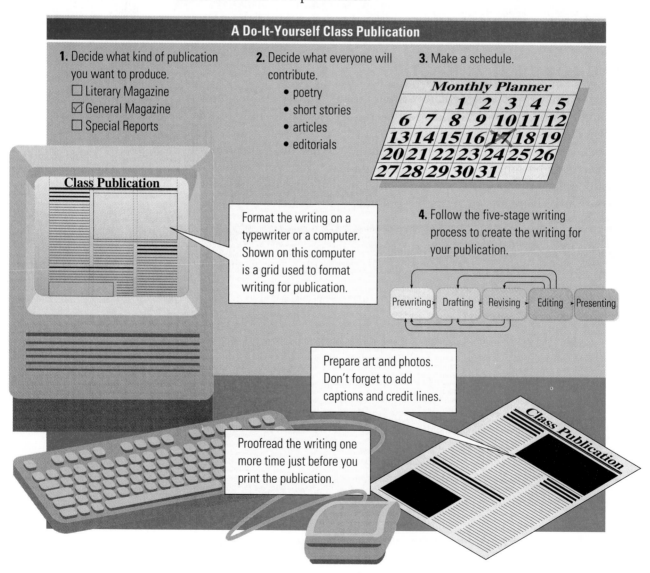

A Do-It-Yourself Class Publication

1. Decide what kind of publication you want to produce.
- ☐ Literary Magazine
- ☑ General Magazine
- ☐ Special Reports

2. Decide what everyone will contribute.
- poetry
- short stories
- articles
- editorials

3. Make a schedule.

Monthly Planner

		1	2	3	4	5
6	7	8	9	10	11	12
13	14	15	16	17	18	19
20	21	22	23	24	25	26
27	28	29	30	31		

Class Publication

Format the writing on a typewriter or a computer. Shown on this computer is a grid used to format writing for publication.

4. Follow the five-stage writing process to create the writing for your publication.

Prewriting ▸ Drafting ▸ Revising ▸ Editing ▸ Presenting

Prepare art and photos. Don't forget to add captions and credit lines.

Proofread the writing one more time just before you print the publication.

Class Publication

2.10 Writing Activities

Present Your Writing

You have taken your report through prewriting, drafting, revising, and editing. Now it's time for the payoff—presenting, publishing, or sharing your writing!

- Prepare your work in the format that is best for your audience and purpose.
- Make your paper as neat and attractive as you can.
- Add illustrations if you wish.
- Give your report a sendoff!

PURPOSE   To present your finished work
AUDIENCE   The audience you chose when you began to write
LENGTH   Whatever is appropriate for your purpose

Cooperative Learning

In a small group, brainstorm a list of magazines and other vehicles, including electronic ones, in which you and your classmates might publish your writings. Have one group member act as a recorder. Begin by considering the diverse audiences that might be interested in individual and class writing samples. Present your list to the class. If time permits, visit your school or public library and collect potential publications to display in the classroom.

Grammar Link

Use correct punctuation for each part of a business letter.

When you submit a piece of your writing to the editor of a publication, you should write a cover letter to go with it. Be sure to use the correct form and punctuation for your letter.

Use commas to separate city from state, day from year, and after the closing. Use a colon after the greeting. Use correct punctuation with abbreviations.

Write the parts of the business letter below using correct punctuation.

[1] 120 N Merrill Street
Park Ridge IL 60068
March 6 1997

[2] Mr. Paul Oscar Feature Editor
The Shore Weekly
1 Sunrise Lane
[3] Westport CT 06880

[4] Dear Mr. Oscar

[5] Sincerely yours

See Lesson 21.4, page 701, Lesson 21.6, pages 711–712, and Lesson 21.13, pages 728–730.

Writing About Literature
Analyzing Point of View

Point of view is the angle from which you see people, objects, or events. In the cartoon you see what is outside the window from the point of view of Gladys Murphy. In other words, you see only what she sees. In a short story or novel, point of view controls what the reader knows.

"Hello, Emily. This is Gladys Murphy up the street. Fine, thanks . . . Say, could you go to your window and describe what's in my front yard?"

Identify Point of View

The paragraphs that follow tell the same story from different points of view. Read them to discover the three main points of view that story writers use: first-person, third-person limited, and third-person omniscient (all-knowing). The paragraph is part of a mystery story involving a police investigation. The characters are the detective, Sergeant Rivera, and the suspect, Carson. For each version ask these questions: Who is the narrator, or the teller of the story? How much is known to the narrator, and therefore to the reader?

First Person

The writer has Rivera tell the story from his own point of view, using the first-person pronouns "I" and "me." This point of view allows readers to know the character better and gives a "you-are-there" feeling.

We walked to the swimming pool. I leaned against the diving board, wondering if now were the moment to spring my trap, to ask Carson just how his emerald stickpin had wound up on the floor of Jasmine Tsing's abandoned car. Carson sank into the *chaise longue,* clearly puzzled by my silence. I knew he thought he'd left no clues, no evidence along that secluded stretch of Evergreen Road. Time and time again, he told me that he'd never even met Jasmine Tsing. Carson had no idea that a small chunk of fiery green crystal was about to call him a liar.

Third-Person Limited

*T*hey walked to the swimming pool. As Rivera leaned against the diving board, Carson sank into the *chaise longue.* Why, he wondered, was Rivera so silent? Carson was certain he had left no clues, no evidence along that solitary stretch of Evergreen Road where Jasmine Tsing's abandoned car had been discovered. No, he told himself, Rivera couldn't possibly suspect him. Hadn't he told the police more than once that he'd never met Jasmine Tsing?

A third-person limited narrator tells the story from one character's point of view—in this case, Carson's. What does the reader learn about other characters' thoughts and feelings? What clues are given?

Third-Person Omniscient

*T*hey walked to the swimming pool. Rivera leaned against the diving board, wondering if now were the moment to spring the trap, to ask how Carson's emerald stickpin had wound up on the floor of Jasmine Tsing's abandoned car. Carson sank into the *chaise longue.* He was puzzled by Rivera's silence but certain he'd left no clues, no evidence along that secluded stretch of Evergreen Road. Hadn't he told the police more than once that he'd never even met Jasmine Tsing?

A third-person omniscient narrator knows the thoughts and feelings of all the characters. How does this affect the way the reader views the characters?

When you are planning an analysis of point of view in a story, your prewriting begins with reading the work closely. Then you are ready to use the following questionnaire.

Questionnaire on Point of View

1. What point of view is used—first-person, third-person limited, or third-person omniscient?
2. How does the point of view affect your attitude toward the characters and the events?
3. How does the point of view affect your overall understanding of the story?
4. How would the story be different if the author had told it from another point of view?
5. What point of view would you use if you were writing this story? Why?

Journal Writing

Use the questionnaire to analyze point of view in a favorite short story. Do you view the story differently now? Explain your answer.

Draft Your Analysis

Once you've completed the questionnaire, you are ready to draft your analysis of the point of view in a story or novel. You've seen that first-person point of view uses the pronoun *I*. Third-person point of view, limited or omniscient, uses *he, she,* and *it*. But as you will see in Katherine Wise's analysis of Willa Cather's *My Ántonia*, point of view goes far beyond grammar.

Willa Cather and Jim Burden were crossing Iowa on the same train. They began talking about the small Nebraska town where they had grown up together. In her introduction to the novel *My Ántonia*, Cather says that the conversation kept centering around a Bohemian girl who, better than anyone else, seemed to epitomize their prairie childhood. Over the years Burden had written down the things he remembered about her, and he showed his manuscript to Cather. He had entitled it *Ántonia* but after a little thought changed it to *My Ántonia*. From there came what is considered Willa Cather's greatest work.

Cather tells the story through Jim Burden's eyes. But they become her eyes, too. The book is so real that you keep flipping back to the introduction to see that yes, this was written by Cather, and that no, this is not a biography—it is a novel.

Cather is able to maintain this feeling of reality because as the narrator she remains completely objective. She describes everything through Jim's eyes, but she never states what his feelings or emotions are. This seems strange at times, but it would not have been as sincere if Cather had tried to apply her own feelings to Jim, or if she had tried to imagine what his feelings might be. Instead her objectivity emphasizes the fact that the book is not about Jim, but about Ántonia.

Burden and Cather had "agreed that no one who had not grown up in a little prairie town could know anything about it." But they proved themselves wrong. Cather took me there—to Black Hawk, Nebraska—swept away on the prairie winds of her words. Her writing is as plain, simple, and harsh as the land it is about, and just as beautiful.

Katherine Jane Wise, Perrysburg High School, Perrysburg, Ohio

Wise provides background by referring to Cather's introduction.

According to Wise, the story is told through whose eyes? What effect does this create?

This paragraph describes the student's strong personal response to a powerful story.

2.11 Writing Activities

Write from a Particular Point of View

Look at the painting and its title below. Write a short description of what might be happening in the scene from one of these points of view: the first-person point of view of one of the people pictured; third-person limited; or third-person omniscient.

- Make the point of view clear.
- Keep the point of view consistent.
- Use pronouns correctly.

PURPOSE To explore point of view
AUDIENCE Your classmates
LENGTH 2 paragraphs

Cooperative Learning

With a small group of classmates select a short story you have all read. Discuss why the particular point of view used in the story might have been chosen by the author.

Consider the points of view of different characters. Discuss which points of view offer the most interesting perspectives on the events of story. Then take turns telling parts of the story as first-person narration by different characters.

Grammar Link

Be consistent about point of view when writing.

When you write in the first person, you use the pronouns *I* and *we*. When you write in the third person, you refer to characters as *he*, *she*, *one*, and *they*. When you write in the second person, use *you*. The writer of the first-person narration in the model on page 94 used pronouns consistently:

*I leaned against the diving board, wondering if now was the moment to spring **my** trap.* . . .

Revise each sentence below to eliminate the incorrect shifts in pronouns.

1. When you analyze first-person point of view, we decide how much we can learn from the first-person narrator.
2. If they are writing from a third-person point of view, you can narrate the actions and words of all the characters.
3. If a story captures one's curiosity, your interest usually follows.
4. When one is interested in a story, I keep on reading.
5. She and I like reading the same kinds of books in their spare time.

See Lesson 17.5, page 606.

Sofonisba Anguissola,
Three of the Artist's Sisters Playing Chess, 1555

WRITING PROCESS IN ACTION

THE WRITING PROCESS

In preceding lessons you learned about the five stages of the writing process—prewriting, drafting, revising, editing, and presenting. You also had an opportunity to practice each of these stages as you produced your written report. Now you will use the writing process to put together a piece of writing about your personal history or heritage.

• Assignment •

Context	*As part of a world history assignment, class members have been asked to write about some aspect of their personal history or heritage. Suggested topics include family histories, descriptions of family or relatives, and autobiographical accounts. The goal of the assignment is to show how you are part of history and of the history-making process.*
Purpose	*To briefly describe a particular aspect of your personal history or heritage*
Audience	*Your teacher and peers, and perhaps your family members*
Length	*1–2 pages*

For advice on how to approach this assignment, you will find the next few pages helpful. You can come back to these pages as you write, getting help where and when you need it. Don't feel limited by the suggestions here. You're in charge of your own writing process.

Prewriting

Do you remember listening spellbound to a tale about your past or your family's past? Maybe you have your own stories—memories that hold their shape and color despite the passage of time. Search your memory for a story you'd like to explore. If you're looking for an idea, try the prewriting suggestions on the notepad.

Next, review the assignment. Your main purpose is to inform your readers about an aspect of your personal history or heritage. Is there anything else you want to accomplish? For example, do you want to persuade your readers to be proud of their own roots? Also keep in mind the needs of your audience. Be sure to provide enough background information so that family relationships and other details that you take for granted will make sense to your teacher and classmates.

Then, work on a main idea statement to help you choose details and keep your writing on track. To find details, start with family photo albums or videos. Interview family members and family friends to get firsthand information. Make notes on what you learn to help you as you draft.

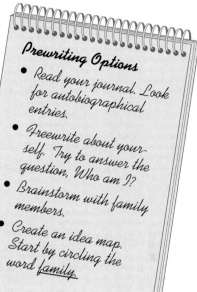

Prewriting Options
- *Read your journal. Look for autobiographical entries.*
- *Freewrite about yourself. Try to answer the question, Who am I?*
- *Brainstorm with family members.*
- *Create an idea map. Start by circling the word <u>family</u>.*

> **Prewriting Tip**
>
> For tips on interviewing, see Lesson 2.5, pages 68–70.

Drafting

Now it's time to start getting your story down on paper. Review your prewriting notes and main idea statement. Then find a place to jump in—either at the beginning, or at the part that is clearest in your mind, even if that's somewhere in the middle. The goal of drafting is to get your ideas down, even if they're not exactly in the right order or in a polished form.

How will you organize your draft? If you're telling a story about your past, chronological order may be your best choice. If you are describing a special place, you may want to use spatial order.

As you write, look for ways you can use details to intrigue your readers. In his autobiography, Alex Haley, the author of *Roots*, introduces his readers to the strange sounding words that were clues to his African heritage. Read the following passage and notice Haley's effective use of details.

> **Drafting Tip**
>
> For examples of different types of supporting details, see Lesson 2.6, page 74.

> ### Literature Model
>
> Anyway, all of this is how I was growing up in Henning at Grandma's, listening from behind her rocking chair as she and the other visiting old women talked of that African . . . who said his name was *"Kin-tay,"* and said *"ko"* for banjo, *"Kamby Bolong"* for river, and a jumble of other *"k"*-beginning sounds that Grandma privately muttered. . . .
>
> Alex Haley, "My Furthest-Back Person—The African"

Once you've got everything down, take a break from your writing, even if you're not particularly satisfied with your draft. You'll be able to evaluate your draft more objectively after a few hours or a day away from it.

Revising

To begin revising, read over your draft to make sure that what you've written fits your purpose and audience. Then have a **writing conference.** Read your draft to a partner or small group. Use your audience's reactions and the Revising Checklist below to help you evaluate your work.

Revising Tip

For advice on how to work with a peer reviewer, see Lesson 2.8, page 81.

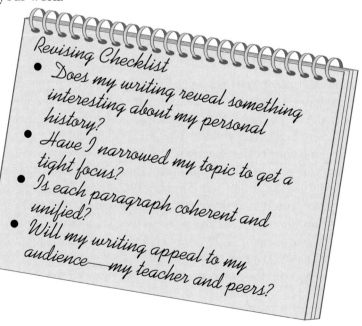

Revising Checklist
- *Does my writing reveal something interesting about my personal history?*
- *Have I narrowed my topic to get a tight focus?*
- *Is each paragraph coherent and unified?*
- *Will my writing appeal to my audience—my teacher and peers?*

Editing

When you have revised your writing for basic content and organization, **proofread** it carefully for grammar, usage, and mechanics errors that can distract readers. Use the questions at the right as a guide.

Now use the Self-Evaluation list below to judge your overall work. When you're satisfied with your personal history, make a clean copy of it and proofread one more time.

Self-Evaluation
Make sure that your personal history—

- describes an aspect of your life or heritage
- uses an appropriate method of organization
- includes supporting details, humor, or suspense to maintain audience interest
- reveals something interesting about your background
- follows correct grammar, usage, mechanics, and spelling

Editing Checklist
- *Have I capitalized proper nouns, especially names of places and people?*
- *Have I made sure that all pronouns are correct?*
- *Have I added commas and semicolons where they are needed?*
- *Have I set off direct quotes with quotation marks?*
- *Have I checked carefully for possible misspellings?*

Presenting

Proofreading

For proofreading symbols, see page 88.

If you choose to do so, share your writing with the class. You also may want to publish your writing in a local history journal or in a magazine which publishes students' writing.

Journal Writing

Reflect on your writing process experience. Answer these questions in your journal: What do you like best about your personal history? What was the hardest part of writing it? What did you learn in your writing conference? What new things have you learned as a writer?

The Writing Process
Literature Model

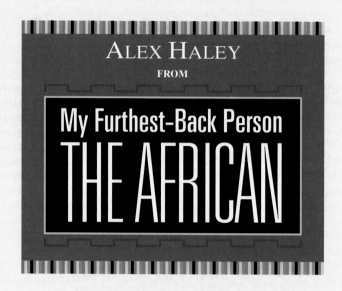

ALEX HALEY

FROM

My Furthest-Back Person
THE AFRICAN

Alex Haley wrote the tremendously popular Roots, *an account of seven generations of his own African American family. In the following autobiographical selection, Haley provides a glimpse of his own writing process as he shows how he got the original idea for* Roots. *As you read, note how he began researching the full story. Then try the activities in Linking Writing and Literature on page 111.*

My Grandma Cynthia Murray Palmer lived in Henning, Tenn. (pop. 500), about 50 miles north of Memphis. Each summer as I grew up there, we would be visited by several women relatives who were mostly around Grandma's age, such as my Great Aunt Liz Murray who taught in Oklahoma, and Great Aunt Till Merriwether from Jackson, Tenn., or their considerably younger niece, Cousin Georgia Anderson from Kansas City, Kan., and some others. Always after the supper dishes had been washed, they would go out to take seats and talk in the rocking chairs on the front porch, and I would scrunch down, listening, behind

Grandma's squeaky chair, with the dusk deepening into night and the lightning bugs flicking on and off above the now shadowy honeysuckles. Most often they talked about our family—the story had been passed down for generations—until the whistling blur of lights of the southbound Panama Limited train whooshing through Henning at 9:05 p.m. signaled our bedtime.

So much of their talking of people, places and events I didn't understand: For instance, what was an "Ol' Massa," an "Ol' Missus" or a "plantation"? But early I gathered that white folks had done lots of bad things to our folks, though I couldn't figure out why. I guessed that all that they talked about had happened a long time ago, as now or then Grandma or another, speaking of someone in the past, would excitedly thrust a finger toward me, exclaiming, "Wasn't big as *this* young 'un!" And it would astound me that anyone as old and grey-haired as they could relate to my age. But in time my head began both a recording and picturing of the more graphic scenes they would describe, just as I also visualized David killing Goliath with his slingshot, Old Pharaoh's army drowning, Noah and his ark, Jesus feeding that big multitude with nothing but five loaves and two fishes, and other wonders that I heard in my Sunday school lessons at our New Hope Methodist Church.

The furthest-back person Grandma and the others talked of— always in tones of awe, I noticed—they would call "The African." They said that some ship brought him to a place that they pronounced " 'Naplis." They said that then some "Mas' John Waller" bought him for his plantation in "Spotsylvania County, Va." This African kept on escaping, the fourth time trying to kill the "hateful po' cracker" slave-catcher, who gave him the punishment choice of castration or of losing one foot. This African took a foot being chopped off with an ax against a tree stump, they said, and he was about to die. But his life was saved by "Mas' John's" brother— "Mas' William Waller," a doctor, who was so furious about what had happened that he bought the African for himself and gave him the name "Toby."

Crippling about, working in "Mas' William's" house and yard, the African in time met and mated with "the big house cook named Bell," and there was born a girl named Kizzy. As she grew up her African daddy often showed her different kinds of things, telling her what they were in his native tongue. Pointing at a banjo, for example, the African uttered, *"ko"*; or pointing at a river near the plantation, he would say, *"Kamby Bolong."* Many of his strange words started with a "k" sound, and the little, growing Kizzy learned gradually that they identified different things.

When addressed by other slaves as "Toby," the master's name for him, the African said angrily that his name was *"Kin-tay."* And as he gradually learned English, he told young Kizzy some things about himself—for instance, that he was not far from his village, chopping wood to make himself a drum, when four men had surprised, overwhelmed, and kidnaped him.

So Kizzy's head held much about her African daddy when at age 16 she was sold away onto a much smaller plantation in North Carolina. Her new "Mas' Tom Lea" fathered her first child, a boy she named George. And Kizzy told her boy all about his African grandfather. George grew up to be such a gamecock[1] fighter that he was called "Chicken George," and people would come from all over and "bet big money" on his cockfights. He mated with Matilda, another of Lea's slaves; they had seven children, and he told them the stories and strange sounds of their African great-grandfather. And one of those children, Tom, became a blacksmith who was bought away by a "Mas' Murray" for his tobacco plantation in Alamance County, N.C.

Tom mated there with Irene, a weaver on the plantation. She also bore seven children, and Tom now told them all about their African great-great-grandfather, the faithfully passed-down knowledge of his sounds and stories having become by now the family's prideful treasure.

The youngest of that second set of seven children was a girl, Cynthia, who became my maternal Grandma (which today I can only see as fated). Anyway, all of this is how I was growing up in Henning at Grandma's, listening from behind her rocking chair as she and the other visiting old women talked of that African (never then comprehended as *my* great-great-great-great-grandfather) who said his name was "*Kin-tay*," and said "*ko*" for banjo, "*Kamby Bolong*" for river, and a jumble of other "k"-beginning sounds that Grandma privately muttered, most often while making beds or cooking, and who also said that near his village he was kidnaped while chopping wood to make himself a drum.

The story had become nearly as fixed in my head as in Grandma's by the time Dad and Mama moved me and my two younger brothers, George and Julius, away from Henning to be with them at the small black agricultural and mechanical college in Normal, Ala., where Dad taught.

To compress my next 25 years: When I was 17 Dad let me enlist as a mess boy in the U.S. Coast Guard. I became a ship's cook out in the South Pacific during World War II, and at night down by my bunk I began trying to write sea adventure stories, mailing them off to magazines and collecting rejection slips for eight years before some editors began purchasing and publishing occasional stories.

1 gamecock (gām' käk') a rooster bred and trained to fight other roosters in events called cockfights

By 1949 the Coast Guard had made me its first "journalist"; finally with 20 years' service, I retired at the age of 37, determined to make a full time career of writing. I wrote mostly magazine articles; my first book was "The Autobiography of Malcolm X."

Then one Saturday in 1965 I happened to be walking past the National Archives building in Washington. Across the interim years I had thought of Grandma's old stories—otherwise I can't think what diverted me up the Archives' steps. And when a main reading room desk attendant asked if he could help me, I wouldn't have dreamed of admitting to him some curiosity hanging on from boyhood about my slave forebears. I kind of bumbled that I was interested in census records of Alamance County, North Carolina, just after the Civil War.

The microfilm rolls were delivered, and I turned them through the machine with a building sense of intrigue, viewing in different census takers' penmanship an endless parade of names. After about a dozen microfilmed rolls, I was beginning to tire, when in utter astonishment I looked upon the names of Grandma's parents: Tom Murray, Irene Murray . . . older sisters of Grandma's as well—every one of them a name that I'd heard countless times on her front porch.

It wasn't that I hadn't believed Grandma. You just *didn't* not believe my Grandma. It was simply so uncanny actually seeing those names in print and in official U.S. Government records.

During the next several months I was back in Washington whenever possible, in the Archives, the Library of Congress, the Daughters of the American Revolution Library. (Whenever black attendants understood the idea of my search, documents I requested reached me with miraculous speed.) In one source or another during 1966 I was able to document at least the highlights of the cherished family story. I would have given anything to have told Grandma, but sadly, in 1949 she had gone. So I went and told the only survivor of those Henning front-porch storytellers: Cousin Georgia Anderson now in her 80's in Kansas City, Kan. Wrinkled, bent, not well

Howardena Pindell, *Autobiography: Water/Ancestors, Middle Passage/Family Ghosts*, 1988

herself, she was so overjoyed, repeating to me the old stories and sounds; they were like Henning echoes: "Yeah, boy, that African say his name was '*Kin-tay*'; he say the banjo was 'ko,' an' the river 'Kamby-Bolong,' an' he was off choppin' some wood to make his drum when they grabbed 'im!" Cousin Georgia grew so excited we had to stop her, calm her down, "You go' head, boy! Your grandma an' all of 'em—they up there watching what you do!"

That week I flew to London on a magazine assignment. Since by now I was steeped in the old, in the past, scarcely a tour guide missed me—I was awed at so many historical places and treasures I'd heard of and read of. I came upon the Rosetta stone[2] in the British Museum, marveling anew at how Jean Champollion, the French archaeologist, had miraculously deciphered its ancient demotic and hieroglyphic[3] texts. . . .

The thrill of that just kept hanging around in my head. I was on a jet returning to New York when a thought hit me. Those strange, unknown-tongue sounds, always part of our family's old story . . . they were obviously bits of our original African "Kin-tay's" native tongue. What specific tongue? Could I somehow find out?

Back in New York, I began making visits to the United Nations Headquarters lobby; it wasn't hard to spot Africans. I'd stop any I could, asking if my bits of phonetic sounds held any meaning for them. A couple of dozen Africans quickly looked at me, listened, and took off—understandably dubious about some Tennesseean's accent alleging "African" sounds.

My research assistant, George Sims (we grew up together in Henning), brought me some names of ranking scholars of African linguistics. One was particularly intriguing: a Belgian- and English-educated Dr. Jan Vansina; he had spent his early career living in West African villages, studying and tape-recording countless oral histories that were narrated by certain very old African men; he had written a standard textbook, "The Oral Tradition."

So I flew to the University of Wisconsin to see Dr. Vansina. In his living room I told him every bit of the family story in the fullest detail that I could remember it. Then, intensely, he queried me about the story's relay across the generations, about the gibberish of "k" sounds Grandma had fiercely muttered to herself while doing her housework, with my brothers and me giggling beyond her hearing at what we had dubbed "Grandma's noises."

2 **Rosetta** (rō zet′ a) stone an ancient tablet found in Egypt with inscriptions in both Greek and Egyptian, thus giving researchers a key to understanding ancient Egyptian writings
3 **demotic** (də mät′ ik), hieroglyphic (hī rō glif′ ik) two ancient Egyptian systems of writing

Dr. Vansina, his manner very serious, finally said, "These sounds your family has kept sound very probably of the tongue called 'Mandinka.'"

I'd never heard of any "Mandinka." Grandma just told of the African saying "*ko*" for banjo, or "*Kamby Bolong*" for a Virginia river.

Among Mandinka stringed instruments, Dr. Vansina said, one of the oldest was the "*kora.*"

"*Bolong,*" he said, was clearly Mandinka for "river." Preceded by "Kamby," it very likely meant "Gambia River."

Dr. Vasina telephoned an eminent Africanist colleague, Dr. Philip Curtin. He said that the phonetic "*Kin-tay*" was correctly spelled "Kinte," a very old clan that had originated in Old Mali. The Kinte men traditionally were blacksmiths, and the women were potters and weavers.

I knew I must get to the Gambia River.

The first native Gambian I could locate in the U. S. was named Ebou Manga, then a junior attending Hamilton College in upstate Clinton, N.Y. He and I flew to Dakar, Senegal, then took a smaller plane to Yundum Airport, and rode in a van to Gambia's capital, Bathurst. Ebou and his father assembled eight Gambia government officials. I told them Grandma's stories, every detail I could remember, as they listened intently, then reacted. " '*Kamby Bolong*' of course is Gambia River!" I heard. "But more clue is your forefather's saying his name was '*Kinte.*' " Then they told me something I would never even have fantasized—that in places in the back country lived very old men, commonly called *griots*, who could tell centuries of the histories of certain very old family clans. As for *Kintes*, they pointed out to me on a map some family villages, Kinte-Kundah, and Kinte-Kundah Janneh-Ya, for instance.

The Gambian officials said they would try to help me. I returned to New York dazed. It is embarrassing to me now, but despite Grandma's stories, I'd never been concerned much with Africa, and I had the routine images of African people living mostly in exotic jungles. But a compulsion[4] now laid hold of me to learn all I could, and I began devouring books about Africa, especially about the slave trade. Then one Thursday's mail contained a letter from one of the Gambian officials, inviting me to return there.

Monday I was back in Bathurst. It galvanized[5] me when the officials said that a griot had been located who told the *Kinte* clan history—his name was Kebba Kanga Fofana. To reach him, I discovered, required a modified safari: renting a launch to get upriver, two land

---

4 compulsion (kəm pul′ sh n) a driving force
5 galvanized (gal′ və nīz′′d) excited, as if by an electric shock

vehicles to carry supplies by a roundabout land route, and employing finally 14 people, including three interpreters and four musicians, since a *griot* would not speak the revered clan histories without background music.

The boat Baddibu vibrated upriver, with me acutely tense: Were these Africans maybe viewing me as but another of the pith-helmets?[6] After about two hours, we put in at James Island, for me to see the ruins of the once British-operated James Fort. Here two centuries of slave ships had loaded thousands of cargoes of Gambian tribespeople. The crumbling stones, the deeply oxidized[7] swivel cannon, even some remnant links of chain seemed all but impossible to believe. Then we continued upriver to the left-bank village of Albreda, and there put ashore to continue on foot to Juffure, village of the *griot*. Once more we stopped, for me to see *toubob kolong*, "the white man's well," now almost filled in, in a swampy area with abundant, tall, saw-toothed grass. It was dug two centuries ago to "17 men's height deep" to insure survival drinking water for long-driven, famishing coffles[8] of slaves.

Walking on, I kept wishing that Grandma could hear how her stories had led me to the "*Kamby Bolong*." (Our surviving storyteller Cousin Georgia died in a Kansas City hospital during this same morning, I would learn later.) Finally, Juffure village's playing children, sighting us, flashed an alert. The 70-odd people came rushing from their circular, thatch-roofed, mud-walled huts, with goats bounding up and about, and parrots squawking from up in the palms. I sensed him in advance somehow, the small man amid them, wearing a pillbox cap and an off-white robe—the *griot.* Then the interpreters went to him, as the villagers thronged around me.

And it hit me like a gale wind: every one of them, the whole crowd, was *jet black*. An enormous sense of guilt swept me—a sense of being some kind of hybrid[9]. . . a sense of being impure among the pure. It was an awful sensation.

The old *griot* stepped away from my interpreters and the crowd quickly swarmed around him—all of them buzzing. An interpreter named A. B. C. Salla came to me; he whispered: "Why they stare at you so, they have never seen here a black American." And that hit me: I was symbolizing for them twenty-five millions of us they had never seen. What did they think of me—of us?

---

6 **pith-helmets** (pith′ hel′ mət) a reference to earlier European explorers of Africa, who wore such helmets

7 **oxidized** (äk′sə dlīz″d) rusted

8 **coffles** (kôf″lz) groups of slaves fastened or driven together

9 **hybrid** (hī′ brid) the offspring of individuals of unlike genetic background, such as of people of different races

Then abruptly the old *griot* was briskly walking toward me. His eyes boring into mine, he spoke in Mandinka, as if instinctively I should understand—and A. B. C. Salla translated:

"Yes . . . we have been told by the forefathers . . . that many of us from this place are in exile . . . in that place called America . . . and in other places."

I suppose I physically wavered, and they thought it was the heat; rustling whispers went through the crowd, and a man brought me a low stool. Now the whispering hushed—the musicians had softly begun playing *kora* and *balafon*, and a canvas sling lawn seat was taken by the *griot*, Kebba Kanga Fofana, aged 73 "rains" (one rainy season each year). He seemed to gather himself into a physical rigidity, and he began speaking the *Kinte* clan's ancestral oral history; it came rolling from his mouth across the next hours . . . 17th- and 18th-century *Kinte* lineage details, predominantly what men took wives; the children they "begot," in the order of their births; those children's mates and children.

Events frequently were dated by some proximate singular physical occurrence. It was as if some ancient scroll were printed indelibly within the *griot's* brain. Each few sentences or so, he would pause for an interpreter's translation to me. I distill here the essence:

The *Kinte* clan began in Old Mali, the men generally blacksmiths ". . . who conquered fire," and the women potters and weavers. One large branch of the clan moved to Mauretania from where one son of the clan, Kairaba Kunta Kinte, a Moslem Marabout holy man, entered Gambia. He lived first in the village of Pakali N'Ding; he moved next to Jiffarong village; ". . . and then he came here, into our own village of Juffure."

In Juffure, Kairaba Kunta Kinte took his first wife, ". . . a Mandinka maiden, whose name was Sireng. By her, he begot two sons, whose names were Janneh and Saloum. Then he got a second wife, Yaisa. By her, he begot a son, Omoro."

The three sons became men in Juffure. Janneh and Saloum went off and found a new village, Kinte-Kundah Janneh-Ya. "And then Omoro, the youngest son, when he had 30 rains, took as a wife a maiden, Binta Kebba.

"And by her, he begot four sons—Kunta, Lamin, Suwadu, and Madi . . . "

Sometimes, a "begotten," after his naming, would be accompanied by some later occurring detail, perhaps as ". . . in time of big water (flood), he slew a water buffalo." Having named those four sons, now the *griot* stated such a detail.

"About the time the king's soldiers came, the eldest of these four sons, Kunta, when he had about 16 rains, went away from this village, to chop wood to make a drum . . . and he was never seen again . . . "

Goose-pimples the size of lemons seemed to pop all over me. In my knapsack were my cumulative notebooks, the first of them including how in my boyhood, my Grandma, Cousin Georgia and the others told of the African "*Kin-tay*" who always said he was kidnaped near his village—while chopping wood to make a drum . . .

I showed the interpreter, he showed and told the *griot*, who excitedly told the people; they grew very agitated. Abruptly then they formed a human ring, encircling me, dancing and chanting. Perhaps a dozen of the women carrying their infant babies rushed in toward me, thrusting the infants into my arms—conveying, I would later learn, "the laying on of hands . . . through this flesh which is us, we are you, and you are us." The men hurried me into their mosque[10], their Arabic praying later being translated outside: "Thanks be to Allah for returning the long lost from among us." Direct descendants of Kunta Kinte's blood brothers were hastened, some of them from nearby villages, for a family portrait to be taken with me, surrounded by actual ancestral sixth cousins. More symbolic acts filled the remaining day.

When they would let me leave, for some reason I wanted to go away over the African land. Dazed, silent in the bumping Land Rover, I heard the cutting staccato[11] of talking drums. Then when we sighted the next village, its people came thronging to meet us. They were all—little naked ones to wizened[12] elders—waving, beaming, amid a cacophony[13] of crying out; and then my ears identified their words: "*Meester Kinte! Meester Kinte!*"

Let me tell you something: I am a man. But I remember the sob surging up from my feet, flinging up my hands before my face and bawling as I had not done since I was a baby . . . the jet-black Africans were jostling, staring . . . I didn't care, with the feelings surging. If you really knew the odyssey of us millions of black Americans, if you really knew how we came in the seeds of our forefathers, captured, driven, beaten, inspected, bought, branded, chained in foul ships, if you really knew, you needed weeping . . .

10 **mosque** (mäsk) a Muslim place of worship
11 **staccato** (stə kät´ō) a pattern of rapid, abrupt sounds with quick, distinct breaks
12 **wizened** (wi zən'd) withered, wrinkled
13 **cacophony** (kə käf´ə nē) jarring, dissonant sounds

Linking Writing and Literature

Readers Respond to the Model

How did Alex Haley's purpose and point of view affect his writing process?

Explore Alex Haley's techniques by answering these questions. Then read what other students liked about Haley's writing.

1. How did Alex Haley come up with the idea to write a book tracing his roots back to his "furthest-back person"?
2. What sources did Haley consult to research his African heritage?
3. How did Haley order and present the information he collected? In what other ways could he have structured and told his story?
4. To which part of Alex Haley's story did you personally relate? Why?

This piece was about Alex Haley becoming more interested in his roots and how he traced them all the way back to a specific Gambian family. The part I remember most clearly was when Haley met his family in Gambia. It was an emotional, climactic scene.

Chris Fickes

This selection was about a person trying to find out about his heritage. Haley wrote in first person because he was talking about his own experience. The mood was one of curiosity. Haley was curious, and as a reader I was, too. I found what the author was looking for as he found it. The writer created this mood by telling his story in chronological order. I enjoyed this selection and would recommend it to people who are interested in their heritage.

Yahna Awazu

Unit 2 Review

Reflecting on the Unit

Summarize what you learned in this unit by answering the following questions.

- What are the five stages of the writing process?

- What are the important elements of each stage?

- What techniques, tools, or procedures can help you successfully complete each stage of the process?

- What are some of the main things to consider when you analyze point of view in literature?

Adding to Your Portfolio

Choose a selection for your portfolio.
Look over the writing you have done during this unit. Select a completed piece of writing to put in your portfolio. The piece you choose should show some or all of the following:

- a specific audience and writing purpose
- a clear topic sentence or sentences supported by appropriate details
- a logical ordering of ideas
- unity and coherence
- careful editing and proofreading

Reflect on your choice.
Attach a note to the piece you chose, explaining briefly why you chose it and what you learned from writing it.

Set goals.
How can you improve your writing? What skill will you focus on the next time you write?

Writing Across the Curriculum

Make a social studies connection.
Scan your government textbook or a magazine or newspaper for topics relating to local, state, or national politics. Choose a subject that interests you. Write two related topic sentences and list details that will help support each. Try to include each type of supporting detail: a concrete detail, an example, a fact or statistic, and a reason. Then follow the other stages of the writing process. Use your topic sentences and supporting details to draft, revise, and edit two unified paragraphs that describe a political issue. You may wish to present your finished writing to an audience of other students.

Descriptive Writing in the Real World

Clarke Follows the Equator

F O C U S: To bring a place to life, travel writers use descriptive writing full of colorful details, conversations, background facts, and strong impressions.

Travel writer Thurston Clarke

It began in 1985 on a "snowy February evening in New York," travel writer Thurston Clarke recalls in the opening of *Equator*, "when I grabbed a globe off a friend's bookshelf and spun it into a whirling bouquet of continents and oceans. Then I held it in front of a frosted window and watched places I might never see race past.

"Most prominent was a triple-thick, brown-and-yellow checkered line coiled like a snake around the middle of the earth. The equator. . . . I traced it with a finger, imagining for the first time a trip along its path."

The spinning globe and the checkered line around its middle captured the imagination of a seasoned writer, the author of five books, both fiction and nonfiction. "I was looking for a large subject that hadn't been done," Clarke said, "something large enough to carry a book. When I saw the equator, something clicked."

Writing a Travel Book

Prewriting	Drafting	Revising/Editing
Researching and Traveling	Putting the Trip into Words	Adding the Finishing Touches

Prewriting

RESEARCHING AND TRAVELING

For a project as large as writing a book about life along the equator, Clarke spent several months organizing his expedition to Brazil, Rwanda, Indonesia, and more than a dozen other countries on the equator. Research was a major part of his job. "I spent two or three months in libraries, reading about each country, especially newspaper articles," he said.

As he read news stories, Clarke jotted down the names of missionaries, politicians, Peace Corps workers, and other people in each country. "It's important to have a couple of people to call who live in a place," he said. "They can give you a briefing about the country, tell you where to go, what to avoid, describe the political situation, and introduce you to other people."

Clarke's research also helped him develop a loose itinerary. "This was too big a book to do on one trip, so I broke [my travels] down by continent," he explained.

> "*A place is very mysterious at night. [Some] cities are very poorly lit, so you don't see much, just pools of light here and there. . . . The next morning you find a great surprise; you're overwhelmed by what makes the city new and different. That's the time to take notes.*"
>
> —Thurston Clarke

Clarke decided to travel west to east, beginning in the small city of Macapá, Brazil. His second trip would take him to equatorial Africa, and his third would cover Asia, followed by several Pacific islands. On his last trip Clarke would return to South America.

Between 1985 and 1987, Clarke spent about eight months using his wits and determination to travel the equator. He saw Pekanbaru, Indonesia, by night from the back of a motorbike and hiked up the southern slope of Cayambe, an Ecuadorian volcano, to reach the highest spot on the equator.

Wherever he went, Clarke captured his first reactions. "First impressions are very important for any writer," he said. "I sched-ule nothing the first day. I take long walks and notice everything new, scary, wonderful. I jot down a few words about something that strikes me. If I hear a conversation I want, I write a summary. In the evening I expand my notes into a para-graph or two about what impressed me."

How did Clarke's first encounter with the equator at Macapá strike him? "I didn't expect anything," he said. "Maybe a little marker." Instead, Clarke found the Park of the Equator. It celebrated the equator with a long, low wall faced in blue

Cayambe, pictured below at left, lies along the Andes Mountains. At right, a river meanders through the grasslands around Kampala, Uganda.

Cayambe •   Macapá •   **EQUATOR**   Libreville •   Kampala •
Quito •   Belém •   • Nairobi
SOUTH AMERICA   *ATLANTIC OCEAN*   AFRICA   Kigali

tiles and a garden. Down the road from the park, Clarke spotted a wooden cabin, which turned out to be the home of José Maria.

José Maria invited Clarke into his cabin and explained that living on the equator was lucky. Before Clarke left, José Maria asked Clarke if he'd be back. "Of course I'll be back," Clarke wrote later. "I was starting here so I had to return to complete the circle."

Drafting

PUTTING THE TRIP INTO WORDS

By the time Clarke got back to Macapá two years later, the Park of the Equator had been replaced by an "eight-story concrete slab," and José Maria was building a motel and soccer field on the equator. Clarke decided it was time to go home and start writing.

When Clarke sat down at his computer, much of the book had already taken shape in his mind. "The trip itself defines the book, so as I experienced and did things they determined the book," he reflected.

Still, Clarke had to choose material from a dozen notebooks and the newspaper clips he collected along the way. "Travel books depend on variety," he said. "So I used my best, most interesting stuff. With those things in mind, Clarke began to write. "I always write a first draft fast, just to get something down. Often the sentences run on, there's a lot of repetition, and the transitions aren't very good. . . . I just keep moving to get a first draft," he said.

Dusk falls over the water surrounding Indonesia.

EQUATOR

Singapore

INDIAN OCEAN

INDONESIA

Revising/Editing

ADDING THE FINISHING TOUCHES

Once he finished a draft, he started revising. "I really think of writing as editing," Clarke explained. "I edit so many times that the writing happens for me when I edit. That's when I put in the transitions and play with the copy. I enjoy editing a lot."

During this phase, Clarke took care to create powerful descriptions, using active verbs—not adjectives. "If you're describing a landscape or a city, there are always things going on; there's always motion and movement," he said. For example, to describe Tarawa, a Pacific island, Clarke wrote: "My first sunset . . . was a classic equatorial one, with the sun hesitating an instant as if taking a deep breath, before jumping into the sea. The wind dropped, clouds froze, and the sails of a native canoe sagged. The sun fell and the lagoon turned silver."

Clarke did between six and eight revisions of the manuscript. After the better part of a year, Clarke had finished the book.

The manuscript Clarke sent to William Morrow ran for 650 well-crafted pages. "I never submit a book until it's absolutely ready. If you're writing for money, you should never give an editor something that is not completely finished, the best you can do," Clarke emphasized. "Editors aren't there to teach you to write."

Clarke had no major changes to make in his book—except to cut it down. "After I handed it in I knew it needed to be shorter, and that's where the editor came in," he said. "I told my editor I was too close to this material," Clarke said. "I asked for some ideas about what to cut." With that help, Clarke did his final job—trimming 20,000 words from *Equator*.

The task of writing does not end with a polished manuscript. Often substantial changes are required before a book can be published.

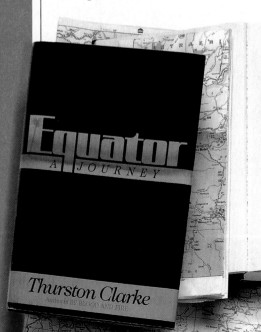

Responding to the Case Study

1. Discussion

Discuss these questions about Thurston Clarke's writing.

- How did Thurston Clarke prepare to write his travel book about life along the equator?
- What functions did research serve in Clarke's preparations?
- What organizational plan did Clarke follow in his travels and note taking?
- Why does Clarke feel that creating powerful descriptions using active verbs is important in travel writing?
- What is Clarke's goal in writing a first draft? In revising his work?

2. Descriptive Writing

Write a paragraph describing a place. Look around carefully at your classroom or some other location in your school or neighborhood. Note any details that particularly interest you. Organize your details. Then write a powerful description using active verbs to describe what you see.

Grammar Link

Use strong verbs.

Thurston Clarke concentrates on using strong verbs, not adjectives, to create powerful descriptions such as this one:

*The wind **dropped**, clouds **froze**, and the sails of a native canoe **sagged**.*

Rewrite the following sentences, replacing weak verbs with stronger ones that will paint a vivid picture. (You may make other changes, too, if you wish.)

1. As the wind blew, the trees moved.
2. A convertible that looked as if it were held together with bandages and tape came in our direction.
3. Its driver had on an orange jumpsuit and matching cap that caught the eye of everyone on the street.
4. When the car got closer to us, the driver motioned.
5. He spoke, but we couldn't hear what he said over the racket his car was making.

See Lesson 10.3, page 415.

CITY HALL   PHILADELPHIA, PENNSYLVANIA

Atlanta

Georgia

THE THREE SISTERS, CA

TAR HEEL ST

Descriptive Writing
Writing to Describe

Good descriptive writing depends on the creation of vivid word pictures and the organization of those pictures into an effective pattern. Note how Stephen King organizes details in the following passage to let the reader "see" the scene.

Literature Model

King helps bring the scene to life with vivid images like "lightning flared in a blue sheet" and "thunder exploded a bare moment later."

L ightning flared in a blue sheet, giving Anderson a shutter-click of what she had come to think of—as her neighbors did—as her dooryard. She saw the truck, with the first drops of rain on its windshield; the short dirt driveway; the mailbox with its flag down and tucked securely against its aluminum side; the writhing trees. Thunder exploded a bare moment later, and Peter jumped against her, whining. The lights went out. They didn't bother dimming or flickering or messing around; they went out all at once, completely. They went out with *authority*.

Anderson reached for the lantern—and then her hand stopped.

There was a green spot on the far wall, just to the right of Uncle Frank's Welsh dresser. It bobbed up two inches, moved left, then right. It disappeared for a moment and then came back. . . .

Is "hearing the tendons in her neck creak like dirty doorhinges" an effective image? Why?

She turned toward Peter, hearing the tendons in her neck creak like dirty doorhinges, knowing what she was going to see. The light was coming from Peter's eye. His left eye. It glared with the witchy green light of St. Elmo's fire drifting over a swamp after a still, muggy day.

Stephen King, *The Tommyknockers*

Organize Details in Spatial Order

Good descriptive writing depends on the effective use of details, and the organization of those details into meaningful patterns. One natural way of organizing descriptive writing is to arrange details in spatial order—that is, left to right, front to back, near to far, clockwise, or counterclockwise. How did Iowa writer Sharon Oard Warner organize the details of her description?

Grammar
Drafting Tip

When you write descriptions, you can use prepositional phrases, as Warner does, to establish spatial relationships between objects. For more information about prepositional phrases, see Lesson 12.1, page 485.

Literature Model

*T*he pediatric waiting room is divided into two unequal sections by a length of Plexiglas that juts out into the middle of the room. A table at one end keeps people from walking into the flat edge. Orange and brown upholstered chairs line both sides of this transparent wall, back to back, as though some enormous game of musical chairs is about to begin. The smaller section of the room is reserved for well patients, and a prominent sign directs the rest of us to the other side.

When I carried Jancey in this morning, I stopped in the entrance, momentarily confused. Some redecorating had gone on since our last visit. A large oval braided rug covered an expanse of institutional carpet in the unwell section, and a baby not much older than Jancey was seated in the middle of it. While I watched, he crawled to the edge and then back again, as though the rug were an island and he was marooned.

Sharon Oard Warner, "A Simple Matter of Hunger"

"Island" and "marooned" reinforce the sense of rigidly divided space.

Journal Writing

Experiment with spatial organization of details by writing a brief description of a special place or secret hideaway where you go to get away from it all.

Organize Details According to Importance

Writers sometimes arrange details in order of importance, from the least important detail to the most important. This lets the description build to a climax, leaving the strongest image for the end. In the passage below, African American writer Eugenia Collier recalls several details about childhood summers that made a lasting impression.

Beverly Buchanan, *Barnesville*, 1989

In this case, order of importance means moving from the general and pervasive—"dust"—to the specific and sharply focused—"a brilliant splash of sunny yellow."

Literature Model

When I think of the home town of my youth, all that I seem to remember is dust—the brown, crumbly dust of late summer—arid, sterile dust that gets into the eyes and makes them water, gets into the throat and between the toes of bare brown feet. I don't know why I should remember only the dust. Surely there must have been lush green lawns and paved streets under leafy shade trees somewhere in town; but memory is an abstract painting—it does not present things as they are, but rather as they *feel*. And so, when I think of that time and that place, I remember only the dry September of the dirt roads and grassless yards of the shanty-town where I lived. And one other thing I remember, another incongruency of memory—a brilliant splash of sunny yellow against the dust—Miss Lottie's marigolds.

Eugenia Collier, "Marigolds"

Focus on the Topic Sentence

Topic sentences are as important in writing descriptions as in any other form of writing. Where you place your topic sentence—at the beginning of the paragraph or at the end—depends upon the effect you want to achieve. The model below begins with a topic sentence, setting the stage for a scary night for two children.

Literature Model

W e were afraid at night in the winter. . . . The upstairs of our house was not finished. A brick chimney went up one wall. In the middle of the floor was a square hole, with a wooden railing around it; that was where the stairs came up. On the other side of the stairwell were the things that nobody had any use for anymore. . . . I had told Laird, as soon as he was old enough to understand such things, that bats and skeletons lived over there; whenever a man escaped from the county jail, twenty miles away, I imagined that he had somehow let himself in the window and was hiding behind the linoleum.

Alice Munro, "Boys and Girls"

The topic sentence states the main idea—the children were afraid at night—and the rest of the paragraph describes why they were afraid.

The next paragraph takes a different approach, beginning leisurely and developing a vivid picture one detail at a time. Everything builds toward the topic sentence at the end.

Model

T all bookshelves stood at attention along the right wall; the books toed a straight line. Two uncomfortable chairs were deployed strategically across the room. Matching brass trays holding paper clips and pens were set up across the front of the desk. Rosa's office clearly revealed her personality.

What can you infer from the description about Rosa's personality?

Journal Writing

Find a paragraph that begins with a topic sentence. Rewrite the paragraph with the topic sentence at the end. Compare the two versions. Explain which you like better.

Put It All Together

After you've created your images and organized them around a topic sentence, you should have an effective description. Notice how student Lonn Rider used specific and vivid details to create a clear image of a favorite place.

The topic sentence states the main idea: to describe Picture Canyon and explain why it has a special effect on people.

In what order does Rider arrange his details in describing Picture Canyon? What details does he use?

Transition words such as "overhead," "on either side," and "looking ahead" help the reader follow the organization.

Student Model

Picture Canyon, though not the most beautiful of places, has a special, enigmatic effect on people. As you enter the canyon, the soft golden sandstone walls begin to build and loom overhead until they meet the electric-blue skyline. Native American drawings etched inside the canyon cover sheer cliff walls on either side, illustrating a past long since forgotten. The rugged floor of the canyon is scattered with multitudes of small, algae-covered ponds with a few weather-beaten, sandstone roadways. Looking ahead, there are small, wind-twisted pine trees with a multitude of squirrels feeding on the pea-sized piñon nuts. Each playfully eats his fill and stores the excess in bulging cheeks. As the sun sets over the horizon, the jagged, golden rock formations on the skyline seem to radiate an eerie, golden energy known only to a few infrequent visitors and to the Native Americans who lived in the canyon centuries ago.

Lonn Rider, Centennial High School, Pueblo, Colorado

Like Rider, you can enhance your descriptions by carefully organizing your ideas and supporting details. Follow these guidelines when you write your own descriptive paragraphs.

Revising Tip

When you revise your writing, add transition words to help the reader follow the organization of your descriptive details. For help refer to Lesson 2.7, page 76.

Guidelines for Descriptive Writing

1. Gather vivid details that will help you re-create a scene or an experience for your readers.
2. Decide which kind of organization will be more appropriate for your subject—spatial order or order of importance.
3. Write a topic sentence, and decide whether it will be more effective positioned at the beginning or the end.
4. Use appropriate transitions to make the organization and relationships among ideas clear.

3.1 Writing Activities

Write a Descriptive Paragraph

Write a description of the painting below that is so specific that someone who has never seen it would immediately recognize it. Use the guidelines on page 124 to help you.

- Use specific details.
- Order details spatially or by order of importance.
- Write and place a topic sentence.

PURPOSE To describe a painting
AUDIENCE Someone who has never seen it
LENGTH 1 paragraph

Cooperative Learning

Write a paragraph about a possession you had in your early childhood. Describe the object's most unusual features, without naming the object. Read your paragraphs aloud in a group, identify the objects, and discuss which specific details helped identify the objects.

Grammar Link

Use prepositional phrases to show spatial relationships.

The literature models in this lesson used prepositional phrases, such as "in the middle of the floor," to establish spatial relationships.

Clarify position or location by adding at least one prepositional phrase to each sentence below.

1. A bookcase stood.
2. An overstuffed blue chair squatted.
3. A patchwork quilt of primary colors covered the bed.
4. Clothes were strewn in heaps.
5. A matching chair and desk of oak faced the window.

See Lesson 12.1, pages 485–486.

Blackbear Bosin,
Prairie Fire, 1953

Descriptive Writing
Observing and Taking Notes

Striking, image-creating details bring a place to life. The most effective way to "capture" such details is through direct observation and note taking. What direct observations were used to enliven this description of an Indian restaurant in Queens, New York?

Literature Model

Specific visual images like "red plastic tables," "yellow turmeric stains," and "styrofoam bowls" evoke a strong sense of place.

What do words like "wheaty," "bitter," and "sting" add to the description of the scene?

Adam is in an Indian restaurant in Queens, little red plastic tables with yellow turmeric[1] stains on them, styrofoam bowls of dal[2] and chicken curry, slippery with orange oil.

Adam's fingers tear a chapati[3] and dip it into the dal. He gulps it down, the smoothness of the dal mixing with the wheaty taste of the chapati. He eats some chicken, carefully licking all the masala[4] from his fingers, almost tasting each spice alone, the sweet cinnamon and cardamom, the bitter cumin and coriander, the sting of the chilies. The smell makes him so homesick his eyes start watering. He thinks of his grandmother's chicken curry.

"Food all right, sir? Not too spicy?"

Adam swallows. The chicken is so sweet. He looks up at the waiter. "It's perfect," he says.

The waiter looks worried. "You want some yogurt, sir? To make it less spicy. Some raita. That is yogurt with cucumber in it. You know, cucumber."

"No, thank you," says Adam, smiling. "I know what raita is."

"Oh yes, a lot of Europeans eat Indian food now. It's very popular in England as well. Yes, I can see you know how to eat like an Indian," leaning on the table now, he hangs the wet cloth over the back of the chair. ➡

1 turmeric (tur´mer ĭk) spice

2 dal (däl) dip

3 chapati (ch ə pät´ē) bread

4 masala (m ə säl´a) sauce

> "Me, I like American food. I never eat here. I eat at McDonald's or Kentucky Chicken. It's so funny, isn't it? Indians like American food and Americans like Indian food."
>
> Ameena Meer, "The Only Living Boy in New York"

Use Direct Observation

Revisiting a scene through memory is one kind of observation, but you can get a better sense of a place if you revisit the location in person. In both cases you will want to consider the same questions as you think about re-creating the scene in words: What is the most striking thing about the scene? What colors do you see? What sounds do you hear? What scents do you smell? What will you have to include in the description so that your readers will see what you saw, feel as you felt?

Take Notes

If you don't have a photographic memory, draw a sketch, make a video, take notes in your personal journal. Do whatever you think will help you re-create the scene later when you sit down to write. Here is a set of notes that student Michelle Kalski took in preparation for writing a description of her favorite getaway spot.

Prewriting Tip

To learn from the techniques travel writer Thurston Clarke used for collecting observations and taking notes, look back at the Case Study on pages 114–118.

Sight

green grass, sunlight and shadows, sun-kissed water, rippling waves, white sails, cobalt-blue sky, cotton-fluffy clouds, snow-white gulls

Sound	*Smell*	*Touch*
chirping birds,	fresh greenery,	soft summer breeze,
whispering trees	fragrant pines	clean dry grass

Journal Writing

Look carefully around you right now. Think about the questions above under "Use Direct Observation." Make notes answering these questions.

Write from Notes

The student model below shows how Kalski used her notes to write a descriptive paragraph. She began with a topic sentence stating the main idea. She then organized the supporting details in order of importance, saving strong, mood-capturing details for the end.

Presenting Tip

You might want to get together with others to create a poster display of your descriptive writing.

Kalski relied on her notes for specific sensory details like "green dry grass," "warm breeze," and "glistening lake."

How do original and unusual details make this passage more effective?

Student Model

School is out in gorgeous weather, and there isn't much to worry about except sleeping too late into the afternoon. I head out to my favorite spot, a small patch of space to separate me from the busy lives of all the bustling people. As I lie there, the green dry grass plays hide and seek with my fingers and toes. Sun and shade spot me like tie-dye configurations, while a warm breeze keeps me company. The trees overhead say "Hello," as if they were old friends; they shade and protect me just in case the sky might fall. I feel a warm sun penetrating through the trees, making conversation with the breeze as if they'd known each other for a thousand years. I'm surrounded and encompassed by nature. I look over the glistening lake and see ripples kissing the water's surface. Scattered cotton clouds on blue wait to absorb everything around in just one season. The only things heard are birds chirping and the breeze and trees discussing old times. Peace is all around until sunset and later on.

Michelle Kalski, Evanston Township High School, Evanston, Illinois

3.2 Writing Activities

Write About Paintings

The paintings on this page portray two artists' versions of the same place. Write a descriptive paragraph for each painting. Take notes on the style, colors, and effect of each painting.

- Compose a topic sentence for each paragraph.
- List the details each artist emphasizes.

PURPOSE To observe and describe paintings
AUDIENCE Your teacher
LENGTH 2 paragraphs

Cooperative Learning

In a small group, explore an outdoor location. Divide the location into sections. Ask each group member to take detailed notes about the plant and animal life in one section. Write a group description of the location, using the combined notes.

Grammar Link

Form possessive pronouns correctly.

Possessive pronouns do not use apostrophes. Do not confuse the possessive pronoun *its* with the contraction *it's* (it is):

"It's perfect," he *[Adam] says.*

Choose the right words to complete each sentence below.

1. (Her's, Hers) is the backpack that's bigger than (your's, yours).
2. This canvas backpack is (he's, his).
3. The backpacks left on the bus must be (their's, theirs).
4. (Our's, Ours) were not on the bus.
5. Ted's backpack is torn; (it's, its) time for him to find (it's, its) replacement.

See Lesson 17.1, pages 599–600.

Childe Hassam, *Fifth Avenue*, 1919

John Marin, *Movement, Fifth Avenue*, 1912

Descriptive Writing
Using Energetic Verbs

Cartoonists highlight words like BAM, POW, and BWHOOOOOSH. You can bring the same kind of energy to your own writing by using specific, action-packed words.

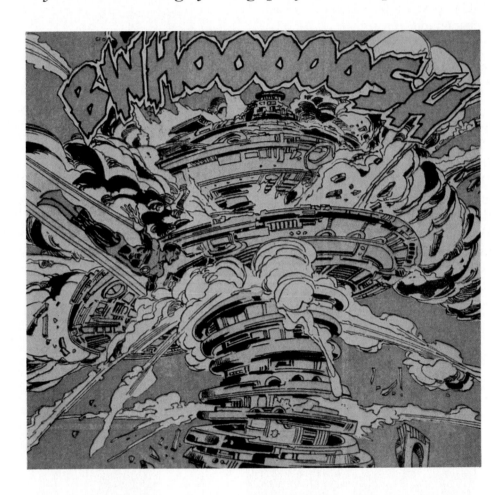

Choose Exact Verbs

Exact verbs create mood and strong mental images in descriptive writing. Notice how the writers of the following models have used energetic verbs.

*T*he nights now are full of wind and destruction; the trees plunge and bend and their leaves fly helter skelter until the lawn is plastered with them and they lie packed in gutters and choke rain pipes and scatter damp paths.

Virginia Woolf, *To the Lighthouse*

*T*he crowds are thick on the sidewalks and street vendors work on nearly every block. The litter baskets—they look like volcanoes of trash that have just erupted—are overloaded from a Sunday's use. Debris is strewn over the pavement and in the gutters. A wind stirs up scraps and creates a funnel of newspaper that swirls up in a mad ballet.

McCandlish Phillips, *City Notebook*

What verbs in these passages create strong mental pictures? What pictures do they create?

Vocabulary
Revising Tip

During the revising stage, replace verb-adverb pairs with a single verb. For instance, change "Pablo smiled happily" to "Pablo beamed."

To choose just the right verb to use in a particular situation, do what many professional writers do—use a thesaurus, which is a collection of synonyms. Just keep in mind that synonyms are not necessarily interchangeable. For example, you wouldn't write "The horse *jogs*" when you mean "The horse *gallops*," even though *jog* and *gallop* are both synonyms for *run*.

Sometimes you may not be certain of the precise meanings of synonyms. See the thesaurus entry at the right, for example: you might have to consult a dictionary to find the exact meanings of *aggrandize* and *augment*.

INCREASE—V.
Increase, enhance, aggrandize, augment; intensify, step up, raise, boost.
    grow, surge, swell, fill out, inflate; skyrocket; overgrow, spread.

Journal Writing

Choose a recent entry in your journal. Underline all the verbs. Replace them with more vivid ones. How does this change your entry?

Revise with Exact Verbs

The best time to check the effectiveness of your verbs is in the revising stage, after you've gotten all your ideas down. Notice how much the replacement verbs in the following model strengthen the images the writer is trying to create. The guidelines below the model provide a plan for systematically checking and improving verbs.

Model

"Pour" gives a better feeling of relentless motion than "flow."

It stopped raining at noon, but clouds con-
tinued to ~~flow~~ *pour* down the craggy mountain into the valley below. Despite the weather, we were determined to hike up at least one mountain in

How is "trudged" better than "climbed"?

Switzerland. We ~~climbe~~ *trudged* up the steep slope behind the Klausen Pass Hotel, picking our way through fields of sharp rock and over spongelike clumps of wet lichen. After an hour of heavy

What does "plopped" tell you?

climbing, we ~~sat~~ *plopped* down on a chilly slab to revive ourselves with water and chocolate. Sud-denly, the clouds that had been moving down the mountain spread over our slope, enveloping us in mist. Like it or not, we knew we had to turn

"Stumbled" calls up a more vivid mental image than "walked." How does "stumbled" build on the impression created by "plopped" and "trudged"?

back. Disappointed, we ~~walked~~ *stumbled* blindly downward until we came to the road to our hotel.

Grammar
Editing Tip

When you get to the editing stage, pay particular attention to consistency of tenses. See Lessons 15.3–15.6, pages 551–561.

Guidelines for Revision

1. Read your first draft carefully, highlighting each verb with a yellow marker.
2. Scrutinize each verb carefully. Does it call up a vivid mental picture? If not, try to substitute one that does.
3. Consult a thesaurus for help.

Write with Energetic Verbs

Close your eyes, and use one of the following verbs to help you visualize a place with which you are familiar:

slide	kick	skip
hoot	giggle	chase
lunge	swoop	shove
shriek	whirl	toss

Picture both the location and the action. Write a description of the place you visualized. First, make a list of striking details you want to include in the description. Then, write a first draft, using your details to create a vivid word picture. Finally, revise your paragraph, replacing simple verbs with high-energy, action-packed verbs. Consult a thesaurus if you need help finding synonyms.

• Use exact verbs

PURPOSE To use action verbs to describe a place
AUDIENCE Yourself and your teacher
LENGTH 1 paragraph

COMPUTER OPTION

If your word processor has an electronic thesaurus, you can use it to help you choose energetic verbs. The electronic thesaurus will quickly give you options for synonyms of verbs, or any other words, that you highlight. The thesaurus may even replace the original word automatically with the new word you have chosen.

Grammar Link

Use verbs correctly.

Even vivid verbs will not be effective if you do not use them correctly. Remember to use the past form without a helping verb (I *went*) and the past participle form with a helping verb (I *have gone*). Remember also to use the correct verb in confusing pairs like *lie* and *lay*.

Rewrite each sentence below, inserting the correct form of the verb in parentheses.

1. I have (grew, grown) up reading English writer Virginia Woolf.
2. She (wrote, written) several excellent novels, including *To the Lighthouse*.
3. I have (read, readed) most of Virginia Woolf's books.
4. I have sometimes (thunk, thought) that they are among my favorites.
5. Occasionally, Woolf's characters have (drove, driven) me crazy.
6. They often seem to have (fell, fallen) into mysterious emotional states.
7. The stream-of-consciousness technique the author (chose, chosen) to use in some of her books makes them difficult to read.
8. I have (began, begun) *Orlando* several times.
9. Each time I have (lain, laid) the novel down without finishing it.
10. The book still (lies, lays) on my bedside table.

See Lessons 15.1 and 15.2, pages 547–550.

Descriptive Writing

Describing from Vantage Points

The term vantage point *refers to the location from which a writer observes a scene. A writer can describe a scene from a stationary vantage point or, if the scene continually changes, from a moving vantage point. Which vantage point would be used to describe the cockpit below? The scene outside it?*

Stationary Vantage Points

A stationary vantage point is a fixed position from which to view a scene. In the following model, American writer Edward Abbey describes a scene from such a vantage point. He is viewing a mountain landscape from a central focus, describing the view to each compass point in turn, first west, then south and north, leaving east for last. The graphic at the right diagrams this spatial organization.

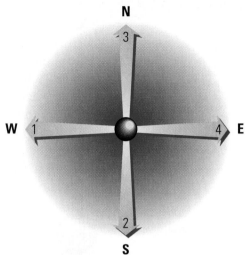

Literature Model

*T*he view is open and perfect in all directions except to the west where the ground rises and the skyline is only a few hundred yards away. Looking toward the mountains I can see the dark gorge of the Colorado River five or six miles away, carved through the sandstone mesa, though nothing of the river itself down inside the gorge. Southward, on the far side of the river, lies the Moab valley between thousand-foot walls of rock, with the town of Moab somewhere on the valley floor, too small to be seen from here. Beyond the Moab valley is more canyon and tableland stretching away to the Blue Mountains fifty miles south. On the north and northwest I see the Roan Cliffs and the Book Cliffs, the two-level face of the Uinta Plateau. . . . To the east, under the spreading sunrise, are more mesas, more canyons, league on league of red cliff and arid tablelands, extending through purple haze over the bulging curve of the planet to the ranges of Colorado—a sea of desert.

Edward Abbey, "The Most Beautiful Place on Earth"

What words give you a sense of direction in this passage?

Prewriting Tip

Creating a diagram before you begin drafting a description can help you focus your writing. Use arrows and numbers to show the ordering of specific details.

Journal Writing

Think about your trip to school every day. List details you would use to describe that trip. In your journal write a few sentences to explain your graphics. Experiment with some kinds of graphics for organizing your trip from a stationary vantage point.

Move the Vantage Point

A moving vantage point occurs when the position of the viewer continually changes. Usually a writer switches to chronological, or time, order when describing a scene from a moving vantage point. The diagram graphically shows the model's chronological organization.

Moving along points on a path, you describe each scene as you come upon it.

Scene 1
Scene 2
Scene 3
Scene 4
Scene 5

You can get a better feel for the chronological nature of Abbey's organization by comparing the description with the diagram.

Literature Model

I drove twelve miles farther north on the highway until I came to a dirt road on the right, where a small wooden sign pointed the way: ARCHES NATIONAL MONUMENT EIGHT MILES. I left the pavement, turned east into the howling wilderness. Wind roaring out of the northwest, black clouds across the stars—all I could see were clumps of brush and scattered junipers along the roadside. Then another modest signboard:

WARNING: QUICKSAND
DO NOT CROSS WASH WHEN WATER IS RUNNING

The wash looked perfectly dry in my headlights. I drove down, across, up the other side and on into the night. Glimpses of weird humps of pale rock on either side, like petrified elephants, dinosaurs, stone-age hobgoblins. Now and then something alive scurried across the road: kangaroo mice, a jackrabbit, an animal that looked like a cross between a raccoon and a squirrel—the ringtail cat. Farther on a pair of mule deer started from the brush and bounded obliquely through the beams of my lights, raising puffs of dust which the wind, moving faster than my pickup truck, caught and carried ahead of me out of sight into the dark. The road, narrow and rocky, twisted sharply left and right, dipped in and out of tight ravines, climbing by degrees toward a summit which I would see only in the light of the coming day.

Edward Abbey, "The Most Beautiful Place on Earth"

Vocabulary
Revising Tip

When you revise descriptions written from a moving vantage point, you can make chronological order clearer by using transitions that suggest the passage of time: *until, later, then, after.*

3.4 Writing Activities

Write from a Moving Vantage Point

Write a description of a place from a moving vantage point, such as a landscape viewed from a train window or a canyon as you climb down into it.

- Select the different scenes you will describe.
- Use chronological order.
- Use transitions when your vantage point changes.

PURPOSE To describe a scene from a moving vantage point
AUDIENCE Your classmates
LENGTH 2–3 paragraphs

Cross-Curricular: Geography

Think of a city that you have studied recently or one with which you are familiar. Choose one stationary vantage point from which to describe it, and write a paragraph telling what you see from that vantage point. Then select an area of the city that you could walk through, and write a paragraph describing sites from that moving vantage point. Decide which description communicates a better sense of the city.

Writing About Literature
Responding to Imagery in Poetry

The images a poet uses enable readers to share the poet's unique experience of the world. How would you respond to the images in the following poem? By writing your own poem? By painting a picture such as the one on page 139?

Literature Model

Corsons Inlet

I went for a walk over the dunes again this morning
to the sea,
then turned right along
    the surf
          rounded a naked headland
          and returned

  along the inlet shore:

it was muggy sunny, the wind from the sea steady and high,
crisp in the running sand,
    some breakthroughs of sun
  but after a bit

continuous overcast:

the walk liberating, I was released from forms,
from the perpendiculars,
      straight lines, blocks, boxes, binds
of thought
into the hues, shadings, rises, flowing bends and blends
      of sight . . .

A. R. Ammons

Respond Creatively

Sometimes people are so affected by a poem that they feel a need to respond in a creative way. For example, some people turn poetic images into pictures—pencil sketches, watercolors, even quilts. Others pick an image and respond by choreographing a dance. The following chart shows four other creative ways of responding to imagery in a poem.

Creative Responses to Poetic Images
1. Create a collage that expresses the image's meaning to you.
2. Use your journal to explore the feelings the image arouses in you.
3. Write a poem based on an image that inspires you.
4. Read the poem aloud for a friend or group of classmates.

Prewriting Tip

You may want to discuss your idea for responding to a poem with a classmate before working it out on your own. Such interaction will help you clarify and focus your own ideas.

Grammar
Revising Tip

When you revise poems you have written as responses, add vivid adjectives to bring images to life. For more information about adjectives, see Lesson 10.4, pages 422–427.

Arthur Dove, *Sunrise*, 1924

Journal Writing

Think about different ways of responding to a favorite poem. In your journal, discuss which of the responses listed above would work best for you.

Respond to Poetry

Sometimes it isn't easy to respond to a poem. New York poet Kenneth Koch found a way to help his students—children as young as 8 and adults as old as 98. Koch taught reading poetry and writing poetry as one subject. The two were brought together by "poetry ideas," suggestions for writing that echo the theme of a poem being studied.

To see how to apply Koch's idea, look back at the selection "Corsons Inlet" on page 138. Notice how Ammons contrasts the changing shapes and movement of nature—the dunes, the sea, the wind, and the sun—with the rigid perpendiculars, straight lines, and binds of his own thinking. One writer took that as his "poetry idea": how thinking often gets in the way of really seeing.

Sonia Terk Delaunay, *Electric Prisms*, 1914

The writer uses Ammons's images of nature as a springboard for the new poem.

Why does the poet suddenly include the image of a diner counter? What does it point to?

In the second stanza the writer details how thinking gets in the way of seeing.

Model

I wish the hard part
would be forms. Catching the trees right,
getting the sea to cooperate.
Or the sun, coaxing the sun out
when everything is right
and you want it shining.
But all this is easy, soothing, and natural.
As bright and spotless as a diner counter.

The real difficulty is eyeing the flat,
plain, and level. Scaffolding,
the high wires, the firefighter's ladders,
disarrange the subject. Then
an ocean has thoughts; the wind
calls collect, a whispering relative. Your signature
is on everything
saying names and hiding shapes.

3.5 Writing Activities

Write a Poem

Write a poem in response to one of the images in the poem at the beginning of this lesson or in another poem of your own choosing. First, find a "poetry idea" in the original poem. Then, freewrite to build on this idea.

- Use vivid adjectives to create your own images.

PURPOSE To respond to a poetic image
AUDIENCE Yourself and your teacher
LENGTH 1 page

COMPUTER OPTION

As you are writing your poem, you might experiment with how the words look on the page. Try breaking your lines at different places. Try a different typeface or size. The shape and size of the letters can affect the "feel" of your poem. Print out different versions of your poem and compare them. If you want to achieve a special effect, change the typeface of only one line or word. Use tabs or alignment commands to scatter your text across the page. See which changes bring the most meaning to your poem.

Grammar Link

Use clear, precise adjectives to improve your descriptions.

Adjectives such as *muggy*, *flowing*, and *soothing* from the models in this lesson help create precise word pictures. Look at this example by A. R. Ammons:

*it was **muggy sunny**, the wind from the sea*
*   **steady** and **high**,*
***crisp** in the **running** sand . . .*

Revise the following sentences by adding at least one vivid adjective to each.

1. I walked over the dunes.
2. The sea grass grew.
3. The sea beckoned me.
4. The waves lapped the shore.
5. A boat bobbed, straining at its anchor.
6. The sun barely penetrated the mist.
7. The air tickled my nose.
8. On the horizon loomed the shadow of a tanker.
9. Clouds scudded before a breeze.
10. I laughed.

See Lesson 10.4, pages 422–427.

Writing About Literature
Analyzing Setting in a Short Story

Setting is the environment—the time and place—in which the action of a story takes place. When you analyze setting, you describe the setting and then look at how it relates to other important elements of the story.

The graphic below illustrates some important uses of setting. Consider these uses when you analyze the setting of any story.

Uses of Setting		
Use	**Example**	**Explanation**
To create mood	During the whole of a dull, dark, and soundless day in the autumn of the year, when the clouds hung oppressively low in the heavens, I had been passing alone, on horseback, through a singularly dreary tract of country, and at length found myself, as the shades of evening drew on, within view of the melancholy House of Usher. Edgar Allan Poe, "The Fall of the House of Usher"	The setting creates a mood of depression and impending doom.
To affect action	The house was very still about me and yet alive, as if it breathed softly. . . . I shivered and crept to the wide-open window. The faint dawn light, scarcely less than darkness, showed only the silhouette of the birch trees. The moon was down. The garden was totally indistinct. Iris Murdoch, "The Italian Girl"	The setting is crucial as a backdrop for the action.
To develop character	"It's pretty over there," she said. . . . "I go there all the time. Ride over. Especially the graveyard. Down where Spring Creek runs into the Clear Fork. Daddy says it's dangerous because of the copperheads but I go there anyway." A. C. Greene, "The Girl at Cabe Ranch"	The setting conveys information about the main character.

Look for Connections

When you look at the connection between the setting of a story and other elements such as mood, plot, and character, you may find that the author uses setting to tell about the other elements. For example, setting may foreshadow disaster or create an atmosphere of terror. The contrast between two settings in a story—a farmhouse and a city apartment, for instance—may be used to reveal a character's feelings. Similarly, the details of setting—color of walls, neatness of a desk, contents of a drawer—may provide important information about a character.

Setting may also be used as an active participant in a story—for example, a mountain that must be scaled. In this case the setting is something that a character must struggle against. Below is a questionnaire that you can use to analyze a story setting.

Grammar

Prewriting Tip

As you analyze story setting, notice if—and how—the author uses adverbs to present a more vivid picture of place. For more information about adverbs, see Lesson 10.5, pages 428–434.

Analyzing a Story Setting

General
1. What is the name of the story?
2. Where does most of the story action take place? When does it take place? Is there historical significance to the setting?

Setting and Mood
3. What is the general mood of the story? Cheerful or gloomy? Comforting or threatening? Hopeful or despairing?
4. How does the story setting contribute to the mood?

Setting and Plot
5. What is the plot in the story?
6. Is the setting crucial to the plot? Would it matter much if the story had a different setting? Does the description of the setting change as the story progresses?

Setting and Character
7. Who is the main character in the story? What is this person like?
8. How do we learn about the main character? Does the author convey any important information about the main character through setting?

Journal Writing

Use the questionnaire to begin analyzing setting in a favorite short story. Answer the questions as thoroughly as possible.

Create Your Analysis

After you identify the connections between setting and the other story elements, plan an effective analysis. Use the questionnaire on page 143 as a guide while developing your main points and the support for your arguments. Notice how the questionnaire relates to the following model. Below the model is a set of guidelines you can use to write your own essay about setting in a short story.

Model

The introductory paragraph points out that setting plays a major role in the story.

How does the writer use direct quotations from the story?

How does the writer use evidence from the story to support the arguments of the analysis?

*I*n some stories setting isn't very important. It's only background to the main action. In other stories, however, setting plays a major role, creating a unifying thread that touches everyone and everything. Such is the case with the setting in "Chee's Daughter."

Chee is a Navaho who always tries to live in harmony with nature. He has a "feeling of wholeness and of oneness with the sun and earth and growing things." As the story begins, we learn that Chee's wife has died, leaving a three-year-old daughter who, according to Navaho custom, now lives with the mother's relatives.

The story revolves around Chee's efforts to get his daughter back, and the plot and the setting are intertwined every step of the way. For example, the story begins in the cold of winter, so when Chee first asks the grandparents if the daughter can stay with him, we know what the answer will be: a frigid no. We soon learn, however, that "springtime transformed the mesas," and we realize immediately that it will transform Chee, too. He has a new plan—to place his trust in the land, grow a bountiful harvest, and exchange the food for the child. In the end, Chee's faith is vindicated, and he gets his daughter back.

Guidelines for Writing About Setting

1. Read the story carefully, completing the questionnaire as you go.
2. Write an introductory paragraph that states the main idea of your essay.
3. Use information from the questionnaire in developing your major points.
4. Cite specific evidence from the story to support your argument.
5. End with a brief paragraph summarizing your conclusions.

3.6 Writing Activities

Allan Crite, *Shadow and Sunlight*, 1941

Write a Setting Analysis

Think of a general plot for a short story that could belong with the painting above. Then write an explanation of how the painting's setting affects the story.

- Describe the mood created by the setting.
- Explain how the setting affects the feelings of various characters.
- Discuss how the setting relates to the story's actions.

PURPOSE To analyze setting
AUDIENCE Your teacher
LENGTH 2–3 paragraphs

Cross-Curricular: History

Read a short story that takes place in a specific historical period. Write an analysis of how the story's setting, including the historical context, affects the story's mood, action, and character development

Grammar Link

Use strong adverbs to make descriptions more precise.

Notice how Edgar Allan Poe uses the adverbs *oppressively*, *alone*, and *singularly* in the model on page 142.

Revise the following sentences by adding at least one vivid adverb to each. (You may make other changes, too, if you wish.)

1. The thunder faded into the distance.
2. Gray clouds raced overhead.
3. The countryside lay sodden and silent.
4. The weary plop of a horse's hooves reached my ears.
5. A solitary rider approached.

See Lesson 10.5, page 428.

WRITING PROCESS IN ACTION

DESCRIPTIVE WRITING

In preceding lessons you've learned how to describe a place by choosing a vantage point, observing and organizing details carefully, and using energetic verbs. You've also had a chance to write a poem and an essay about story setting. In this lesson you'll put together what you've learned by describing a place that you know well.

• Assignment •

Context	A student from another state is moving to your school. Your principal has sent the student a variety of orientation materials—class schedules, copies of the school newspaper, last year's yearbook. The student writes back, politely explaining that what she or he really wants is a description of the new school that will allow her or him to "see" the place and the people in it. You've been asked to respond to this request.
Purpose	To write a description of your school that will convey what it's like from a student's point of view
Audience	A student moving to your school from another state
Length	1 to 2 pages

You will find the next few pages helpful as you plan and write your description. Read through the pages, and refer to them as you need to, but remember that they are only guidelines. After all, you're in charge of your own writing process.

Prewriting

How will you describe your school? What details will you use to present a picture of the building? What details will bring the people in the school to life for your future schoolmate? The questions on the notepad may help you choose details and a method of organizing the details that will help you write a vivid description.

Jot down notes of details as they occur to you. If you decide that you want to describe the school from a moving vantage point, walk through the building, noting any striking images that will help you write your description. If necessary, research facts by checking with the school administration.

Once you've collected your details, decide which ones you want to use, and organize your notes. Is there a fact or an image that stands out? If so, that's what you want to use for your lead—the first sentence or two that will grab and hold your reader's attention. Look at the lead that Gretel Ehrlich uses in this description of her subject, Wyoming. Note how this passage marries a generalized picture with a quotation that creates a vivid snapshot.

Prewriting Questions
- What images—verbal snapshots—will allow my reader to see the school as I see it?
- What personal anecdotes or quotations can I include?
- What facts and statistics will provide useful information?
- What vantage point would give life to my description?

Literature Model

*T*o live and work in this kind of open country, with its hundred-mile views, is to lose the distinction between background and foreground. When I asked an older ranch hand to describe Wyoming's openness, he said, "It's all a bunch of nothing—wind and rattlesnakes—and so much of it you can't tell where you're going or where you've been and it don't make much difference."

Gretel Ehrlich, *The Solace of Open Spaces*

Drafting

Drafting Tip

To review how to organize details, see Lesson 2.7, pages 76–78, and Lesson 3.1, pages 121–124.

To begin drafting, imagine where you are—the place you'll begin your tour or where you will stand to describe all that you see around you—or look at your lead. Then just start writing.

As you write, be aware of details unique to your school that might need special explanation. Try to look at your school with a "fresh" eye so you can make the description clear for the new student.

Visualize what you are describing. Use your notes to remember details, but don't stop writing at this stage to find the perfect verb or image. If you get stuck, take a break, talk about your description with a friend, or start over.

Revising

To begin revising, read over your draft to make sure that what you've written fits your purpose and audience. Then have a **writing conference**. Read your draft to a partner or small group. Use your audience's reactions and the Revising Checklist below to help you evaluate your work.

Revising Tip

If you are having trouble with word choice, consult the Guidelines for Revision chart, Lesson 3.3, page 132

Revising Checklist
- Did I use a lead that grabbed the reader?
- Did I select good details and organize them logically around topic sentences?
- Were the images I used clear and striking?
- Did I use exact, energetic verbs to enliven my description?
- Did I write from a vantage point that made sense?

Editing

When you are satisfied with your description, **proofread** it carefully for errors in grammar, usage, mechanics, and spelling. Use the questions at the right as a guide.

In addition to proofreading, use the Self-Evaluation to make sure your writing describes the school well. When you feel that it does, make a clean copy of your description and proofread it one more time.

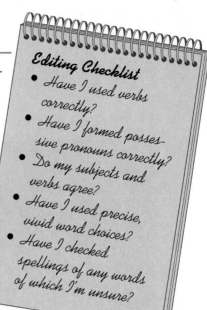

Editing Checklist
- *Have I used verbs correctly?*
- *Have I formed possessive pronouns correctly?*
- *Do my subjects and verbs agree?*
- *Have I used precise, vivid word choices?*
- *Have I checked spellings of any words of which I'm unsure?*

Self-Evaluation
Make sure your description—

- focuses on interesting aspects of school or school life
- uses a strong lead
- uses different kinds of vivid supporting details
- uses strong verbs and good transitions
- follows correct grammar, usage, mechanics, and spelling

Editing, like revising, is done best in a series of passes through your work. It's easier to watch for one type of error than to be on the lookout for ten kinds. The guidelines for editing presented in Lesson 2.9, pages 87–88, can also help. Don't let the fact that you know your work lull you into missing obvious errors.

Presenting

You might want to have someone from another state read your description. Your reader might be a friend who has moved away, a relative, or a pen pal. Feedback from such a reading would tell you how well your description works.

> **Proofreading**
>
> For proofreading symbols, see page 88.

Journal Writing

Reflect on your writing process experience. Answer these questions in your journal: What do you like best about your description? What was the hardest part of writing it? What did you learn in your writing conference? What new things have you learned as a writer?

Descriptive Writing
Literature Model

GRETEL EHRLICH

FROM

*The Solace of
Open Spaces*

In this excerpt from her book The Solace of Open Spaces, *Gretel Ehrlich, who lives on a
ranch in Wyoming, uses descriptive writing to portray her adopted home state, its land, and
its people. Pay particular attention to the images, the facts, and the anecdotes Ehrlich uses to
engage the reader in her description. Then try the activities in Linking Writing and
Literature on page 155.*

To live and work in this kind of open country, with its
hundred-mile views, is to lose the distinction between background and foreground. When I asked an older ranch hand to
describe Wyoming's openness, he said, "It's all a bunch of nothing—
wind and rattlesnakes—and so much of it you can't tell where
you're going or where you've been and it don't make much difference." John, a sheepman I know, is tall and handsome and has an
explosive temperament. He has a perfect intuition about people and
sheep. They call him "Highpockets," because he's so long-legged;
his graceful stride matches the distances he has to cover. He says,
"Open space hasn't affected me at all. It's all the people moving in

on it." The huge ranch he was born on takes up much of one county and spreads into another state; to put 100,000 miles on his pickup in three years and never leave home is not unusual. A friend of mine has an aunt who ranched on Powder River and didn't go off her place for eleven years. When her husband died, she quickly moved to town, bought a car, and drove around the States to see what she'd been missing.

Most people tell me they've simply driven through Wyoming, as if there were nothing to stop for. Or else they've skied in Jackson Hole, a place Wyomingites acknowledge uncomfortably because its green beauty and chic affluence[1] are mismatched with the rest of the state. Most of Wyoming has a "lean-to" look. Instead of big, roomy barns and Victorian houses, there are dugouts, low sheds, log cabins, sheep camps, and fence lines that look like driftwood blown haphazardly into place. People here still feel pride because they live in such a harsh place, part of the glamorous cowboy past, and they are determined not to be the victims of a mining-dominated future.

Most characteristic of the state's landscape is what a developer euphemistically[2] describes as "indigenous growth right up to your front door"—a reference to waterless stands of salt sage, snakes, jack rabbits, deerflies, red dust, a brief respite of wildflowers, dry washes, and no trees. In the Great Plains the vistas look like music, like Kyries[3] of grass, but Wyoming seems to be the doing of a mad

Frederic Remington, *The Fall of the Cowboy*, 1895

1 chic affluence (shēk´ af´ loo wəns) stylish wealth

2 euphemistically (yōō fə mis´ tik lē) using a word or phrase in place of another that is distasteful or offensive

3 Kyries (kir´ ē āz) parts of the Roman Catholic mass, often set to music architect—tumbled and twisted, ribboned with faded, deathbed colors, thrust up and pulled down as if the place had been startled out of a deep sleep and thrown into a pure light.

I came here four years ago. I had not planned to stay, but I couldn't make myself leave. John, the sheepman, put me to work immediately. It was spring, and shearing time. For fourteen days of fourteen hours each, we moved thousands of sheep through sorting corrals to be sheared, branded, and deloused.[4] I suspect that my original motive for coming here was to "lose myself" in new and unpopulated territory. Instead of producing the numbness I thought I wanted, life on the sheep ranch woke me up. The vitality of the people I was working with flushed out what had become a hallucinatory[5] rawness inside me. I threw away my clothes and bought new ones; I cut my hair. The arid country was a clean slate. Its absolute indifference steadied me.

Sagebrush covers 58,000 square miles of Wyoming. The biggest city has a population of fifty thousand, and there are only five settlements that could be called cities in the whole state. The rest are towns, scattered across the expanse with as much as sixty miles between them, their populations two thousand, fifty, or ten. They are fugitive-looking, perched on a barren, windblown bench, or tagged onto a river or a railroad, or laid out straight in a farming valley with implement stores and a block-long Mormon church. In the eastern part of the state, which slides down into the Great Plains, the new mining settlements are boomtowns, trailer cities, metal knots on flat land.

Despite the desolate look, there's a coziness to living in this state. There are so few people (only 470,000) that ranchers who buy and sell cattle know one another statewide; the kids who choose to go to college usually go to the state's one university, in Laramie; hired hands work their way around Wyoming in a lifetime of hirings and firings. And despite the physical separation, people stay in touch, often driving two or three hours to another ranch for dinner.

Seventy-five years ago, when travel was by buckboard or horseback, cowboys who were temporarily out of work rode the grub line—drifting from ranch to ranch, mending fences or milking cows, and receiving in exchange a bed and meals. Gossip and messages traveled this slow circuit with them, creating an intimacy between ranchers who were three and four weeks' ride apart. One old-time couple I know, whose turn-of-the-century homestead was used by an outlaw gang as a relay station for stolen horses, recall that if you were traveling, desperado or not, any lighted ranch house was a

4 deloused (dē lous′ d) rid of lice

5 hallucinatory (hə lōōs′ sə nə tôr′ ē) characterized by or producing sights or sounds that are not really present welcome sign. Even now, for someone who lives in a remote spot, arriving at a ranch or coming to town for supplies is cause for celebration. To emerge from isolation can be disorienting.[6] Everything looks bright, new, vivid. After I had been herding sheep for only three days, the sound of the camp tender's pickup flustered me. Longing for human company, I felt a foolish grin take over my face; yet I had to resist an urgent temptation to run and hide.

Things happen suddenly in Wyoming, the change of seasons and weather; for people, the violent swings in and out of isolation. But good-naturedness is concomitant with severity.[7] Friendliness is a tradition. Strangers passing on the road wave hello. A common sight is two pickups stopped side by side far out on a range, on a dirt track winding thought the sage. The drivers will share a cigarette, uncap their thermos bottles, and pass a battered cup, steaming with coffee, between windows. These meetings summon up the details of several generations, because, in Wyoming, private histories are largely public knowledge.

Because ranch work is a physical and, these days, economic strain, being "at home on the range" is a matter of vigor, self-reliance, and common sense. A person's life is not a series of dramatic events for which he or she is applauded or exiled but a slow accumulation of days, seasons, years, fleshed out by the generational weight of one's family and anchored by a land-bound sense of place.

In most parts of Wyoming, the human population is visibly outnumbered by the animal. Not far from my town of fifty, I rode into a narrow valley and startled a herd of two hundred elk. Eagles look like small people as they eat car-killed deer by the road. Antelope, moving in small, graceful bands, travel at sixty miles an hour, their mouths open as if drinking in the space.

The solitude in which westerners live makes them quiet. They telegraph thoughts and feelings by the way they tilt their heads and listen; pulling their Stetsons into a steep dive over their eyes, or pigeon-toeing one boot over the other, they lean against a fence with a fat wedge of Copenhagen beneath their lower lips and take in the whole scene. These detached looks of quiet amusement are sometimes cynical, but they can also come from a dry-eyed humility as lucid as the air is clear.

Ann Taylor, *Red Riding*, 1982

6 disorienting (dis ôr´ ē ent´ iŋ) causing one to lose one's bearings

7 is concomitant with severity (kən käm´ ə tənt) (se ver´ ə tē) is related to harshness

Conversation goes on in what sounds like a private code; a few phrases imply a complex of meanings. Asking directions, you get a curious list of details. While trailing sheep I was told to "ride up to that kinda upturned rock, follow the pink wash, turn left at the dump, and then you'll see the water hole." One friend told his wife on roundup to "turn at the salt lick and the dead cow," which turned out to be a scattering of bones and no salt lick at all.

Sentence structure is shortened to the skin and bones of a thought. Descriptive words are dropped, even verbs; a cowboy looking over a corral full of horses will say to a wrangler, "Which one needs rode?" People hold back their thoughts in what seems to be a dumbfounded silence, then erupt with an excoriating[8] perceptive remark. Language, so compressed, becomes metaphorical. A rancher ended a relationship with one remark: "You're a bad check," meaning bouncing in and out was intolerable, and even coming back would be no good.

What's behind this laconic[9] style is shyness. There is no vocabulary for the subject of feelings. It's not a hangdog[10] shyness, or anything coy—always there's a robust spirit in evidence behind the restraint, as if the earth-dredging wind that pulls across Wyoming had carried its people's voices away but everything else in them had shouldered confidently into the breeze.

I've spent hours riding to sheep camp at dawn in a pickup when nothing was said; eaten meals in the cookhouse when the only words spoken were a mumbled "Thank you, ma'am" at the end of dinner. The silence is profound. Instead of talking, we seem to share one eye. Keenly observed, the world is transformed. The landscape is engorged with detail, every movement on it chillingly sharp. The air between people is charged. Days unfold, bathed in their own music. Nights become hallucinatory; dreams, prescient.[11]

---

8 **excoriating** (ik skôr´ ē āt´ iŋ) harsh; abrasive

9 **laconic** (lə kän´ ik) brief or succinct in speech

10 **hangdog** ashamed; cringing

11 **prescient** (prē´ shē ənt) able to know of things before they occur

Linking Writing and Literature

Readers Respond to the Model

What makes Gretel Ehrlich's description effective?

Explore Gretel Ehrlich's description by answering these questions.
Then read how other students reacted to Ehrlich's narrative.

1. How did Ehrlich convey a "sense of place" in this selection?
2. Choose one descriptive paragraph that you particularly liked. What specific details or images made this description work?
3. What mood does Ehrlich's description evoke? How?

4. Explain how the following description of the geography contrasts with Ehrlich's description of the people: . . . "Wyoming seems to be the doing of a mad architect—tumbled and twisted, ribboned with faded, deathbed colors, thrust up and pulled down as if the place had been startled out of a deep sleep and thrown into a pure light."

I truly admire Gretel Ehrlich's passion for Wyoming's desolate country and her ability to make such a seemingly barren land come to life. Her description was phenomenal; it made me see the whole state. Ehrlich's first-person point of view made the selection very lyrical and personal, without being clichéd. Her writing had a real human quality. I believe the author wrote as she did because she is akin to the land and its people.

The part I remember best was when Ehrlich talked about how the people rarely spoke, about their having a silent language. It seemed both straightforward and cryptic; it made me feel somehow included in the private, secretive lives of the ranchers. I would recommend this selection to a friend because it is so personal and truthful. It made me understand how someone can have so much love for a place.

Rachel Hansen

Although Ehrlich's descriptions were good, this selection did not interest me very much— perhaps because of the quiet and peaceful nature of the place. The writer simply failed to keep my attention.

Claire Monty

Unit 3 Review

Reflecting on the Unit

Summarize what you learned in this unit by answering the following questions.

- How can you gather details for descriptive writing?

- What are some effective ways to organize descriptive details to create effective images?

- How can choice of verbs affect the vitality of your writing?

- How does vantage point relate to description of a place?

- What are some important elements in analyzing the setting of a story?

Adding to Your Portfolio

Choose a selection for your portfolio.
Look over the descriptive writing you have done during this unit. Select a completed piece of writing to put into your portfolio. The piece you choose should show some or all of the following:

- descriptive details arranged in an effective order
- a basis in observation and note taking
- precise, vivid verbs
- the use of a clear vantage point

Reflect on your choice.
Attach a note to the piece you chose, explaining briefly why you chose it and what you learned from writing it.

Set goals.
How can you improve your writing?
What skill will you focus on the next time you write?

Writing Across the Curriculum

Make a geography connection.
Think about the description of your school that you wrote and about Gretel Ehrlich's description of Wyoming. What images spring to mind when you think about your town or county? Take notes and organize your descriptive details. Create a lead using colorful images, quotations, anecdotes, or background facts. Then write a two- or three-paragraph description of your town or county. Use topic sentences to focus the details in your paragraphs and action-packed verbs to make your vision come to life for the reader.

Narrative Writing in the Real World

Norfolk Tells Tales

F O C U S: Like a written narrative, a told story has a plot, character, and setting; a storyteller usually emphasizes character and plot over setting.

I n 1986 Bobby Norfolk resigned from the National Park Service to become a full-time storyteller. "I've never looked back," he says with a smile.

Bobby Norfolk's success as a storyteller would never have been predicted by his grammar school teachers. "I stuttered all through grade school," Norfolk recalls. "It did nothing for my social life, so I retreated into books. Literature increased my vocabulary and evoked my imagination. Then, in high school drama, I found I could be all these different personas. High school drama plus learning relaxation techniques finally ended my stuttering."

The many personas Bobby Norfolk discovered in acting he now employs in his storytelling career. Norfolk has entertained audiences (sometimes as large as three thousand) in forty-three states and Canada. The storyteller has produced two award-winning audio-cassette tapes and has also starred in an Emmy award-winning television show, *Gator Tales,* which aired on a CBS affiliate station in Saint Louis.

Storyteller Bobby Norfolk

> *"I didn't seek storytelling. It sought me. I'd worked as a stand-up comedian, an actor, an investigative reporter, a car salesman, a substitute teacher, and a national park ranger. In 1978 Saint Louis held its first annual storytelling festival under the Arch, where I was a park ranger. I saw that I could blend all my skills into storytelling."*
>
> —Bobby Norfolk

Prewriting

FINDING THE STORY

Some tellers write their own stories. Others retell narratives they've heard from family and friends. Like many storytellers, Bobby Norfolk finds most of his stories in books. "I live in libraries and bookstores," says Norfolk.

After poring over Edith Hamilton's *Mythology*, the story-teller chose the tale of Perseus, one of the heroes of Greek mythology, "because it was the most visual of all the myths. This one gets as close as you can to classic horror, so I knew kids would relish it."

As told by Edith Hamilton, the story of Perseus unfolds like a fairy tale. Perseus's extraordinary adventures begin with his boast that he will slay Medusa, a Gorgon, or monster, who has snakes for hair and turns anyone who looks at her into stone. Naturally, Perseus needs help in his quest, and he gets it from three witches and several Greek gods. Norfolk says, "As I read the story, I visualized the three witches who had to share one eye, and Perseus's meeting with the Greek gods. I knew I could convey these vivid images to my listeners."

| Storytelling | | | |

Prewriting

Finding
the Story

Drafting

Adapting
the Story

Revising

Fine-tuning
the Story

Presenting

Performing
the Story

Drafting

The foundation of world literature lies in the stories of ancient mythology.

ADAPTING THE STORY

To adapt Hamilton's version of the myth for the stage, the storyteller says, "I added a lot of dialogue to the original tale." Norfolk also supplied details to emphasize the scene that he considered the climax of the story. In Hamilton's version, the king and his court are turned into stone all at once. In Norfolk's adaptation, a series of pantomime freezes shows five or six courtiers becoming petrified in turn. This technique extends the action and underlines the climactic moment.

In addition to adding dialogue and highlighting plot elements, Norfolk also enlarged on several character descriptions. Hamilton describes Medusa's "snaky hair, most horrible to mortals." Norfolk's version supplies many other vivid details his listeners can visualize as he speaks:

Medusa stood about eight feet tall and had scales of green hue. Her fingernails were long and sharp, and she had canine teeth that hung from her mouth—used for tearing flesh from bone. Her hair was a mass of living snakes, hissing and twirling about constantly. Medusa had a long serpentlike tail that dragged behind her for six feet. That was not the most hideous thing about Medusa, however. She had blood-red eyes that lit up when any person looked upon her. That person would immediately turn into stone.

Bobby Norfolk

Norfolk pantomimes Medusa's snaky hair.

Revising

FINE-TUNING THE STORY

No matter how much a storyteller has practiced beforehand, storytelling is an improvisational art. Many storytellers make changes while the telling is in process. Bobby Norfolk says, "As I tell my story, I look around the audience and gauge their response. Sometimes I insert a modern reference, as in describing Perseus. I say he's built like Hulk Hogan, and then I growl and flex my muscles.

"The first time I told this story, I made clicking noises as the three witches in turn plucked the eye out of their forehead.

The kids all said 'oooh,' so I knew that part had to stay. They also loved the part where I act out Medusa. I made my ten fingers the snakes wriggling on my head. I hissed like a snake, and then I did hand movements like silhouettes on the wall, rising through the air."

Observing the audience to fine-tune a story is similar to the revising process any writer must go through. Bobby Norfolk says, "If I don't get a satisfactory reaction, I know I have to revamp or rework my story. I usually get an audience's rapt attention. If people are glancing off, I know they have mentally strayed. But if the story is hot, if the audience is very upbeat, then I know I've done the right thing. That's how I critique myself."

Edith Hamilton's book Mythology *inspired Norfolk to create his version of the Perseus tale.*

Portraying various moods and gestures, Norfolk performs the tale of Perseus.

Presenting

PERFORMING THE STORY

The way a storyteller delivers the final version of a story is comparable to a writer's style. Some successful writers write simply, just as some storytellers tell their tales sitting in a chair. Not Bobby Norfolk. Norfolk's dramatic storytelling style incorporates his skills in acrobatics and sound effects so that his audience can "see, hear, taste, touch, and smell the story."

Norfolk's physical style added comic relief to the tale of Perseus in a scene where a cruel king discovers his daughter is hiding her infant son, Perseus. In performance, Norfolk mimes the crown jumping off the shocked king's head. "And when Perseus kills Medusa, I pretend to be the Gorgon's head and do two and a half somersaults."

Unless a storyteller chooses to publish his story in print or on tape, the story may continue to evolve with each telling. Bobby Norfolk has written down his version of "Perseus and the Gorgon," but the storyteller says, "I've revised the story since I originally performed it. If you saw it, you would probably notice some parts that are different from my written version."

Norfolk performs at Miller Plaza in Chattanooga to celebrate the county library's summer reading program.

162

Responding to the Case Study

1. Discussion

Discuss these questions about Bobby Norfolk's storytelling.

- What are some basic similarities between telling a story as Bobby Norfolk does and writing a story? Some differences?
- How and why does Norfolk conduct research?
- What major changes does Norfolk say he made to Edith Hamilton's written myth of Perseus to adapt it for oral storytelling? Why do you think he made these changes?
- Why might a storyteller revise his or her story?

2. Narrative Writing

Write and perform a three-minute story.

Write a story of your own or adapt a published one. Include dialogue and descriptive details of character and setting. If you choose to adapt someone else's writing, make changes appropriate for your audience—your classmates, family, or friends. Consider how sound effects, voice changes, gestures, and acrobatic movements may enhance the telling of your tale. Finally, arrange to tell your story.

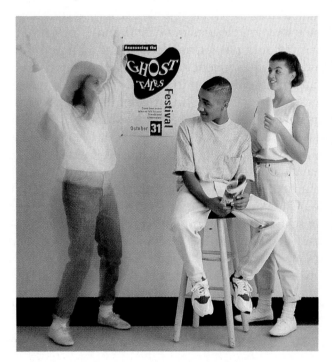

Grammar Link

Use participles, correctly punctuated, to add lively details to a story.

A *participle* is a verb form used as an adjective. Introductory participles and participial phrases and those that are not essential to the meaning of a sentence are set off by commas.

*Her hair was a mass of **living** snakes, **hissing** and **twirling** about constantly.*

Use each present participle below in a sentence. Insert commas where necessary.

1. screeching
2. whining
3. snaking
4. clutching
5. hammering
6. honking
7. snarling
8. glistening
9. sprinting
10. rumbling

See Lesson 12.3, pages 489–490, and Lesson 21.6, pages 707–709.

Narrative Writing
Narrating a Personal Experience

A personal narrative allows you to focus on important events of your life and their significance. Notice how Amber Sumrall uses first person and chronological order in relating an event from early childhood.

Literature Model

After setting the scene, Sumrall narrates the event vividly and dramatically.

When I was five we went to Yosemite for our first vacation. As my mother and father sat outside our cabin in Tuolomne Meadows reading the newspaper I played near the river with Bear, dipping his furry feet into the icy water. He was my best friend; I took him everywhere, could not fall asleep at night without him. Suddenly the current swept him out of my hands. I ran screaming and crying to my father, "Daddy, hurry, Bear's gone down the river." In a matter of seconds he'd tossed his newspaper aside and followed me to the place where I last saw Bear. Leaping from boulder to boulder he seemed to be flying down the creek, his red flannel shirt billowing like a flag, finally disappearing from view. When he returned an hour later, drenched and disheveled, he had Bear in his hands. Until that moment I had never been conscious of loving my father. I wonder if he realized then just how thoroughly Bear had taken his place. And if he knew what a disaster it would be for both of us if he'd returned empty-handed.

What meaning did the event have for the writer? Why does she remember it so vividly? Explain in your own words.

Amber Coverdale Sumrall, "Home Stretch"

Find Ideas for Your Personal Narrative

A personal narrative, such as the one you just read, comes directly from the writer's experience; it tells a real-life story. It also takes readers beyond the events to the meaning of those events. Two strategies—charting and mapping—can help you find ideas for personal narratives.

Charting involves making a chart of events grouped in categories. It includes such categories as important firsts, like the first day of school or a first date; turning points, like moving or joining a team; worst times, such as a disastrous summer job or an unfriendly sleepover.

Mapping involves making a map of your life. Draw a winding path showing high and low points, turning points, roads not taken. How would your personal map compare with the one below?

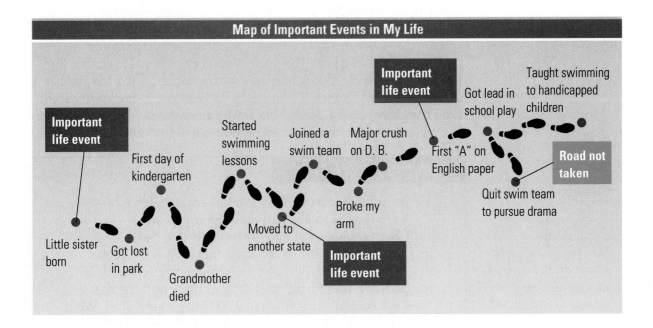

Map of Important Events in My Life

Important life event — Little sister born

Got lost in park

First day of kindergarten

Grandmother died

Started swimming lessons

Moved to another state — Important life event

Joined a swim team

Broke my arm

Major crush on D. B.

Important life event — First "A" on English paper

Got lead in school play

Taught swimming to handicapped children

Quit swim team to pursue drama — Road not taken

Journal Writing

Explore ideas for a personal narrative by charting and mapping. In your journal try out each strategy for about ten minutes. Compare the results. Write a few sentences about which strategy uncovered more of your memories and why.

Write Your Personal Narrative

Grammar
Revising Tip

When you revise your personal narrative, check for correct use of first-person pronouns. For help, see Lesson 17.1, pages 599–600.

After you find a personal experience to write about, use a prewriting strategy such as brainstorming to recall as many details as possible. Complete your prewriting by deciding what meaning your experience had for you. Then follow these guidelines to write your narrative.

Guidelines for Writing a Personal Narrative

1. In prewriting, list the events chronologically—the order in which they happened.
2. Maintain a first-person point of view, using the pronoun *I*.
3. Enliven your narrative with specific facts and details.
4. Use language—concrete nouns, vivid verbs, precise adjectives—to help readers share your excitement, sorrow, or anger.
5. Build a conclusion that expresses your thoughts and feelings about your experience and tell what it means to you.

Van Ngo followed this last guideline in her personal narrative. She related an experience that happened six years earlier, when she and her family fled from Vietnam. Their voyage in her uncle's small boat meant many hardships, even a death—but finally a new home. Following is her conclusion, in which the writer gives meaning to her experience.

Student Model

Here Van provides information she had intentionally omitted earlier in order to focus on the sea voyage.

Mimi, wake up. You're going to be late for school," my mom's voice cut through my dream.

I got slowly out of bed, dazed and disoriented. For a few moments, I didn't even know where I was. Then I remembered, and my dreams and memories came flooding back. I remembered that long journey and the day after my cousin's death when we finally found land. We'd landed on a Malaysian island and stayed for sixteen months before being sponsored by St. Mary's Church in Ohio. The Lord had answered all our prayers!

The experience has more than one meaning for Van. What does she say is the most important lesson she learned?

Six years have passed, but I still occasionally have dreams about my long journey to America. I feel so lucky and grateful that we found land and a new life in America. I learned that life should be appreciated and loved. Above all, I learned never to give up hope.

Van Ngo, Thomas Jefferson High School, Alexandria, Virginia
First appeared in *Merlyn's Pen: The National Magazine of Student Writing*

4.1 Writing Activities

Write a Personal Narrative

Charles Dickens began his famous novel *A Tale of Two Cities* with these words: "It was the best of times, it was the worst of times." Write a narrative about your own personal best time or worst time. Use mapping or charting to choose an event.

- Present events chronologically.
- Maintain first-person point of view.
- Build a conclusion that explains what the experience meant to you.

PURPOSE To write a personal narrative
AUDIENCE English class
LENGTH 3–4 paragraphs

Cross-Curricular: Science

Some personal experiences are humorous. Read James Thurber's account of his continuing failure in biology class.

I never once saw a cell through a microscope. This used to enrage my instructor. He would wander around the laboratory pleased with the progress all the students were making in drawing the involved and, so I am told, interesting structure of flower cells, until he came to me. I would just be standing there. "I can't see anything," I would say. He would begin patiently enough, explaining how anybody can see through a microscope, but he would always end up in a fury, claiming that I could too see through a microscope but just pretended that I couldn't.

James Thurber, *My Life and Hard Times*

Write a short humorous narrative about an experience you've had in a science class. Your audience is your fellow students. Read your narrative aloud to a small group.

Grammar Link

Use *I* and *me* correctly.

Personal writing involves much use of first-person pronouns.

*. . . followed **me** to the place where **I** last saw Bear.*

In compound constructions be particularly careful to use *I* for subjects and *me* for objects.

Complete each sentence below by adding *I* or *me*.

1. Chin and ____ have bicycled together before.
2. Yet this was a major trip for both him and ____ .
3. Vanessa's description of a family bike trip had so impressed Chin and ____ that we decided to follow the same route.
4. My parents made my friend and ____ sandwiches for two days' lunches.
5. Since we had arranged to stay with Chin's uncle overnight, Chin and ____ planned to eat dinner and the next day's breakfast with his uncle's family.

See Lesson 17.1, pages 599–600.

Narrative Writing
Developing a Fictional Narrative

Like any other narrative, a fictional narrative tells a story. A short story is a tightly constructed narrative built around a complication. Note the characters, the setting, the events that form the plot, and the point of view from which the story below is told.

Literature Model

They went out from the house. The sun turned the sweat of Durante to hot water and then dried his skin so that his clothes felt transparent. "Tony, I gotta be mean," said Durante. "Stand right there where I can see you. Don't try to get close. Now listen. The sheriff's gunna be along this trail sometime today, looking for me. He'll load up himself and all his gang with water out of your tanks. Then he'll follow my sign across the desert. Get me? He'll follow if he finds water on the place. But he's not gunna find water."

"What you done, poor Dick?" said Tony. "Now look, I could hide you in the old wine cellar where nobody—"

"The sheriff's not gunna find water," said Durante. "It's gunna be like this."

He put the rifle to his shoulder, aimed, fired. The shot struck the base of the nearest tank, ranging down through the bottom. A semicircle of darkness began to stain the soil near the edge of the iron wall.

Tony fell on his knees. "No, no, Dick! Good Dick!" he said. "Look! All the vineyard. It will die. It will turn into old, dead wood, Dick. . . ." ➡

Someone fleeing from someone else has formed the basic action in countless fictional narratives, both short stories and novels.

Durante, ruthless and single-minded, confronts kind, trusting Tony. Through the ages, writers have told stories about the struggle between good and evil.

"Shut your face," said Durante. "Now I've started, I kinda like the job."

Max Brand, "Wine on the Desert"

The Elements of a Short Story

This lesson will focus on the short story, one kind of fictional narrative. It is created in the writer's imagination and tells about some made-up event or occurrence. In a short story, an event or series of events forms the **plot.** The events happen to **characters,** usually people. They happen in a time and place—**the setting**—and are told from a certain angle, or **point of view.** In the chart below, examine the elements that make up the short story "Wine on the Desert."

Prewriting Tip

A story's point of view is usually chosen during prewriting. For more about point of view, see Lesson 2.11, on pages 94–96.

Elements of a Narrative		
Element	**Explanation**	**Example**
Plot	The plot is the story's action and events. Most plots focus on a problem faced by the main character.	Durante is being pursued by the sheriff. He destroys Tony's water tanks to solve this problem.
Character	The characters of a story are the people or animals involved in the plot.	Tony and Durante are the characters. The sheriff is pursuing Durante, but doesn't appear in the story.
Setting	The setting is the time and place in which the events of a story happen. Setting can create mood or atmosphere.	The desert setting of "Wine on the Desert" creates an atmosphere of starkness and danger.
Point of View	Point of view is the particular vantage point from which the story is told.	"Wine on the Desert" is told from Durante's viewpoint, using the third-person pronouns *he* and *him.*

Journal Writing

Think of a short story you've read recently. In your journal summarize the plot, characters, setting, and point of view. Explain how any one of these elements contributes to the short story.

Add Other Story Elements

Plot, character, setting, and point of view provide the basic language for talking about a story. But there are other, equally important, story elements. Jon Franklin, Pulitzer-Prize-winning feature story writer, says that a story "consists of a sequence of actions that occur when a sympathetic character encounters a complicating situation that he [or she] confronts and solves." In other words, a story centers around a problem, or **complication,** and its solution, or **resolution.**

The Complication   The most attention-grabbing element of a story is the complication. The complication may be external: Leo struggles to keep his boat afloat in a storm. Or it may be internal: Lisa is torn between loyalty and honesty when her friend shoplifts. Above all, the problem must be basic to human experience, and the central character must care deeply about it.

Kristi Yamaguchi, 1989 U.S. Olympic Sports Festival, Oklahoma

The Resolution   A story's plot moves forward in a series of actions resulting from the complication and moving toward the resolution, which is the solution to the character's problem. The resolution must grow out of the story; a character's problem can't be solved by having the roof cave in on the villain. Often, the resolution teaches the character—and the reader—a lesson about coping with the world.

News photos that present actual events can spark ideas for fictional narratives. A photo of a disabled bus or a homeless dog illustrates a problem in someone's life. A photo of a daring rescue from a burning building illustrates both a problem and a solution. To a writer, the photo of a skating competition on this page could suggest a story complication; the photo of the winner could suggest a resolution.

Find a Story Idea

For many short-story writers, thinking of a good idea is the hardest part about writing. However, good ideas are everywhere, in other people's lives and in your own life. Behind almost every action in real life lies an attempt to solve a problem or conflict. The chart below shows some strategies for using real-life problems and solutions to find and evaluate story ideas.

Using Complications To...	
Find Story Ideas	**Evaluate Story Ideas**
• Look for external problems: Kelly's father was ill. • Look for internal problems: Ana had to make a moral decision. • Look for action: What action did Otis take to solve a problem? • Look for motivations: Why did Anita quit her job?	• Does the complication concern basic human experiences such as love, hate, loyalty, faith, sorrow, pain, survival, death? • Does the complication matter deeply to the character? • Does the complication create an opportunity for the character to learn something?

Using Resolutions To...	
Find Story Ideas	**Evaluate Story Ideas**
• Look for newspaper stories about achievement. • Look for changes in a person, condition, or situation. • Work backward from a resolution to a complication—if someone received an award, ask how.	• Does the resolution grow directly out of the complication? • Is the resolution the result of a character's own efforts? • Does the resolution teach readers a lesson about how to deal with life? • Does the character change or grow by resolving the complication?

Journal Writing

List four or five problems that would make interesting stories. Then list possible solutions for each problem. Ideas might come from your own experience, from photos, or from other sources.

Develop Your Story

Drafting Tip

In drafting your story, you usually relate the events in chronological order—but not always. "Summer's End," for example, tells the central event through a flashback that "looks back" at an earlier event.

A short story can start with a problem or solution. You decide who the characters are, what problems they confront, how they solve them, and what they learn. Refer to the chart and the excerpt from Jeanine Skendzel's "Summers' End" for development ideas.

How to Write a Story	
• Create a character.	• Show the character reacting to the situation.
• Confront the character with a problem.	• Allow the character to resolve the problem.

Student Model

How does Skendzel prepare you in this paragraph for the problem that is the basis of her story's plot?

What details demonstrate that Skendzel is interested not only in the actions and events but also in how actions and events affect her characters?

W e're heading to our cottage on Scenic Lake. A dull ache pounds in my head, and my stomach churns in rhythm with the motor. I stretch out comfortably halfway across the seat until I accidentally hit my sleeping sister, Tracy. Just a few months ago we could hardly fit in this back seat: that's when my brother, Drew, was here. He would take up half the seat alone. The pain stabs me and the memories quickly flood back.

We're diving for Drew's waterproof wristwatch as we do every year. Drew or I throw the watch as far as possible and the other person dives to find it. Since Drew is seventeen and I'm only fourteen, he holds an unfair advantage, but I never complain. This time it's my turn to throw it. He has already beaten me three times today by thirty seconds each, so this particular time I secretly throw the watch behind me. Drew bobs up and down the dock, searching for a glint of silver in the hot summer sun.

"Come on, Ben! What'd ya do with it?" he frustratedly whines. I foolishly grin back, pleased that I have finally outwitted him at something. Grabbing my arm, he strongly twists it into a horrible snake bite.

"Tell me, Ben, or you know what's coming," he whispers, checking for our parents. We glare at each other, flashing our ugliest poses. Finally, we break down laughing and I point happily toward the watch.

"You little . . ." is all I hear before he sprints off the dock and pulls into a flawless dive.

Jeanine Skendzel, Traverse City Senior High School, Traverse City, Michigan
First appeared in *Merlyn's Pen: The National Magazine of Student Writing*

Write the Solution for a Story Problem

In his short story "The Lady or the Tiger?" Frank Stockton presents the following unresolved complication:

A young man dared to love a princess. He was brought to an arena, where he must open one of two identical doors. Behind one a fierce, hungry tiger was waiting; behind the other, a beautiful lady—not the princess—was waiting to marry him.

Write an ending to the story.

- Develop the characters.
- Resolve the complication by specifying whether the young man opens the door on death or an unwanted marriage.

PURPOSE To create a story resolution
AUDIENCE Your English class
LENGTH 1 paragraph

José Gamarra, *Five Centuries Later*, 1986

Cross-Curricular: Geography

Freewrite about the lush jungle scene in the painting shown. Consider the plants, trees, water, lighting, and other natural elements. Jot down some story ideas that the painting suggests. Choose one idea, and plan a short story about it.

Grammar Link

Make verbs agree with compound subjects.

When you have a compound subject joined by *or* or *nor* or *either . . . or* or *neither . . . nor,* the verb always agrees with the subject nearer the verb.

*Drew or I **throw** the watch. . . .*

Choose the correct form of the verb for each sentence below.

1. Fur or feathers (covers/cover) many living creatures.
2. Neither people nor a bird (is/are) cold-blooded.
3. Either feathers or hair (keeps/keep) the body warm.
4. However, neither a fur coat nor feathers nor warm blood (identifies/identify) a mammal.
5. The distinguishing feature or identifying factors (is/are) a hair or fur covering, warm blood, and the ability to suckle young.

See Lesson 16.5, page 582.

Narrative Writing
Organizing a Fictional Narrative

After you've identified your story idea, a main character, and a problem, you're ready to plan your story. Creating a story outline or diagram can help you organize the events for your plot.

Plan Your Story

Look at the outline for a story called "Same Difference," written by student Yannie ten Broeke. Note how it orders the events of the plot.

1. Introduce a main character.	Mrs. Kreager, a poor, elderly woman
2. Introduce a problem (complication, conflict).	Mrs. Kreager, who lives alone in a city apartment, walks to the park on her birthday to feed the pigeons.
3. List the actions and events (in chronological order, the order in which they happen).	1. Mrs. Kreager gathers bread crumbs in a small bag. 2. She goes to the park to feed the pigeons. 3. She tries to feed Henry, her pet pigeon.
4. Tell the climax (the point of highest tension in the story).	When Sam, a younger pigeon, keeps Henry from eating, Mrs. Kreager accidentally hits Henry. Henry will never recover.
5. Suggest the resolution (how the problem is solved or not solved).	Mrs. Kreager leaves the park, never to return.

With the elements shown in the outline, Yannie ten Broeke has forged a moving story that focuses on cheerful, plucky Mrs. Kreager, whose one pleasure is feeding pigeons in the park. Read from her story's ending.

H enry fell over on his side, stunned, and made no attempt to get to his feet. Mrs. Kreager's eyes opened wide with horror, and her hands covered her mouth. She lurched with such quickness that all the pigeons scattered, leaving an immobile Henry. She put him in her hands, and although he was not dead, it seemed he had given up life. . . .

She stood up, still clutching the warm little body, and began to walk home, leaving the bag on the bench to be thrown away by the Park Service and the stick to be found by some child in search of an imaginary Excalibur. She knew she would not be back.

Yannie ten Broeke, Rutgers Preparatory School, Somerset, New Jersey
First appeared in *Merlyn's Pen: The National Magazine of Student Writing*

Do you think the resolution solves the problem? Why or why not?

A plot diagram like the one below can be a handy tool to help you visualize the structure of the story you will write. Notice how the diagram reflects the basic structure of a story.

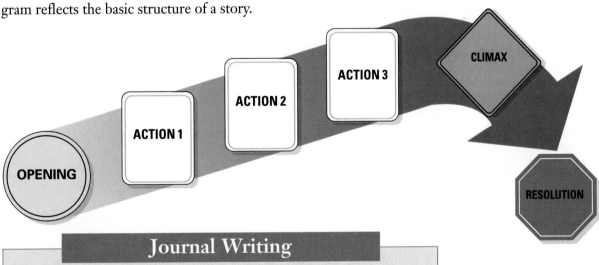

Journal Writing

Use the diagram above to examine a short story you've read. List the main character, the complication, the main events, the climax, and the resolution.

Draft Your Opening

Once you have a story outline, your next step is to draft your opening. Does the story opening below snag your interest? If so, how?

Literature Model

I reached over and shut off the insistent buzzing of my bedside alarm clock. I sat up, swung my feet over the edge of the bed, and felt for my slippers on the floor. Yawning, I walked toward the bathroom. As I walked by the corner of my room, where my computer table was set up, I pressed the on button, slid a diskette into the floppy drive, then went to brush my teeth. By the time I got back, the computer's screen was glowing greenly, displaying the message: *Good Morning, Kevin.*

I sat down before the computer table, addressed the keyboard and typed: *Good Morning, Louis.* The computer immediately began to whirr and promptly displayed a list of items on its green screen.

```
Today is Monday, April 22, the 113th day of the
year. There are 254 days remaining. Your 14th
birthday is five days from this date.
Math test today, 4th Period.
Your history project is due today. Do you wish
printout: Y/N?
```

I punched the letter *Y* on the keyboard and flipped on the switch to the computer's printer. At once the printer sprang to life and began *eeeek*ing out page one. I went downstairs to breakfast. . . .

When I returned to my room to shower and dress for the day, my history project was already printed out. I had almost walked by Louis, when I noticed there was a message on the screen. It wasn't the usual:

```
Printout completed. Do you wish to continue: Y/N?
```

Underneath the printout question were two lines:

```
When are you going to get me my voice module,
Kevin?
```

I blinked. It couldn't be. There was nothing in Louis's basic programming that would allow for a question like this.

T. Ernesto Bethancourt, "User Friendly"

Write a Story Opening

Plan an original short story for your school's literary magazine. You will base your story on the painting shown here. Write a plot diagram and the opening for the story you will submit.

- Chart the complication, action, climax, and resolution of the plot.
- Draft your opening—identify character, establish setting, point of view, and hint at complication.

Richard Bosman, *Flight*, 1981–82

PURPOSE To write a story opening that introduces character, setting, and complication
AUDIENCE Student, parent, and teacher readers of the school literary magazine
LENGTH 3–4 paragraphs

Cooperative Learning

In a small group, find a short story in your literature book or another source. After reading the story, discuss the author's resolution to the problem. Discuss alternative possible resolutions. Which seems most satisfactory? Why?

Grammar Link

Use commas to separate three or more items in a series.

Note how Bethancourt uses commas to separate parts of a series in this sentence from "User Friendly."

I sat up, swung my feet over the edge of the bed, and felt for my slippers on the floor.

Rewrite the following sentences, inserting commas as necessary.

1. My little brother scowled stamped his right foot stuck out his lower lip and announced that he was mad.
2. His face was pale wrinkled and angry.
3. He cast furious glances at me at our mother and toward the cat.
4. I bristled my mother looked puzzled and the cat stalked away.
5. "I want milk bread jelly and peanut butter right now," announced the little tyrant.

See Lesson 21.6, page 705.

It's about time they let us speak for ourselves! If I hear myself described one more time as a puffed-up, blustering fool, I'll . . .

At least they gave you a personality. I'm portrayed so vaguely that if I ever get to open my mouth, I won't know what to say, much less how to say it.

A dialogue is a conversation between two or more persons. Note how Mary Lavin uses dialogue in the model below to bring characters and events to life.

How does the dialogue create a vivid sense of time and place?

The dialogue shows the widow's deep pride in Packy.

The dialogue contains a subtle foreshadowing, or hint of possible trouble to come. What is it?

Where does the dialogue contain another hint of possible danger?

Literature Model

A neighbor passed.

"Waiting for Packy?" said the neighbor, pleasantly, and he stood for a minute to take off his hat and wipe the sweat of the day from his face. He was an old man.

"It's a hot day!" he said. "It will be a hard push for Packy on that battered old bike of his. I wouldn't like to have to face into four miles on a day like this!"

"Packy would travel three times that distance if there was a book at the other end of the road!" said the widow, with the pride of those who cannot read more than a line or two without wearying.

The minutes went by slowly. The widow kept looking up at the sun.

"I suppose the heat is better than the rain!" she said, at last. "The heat can do a lot of harm too, though," said the neighbor, absent-mindedly, as he pulled a long blade of grass from between the stones of the wall and began to chew the end of it. "You could get sunstroke on a day like this!" He looked up at the sun. "The sun is a terror," he said, "It could cause you to drop down dead like a stone!"➡

The widow strained out further over the gate. She looked up the hill in the direction of the town.

"He will have a good cool breeze on his face coming down the hill, at any rate," she said.

The man looked up the hill. "That's true. On the hottest day of the year you would get a cool breeze coming down that hill on a bicycle. You would feel the air streaming past your cheeks like silk. And in the winter it's like two knives flashing to either side of you, and peeling off your skin like you'd peel the bark off a sally-rod [willow twig]." He chewed the grass meditatively. "That must be one of the steepest hills in Ireland," he said. "That hill is a hill worthy of the name of a hill." He took the grass out of his mouth. "It's my belief," he said, earnestly looking at the widow—"it's my belief that that hill is to be found marked with a name in the Ordnance Survey map!"

"If that's the case," said the widow, "Packy will be able to tell you all about it. When it isn't a book he has in his hand it's a map."

"Is that so?" said the man. "That's interesting. A map is a great thing. A map is not an ordinary thing. It isn't everyone can make out a map."

The widow wasn't listening.

"I think I see Packy!" she said, and she opened the gate and stepped out into the roadway.

Mary Lavin, "The Story of the Widow's Son"

> *The dialogue adds liveliness and realism. Even this unnamed old man has a personality—warm, friendly, interested in people and places.*

> *How does this part of the dialogue advance the plot?*

Use Dialogue to Advance Your Story

Good dialogue can serve many purposes in a narrative. Mary Lavin uses it to create a sense of time and place, tell about character, foreshadow possible trouble, and move the plot along. When you write a story, you can use dialogue for all these purposes—and more.

Revising Tip

In revising, read your dialogue aloud to test whether it sounds like real conversation. Keep revising and rereading until your characters' words sound right.

Journal Writing

Find and examine some dialogue in a novel or short story. Explore the purposes of the dialogue by writing what it reveals about the setting, the characters, or the plot.

Write Dialogue

Essentially, a dialogue is a series of direct quotations. A direct quotation is a character's own words enclosed in quotation marks. An indirect quotation is a report of what someone said. Compare the following quotations.

> Direct quotation: "I think I see Packy!" she said.
> Indirect quotation: The widow said that she thought she saw Packy.

In a dialogue, the words that identify the speaker, such as "said the widow," are called tag lines. Without tag lines, readers might have trouble figuring out who is saying what. Too few tag lines can make a dialogue confusing; too many tag lines can make it choppy.

Mary Lavin uses the verb *said* eleven times in the passage you read. You might think that the story would be more interesting if she had substituted synonyms such as *replied* and *remarked*. However, Lavin chose her verbs carefully. Later, to emphasize the difference in the widow's tone of voice, she used vivid verbs in her tag lines:

> "He's only in a weakness!" *screamed* the widow. . . . "Get a doctor!" she *cried*.

In addition to tag lines, your dialogue can include descriptions of characters' facial expressions, tone of voice, gestures, and mannerisms. Here is an example:

> "The heat can do a lot of harm too, though," said the neighbor, absent-mindedly, as he pulled a long blade of grass from between the stones of the wall and began to chew the end of it.

The following guidelines will help you write effective dialogue in your fictional narratives.

Grammar

Editing Tip

If you need to review the mechanics of writing dialogue, see Lesson 21.9, page 717.

Guidelines for Writing Dialogue

1. Make sure your dialogue has a purpose: to reveal character, to highlight the relationships between characters, to intensify the action, to add suspense, or a combination.
2. Write dialogue in words and phrases appropriate to each character. Consider the character's age, personality, and educational background. Consider the character's emotional state.
3. Use dialogue to reveal character and personality. What are this character's beliefs? Desires? Fears? Is the character shy? Honest? Nervous? Ignorant? Boastful?
4. Make your dialogue sound like real conversation by using interruptions and pauses.
5. Make your dialogue easy to follow by using clear tag lines and correct paragraphing and punctuation.

4.4 Writing Activities

Write a Dialogue

Recall an interesting conversation you heard or took part in. Write it down as you remember it. Then turn it into a fictional dialogue. Change the real dialogue in any way necessary to add interest and liveliness.

- Use the dialogue to reveal something about your speakers.
- Use words and phrasing appropriate for each speaker.
- Use clear tag lines and correct paragraphing, punctuation, and capitalization.

PURPOSE To create a dialogue
AUDIENCE Your teacher and classmates
LENGTH 1–2 pages

Gilberto Ruiz, *The Good News Call*, 1986

Cooperative Learning

In a small group, brainstorm about the painting on this page. Have each group member assume the role of a character, and ad-lib dialogue for a short dramatic scene, with one group member serving as recorder. Read the script aloud, and revise it to make it more realistic. Finalize the script and present it.

Grammar Link

Capitalize and punctuate direct and indirect quotations correctly.

Reread Mary Lavin's dialogue and page 180. Then rewrite the following sentences correctly. Write *correct* for any sentence that needs no changes.

1. Abraham Lincoln gave a speech in which he said the ballot is stronger than the bullet.
2. In a later speech, Lincoln said that nobody had ever expected him to be President.
3. I feel somewhat like the boy in Kentucky who stubbed his toe while running to see his sweetheart Lincoln replied in answer to a question in 1862. The boy said he was too big to cry, and far too badly hurt to laugh.
4. These words of Lincoln are in John Bartlett's *Familiar Quotations* my teacher said. do you know what that book is?
5. I've heard of it I admitted but I don't know whether I've ever seen it.

See Lesson 20.1, page 675 and 21.9, page 717.

Narrative Writing
Theme and Anecdote

An anecdote is a brief story that makes a point. The theme of a work is its main idea or underlying message. Look for the point that Will Steger makes with this anecdote.

How is this anecdote a story within a story? Why do you think Steger decided to use it as his introduction?

Why does Steger use a direct quotation in his anecdote? Why not just say "I called Keizo by name"?

Literature Model

Tears of frustration and despair blinded me more than the stinging wind or snow. For 24 hours a storm had pinned us in our camp only 16 miles from our goal—the far edge of Antarctica. We had come too far, endured too much suffering, to lose a man now, I thought bitterly. We had to find him.

We clung to a long rope as we searched; the end was tied to a sled to keep us from straying, as he had, into the raging whiteout. "Keizo!" I yelled into the blizzard. "Keizo! . . . Keizo!"

Faintly I heard the others shouting his name as they too groped in a tethered arc around the tents and sleds. Our Japanese teammate, Keizo Funatsu—gentle, compassionate Keizo—had crawled out of his tent at 4:30 the afternoon before to check on his dogs. By six we knew he was lost. We searched into the night, calling and listening, flashlight beams futile against the swirling snow.

Now in the first faint wash of daylight we were searching again.

It was unthinkable that one of us could be gone after what we had come through together for nearly seven months: Trudging, antlike, across 3,700 miles of brutal terrain, from sea level to lonely elevations above 11,000 feet . . . battered for weeks by continuous storms . . . winds that howled at 90 miles an hour.

We had challenged a foreign place, a place not meant for warm-blooded animals. Antarctica's terrible interior tries to turn men into its own image—frozen. Yet this endurance test had forged a deep and permanent bond among us: six dissimilar men from six nations, attempting to complete the first crossing of the continent by dogsled. ➡

I envisioned the worst—carrying Keizo these last few miles wrapped in the flag of his homeland—and my stomach knotted in anguish. "Keizo!" I bellowed, over and over again.

I couldn't believe it when I glimpsed him—a wraith emerging from the driving curtain of snow. "I am alive," he said. In seconds we were clutching each other. Both of us were crying.

Keizo is a skilled survivor. Once lost, he scraped a shallow trench with pliers, the only tool he had, and curled up in it like a sled dog, allowing the blizzard to bury him. And there, with Zen-like calm, he waited for 13 hours, until he heard our calls.

It was then—but only then—that I was certain our expedition was a success.

Will Steger, "Six Across Antarctica," *National Geographic*

How does this last sentence suggest the point of the anecdote?

Understand the Theme

Steger's anecdote forcefully introduces his article. It also illustrates his theme, or main idea: Six men from dissimilar cultural backgrounds could work together under some of the cruelest conditions on the planet.

The chart below explains some of the characteristics of a theme. Notice that it discusses themes in fiction as well as nonfiction.

The Characteristics of a Theme	
A Theme is . . .	**A Theme is Not . . .**
• A theme is a general insight about life or people. • In nonfiction, a theme is often stated, as in Steger's article. • In fiction, a theme is usually implied, as in a story in which the events show how love overcomes prejudice.	• A theme is not the topic or subject of the work. • A theme is not a summary of a plot or story line. • A theme is not a moral or lesson about life, though it may suggest one.

Journal Writing

Find a theme in something you have written. In your journal express the theme as a general statement about life or human nature.

Use Anecdotes to Support the Theme

An anecdote in fiction is a story within a story. Claire Edwards has included the following anecdote in "Kay," a fictional story about the death of the narrator's best friend, an event that happened when both girls were teenagers. Underlying Edwards's story is a theme about a strong friendship that the narrator believes will endure forever. Notice how this anecdote supports the theme.

Student Model

This anecdote has all the elements of any narrative. Can you identify the characters, the setting, the complication, and the resolution?

Kay and I met on the first day of third grade. Fate brought us together—literally! We collided on the front steps of our school building, and I ended up dropping all my new books. A freckled face peered into mine and gasped, "Oh, I'm sorry! Would you believe this is the second time today I've bumped into someone? I'm not always this clumsy, but I woke up late, and my mom made me eat all my breakfast, bite by bite. It took such a long time, and I don't think I'm quite fully awake yet. By the way, my name's Katherine Montgomery, but all my friends call me Kay." It was only a matter of weeks before Kay and I were inseparable.

This last sentence expresses the point of the anecdote. How does the anecdote support the theme of the whole story?

Claire Edwards, New Trier East Township High School, Winnetka, Illinois
First appeared in *Merlyn's Pen: The National Magazine of Student Writing*

When writing either nonfiction or fiction, think of anecdotes you might use to support your theme. For example, a nonfiction article about the importance of animals to children could include an anecdote about the writer's own pet. A fiction story about a teenager who works in a restaurant could include a humorous anecdote showing how his job teaches him valuable lessons about people. Once you have an idea for an anecdote, answer the following questions to plan it.

Revising Tip

In revising, make your anecdote short and lively. Cut out unnecessary details, but keep those that make your writing interesting. A peer reviewer can help you make cuts.

Prewriting Your Anecdote

- What is the setting?
- Who are the characters?
- What problem, challenge, or conflict do they face?
- How is the problem solved?
- What's the point?

4.5 Writing Activities

Write an Anecdote

Adults often tell young children stories about lessons learned through experience. These stories are anecdotes. Write an anecdote for young children based on your own experience.

- Illustrate a theme or lesson.
- Explain setting, characters, complication, and resolution.
- Make the point of your anecdote clear.

PURPOSE To write an anecdote
AUDIENCE Young children
LENGTH 4–6 paragraphs

COMPUTER OPTION

Anecdotes, like jokes, benefit in special ways from revision, since they succeed best when they are brief and lively, saying much in little space. Use the copy feature of your word-processing program to help you revise your anecdotes. Make several copies of the original, and revise each one, creating different versions. Compare them, and select the best version. If you're unsure which is really your best, print out two you like, and ask a peer reviewer to read and respond to them.

Grammar Link

Use and punctuate appositives and appositive phrases correctly.

An *appositive* is a noun or pronoun placed next to another noun or pronoun to provide additional information. An *appositive phrase* is an appositive plus any words that modify it. Note how Will Steger uses a comma to set off the appositive phrase because it is not essential to the meaning of the sentence.

. . . *a foreign place,* **a place not meant for warm-blooded animals.**

Add at least one appositive or appositive phrase to each sentence below. Use commas as needed.

1. In 1832, Charles Darwin sailed from England on the HMS *Beagle*.
2. Darwin collected 68 different species of small beetles in a forest outside Rio de Janeiro.
3. During the next three years, the *Beagle* sailed south to round Cape Horn and north again up the coast of Chile.
4. The expedition eventually came to the Galápagos Islands where Darwin made more studies of wildlife.
5. There Darwin found cormorants, iguanas, and tortoises that were very different from those on the mainland.

See Lesson 12.2, page 487.

Writing About Literature
The Plot Summary

A plot summary is a shortened version of a story built around the main character's problem. Like a traveler's passport, it shows important stopping points but does not tell whether the trip was enjoyable. As you read the plot summary of "The Most Dangerous Game," note how it summarizes the narrative elements of the story.

Model

What elements of the plot does the summary introduce in the first paragraph?

The short story "The Most Dangerous Game," by Richard Connell, pits two great hunters against each other. Rainsford, the main character, falls from a yacht and swims to an island owned by General Zaroff. We as readers see the events through Rainsford's eyes. Zaroff, bored with hunting animals, hunts men instead. Rainsford's horror grows as he finds himself the unwilling quarry in Zaroff's deadly game. ➡

According to the rules of that game, Rainsford must elude his foe for three days or be killed. He begins his flight in panic, then gathers his wits and draws on his vast knowledge of hunting. Rainsford knows terror when Zaroff tracks his intricate trail but deliberately saves him for another day's sport. The next day, Rainsford escapes death and wins his foe's respect by building ingenious traps that wound Zaroff and kill one of his dogs. The third day, Zaroff pursues him with a pack of ferocious dogs led by his savage servant, Ivan. Rainsford's last trap misses its intended victim but kills the servant. Finally, knowing he cannot outrun the dogs, Rainsford leaps into the sea.

The climax comes later that night. Retiring to his bedroom, Zaroff finds himself face to face with Rainsford, who swam across the cove to the chateau. Surprised, the general congratulates Rainsford for winning the game. Rainsford lets his enemy know the game isn't over, and both men realize that the loser will be fed to the dogs. We know who that is in the last sentence, when Rainsford decides that he "never slept in a better bed."

> *Notice that the second paragraph sums up the main events that build suspense.*

> *What is the writer's purpose in this third paragraph?*

Why Write a Plot Summary?

A plot summary is intended to sum up the main events in a story—specifically, the main character's problem and how it is resolved. It does not include personal opinion or evaluation.

Plot summaries can be valuable in a number of ways. Read the chart for ideas of how to use summaries.

Uses of a Plot Summary

- Preparing a plot summary will help you recognize the story line and other narrative elements.
- Writing the summary will help you clarify your understanding of action, complication, resolution, and theme.
- Reading the plot summary later will help you review for a test.

Journal Writing

Think of a movie or TV program you saw recently. How would you summarize it in two or three sentences for a friend? Write your summary in your journal.

Write a Plot Summary

As with most writing you do, prewriting is crucial to preparing a plot summary. The first step is to read the work carefully. As you read, take notes regarding the elements listed in the chart below. Most plot summaries, including both of the models in this lesson, are organized as shown. Notice the focus on the main character's problem.

Paragraph 1
List the title, author, main character(s), setting, and point of view. Then describe the main character's problem.

Paragraph 2
Explain the main events in chronological order (the order in which they happen).

Paragraph 3
Describe the climax or turning point, when readers know how the problem will be solved and how the story ends.

Literary terms, such as *complication* and *climax*, can help you summarize the story line, but their use isn't necessary. In her plot summary below, Laurie Valle used very few literary terms.

Although the plot summary is written in Valle's own words, it includes this brief quotation. Why did Valle choose to use these words from the story?

How does Mrs. Mallard's story illustrate irony, a contrast between what appears to be true and what really is true?

Student Model

"The Story of an Hour" by Kate Chopin begins with a delicate situation. Louise Mallard, who has a serious heart condition, must be told that her husband is dead. Her sister Josephine and her husband's friend Richards have come to her home, where they gently break the news of the tragic railroad accident.

Louise retires to her bedroom, overcome with weeping. Alone, she thinks about the accident and the effect it will have on her life. The reader learns that she did not love her husband. She feels no grief at his death but rather, exultation. Now she is free, able to run her own life.

Then Brently Mallard walks through the door unscathed. He was not on the train at all and was, in fact, very far from the accident. The irony of the situation is in the way Louise Mallard dies. The doctor says her sudden death is from "heart disease—joy that kills." But the reader knows it isn't joy that kills Louise Mallard. Instead, seeing her husband alive has destroyed her new sense of freedom, killing her joy and causing her death.

Laurie Valle, Edison High School, Edison, New Jersey

4.6 Writing Activities

Write a Plot Summary

Summarize the plot of a short story you read or a movie you saw recently.

- Describe setting, point of view, and the main character's problem.
- Explain the important events up through the climax and resolution.
- Do not include personal opinions of the story.

PURPOSE To summarize a short story or movie
AUDIENCE Your classmates
LENGTH 3 paragraphs

Cross-Curricular: World History

History is usually told as a narrative, with the events related in chronological order. Summarizing requires in-depth reading, so a useful technique for studying history is to summarize the story line of a chapter or unit in your history text. Try it. Write a one- to two-page summary of the material that will be covered on your next history test.

Grammar Link

Avoid unnecessary shifts in verb tenses.

When summarizing or analyzing literature, use verbs in the present tense. Note how Laurie Valle uses the present tense when speaking of Louise Mallard.

*Louise Mallard . . . **has** a serious heart condition.*

Then note the verbs in the rest of Valle's plot summary.
   Revise the plot summary below, correcting shifts from the present tense.

1. In "The Most Dangerous Game," General Zaroff played a deadly game in which he hunts people, not animals.
2. Rainsford, the main character, tried to escape from Zaroff, who hunted him.
3. Although Zaroff finds Rainsford on the first day, Rainsford is not killed because Zaroff wanted to track him for one more day.
4. On the second day Rainsford fought back and made a clever trap, which kills one of Zaroff's tracking dogs.
5. On the final day of the hunt, Rainsford escaped from the dogs and jumps into the sea.
6. He will be the victor, though, because he will become the hunter and confront Zaroff when he least expected it.

See Lesson 15.6, page 560.

Writing About Literature
Analyzing Conflict

One way to understand a story is to examine its conflict, or the struggle between opposing forces. Read the analysis below of W. W. Jacobs's "The Monkey's Paw." Who or what are the opposing forces in the conflict?

Edvard Munch, *The Scream*, 1893

Model

The analysis begins with this thesis sentence, which is a statement about the nature of the conflict.

1 fakir: (fə kir′) a Hindu or Muslim holy man

According to the analysis, readers can predict which side of this conflict will win. What causes the suspense that makes readers want to read on?

*I*n the short story "The Monkey's Paw," members of an ordinary family come into conflict with fate. The family suffers because they try to change their lives by using the magic in the monkey's paw.

Mr. White is intrigued with magic and the unknown, so he rescues the paw when his guest, Morris, throws it into the fire. Later, Mr. White's first wish is granted. When the Whites hear of their son's death, they realize the awful truth of the fakir's[1] words: "that fate ruled people's lives, and that those who interfered with it did so to their sorrow."

As readers, we know that the monkey's paw always brings tragedy. Before the action of the story, the paw had caused one death and left Morris with terrible memories. Still, much of our interest in this story is created by its suspense. We don't know what the tragedy will be, or how it will happen, and we care about this family. We identify with Mrs. White in her desire to get her son back, but we know the monkey's paw can bring nothing good, even if he returns. In the end, the Whites have learned a great deal about fate, but with their knowledge has come the sorrow that the fakir had promised.

Recognize Conflict

Most stories focus on a complication, a problem in the main characters' lives. Usually, the complication is a conflict, a struggle between opposing forces. The conflict can be important (two soldiers fight to the death) or petty (a sister and brother argue over their inheritance). The conflict can be external (a family fight to save their house from a flood) or internal (a girl is torn between love for her mother and desire for independence). Conflict engages readers by creating suspense, a desire to find out what happens. The suspense ends when the conflict is resolved and readers know which opposing force will prevail.

Near the story's beginning, the conflict motivates the characters, leading them to act. By the story's end, the characters have usually learned something significant. The chart below gives examples of conflicts found in fiction.

Revising Tip

In prewriting a conflict analysis, you may find it helpful to discuss the story with another person who has read it.

Conflicts in Fiction		
Kind	**Example**	**Plot**
Person vs. Person	"The Most Dangerous Game" by Richard Connell	Rainsford, who has become General Zaroff's unwilling prey, must elude his hunter for three days or be killed.
Person vs. Nature	"To Build a Fire" by Jack London	A man struggles to keep from freezing to death in the extreme cold of winter in the Klondike region of western Canada.
Person vs. Society	"The Lottery" by Shirley Jackson	A woman is selected by lot for death by stoning in a ritual mandated and carried out by the community.
Person vs. Self	"Through the Tunnel" by Doris Lessing	A boy struggles to overcome his fear of drowning in order to satisfy his desire to swim through an underwater tunnel.
Person vs. Machine	"Trucks" by Stephen King	People who are being held hostage by trucks must decide whether to meet the trucks' demands.
Person vs. the Supernatural	*The Odyssey* by Homer	Odysseus is delayed in his return to Ithaca by various characters, including the sea god Poseidon.

Journal Writing

Why do you think conflict is an element of most good fiction? Is it because readers can identify with conflicts they have experienced? Is it because the resolution of conflict gives meaning to events? Explore these questions in your journal.

Write About Conflict

Grammar
Editing Tip

When you revise your analysis, you might discover places to use direct quotations to support your ideas. For information about punctuating direct quotations, see Lesson 21.9, page 717.

As you prepare to write a conflict analysis, first pinpoint the conflict. Then reread the story with that conflict in mind. Finally, use the questions in the chart below to help you plan your analysis.

Questions About Conflict
1. What are the opposing forces in the conflict?
2. Is the conflict external, internal, or both?
3. How does the writer create and maintain interest in the conflict?
4. How is the conflict resolved?
5. What new understanding do the characters reach as a result of the conflict and its resolution? What new understanding do readers discover?
6. How does the conflict help the author develop the story's theme?

A conflict analysis is not a plot summary. Refer to the plot only as it relates to the conflict, as Cary Chaffee does in the analysis below.

Student Model

What is the thesis statement in Chaffee's analysis, and what is its purpose?

In the short story "Eveline," from James Joyce's *Dubliners,* the conflict is internal; it is Eveline versus herself. Eveline's dilemma—whether to stay in an unhappy home or seize an opportunity to escape to another place and a better life—is with herself alone. It is a conflict that many readers will recognize. Like many people, Eveline must choose between security and happiness.

Eveline lives a terrible life. On her job she is unappreciated, and in her home she is little more than a household drudge. Her father, a drunkard, has recently begun to threaten her with the same kind of violence he once used on her brothers. Now she has a chance to escape. "Why should she be unhappy? She had a right to happiness."

Why do you think the writer chose to quote from the story? What do the direct quotations add to her analysis?

Eveline realizes, though, that no matter how bad things are, she is secure at home with her father. "It was hard work—a hard life—but now that she was about to leave it she did not find it a wholly undesirable life." Eveline's inner struggle makes readers want to urge her to marry her lover and be happy. Her uncertainty creates suspense. In her decision to stay, readers can discover a theme: you can become happy only by taking risks.

Cary Chaffee, Quartz Hill High School, Quartz Hill, California

4.7 Writing Activities

Write a Conflict Analysis

Write an analysis of the conflict in one of the following short stories: "The Use of Force" by William Carlos Williams; "Barn Burning" by William Faulkner; or "Through the Tunnel" by Doris Lessing.

- Identify the conflict and the forces involved in it.
- Explain the development of the conflict and its resolution.
- Tell what new understandings the characters and the reader reach.

PURPOSE To analyze conflict in a short story
AUDIENCE Your teacher and classmates
LENGTH 3–4 paragraphs

Melissa Miller, *Salmon Run*, 1984

Cooperative Learning

In a small group discuss the elements of conflict in the painting *Salmon Run*. Then brainstorm to list varied examples of conflict in nature: animal vs. environment; one animal species vs. another; conflict among animals of the same species. What kinds of resolution are possible in these conflicts? As a group, plan an effective way to organize your ideas in a display for other students.

Grammar Link

Form possessive nouns correctly.

The writer of the conflict analysis of "The Monkey's Paw" used a number of singular possessive nouns:
monkey's paw
Mr. White's *first wish*
fakir's words

Remember that to refer to the paws of more than one monkey, you would write "*monkeys'* paws."

Complete each sentence below with the correct possessive form.

1. The teacher collected one (class's, classes') papers.
2. She announced that all (student's, students') writing had improved.
3. Each (paper's, papers') subject was conflict.
4. Many (paper's, papers') thesis statements related to the nature of the conflict analyzed.
5. Mrs. (Harris's, Harris') comments were generally favorable.

See Lesson 21.11, pages 722–723.

UNIT 4

WRITING PROCESS IN ACTION

NARRATIVE WRITING

In preceding lessons you've learned about the basics of narrative writing—character, setting, plot, point of view, conflict, and resolution. You've also had a chance to practice writing parts of narratives, as well as plot summaries and conflict analyses. Now it's time to put together everything you've learned. In this lesson, you're invited to plan a short story of your own and to write the beginning of it.

• Assignment •

Context	You are a faithful reader of _To Be Continued_ . . ., a magazine that publishes serialized student fiction in short monthly installments. You plan to submit a story to the magazine. In the first installment of your story, you will introduce the characters, setting, plot, and the complication you plan to develop in the succeeding installments.
Purpose	To write a narrative that could serve as an introduction to a longer work of fiction
Audience	Editors and teenage readers of _To Be Continued_ . . .
Length	1–2 pages

You will find the next few pages helpful for planning your story and writing its first installment. Begin by reading through the pages, but don't feel you have to remember everything on them. You can refer back to the pages as you need to. After all, you're in charge of your own writing process.

Prewriting

Ideas for stories are everywhere, in other people's lives and in your own. If you have trouble coming up with an idea, the suggestions on the notepad may help you think of a good story idea to explore.

After you've chosen your story idea, do the following:

- Make notes to identify characters, setting, point of view, and the basic events of your plot.
- Do some freewriting about the complication of your story and how your characters will resolve it.
- Organize the basic events of your story, perhaps by outlining them or creating a plot diagram.
- Decide whether you will use a first-person, third-person limited, or third-person omniscient narrator, and, if limited, from which character's point of view you will tell the story.

Prewriting Options
- *Skim your journal for ideas.*
- *Brainstorm with family members or friends.*
- *Browse through newspapers and magazines to find references to interesting characters or real-life problems and solutions.*
- *Select a theme, conflict, or character type that interests you.*

Drafting

Although you are writing the first installment of your story, that doesn't necessarily mean you are telling the story from its beginning. Look at what Rudolfo A. Anaya does in these opening paragraphs of his novel *Tortuga*.

Prewriting Tip

If you want to review creating a story outline or plot diagram, see Lesson 4.3, pages 174–175.

Literature Model

I awoke from a restless sleep. For a moment I couldn't remember where I was, then I heard Filomón and Clepo talking up front and I felt the wind sway the old ambulance. I tried to turn my body, but it was impossible. Upon waking it was always the same; I tried to move but the paralysis held me firmly in its grip.

I could turn my head and look out the small window. The cold winter rain was still falling. It had been only a gray drizzle when we left the hospital, but the farther south we went into the desert the sheets of icy rain became more intense. For a great part of the trip we had been surrounded by darkness. Only the flashes of lightning which tore through the sky illuminated the desolate landscape.

Rudolfo A. Anaya, *Tortuga*

Drafting Tip

For help in structuring your introduction as an anecdote, see Lesson 4.5, pages 182–184.

Anaya introduces the main elements of his narrative—the character and complication—in the first paragraphs of his book. Later he will have to go back in time to explain the origin of the complication—how the boy came to be paralyzed—and move forward in time to resolve the complication.

However you start your story, you need to construct a beginning that grabs your reader, moves the story along, lets readers get to know your characters, and gives them some idea of what lies ahead. Since you are writing the first installment of a continuing narrative, you can't really wrap up your story at the end. You can and should, however, leave your readers eager to find out more. Think about raising a compelling question, introducing a mysterious character, or even creating a suspenseful cliff-hanger.

Revising

Revising Tip

If your peer reviewers suggest that more or better dialogue would improve your story introduction, see Lesson 4.4, pages 178–180.

To begin revising, read over your draft to make sure that what you've written fits your purpose and audience. Then have a **writing conference.** Read your draft to a partner or small group. Use your audience's reactions and the Revising Checklist below to help you evaluate your work.

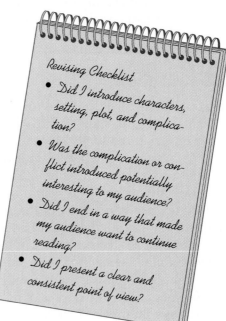

Revising Checklist
- *Did I introduce characters, setting, plot, and complication?*
- *Was the complication or conflict introduced potentially interesting to my audience?*
- *Did I end in a way that made my audience want to continue reading?*
- *Did I present a clear and consistent point of view?*

Editing

When you are satisfied with your story introduction, **proofread** it carefully for errors in grammar, usage, mechanics, and spelling. Use the questions at the right as a guide.

In addition to proofreading, use the self-evaluation list below to make sure your story introduction does all the things you want it to do. When you feel that it does, make a clean copy of your story and proofread it one more time.

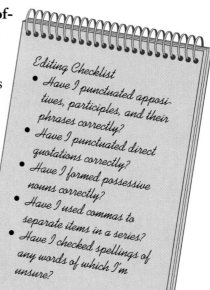

Editing Checklist
- *Have I punctuated appositives, participles, and their phrases correctly?*
- *Have I punctuated direct quotations correctly?*
- *Have I formed possessive nouns correctly?*
- *Have I used commas to separate items in a series?*
- *Have I checked spellings of any words of which I'm unsure?*

Self-Evaluation
Make sure your narrative introduction—

- focuses on an interesting complication
- establishes setting, characters, and conflict
- has a compelling beginning and ending
- ends in a way that keeps the reader guessing
- uses dialogue and/or anecdotes effectively
- is written from a consistent point of view
- follows correct grammar, usage, mechanics, and spelling

Presenting

Proofreading

For proofreading symbols see page 88.

Many magazines publish student writing. Check such references as *Writer's Market* to identify publications and determine their policy for submissions. If you decide to send your chapter to a real magazine, attach a brief letter informing the editors that you are submitting your story for publication. Be sure to include your address and phone number so that they can respond to your work.

Journal Writing

Reflect on your writing process experience. Answer these questions in your journal: What do you like best about your narrative introduction? What was the hardest part of writing it? What did you learn in your writing conference? What new things have you learned as a writer?

Rudolfo A. Anaya

FROM

TORTUGA

Mexican American writer Rudolfo A. Anaya, who was born in New Mexico, says he learned
"from the old storytellers" in his native state "how to re-create the narrative and pass it on."
In this beginning to the third novel of his trilogy about growing up a Mexican American in
the Southwest, notice how the author creates mood while introducing characters and plot.
Then complete the activities in Linking Writing and Literature on page 205.

I awoke from a restless sleep. For a moment I couldn't remember where I was, then I heard Filomón and Clepo talking up front and I felt the wind sway the old ambulance. I tried to turn my body, but it was impossible. Upon waking it was always the same; I tried to move but the paralysis held me firmly in its grip.

I could turn my head and look out the small window. The cold winter rain was still falling. It had been only a gray drizzle when we left the hospital, but the farther south we went into the desert the sheets of icy rain became more intense. For a great part of the trip we had been surrounded by darkness. Only the flashes of lightning which tore through the sky illuminated the desolate landscape.

I had slept most of the way; the rain drumming against the ambulance and the rumble of the distant thunder lulled me to sleep. Now I blinked my eyes and remembered that we had left at day-break, and Filomón had said that it would be mid-afternoon before we arrived at the new hospital.

Your new home, he had said.

Home. Up north, at home, it would be snowing, but here it was only the dark, dismal rain which swept across the wide desert and covered us with its darkness. I tried to turn again, but the paralysis compounded by the bone-chilling cold held me. I cursed silently.

"It's never been this dark before," I heard Clepo whisper.

"Don't worry," Filomón answered, "it'll get better before it gets worse. You have to know the desert to know rain don't last. It can be raining one minute and blowing dust devils[1] the next. But the clouds are beginning to break, see, to the west."

I turned my head and looked out the window. In the distance I could see the bare outline of a mountain range. Around us the desert was alkaline[2] and white. Only the most tenacious shrubs and brittle grasses seemed to grow, clinging to the harsh land like tufts of mouldy hair. Overhead, the sun struggled to break through the clouds. To the east, a diffused, distorted rainbow stretched across the vast, gray sky.

I remembered the rainbows of my childhood, beautifully sculptured arches reaching from north to south, shafts of light so pure their harmony seemed to wed the sky and earth. My mother had taught me to look at rainbows, the mantle[3] of the Blessed Virgin Mary she called them. When a summer thunderstorm passed she would take me out and we would stand in the thin drops which followed the storm. We would turn our faces up to the sky, and the large, glistening drops of rain would pelt our faces. She would open her mouth and hold out her tongue to receive the large, golden drops. She would stir the muddy ponds and pick up the little frogs which came with the rain. "They are like you," she told me, "blessed by the rain, children of the water." When I was hurt she would take me in her arms and sing . . . .

1 dust devils small whirlwinds of dust

2 alkaline (al′ kə lin) containing mineral salts

3 mantle a cloak or cape

> Sana, sana
> colita de rana
> Si no sanas hoy
> sanarás mañana . . . **4**

And her touch could drive away the worst of pains. But then the paralysis had come, and suddenly her prayers and her touch were not enough. Her face grew pale and thin, her eyes grew dark. "It is God's will," she had said.

"It's clearing now," Filomón said, "see, the sun is beginning to break through!"

"Yes, the sun!" Clepo shouted. He was Filomón's assistant, a small impish man with hunched shoulders. I noticed he limped when they loaded me on the ambulance.

"I think I see the top of the mountain!" Filomón cried cheerfully.

I was fully awake. The last images of the dreams faded as the darkness of the rain moved over us and eastward. Only occasional peals of thunder rumbled across the sky. Beneath us the ambulance rocked like a ship. Memories of my life moved in and out of my troubled consciousness. My mother's face appeared again and again. She had cried when they loaded me on the ambulance, but she knew it was necessary. The doctors there had helped as much as they could. Now, they insisted, they had to move me to this new hospital in the south where they specialized in taking care of crippled children. If there was any hope of regaining the use of my stiff limbs, it was there. So early in the morning they wheeled me on a gurney[5] to the outpatient area, loaded me onto Filomón's ambulance and the journey began.

"There!" Filomón shouted again, "There's the mountain!"

I tried to turn my head to see, but I couldn't. "What mountain?" I asked.

"Tortuga Mountain," he said and looked back, "it's right by the hospital. Don't worry, I'll stop so you can see it." He sounded happy, revived, after the long, monotonous drive across the desert. I felt a sense of urgency as he pulled the ambulance onto the shoulder of the road. We bounced along until he found the right spot, then he stopped the ambulance and turned off the motor. He climbed over the seat to where I lay strapped on the small cot.

---

4 Sana, sana / colita de rana / Si no sanas hoy / sanarás mañana . . .
Spanish for: Get well, get well / little frogtail / If you don't get well today / you will tomorrow . . .

5 gurney (gʉr' nē) a wheeled stretcher or cot used to move hospital patients

"Ah, Filo," Clepo grumbled, "you've stopped here every time we bring a new kid. Don't you ever get tired of showing them that . . . mountain?"

"It's always a new kid," Filomón smiled as he loosened the straps that held me, "and each kid deserves to see the mountain from here. I want the boy to see it."

Filomón was an old man with a deep wrinkled face and rough, calloused hands, but he moved like a younger man as he lifted me tenderly so I could look out the window and see the mountain.

"There it is," he nodded, "that's Tortuga." His eyes sparkled as he looked at the volcanic mountain that loomed over the otherwise empty desert. It rose so magically into the gray sky that it seemed to hold the heavens and the earth together. It lay just east of the river valley, and the afternoon sun shining on it after the rain covered it with a sheen of silver.

"It's a magic mountain," Filomón whispered, and I felt his heart beating against me as he held me. "See!" he whispered, "See!" I tried to see beyond the volcanic slabs and granite boulders which formed the outline of a turtle, I tried to sense the steady rhythm of his pulse which seemed to be draining into the giant mountain, but I couldn't. I was too tired, and my faith in magic had drained out the night the paralysis came and in the ensuing nights and days which I spent without movement on the hospital bed.

I shook my head.

"That's okay," he smiled, "it comes slowly sometimes. But now at least you know it's there—" He seemed very tired. It had been a long trip for him too. He had had to keep the ambulance on course through one of the worst storms I could remember. But now we were almost there.

"Where's the hospital?" I asked.

"It's on this side of the river, you can't see it from here. See the smoke rising in the valley? That's Agua Bendita.[6] It's a small town, but people come from all over to bathe in the mineral waters from the springs which drain from the mountain—"

"It's a town full of old arthritics," Clepo giggled, "old people who think they can escape the pains of old age by dipping themselves in the mountain's water, but they can't run fast enough from death!" He slapped his thigh and laughed.

Filomón didn't answer. He sat beside the cot and looked out the window into the desert. "Even as terrible as the storm was for us, it will be good for the plants in the spring. After a good, wet winter the desert blooms like a garden," he nodded and rolled a cigarette. There was something about the way he spoke, the strength of his

6 Agua Bendita (ä' gwə ben dē' tə) Spanish for "holy water"

face, that reminded me of someone I had known—my grandfather perhaps, but I hadn't thought of him in years.

"These old villages cling to the river like the beads of a rosary,"[7] he continued, thinking aloud.

"Whoever crosses this desert has a lot of praying to do," Clepo agreed, "it's a journey of death."

"No, a journey of life. Our forefathers have wandered up and down this river valley for a long, long time. First the Indians roamed up and down this river, then others came, but they all stopped here at this same place: the springs of Tortuga, the place of the healing water—"

He talked and smoked. The dull sun shone through the window and played on the swirling smoke. I was fully awake now, but I felt feverish, and I couldn't help wondering what a strange day it had been to ride all this way with the old man and his assistant. I shivered, but not from the cold. The inside of the ambulance was now stifling. It glowed with white smoke and golden light which poured through the window. Filomón's eyes shone.

"How long have you been bringing kids to the hospital?" I asked.

"As long as I can remember," Filomón answered. "I bought this old hearse[8] in a junk yard and I fixed it up like an ambulance. I've been transporting kids ever since."

"We get thirty dollars a kid, dead or alive," Clepo laughed. "And we get to hear a lot of interesting stories. We've taken every kind of diseased body there is to the hospital. Why, Filo and I could become doctors if we wanted to, couldn't we Filo? But we don't know anything about you. You slept most of the way." He leaned over the seat and peered at me.

"He's tired," Filomón said.

"Yeah, but he's awake now," Clepo grinned. "So how did he get crippled? I know it ain't polio, I know polio. And how come his left hand is bandaged, huh? There's quite a story there, but he hasn't said a word!"

He seemed put out that I had slept most of the way and had not told the story of my past. But since the paralysis the past didn't matter. It was as if everything had died, except the dreams and the memories which kept haunting me. And even those were useless against the terrible weight which had fallen over me and which I cursed until I could curse no more.

"Do you take the kids back?" I asked.

"No, we don't!" Clepo said, "That's against the rules!"

"I picked you up," Filomón reminded him.

7 rosary (rō′ zər ē) a string of beads used in prayer to keep count

8 hearse an automobile used to carry the corpse during a funeral

Rufino Tamayo, *Interior with Alarm Clock*, 1928

"I was hitch-hiking," Clepo said smartly, "somebody would have picked me up."

"You were lost. I found you in the middle of a sandstorm, crying. Lucky for you I came along."

"I wasn't crying, I had sand in my eyes," Clepo insisted.

Filomón smiled. "It doesn't matter, you've been a good assistant." That seemed to satisfy Clepo, he grunted and sat back down. Filomón drew close and looked at me. "We can't take anybody back, that's not our job. But when you get better you can make the trip back home by yourself. Just wait till spring, and you'll be better. I know it looks bad now, but in the spring the river comes alive and the desert dresses like a young bride. The lizards come out to play in the warm sun, and even the mountain moves—" He touched my forehead with his fingers, then he leaned close to me and I felt his forehead touch mine, perhaps he was just leaning to retrieve one of the straps to tie me up again, but I felt his forehead brush mine, and I felt a relief from the paralysis which I hadn't felt since it came. Then he tied the strap and climbed back into the driver's seat.

"Filomón says you gotta keep your eyes on the mountain," Clepo said to fill in the silence.

"Well, it's helped us," Filomón answered, "it's been our faith in this wasteland . . . and it's helped a lot of kids. There's a strong power there."

He started the ambulance and let it coast down the long slope of the hill into the valley. I knew he was still looking at the mountain, still feeling the strange power that resided there for him.

"The water from the mountain springs is holy," he mused aloud, "long ago the place was used as a winter ceremonial ground by the Indians. They came to purify themselves by bathing in the warm waters . . . the water of the turtle . . . Later, when the Spaniards came, they called the springs Los Ojos de la Tortuga,[9] and when they discovered the waters could cure many illnesses they called the village Agua Bendita . . ."

"Who lives here?" I asked. We had entered the edge of the small town. Through the window I could see the tops of rundown gas stations, motels and cafes. There was a dilapidated movie house, a brownstone hotel, and many signs which creaked in the wind as they advertised the hot mineral baths.

"Mostly old people who come for the baths, people who work at the hospital, and a few of the old people who try to make a living from the small farms along the river—"

Filomón turned the ambulance and I caught a glimpse of a weathered sign that read *Crippled Children and Orphans Hospital*. The arrow pointed up the hill, so from the highway which ran through the small town we had to turn up the hill again towards the washed-out buildings which huddled together at the top. I struggled to turn to see more, instinctively, as I had so many times before, but it was useless, I couldn't move. I could only turn my head and watch the mountain across the valley. An air of hopelessness brooded over the dull mountain as the remaining winter clouds huddled at its peak. It seemed lost and out of place in the immense desert which surrounded it, and I wondered what secret rested in its core. Whatever it was, it was something that made Filomón's voice ring with hope and made his eyes sparkle even after the fatigue of the long journey.

9 Los Ojos de la Tortuga (lōs ō′ hos dā lä tôr tōō′ gə) Spanish for "the eyes of the turtle"

Linking Writing and Literature
Readers Respond to the Model

How does Rudolfo A. Anaya use character and complication to create mood in his narrative?

Explore Rudolfo A. Anaya's narrative by answering these questions. Then read what other students liked about Anaya's narrative.

1. Choose a character that you particularly liked. Explain how Anaya's description of this character contributes to the narrative.

2. What is the basic complication or conflict in Anaya's narrative? What background information does the author provide to set up this complication and make it appear realistic?

3. How did the author use setting to create mood?

4. How would the story have changed if the author had told it in the third person rather than the first?

The boy was my favorite character because, although he had a handicap, he still believed he would be healed someday. These details made the boy's character very realistic. The vivid description of Clepo, from his little limp to his facial expressions, also made that character seem real. I liked Filomón's story about the first inhabitants of the land and about the significance of Tortuga Mountain because it showed the importance of knowing your background. I would recommend this selection to a friend because it gives you an idea of how other cultures tell stories about healing and myths.

Torré Triplett

The dominant mood of the selection was uneasiness. The author set up that mood from the beginning by showing the boy thinking about how different and unfamiliar the weather was in the desert than at his home. Just as the setting was unfamiliar, the hospital where the boy was being taken was also unfamiliar. The boy had no idea what awaited him.
Lucino Vences

Unit 4 Review

Reflecting on the Unit

Summarize what you learned in this unit by answering the following questions.

- What are the characteristics of personal narrative writing, and what strategies can help you find ideas for your personal narratives?

- What are the basic elements of a work of fiction, and what characterizes plot?
- How does dialogue serve narrative writing?
- What is an anecdote? How can anecdotes serve theme in fiction and nonfiction?
- What are the important aspects of plot summary and conflict analysis and the uses of each?

Adding to Your Portfolio

Choose a selection for your portfolio.
Look over the narrative writing you have done during this unit. Select a completed piece of writing to put into your portfolio. The piece you choose should show some or all of the following:

- the basic narrative elements—characters, setting, plot, and point of view
- a character in a conflict or complication that leads to a climax and a resolution
- dialogue that advances plot or reveals character
- an anecdote that reinforces the theme of the story

Reflect on your choice.
Attach a note to the piece you chose, explaining briefly why you chose it and what you learned from writing it.

Set goals.
How can you improve your writing? What skill will you focus on the next time you write?

Writing Across the Curriculum

Make a literature connection.
Select a work of literature you read in class this year—a story, novel, or personal narrative. Then write a one-or two-page story introduction that would get someone interested in reading the story. Include setting, characters, complication, and resolution.

Expository Writing in the Real World

Behind the Science Feature

F O C U S: Like other kinds of exposition for a general audience, science writing uses plain talk and everyday examples to bring its subject to life.

Time *editor
Anastasia Toufexis*

I t was a May 1990 news conference on insomnia and sleep deprivation that finally did it. For years Anastasia Toufexis, health and behavior editor at *Time* magazine, had been pushing for a cover story on sleep—a hot topic in the early 1980s that seemed to cool during the middle of that decade.

In the late 1980s, though, reports came out that indicated the potential for human error increases when the factor of sleep deprivation is added to the equation. Analyses indicated that when people work horrendous hours, lack of sleep can affect all aspects of their lives, including performance on the job and at school.

During the same period, Toufexis began to see more studies on sleep, including figures showing that, next to alcohol, lack of sleep was a major factor in road accidents. Sleep had also become a personal issue for Toufexis and many others. Everywhere Toufexis turned she heard friends and colleagues—even herself— moaning about how groggy they were. "I was keep-

Writing the Science Feature

Prewriting	Drafting	Editing/Presenting
Getting the Facts	Selecting and Condensing Facts	Checking Accuracy and Sense

ing lousy hours because of our work schedule," Toufexis said. "I wondered, after thirteen years at *Time*, wasn't a lack of sleep taking a toll on me?"

It was the news conference on sleep that clinched things, though. Among the top national sleep researchers who spoke at the New York City conference was Dr. William Dement, director of the sleep center at Stanford University. Dement synthesized the growing body of research and everyday complaints into a disturbing statement: sleep deprivation had become a public health hazard.

After hearing Dement's remarks, Toufexis was convinced that the time had come for a "big act"—a *Time* cover story on sleep.

Press conferences, such as the one on "America's Sleep Debt," sometimes offer a forum for individuals to present their research on a topic.

"What does it take to write about science? Curiosity. A willingness to ask what may sound like stupid questions. The ability to translate jargon into common English, to make science vivid, related to the personal lives of your readers."

—Anastasia Toufexis

Prewriting

GETTING THE FACTS

In late October, Toufexis enlisted the help of correspondents in six *Time* bureaus around the country. She sent each one a query explaining the gist of the story, a list of questions to research, and the names of a few information sources.

Toufexis worked with a team on this story to get quick national coverage, a must for a magazine with readers from Maine to southern California. "There

For timely research and analysis needed in their stories, national magazines rely on their correspondents located in bureau offices in different cities across the country.

would be no way to get national coverage unless we had an enormous amount of time [for me to] travel around the country, stop-

ping in each and every place to get experts' views and analyses of their research plus finding people locally," she explained.

Those local people—pilots, students, stockbrokers, truck drivers, working moms—were critical to the story. "We didn't want a dry academic treatise on the lack of sleep," Toufexis said. "We wanted to humanize the problem, make it alive."

Through November, Toufexis did considerable reading herself, in books, *Time*'s clip folder of articles on sleep, professional journals, and her bulging file of reports on sleep research. She also interviewed several top sleep researchers.

After a month of detective work, Toufexis and her team had a wealth of data revealing a serious national problem—from scary tales of sleepy pilots to statistics showing that up to 200,000 truck accidents a year may be related to fatigue. The stack of research material stood a foot and a half high.

Drafting

SELECTING AND CONDENSING FACTS

Before trying to turn this mountain of data into a lively article, Toufexis laid some important groundwork. She organized her notes into topics. Then she typed the most important facts, studies, and quotes for each topic into her computer. The result: three or four pages of information for each topic. Next Toufexis noted the length her story should be— 4,000 to 5,000 words.

Toufexis's first challenge was to write a gripping lead. "Within the first two or three paragraphs, I have to be clear about why I'm doing the story, so I can get people interested," she said. "Then I try to hit them with the billboard: Why is this important? How does it affect you?" For this article, Toufexis turned to everyone's common experience with sleep.

With her lead resolved, Toufexis began writing. She selected key information, explained the research clearly, and connected it to the best examples from interviews all over the country. For instance,

Toufexis cited one study that found that adolescents need nine and a half or more hours of sleep each night. Do they get it? Toufexis illustrated this point with two examples: a quote from fifteen-year-old Kimberly Erlich from Van Nuys, California, who was horrified at the notion of sleeping nearly ten hours a night, and interviews with teachers who described "sleepy youngsters arriving late to class. . . . "

After selecting and condensing material, Toufexis had a complete draft. It was "way too long, portions were unbalanced, but it was finished," Toufexis said. She let the draft sit for a couple of days before starting to revise.

All over the country, the correspondents found that school, part-time work, and social demands keep teens from getting necessary sleep.

Editing/Presenting

CHECKING ACCURACY AND SENSE

After a week of writing and revising, Toufexis released her story to the senior editor for sciences, who edited it for interest and sense. *Time's* managing editor and other high-level editors also reviewed Toufexis's story.

Copies of the edited story were also sent to the correspondents, along with a list of fact-checking questions for them to answer.

The week before Toufexis's story ran, she and a researcher worked long hours correcting the story and answering questions of grammar, punctuation, sense, and style raised by *Time's* copy desk. As the deadline neared, Toufexis and her researcher fit the story to the

layout, wrote captions, and held a final review with the sciences editor. Finally, "Drowsy America" was ready.

Was all the effort worth it? "I hope my work has an impact," Toufexis said. "But for the most part, I work to get a piece of information across. If I make people aware that a subject is something they should think of, I've done my job."

By her own standards, Toufexis did a stellar job. "For a week and a half after the story ran, I got the most requests for radio interviews that I've ever had," she said. "I must have touched a nerve."

Through collaborative effort, a large group of people made this cover story possible.

Responding to the Case Study

1. Discussion

Discuss these questions about Anastasia Toufexis's science writing.

- What was Anastasia Toufexis's purpose for writing her scientific article about sleep?
- How did Toufexis and her team gather information on sleep deprivation?
- How did Toufexis go about organizing the wealth of data she had collected?
- What was the role of each editor who reviewed Toufexis's article before it was published?

2. Expository Writing

Write a review of a science story. Write a review of a science article or special feature from a newspaper or magazine. Explain the article's purpose, the scientific research that provided data, and how the writer presented technical information in an appealing way. For example, did the writer start with a gripping lead or include graphics such as the photograph below?

Grammar Link

Vary sentence structure to create interest.

Reread the case study. Note how the sentences vary in structure and in length. In addition to simple sentences, there are compound sentences: *It was "way too long, portions were unbalanced, but it was finished," . . .* There are also complex sentences: *As the deadline neared, Toufexis and her researcher fit the story to the layout. . . .*

Create different types of sentences.

1. Write a simple sentence or choose one in the case study.
2. Rework it, making it a compound sentence.
3. Rework the simple sentence again to make it part of a complex sentence.
4. Rework your compound sentence into a compound-complex sentence.
5. Write a fifth related sentence, and tell what type of sentence it is.

See Lesson 13.3, pages 507–508, and Lesson 13.4, pages 509–510.

Expository Writing
Writing to Inform and Explain

Expository writing is what you use to give directions, explain a new term or idea, compare one thing to another, or explain how to do something. In the model below, Mary Crow Dog and Richard Erdoes explain the importance of the tiyospaye[1] *in Lakota Sioux society.*

The topic sentence defines "tiyospaye."

Supporting sentences use comparison and several examples to explain the specific qualities of a tiyospaye.

Literature Model

At the center of the old Sioux society was the *tiyospaye,* the extended family group, the basic hunting band, which included grandparents, uncles, aunts, in-laws, and cousins. The tiyospaye was like a warm womb cradling all within it. Kids were never alone, always fussed over by not one but several mothers, watched and taught by several fathers. The real father, as a matter of fact, selected a second father, some well-thought-of relative with special skills as a hunter or medicine man, to help him bring up a boy, and such a person was called "Father" too. And the same was true for the girls. Grandparents in our tribe always held a special place in caring for the little ones, because they had more time to devote to them, when the father was out hunting, taking the mother with him to help with the skinning and butchering.

Mary Crow Dog and Richard Erdoes,
Lakota Woman

1 **tiyospaye** tē′ yō shpä′ yā

Choose a Kind of Expository Writing

An essay is the most general form of expository writing. The introduction of an essay includes a thesis statement, a one-sentence summary of purpose. The body is made up of one or more paragraphs of details that support the thesis. The conclusion states the implications of the thesis. Within the general essay format, the specific kind of exposition you write depends on your goal, as the chart shows.

Six Kinds of Expository Writing		
Kind	Attribute	Examples
Process Explanation	Uses step-by-step organization to explain how something happens, works, or is done	How do you run a computer program? How are homes built? How does the human body process food?
Cause and Effect	Identifies the causes and/or effects of something and examines the relationship between causes and effects	What causes freckles? What causes sunspots? What are the effects of poverty on children?
Comparison and Contrast	Examines similarities and differences to find relationships and draw conclusions	Compare jazz and rap, or blues and country music. Compare and contrast basketball and ballet.
Definition	Explains a term or concept by listing and examining its qualities or characteristics	What is hypothermia? What is "grandstanding"? What was the Harlem Renaissance?
Classification	Organizes subjects into categories and examines qualities or characteristics of those categories	What organisms are considered fungi? How would you characterize the writing of Stephen King?
Problem and Solution	Examines aspects of a complex problem and explores or proposes possible solutions	How can your community increase literacy? What can be done to protect wilderness areas?

Grammar
Editing Tip

In the editing stage, check that words used to represent themselves have been italicized or underlined. For more information about italics, see Lesson 21.10, pages 720–721.

Journal Writing

If you were to be asked to write about any aspect of school life for your school's newspaper, what would you write about? Choose a topic and tell which kind of expository writing would help you meet your goal.

Combine Various Kinds of Exposition

Revising Tip

Whenever you revise expository writing, ask yourself whether using a different kind of exposition would help you develop your topic more clearly or completely.

To fully explore the qualities and characteristics of a topic, you will most often need to use a combination of expository types. In the following passage, authors Betsy Armstrong and Knox Williams write about an avalanche-prone area in Switzerland. The authors begin by explaining how forests tend to inhibit avalanches. Then they discuss what happens when areas are deforested for building or heating purposes. Finally, the authors describe how reforestation can prevent avalanches. As you read, try to pick out the specific kinds of expository writing the authors use.

What is the cause-and-effect relationship between human settlement and an increase in avalanches?

How do the writers explain reforestation in Ursental, Switzerland, as the solution to a problem?

Literature Model

In many cases, the villagers made the avalanche problem worse. Before settlement, dense forests covered many of the steep slopes above the valleys. The forests inhibited large avalanches, since catastrophic avalanches do not originate in a heavy forest, and avalanches traveling into such a forest will often slow as the snow encounters the trees. [A forest] tends to diminish the speed of the snow and break up the avalanche. However, villagers often cut down the forests for building and heating purposes. In many areas the trees never grew back, leaving the slopes bare and smooth—a perfect track for the run of a snow avalanche. A prime example of deforestation is in the valley of Ursental in central Switzerland. Above the town of Andermatt, there remains just a wedge of trees, while the remainder of the steep slope is bare. Up valley, near the Furka Pass, is the town of Hospental, which also maintains its own protective wedge of trees. As the story is told, the inhabitants of the valley systematically cut down the forests that covered the steep slopes on both sides. Almost too late they realized their mistake: they saw that on the bare, treeless slopes, huge avalanches began descending to the valley floor, making travel between towns extremely dangerous. All tree-cutting stopped and the wedges of trees above the towns were preserved. Reforestation, the systematic planting of trees, continues today in the Ursental, to thicken the wedges that are periodically thinned by avalanches.

Betsy Armstrong and Knox Williams, *The Avalanche Book*

5.1 Writing Activities

Write an Explanation of an Event

Examine the painting *Castle of Cards*. Who do you think the four people are, and how might they be related? What's going on? Write an essay explaining the event you see in the painting.

- Combine the kinds of exposition you use.
- Include an introduction, body, and a conclusion.

PURPOSE To explain an event portrayed in a piece of art
AUDIENCE Your teacher and classmates
LENGTH 2–3 paragraphs

Zinaida Serebriakova, *Castle of Cards*, 1918

Cooperative Learning

In a small group, select a natural phenomenon: a hurricane, earthquake, glacier, iceberg, sunspots, or any other you'd like to explore. Work together to compile a list of questions based on the six kinds of exposition. Divide the questions among group members. Do some basic research using your science textbook, and write a paragraph answering your question. Then combine the paragraphs into a fact sheet on your subject to share with the class.

Expository Writing
Knowing Your Audience

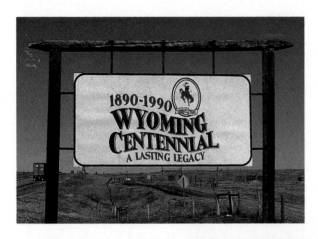

Identifying your audience will help you focus your writing and choose details. In the model below, one-time California filmmaker Gretel Ehrlich explains her attraction to a place that her audience, most of them city dwellers, regard as isolated and desolate.

Erlich provides two examples to show what she means when she says the people are "tender-hearted about quirky behavior."

This quotation brings a sense of immediacy to the writing. How might Cliff's comment help Erlich's readers to understand her words "strong on scruples"?

Literature Model

*I*n all this open space, values crystallize quickly. People are strong on scruples but tenderhearted about quirky behavior. . . . A friend, Cliff, who runs a trapline in the winter, cut off half his foot while chopping a hole in the ice. Alone, he dragged himself to his pickup and headed for town, stopping to open the ranch gate as he left, and getting out to close it again, thus losing, in his observance of rules, precious time and blood. Later, he commented, "How would it look, them having to come to the hospital to tell me their cows had gotten out?"

Accustomed to emergencies, my friends doctor each other from the vet's bag with relish. When one old-timer suffered a heart attack in hunting camp, his partner quickly stirred up a brew of red horse liniment and hot water and made the half-conscious victim drink it, then tied him onto a horse and led him twenty miles to town. He regained consciousness and lived.

Gretel Ehrlich, *The Solace of Open Spaces*

Write to Someone

Thinking about your particular audience for each piece of expository writing will help you zero in on what your readers need to know. Even if your main readers are your teachers, you should remember every teacher is different. Think about what each teacher is looking for as you complete your assignments.

Besides teachers, classmates and other peers will often read and critique your writing. In addition, when you write personal notes, letters to friends, job or college applications, or news stories for the school paper, you must consider various readers. The following questions can help you develop a feel for your audience.

Revising Tip

A peer editor can give you valuable feedback on how well you have responded to the needs of your audience.

Understanding Your Audience

Interest
- Does this audience care about my topic already, or must I convince them of its importance?
- Will I need to find ways to overcome apathy or dislike of my topic?
- If this audience has a strong interest in my topic, how can I move forward swiftly to maintain their interest?

Background
- How much does this audience already know about my topic?
- Do I need to define basic terms and concepts?
- Do I need to probe deeply for new insights in order to tell this audience something it doesn't already know, or should I concentrate on clarifying the main points?

Vocabulary
- Should I use formal or informal language to reach this audience?
- Should I present my points in nontechnical language?
- Will my audience be able to follow complex explanations, or should I keep sentences short and simple?

Journal Writing

Using the chart above, analyze a piece of writing you have already completed. Would you change anything now? Record your reactions in your journal.

Use Details to Appeal to Your Audience

Identifying your audience is just the first step. Here are some strategies you can use to support your main ideas and make connections clear to your audience.

Supporting Details and Good Connections	
Examples	Support main ideas with vivid, interesting examples to help readers grasp unfamiliar information or relate information to their own experiences.
Facts and Statistics	Use facts and statistics to help readers understand the magnitude of an issue, set the time frame, provide historical background, or support technical points.
Comparisons	Use analogies, metaphors, similes, and other forms of comparison to help readers understand unfamiliar concepts by relating them to something readers *do* understand.
Quotations	Use engaging quotations from experts on your topic to clarify meanings or lend authority to your writing. Or use a relevant quotation at the beginning of your writing to set the tone.

Grammar
Editing Tip

When editing expository writing, check that all proper nouns and proper adjectives are capitalized, as in the literature model. To review capitalization rules, see Lessons 20.2 and 20.3, pages 677–687.

Literature Model

Statistics help give readers a sense of the vastness of the continent.

Lamb compares the size of the Sahara and the United States. What does this comparison tell you that statistics alone cannot?

*A*frica occupies 20 percent of the earth's land surface, or 11.7 million square miles. Only Asia is larger. Africa is 5,000 miles long, reaching from the God-forsaken deserts of the north to the lush wine country in the south, and 4,600 miles wide. Its coastline measures 18,950 miles—shorter than Europe's because of the absence of inlets and bays—and the equator cuts Africa just about in half. Africa's climate varies wildly, from temperate in the high plateaus, to tropical along the coastal plains to just plain intolerable in the sizzling deserts.

The coastal strip around Africa is narrow, and the interior plateaus are characterized by wide belts of tropical rain forest, wooded savanna and grassland plains. In the far north is the Sahara, the world's largest desert. It covers one quarter of the continent, an area as large as the United States mainland. In the far south is the Kalahari Desert, the world's seventh largest. The highest point in Africa is Mount Kilimanjaro in Tanzania, 19,340 feet tall and snow-capped the year round. . . .

David Lamb, *The Africans*

Write an Explanation of a Painting

Look carefully at the painting on this page and read the title. Write a short explanation of what is happening in the picture. Your audience is a foreign exchange student unfamiliar with the game of baseball. Think about what your audience needs to know.

- Use language that your audience will understand.
- Use details to support your main ideas.
- Make good, clear connections.

PURPOSE　To explain baseball to someone unfamiliar with the game
AUDIENCE　A foreign exchange student
LENGTH　2–3 paragraphs

Jacob Lawrence, *Strike*, 1949

Grammar Link

Avoid sentence fragments.

A *sentence fragment* is an incomplete sentence punctuated as if it were a complete sentence.

Rewrite the following items, correcting all sentence fragments.

1. Expository writing can be dry and boring. Often lacks feeling.
2. Your readers have different levels of knowledge. And varying degrees of interest in your topic.
3. What kind of language should you use to reach a younger audience? Probably informal.
4. Regardless of their background. Make sure that your audience understands technical terms you introduce.
5. Support your main ideas with comparisons. For example, analogies, metaphors, and similes.

See Lesson 13.9, pages 519–520.

Cooperative Learning

In a small group, choose a complex biological term, such as *ecosystem, conservation,* or *pollution.* Each of you should choose a different audience: for example, a younger child, a parent, or a biology teacher, and write a paragraph defining the term. Later, compare your definitions, analyzing and evaluating the techniques each writer used to reach a particular audience. Consider with your group how to present the completed paragraphs to the appropriate audience.

Expository Writing
Writing About a Process

When you explain a process, you explain the steps involved in completing it. Notice the details James Wagenvoord uses in his explanation.

Literature Model

Wagenvoord discusses several different variations of stickball, beginning with the basic version.

S tickball's a little closer to the big game than stoopball. Instead of playing the width of a street, it stretches down the block as far as a hollow Spaldeen can be powered with a cut-off broom handle. It's often an impressive distance. There are neighborhood variations upon variations. If there's a basic version it's the street game—the hitter flipping the ball into the air, fixedly eyeing its bounce in front of him, and then, as it rises to its apex, stepping into the ball to slash at it with the bat. When the ball is smashed into the playing area, the standard baseball rules take over—again with variations. A ball landing and staying on the rooftop—fair or foul—is an automatic out. But a fair ball skimming off fire escapes, window frames, and dribbling down building faces is in play. There's a version of the game called slow pitch which, with a pitcher, becomes baseball except for the size of the ball and the narrow bat. And there's "off the wall," a tailoring of the classic to interior courtyards, a reversed mirror-image form. The pitcher stands behind the batter, outfielders ranging behind them and all facing the same wall, as the batter waits for his crack until a pitch has been flung at the wall and rebounds to him. His hit is in play the moment that, on the fly, it again strikes the wall. Then stoopball bounce rules take over. One bounce before being caught is a single, and a home run is four bounces or a smash hopelessly beyond reach of the defenders.

What kind of details does Wagenvoord use to characterize stickball?

James Wagenvoord, *Hangin' Out: City Kids, City Games*

Explain One Step at a Time

When you write about a process, you must take care to remember all the little details involved. Unless you can describe the process completely and accurately, your readers will be left in the dark. You must also take into consideration the level of knowledge of your readers. If they know little about the process, you may need to define basic terms and concepts. If your readers are familiar with the process, you don't want to bore them with general information they already know. The following steps can help you write about a process.

Explaining a Process

1. Investigate	Watch someone perform the process, do it yourself, ask questions about it, or read about it. Take notes as you go.
2. Observe	Identify the main parts of the process and the specific steps needed to carry it out.
3. Arrange	Put the steps in chronological order. You may wish to "walk through" the process mentally to make sure nothing is missing.
4. Elaborate	Decide what background information and examples you need to include so that your audience will understand your explanation. Be sure to define any unfamiliar terms.
5. Polish	Use transitions such as *first, next, meanwhile, then, finally*, and *last* to point the way as you write.
6. Review	Check to make sure your explanation is complete, clear, and accurate.

Journal Writing

What steps do you take to get ready for a party or a school dance? Try listing the steps in your journal. Be careful not to leave anything out or take anything for granted. You may be surprised at how complex such a routine process turns out to be.

Revise Your Explanation

Prewriting Tip

Explaining a process to a peer editor before writing can help you identify steps or essential background information you may have overlooked.

When you revise an explanation, your main goals are clarity, completeness, and accuracy. Make sure that the information you present and the way you present it are appropriate for your audience.

The first draft below is taken from an essay that explains the stages of building a house. It is intended for a general audience with no specific background in home building. What changes would you make in order to improve the passage's clarity and appropriateness for that audience?

Grammar

Drafting Tip

When describing a process, be sure to use the same verb tense throughout the explanation. For help, see Lesson 15.6, pages 560–561.

> **Model**
>
> *N*ext, workers bolt wooden sills to the top of the foundation. Floor joists are placed across the foundation on the sills, and the floorboards are nailed to the top of the joists, forming the bottom layer of the floor. Each wall frame is lifted into place along the sill and braced temporarily. When all the outside walls have been set in place, they are nailed together and braced permanently.

When the writer reviewed the draft, she made some vocabulary changes. She realized her readers might not know some basic terms, such as *sills* and *joists*. Also, they might understand the process more easily if she drew attention to the distinct stages of the process. Notice the changes she made.

How does the topic sentence in each paragraph make the steps of the process clearer?

The writer also defines terms that she knows might be unfamiliar.

> **Model**
>
> *T*he next step is to build the frame. Workers start by bolting wooden sills, called base plates, to the top of the foundation. These sills support the outside walls. Next, floor joists, or support beams, are placed across the foundation on the sills, and the floor boards are nailed to the top of the joists, forming the bottom layer of the floor.
>
> At this point the structure is solid enough to hold the wall frames. Carpenters assemble each wall frame separately. Then each one is lifted into place along the sill and braced temporarily. When all the outside walls have been set in place, they are nailed together and braced permanently.

5.3 Writing Activities

Write a "How-to" Article

Write a 2- to 3-paragraph explanation of a process you are very familiar with, such as how to care for tropical fish or how to train for a 10K race. Assume that your audience is fellow students who are unfamiliar with the process. Perform or observe the activity and note the steps.

- Arrange the steps in chronological order.
- Explain one step at a time.
- Tailor your explanation to the background level of your audience.

PURPOSE To explain a familiar process to somebody unfamiliar with it
AUDIENCE Other students
LENGTH 2–3 paragraphs

Cooperative Learning

In a small group, discuss processes in M. C. Escher's *Day and Night* shown on this page. Refer to a process that is portrayed in the picture, a process used by the artist to achieve his effects, or both. After the discussion each group member should write a paragraph about the picture. Share and compare responses.

Maurits Cornelis Escher,
Day and Night, 1938

Expository Writing

Writing About Cause and Effect

Cause-and-effect writing explains relationships between events or facts—specifically, that one event or fact caused another. In the model below, reporter Frank Trippett describes several revolutionary effects of air conditioning.

Literature Model

Trippett begins by identifying the cause and then explains the effects.

Trippett gives details about a series of effects of air conditioning.

I n fact, air conditioning has substantially altered the country's character and folkways. . . . Many of its byproducts are so conspicuous that they are scarcely noticed. To begin with, air conditioning transformed the face of urban America by making possible those glassy, boxy, sealed-in skyscrapers on which the once humane geometries of places like San Francisco, Boston and Manhattan have been impaled. It has been indispensable, no less, to the functioning of sensitive advanced computers, whose high operating temperatures require that they be constantly cooled. Thus, in a very real way, air conditioning has made possible the ascendancy of computerized civilization. . . . It has also reshaped the national economy and redistributed political power simply by encouraging the burgeoning of the sultry southerly swatch of the country, profoundly influencing major migration trends of people and industry. Sunbelt cities like Phoenix, Atlanta, Dallas and Houston (where shivering indoor frigidity became a mark of status) could never have mushroomed so prosperously without air conditioning; some communities—Las Vegas in the Nevada desert and Lake Havasu City on the Arizona-California border— would shrivel and die overnight if it were turned off.

Frank Trippett, "The Great American Cooling Machine"

Identify the Relationship

In a simple chronological relationship, one event simply follows another in time. In a cause-and-effect relationship, however, one event *causes* another—for example, according to Frank Trippett, the birth of skyscrapers occurred because of air conditioning. You can test for a cause-and-effect relationship by asking the following: If the "cause" hadn't happened, would the "effect" have happened?

Cause-and-effect relationships are not always simple and straight-forward. One cause can have several effects; one effect can result from several causes. Individual causes and effects can also form a chain of events, each one leading to the next. The graphic below will help you to visualize these relationships.

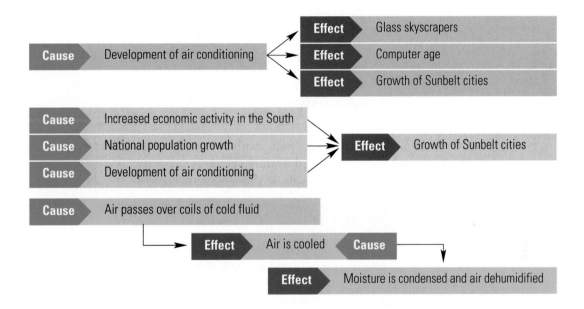

When you write about cause-and-effect relationships, you generally use one of two patterns of organization. With the cause-to-effect pattern, you start by explaining the cause (or causes) and then proceed to the effects. In the effect-to-cause pattern, you examine the effect (or effects) first and then explain what caused them.

Journal Writing

In your journal brainstorm a list of positive and negative effects of the computer. Then write a short paragraph exploring this question: On the whole, have the effects of the computer on modern society been beneficial or harmful?

Explore Relationships

Examining causes and effects is a skill frequently used in the natural and social sciences and in journalistic writing. The following guidelines can help you explore cause-and-effect relationships.

Vocabulary

Revising Tip

Transitions such as *accordingly, as a result, consequently, therefore,* and *thus* can help you show connections between causes and effects.

Guidelines for Writing a Cause-and-Effect Essay

1. Test the cause-and-effect relationship. Does one action actually *cause* another to happen, or does one merely follow the other?
2. Explore the cause-and-effect relationship. How are causes and effects related? What are the most significant aspects of the relationship?
3. Choose a focus. Do you want to emphasize causes, effects, or both?
4. Gather details. Find examples, facts and statistics, and other details to explain the cause-and-effect relationship. Keep in mind the interest level and prior knowledge of your audience.
5. Organize your writing. Should you use cause-to-effect order or effect-to-cause order? Or should you explain a chain of causes and effects in chronological order?
6. Clarify relationships. Use paragraphing and transitions to draw distinctions between causes and effects.

This cause-and-effect paragraph is from an essay about the benefits and drawbacks of air conditioning. What is the cause? What are the effects? What transitions show these relationships?

Model

Which phrases help to show the relationship between causes and effects?

Despite its benefits, air conditioning has caused its share of problems as well. Air conditioners require tremendous amounts of power. Consequently, as more homes and businesses installed air conditioning, power utilities were forced to increase their capacities. Some coal-burning utilities began burning far more fuel to meet the demand. As a result, pollution increased. Other utilities began ambitious nuclear power projects. Some citizens, concerned about the safety of nuclear power, protested. As a result, many of these projects were halted or forced to exceed their budgets to meet new safety requirements. In many large cities, even increased utility capacity could not keep up with the demand. Summer became a time of frequent "brownouts," when certain parts of a city would experience brief periods of reduced power. In some cases, power would be lost completely.

This specific example elaborates on one effect.

5.4 Writing Activities

Write a Cause-and-Effect Paragraph

The following poems, both by Robert Frost, contain causes and effects. In the first poem the cause and effect are momentous, concerning the world and everyone in it. In the second the cause and effect are private, concerning only the speaker. Choose one of the poems, and write a paragraph explaining its meaning in terms of cause and effect.

- Identify the cause-and-effect relationship.
- Use a pattern of organization from the chart on page 227.
- Clarify relationships with transitions.

Fire and Ice
Some say the world will end in fire,
Some say in ice.
From what I've tasted of desire
I hold with those who favor fire.
But if it had to perish twice,
I think I know enough of hate
To say that for destruction ice
Is also great
And would suffice.

Dust of Snow
The way a crow
Shook down on me
The dust of snow
From a hemlock tree

Has given my heart
A change of mood
And saved some part
Of a day I'd rued.

PURPOSE   To explain a cause-and-effect relationship in poetry
AUDIENCE   Your English teacher
LENGTH   1 paragraph

COMPUTER OPTION

Many word-processing programs include an outlining feature that enables you to create an outline and a skeleton "draft" at the same time. If you revise your outline, the draft changes along with it. If your PC has this outlining feature, use it as you organize your material for the above assignment.

Grammar Link

Make verbs agree with indefinite pronoun subjects.

Some indefinite pronouns are singular and require singular verbs; others are plural and take plural verbs. Note how the indefinite pronoun subject *many* is used in this sentence from the model on page 226: "*Many* of its byproducts *are* . . . scarcely noticed." There are also indefinite pronouns whose number depends on the nouns to which they refer.

Write sentences using each of the ten indefinite pronouns below as the subject. Make each subject agree with a present-tense verb.

1. nothing   2. some
3. several   4. one
5. each   6. few
7. both   8. everyone
9. most   10. either

See Lesson 16.7, pages 585–587.

Expository Writing
Comparing and Contrasting

高
等
学
校

When you compare two or more subjects, you explain how they are similar. When you contrast them, you explain how they are different. Note how writer Phil Sudo uses comparison and contrast to discuss the likes and dislikes of a Japanese exchange student studying in the United States.

The first sentence introduces the main idea— "the radical differences" between Japanese and U.S. schools.

Sudo compares features of Japanese and U.S. schools: study habits, teacher-student relationships, social life.

Literature Model

L ife in America has exposed Naohiko to the radical differences between Japanese and U.S. schools. [In the United States] students rarely study more than two hours a night. In part, that's because so many have part-time jobs. "In my high school in Japan, they said we couldn't get jobs. 'If you get a job, you can't study,' they said." But also, he says, some students [in the United States] take advantage of the free environment. "I don't understand why it's so easy to skip class," says Naohiko. . . .

On the positive side, . . . is the open curriculum. "Here we can choose our classes and choose our teachers. In Japan, I didn't like teachers and they didn't like students. In America, a teacher is like a friend."

He also likes the social aspects of school. He has an American girlfriend, and goes to school dances. "In Japan, school is for studying. There's not many good experiences. In America, we get a lot of good experiences. It makes a lot of nice memories."

Phil Sudo, *Scholastic Update*

When comparing and contrasting, you do more than list similarities and differences. You investigate relationships and draw conclusions.

Create Graphic Organizers

In preparing to write a comparison-contrast, you may find two kinds of graphic organizers particularly useful.

Venn Diagrams   A Venn diagram can help you explore similarities and differences in your subjects. Here's how to create a Venn diagram:

1. Draw two intersecting circles.

2. In the left-hand circle, list features unique to Subject A. In the right-hand circle, list features unique to Subject B.

3. Where the circles overlap, list the important features that both subjects share.

Japanese Schools
- More than two hours of homework; no jobs
- No choice of classes or teachers
- School for studying; no socializing

Similarities
- Standardized tests
- Competitive environment

U.S. Schools
- Limited homework because of part-time jobs and extracurricular activities
- Some required courses, some electives; some choice of teachers
- Social life a big part of school

Comparison Frames   If you know the categories you want to compare and contrast, you may wish to use a comparison frame. Follow these steps:

1. Write the two subjects being compared as headings.

2. List the categories you will compare and contrast.

3. Fill in the boxes.

Categories	Subjects	
	U.S. Schools	**Japanese Schools**
Study Habits	Limited homework because of activities and jobs	Often more than two hours of homework; no jobs
Student Choice	Some required courses and some electives	Courses prescribed by government
Social Life	Social life an important aspect of school	School for studying, not socializing

Grammar

Drafting Tip

When comparing two items, use the comparative form of a modifier. For help, see Lesson 18.1, pages 625–626.

Journal Writing

How would you compare and contrast three things such as baseball, basketball, and football, or three movies? In your journal, create a Venn diagram or comparison frame.

Organize Your Comparison

Sudo's comparison of Japanese and U.S. high schools shows one method of organization, comparing the subjects feature by feature. Another method, shown here, is to discuss all aspects first of one subject, then of the other. The chart below clarifies each method.

Model

How do the first two sentences set the stage for a contrast?

The writer compares by presenting subjects separately. The first subject is her expectations. The second subject is her actual observations.

What is the purpose of the last sentence?

The only reason I cared about going to Florida on vacation with my family was to see the killer whales at Sea World. But what I saw was not what I had expected. I pictured the killer whales I had seen on television, huge creatures—twenty to thirty feet long—with shiny backs and white bellies. I recalled them swimming freely through ocean waters at speeds as fast as twenty-five miles an hour in groups as large as twenty or more, stopping occasionally for a joyful roll through the water or a leap above the surface.

The killer whales I saw at Sea World certainly looked as I had expected, but everything else about them surprised and disappointed me. They lived in tanks—gigantic to you and me, but puny compared to the vast ocean. They traveled at rates that never even approached their top ocean speeds and were alone or in pairs rather than in large groups. Their flips and leaps were commanded by the trainer and didn't seem quite so joyful and free. After a short time, all I felt was sadness for these captives of an environment not their own.

Grammar

Editing Tip

Eliminate any double comparisons—that is, comparisons that add both the ending -er or -est and the word more or most to the modifier. See Lesson 18.3, pages 630–631.

How to Organize a Comparison-Contrast

Feature by Feature	Subject by Subject

1. Study Habits
  A. Japan
  B. United States
	1. What I expected
	  A. Swimming in ocean
	  B. Groups of twenty or more
	  C. Free, joyful actions

2. Student Choice
  A. Japan
  B. United States
	2. What I observed
	  A. Confined to tanks
	  B. Alone or in pairs
	  C. Actions on command

3. Social Life
  A. Japan
  B. United States	

Write a Comparison-Contrast Article

Write an article about the abstract painting below, comparing and contrasting it with the realistic floral painting on page 237 in regard to color, composition, and total effect on the viewer. First, explore similarities and differences in a Venn diagram. Then, list your categories and information in a comparison frame.

- Use a method of organization shown on page 232.
- Draw conclusions.

PURPOSE To compare and contrast two paintings
AUDIENCE Your classmates and teacher
LENGTH 2–3 paragraphs

Alma Thomas, *Iris, Tulips, Jonquils and Crocuses*, 1969

Grammar Link

Avoid double comparisons.

The comparative form of an adjective or adverb is formed with *-er* or *more/less*. Using both together creates an incorrect double comparison.

Rewrite each sentence below to eliminate the double comparison.

1. U.S. schools are more easier than Russian schools.
2. Russian students have homework more frequenter than American students.
3. Russian teachers are less friendlier than American teachers.
4. Russian schools offer more fewer electives than U.S. schools.
5. American students attend social events more oftener than do Russian students.

See Lesson 18.3, pages 630–631.

Cross-Curricular: Science

As the editor of a conservation newsletter, you will write an editorial about how different kinds of people view the future of the planet. Use the following notes to write a comparison and contrast essay.

The Optimist Thinks the environment will be saved, believes people will learn to recycle and end pollution, sees today's efforts as a strong foundation, inspires confidence in friends

The Pessimist Assumes the environment will get worse, does not trust human nature to care for the planet, sees today's efforts as having doomsday consequences, inspires gloom and doom in friends

Expository Writing
Writing Effective Definitions

Basic definitions of words can be found in dictionaries. To present more elaborate concepts of words, however, lengthier writing is often needed. Notice how Wendell Berry gives both a formal and a personal definition of "family farm" in this excerpt from an essay.

Literature Model

What is Berry's definition of a family farm?

What I shall mean by the term "family farm" is a farm small enough to be farmed by a family and one that *is* farmed by a family, perhaps with a small amount of hired help. I shall *not* mean a farm that is owned by a family and worked by other people. The family farm is both the home and the workplace of the family that owns it. . . .

Furthermore, the term "family farm" implies longevity in the connection between family and farm. A family farm is not a farm that a family has bought on speculation and is only occupying and using until it can be profitably sold.

What two types of farm does Berry exclude from his definition?

Wendell Berry, "A Defense of the Family Farm"

Write a Formal Definition

A formal definition places a word or subject in a general category and examines how it differs from other words in its category. One way to get started in writing a formal definition is to create a word map.

Word Map

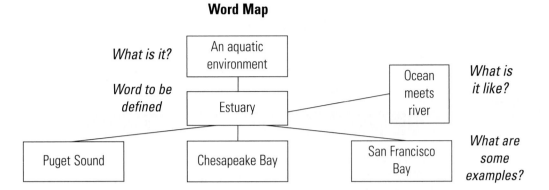

Naming your word's general category (What is it?) helps identify its broadest, most basic meaning. Naming other words in the same category (What is it like?) helps pinpoint the meanings that are unique to your word. Citing examples helps clarify the specific qualities included in the meaning of your word.

The word map above was helpful in writing this definition of *estuary*. As you read the definition, refer to the word map.

Model

Puget Sound, San Francisco Bay, and Chesapeake Bay may seem to be just busy waterways in the middle of large urban areas, but they have something else in common as well. They are all estuaries, aquatic environments with unique combinations of physical surroundings and life forms.

Estuaries are located where rivers and oceans meet, and the mixing of salt water from the ocean and fresh water from the river produces a unique environment. In addition, the action of ocean tides creates currents that deposit sediments and organic debris, making estuaries rich in minerals and nutrients. These conditions also make estuaries productive breeding grounds for shellfish.

Familiar examples help readers picture the meaning of the term being defined.

The explanation about oceans and rivers shows how estuaries are related to these other aquatic environments.

Journal Writing

Experiment with writing formal definitions. Create a word map for one or more of the following words: *horror movie, personal computer, frog, medicine.*

Write a Personal Definition

Formal definitions of words like *love* only scratch the surface. An informal definition—involving your language, your style, your meaning—can often do a better job. Look at the guidelines below.

Vocabulary
Drafting Tip

You may find that you need to combine the techniques of writing formal and personal definitions to fully explore the meaning of some words.

Guidelines for Writing Personal Definitions

1. Examine what the word means to you personally. How does the word affect you? What feelings or experiences does the word bring to mind?
2. Examine other viewpoints. What is the dictionary definition? What other personal definitions can you find? How is your definition different from others?
3. Find details to support your definition.

Notice the techniques this writer used to develop a personal definition of the term *environmentalist*.

Model

A dictionary definition "anchors" the personal definition and provides a basis for comparison.

I consider myself an environmentalist. According to the dictionary, an *environmentalist* is interested in preserving and improving the environment, and I certainly fit that description. To me, however, being an environmentalist requires a greater commitment than just being "interested."

Examples elaborate on the personal definition.

For me, every day is Earth Day. I try to buy only those products that are packaged in biodegradable materials. I recycle paper, aluminum, and plastics. I persuaded my brother and sister-in-law to stop buying disposable diapers for my nephew Mark. My biggest accomplishment, however, was getting my parents to stop using weed killers on our lawn. No more pesticides for us. If we see a few weeds, that's OK. We can live with weeds.

Some environmental activists are more extreme. They chain themselves to trees in the forest to keep them from being cut down. They lie down in front of bulldozers. They ride out in boats to interfere with commercial fishing and nuclear testing. I support their goals, but not their tactics. I believe we've done enough violence to the environment without doing more harm to one another. I just want future generations to live in a world that is a little cleaner and a little less threatening than the one I am growing up in.

5.6 Writing Activities

Write a Definition

The style of the realistic painting shown on this page is sometimes called *photorealism.* Look at the painting closely, and use it to write your own definition of photorealism. Before you write your definition, prepare a word map.

- Identify feelings and experiences the word or painting brings to mind.
- Find details to support your definition.

PURPOSE To define *photorealism,* using a painting as an example
AUDIENCE Your teacher and classmates
LENGTH 1–2 paragraphs

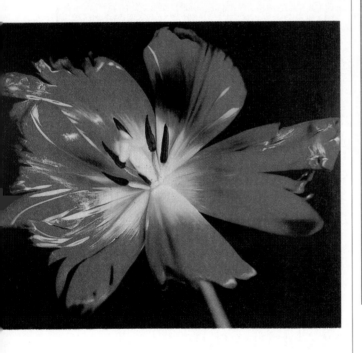

Ben Schonzeit, *Parrot Tulip,* 1976

Cooperative Learning

In a small group, prepare a dictionary of current teenage slang. Brainstorm to generate a list of entries, starting with words for *good* and *bad.* Set a length for the definitions, and assign several definitions and example sentences to each student. Work with a peer editor to edit and proofread your part of the dictionary. Finally, assemble your dictionary.

Grammar Link

Use precise nouns to clarify meaning.

When you write definitions, use specific nouns to make clear what you mean. Note how precise nouns are used as supporting details in the model definitions.

Rewrite the definitions for the italicized words below, replacing the general nouns with nouns that are more exact.

1. A *community* is a collection of things.
2. A *habitat* is a place where things live and grow.
3. *Ecologists* are people who study science.
4. *Air* is the item all things breathe.
5. *Water* is another thing all things need to live.

See Lesson 10.1, pages 401–406.

Expository Writing
Using Graphs in Exposition

Expository writers often use graphs to present information that may be too difficult or boring to present in words. Notice how the graph below shows that the population of Phoenix more than doubled from 1960 to 1990.

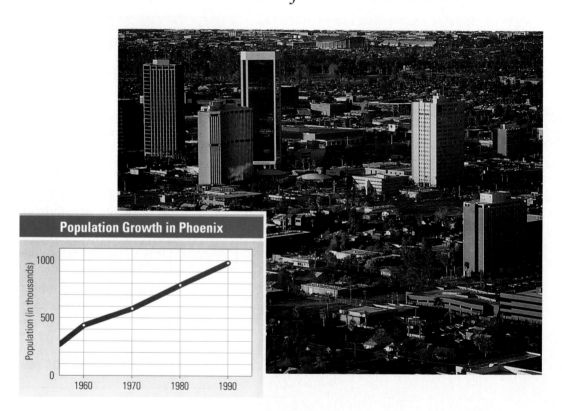

Population Growth in Phoenix

Use Graphs for Clarification

Writing filled with statistics can be deadly, with numbers cluttering up the sentences, making them hard to read and understand. Study the two examples on the next page carefully. Which model does a better job of presenting the information about the 10 largest cities in the United States—the one with the graph or the one without?

*T*he census figures show that New York is still the nation's largest city, with 7.3 million people, even though the city's population shrank by almost a half million between 1960 and 1990. Los Angeles became the second largest city, growing by one million people to 3.5 million, and Chicago dropped to third. Houston edged past Philadelphia—now in the fifth position—to become the fourth largest city, and San Diego jumped to sixth place, ahead of Detroit, Dallas, Phoenix, and San Antonio. Phoenix, number 29 on the list in 1960, rose to ninth.

Burying statistics in a paragraph makes the data hard to find and hard to follow.

Model: Text and Graph

*T*he latest census figures reveal a reshuffling of the order of the nation's largest cities. As the graph below shows, New York remains by far the nation's most populous city, and Los Angeles has moved past Chicago into second place. Other cities to make the top ten were Houston, Phoenix, and San Diego. Baltimore, which was sixth in 1960, failed to make the top ten this time around.

Presenting the statistics in a graph enables the reader to take in the information at a glance.

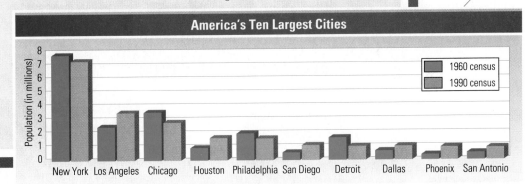

America's Ten Largest Cities

Population (in millions) — New York, Los Angeles, Chicago, Houston, Philadelphia, San Diego, Detroit, Dallas, Phoenix, San Antonio; 1960 census, 1990 census

The bar graph helps readers visualize the information. It allows readers to see which cities are larger and also how much larger.

Journal Writing

List some kinds of data that can be graphed, such as height, weight, test scores, and so on. What is the advantage to presenting this kind of information in a graph?

Choose the Right Graph

Presenting Tip

Include a graph, diagram, map, or other graphic with your final draft to enhance a reader's understanding of your exposition.

You can choose specific types of graphs to clarify different relationships among statistics. Examine the models below. Then use the guidelines below the models to determine when and how to include graphs in your expository writing.

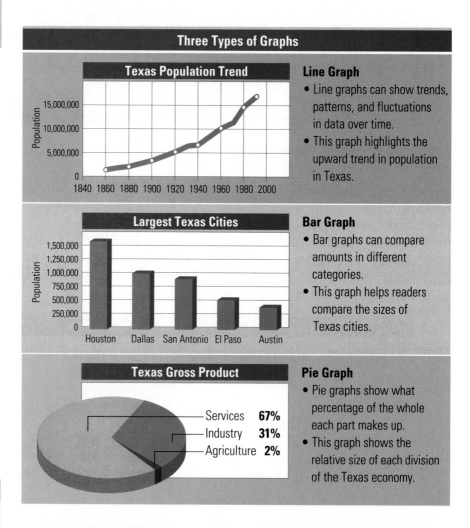

Three Types of Graphs

Texas Population Trend

Line Graph
- Line graphs can show trends, patterns, and fluctuations in data over time.
- This graph highlights the upward trend in population in Texas.

Largest Texas Cities

Bar Graph
- Bar graphs can compare amounts in different categories.
- This graph helps readers compare the sizes of Texas cities.

Texas Gross Product

Services **67%**
Industry **31%**
Agriculture **2%**

Pie Graph
- Pie graphs show what percentage of the whole each part makes up.
- This graph shows the relative size of each division of the Texas economy.

Revising Tip

Make sure that readers recognize how the graph relates to the text. If necessary, add a specific reference or caption to make the connection clear.

Guidelines for Making Graphs

1. Examine your data to determine whether or not a graph will help. Can you present the data more clearly in a graph than in sentences alone?
2. Decide whether you want to emphasize trends, comparisons, or parts of a whole. Choose the type of graph that meets your needs.
3. Add titles and labels that explain the information you are presenting.

Write to Compare Information

Write a paragraph in which you compare and contrast the average high and low temperatures in Flagstaff and Phoenix and their implications for travelers. Use the graph for information.

- Include facts from the graph.
- Organize your information in a meaningful manner.

PURPOSE To compare and contrast high and low temperatures using a graph to present information
AUDIENCE Travelers
LENGTH 1 paragraph

COMPUTER OPTION

Any article has a better chance for publication if it has been carefully proofread. Your electronic spell-checker can help you, but you have to be careful with certain kinds of words. For example, if you've used the wrong homonym, such as *here* when you meant *hear*, your spell-checker will not catch the error. Be sure to check manually the proper nouns not in the spell-checker. Then, if the program permits, add these nouns to your spell-checker.

Temperature Averages (High/Low)

Grammar Link

Capitalize names and titles in a graphic correctly.

Capitalize all proper nouns in a graphic, including the beginning and key words in its title.

Rewrite the following sentences, adding capital letters as necessary.

1. The time line shows the establishment of the massachusetts bay colony, virginia, maryland, and other english colonies.
2. The title of the diagram is how a bill becomes a law.
3. The map shows bull run, gettysburg, vicksburg, and other battle sites of the civil war.
4. The line graph compares the population growth rate of hispanics, african americans, asians, and other ethnic groups.

See Lesson 20.2, pages 677–683 and Lesson 20.3, pages 684–685.

Expository Writing
Writing a News Article

The primary purpose of a news story is to inform; thus, it presents its most important information first. Note the organization of the following article.

The first paragraph— the lead—captures attention and summarizes the main points of the story.

In what order are paragraphs arranged in this article?

2 Condors to Fly Free Late in '91

Release plans follow unexpected success of captive breeding

By Gina Lubrano
Staff Writer

LOS ANGELES — Two California condors will be reintroduced into the wilds of Ventura County late this year in a gamble that the once nearly extinct birds can live free, officials said yesterday.

"The time is now for the condors' return," said Marvin Plenert, Pacific regional director of the U.S. Fish and Wildlife Service.

"We have the birds. We have the site. We have the expertise, and we have the dedication."

Chocuyens, hatched at the San Diego Wild Animal Park on May 29, and Hoi-Ne-Wut, hatched at the Los Angeles Zoo three weeks earlier, are the million-dollar babies selected for release.

"Frankly, we will be taking a gamble," Plenert said. "The chance of losing a young condor faced with the uncertainties of life in the wild is extremely high."

Marc Weitzel, manager of the Hopper Mountain National Wildlife Refuge in Ventura County, tells where two endangered California condors will be released into the wild.

Get the Facts

Most of the details in a news story are facts—statements, events, and observations that can be proved or disproved. The readers of news articles—a broad, general-interest audience—want to know what happened, not what the writer's opinions are. The goal of a news article is to answer six basic questions, the five *W*s and an *H*.

5 *W*s and *H*	
Who?	Who did it? Who caused the action? Who else is affected?
What?	What happened? What was the action? What were the reactions?
When?	When did it take place? When will related actions occur?
Where?	Where did it happen? What was the scene like?
Why?	Why did it happen? Why is it significant?
How?	How did it happen? How does it work? How will it affect people?

Start with a Lead

An effective lead, or opening paragraph, attracts attention and provides a capsule summary of the article—all in the space of a sentence or two. The lead presents the essential facts, answering some or all of the six basic questions. Notice which questions are answered in this lead.

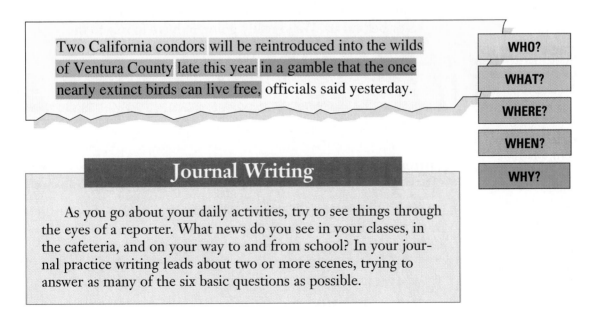

Two California condors will be reintroduced into the wilds of Ventura County late this year in a gamble that the once nearly extinct birds can live free, officials said yesterday.

WHO?
WHAT?
WHERE?
WHEN?
WHY?

Journal Writing

As you go about your daily activities, try to see things through the eyes of a reporter. What news do you see in your classes, in the cafeteria, and on your way to and from school? In your journal practice writing leads about two or more scenes, trying to answer as many of the six basic questions as possible.

Present the Details

The events in a story usually build up to a climax or turning point, often the most important event in the story. Reporters turn this pattern upside down. They start with a lead that sums up the most important event and relate other events in decreasing order of importance. This organization makes it easier for editors to make last-minute cuts in the story. Read Michael Han's story to see how it follows this pattern. Then review guidelines for writing a news article.

How does Michael's lead draw readers into the story? Which of the five Ws does he answer in the lead?

After presenting the most important part of the story at the beginning, Michael adds less important material.

Grammar
Prewriting Tip

As you gather information for a news article, listen for direct quotations, which will add authority and interest to your writing. Set off direct quotes with quotation marks. For information on using quotation marks, see Lesson 21.9, pages 717–719.

Student Model

*T*he Cookeville Cavaliers head into their game at Warren County tonight with a new football coach and a new enthusiasm.

"I'm looking forward to the season," said senior Jerald Bryant. "I think it's going to be a great one."

Jake Libbey begins his second stint as the head football coach of the Cavaliers with what could best be described as a "rebuilding" year. The team has only 32 players, 17 of them seniors.

The season began last Friday here in Cookeville with a win against Hillsboro. The Cavaliers are staring at a demanding schedule with five away games, including Oakland and McGavock. The Homecoming game will be against Riverdale on October 5.

"We are just going to have to take this schedule one game at a time," said Coach Libbey. "We can't look before us or behind us. We're really going to have to rise to the occasion with courage and desire."

Michael Han, Cookeville High School, Cookeville, Tennessee

Guidelines for Writing a News Article

1. Gather information that will add authority and interest to your writing.
2. Write a strong lead. Grab the reader's attention and summarize your main points.
3. Present information in order of importance. Start with the most important points.
4. Be fair. Cover all sides of the story, and keep your own opinions out of your article.
5. Make sure your facts are accurate and that proper names are spelled correctly.

Write a News Article

Imagine you were a reporter who was present on the historic day when the Berlin Wall was opened. Here are the facts:

- Wall is opened November 9, 1989.
- A massive, all-night celebration is held on the wall itself.
- People travel freely between East and West Berlin for the first time since 1961.
- At exactly midnight, people begin crossing.
- The wall is twenty-six miles long.
- People celebrate its opening by tooting trumpets and dancing on the wall.
- Tens of thousands of East and West Berliners swarm across the wall.
- Many people bring hammers and chisels and start tearing down the wall for souvenirs.
- One elderly East Berliner who crosses over the wall is overheard saying, "I can't believe I'm here. This is what we have dreamed of all these years."

Write a news article using these facts.

- Write a strong lead.
- Present details in decreasing order of importance.
- Avoid offering personal opinions.

PURPOSE To write a news story about a major historical event

AUDIENCE Readers of your local newspaper, all ages

LENGTH 2–3 paragraphs

COMPUTER OPTION

The Search and Replace feature of your word-processing program can help you prepare clean copy for your article. Suppose that in revising, you discover a misspelled word—perhaps a proper noun such as *Berlin*. Since you referred to that city again and again, you can save time by instructing your PC to find and correct the name each time it appears.

Grammar Link

Punctuate direct quotations correctly.

Note how the writer punctuated this direct quote in her news article about condors:

*"Frankly, we will be taking a gamble,"
Plenert said. "The chance of losing a young
condor . . . is extremely high."*

Rewrite the following sentences, adding or correcting punctuation as necessary.

1. For years, the Japanese assumed that their cities were earthquake resistant, a news reporter commented.
2. "Twenty seconds of terror shattered that belief" said one reporter, "when a 7.2 earthquake hit Kobe, Japan, in 1995"
3. A government official admitted, I never felt so powerless in my life
4. A second official confessed, "The government's initial response was pure panic and confusion".
5. "Revamping disaster-relief plans and revising building codes are the only way to avoid future disasters" seismologists warn.

See Lesson 21.9, pages 717–719.

Expository Writing
Taking an Essay Test

Do you react like the character in the cartoon when you have to take an essay test? In this lesson you will learn some ways to examine test questions and compose illuminating answers.

Look at the sample test below. How would you go about answering the following questions?

> Answer all the questions below. You will have one hour to complete this test.
> 1. Define the term <u>biome</u>. (20 points)
> 2. Discuss the characteristics of desert biomes. (20 points)
> 3. Compare the qualities of tropical savannas to those of temperate grasslands. (20 points)
> 4. Analyze the factors that affect the distribution of biomes. (40 points)

Develop a Plan of Attack

When you sit down to take a test like the one on the previous page, don't jump right in and start writing answers. Instead, take a moment to look over the individual questions and the test as a whole. That way you can make plans that will help you answer all the questions in the time available. Keep the following steps in mind.

Read the directions. Are you expected to answer *all* the questions, or do you have a choice? How much time do you have to complete the test?

Read each question. Which ones will be easier or will take less time to answer? Are you unprepared to answer any of the questions?

Note the point value for each question. Are some questions worth more than others? Does the test include any extra credit questions?

To avoid the problem of time being up while you are still writing answers, estimate how much time you will need for each question. Consider both how much you know about the subject and how many points the question is worth. The greater the point value, the more time you should plan to devote to the question, especially if it's one about which you know a great deal. The graphic below shows one way to divide your time among four unequally weighted questions. How might your time allotment vary if you knew little about question 2?

Time allotted for test:
1 hour

Question Value:
#1: **20 points**
#2: **20 points**
#3: **20 points**
#4: **40 points**

9:00 A.M.	9:12 A.M.	9:24 A.M.	9:36 A.M.	10:00 A.M.
Start 1	Start 2	Start 3	Start 4	Finish

Journal Writing

In your journal, reflect on your test-taking experiences. Write about some ways that previewing tests and budgeting your time could help you improve your performance.

Understand the Questions

Make sure you understand each question before you start to respond. Focus on key words that tell exactly what you have to do. Below are some questions that include common key words and some strategies for answering them.

Key Words in Essay Questions		
Question	**Key Word**	**Strategy for Answering**
Define the term *biome*.	**Define**	Tell what the term means, and explain what distinguishes it from other similar terms.
Discuss the characteristics of desert biomes.	**Discuss**	Look at your subject from several viewpoints, and provide facts and other details to explain its characteristics or qualities.
Compare the qualities of tropical savannas with those of temperate grasslands.	**Compare**	Tell how two or more subjects are alike and how they are different. Support your ideas with details and examples.
Analyze the factors that affect the distribution of biomes.	**Analyze**	Identify the important parts of your subject, examine each part, and explain how each part relates to the others.
Describe the vegetation found in tropical rain forests.	**Describe**	Create and organize concrete sensory images that vividly illustrate the qualities of your subject.
Summarize the problems facing tropical rain forests today.	**Summarize**	Present the main points or concepts of your subject, and give a brief explanation for each.

Write a Thesis Statement

An effective thesis statement, a sentence that communicates the main idea you intend to develop in an answer, can point you in the right direction as you begin writing. Such a statement also tells the reader how you will respond to the key word in the question and helps you determine what types of details you must include to develop your essay. Often you can rephrase the question as a statement and indicate how you will respond to it, as in the example below.

> 2. Discuss the characteristics of desert
>   biomes. (20 points)
>   *Desert biomes are characterized by a variety of harsh conditions, chief of which is a lack of water.*

Create a Plan

Since you probably will not have much time to revise your answer, it pays to plan what you intend to say before you start writing. Your plan should be simple, logically organized, and easy to follow. Create an outline, a cluster diagram, or a comparison-contrast chart to identify and organize your main points. Notice how brief your organizing plan can be.

Drafting Tip

As you write, keep looking back at your thesis statement to remind yourself of your focus.

> 2. Discuss the characteristics of desert
>   biomes. (20 points)
>   A. *Amount of precipitation*
>   B. *Range of temperatures*
>   C. *Types of plants*
>   D. *Types of animals*

Journal Writing

Look at the questions in the chart on page 248. In your journal, write thesis statements for several by rewording the questions and anticipating how you might respond to them.

Draft Your Answer

Because your time is limited, you need to use a simple, straightforward format for writing your answer. Your thesis statement, which introduces your main idea, can serve as your first sentence. Then you can let your outline or graphic aid guide you as you compose your answer, adding solid facts and other supporting details that elaborate on your thesis. Remember to use appropriate transition words and phrases to connect ideas. Finally, end your answer with a brief conclusion that restates your main idea.

The answer begins with the thesis statement. Each paragraph addresses a topic that supports the thesis. The conclusion restates the main point.

What specific details are used to support generalizations?

2. Discuss the characteristics of desert biomes. (20 points)

Desert biomes are characterized by harsh conditions, including a lack of water. Deserts get little rain, so plants are few and widely scattered. The soil is often mainly sand. The lack of ground cover affects temperatures. The land heats up rapidly during the day and cools off rapidly at night, so temperature ranges are extreme.

Plants and animals have adapted to the desert in various ways. Some plants, such as the saguaro cactus, store water in their tissues during rains and use it later in dry periods. Others, such as the desert dandelion, grow only when there is enough moisture. Many desert animals are nocturnal, sleeping in the shade during the day.

In the harsh conditions of desert biomes, only hardy plants and animals survive.

There's no getting away from essay tests; you will face them throughout your school years. By following the steps summarized below, you can probably improve your performance.

Editing Tip

Even though time is limited, be sure to proofread your work. Pay special attention to the spelling and usage of those key terms and concepts on which you are being tested.

Guidelines for Taking an Essay Test

1. Preview the test by reading all directions and questions.
2. Budget your time, using the point value of each question as a guide.
3. Prepare a thesis statement and brief outline or graphic aid before you begin drafting your essay.
4. Start your essay with your thesis statement, follow your outline, and support each point with specific facts and details. Conclude by restating your thesis.

5.9 Writing Activities

Write an Essay Answer

Read the following excerpt from *Sand County Almanac*, and take the essay test that follows it. Allow yourself thirty minutes. Read the whole test before you begin.

- Budget your time.
- Study the key words in each question.
- Write thesis statements.
- Plan out each answer.

When I was a boy, there was an old German merchant who lived in a little cottage in our town. On Sundays he used to go out and knock chips off the limestone ledges along the Mississippi, and he had a great tonnage of these chips, all labeled and catalogued. The chips contained little fossil stems of some defunct water creatures called crinoids. The townspeople regarded this gentle old fellow as just a little bit abnormal, but harmless. One day the newspaper reported the arrival of certain titled strangers. It was whispered that these visitors were great scientists. Some of them were from foreign lands, and some among the world's leading paleontologists. They came to visit the harmless old man and to hear his pronouncements on crinoids, and they accepted these pronouncements as law. When the old German died, the town awoke to the fact that he was a world authority on his subject, a creator of knowledge, a maker of scientific history. He was a great man—a man beside whom the local captains of industry were mere bushwhackers. His collection went to a national museum, and his name is known in all the nations of the earth.

Aldo Leopold, *Sand County Almanac*

Essay Test

- Compare and contrast what the German merchant was like with what people in the town thought he was like. (60 points)
- Summarize Leopold's main point in telling this story. (40 points)

PURPOSE To take an essay test on literature
AUDIENCE Your English teacher
LENGTH 3–6 paragraphs

Cross-Curricular: Science

Brainstorm with a classmate for essay questions on a science topic you are studying. Write individual answers; then evaluate each other's for completeness.

Grammar Link

Use commas in compound sentences to avoid run-ons.

Commas and coordinating conjunctions are needed between the clauses in a compound sentence.

Rewrite the following compound sentences, adding commas as necessary.

1. Energy cannot be created or destroyed yet it can change form.
2. Energy is needed to maintain all aspects of life for you use it even when you sleep.
3. All living things get their energy from the sun but plants get it directly.
4. Energy conversions always involve a loss nor is any conversion 100-percent efficient.

See Lesson 21.6, page 706.

Writing About Literature
Comparing and Contrasting Literature

There are many approaches you can take in comparing and contrasting works of literature. For example, you might compare this modern fable with a traditional fable.

Literature Model

*T*here was once a town in the heart of America where all life seemed to live in harmony with its surroundings. The town lay in the midst of a checkerboard of prosperous farms, with fields of grain and hillsides of orchards where, in spring, white clouds of bloom drifted above the green fields. In autumn, oak and maple and birch set up a blaze of color that flamed and flickered across a backdrop of pines. Then foxes barked in the hills and deer silently crossed the fields, half hidden in the mists of the fall mornings.

Along the roads, laurel, viburnum and alder, great ferns and wildflowers delighted the traveler's eye through much of the year. Even in winter the roadsides were places of beauty, where countless birds came to feed on the berries and on the seed heads of the dried weeds rising above the snow. The countryside was, in fact, famous for the abundance and variety of its bird life, and when the flood of migrants was pouring through in spring and fall, people traveled from great distances to observe them. Others came to fish the streams, which flowed clear and cold out of the hills and contained shady pools where trout lay. So it had been from the days many years ago when the first settlers raised their houses, sank their wells, and built their barns.

Then a strange blight crept over the area and everything began to change. Some evil spell had settled on the community: mysterious maladies swept the flocks of chickens; the cattle and sheep sickened and died. ➡

The first sentence introduces a style and tone similar to those of traditional fables.

Everywhere was a shadow of death. The farmers spoke of much illness among their families. In the town the doctors had become more and more puzzled by new kinds of sickness appearing among their patients. There had been several sudden and unexplained deaths, not only among adults but even among children, who would be stricken suddenly while at play and die within a few hours.

There was a strange stillness. The birds, for example—where had they gone? Many people spoke of them, puzzled and disturbed. The feeding stations in the backyards were deserted. The few birds seen anywhere were moribund; they trembled violently and could not fly. It was a spring without voices. On the mornings that had once throbbed with the dawn chorus of robins, catbirds, doves, jays, wrens, and scores of other bird voices there was now no sound; only silence lay over the fields and woods and marsh. . . .

No witchcraft, no enemy action had silenced the rebirth of new life in this stricken world. The people had done it themselves.

Rachel Carson, *Silent Spring*

Most traditional fables end with a moral; Carson's fable ends with an accusation. How does her accusation serve as a kind of moral?

Evaluate Literary Elements

Depending on what your precise topic is, your literary analysis will examine some or all of the elements listed below.

Analyzing Basic Elements of Literature	
Element	**Question to ask**
Theme, or central focus	Does the work address a univeral problem or teach a moral?
Style	Is the language formal or informal, figurative or objective?
Tone	Is it serious? Sad? Humorous?
Setting	What is the role of time and place?
Plot	What is the main conflict?
Characters	How do we know what the characters are like?

Prewriting Tip

It is often helpful to write down your initial impressions about a piece of literature as you read.

Journal Writing

Reread a short literary piece you've read recently. In your journal, note what you see now that you hadn't seen before.

When comparing
literary pieces, use
quotation marks to set
off the titles of short
works, such as short
stories and poems.
Italicize, or underline,
the titles of longer
works, such as novels.
See Lessons 21.9,
page 719, and 21.10,
page 720.

Make Your Point

After you've identified the elements on which you will focus, examine similarities and differences about each element. Look also for direct quotations you can use to help you make your points. Use these guidelines to help you.

Guidelines for Writing a Literary Comparison and Contrast

1. Write an introductory paragraph stating your main idea.
2. Use information from your reading to shape your writing.
3. Include quotations, when appropriate, to support your points.
4. Write an effective conclusion, summing up your main idea in a sentence or two.

The following model compares and contrasts Rachel Carson's fable with the traditional form of the fable. Note how it uses the guidelines.

Model

The form of Carson's fable is compared to that of traditional fables.

How does this quotation contribute to the overall passage?

What does the writer contrast at the end? How does the writer achieve this effect?

*F*or thousands of years, people have told fables to teach a lesson or to pass on wisdom. Fables were part of the oral tradition of many early cultures, and the well-known Aesop's fables date to the sixth century B.C. Yet, the form of the fable still has value today, as Rachel Carson demonstrates in "A Fable for Tomorrow."

Carson uses a simple, direct style common to fables. In fact, her style and tone are seemingly directed at children. "There was once a town in the heart of America where all life seemed to live in harmony with its surroundings," her fable begins, borrowing some familiar words from many age-old fables. Behind the simple style, however, is a serious message intended for everyone.

In contrast to traditional fables, Carson's story ends with an accusation instead of a moral. She warns of the environmental dangers facing society, and she teaches that people must take responsibility for saving their environment.

The themes of traditional fables often deal with simple truths about everyday life. In contrast, Carson's theme is a more weighty warning about environmental destruction. Nevertheless, Carson proves that a simple literary form that has been passed down through the ages can still be used today to draw attention to important truths.

5.10 Writing Activities

Write a Comparison-Contrast Essay

The two poems on this page were both written by William Carlos Williams. Write a comparison-contrast essay about the two poems.

- Identify key elements in each poem.
- Explore similarities and differences for each element.
- Identify quotations to support your points.

This Is Just to Say

I have eaten
the plums
that were in
the icebox

and which
you were probably
saving for breakfast

Forgive me
they were delicious
so sweet
and so cold

The Red Wheelbarrow

so much depends
upon

a red wheel
barrow

glazed with rain
water

beside the white
chickens

William Carlos Williams

PURPOSE To compare and contrast works of a poet
AUDIENCE Your English teacher and classmates
LENGTH 2 paragraphs

COMPUTER OPTION

To write effective literary criticism, you must find the right words to express your meaning. If your word-processing program has an electronic thesaurus, be sure to use it, especially in revising.

Grammar Link

Make clear and complete comparisons.

In the model, note how the student clearly states one difference between Rachel Carson's fable and more traditional fables:

In contrast to traditional fables, Carson's story ends with an accusation instead of a moral.

Rewrite the sentences below to correct the unclear comparison in each.

1. Rachel Carson, a marine biologist, wrote more books on the environment than any scientist.
2. She has had more influence on environmental beliefs than anyone.
3. Carson portrayed people's role in silencing the rebirth of new life as greater than witchcraft or enemy action.
4. Traditional fables deal with simpler truths than Carson.
5. Still, in their own way yesterday's fables are as valuable as today.

See Lesson 18.4, page 632.

WRITING PROCESS IN ACTION

EXPOSITORY WRITING

In preceding lessons you learned about the different kinds of expository writing, the purpose of each, and ways to make exposition informative and engaging. You've had a chance to write comparison-contrasts, definitions, and news articles. Now you are invited to write a practical or whimsical explanation of a process that is familiar and enjoyable for you.

• Assignment •

Context	You are a member of a team of writers selected to write a book entitled _How to Do Just About Anything._ You have been asked to write an entry explaining a process with which you are familiar and that you enjoy. The subject you select can be practical or whimsical, and your writing style should be light and engaging.
Purpose	To write a practical or whimsical explanation of a familiar process
Audience	Teenagers and adults who read general-interest books
Length	1–2 pages

The guidelines on the following pages can help you plan and write your book entry. Read through the guidelines, and then refer back to them as you complete this assignment. However, don't feel tied down by them. Remember, you're in charge of your own writing process.

Prewriting

A good way to find a topic is to think about your talents and your interests. Let your mind wander for a few minutes. Additional ways to probe your thoughts are listed on the notepad.

Once you've found a topic, think about what you want to accomplish with this piece. You might want to clear up misconceptions about something, persuade readers to look at your process in a new light, or just entertain your readers. Try freewriting to explore how you really feel about your topic; develop a main idea statement.

Next, think about your audience. The fact that you will be writing for a general readership means you can't assume readers will have any prior knowledge of your process. It also means they probably won't have enough interest to wade through piles of dry facts.

Prewriting Options
- Freewrite about your areas of expertise. Explore jobs, hobbies, sports, and school subjects.
- List "how to" topics.
- Hold a brainstorming session with your classmates.

Drafting

The challenge in explaining a process is to make your writing more than just a monotonous list of steps. The key is finding a way to make your writing flow. Start by figuring out how to break down your subject. What are the major terms and concepts you need to explain? What are the processes related to these concepts?

Next, think about how you can weave the concepts and processes into an engaging expository essay. Don't let yourself get bogged down in technicalities. Keep your audience in mind, and consider what details will grab their attention and maintain their interest. Note how naturalist writer Sue Hubbell mixes factual data with first-person observations in the model below.

Prewriting Tip

To gain better understanding of your audience, ask yourself the questions listed in Lesson 5.2, page 219.

Drafting Tip

For tips on writing about a process, see Lesson 5.3, pages 222–224.

Literature Model

*I*n early springtime, the bees' need for pollen may be greater than what is available, and then they will compulsively gather up almost any fine granular material— sawdust, bits of plastic packing materials, ashes— whether it is useful to them or not. I often see them at the bird feeder, picking through the wild bird feed. At that time of year, I often get a telephone call from a dairy farmer who lives near one of my beeyards. ➡

> "Hey, Sue," he says. "How about coming over and feeding your bees? They're in the calf feed again."
>
> Sue Hubbell, *A Book of Bees . . . and How to Keep Them*

Revising Tip

For additional tips on revising expository writing, see Lesson 5.3, page 224.

Revising

To begin revising, read over your draft to make sure that what you have written fits your purpose and your audience. Then have a **writing conference.** Read your draft to a partner or small group. Use your audience's reactions to help you evaluate your work so far. The questions in the Revising Checklist can help you and your listeners.

An easy way to check your explanation for completeness is to visualize yourself actually doing the process. Walk through each step of the process mentally, checking your work as you go. Sharing your draft with a peer reader is another way to identify holes in your explanation. Ask for feedback about steps that are unclear, terms that are unfamiliar, background information that would be helpful.

Next, look closely at how your explanation flows. Make sure you use strong topic sentences to tell readers where you are headed with each paragraph. Within paragraphs, use transitions to move readers along the steps of the process.

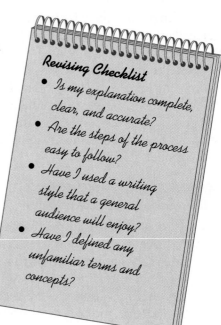

Revising Checklist
- Is my explanation complete, clear, and accurate?
- Are the steps of the process easy to follow?
- Have I used a writing style that a general audience will enjoy?
- Have I defined any unfamiliar terms and concepts?

Editing

Once you have revised your article for basic content and organization, **proofread** it carefully for errors in grammar, usage, mechanics, and spelling. Use the questions at the right as a guide.

In addition to proofreading, use the Self-Evaluation list below to make sure your explanation does all the things you want it to do. When you're satisfied, make a clean copy of your explanation and proofread it one more time.

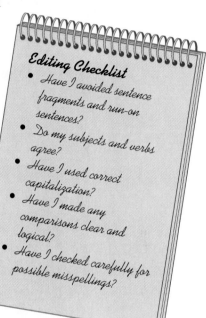

Editing Checklist
- Have I avoided sentence fragments and run-on sentences?
- Do my subjects and verbs agree?
- Have I used correct capitalization?
- Have I made any comparisons clear and logical?
- Have I checked carefully for possible misspellings?

Self-Evaluation

Make sure your exposition—

- focuses on explaining a process
- presents steps in a clear, easy-to-follow order
- uses terms and concepts related to the process in an appropriate way
- uses a light, engaging style of writing
- follows correct grammar, usage, mechanics, and spelling

Presenting

With your classmates, compile a class "how to" book. Create a cover, table of contents, and an introduction for the volume. Have interested classmates either draw or find illustrations to include in the book.

For proofreading symbols, see page 88.

Journal Writing

Reflect on your writing process experience. Answer these questions in your journal: What do you like best about your process explanation? What was the hardest part of writing it? What did you learn in your writing conference? What new things have you learned as a writer?

Expository Writing
Literature Model

Sue Hubbell

FROM

A Book of Bees

Sue Hubbell, a self-taught naturalist, spends much of the year on her Missouri farm, taking care of her 300 beehives and approximately 12 million bees. As you read the selection below from A Book of Bees . . . and How to Keep Them, *note how Hubbell reaches out to her readers as she guides them through the beekeeper's year. Then try the activities in Linking Writing and Literature on page 267.*

Spring for bees, and so for beekeepers as well, has nothing to do with the calendar. In protected hollows even in the Missouri winter, bees can find a bit of springtime in flowers with enough pollen to feed the first young bees growing from the eggs the queen has begun to lay.

Various species of maples, all members of the genus *Acer,* with their delicate blossoms ranging from yellow-green to red, are one of the earliest to bloom. Maples are tall trees, and their blossoms are borne high in the crowns, where they often are not seen by humans. The bees, of course, have no trouble in finding them. The American hazel, *Corylus americana,* is a smaller tree—hardly more than a shrub—that is another early source of pollen, and easier for us to see. It grows wild throughout most of temperate North America and produces the nuts we call filberts. In late winter and early spring when most other plants are at rest, hazel generously produces pollen on long, dangling catkins.[1] In the winter, I like to stop on my walk down to the mailbox and draw one of the yellowish brown catkins between my thumb and forefinger and watch the powdery golden pollen collect in my palm. On days warm enough, bees, having declared it springtime, will be on the catkins collecting pollen.

Skunk cabbage, *Symplocarpus foetidus,* with its coarsely sheathed flower and supposedly vile odor, makes spring for bees in February in northern parts of the country. If a walker in the wet woods or swamps takes the time to look inside the skunk-cabbage spathe[2] on a mild day, he will usually find a honeybee there, packing pollen into the carrying baskets on her back legs.

Mature adult bees are carbohydrate feeders. They live on nectar and honey, which are almost exclusively carbohydrate in composition except for a few traces of minerals, vitamins and other materials. But young and developing bees need protein to grow muscles, glands and other tissues, and it is pollen—variously rich in protein, depending on its source—that provides it.

It takes about three weeks for a bee to grow from egg to adult. Three days after the queen bee has laid an egg, it hatches out into a nearly white larva that, throughout its instars, or developmental stages, has a ferocious need for food high in protein. Bee larvae don't move around looking for food as some insects do in their early stages; they are not wriggly caterpillars as are those of moths or butterflies. They merely lie passively in their cells, growing, changing. They are small animals, with disproportionately large stomachs waiting to be filled by nurse bees—young adults just emerged from pupation.[3] These nurse bees feed on the gathered pollen and

1 **catkins** (kat´ kinz) drooping, scaly spikes that hang down from trees such as poplars and birches
2 **spathe** (spāth) a leaflike part of a plant that encloses a fleshy spike of tiny flower
3 **pupation** (pyoo pā´ shən) the developmental stage between larva and adult insect

Vincent van Gogh, *View of Arles*, 1889

produce secretions from their hypopharyngeal[4] glands (glands under the pharynx), which they will use as food for the developing larvae.

In recent years, vendors of nostrums[5] to the health-food industry have been delighted by Ronald Reagan's public consumption of pollen, and pollen has become a hot item in health-food stores. Claims are made that humans who eat pollen are stronger, sexier, livelier and more cheerful, but there is no good medical evidence to back up these claims so far. And as a matter of fact, some people have experienced severe allergic reactions after eating it. Pollen from a hay-fever sufferer's local area is also said to cure him of his allergy. I have an open mind. I am an empiricist.[6] I have hay fever. And, after all, bee venom[7] does help my arthritis. So one summer, when my eyes were running and I was sneezing exquisitely from ragweed, I gathered and ate pollen from my bees. Pollen has a bitter taste. It is no fun to eat, but in the interests of testing the efficacy[8] of the stuff I dutifully continued to eat it—and to sneeze. It is possible pollen may cure someone else's hay fever, but it doesn't cure mine.

4 **hypopharyngeal** (hī´ pō fə rin´ jē ə l) [for pronunciation only; see above for definition]

5 **nostrums** (näs´ trəmz) medicines, sometimes sold with exaggerated claims of what they can do

6 **empiricist** (em pir´ ə sist) one willing to learn through experiment and observation

7 **venom** (ven´ əm) a secreted poison

8 **efficacy** (ef´ i kə sē) effectiveness

I am always too eager to start working with the bees in the spring. I miss them in the winter and want to be back with them again. But I sternly remind myself I can do more harm than good if I open their hives before the daffodils bloom, so when the crocuses flower around my cabin I have to content myself with crouching down beside those purple, white and yellow blossoms to watch the field bees gathering pollen.

Each worker bee is covered with stiff hairs. These catch the granules when the bee brushes against the flower's pollen-bearing anthers.[9] She is soon covered and stops to use her two front pairs of legs to comb the sticky pollen from her body and pack it into the baskets on her rear pair of legs. When her legs are heavy with their wads of pollen she returns to her hive to unload. House bees arrange the pollen granules in the honeycomb cells around the developing bee larvae, where it is conveniently available to the nurse bees.

In the springtime, a typical frame of brood—as beekeepers call developing bees—contains a large central semicircle of cells containing eggs and larvae in various stages. The eggs and larvae are there to see, but the oldest brood, stomachs full, have spun themselves cocoons in which to pupate, and are hidden from human eyes, sealed in their cells by a tough, velvety brown covering, from beneath which they will emerge as adults. The entire semicircle of brood is bordered by a ring of pollen-filled cells, which in turn is surrounded by honey, or, as the season progresses, nectar.

In this part of the country most of the early pollen collected is yellow and makes a bright ring around the fuzzy brown sealed brood area. But as the season advances and the days lengthen, more pollen sources are available. Serviceberry, *Amelanchier arborea*, frosts the slopes of the hills near the rivers with white blossoms. Redbud, *Cercis canadensis*, flourishes in the wood's understory, with dramatic purplish red clusters of blossom. Henbit, *Lamium amplexicaule*, which everyone except beekeepers think of as an unwelcome weed, covers the ground with a low-growing thatch of purple-blue flowers. The wild fruit trees—plum, cherry and peach—bloom extravagantly. These flowers all have different-colored pollens, and the pollen cells ringing the bees' brood are as various: scarlet, pale green, yellow and orange—as beautiful as a stained-glass window.

In early springtime, the bees' need for pollen may be greater than what is available, and then they will compulsively gather up almost any fine granular material—sawdust, bits of plastic packing material, ashes—whether it is useful to them or not. I often see them at the bird feeder, picking through the wild bird feed. At that time of year, I often get a telephone call from a dairy farmer who lives near one of my beeyards.

9 anthers (an´ thərz) pollen sacs

"Hey, Sue," he says. "How about coming over and feeding your bees? They're in the calf feed again."

He's always a little embarrassed. The first time he called me, years ago, was on a day in autumn. There were, he insisted, bees flying all around the inside of his milking shed. He didn't want to spray them with insecticide, but he was going to have to do that unless I could lure them out.

It sounded like an odd way for bees to behave, but I drove over to his place. There they were, golden-striped fuzzy insects flying around inside his barn, darting here and there. They looked like bees, but they didn't act like bees, so I captured one in my hand. The creature did not sting me as a honeybee would have done and on close scrutiny its beelike appearance disappeared. Moreover, the insect had only a single pair of wings, not two sets, as a bee has. The two wings, a single pair, puts any insect into the zoological order Diptera (which means two-winged), the order of flies. Honeybees belong to the order Hymenoptera (or membrane-winged), which includes not only all the bees but also wasps, ants and other similar insects.

I wasn't sure which flies these were in the milk barn, because I don't know much about Diptera, but I know that there were a number of fly species that mimic bees in appearance. I showed the farmer the single pair of wings and told him that this and the others in the air were flies, not bees. He was interested, and asked more questions than I could answer. When I got home, I photocopied as much information about bee-mimicking flies as I could find on my bookshelves and sent it to him. Now when he calls he always makes sure that the insect about which he is lodging a complaint is indeed a honeybee.

The first time he found bees in his calf feed he was worried that they were after the calves, and might sting and frighten them. I assured him that the bees were not the least concerned with the calves but were looking for the pollen they needed as food in the springtime. As soon as some pollen-bearing flower bloomed, I told him, the bees would disappear from the calf feed, but in the meantime I'd try giving them a pollen substitute that might satisfy them.

Beekeeping-supply companies sell a commercial pollen substitute made of a combination of protein-rich materials such as soy flour and brewers' yeast. This powder can be mixed with honey to make into patties, which can be squished down between the top bars on the frames of the upper hive bodies. Many beekeepers recommend the feeding of pollen substitute as a regular routine, and for a number of years I made up patties and fed them to all my hives. In some parts of the country where there is not a dependable source of pollen this may be a good practice, but I have concluded that it is not worth the expense or time here in the Ozarks. Bees prefer the real thing—fresh pollen—and although a day or two in these

Vincent van Gogh, *View of Arles with Irises*, 1888

hills may pass when they can't find any, something usually bursts into bloom and they scorn the substitute, leaving it to molder inside the hives. So I stopped feeding pollen substitute, and find that productivity of my hives is no poorer for doing so. Indeed, the per-hive yield of honey from my bees has grown greater in what appears to be a direct relationship to the decrease in the number of times I open the hives. The less I disrupt and fiddle with the bees, the more they can concentrate on making honey.

Now when the dairy farmer calls, more as a public-relations gesture then anything else, I go to the health-food store and buy fifty-nine cents' worth of soy flour, take it over to the hives near his place, lift off the outer cover of each hive and sprinkle some of it on the inner cover. I did that a few days ago, and today I stopped by his place to give him a jar of honey as a recompense[10] for the nuisance my bees had caused him.

I asked if the bees had stopped coming to the calf feed.

"Yep. They've left. Thank you kindly for feeding them."

"No trouble. Thank you for calling me and letting me know. I don't like the bees to be a bother to you."

Then I drove over to the hives and lifted up the telescoping covers. The soy flour stood unused on the inner covers, and I shook it off on the grass. The bees had not wanted it. Flowers have begun to bloom somewhere, and the bees, their rear legs wadded with golden pollen, are flying into the hives so heavily loaded they find it hard to stay airborne.

The farmer is happy. The calves are happy. The bees are happy.

I sit down beside the end hive and watch the bees flying in with their loads of pollen, which will assure the development of the thousands of young bees needed to gather nectar and make honey in the months to come.

The sun is shining on my back as I watch, and I can feel its warmth. The air is fragrant. There are flowers in bloom everywhere today.

And I am happy.

Ernest Lawson, *Garden Landscape*, ca. 1895

10 recompense (rek′ əm pens′) something given to make up for an inconvenience

Linking Writing and Literature

Readers Respond to the Model

How does Sue Hubbell convey in-depth information in a lively and appealing way?

Explore Sue Hubbell's exposition by answering these questions. Then read what other students liked about Hubbell's writing.

1. Hubbell mixes personal anecdotes with factual information. How does this mix affect her writing?

2. What different kinds of exposition does Hubbell use in her essay? Give an example of each.

3. How would you describe the mood of this selection? What specific words and images help to create this mood?

I liked the springlike mood the author created through her imagery. I think that even though her writing was informational and documentary-like, the author wrote in first person because she was telling her own experieinces. The part I remembered most clearly was about pollen's health benefits. Hubbell stated that some people consider pollen a healthy, positive substance. I found the detail about Ronald Reagan eating pollen amusing, and it held my attention.
Chris Fickes

I liked how Hubbell balanced the social and factual parts of her piece. She obviously has love and admiration for a largely misunderstood insect. Through her facts and stories, she was able to make anyone feel more comfortable around bees. However, if I had written the piece, I don't think that I would have included as many facts about the bees while telling the "bee stories."
Yahna Awazu

Unit 5 Review

Reflecting on the Unit

Summarize what you have learned in this unit by answering the following questions.

- What are six kinds of expository writing, and what is the basic purpose of each?

- What are some of the ways cause-and-effect writing can be organized?

- What types of graphic organizers can help you organize information for a compare-contrast essay?

- How do graphs and charts clarify explanations?

- How can you use the words in essay questions to plan your answer?

- What steps can you take to improve your performance on essay tests?

Adding to Your Portfolio

Choose a selection for your portfolio.
Look over the expository writing you have done during this unit. Select a completed piece of writing to put in your portfolio. The piece you choose should show some or all of the following:

- a specific audience and writing purpose
- a well-expressed thesis statement
- supporting details that appeal to readers' level of knowledge and interest
- logical organization and clear connections
- a combination of expository types

Reflect on your choice.
Attach a note to the piece you chose, explaining briefly why you chose it and what you learned from writing it.

Set goals.
How can you improve your writing? What skill will you focus on the next time you write?

Writing Across the Curriculum

Make a history connection.
Scan your history textbook for a historical event or occurrence that can be described as a process, such as the building of a stockade or the election of a president. Write a brief essay explaining the process. Be sure to explain any unfamiliar terms.

Persuasive Writing

Persuasive Writing in the Real World

"What Will It Do to You?"

FOCUS: Effective persuasive writing is unified by one central, main idea.

Each year, Chicago's Museum of Contemporary Art (MCA) had been asking a different advertising agency to donate an advertising campaign to boost museum attendance and membership. In 1989 the ad agency Mitchiner, Ross and Kahn took on the job.

Mitchiner, Ross and Kahn's ads for the Museum of Contemporary Art were supposed to run for only a year. Within eight months museum attendance had skyrocketed by 42 percent and membership by 16 percent. These rises represented the biggest jumps in the history of the museum. The ads were slated to continue indefinitely.

Amy Krouse Rosenthal, assistant creative director,
Steven Wohlwender, senior art director,
and Marshall Ross, creative director

Steven Wohlwender—Mitchiner, Ross and Kahn's senior art director—described how the successful ad campaign began. "When we started, we looked at other campaigns for art museums. Basically, they were just announcements that showed some of the art. We knew we didn't want to do that because modern art doesn't reproduce very well in newspaper ads. It's not a great way to see this art for the first time.

"We're firm believers in doing our homework up front. So we got a breakdown from the museum about who visits—by age, income, and so on. And then we went to the museum ourselves so we could see how to get your average Joe to come look at contemporary art."

"The first time I went to the Museum of Contemporary Art, I noticed people . . . were really involved, getting their noses right up to the art. I overheard some people saying, 'What's that?' some saying, 'That's great,' and some saying, 'That's awful!' In our ad campaign we wanted to show people that the museum will get some kind of reaction out of you. . . ."

—Steven Wohlwender

To develop the main idea of the ad campaign, Mitchiner, Ross and Kahn needed to find out about its audience—the museum's patrons.

An Ad Campaign

Prewriting	Drafting	Revising and Presenting
Creating the Main Idea	Seeing the Picture	Getting the Message Out

The idea generated in Wohlwender's sketch of a goofy face was carried through several design stages and ultimately appeared in a variety of formats, from T-shirts to café table tents.

Prewriting

CREATING THE MAIN IDEA

Wohlwender explains how the main theme for this campaign emerged. "I'd drawn this goofy little face with a strange reaction on it, based on the people I'd seen at the museum. And Marshall Ross, our creative director, simply said, 'What will it do to you?'

"That question started out being a headline for just one ad, but then Ross said, 'This should be the main theme because it works for everything.' And the rest of us saw the light."

Assistant creative director Amy Krouse Rosenthal calls "What will it do to you?" an idea with "legs." That expression means the idea can "walk into other areas," serving as well for brochures, banners, and bus posters as it does for newspaper ads. She adds, "We want the people who see these ads to get off their bottoms, go to the museum, and get zapped in the brain."

272

Drafting

SEEING THE PICTURE

The advertising team decided to use photographs of real faces instead of sketches because they believed photos would be more persuasive than drawings. As Wohlwender puts it, "Photography is real. These people look real. The photographer even picked people off the street and told them to give a reaction as if they were looking at art."

He continues, "We wanted to make the ads appeal to as broad a group as possible. The museum told us what kind of people they wanted shown in terms of the range of ages and ethnic groups they were targeting. The photographer went out and got ten people in each category. You don't want people who look like models, of course. These people look real. We wanted people looking at any one of these ads to be able to say, 'This museum is for me.'"

Revising/Presenting

GETTING THE MESSAGE OUT

For the MCA ad campaign, it was crucial to use humor and informal language.

The booklet sent to prospective members is filled with funny, irreverent questions that all relate to the main idea of the campaign, "What will it do to you?" Wohlwender says, "Usually people will read just one line and throw away a piece of junk mail. We tried to write it so people would keep turning the pages."

Every word used in an ad must contribute to persuading the audience. For example, Krouse Rosenthal says the word *you* was crucial to this campaign because "it makes you think about yourself." In planning the other words for the MCA campaign, the ad team at Mitchiner, Ross and Kahn made a conscious decision to keep the language informal. Krouse Rosenthal explains that if the ads had used lofty language, some readers might have felt excluded from the museum experience.

Responding to the Case Study

1. Discussion

Discuss these questions about Mitchiner, Ross and Kahn's ad campaign.

- What was the purpose of the MCA ad campaign?
- What was the campaign's unifying idea?
- How did the advertising team come up with this idea?
- Why did the team decide to use informal language throughout the campaign?
- In addition to informal language, what other elements made the ad campaign so successful?

2. Persuasive Writing

Write about an ad.

Advertisements persuade particular groups of people to buy products and services and engage in—or avoid—certain activities. Ads achieve their results by means of words and pictures. Choose an ad that you find especially persuasive *or* especially ineffective, or use the ad on this page. Argue for or against the ad's effectiveness. Explain what group (age, gender, income) the ad seems to target and how its words and pictures do or do not work together to persuade this group.

Grammar Link

Make pronouns agree with antecedents.

A pronoun must agree with its antecedent in gender, number, and person.

*The advertising **team** decided to use photographs . . . because **they** believed . . .*

Rewrite each sentence to correct the pronoun use.

1. Our class wants to go to the Museum of Contemporary Art, where you can see an exhibit of Georgia O'Keeffe's paintings.
2. I always rent an audiotape so that you know what to look for when you study a painting.
3. My friend and I plan to visit the museum gift shop, where you can buy prints of your favorite paintings.
4. Many students recognize that you can do firsthand research for a report in a museum.
5. Do you think that someday you'll visit the museum?

See Lesson 17.5, pages 606–610.

Persuasive Writing
Understanding Persuasive Writing

In persuasive writing, you try to convince readers to agree with your opinion and possibly to take action. In the following excerpt a former Federal Communications Commission chairman appeals to both reason and emotion to persuade broadcasters that television is a "vast wasteland."

How would you summarize Minow's opinion in your own words?

What specific examples does Minow use to support his opinion?

In what way does this final question challenge the particular audience to whom Minow spoke?

1 rating book: a book that rates TV programs by the number of households viewing them

Literature Model

When television is bad, nothing is worse. I invite you to sit down in front of your television set when your station goes on the air and stay there without a book, magazine, newspaper, profit-and-loss sheet, or rating book**1** to distract you—and keep your eyes glued to that set until the station signs off. I can assure you that you will observe a vast wasteland.

You will see a procession of game shows, violence, audience participation shows, formula comedies about totally unbelievable families, blood and thunder, mayhem, violence, sadism, murder, Western badmen, Western good men, private eyes, gangsters, more violence and cartoons. And, endlessly, commercials—many screaming, cajoling, and offending. And, most of all, boredom. True, you will see a few things you will enjoy. But they will be very, very few. And if you think I exaggerate, try it.

Is there one person in this room who claims that broadcasting can't do better?

Newton Minow, Address to the Broadcasting Industry

Recognize Persuasive Writing

Persuasive writing expresses a writer's opinion and tries to make readers agree with it, change their own opinion, and sometimes take action. In persuasive writing, audience is all-important, as the speech about television illustrates. Commissioner Minow aimed his message at broadcast executives, the very people responsible for television programming.

Every day you see and hear countless persuasive messages: a billboard ad for a popular brand of jeans, a radio spot for a movie the critics are raving about, bumper stickers calling attention to a cause or a candidate. Below are some of the places where you encounter persuasive messages. Can you think of others?

Persuasive Writing

Television · Billboards · Other students · Teachers · Posters · Junk mail · Bus advertisements · Newspapers · Radio · T-shirts · Books · Buckle Up · Visit the ZOO · Linda C. 4 Student President

Journal Writing

Persuasive appeals are so widespread that you probably tune many of them out as you go about your business. Think back over the past day, and try to remember all the persuasive appeals you heard or saw. List them in your journal.

Give Your Persuasive Writing an Edge

Grammar

Revising Tip

When revising a piece of persuasive writing, determine whether the modifiers you have used are vivid and strong enough to support your opinion. For basic information on modifiers, see Lessons 10.4 and 10.5, pages 422–434.

Like other types of writing, persuasive writing consists of a topic, a main idea about that topic, and supporting details. However, your main idea in persuasive writing has an edge to it. It's an opinion that you want others to adopt. Therefore, you need to pay special attention to your audience, presenting your supporting ideas in a way that will persuade your audience to accept your opinion.

You can support your opinion with two main kinds of details: appeals to reason and appeals to emotion. To appeal to reason, use facts, statistics, expert opinions, and examples that validate your position. To appeal to emotion, use words that generate strong positive or negative responses. For example, if you want to persuade readers to favor a candidate, you might applaud his "courageous" stand on the issues; if you want to discredit that same candidate, you might attack his "foolhardy" position.

Often you will want to appeal to both reason and emotion in the same piece of persuasive writing. Look at the advertisement below. What kind of appeal does the headline make? What part of the ad appeals to reason? To emotion?

AND ON THE EIGHTH DAY, WE BULLDOZED IT.

Elusive jaguars, rarest orchids, colorful birds-of-paradise.

Rainforests are haven to half of all the plant and animal species on earth. But how much time do they have left?

Fifty thousand rainforest acres are lost each day worldwide. At that rate, the last traces of original, irreplaceable paradise will vanish in a single human lifespan.

To preserve the splendid variety of life we must save the endangered rainforests.

Please support our efforts to conserve a miracle of creation. Tomorrow won't wait.

Save the rainforests and safeguard the survival of half of the species on earth, including our own. Here's my donation of ☐ $25 ☐ $50 ☐ $75 ☐ $100 ☐ _____ .

NAME _____
ADDRESS _____
CITY _____ STATE _____ ZIP_____

RAINFOREST ACTION NETWORK

300 BROADWAY, SAN FRANCISCO, CA 94133

Public Media Center

6.1 Writing Activities

Write an Opinion

Express your opinion of the painting below in a brief essay that could be published in an art gallery brochure. Use the details in the painting to support your opinion.

- Present your opinion in a main idea statement.
- Use supporting ideas that appeal to both reason and emotion.
- Pitch your argument to your particular audience.

PURPOSE To express and support an opinion
AUDIENCE Visitors to an art gallery
LENGTH 2–3 paragraphs

Cooperative Learning

In a small group, evaluate the quality of commercial TV programming. Assign each member to either read a recent article on current TV programming or view a different channel for several hours. Meet to discuss your findings, and collaborate on a one-page response to Newton Minow's statements.

Jonathan Franklin, *Mad Hatters*, 1990

Grammar Link

Avoid sentence fragments in your writing.

A *sentence fragment* is an incomplete sentence punctuated as if it were a complete sentence:

Elusive jaguars, rarest orchids, colorful birds-of-paradise.

Though sentence fragments may be effective in advertising, do not use them in formal writing.

Rewrite to correct the fragments.

1. Television, labeled a "vast wasteland" by Newton Minow.
2. Insulting comedies, violent detective shows, irrelevant talk shows, and endless commercials. The list goes on.
3. There are a few shows that entertain and inform. Such as *Sixty Minutes*.
4. Cable television, supposedly an improvement over network programs.
5. Soon to be a major player on the information superhighway.

See Lesson 13.9, pages 519–520.

Persuasive Writing
Evidence in Persuasive Writing

In persuasive writing you need to support your viewpoint with facts and relevant opinions. As you read these two contrasting views of MTV, look for supporting evidence.

Literature Model

Which of Shales's word choices helps to reinforce his negative opinion of MTV?

MTV is primarily a triumph of marketing. Who would have thought, say, eleven years ago, that TV audiences would sit still for a channel showing nothing but commercials separated by commercials? Those music videos are essentially ads designed to sell records. In between them, MTV places real commercials to sell seven thousand different kinds of jeans and hair glop.

Not for nothing has MTV earned the nickname "Empty-V." Instead of denying that emptiness, however, MTV celebrates it. Members of the viewing audience are frequently assured that they are not to be bothered with matters of consequence. "MTV News," which is shown frequently each day, is "news" about rock stars, pop stars and silly celebrities—puff and fluff spun in the hype mills of Hollywood.

Tom Shales, "MTV Has Shallow Look of Success"

*A*lmost since its inception, MTV has been rightly applauded by a grateful record industry for revitalizing pop music, boosting album sales and creating a thriving new market for home music videos. (MTV helped boost sales of music videos to a record $172.3 million last year, up $55 million from 1989. . . .)

MTV has also been hailed for revolutionizing TV (it is largely credited with inspiring the tone of the "Miami Vice" series), and for making its 1981 slogan "You'll never look at music the same way again," a reality. . . .

Eager to counter the many charges of vacuousness and puffery that have plagued it, MTV has also aired public service programs about political, social and environmental issues, even winning a prestigious Peabody Award for its two-hour retrospective on the '80s, "Decade."

George Varga, "Is It MTV, or Is It 'Empty-V'?"

What facts does Varga use to portray MTV in a more positive light?

Use Facts and Opinions

Persuasive writing is more than just a statement of your opinion. You need to back up your opinion with evidence—facts and opinions that support your viewpoint. Facts are statements, statistics, observations, and examples that can be verified, or proved true or false. Evaluate a fact by answering these questions: Is it accurate? Is it up to date? Is it relevant?

Opinions are personal judgments. They may be supported by facts, or they may be simply personal preferences. Their value depends upon the qualifications of the person stating them. Evaluate an opinion by answering these questions: Is the opinion-giver qualified, with specific knowledge of the subject? Is the opinion-giver biased, with something to gain from supporting a certain viewpoint?

Both facts and opinions are open to interpretation. Different people draw different conclusions from the same evidence. The key is to decide how valid the evidence is.

Prewriting Tip

Both clustering and brainstorming can help you generate facts and opinions for persuasive writing, but you need to evaluate the evidence you generate.

Journal Writing

What's your opinion on MTV? In your journal, list several facts and opinions that you could use to support your view.

Prepare Arguments

Grammar
Editing Tip

When editing, check that verbs and indefinite pronouns, such as *one* and *some*, agree in number. For more information about indefinite pronouns as subjects, see Lesson 16.7, pages 585–587.

In persuasive writing, an argument is the position you take on an issue, along with the evidence you use to support your position. Often your evidence will include a mix of facts, statistics, expert opinions, and personal opinions that anticipate opposing viewpoints.

The excerpt below is from an ad by the makers of jewel boxes, the plastic packages in which compact discs are sold. The ad writer seeks to convince record companies that jewel boxes are the best packaging for CDs. What evidence supports the position? Is it convincing?

Literature Model

THE PEOPLE'S CHOICE

As the makers and advocates of the jewel box, we believe the best alternative to the longbox already exists. One that's proven internationally—sell CDs in the jewel box, alone.

We're not the only ones who believe this. Peter Gabriel and Raffi are just two of the artists who agree. And with successful "jewel box-only" releases, they've proved the viability of that option.

But most important is the opinion of CD buyers like you—the people who should have the final say in any CD packaging decision. In a recent survey by *CD Review* magazine, they found that 84% of CD buyers preferred the sturdy, plastic jewel box to an alternative, paperboard package. . . .

ENVIRONMENTAL PROTECTION

Of course, some argue that an alternative package will be better for the environment. But the facts don't support their position.

Consider that last year alone at least 50 million unsold CDs were returned by retailers. Not a problem with the jewel box—the discs, artwork and booklets can be removed, and the jewel boxes could be re-used or recycled.

But proposed alternative CD packages can't be re-used or recycled, because they're made of paperboard and plastic glued together and pre-printed for just one release. If those 50 million returns were in an alternative package, the packages would have only one place to go—into the garbage.

JAM (Jewelbox Advocates and Manufacturers)

Write an Editorial

Write an editorial for your school newspaper on security measures, testing student athletes for drug use, or some other controversial school issue of your choice.

- State your position on the issue.
- Support your position with facts and valid opinions.
- Anticipate and respond to possible opposing viewpoints.

PURPOSE To express and support an opinion on a school issue
AUDIENCE Readers of the school newspaper
LENGTH 3–4 paragraphs

Cross-Curricular: Art

The painting below is by Mandy Martin, an Australian known for expressing her views on environmental issues through her art. In this painting, she set out to show the negative effect of the mining industry on the environment. Does she succeed? Use facts about the painting along with your personal judgment to write an evaluation of how the painting fulfills its purpose.

Grammar Link

Make collective noun subjects and verbs agree.

A collective noun can be singular or plural. When writing about MTV's *audience*, for example, you would use a singular verb to refer to a group as a whole but a plural verb to refer to individual group members.

Write the correct form of the verb in parentheses.

1. The crowd (roar, roars) its approval.
2. The crowd (have, has) to pass through the gate, one at a time.
3. The band (is, are) warming up.
4. The band (take, takes) their places on stage.
5. Our whole group (is, are) shocked by the news about the lead singer.

See Lesson 16.4, page 580.

Mandy Martin, *Powerhouse*, 1988

Persuasive Writing
Presenting an Opinion

The models below present opposing viewpoints on the issue of high school classes watching commercial television programs. Try to identify the position each writer takes and the audience to which each argument is targeted.

Literature Model

I have no objection to television commercials being shown to a "captive" audience of students in school, especially when the commercials are tastefully done. . . .

The furor over Channel One advertising baffles me. Ads are everywhere in our building and have been for years. The clocks, the No. 2 pencils, the computers, even the footballs have company logos. . . .

The things we use have to be paid for by somebody. Many school systems like mine would never have this kind of equipment except through a program like this.

Betty Berry, *NEA Today*

> Summarize Berry's opinion in one sentence.

Literature Model

S chools are marketplaces for ideas, not commercial turf. The opposite concept—that schools should provide a captive audience for commercials "endorsed" by educators—is repulsive. *Educators present all sides of an issue—we don't "sell" one point of view.* . . .

The *Wall Street Journal* reports that American teenagers spent $55 billion in 1988. Harnessing that purchasing power can give an advertiser a big advantage in the marketplace.

Jennifer March, *NEA Today*

> Summarize March's opinion in one sentence.

Take a Meaningful Stand

To write persuasively, you must take a stand on a topic you have some knowledge of and then support your position with relevant evidence. For instance, both Berry and March drew on their many years of teaching experience to present specific arguments for and against commercials in classroom programs.

In addition to knowing your subject, you need to make sure that a genuine difference of opinion exists between you and your audience. Taking a stand against pollution would probably not be worth your time, since few people would disagree. Taking a stand in favor of a specific antipollution measure, such as mandatory carpooling, is more plausible, since some people may oppose your position. Once you have an arguable topic, express your opinion in a clear thesis statement such as this: Mandatory carpooling regulations should be adopted to ease air pollution.

Prewriting Tip

Discuss your opinion and your audience with a peer. Ask for ideas about how to get through to the audience you have in mind.

Examine Your Audience

Knowing your audience is the essence of persuasive writing. After all, you're trying to influence their opinions and sometimes even change their actions. The questions in the chart may help you decide what you need to know about your audience.

Drafting Tip

For examples of the kinds of details to use to support a position, see Lesson 5.2, page 220.

Evaluating Your Audience

- What is the current attitude of my audience? Are they likely to agree or disagree? Do they care about the issue, or will I have to overcome their apathy?
- What do they already know about the issue? Do I need to provide background or clear up misconceptions?
- What types of evidence will have the strongest impact on my audience? Will facts and statistics do the job? Should I include informed opinions?
- What do I want my audience to do: change their thinking, take action, or simply recognize the validity of my viewpoint?

Journal Writing

Make notes in your journal about some audiences you could write for, including how your choice of an audience affects your argument. If you presented your opinion about watching commercials in school, what information would appeal to your classmates, your teachers, your parents, and the members of your school board?

State Your Case

Drafting Tip

As you draft persuasive writing, think about the order of your arguments. You can leave your readers with a stronger impression if you save your best argument for last.

Your success in persuasive writing will depend on stating your case well, and that means organization. Persuasive writing often follows the four-step plan below.

Guidelines for Persuasive Writing			
Introduce the issue	**State your opinion**	**Support your position**	**Draw your conclusion**
Describe the issue, and supply any background needed to help readers understand it.	Take your stand in a clear, direct thesis statement.	Present your evidence—facts, opinions, or both—and respond to opposing viewpoints.	End by summarizing your ideas and, if appropriate, giving a clear call to action.

Public-service advertisements often use the approach suggested above to draw attention to a cause or to seek financial support. In your opinion, how well does the following ad make its case?

How effective is this headline and why?

What facts does this ad include, and how do they provide strong support for the ad's purpose?

What specific action does this ad call for in its conclusion?

Back By Popular Demand.

At one time, peregrine falcons nested by the thousands throughout the United States. But with the widespread use of the insecticide DDT in the 1940s and 1950s, the species suffered greatly. In the eastern U.S., the peregrine falcon disappeared entirely.

Now peregrine falcons have made a comeback, thanks to efforts by conservationists.

Since 1975 when recovery programs were established, 752 peregrines have been released in the eastern U.S., and there has been a steady increase in the nesting population.

With wise conservation policies, other once rare species such as the American alligator and the bald eagle have also made comebacks. Help save our endangered species. Join the National Wildlife Federation, 1412 16th Street, NW, Washington, DC 20036-2266.

Working for the Nature of Tomorrow℠
NATIONAL WILDLIFE FEDERATION

Wayne Lynch

6.3 Writing Activities

Write a Letter

Write a letter to your school principal stating your position on this topic: Your school should (should not) receive daily television news broadcasts. (If your school currently uses news broadcasts, change "receive" to "continue to receive.") As your evidence, use the information below, the information on page 284, and your own ideas.

- Explain the issue.
- State your position in a thesis statement.
- Support your position.
- Draw your own conclusion.
- Gear your argument to your audience.

Pro
— In exchange for requiring students to watch the television news, with commercials, schools are loaned TV equipment.
— Many high school students lack knowledge of current events.
— A study by the producer of the news program found that students who had watched it had a "significantly better" knowledge of world and national events than other students.

Con
— The contract requires students to watch the news program every day.
— When the contract expires, the television equipment must be returned.
— Schools have no control over what kinds of information and commercials are presented during the broadcasts.

PURPOSE To write a letter supporting or opposing TV news in the classroom
AUDIENCE Your school principal
LENGTH 2–3 paragraphs

COMPUTER OPTION

Your word-processing program can help you record and store the facts and opinions you will use to support your position. First, enter the information, give it a heading, and box it so that it looks like a note card. Organize your notes just as you would arrange note cards, grouping them under the main ideas or headings of your paper. In the drafting stage, copy the information from your notes and paste it down in your draft.

Grammar Link

Use specific nouns and strong modifiers.

Jennifer March uses precise language in her argument on television commercials.

*Schools are **marketplaces** for ideas, not **commercial turf**.*

Revise the sentences below, using specific nouns and adding strong modifiers.

1. Students in some towns should have the same educational opportunities as students in others.
2. Some schools have a lot of things and some don't.
3. School funds should come from many sources.
4. Taxes on many items could be raised.
5. Certain people think that a new tax plan will result in better schools.

See Lesson 10.1, page 401; Lesson 10.4, page 422; and Lesson 10.5, page 428.

Persuasive Writing
Writing a Product Evaluation

FREEBLADES
Come alive with Freeblades. Cool and in-line.

Using persuasive writing techniques, writers prepare evaluations on a broad range of products and services. Reading a product evaluation such as this one could help you find the right in-line skates.

Literature Model

T he hottest roller skates around don't look much like the skates most grownups remember from their childhood. The hardware most resembles flashy ski boots with a line of plastic wheels down the center of the sole. They're known formally as in-line skates. . . .

We tested nine skates in time trials around a paved running track, in our parking lot, and along some country roads. We also rolled on an exercise treadmill and measured the amount of force needed to keep rolling along. . . .

The hard, molded-plastic boots provide good ankle support—provided you can pull the laces tight enough. That wasn't always easy to do, we found. . . .

Beginners might well look low in the Ratings [of specific models], to skates at less than $100. (Just make sure the boots feel comfortable to you.)

Those skates may not roll quite as easily or rapidly as higher-priced models. But then, you may not want a lot of speed as a beginner. Once the original wheels and bearings wear out, you can swap them for a good set for about $100. Changing wheels is fairly easy.

"In-Line Skates: They Aren't Just for Kids," *Consumer Reports*

The article begins by explaining what the product is.

What kind of testing did the evaluators do?

What are the report's recommendations? How might they help a consumer?

Set a Goal

Product evaluations that you write can serve various purposes. You can judge the quality of a particular brand or service; you can compare several brands or services for the purpose of rating them; or you can evaluate the usefulness of a product itself, making a judgment about whether it's worth purchasing *any* brand. Setting a goal at the outset will help you determine what types of evidence you need to gather.

Develop Standards for Evaluation

A product evaluation must be backed up with evidence. You need to develop standards you can use to evaluate the product and then determine how well the product measures up to your standards. *Consumer Reports* evaluates products by running them through a series of tests. You yourself can't conduct that type of evaluation, but you *can* go to product users for evidence. Conduct an informal survey, asking your friends, neighbors, and family to answer questions about the product you plan to evaluate. You can adapt the chart below to fit your product.

Prewriting Tip

A comparison frame can help you organize your evidence for a product evaluation. See Lesson 5.5 on page 231.

Standards for Evaluating Products

Price	Is the price reasonable? How does it compare with those of similar products?
Features	What are its most important features? Are any desirable features missing? Are any of its features unnecessary?
Workmanship	Is the product well made? Is anything easily broken?
Design	Is it good-looking? Is it easy to use?

Based on the information from your survey, you can make informed judgments about the product. You can then prepare a written report to help other consumers make the right choices.

Journal Writing

Think of a product you bought recently, and evaluate it according to the standards in the chart above for price, features, quality, and design. Would you have purchased the product if you first had evaluated it according to these standards? Write your answer in your journal.

Use Visual Evidence

Photos and other illustrations can add vital information about a product. For example, the *Consumer Reports* evaluation of film-processing services noted that photographers sometimes blame themselves for what are actually problems in processing. To illustrate processing problems, *Consumer Reports* used the following photos as visual evidence.

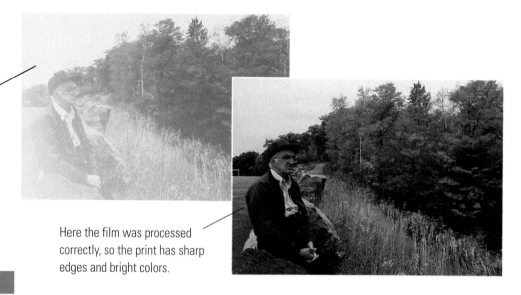

The film was underexposed in printing, so the print has low contrast and washed-out colors.

Here the film was processed correctly, so the print has sharp edges and bright colors.

Grammar
Editing Tip

When editing a product evaluation, check that antecedents of pronouns such as *this, that, which,* and *it* are clearly stated. For more information about pronoun references, see Lesson 17.6, page 611.

Once you've completed your investigation, you'll need to present your findings. Here are some guidelines you can follow to make your evaluation helpful to your readers.

Writing a Product Evaluation	
Introduce it	What product or service are you evaluating?
State your main idea	Are you judging one product or service? Are you comparing two or more?
Explain your methods	Did you examine the product or service? Did you survey its users?
State your findings	What are your standards? How well did the product or service measure up?
Make a recommendation	Should people buy the product or use the service?

6.4 Writing Activities

Write an Evaluation of a Place

Write an article for a travel magazine evaluating a place you have visited, such as an amusement park, a museum, a zoo, or a national park.

- State your main idea.
- Identify your standards for evaluating the place.
- Explain how you gathered your data.
- State your findings and make a recommendation.
- Provide visual evidence if possible.

PURPOSE To write an evaluation of a travel destination

AUDIENCE Readers of a travel magazine

LENGTH 3–4 paragraphs

Cooperative Learning

Work in a small group to evaluate a product or service popular among teenagers—for example, jeans, CD players, or fast-food restaurants. Draw up a list of standards for evaluating your product or service. Then have each member use the standards to conduct an informal survey of friends and classmates. If possible, try out the product or service on your own as well. Record individual findings, and pool the results of the surveys. Then prepare a product evaluation, having each member write one part of the report. For example, one member can write about the standards; another, the survey findings; and a third, the group's recommendation.

Grammar Link

Use *good/well* and *bad/badly* correctly.

Good and *bad* are adjectives. They precede nouns and follow linking verbs. Use *well* as an adjective to mean "in good health." Otherwise *well* and *badly* are adverbs and modify action verbs.

> *Beginners might **well** look . . . in the ratings. . . . swap them for a **good** set. . . .*

Complete each sentence below by adding *good, well, bad,* or *badly*.

1. We have recently been told that margarine may be as ____ for us as cholesterol-laden butter.
2. Eating a bucket of unbuttered popcorn is not ____ for you either.
3. Foods saturated with fat or brimming with salt can make you feel ____.
4. Nutrition experts debate whether people should take vitamin supplements or simply eat ____.
5. The few federal standards that do exist for nutrition supplements are enforced ____.
6. Price differences for vitamins are great, so shop carefully for a ____ buy.
7. Studies show that in moderate doses, nutrition supplements are ____ for you.
8. Many questions remain, however, and more research is ____ needed.
9. To look ____ and feel ____, do you need daily doses of beta carotene?
10. How ____ do vitamin or mineral products fare in the treatment of disease?

See Lesson 18.5, pages 633–634.

Persuasive Writing
Creating an Ad

A strong ad is carefully worded to grab the attention of its intended audience. At what audience is the ad below aimed? Do you think it successfully "sells" advertising?

> How does the headline grab your attention?

THIS AD IS FULL OF LIES.

LIE #1: ADVERTISING MAKES YOU BUY THINGS YOU DON'T WANT.
Advertising is often accused of inducing people to buy things against their will. But when was the last time you returned home from the local shopping mall with a bag full of things you had absolutely no use for? The truth is, nothing short of a pointed gun can get *anybody* to spend money on something he or she doesn't want.

No matter how effective an ad is, you and millions of other American consumers make your own decisions. If you don't believe it, ask someone who knows firsthand about the limits of advertising. Like your local Edsel dealer.

> The ad appeals to reason and emotion as it answers common arguments against advertising.

LIE #2: ADVERTISING MAKES THINGS COST MORE. Since advertising costs money, it's natural to assume it costs *you* money. But the truth is that advertising often brings prices down.

Consider the electronic calculator, for example. In the late 1960s, advertising created a mass market for calculators. That meant more of them needed to be produced, which brought the price of producing each calculator down. Competition spurred by advertising brought the price down still further.

As a result, the same product that used to cost hundreds of dollars now costs as little as five dollars.

LIE #3: ADVERTISING HELPS BAD PRODUCTS SELL.
Some people worry that good advertising sometimes covers up for bad products.

But nothing can make you like a bad product. So, while advertising can help convince you to try something once, it can't make you buy it twice. If you don't like what you've bought, you won't buy it again. And if enough people feel the same way, the product dies on the shelf.

In other words, the only thing advertising can do for a bad product is help you find out it's a bad product. And you take it from there.

> Does the ad present its strongest argument at the end? Support your opinion.

LIE #4: ADVERTISING IS A WASTE OF MONEY. Some people wonder why we don't just put all the money spent on advertising directly into our national economy.

The answer is, we already do.

Advertising helps products sell, which holds down prices, which helps sales even more. It creates jobs. It informs you about all the products available and helps you compare them. And it stimulates the competition that produces new and better products at reasonable prices.

If all that doesn't convince you that advertising is important to our economy, you might as well stop reading.

Because on top of everything else, advertising has paid for a large part of the magazine you're now holding.

And that's the truth.

ADVERTISING.
ANOTHER WORD FOR FREEDOM OF CHOICE.
American Association of Advertising Agencies

Get Your Audience's Attention

Advertisements have a clear purpose—to persuade people to buy a product or service or to support a point of view, idea, or candidate. The goals of advertising can be summed up in the acronym AIDA: a good ad must attract *Attention*, arouse *Interest*, create *Desire*, and get *Action*. Study this chart to see how AIDA works.

AIDA	
Attention	Use an attention-getting headline or striking design to draw readers in.
Interest	Present evidence to show why readers should be interested. Use facts and opinions to explain the product's features and show how it's different from the competition—and better.
Desire	Appeal to your readers' reason and emotion to make them want your product.
Action	End with a clear call to action — buy the product, give money to the cause, vote for the candidate.

Create an Audience Profile

You want your ad to succeed, and that means reaching the right audience: those who are likely to use your product, service, or idea. An audience profile gives you the information you need to tailor your ad to the desired audience. All it takes is asking a few simple questions.

Audience Profile	
Age group	How old are the people who might use your product or service?
Education level	Does your product or service appeal to people with a certain level of education?
Buying power	Does your product or service appeal to people with a certain level of income?
Attitudes	What opinions and interests characterize your audience?
Life style	What entertainment characterizes your audience?
Needs	What are the needs of your audience?

Journal Writing

Find a magazine or newspaper ad that you think is effective, and paste it in your journal. Prepare an audience profile for the ad, answering as many questions as you can from the chart above.

Choose the Right Words

Vocabulary
Revising Tip

When looking for the right word, you may want to use a the-saurus. For information about how to use this reference, see Lesson 24.2, pages 776–777.

To arouse your audience's interest and create desire for the product, you need to use the right words. Mark Twain once said, "The difference between the right word and the nearly right word is the same as that between lightning and the lightning bug."

Use Precise Words   Ad writers choose words carefully. Wear Champions running shoes, and you won't just run fast; you'll "glide effortlessly." Devine Cookies aren't simply delicious; they're "honey-sweet and taste-tempting." The Rapmaster isn't just a new radio; it's "a state-of-the-art sound system." Concrete nouns, strong action verbs, and colorful adjectives and adverbs help to create a desire for your product, service, or idea.

Grammar
Editing Tip

When editing copy for an ad, make sure that a noun of amount, such as *hundreds,* agrees in number with its verb. For more information about verb agreement with special subjects, see Lesson 16.4, page 580.

Recognize Connotations   You're writing an ad for the Fataway exerciser. Do you promise customers a "scrawny body" or a "lean body"? *Scrawny* and *lean* have similar meanings; both are synonyms of *thin*. But the connotations of the words—their positive or negative associations—are strikingly different. Since persuasive writing appeals to emotion as well as reason, you can enhance your message by keeping connotations in mind. What word choices help to make the following ad effective?

Words paint an attractive picture of Idaho's lakes and suggest a relaxing travel destination.

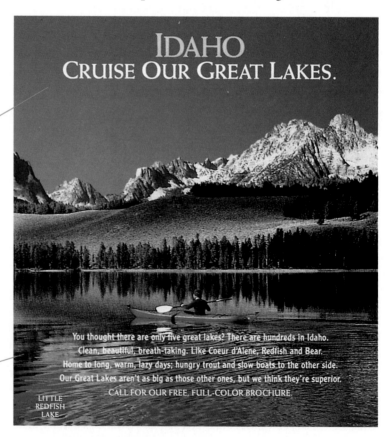

IDAHO
CRUISE OUR GREAT LAKES.

You thought there are only five great lakes? There are hundreds in Idaho.
Clean, beautiful, breath-taking. Like Coeur d'Alene, Redfish and Bear.
Home to long, warm, lazy days; hungry trout and slow boats to the other side.
Our Great Lakes aren't as big as those other ones, but we think they're superior.
CALL FOR OUR FREE, FULL-COLOR BROCHURE.

LITTLE
REDFISH
LAKE

Ad writers capitalize on double meanings. How does this ad play on two meanings of "great lakes"?

6.5 Writing Activities

Write an Ad

Write a one-page ad for your local newspaper with the painting on this page as your center-piece. You can create an ad for an exhibit of paintings, for a travel agency, a soap, a perfume, a cleaning service, or for a product, service, or idea of your choice.

- Appeal to your desired audience.
- Write an attention-getting headline.
- Present evidence.
- Appeal to readers' reason and emotion.
- End with a clear call to action.
- Use precise words with appropriate connotations.

PURPOSE To create an advertisement using a painting as the visual
AUDIENCE Readers of the local newspaper
LENGTH 1 page

Claude Monet, *Les Coquelicots (Wild Poppies)*, 1873

Cross-Curricular: Government

You are working on an advertising campaign urging citizens to register to vote in the upcoming election. Your task is to create an ad targeted specifically to people who have just turned 18 and are eligible to vote for the first time. Write the ad copy, and design a full-page ad including an appropriate graphic.

Grammar Link

Make indefinite pronouns and personal pronouns referring to them agree in number and person.

Pronouns referring to indefinite pronouns should be singular if the indefinite pronoun is singular and plural if it is plural. If the gender of a singular indefinite pronoun is unknown, you may wish to rephrase to avoid "he or she."

Rewrite the sentences to make the personal and indefinite pronouns agree.

1. Most of the consumers assume that you cannot be swayed by advertising.
2. Few of the men think that he has been forced to buy products or services against their will.
3. Others of them have purchased an item because he or she was influenced by an ad.
4. Neither of the girls bought this item because they believed the ad.
5. None of us should blame the advertiser, however, if they buy a shoddy product twice.

See Lesson 17.5, page 609–610.

Persuasive Writing
Writing a Letter of Complaint

"Try to imagine how much I care!"

When you write a letter of complaint, you usually want to persuade someone to solve a problem. In the letter below, notice how the writer calmly identifies the problem, offers evidence, and proposes a reasonable solution.

Student Model

Summarize Reis's complaint in a sentence.

What evidence does Reis present to justify her complaint?

What solution does Reis suggest? Is her suggestion reasonable?

I purchased an automatic dishwasher, model 98765, from B & A Appliance Service Center on April 18. On May 2 the washer began leaking water from the bottom.

Right away, I called B & A and explained the problem. I also explained my warranty, which entitles me to parts and labor for a full year from the purchase date. The next day B & A sent two repairmen, but they were unsuccessful, and the washer still leaked. I called again, and on May 6 the same men came back but still could not fix the washer. On May 8, I received a bill for $59.03 from B & A for parts and labor. I now have called and visited your store on several occasions. Mr. Black, the department manager, insists that I am responsible for paying the bill.

I am enclosing a copy of my original receipt, my warranty, and the repair bill. I believe I am not responsible for these charges. My washer still leaks, so I request that B & A live up to the terms of the warranty and fix it. If it cannot be fixed, please replace it with another washer of the same make and model. I hope we can come to an agreement on this matter.

Teresa Reis, Quartz Hill High School, Quartz Hill, California

Identify the Problem and a Solution

When you write a letter of complaint, you are trying to solve a problem. Your goals are to explain your problem, convince your reader that you have a valid complaint, and propose a reasonable solution. Your letter can follow this simple pattern.

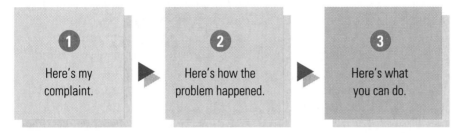

In the model letter on the opposite page, Teresa Reis has presented these three ideas in three paragraphs. Some complaints have a long history, and the letter must be longer. Other complaints can be explained in one paragraph. Whatever its length, your letter should have the same three parts.

First open with a clear statement of the problem, usually in a sentence or two. Make it brief but complete. No one can help you without understanding what your problem is.

Next tell your story. In a paragraph or two, explain what happened, describing any previous attempts to correct the problem. This middle section is usually a narrative, so arrange the details in chronological order, the order in which they happened. Include dates and names, but avoid unnecessary details. Enclose any relevant evidence, such as a photocopy of the manufacturer's warranty.

In your final paragraph, explain specifically what you want done. If the solution you propose is a reasonable one, you are likely to get the results you want. The key word here is *reasonable*. A reasonable solution is one that the person or company can agree to without going to an excessive amount of trouble or expense.

Journal Writing

Set aside a page in your journal. Label the page "Complaints," and keep a running list of ideas for complaint letters. Over a period of time, you may find that the same complaint appears again and again. When that happens, it may be time to compose and mail that letter of complaint.

Use a Businesslike Tone and Form

When you are writing a letter of complaint, chances are you're angry. Your first impulse may be to strike back with sarcasm, insults, even threats. ("I'll never shop in your stupid store again, and I'll tell all my friends to stay away, too.") To write an effective letter of complaint, you need to keep your emotions under control. Remember, your goal is to get the problem corrected. Your tone of voice comes through in writing just as it does in speech. You're more likely to accomplish your goal if your letter has a calm, businesslike tone. That way, you allow the other side to respond calmly and reasonably as well.

Another way to ensure that your letter will get a sympathetic reading is to use proper form. The letter below illustrates the semiblock form, a popular style for a business letter that will help you get results.

123 Washington Way
Irving, NY 12034
July 27, 1992

Sales Manager
Bemus Music Store
1 Trailblazer Way
Portland, OR 97202

Dear Sir or Madam:

On July 15, I ordered the tape <u>Ice Rink</u>, by Carrie Carey. Today it came, but it broke the first time I played it.

When I inserted the tape and pushed the play button on my tape player, I heard the beginning of the first number, but no more. When I removed the tape, I could see that it was broken. I played some other tapes to make sure my player had not caused the problem, but it worked perfectly.

I am enclosing a copy of the receipt, and I am returning the defective tape in a separate package. Please send me another copy.

Yours truly,

Peter Bianco

Peter Bianco

Write a Complaint Letter

Think about problems with products and services you or members of your family have had. Write a letter of complaint about a problem of your choice or one listed below. Follow correct business-letter format.

> (1) You paid $299 for a new camera. The next week the manufacturer announced that it was discontinuing the model and replacing it with a more advanced one at an introductory price of $250.
>
> (2) You washed a new sweater as directed on the label, but the sweater shrank two sizes.
>
> (3) You and some friends waited to be served in a restaurant for almost an hour. When the food came, it was cold.

- State the complaint clearly and briefly.
- Explain what happened.
- Propose a reasonable solution.
- Use a businesslike tone.
- Use correct business-letter form.

PURPOSE To write a letter of complaint
AUDIENCE Person or company
LENGTH 3 paragraphs

COMPUTER OPTION

Proofreading is especially important in letters of complaint because your reader is more likely to take your complaint seriously if you write it correctly. The electronic spell-checker in your word-processing program can be a great help in proofreading. Be especially careful, though, since your spell-checker won't help you if you've misspelled a proper noun such as the name of the company, or if you've used the wrong homonym, such as *you're* instead of *your*.

Grammar Link

Use the past and past perfect tenses correctly.

Use the *past tense* to describe an action that was started and completed in the past. Use the *past perfect* tense to show that a past action began and ended before another past action began. Note how Peter Bianco used verb tenses in his complaint letter.

*I **played** some other tapes to make sure my player **had** not **caused** the problem. . . .*

Write the correct form of each verb in parentheses.

1. By the time I (go) shopping for a cordless phone, I (research) the product in several consumer magazines.
2. However, the sales clerk (convince) me to buy a different model than the one that I (choose).
3. When I (arrive) home, I knew that I (make) a terrible mistake.
4. I (buy) a phone that (lack) two important features—speed dialing and call forwarding.
5. I (want) these special features long before they (become) popular.

See Lesson 15.3, page 552, and Lesson 15.4, page 556.

Writing About Literature
Reviewing a Nonfiction Book

Book reviews are a type of product evaluation. The reviewer gives an opinion, supported with evidence, about whether a book is worth a reader's time and money.

Answer Questions in a Review

Readers ask two basic questions about any nonfiction book: What's it about? and Is it any good? As a reviewer, your job is to answer those questions. Begin by assuming that your readers are unfamiliar with the book. Summarize the book's contents—its subject and the author's purpose in writing. You may also need to provide background information about the author and subject, though such information isn't always necessary. Reviewers who write for *Rolling Stone*, for example, can assume that their readers have a basic knowledge of rock-and-roll, so they spend less time on background than they would for the general public.

Prepare by Taking Notes

A good nonfiction review says more than whether the reviewer liked the book; it explains why, presenting specific reasons to support its position. The best way to write such a review is to respond to the book as you are reading it. Take notes—in your reader-response journal if you have one—about ideas and opinions. Quote whole sentences that are striking. Also take notes on your own responses: Do you agree or disagree with the author? Are you surprised, angered, encouraged, or discouraged by the book's message? You may wish to reread the book, or key parts of it, to grasp the author's meaning fully. The questions below can help you reflect on your reading.

Grammar
Drafting Tip

When quoting whole sentences from a book, use quotation marks to set off direct quotes. When summarizing statements in your own words, you do not need quotation marks. For information on how to use punctuation with quotations, see Lesson 21.9, pages 717–719.

Questions for Book Reviewers

1. Why do I think the author wrote this book and what did I learn from it?
2. What would I like to know more about? Less about?
3. What was memorable about the book?
4. Did I find the book factual? Believable?
5. Was I persuaded to agree with the author?
6. How has the book affected my attitude on the topic?
7. How did the author's style affect the book's message?
8. Who would benefit most from reading this book?
9. Would I choose to read other books by this author?

Journal Writing

You and your friends probably give each other mini-reviews of books, movies, and music. Think about discussions you've had. In your journal explain what information helps you the most in choosing books, movies, and music for yourself.

Find a Focus

Once you've finished reading, use your notes to help you write a statement of opinion—a thesis statement—to focus your book review. For a nonfiction book, your statement of opinion will sum up the author's purpose and state whether you recommend the book. Then in the body of the review consider these points: Was the purpose a worthy one? How well did the author achieve it? Should others read the book?

Keep in mind that reading is a personal matter. The best reviews present not only reasoned evidence but also the reviewer's own responses. In the review below, notice how David Fricke's enthusiasm comes through.

Grammar
Drafting Tip

When you use the book's title in your review, remember to underscore it to indicate italics. For more about writing titles, see Lesson 21.10 on pages 720–721.

The first paragraph provides important historical background and an overview of the book's content.

What details in the review give readers a feel for the liveliness of the author's style?

Explain the purpose of the last sentence, referring to both its content and its style.

Literature Model

Sam Phillips did not set out to make rock & roll history when he founded Sun Records in 1952. History came to him, walking through the doors of his converted storefront studio, the Memphis Recording Service, in the form of Elvis Presley, Jerry Lee Lewis, Roy Orbison, Johnny Cash and Carl Perkins, among others. But as Colin Escott and Martin Hawkins explain in *Good Rockin' Tonight*, Phillips presided over the birth of rock & roll because he had the instinctive wisdom to recognize the wealth of talent at his doorstep, the indefatigable energy to record as much of it as possible and the discriminating genius to select the pick of the litter to bear Sun's immortal yellow rooster-at-dawn logo. . . .

But the most impressive thing about *Good Rockin' Tonight* is that its narrative drive is every bit as contagious as the music it celebrates. "Long on feel and short on contrivance" is how Escott, in his preface, describes the explosive hybrid of blues, country, gospel and rockabilly that came to be known as the Sun Sound. It is an apt description of the book as well. *Good Rockin' Tonight* reads like a day at Phillips's office, with its breathless parade of frantic farm-boy rockers, blustery blues singers and hillbilly crooners passing daily in front of the Sun microphones. . . .

Phillips . . . wasn't a great businessman; his biggest stars had all left the label by 1963. But the breadth of his vision and the depth of his faith in the music he recorded and released is eloquently documented here. From Sun-rise to Sun-set, *Good Rockin' Tonight* is the last word on the first great rock & roll record label.

David Fricke, "Sam Phillips and the Birth of Rock & Roll," *Rolling Stone*

6.7 Writing Activities

Write a Book Review

Select a nonfiction book you have read, and write a review of it for your school newspaper. First, consider your audience's knowledge and interest level. Then, make notes about the author's opinions and ideas and about your responses.

- Write a thesis statement summarizing the author's purpose and your opinion of the book.
- Include your own response to the book.

PURPOSE To write a book review
AUDIENCE High school students and teachers
LENGTH 1–2 paragraphs

Cross-Curricular: Music

Find a review of any nonfiction book, including a biography or autobiography, on a topic related to music. Read the review carefully. Then use the information in the review to write 100–200 words of text for the jacket of the book. If necessary, provide background information about the author and the subject, and quote striking sentences from the book or review.

Grammar Link

Punctuate and capitalize titles correctly.

BOOK TITLE: *Good Rockin' Tonight*
BOOK REVIEW: "Sam Phillips and the Birth of Rock & Roll"

Write the titles listed below correctly. Underline the titles that should be italicized.

1. one writer's beginnings [book]
2. an electronic job hunt [magazine article]
3. U.S. news & world report [magazine]
4. the charge of the light brigade [poem]
5. great lady on a white horse [short story]
6. playing through [magazine article]
7. new forces of nationalism [chapter in a book]
8. the world almanac and book of facts [book]
9. the new york times [newspaper]
10. long day's journey into night [play]
11. the new york public library desk reference [book]
12. the rime of the ancient mariner [poem]
13. a midsummer night's dream [play]
14. a perfect day for bananafish [short story]
15. the waves [book]

See Lesson 20.2, pages 682–683; Lesson 21.9, pages 718–719; and Lesson 21.10, pages 720–721.

WRITING PROCESS IN ACTION

PERSUASIVE WRITING

In preceding lessons, you have learned the techniques of persuasive writing. You have had the chance to present and support an opinion, create an ad, and write a product evaluation and a complaint letter. Now it's time to apply what you've learned. In this lesson you're invited to write a letter persuading someone in authority to change a rule in a game or sport that you enjoy playing or watching.

• Assignment •

Context	Years of playing or watching have convinced you that a rule change would enhance a certain sport or game. You have decided to write a letter to the people who have the power to change the rules. You want to persuade them to adopt the rule change you propose.
Purpose	To write a brief persuasive essay on a rule change you propose for a sport or game you play or enjoy watching
Audience	The rules committee, governing body, or manufacturer of the sport or game you want to change
Length	1 to 2 pages

The following pages can help you plan and write your letter. Read through them and then refer back to them as you write. However, do not feel tied down by these guidelines. Remember, you're in charge of your own writing process.

Prewriting

Should professional football reinstate the use of instant replays? Should Pin the Tail on the Donkey be changed to Tape the Tail on the Donkey to avoid cruelty to animals? Maybe an idea for a rule change came to mind the minute you read this assignment. If not, the suggestions on the notepad may help you.

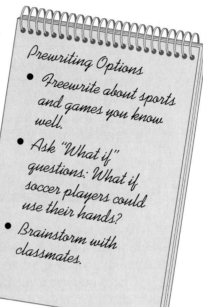

Prewriting Options

- *Freewrite about sports and games you know well.*
- *Ask "What if" questions: What if soccer players could use their hands?*
- *Brainstorm with classmates.*

When you have identified a rule change to propose in your letter, spend some time exploring the change to see if it is a reasonable one. Consider potential short- and long-term consequences and the effect of the change on players and spectators.

Once you have chosen your topic, express your position clearly and directly in a thesis statement. Then think about how to approach your audience. You will be writing to the people responsible for the rules of the game, so you know that you won't need to provide background information and clarify terms. You will, however, need to present compelling and convincing evidence to support your position.

When gathering evidence, look for facts and valid opinions. Although facts are generally the stronger kind of evidence, it might be difficult to find hard facts to support your position. Therefore, you may have to cite the opinions of experts who have specific knowledge of your sport or game.

Prewriting Tip

To gain a better understanding of your audience, use the questions in Lesson 6.3, page 284.

Drafting

In persuasive writing more than in other kinds of writing, your effectiveness depends upon both what you say and how you say it. Choose a tone that is appropriate for the point you want to make. Then, as you write, choose specific words with strong positive or negative connotations to bolster your argument.

Now you are ready to state your case. Begin with an introduction that will create interest in your topic and motivate your audience to read on. Then state your position clearly and precisely. In the model on the next page, note how Mark Mathabane introduces his position on the emergence of power rackets on the professional tennis circuit.

Drafting Tip

For suggestions about using precise words and words with strong connotations, see Lesson 6.5, page 292.

Literature Model

*T*he U.S. Open, America's premier tennis event, is under way and at the end of its two hectic weeks of fierce competition, new champions will be crowned in the men's and women's fields. But one of the hottest controversies on the professional tennis circuit will remain unresolved: the threat to the integrity of the game proposed by the new breed of power rackets. . . . Over the past three or four years, these rackets have transformed the sport of tennis from one of skill and finesse to one of sheer power.

Mark Mathabane, "A Plague on Tennis"

As you provide evidence in support of your position, be sure to respond to opposing viewpoints. Ignoring arguments against your viewpoint gives readers an excuse to dismiss it.

Once you have presented your evidence, write a conclusion that puts an exclamation point on your argument. You want your readers to act on your proposal, so you need to leave them with a convincing call to action.

Revising Tip

When revising your letter, you may need to qualify or limit your arguments to avoid generalizations. For example, state that "*Some* experts believe . . . ," not "*Everyone* believes . . ."

Revising

To begin revising, read over your draft to make sure that what you've written fits your purpose and audience. Then have a **writing conference.** Read your draft to a partner or small group. Use your audience's reactions to help you evaluate your work so far. The Revising Checklist can help you and your listeners.

Revising Checklist

- *Is my position stated in a clear thesis statement?*
- *Is the supporting evidence convincing? Have I addressed opposing viewpoints?*
- *Are the facts and opinions relevant and credible?*
- *Does the conclusion relate to the evidence?*
- *Is the tone appropriate?*

Editing

Once you are happy with the content of your letter, **proofread** it carefully for errors in grammar, usage, mechanics, and spelling. Use the questions at the right as a guide.

In addition to proofreading, use the Self-Evaluation list below to assess your letter. When you're satisfied, make a clean copy and proofread it one more time.

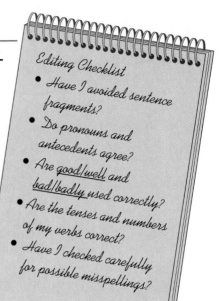

Editing Checklist
- *Have I avoided sentence fragments?*
- *Do pronouns and antecedents agree?*
- *Are good/well and bad/badly used correctly?*
- *Are the tenses and numbers of my verbs correct?*
- *Have I checked carefully for possible misspellings?*

Self-Evaluation

Make sure your persuasive letter—

- focuses on a rule change in a sport or game you know well
- addresses potential problems and consequences of the rule change
- follows a plan that includes a strong thesis statement and a clear call for action
- uses valid evidence and logical reasoning
- follows correct grammar, usage, mechanics, and spelling

Proofreading

For proofreading symbols, see page 88.

Presenting

You're almost ready to send your letter off to the powers that be. But what if your proposal is rejected? That doesn't have to be the end. How about submitting a letter to the editor of a newspaper or a magazine that is read by fans of the sport or game of your choice?

Journal Writing

Reflect on your writing process experience. Answer these questions in your journal: What do you like best about your persuasive letter? What was the hardest part of writing it? What did you learn in your writing conference? What new things have you learned as a writer?

Persuasive Writing
Literature Model

In his autobiography Kaffir Boy in America, *Mark Mathabane, a black South African,*
describes how he "escaped" his country's oppressive apartheid system on a tennis scholarship
that sent him to the United States. As you read the excerpt below, look for evidence
Mathabane uses to support his views on the emergence of power rackets in professional
tennis. Then try the activities in Linking Writing and Literature on page 311.

The U.S. Open, America's premier tennis event, is under way
and at the end of its two hectic weeks of fierce competition,
new champions will be crowned in the men's and women's
fields. But one of the hottest controversies on the professional tennis
circuit will remain unresolved: the threat to the integrity of the game
posed by the new breed of power rackets.

A power racket is much bigger than a traditional racket. It's
almost two rackets welded together. Its "sweet spot"—the best
place for the ball to be struck, in the center of the racket head—is
abnormally large.

Over the past three or four years, these rackets have transformed the sport of tennis from one of skill and finesse to one of sheer power. They have removed a compelling reason for players to develop all-round games, as did champions of the past.

"Power-hitters" like Andre Agassi, Ivan Lendl, Jennifer Capriati and Monica Seles typify this change. Some tennis experts, among them the commentator Bud Collins and the champion Jimmy Connors, have gone so far as to call for a ban on power rackets at high levels of competition.

When I took up tennis in the early 1970's the sport was synonymous with wooden rackets. The players I idolized, enjoyed watching, and sought to emulate—Arthur Ashe, Stan Smith and Rod Laver—all relied on wooden rackets to carve out illustrious careers and win major championships, including Wimbledon and the U.S. Open.

Their talent and finesse on the court were unmistakable. They served, volleyed and hit ground-strokes flat, sliced or with topspin, and whenever the occasion demanded, they played delicate touch strokes, such as angled drop shots. In sum, they possessed all-round games. They were the closest thing to the "complete player" and a delight for spectators to watch.

The demise of wooden rackets changed all that. The nature of tennis today is, in a word, power. The new rackets can generate so much power in the hands of just about anyone that players of modest abilities are transformed into giant-killers on the court, capable on any given day, usually in the early rounds, of defeating the game's finest.

Are power rackets good for tennis? The weekend player has certainly benefited from them. Their large "sweet spot" can compensate for poor vision, awkward footwork and lapses in concentration.

Charles March Gere, *The Tennis Party*, 1900

But at the professional level these rackets have had a ruinous effect. After all, the true test of a champion is not whether he or she can hit the ball at 100 miles an hour. Racket control, variety of strokes, footwork, concentration, conditioning and above all, the ability to out-think one's opponent, are the marks of great champions.

One need only recall the impeccable styles and court acumen[1] of players like Althea Gibson, Don Budge, Margaret Court, Yvonne Goolagong and Billie Jean King to get the point.

Most tennis fans I know would rather watch the symphonic[2] play that was characteristic of these players than the "boom-boom" tennis matches of their modern replacements. With a few notable exceptions such as John McEnroe, Martina Navratilova, Boris Becker and Zina Garrison, most tennis professionals today play predictable, insipid[3] and monotonous tennis.

Their robotic games are hopelessly lacking in variety. Armed with rackets that behave like cannons on the court, all these players are content to do, all day if need be, is keep firing the same "boom-boom" missiles until their opponents drop dead.

Some people have argued that power rackets are a great equalizer and enable small players like Michael Chang to compete with big, tall players like Boris Becker. I disagree. I believe that a player of Michael Chang's talents can compete with the best using any racket.

I know it's unrealistic to expect a return to wooden rackets. For players and racket manufacturers, there's simply too much money in the new rackets. But one would hope that for the sake of the lovely sport of tennis, already tarnished by commercialism and unsportsmanlike behavior, professional tennis players and racket makers would curb the mania[4] for more powerful rackets.

Something can be learned from major league baseball's insistence on wooden bats. The rule recognizes that it should be the batter's ability, not the bat, which drives that pitch out of the ball park. The same should apply to tennis. Fans at the U.S. Open and other major tournaments around the world deserve to watch tennis at its best. And the best tennis remains that provided by players with complete games.

1 acumen (əkyoo′ mən) shrewdness

2 symphonic (sim fän′ ik) harmonious; having all parts combined in a pleasing arrangement

3 insipid (in sip′ id) dull and lifeless

4 mania (mā′ nē ə) a persistent enthusiasm; a craze

Linking Writing and Literature

Readers Respond to the Model

What central idea unifies Mark Mathabane's writing, and how persuasive is his argument?

Explore Mark Mathabane's persuasive writing by answering these questions. Then read what other students thought about his writing.

1. How does Mathabane view the use of power rackets in recreational tennis? on the professional tennis circuit?
2. What kind of background information does he provide his audience?

3. What are two facts and two opinions Mathabane uses as evidence to support his position?
4. What specific action does Mathabane call for in his conclusion?

This selection was about the new power rackets being used in professional tennis matches. I liked that the writer backed up his opinions with more than one fact. I most enjoyed the part where he talked about the finesse earlier tennis players had when they played with the wooden racket. The author seemed very concerned about real tennis fans and the game of tennis itself. I think he must be a true tennis fan because he feels so strongly about this topic. Tennis is my favorite sport, and I agree with the author. It's refreshing to hear this point of view.

Torré Triplett

The part that really got my attention was when Mathabane said that the player's ability counts most in the game. I disagree. I think that good sportsmanship and having a good time are more important. If I had written this selection, I would have made this point. I would not recommend this selection to a friend because I disagree with the opinion it expresses.

Maritza Pagán

Unit 6 Review

Reflecting on the Unit

Summarize what you have learned in this unit by answering the following questions.

- What are some characteristics of good persuasive writing?

- Why is knowing your audience so important in this type of writing?

- When creating an ad, what four goals should you keep in mind?

- What is an effective three-step plan to follow when writing a letter of complaint?

- How is a book review like a product evaluation?

Adding to Your Portfolio

Choose a selection for your portfolio.
Look over the persuasive writing you have done during this unit. Select a completed piece of writing to put in your portfolio. The piece you choose should show some or all of the following:

- a position supported with facts and opinions that have been evaluated
- evidence that appeals to both reason and emotion
- an awareness of the audience to whom the writing is targeted
- a clear thesis statement, supporting details, and a conclusion calling for action
- precisely chosen words with appropriate connotations

Reflect on your choice.
Attach a note to the piece you chose, explaining briefly why you chose it and what you learned from writing it.

Set goals.
How can you improve your writing? What skill will you focus on the next time you write?

Writing Across the Curriculum

Make a history connection.
Scan the opinion page in your local and national newspapers. Find an editorial or a letter to the editor on a historical or political topic of interest to you. Read the editorial carefully and then draft a letter composed of two or three paragraphs to the editor of the paper, supporting or opposing the writer's position.

Skills and Applications

Unit 7 Review

Research Paper Writing
Prewriting: Planning and Researching

Like a detective, the writer of a research paper must search for the facts. You need to gather data and let the evidence lead you to a conclusion.

Types of Research Papers

Research papers come in many forms. The following chart lists the most common forms.

Types of Research Papers	
Summary	The writer explores a topic by summing up the opinions of other writers but does not express an opinion about it.
Evaluative	The writer states an opinion and backs it up with evidence found in primary and secondary sources.
Original	The writer does original research on a topic and reports on his or her findings.
Combination	The writer combines approaches, such as evaluating the research of others and then conducting original research.

Draw Up a Schedule

After choosing a type of paper, sketch a schedule. A good research paper can't be written in a weekend. Since the paper requires research, schedule ample time for gathering information, as shown below.

Four Weeks	Three Weeks	Two Weeks	One Week
Planning, researching, and outlining	Drafting	Revising	Editing and presenting
April 8	April 15	April 22	April 29

May
6
paper due!

Select a Topic

After making a schedule, select a topic. Spend a little time in the library skimming books and encyclopedia articles. Researching and writing will be easier if you are curious about the topic you choose.

Amy Colleen Bryan, a student at Lexington High School in Lexington, Virginia, was interested in the dramatic tale of the sinking of the *Titanic* in 1912. Throughout this unit, you will see examples of notes, outlines, and drafts leading to a finished research paper about the *Titanic*. You can read Amy's final paper in Lesson 7.6.

Besides your interests, consider what resources are available. If you have only one source on a topic, you will have only one viewpoint. On the other hand, selecting, condensing, and interpreting a mountain of information about a broad topic is difficult. This diagram shows how to identify an appropriate research paper topic.

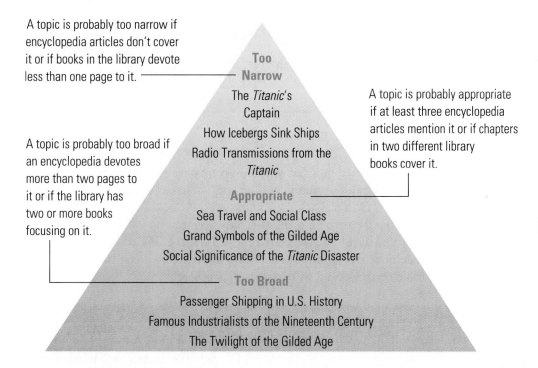

A topic is probably too narrow if encyclopedia articles don't cover it or if books in the library devote less than one page to it.

A topic is probably appropriate if at least three encyclopedia articles mention it or if chapters in two different library books cover it.

A topic is probably too broad if an encyclopedia devotes more than two pages to it or if the library has two or more books focusing on it.

Too Narrow
The *Titanic's* Captain
How Icebergs Sink Ships
Radio Transmissions from the *Titanic*

Appropriate
Sea Travel and Social Class
Grand Symbols of the Gilded Age
Social Significance of the *Titanic* Disaster

Too Broad
Passenger Shipping in U.S. History
Famous Industrialists of the Nineteenth Century
The Twilight of the Gilded Age

Examine the Topic

As you continue to read about your topic, you will begin to determine your central idea. Examine your topic from various points of view. Amy might have considered the following perspectives: How did the owners of the *Titanic* respond to the disaster? What did survivors recall about the sinking? Whom did investigators blame for the tragedy? Don't worry if some angles lead to dead ends. For now just try to think critically about the topic from several perspectives.

> **Drafting Tip**
>
> As you define special terms in your paper, you may want to review the characteristics of a good definition. See Lesson 5.6, pages 234–236.

To set a clear path for research, identify three to seven questions to answer first. In trying to answer these questions, you will discover other questions, as the diagram below shows. Let your central idea guide you in selecting questions but not in arriving at answers.

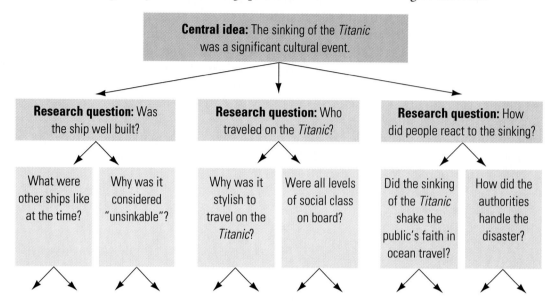

Locate Information

You may use two types of sources—primary and secondary. A primary source is a firsthand account of an event, such as a *Titanic* survivor's testimony before Congress. A secondary source is a secondhand account, such as an article analyzing the survivor's comments. When available, use primary sources to give your report a degree of authority that's hard to achieve using only secondary sources. The chart below lists some basic sources used in social studies research.

Sources of Information on Social Studies Topics		
Type	**Definition**	**Examples**
Periodicals	Magazines and journals devoted to history and written for nonscholarly audiences	*American Heritage* focuses on topics in United States history. *Zillions* covers consumer and economic issues of interest to many students.
Reference Books	Specialized works that provide excellent background information on social studies topics	*Encyclopedia of American History* lists and describes events in U.S. history. *Encyclopedia of World History* lists significant world events in chronological order.
News Updates	Publications that provide information on current events and people	*Facts on File* is an up-to-date review of current events. *Current Biography* provides detailed biographies of important people in the news.

Develop a Working Bibliography

As you begin your research, you will need to develop a working bibliography, a record of the books, articles, and other sources you will consult for your paper. When you have found a source, skim it to see if it has any useful information. If it does, record the publication data—the publishing company, the city, and date of publication—on an index card, as shown below. You will then be able to find the source easily when you conduct research in more detail. Writing complete bibliography cards now will make it easier to write the final bibliography, referred to as the list of works cited, later on. Number your cards in the upper right-hand corner so you can keep them in order. You can also write yourself notes, as shown on the magazine note card below.

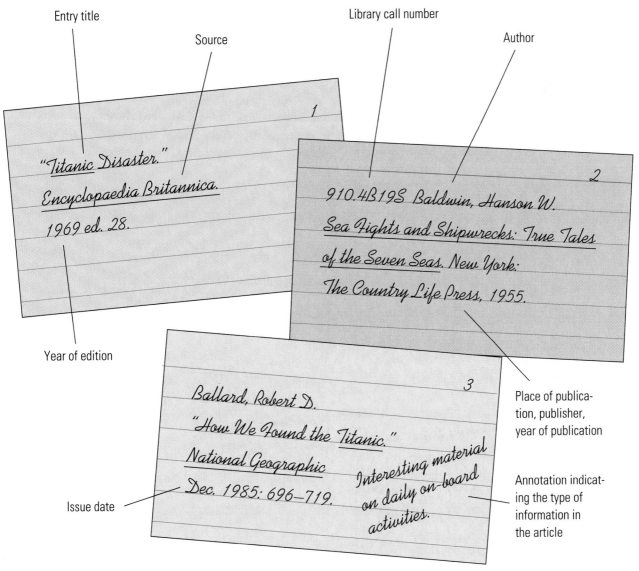

Entry title

Source

Library call number

Author

1

"Titanic Disaster."
Encyclopaedia Britannica.
1969 ed. 28.

Year of edition

2

910.4B19S Baldwin, Hanson W.
Sea Fights and Shipwrecks: True Tales
of the Seven Seas. New York:
The Country Life Press, 1955.

3

Ballard, Robert D.
"How We Found the Titanic."
National Geographic
Dec. 1985: 696–719.

Interesting material on daily on-board activities.

Issue date

Place of publication, publisher, year of publication

Annotation indicating the type of information in the article

Take Notes

Grammar
Prewriting Tip

When taking notes, remember to use quotation marks to enclose direct quotes. For more information about quotation marks, see Lesson 21.9, pages 717–719.

Just as you use three-by-five cards when developing your working bibliography, you can use cards when taking notes. As you find a piece of information that you can use, write it on a note card. In the upper right-hand corner of the note card, write the number of the source from the working bibliography.

You might want to put your initial by any of your own thoughts that you jot down on note cards. By initialing your own comments, you will be able to keep straight which information comes from other sources and which comes from your own interpretation.

Three ways of taking notes—paraphrasing, summarizing, and writing direct quotations—are shown below.

> Nor did Congress care what happened to Third Class. Senator Smith's *Titanic* investigation covered everything under the sun, including what an iceberg was made of ("Ice," explained Fifth Officer Lowe), but the steerage [another name for Third Class] received little attention. Only three of the witnesses were Third Class passengers. Two of these said they were kept from going to the Boat Deck, but the legislators didn't follow up. Again, the testimony doesn't suggest any deliberate hush-up—it was just that no one was interested.
>
> The British Court of Enquiry

Third-class passengers
Fate of Third Class passengers was not considered important in official inquiries.
— only three Third Class witnesses appeared before Congress; none before British Court of Enquiry.
— no follow-up

Summarizing: condensing the main ideas and important details.

Third-class passengers   8
Disaster investigations were thorough, but no one cared about Third Class passengers.
Congress failed to follow up on stories of discrimination against Third Class passengers.
British court found no discrimination, although no Third Class passengers testified. Page. 108

Paraphrasing: restating the information in your own words.

Third-class passengers
"Only three of the witnesses were Third Class passengers. Two of these said they were kept from going to the Boat Deck, but the legislators didn't follow up."

Page 108

Direct quotation: writing the passage exactly as it appears in your source and putting it in quotation marks on your card.

Examine Sources Critically

Because each source you use is written by a person with particular interests, knowledge, and values, be alert to each author's perspective. Try to get sources that approach your topic from different angles. Asking the following questions will help you evaluate your sources.

Questions About Sources
1. What is the author's purpose in writing the book or article?
2. Has new information been discovered since the source was written?
3. Are the views of the author often disputed by others knowledgeable on the topic?
4. Would someone from another culture, religious group, economic class, or time period view the events differently?

Grammar
Editing Tip

When editing, you will be correcting capitalization and punctuation. To make this task easier, be sure to use correct capitalization and punctuation in your notes.

Avoid Plagiarism

Plagiarism occurs when a writer uses someone else's ideas or statements and presents them as his or her own. Even when unintentional, plagiarism is a serious offense. You must give credit to the sources of information you use in your paper. To avoid plagiarism, keep clearly documented notes so you know where you got each piece of information. Lesson 7.4 will teach you how to credit your sources accurately.

7.1 Writing Activities

Skills Practice

1. Write an explanation of why each topic below is too broad, too narrow, or about right for a seven-page research paper.

- the Mongol Empire under Genghis Khan
- the controversy over the death penalty
- the childhood of Indira Gandhi
- African independence movements since 1945

2. For each general area, suggest two topics appropriate for a seven-page research paper:

- great leaders in African history
- relations between China and Japan
- cultural diversity in South America
- railroads in United States history

3. Choose one of the topics you developed above. Write research questions about the topic that reflect each of the following areas of interest: economics, politics, geography, religion, and military.

Your Research Paper

Select a topic for your own research paper, and write three to seven research questions about it. Begin to develop a working bibliography and to take notes on this topic, following the format you learned in this lesson.

Research Paper Writing
Prewriting: Outlining

Your rapidly growing pile of note cards is threatening to bury you. What do you do? It's simple. You learn the lesson that military generals throughout history have learned. If you can break up your opposition into smaller units, you can quickly take control of the situation.

Develop an Outline

An outline is a summary of the main points and the ideas that support them. Soon after you have begun your research—before your pile of note cards is too big—you can start to outline your paper. Outlining will help you organize your information and further focus your research efforts.

A Working Outline As you take notes, look for ways to classify the facts and ideas you find. For example, look for similar features, such as two facts about the role of an individual in a historical event. Begin to group the note cards as you classify them.

As you make decisions on how to organize your cards, you are developing the information you need to write a working outline. The reasons you use to categorize your cards will become the headings on your working outline. If some cards do not fit under the headings, set them aside. Later you can decide whether to keep or discard them.

Think of this first outline as a preliminary sketch. As you continue your research, revise your working outline and your central idea to reflect new information. If a heading seems to be less important than it did earlier, try making it a subheading or discarding it altogether. The annotations on the example outline show how to organize headings and information.

The Impact of the Titanic's Sinking

I. The Gilded Age
   A. Growth of prosperity
   B. Unprecedented wealth for a few people

II. Development of Technology
   A. Titanic symbolized the era
      1. Four blocks long, eleven stories high
      2. Facilities
   B. Trial voyage, 5–11–1911

III. Maiden Voyage, 4–10–1912
   A. Passenger list
      1. Illustrious, wealthy patrons
      2. Modest passengers and poor immigrants
   B. Distinguished crew
   C. Ship considered unsinkable

IV. The Disaster
   A. All iceberg warnings ignored
   B. Iceberg rips 300-foot gash in ship's hull
   C. Rescue calls go out to other ships
   D. Lifeboats lowered
      1. Confusion because drills had never been held
      2. Lifeboats sent off half-filled

Designate main headings by Roman numerals.

Indent subheads under main headings, and label with capital letters.

Beneath subheads, further label and indent items.

Never have just one numeral or letter at a given level of organization. For example, if you have a (1), you must have a (2) as well.

Three Methods of Organization As you categorize your note cards, begin to consider ways to organize the information within each category. Three of the most common methods of organization are described below.

Methods of Organization		
Method	**Description**	**Example**
Chronological	Information arranged according to when it happened; often used in papers describing historical changes	A paper surveying the changing policies of China under Mao Zedong toward the Soviet Union
Cause and Effect	Items arranged showing how one development directly influenced another; often used in papers explaining why something happened	A paper analyzing how each new idea led to another during the Industrial Revolution
Cumulative	Items arranged according to how important or how familiar each one is; often used in papers evaluating results	A paper evaluating the impact of the Gulf War of 1991

Prewriting Tip

For further help in developing a thesis statement, you may wish to review Lesson 2.3, page 60.

Develop a Thesis Statement

When you have completed your research, prepare a final version of your outline, showing the organization of your paper. You can now rewrite your central idea into a concise, tightly focused thesis statement —a single sentence describing your topic and your approach to it. Even though the thesis statement may change slightly in later stages, it will provide a clear direction for your writing.

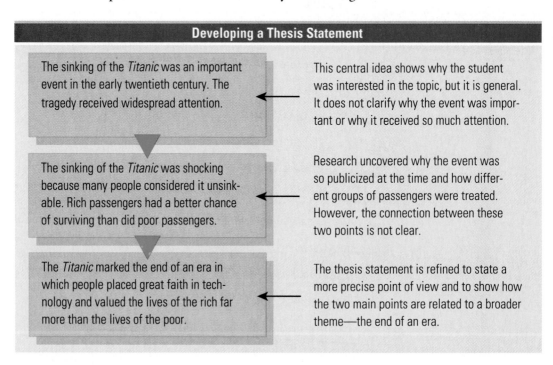

Developing a Thesis Statement

The sinking of the *Titanic* was an important event in the early twentieth century. The tragedy received widespread attention.

This central idea shows why the student was interested in the topic, but it is general. It does not clarify why the event was important or why it received so much attention.

The sinking of the *Titanic* was shocking because many people considered it unsinkable. Rich passengers had a better chance of surviving than did poor passengers.

Research uncovered why the event was so publicized at the time and how different groups of passengers were treated. However, the connection between these two points is not clear.

The *Titanic* marked the end of an era in which people placed great faith in technology and valued the lives of the rich far more than the lives of the poor.

The thesis statement is refined to state a more precise point of view and to show how the two main points are related to a broader theme—the end of an era.

The type of thesis statement you use will depend upon the type of paper you write. The chart below lists some types of thesis statements.

Four Types of Thesis Statements	
Original	Used to demonstrate new information that you have developed
Evaluative	Used when stating your opinion on a topic
Summary	Used when your paper primarily reports the ideas of others
Combination	Utilizes two of the three other categories listed in this chart

7.2 Writing Activities

Skills Practice

1. Create a chronological outline by organizing the statements below under the given headings.

Headings
I. Pre-Berlin Wall Political Divisions
II. The Wall as a Physical Barrier
III. Beginnings of Reunification

Statements
• The Berlin Wall was erected in 1961.
• After World War II ended in 1945, Berlin was divided and occupied by the four major Allied powers: the United States, Britain, France, and the Soviet Union.
• Many people defected from East Germany by escaping to West Berlin in the 1950s.
• The Berlin Wall prevented free movement between East Germany and West Berlin until 1989.
• The Berlin Wall was dismantled in December 1989.
• East Germany became a separate state in 1949.
• In the 1980s, the Soviet Union reduced its influence over East Germany.

2. Organize the following notes into cause-and-effect order.
• Because of trade, Mali prospered.
• Because of scholars, Mali became an intellectual center.
• In the 1300s, the West African kingdom of Mali controlled trade across the Sahara.
• Because of its prosperity, Mali was able to recruit scholars to live there.

3. Organize the following notes in order of importance, beginning with the most important.
• People today do not dress like ancient Romans.
• Roman architecture still has influence today.
• Compared to the Greeks, the Romans produced few significant philosophers.
• Latin, the Roman language, has had a great impact on European languages.

4. Write a thesis statement for each of the outlines you developed in 2 and 3 above.

Your Research Paper

Prepare a working outline for your own research paper, and draft a thesis statement.

Research Paper Writing
Drafting

According to legend, in London in the middle of the 1800s, there lived a historian who would not begin writing until he had read every book available on the topic he was researching. Today that task would be nearly impossible. So many books—not to mention journals, magazines, and newspapers—exist that it would be ambitious to read everything written about even a narrow topic. At some point, like every researcher, you must begin to write.

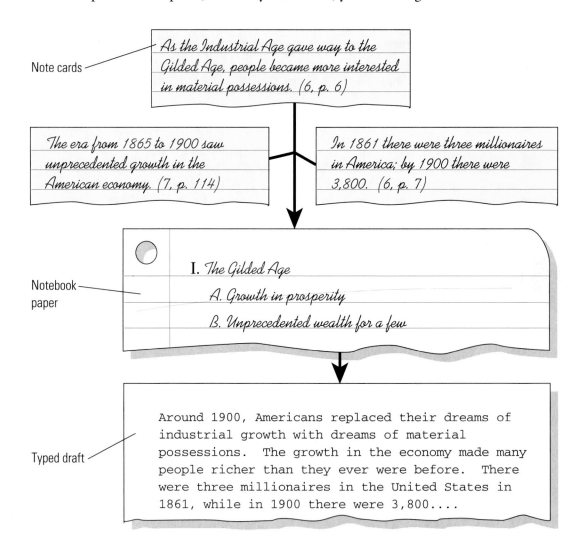

Note cards

As the Industrial Age gave way to the Gilded Age, people became more interested in material possessions. (6, p. 6)

The era from 1865 to 1900 saw unprecedented growth in the American economy. (7, p. 114)

In 1861 there were three millionaires in America; by 1900 there were 3,800. (6, p. 7)

Notebook paper

I. The Gilded Age

A. Growth in prosperity

B. Unprecedented wealth for a few

Typed draft

Around 1900, Americans replaced their dreams of industrial growth with dreams of material possessions. The growth in the economy made many people richer than they ever were before. There were three millionaires in the United States in 1861, while in 1900 there were 3,800....

Write from an Outline

In writing your first draft, use your outline as a map to guide the direction of your writing. Write at least one paragraph for each main heading in your outline. As shown on the preceding page, you can combine information from several cards to help you state one idea. Try to keep your ideas flowing logically from one to the next, but don't get bogged down by details or by trying to find the perfect words to express your ideas. This is only your first draft—you will revise it later.

As you take information from note cards and insert it into your draft, also insert the number of the note card next to the information. This way you will have a clear and accurate record of your sources to use in the final version of your paper.

As you write, you may run into some difficulty in handling a large quantity of information. The chart below gives advice for overcoming some problems that commonly occur in the early stages of drafting.

Grammar

Revising Tip

Your paper will be more interesting to read if you vary your sentences. Before you revise your first draft, look at examples of sentence structures you might use. See Lessons 13.3 and 13.4, pages 507–510.

Drafting: Problems and Solutions	
Problem	**Solution**
I have a large stack of note cards. How do I handle so many notes?	Read through them, and remove anything that duplicates another note or that contains only irrelevant material. Set them aside for possible use later.
I have many notes on some aspects of my topic but very few on others. What should I do?	Conduct more research, or look again at your outline to see if you can write a good paper with the notes you now have. If so, revise your outline.
Do I have to write the first part of the paper first, the second part second, and so on?	Write in whatever way is easiest for you. If you write sections out of sequence, when you revise, pay close attention to the transitions between sections and to how forcefully you are building your argument.
How can I overcome writer's block when I sit down to write my first draft?	Don't worry about finding the perfect words. Just get the ideas down. You can always improve your writing in your next revision.
I seem to run out of time before I get very far into my writing. How should I plan my study time?	Set aside at least three hours for nothing but writing your paper. Eliminate distractions by going to the library or asking your family not to disturb you.

Write an Introduction and a Conclusion

A good paper has an identifiable introduction and conclusion. An effective introduction attracts and holds the reader's attention; it should also contain your thesis statement, which clearly describes the topic or central idea of the paper. A few suggestions for how to start your introduction are shown below. Each describes a way to capture the attention of your readers.

Tips for Writing Introductions	
Summarize	Providing an overview of the main headings in your outline will make your reader comfortable with the topic.
Describe	Include an unusual fact or amusing anecdote about your topic. This will entertain your reader and show your topic from a new perspective.
Pose a Question	If you are writing about the Civil War, for example, ask your reader to imagine what the United States would be like today if the South had won.
Use a Quotation	An eyewitness opinion often is more emotional and gripping than comments by later analysts.
Describe a Scene	In the model paper for this lesson, the writer describes the eerie underwater wreckage of the *Titanic*, transporting the reader to the decks of the once elegant ship.

Your conclusion needs to pull the paper together and alert the reader that you are finishing your argument. As with the introduction, a conclusion can be written in many different ways. Since it is the last part of your paper, you can use the conclusion to impress your main points in your reader's mind.

Tips for Writing Conclusions
1. Summarize your main points to refresh the reader's memory of your arguments.
2. Reexamine the topic and its effects. Did your opinion on the topic change as you researched it? Did any part of your research surprise you?
3. Consider the future. How does your research put your topic in a new light? What questions for further research can you think of? How will you personally approach this topic in the future?

7.3 Writing Activities

Skills Practice

Based on the following outline entries and note cards, write a cohesive paragraph about the early life of South African president Nelson Mandela. Imagine that your audience is a group of seventh-grade students who are just beginning to study South Africa in their social studies class. Use only the entries and note cards that you need to write one good paragraph.

Outline Entries

I. Early years marked Mandela as a leader and a lover of democracy
A. Adopted by the chief of the Thembu
  1. Listened to many legal cases
  2. Went to school to study law
B. Suspended from school for leading a student strike
C. Urged by adoptive father to stop the strike
  1. Father wanted him to become chief of the Thembu
  2. Father had arranged a marriage for him
D. Moved away to go to school in Johannesburg

Note Cards

Mandela's father was the second-most-important leader of the Thembu. On his deathbed, his father asked Chief David Dalindyebo to take Mandela into his care.

———

The Thembu, though governed by a chief, had a long heritage of democracy. Mandela heard these stories at tribal meetings with his father.

———

Despite the South African government's attempts to diminish the authority of the tribal leaders, Dalindyebo still heard and decided on many legal issues. Mandela often sat in on the court deliberations.

———

Chief Dalindyebo was grooming Mandela to become chief of the Thembu.

———

Mandela went to Fort Hare College in 1938 to get a bachelor of arts degree, the first step toward getting a law degree.

———

In 1940 the authorities at Fort Hare College decided to lessen the responsibilities of the student council.
- Mandela was a member of the council.
- He led a student strike in protest and was suspended.

———

Chief Dalindyebo urged him to stop the strike and return to class. The chief also had chosen a wife for Mandela.

———

As a result, Mandela left home and moved to Johannesburg.

———

"My guardian felt it was time for me to get married. He loved me very much and looked after me as diligently as my father had. But he was no democrat and did not think it worth while to consult me about a wife." From page 21 of *Nelson Mandela, the Man and the Movement* by Mary Benson (New York: Norton, 1986).

Your Research Paper

Write a first draft of your own research paper, including an introduction and a conclusion. Follow your working outline.

Research Paper Writing
Citing Sources

When did Christopher Columbus first sail to the Americas? The answer is common knowledge: 1492. When did the industrial revolution begin? Not everyone can answer that—and even those who can might give different answers. When you write a research paper, you must know when to tell your readers where you got your information and when you can assume they know and accept your information.

Document Appropriately

The information you include in your research paper must be properly documented. In other words, you need to identify where you found the information. By citing the sources of all ideas, statements, and quotations that you used, you allow your reader to judge the validity of the information. For example, information quoted from a respected historical journal will carry more weight than a statement quoted from a television dramatization.

Why Document   By citing your sources properly, you acknowledge those people whose ideas you are using. Since they developed the facts, opinions, and analyses that you have borrowed, they deserve a mention in your work.

In addition, by citing your sources properly, you avoid plagiarism—the presentation of someone else's ideas or statements as your own. You should cite your source whether you use the information word for word or you paraphrase it.

What Not to Document   While you want to credit others for their work, you don't have to cite the source of common knowledge. Examples of common knowledge include widely accepted facts, such as that the Andes are in South America or that the Magna Carta was signed in 1215. Widely known proverbs, famous quotations, and simple definitions are also common knowledge. The following chart gives examples of statements and whether or not they need documentation.

Deciding What to Document		
Type of Information	Citation?	Explanation
Direct quotation: The sinking of the *Titanic* "signaled the end of the Edwardian era in all its cocky opulence."	Yes	The source of each direct quotation should be given because the words are clearly borrowed from someone else.
Opinion: Americans equated size with security and excess with success.	Yes	This is a paraphrase of another author's conclusions. Sources of conclusions and other opinions should be cited.
Opinion: Completed in 1912, the *Titanic* was considered the most luxurious ship of its day.	No	The luxuriousness of the ship is an opinion widely enough accepted that it is common knowledge.
Statistics: The *Titanic* was 4 city blocks long and 11 stories high.	Yes	Phrasing the measurements in terms familiar to general readers was the work of another writer, so the source should be cited.
Data: The ship sailed out of London and was to reach New York one week later.	No	General information about the trip could be found in several reference works. None of this information comes from one particular work.

Revising Tip

As you revise your paper and move information from one part of the paper to another, be careful to move the documentation with the information.

Format Citations Properly

Three basic formats exist for citing sources. You may use parenthetical documentation with a Works Cited list, footnotes, or endnotes.

Parenthetical Documentation   The model paper in Lesson 7.6 uses parenthetical documentation to credit sources. In this method, you place a short citation, usually the writer's last name and a page reference, in parentheses, immediately after the information that requires citation. If they wish, readers can find the author's full name and the complete title of the source listed at the end of the paper in the Works Cited list.

In 1861 there were three millionaires in the United States; in 1900 there were 3,800 (Wade 7).

What do you do if the source has two or more authors? Or no author? The chart below shows how to handle these and other common situations when using parenthetical documentation. Several of the examples are taken from Amy Bryan's paper. Note that book and magazine titles are printed in italics; titles of articles and shorter works are set in quotation marks. If your typewriter or computer does not have italic type, underline book and magazine titles.

Drafting Tip

For more information about italicizing (underlining) titles or using quotation marks, see Lessons 21.9, page 719, and 21.10, page 720.

Examples of Parenthetical Documentation	
Type of Source	**Note in Text**
A work by one author when the research paper uses only one work by that author, such as *A Night to Remember* by Walter Lord	Give the author's last name and the page number: (Lord 108).
A work by one author when the paper uses more than one work by that author, such as "Haunting Images of Disaster," one of two articles by Natalie Angier used in the paper	Use the author's name, an abbreviation of the title, and the page number: (Angier, "Haunting Images" 58).
A work by one author when the author's name is mentioned in the text, such as, "Mrs. H. D. Bishop observed . . ."	Use only the page number: (437).
A work by two or three authors, such as *Catastrophe and Crisis* by Jeremy Kingston and David Lambert	Give authors' names and the page number: (Kingston and Lambert 145).
A work with no author or editor listed, such as "*Titanic* Disaster," an article in *Encyclopaedia Britannica*	Give the title of the article, or an abbreviation of it, and the page number: ("*Titanic* Disaster" 28).

Preparing your citations should be simple if your note cards and bibliography cards are carefully organized. In your first draft, whenever you included anything from your note cards, you wrote the numbers of the card and the page immediately after. Now you can replace those numbers with your parenthetical documentation.

Footnotes Another form of citation is the footnote. In footnoting, a single number follows the information cited in the text. This number refers to a note at the bottom of the page. The first footnote from a source includes the author's full name, the complete title of the work, place of publication, publisher, copyright date, and page reference. All other footnotes from the same source include only the author's last name and the page reference. Since the number in the text and the number at the beginning of the footnote are usually printed slightly above the regular text line, they are known as superscripts. Footnotes are numbered consecutively throughout the paper. If you use footnotes, be sure to keep them on the same page as the cited information.

Examples of Footnote and Endnote Styles

1. **For a book with one author:**
   Lawrence Beasley, <u>The Loss of the Titanic</u>
     (London: Phillip Allan, 1929) 174.

2. **For a book with more than one author:**
   Jeremy Kingston and David Lambert, <u>Catastrophe</u>
     <u>and Crisis</u> (New York: Facts on File, 1979) 145.

3. **For a magazine article:**
   Natalie Angier, "Haunting Images of Disaster,"
     <u>TIME</u> 23 Sep. 1985: 58.

4. **For a newspaper article:**
   "<u>Titanic</u> in Peril on Leaving Port," <u>New York</u>
     <u>Times</u> 11 Apr. 1912: A1.

5. **For an encyclopedia article:**
   "<u>Titanic</u> Disaster," <u>Encyclopaedia Britannica</u>,
     1969 ed.

Vocabulary
Editing Tip

When you edit your paper, check the spelling of the names of authors you cite against your list of works cited for possible misspellings.

Endnotes Endnotes appear at the end of the paper instead of on every page. They are placed on a separate page under the heading "Notes," with a double space between each notation. Superscript numbers identify both the citation in the text and the endnote.

Include a List of Works Cited

Whichever form of citation you use, at the end of the paper you should include a list of works cited. The following are some general tips for formatting works-cited lists.

Preparing a List of Works Cited

1. Arrange entries in alphabetical order according to the author's or editor's last name. Write the name in reverse order—last name first. For works with two or more authors, reverse only the first author's name.

2. If no author or editor is given, alphabetize the entry by the title, disregarding the word *a, an,* or *the* at the beginning of a title.

3. When more than one work by an author is listed, use three hyphens followed by a period rather than repeat the author's name.

4. If an entry runs more than one line, indent every line five spaces after the first.

5. Book and magazine titles should be in italics or else underlined.

6. Article titles should be enclosed in quotation marks.

The chart below shows how to organize and punctuate different types of entries in a works-cited list. Some examples are taken from Amy Bryan's paper.

Works-Cited Entries	
Source	**Example of Entry**
Book with one author	Baldwin, Hanson W. *Sea Fights and Shipwrecks: True Tales of the Seven Seas.* New York: Country Press, 1955.
Book with two or three authors	Kingston, Jeremy, and David Lambert. *Catastrophe and Crisis.* New York: Facts on File, 1979.
Book with four or more authors	Brown, Lester, et al. *State of the World 1990.* New York: Norton, 1990.
Government publications	United States Bureau of the Census. *Statistical Abstract of the United States: 1989.* 109th ed. Washington: GPO, 1989.
A selection in an anthology	Bishop, Mrs. H. D. "The *Titanic:* From a Lifeboat, 15 April 1912." *Eyewitness to History.* Ed. John Carey. Cambridge: Harvard UP, 1987. 436–437.
Encyclopedia article	"*Titanic* Disaster." *Encyclopaedia Britannica.* 1969 ed.
Magazine article	Ballard, Robert D. "How We Found the *Titanic.*" *National Geographic* Dec. 1985: 696–719.
Newspaper article	"New Liner *Titanic* Hits an Iceberg; Sinking by the Bow at Midnight; Women Put Off in Lifeboats; Last Wireless at 12:27 A.M. Blurred." *New York Times* 15 Apr. 1912: A1.
Letter to the editor	Drelicharz, Sue. Letter. *Chicago Tribune* 3 Oct. 1991, sec. 1: 26.
Lecture, address, or sermon	Baker, Reverend A. B. Sermon. Trinity Church. Princeton, 21 Apr. 1912.
Television or radio program	*"The War We Left Behind."* Narr. Leslie Cockburn. Prod. Leslie and Andrew Cockburn. *Frontline.* PBS. WTTW, Chicago, 29 Oct. 1991.

Not all sources fit the categories listed above. To cite such sources, adapt one of the above entries, arranging the information in the following order:

• **Author information** should appear at the beginning of the entry, with the author's last name first. If the source has two or more authors, reverse only the first author's name. If no author is listed, list the editor. If no editor is listed, begin with the title.

- **Title information** follows any author information and lists the title of the article, essay, or other part of the book first if needed, then the title of the book.

- **Publication information** follows the author and title and, as needed, lists the editor's name, edition number, volume number, and series name. Always list the place of publication, publisher's name, and publication date. If appropriate, list page numbers.

7.4 Writing Activities

Skills Practice

1. For each piece of information below, tell whether you think source documentation is necessary. Explain the reasons for your answer.

- Kemal Ataturk ruled Turkey from 1923 to 1938.
- Ataturk declared, "Our thoughts and our mentality will become civilized from head to toe."
- According to one historian, Ataturk was more concerned with reforming his country than with increasing his power.
- The status of Turkish women was raised during Ataturk's rule.
- Radical changes instituted by Ataturk threatened to destroy traditional Turkish culture.

2. Each of the following entries from a list of works cited contains two mistakes in punctuation. Copy each entry, correcting the punctuation as you do so.

- Ghareeb, Edmund. *The Kurdish Question in Iraq*. Syracuse, Syracuse University Press. 1981.
- "British Views of Disunion." *New York Times*: 8 February 1861: 8

- Koch, Adrienne and William Peden. eds. *The Life and Selected Writings of Thomas Jefferson*. New York: The Modern Library. 1944.
- Lih, Lars T. "Gorbachev and the Reform Movement." *Current History* October 1987: 310

3. Using parenthetical documentation, write the citation that would appear in the text for each of the following sources:

- a quotation from page 21 of *Abuse of Power* by Theodore Draper
- a quotation from page 17 of *England Under the Tudors* by G. R. Elton, one of three books by Elton used in the paper
- a quotation from page 100 of *The Mau Mau from Within*, by Donald J. Barnett and Karari Njama
- a quotation from page 19 of an article in *Time* magazine, "Six Minutes," with no author listed

Your Research Paper

Prepare five samples of the documentation of information in your research paper and five samples of your works cited entries.

Research Paper Writing
Revising

Even the Declaration of Independence, one of the most powerfully written documents in United States history, needed revision. Thomas Jefferson, the Declaration's author, knew what every good writer knows: almost anything you write can be improved through revision. Your first draft is an important beginning, but you should plan to make changes to it.

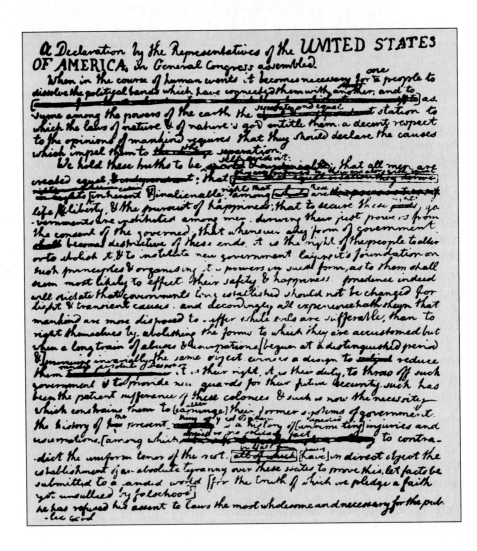

Improve Your Paper

After writing your first draft, take a break. By setting your paper aside for a few hours, or even days, you give yourself a chance to return to it with a fresh eye. You should be able to sharpen your choice of words, to improve the flow of ideas, and to correct mistakes in grammar, spelling, and punctuation that you missed as you were drafting. By asking yourself questions such as the ones listed in the following chart, you can identify what to revise in your paper.

Drafting Tip

As you revise your paper, try to keep a mental note of the types of changes you make most often. This can help you when you begin drafting another paper.

Revising: Questions and Answers	
Questions	**Identifying What Needs Revising**
Have I given the first draft a clear focus?	Review your thesis statement to be sure it is clearly stated.
Have I accomplished what I set out to do in this paper?	Skim your paper, looking for and deleting irrelevant information. Add ideas that readers might need to follow your reasoning.
Do my paragraphs flow logically and smoothly?	Read the last sentence of each paragraph and the first sentence of the following paragraph. If the flow of ideas is not smooth, add transitions.
Have I used someone else's ideas without credit?	Scan your paper, reading each sentence that does not contain a citation. Add documentation if necessary.
Do my examples and supporting details help clarify my main point?	Replace the questionable examples or details with direct and appropriate ones.
Have I used terms that are not familiar to the average reader?	Scan your paper, picking out specialized terms or unusual words. Review your definitions or explanations of each of these terms or words.
Is my choice of words interesting and appropriate?	Delete redundant words and phrases. If a word is repeated often, find synonyms for it. Replace vague terms with more precise ones.
Are my introduction and conclusion effective?	Read your first and last paragraphs. Each should highlight the main point of the paper.

Revising Tip

For examples of different kinds of supporting details you can use when revising your first draft, see Lesson 2.6, page 74.

Using proofreading marks, like the ones shown on the next page, saves time during revision and makes your copy easier to read. To review proofreading symbols, see page 88.

The ~~Titanic~~ [ship] also ~~had~~ carried a ~~good~~ [distinguished]
crew. The captain of the Titanic was
Edward Smith. [and] ~~He~~ was a favorite among
high-society American. ~~He~~ ~~also~~ [who] had been
captain of the Olympic, the Titanic's
sister ship, Upon sailing, ~~it was reported~~
~~that~~ Second Officer C. H. Lightoller [reportedly]
said, "It was clear to everyone on board
that we had a ship that was going to
create the greatest stir British shipping
circles had ever known" (218). When a woman
asked a deckhand ~~was~~ [if] the Titanic [was] really
"unsinkable," ~~the deckhand~~ [he] replied, "God
himself could not sink this ship"
(Friedrich 70).

[This overconfident attitude was matched by] ~~They~~ had perfect weather for the first
four days of sailing. Then at 9:00 [A.M.] ~~in the~~
~~morning~~ on April 14, the Titanic receive[d]s
iceberg warnings from ~~another ship,~~ the
Coronia. Two more warnings ~~was~~ [were] received
that afternoon, yet Captain Smith dismissed
all three. ~~He~~ never decreas[ing]ed the ship's
speed of 22 knots or changed [ing] its course.
At 7:30 P.M. ~~another ship,~~ the Californian,
warned the Titanic of ice.

Revise a Social Studies Paper

Certain writing problems are common in social studies papers. The chart on the next page discusses several of these problems.

Solving Problems in Social Studies Papers	
Problem	**Solution**
History papers often include many specific dates. The numerals in dates can easily be confused or written down or typed incorrectly.	Double-check all dates in an almanac or encyclopedia.
History papers may use words with out-of-date meanings.	Check the usage of terms in a dictionary that includes extensive usage information.
Economics, sociology, and psychology papers often use terms with precise, specialized meanings.	Check the usage of terms in a specialized dictionary for that particular field of study or in a college or unabridged dictionary.
Papers on foreign cultures often are based on sources written by people from outside that culture.	Try to include the viewpoint of people from the culture about which you are writing.
Papers on current events often quote people who are consciously trying to influence public policy and hence are not objective observers.	Try to find contrasting points of view about any given issue.

7.5 Writing Activities

Skills Practice

Each of the following pairs of statements includes an excerpt from a first draft of a social studies paper and a new bit of information that the writer found after completing the first draft. Use the new information to help you revise the italicized information in each first-draft excerpt.

- **First draft:** In 1960, forty-three-year-old John Kennedy became the youngest person elected president of the United States. *As the youngest person ever to serve* as president, he brought great energy to government.
  New information: Theodore Roosevelt was only forty-two years old when, following the assassination of President McKinley, he became president in 1901.

- **First draft:** Jimmy Carter defeated Gerald Ford in the 1976 presidential election. Carter served as president *until 1980.*
  New information: Carter served only one term as president, from 1977 to 1981.

- **First draft:** *Between 1400 and 1450,* many English peasants raised only enough corn for their own use.
  New information: At the time Columbus reached the Americas in 1492, Native Americans were growing corn, cacao, and potatoes. These were important new crops that Europeans learned how to grow at the beginning of the 1500s.

Your Research Paper

Revise the first draft of your research paper according to the guidelines in this lesson.

Research Paper Writing
Editing and Presenting: A Model Paper

IN CONGRESS, JULY 4, 1776.

Do you know how to impress an audience? Thomas Jefferson did. After Jefferson revised the Declaration of Independence, he commissioned a final version in elegant, flowing handwriting. Although the ideas in the Declaration were powerful, Jefferson still took time to prepare a document that would help him win support for his ideas. To win the most support for your research paper, you should follow Jefferson's example.

Prepare the Final Copy

After you have made your paper as clear, logical, and coherent as you can, focus your attention on editing issues. Proofread your paper, watching for mistakes in citations, grammar, spelling, punctuation, and word usage. If you read your paper aloud, your ear will help you catch many mistakes that you might miss by reading silently. Once this is done, you can type or print your final copy. The checklist below can help you remember to examine all the important aspects of your final version.

Editing and Presenting Checklist
1. Have I checked the paper for missing words or letters?
2. Have I considered the proper meaning of the words I've used?
3. Have I corrected all grammar and punctuation mistakes?
4. Is each word spelled and capitalized correctly?
5. Is the paper neat and easy to read?

Present Your Paper

Check that your paper includes all necessary elements. The following list describes some elements often required by teachers.

Editing Tip

Sentences constructed in the active voice are usually stronger than those constructed in the passive voice. To review active voice, see Lesson 15.7, page 562.

Elements of a Complete Paper

1. A title page should contain the title of the paper, your name, your teacher's name, the course name or number, and the date. Center the title and your name in the middle of the page, and list the other information in the lower right corner.
2. A table of contents contains the final outline of the paper.
3. The text should be cleanly typed and double-spaced, with 1.5-inch margins on the sides and 1-inch margins at the top and bottom. Be sure to number your pages.
4. If endnotes are used, they should immediately follow the text.
5. A list of works cited, listing all sources of information used in the final version of your paper, should appear at the end of the paper.

The remainder of this lesson presents a model paper, "The *Titanic*: Was It the End of an Era?" by Amy Colleen Bryan, a student at Lexington High School, in Lexington, Virginia. The callouts in the margins highlight the items discussed throughout this unit.

7.6 Writing Activities

Skills Practice

1. On a separate paper, rewrite the following sentences to make them clearer.

- Each of the United States is represented by two people in the Senate.
- The first Europeans to explore the Great Lakes were missionaries and fur-trapping operations.

2. Copy the following sentences, and correct the problems of word usage and writing style.

- The Great Depression through millions of people out of work.
- Andrew Jackson was tough, shrewd, and had experience as a soldier.

3. Read these sentences, and identify misleading comments or poorly constructed thoughts.

- Because he owned slaves, Thomas Jefferson probably would have sided with the Confederates in the American Civil War.
- Gandhi was beloved by the Indian people because of his nonviolent principles, and he had admirers around the world as well.
- The purchase of Alaska increased the mineral wealth of the United States, and gold was soon discovered in the Canadian Yukon.

Your Research Paper

Prepare the final version of your research paper, and hand it in to your teacher.

THE *TITANIC:*
WAS IT THE END OF AN ERA?

Amy Colleen Bryan

Bryan grabs her reader's attention by describing vivid scenes of the wreck.

"All around us there was this twisted mass of wreckage and tons of coal spread around. And then there was this lady's shoe. It was incredible, just haunting" (Lemonick 70). On September 1, 1985, marine geologist Dr. Robert Ballard, with the help of U.S. and French researchers, found the *Titanic* 13,000 feet below the surface of the Atlantic Ocean. Using sonar and a robot submarine, Dr. Ballard located the ship about 500 miles south of Newfoundland, where it had sunk seventy-three years before. Thirteen thousand feet below the surface the water is totally black with no marine life and a temperature of 39° F, yet the *Titanic* had been well preserved. It was sitting upright covered with silt, and although it split in half during the sinking, the grand staircase, railings and wooden deck were still intact, the planks still visible. On closer investigation, Ballard's crew found five cases of wine with the corks still in them, china plates, wash basins, chamber pots, and luggage.

How does this background information help the reader?

Completed in 1912, the *Titanic* was considered the most luxurious ship of its day. The *Titanic* has been called a "monument to the Gilded Age" (Marbach 46) and its sinking "signaled the end of the Edwardian era in all its cocky opulence" (Angier, "*Titanic* Find" 68). Was the sinking of the *Titanic* really the end of an era?

Bryan states her thesis as a question she is trying to answer in her paper.

The two decades before World War I have been labeled the Gilded Age for a number of reasons. After the American Civil War, as westward expansion resumed, industry expanded and many Americans discovered wealth for the first time. Around 1900 the optimistic "dream" for industrial growth turned into an optimistic dream for material possessions (Wade 6). Many people were richer than ever before. In 1861 there were three millionaires in the United States; in 1900 there were 3,800 (Wade 7). Americans equated size with security and excess with success (Wade 299). They wanted to expand ➡

technologically and materially. They prized business success and placed faith in extravagance.

In the beginning of the 1900s there were no movie, radio, or television stars to idolize, so "the public depended on the socially prominent people for all the vicarious glamour that enriches drab lives" (Lord 109–110). In fact the rich lifestyle of the Gilded Age existed for very few. Those who did fit the description held a wealth almost beyond comprehension, a wealth that has never quite been repeated. The life and fate of the rich and famous received the most attention. John Jacob Astor IV, the richest man in America, possessed thirty million dollars (an amount almost equivalent to $350,000,000 in today's money). Benjamin Guggenheim followed with twenty million and Isidor Straus and George Widener each had ten million (Davie 45).

Besides material growth, the time around 1900 was full of invention and technology, from automobiles to rubberbands (*Secrets*), and it seemed like the *Titanic* was the epitome of this era, symbolizing all that this time had to offer.

Work began on the *Titanic* in 1909 at Harland & Wolff's shipping yards in Belfast, Ireland. It took three thousand men two years to build. When completed, the ship was made of 46,000 tons of steel and measured 882.5 feet long and 105.7 feet high. Comparatively speaking, the *Titanic* was four city blocks long and eleven stories high (Lord 170). The inside of the ship contained facilities ranging from Turkish baths and tennis courts to sun parlors, a theater, and a miniature golf course.

As news of the extravagant technological wonder spread throughout the world, it soon became known as the "unsinkable" *Titanic*. Experts considered the ship "unsinkable" because of its vast size and the strength and stiffness of the floor; the keel, longitudinals, and inner and outer bottoms were greater in size, weight, and thickness than in any other ship; the floor extended up the sides of the ship so as to "frame" it; the whole length of the hull was stiffened by deep web frame girders; the hull was divided into sixteen watertight compartments, four of which could be flooded and the ship would still float; the deck beams were ten inches thick and held to the sides with steel; and the elaborate pipe systems could delay the rise of water ("Experts" 981). The structural ➡

Transitions help the reader follow the course of events.

Why do you think Bryan put the dimensions of the Titanic *in these terms?*

Presenting Tip

Including a diagram or a photograph of the *Titanic* in the final draft would enhance a reader's understanding of the dimensions of the ship.

stability of the ship, unparalleled for its time, was ready to be tested in open waters.

The *Titanic* set sail from Belfast Harbor on May 11, 1911. Her trial voyage lasted eight hours, and upon her return, her builders were confident that she was indeed "unsinkable." She left Southampton at twelve noon on April 10, 1912, on her maiden voyage. She was to reach New York City one week later.

There were approximately 2,207 passengers on board when the *Titanic* left the harbor (Friedrich 70), 706 of whom were immigrants traveling to the United States for the first time (Baldwin 47). About 350 of the biggest names in American and British society were on the first-class list ("*Titanic* in Peril"). These people paid $4,350 for their seven-day trip, an amount almost equivalent to $50,000 in today's money (Ballard 712). The passenger list included: General John Jacob Astor IV and his wife; Major Archibald Butt, military aide to President William Howard Taft; John B. Thayer, Vice-President of the Pennsylvania Railroad; Charles M. Hays, President of Grand Trunk Railways in Canada; Mr. and Mrs. Isidor Straus, owners of Macy's Department Store; and J. Bruce Ismay, chairman and managing director of the White Star Line.

The ship also carried a distinguished crew. The captain of the *Titanic* was Edward Smith, who had been a captain of the *Olympic*, the *Titanic's* sister ship, and was a favorite among high-society Americans. Upon sailing, Second Officer C. H. Lightoller reportedly said, "It was clear to everyone on board that we had a ship that was going to create the greatest stir British shipping circles had ever known" (218). When a woman asked a deckhand if the *Titanic* was really "unsinkable," he replied, "God Himself could not sink this ship" (Friedrich 70).

This over-confident attitude was matched by perfect weather for the first four days of sailing. Then at 9:00 A.M. on April 14, the *Titanic* received iceberg warnings from the *Coronia*. Two more warnings were received that afternoon, yet Captain Smith dismissed all three, never decreasing the ship's speed of 22 knots or changing its course. At 7:30 P.M. the *Californian* warned the *Titanic* of ice. Second Operator Harold Bride ignored these signals because he was figuring accounts. Around 9:30 P.M. Commander Lightoller ordered Frederick Fleet to get up in the crow's nest to watch for icebergs. At 11:00 P.M. the ➡

Bryan converts amounts of money to modern equivalences so the reader can understand their significance.

Grammar

Editing Tip

When editing your paper, check that you have used commas correctly. For information about comma usage, see Lesson 21.6, pages 705–713.

What form of organization does Bryan use in describing the voyage?

Californian again warned the *Titanic* about ice. First Operator Phillips, who relieved Bride, told the *Californian* operator to shut up and leave him alone because he was busy (Baldwin 49). The *Titanic* still steamed full speed ahead at 22 knots.

Up in the crow's nest, at 11:40 P.M., 1300 miles from New York City, Fleet saw an iceberg looming in the · distance. The officer on the bridge gave the order to turn the ship hard to starboard. The orders were too late. There was a faint jarring that lasted for ten seconds. The result was a 300-foot gash along the starboard side of the hull. Five water-tight compartments had been flooded, enough to sink the ship. The first wireless call for help went out at 12:15 A.M. The *Virginian*, the *Carpathia*, and the *Baltic* received the call and started for the ship. Evans, the wireless operator for the *Californian*, had turned off his signals and retired to bed fifteen minutes before. Ironically, the *Californian* was less than ten miles from the *Titanic* (Angier, "Haunting" 58).

At 12:45 A.M. the first distress rocket was fired, and the first lifeboat was lowered. Launching arrangements were confused; because no lifeboat drills had been held beforehand, loading was random. Women and children were given first priority along with the first-class passengers in general (Kingston and Lambert 145). Half-filled boats were asked to take more passengers but did not; they feared tipping and sinking once they got into the water (Baldwin 53). Lifeboat 6 had a capacity of sixty-five passengers but left with only twenty-eight (Baldwin 53). Lifeboat 1 had a capacity of forty people but left with only twelve (Friedrich 70). Two of these passengers were women, the rest men—among them were three millionaires and J. Bruce Ismay.

At 1:40 A.M. the crew fired the last rocket into the air and at 2:05 A.M. lowered the last lifeboat, "collapsible D," into the water. Benjamin Guggenheim and his valet came on deck in full evening dress, saying "We've dressed in our best and are prepared to go down like gentlemen" (Friedrich 70). When Astor tried to board a lifeboat with his wife, he was refused; he told her he would meet her later.

Around 2:10 A.M. the wireless operator sent the last call for help. As the ship sank at 2:20 A.M., Mrs. H. D. Bishop observed from a lifeboat, "It began to slide gently downwards. Its speed increased as it went down head ➡

Eyewitness descriptions carry more power than an analysis from a secondary source.

first, so that the stern shot down with a rush. . . . As the ship sank we could hear the screaming a mile away. Gradually it became fainter and died away" (437).

Many lifeboats made little attempt to help other survivors in the water. Fireman Harry Senior was swept off the ship as it went down. Later he explained, "I tried to get aboard a boat, but some chap hit me over the head with an oar. There were too many people in her" (435).

The *Carpathia* arrived at dawn to pick up survivors. By 8:50 A.M. the *Carpathia* was headed for New York City with 705 *Titanic* passengers (Lord 171–172; Secrets). The total death count was 1,502.

When the news reached American newspapers, the New York Times was so confident that the *Titanic* was unsinkable that it carried only a small front page story about the accident ("New Liner"). However, on April 16 when the news was confirmed, the stories filled up the entire front section of the New York Times for five consecutive days. New York City swarmed with people trying to find out who had survived. The New York Times ran front page stories on the rich and famous who were on board, with an entire article devoted to John Jacob Astor alone; almost as an afterthought the 1,800 others who might have died were listed (Lord 110).

The shock of this calamity raised many questions. Almost immediately after the disaster, both the United States and Great Britain set up investigations. Through these investigations, the injustices that occurred on the *Titanic* that night were made public. These were conditions that would "never get by the social consciousness (or news sense) of today's press" (Lord 108). There were lifeboats for only half the passengers on board, and of the 1,500 people in the water, only 13 were picked up by lifeboats (Kingston and Lambert 145). Greatly debated was the treatment of the second-class, third-class, and steerage passengers. Of the women in first-class, only 4 of 143 drowned (3 by choice); 15 of 93 women in second-class drowned; and 81 of 179 women in third-class drowned. All except 1 of 30 children in first- and second-class survived, but only 23 of the 76 children in steerage survived (Lord 107).

For the most part the third-class passengers had to fend for themselves. Some in third-class thought that access to the lifeboats was a privilege of the first- and ➡

How does this sentence help the reader?

Why is this sentence a helpful lead-in to the paragraph?

second-classes (Lord 108–109). Unbelievably, there was a higher loss of third-class children than first-class men (Lord 108). A steward stationed on the third-class deck testified that some men were kept locked below deck until almost 1:15 A.M. Thirty-four percent of the first-class men were saved, while only eight percent of the second-class and twelve percent of the third-class survived (Davie 45). When lawyers investigated the situation, however, White Star Line was indifferent, as were the press and even Congress. The British enquiry said it found no discrimination (Lord 108).

The investigation procedures for each country were very different but ultimately resulted in the same conclusions. Some recommendations that resulted from the investigations were: life preservers and regulation lifeboats for all passengers on board, lifeboat drills, a wireless operator on duty at all times, and a double-skin for the hull, longitudinal bulkheads, and water-tight decks. The United States and British governments set up the International Ice Patrol and the first International Convention for the Safety of Life at Sea was begun in London in 1913 ("*Titanic* Disaster" 28).

Laws at sea changed, but also Americans realized that in their haste to progress, they had sacrificed safety; in their quest for material possessions, they had forgotten the spiritual. In a sermon given at Princeton University the Sunday after the *Titanic* disaster, Reverend A. B. Baker said:

> Was there not something of self-confidence and self-sufficiency in the contention that it was perfectly safe, that it could outride any ocean storm and come unharmed through any danger to which it might be exposed? . . . It will not do to put our confidence in ships nor in anything that represents the boastful progress of the age.

In this disaster the world had lost a number of the noted wealthy. As a result many Americans changed their view of wealth and success. The *Titanic* was the "last time the special position of First Class was accepted without question" (Lord 109). Many Americans quickly realized that prominent people under stress could be selfish and conceited (Lord 109). As Walter Lord noted, "The *Titanic* was the last stand of wealth and society in the center of public affection" (109). The First World War and later the Depression made sure of that. After the *Titanic* disaster it ➡

Set off any quotations longer than three lines by indenting the entire passage.

Since the author's name is given in the text, only the page number is needed in the citation.

was more difficult for Americans to be as confident of technology and progress. The *Titanic* "mirrored" the Gilded Age. It had seemed to be the peak of all technology, wealth, and luxury. Life after its sinking was never the same.

Many people have tried to pinpoint reasons for the *Titanic* disaster. The chance is one in a million that a ship will hit an iceberg and sink to the ocean floor (Beasley 174). Was this disaster destined by fate? Had people become so sure of themselves that Divine Intervention was needed to put them back in their place?

The Gilded Age was a period of extremes—growing wealth and growing technology. The sinking of the *Titanic* shocked Americans back to reality. It made them retrace their steps and look at the world in a different light, a world where it was harder to be so confident and sure of oneself. Dr. Charles H. Parkhurst tried to explain the reason for this tragedy by saying:

> The two sore spots which really run into one another and which constitute the disease that is gnawing into our civilizations are the love of money and the passion for luxury. These two combined are what sunk the *Titanic* and sent 1500 souls prematurely to their final account ("Religious Views" 939).

Bryan ends her paper with a strong quotation.

Presenting Tip

In your final bibliography, cite only those sources from which you actually used information in your research paper. Your teacher may ask you to include a brief annotation for each work cited in which you explain the source's content and usefulness.

Works Cited

Angier, Natalie. "After 73 Years, A *Titanic* Find." *Time* 16 Sep. 1985: 68.

—. "Haunting Images of Disaster." *Time* 23 Sep. 1985: 58.

Baker, Reverend A. B. Sermon. Trinity Church. Princeton, 21 Apr. 1912.

Baldwin, Hanson W. *Sea Fights and Shipwrecks: True Tales of the Seven Seas.* New York: Country Life Press, 1955.

Ballard, Robert D. "How We Found the *Titanic*." *National Geographic* Dec. 1985: 696–719.

Beasley, Lawrence. *The Loss of the* Titanic. London: Philip Allan, 1929. ➡

Bishop, Mrs. H. D. "The *Titanic:* From a Lifeboat, 15 April 1912." *Eyewitness to History*. Ed. John Carey. Cambridge: Harvard, 1987. 436–437.

Davie, Michael. Titanic: *The Death and Life of a Legend*. New York: Alfred A. Knopf, 1986.

"Experts on the *Titanic* Wreck." *Literary Digest* 11 May 1912: 981.

Friedrich, Otto. "When the Great Ship Went Down." *Time* 16 Sep. 1985: 70.

Kingston, Jeremy, and David Lambert. *Catastrophe and Crisis*. New York: Facts on File, 1979.

Lemonick, Michael D. "Treasures Reclaimed from the Deep." *Time* 2 Nov. 1987: 70.

Lightoller, Commander. Titanic *and Other Ships*. London: Ivor Nicholson and Watson, 1935.

Lord, Walter. *A Night to Remember*. New York: Henry Holt, 1955.

Marbach, William D. "The Sea Gives Up a Secret." *Newsweek* 16 Sep. 1985: 46.

"New Liner *Titanic* Hits an Iceberg; Sinking by the Bow at Midnight; Women Put Off in Lifeboats; Last Wireless at 12:27 A. M. Blurred." *New York Times* 15 Apr. 1912: A1.

"Religious Views of the *Titanic*." *Literary Digest* 4 May 1912.

Secrets of the Titanic. Videocassette. Dir. Nicholas Nixon. With Martin Sheen. National Geographic Society Video, 1986, 58 min.

Senior, Harry. "The *Titanic:* A Fireman's Story, 15 April 1912." *Eyewitness to History*. Ed. John Carey. Cambridge: Harvard, 1987. 434–435.

"*Titanic* Disaster." *Encyclopaedia Britannica*. 1969 ed.

"*Titanic* in Peril on Leaving Port." *New York Times* 11 Apr. 1912: A1.

Wade, Wyn Craig. *The* Titanic—End of a Dream. New York: Rawson, Wade, 1979.

Unit 7 Review

Reflecting on the Unit

Summarize what you learned in this unit by answering the following questions.

- What are the important elements of planning and researching a paper?
- How and why do you outline the information gathered during your research?
- What is the purpose of a thesis statement?
- What are the important steps to follow when you draft a research paper?
- How and why should you document information you use in your paper?
- What techniques can help you revise and present your paper effectively?

Adding to Your Portfolio

Look over the research paper you prepared during this unit and put it into your portfolio. The final draft of your paper should show some or all of the following:

- an appropriate research topic and a useful working bibliography
- a clear thesis statement supported with adequate details
- an effective introduction and a strong conclusion
- clarity, logic, and coherence
- proper documentation of sources

Reflect on your choice.
Write a brief note to explain what you learned from writing your research paper. Attach the note to your paper.

Set goals.
How can you improve your writing? What skill will you focus on the next time you write?

Writing Across the Curriculum

Make a science connection.
One type of research paper is an evaluative paper. In such a paper, the writer states an opinion and backs it up with evidence found in primary and secondary sources. Scan the newspaper, a weekly newsmagazine, or a science journal, and choose an issue or topic that interests you. Draft a central idea statement presenting your opinion on the topic. Locate supporting evidence—facts and educated opinions—in primary and secondary sources. Then outline the contents of the paper, and write a thesis statement and opening paragraph for it.

Sentence Combining

Lessons

Sentence Combining
Style Through Sentence Combining

What do you have in common with writers such as Bill Cosby, Annie Dillard, Martin Luther King Jr., Amy Tan, and Rudolfo Anaya? Like them, you have a distinctive writing style, a way of communicating your personality. Developing a clear, expressive writing style requires practice, of course. By writing regularly in your journal and trying out different types of writing—poems, essays, stories, letters to the editor— you develop a range of skills. Another excellent approach for developing style is sentence combining.

Unlock Your Style

Sentence combining is a research-tested writing strategy that enables you to explore options, make choices, and develop style. This process of combining short sentences into more complex ones is the focus of this unit. Your goal, however, is not to make long sentences, but to make good ones. Sometimes you will find that longer, more complex sentences enable you to express your ideas with precision and clarity. At other times, shorter is better.

The point is that sentence combining helps you understand your stylistic options. Instead of being locked into one type of sentence and "playing it safe" with a short, choppy style that reads like a first-grade reader, you can make choices as a writer. Practice in combining unlocks your style by making you aware of writing choices.

Learn the Drill

In sentence combining, you express the same information in different ways by using four combining strategies: (1) deleting repeated words; (2) using connecting words; (3) rearranging words; and (4) changing the form of words. Consider this cluster of short, basic sentences to see how they might be combined differently.

Sentence combining is a writing strategy.
The strategy has been tested by research.
It enables students to explore options.
It enables students to make choices.
It enables students to develop style.

As you scan these sentences, your brain goes to work, drawing upon your built-in knowledge of language. You can use the four combining strategies to express these ideas in fewer words. For example, take a look at one way of combining illustrated below:

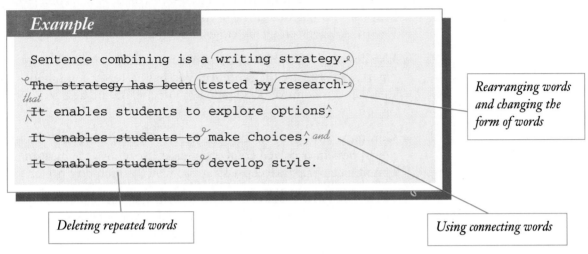

Example

Sentence combining is a (writing strategy.)

~~The strategy has been~~ (tested by research.)
that
^It enables students to explore options;

~~It enables students to~~ make choices; *and*

~~It enables students to~~ develop style.

Rearranging words and changing the form of words

Deleting repeated words

Using connecting words

Notice how editing produces the sentence that starts the section headed "Unlock Your Style" on page 350. But there are many other ways to combine these sentences. Read the ones below aloud, listening to differences in style:

1. Sentence combining is a writing strategy that has been tested by research; as options are explored and choices are made, students develop style.

2. Sentence combining, a writing strategy that has been tested by research, enables students to develop style by exploring options and making choices.

3. Enabling students to explore options, make choices, and develop style, sentence combining is a strategy for writing tested by research.

All of these sentences communicate basically the same message, but each one has a different emphasis. Which is "best"? The answer to that question depends on the *context*, your *purposes* as a writer, and your sense of *audience*. Put simply, your choice of the "best" sentence depends on what sounds right to you.

Follow the Hints

Sentence combining is easy and fun. Here are some basic suggestions that have worked for other high school students—suggestions you might try as you explore style.

1. **Whisper sentences to yourself.** As you work with clusters of sentences, try saying them aloud. This process is faster than writing, and it helps you decide on a "best sentence" to write down.

2. **Work with a partner.** By trying out sentences on a partner—and hearing your partner's ideas—you often discover new, interesting ways to solve specific challenges. Feel free to borrow ideas.

3. **Use context when choosing sentences.** Each paragraph has an emerging context—the sentences you have already combined. Reading this context aloud helps you decide on the best sentence option.

4. **Compare your sentences with those of other students.** Seeing how others have solved combining tasks broadens your awareness of sentence options. Keep asking yourself, "Which do I prefer?"

5. **Look for stylistic patterns in your writing.** Calculate the average number of words per sentence; study your sentence openers; listen to rhythms in your style. Try new patterns to stretch yourself.

6. **Take risks.** Learning to make clear, effective sentences also means taking risks and making mistakes. It actually makes *sense* to accept mistakes—even *welcome* them—as you combine sentences. After all, mistakes provide feedback for your language learning. As you learn from them, you develop an expressive style, a voice of personal authority. You come to know yourself as a writer.

As you can see, sentence combining involves the skills of talking to yourself, making judgments, and holding what you say in your short-term memory so that you can transcribe it. These are oral skills as much as they are writing skills. Good writers trust their "inner voices."

Style and Focus Workshop

Looking ahead in this unit, you will find two kinds of sentence combining. The exercises in sections 8.1 through 8.4 present clusters of short sentences, with spaces between the clusters. The exercises in section 8.5, drawn from literature selections in this book, are set up in an unclustered format.

Sections 8.1 to 8.4 give you practice in making descriptive, narrative, expository, and persuasive paragraphs. You can combine each cluster into a single sentence, but you can also leave a cluster partially combined—or combine clusters with others. The idea, always, is to take risks and create the best sentences you can. The exercises on facing pages deal with the same topic or situation. Think of these exercises as "bookends" for the writing you will do. After you have combined sentences, your task is to connect the paragraphs into a longer essay or story. Doing so will help you transfer sentence-combining skills to your own writing.

Section 8.5 invites you to test your skills against those of professional writers. As you do these unclustered exercises, you will need to figure out which ideas logically belong together. After you have done the sentence combining, you can check your version against the author's original. By studying the similarities and differences of the two passages, you will learn a great deal about your own style. Sometimes you will prefer the professional writer's sentences. Why, specifically, are they "better" than yours? However, you will sometimes prefer your own style. Can you build on this writing skill, trying it out in your own stories and essays? Either way, you will learn to write better.

Explore Your Own Style

The whole point of sentence combining practice is to improve your revising and editing skills. Practice in sentence combining helps you see that sentences are flexible tools for thought, not rigid structures cast in concrete. The simple fact that you feel confident in moving sentence parts around increases your control of revising and editing. To acquire this sense of self-confidence—one based on your real competence in combining and revising sentences—you can try strategies like those shown below.

1. **Vary the length of your sentences.** Work for a rhythmic, interesting balance of long and short sentences, remembering that short sentences can be dramatic.

2. **Vary the structure of your sentences.** By using sentence openers on occasion—and by sometimes tucking information in the middle of a sentence—you can create stylistic interest.

3. **Use parallelism for emphasis.** Experiment with repeated items in a series—words, phrases, and clauses—to understand how structural patterns work and how you can use them to advantage.

4. **Use interruption for emphasis.** Colons, semicolons, dashes, commas, parentheses—all of these are useful tools in your stylistic toolkit. Knowing how to use them well will help you.

5. **Use unusual patterns for emphasis.** That you might sometimes reverse normal sentence patterns may never have occurred to you, but such a strategy can work—if you know how to do it right.

When it comes time to rework a draft, it's important to apply what you have learned about combining and revising. The same holds true when doing peer response. If you spot a passage that could be improved with stylistic tinkering, simply write SC (for sentence combining) in the margin. This will provide a cue to apply some of the skills practiced in this unit.

8.1 Description

Exercise A: Playoff Game

Directions   Combine each cluster of numbered items into one or more sentences. Combine clusters if you wish.

1.1 The gym was jammed with students.
1.2 The gym was jammed with townspeople.
1.3 The gym was jammed with TV equipment.
1.4 The gym was sweltering.

2.1 Signs festooned the walls.
2.2 The signs were made of butcher paper.
2.3 The signs were huge.
2.4 The walls were cinderblock.

3.1 A hometown band erupted into sound.
3.2 The sound was brassy.
3.3 The sound was discordant.
3.4 Cheerleaders bounded into action.
3.5 They were like marionettes.
3.6 The marionettes were perky.

4.1 They danced in syncopation.
4.2 Their syncopation was well-rehearsed.
4.3 They danced from left to right.
4.4 They brought the crowd to its feet.

5.1 Voices chanted in unison.
5.2 The voices were hoarse.
5.3 The voices were excited.
5.4 Voices finally became a chorus.
5.5 The chorus was screaming.
5.6 The chorus had one mind.

6.1 The score was tied.
6.2 It was the fourth quarter.
6.3 There were only minutes left to play.

7.1 Noise rose in a crescendo.
7.2 The crescendo was thundering.
7.3 It was like a tidal wave of sound.

Grammar
Drafting Tip

Try opening either cluster 4 or 5 with a participial phrase. For more on participial phrases, see page 489.

Extension   What else do you picture happening in this scene? Use your description to link "Playoff Game" to "Final Seconds."

Exercise B: Final Seconds

Directions Combine each cluster of numbered items into one or more sentences. Combine clusters if you wish.

1.1 A referee's whistle made a shriek.
1.2 The shriek was high-pitched.
1.3 It pierced the jeers.
1.4 It pierced the groans.
1.5 The groans came from local fans.

2.1 Police braced themselves.
2.2 Security guards braced themselves.
2.3 They were braced for any move.
2.4 The move might signal trouble.

3.1 The hometown coach paced restlessly.
3.2 He chewed a thumbnail.
3.3 He was on the sidelines.
3.4 Both teams took positions downcourt.
3.5 They were awaiting a foul shot.
3.6 It could decide the conference title.

4.1 The opposing star was cocky.
4.2 The opposing star was grinning.
4.3 The opposing star toed the foul line.
4.4 He bounced the ball twice.
4.5 He spun it through his fingertips.

5.1 He shrugged off the catcalls.
5.2 He barely eyed the basket.

6.1 The shot lofted up in an arc.
6.2 The arc was soft.
6.3 The arc was high.
6.4 It dragged the crowd to its feet.

7.1 It hit the back of the rim.
7.2 It bounced against the backboard.
7.3 The backboard was glass.
7.4 The backboard was like a rising moon.

Extension Describe what you see happening after this scene. Share your text with a writing partner.

Exercise C: Canyon Trail

Directions Combine each cluster of numbered items into one or more sentences. Combine clusters if you wish.

1.1 The canyon trail crossed logs.
1.2 The trail was shadowy.
1.3 The logs were moss-covered.
1.4 It passed through thickets of ferns.

2.1 Wildflowers grew in clumps of yellow.
2.2 Wildflowers grew in clumps of purple.
2.3 The clumps were cheerful.
2.4 The clumps were bright.
2.5 The clumps were along the river's edge.

3.1 Huge boulders lay in the white water.
3.2 The water was rushing.
3.3 They were like hippos.
3.4 The hippos were sleeping.

4.1 The trail finally became a clearing.
4.2 The clearing was grassy.
4.3 It was filled with sunlight.
4.4 It was filled with insects.
4.5 The insects hummed.

5.1 Maple trees swelled with life.
5.2 Aspen trees swelled with life.
5.3 Leaves uncurled from buds.
5.4 The leaves were golden.
5.5 The buds were tiny.

6.1 The sky above was like a hole.
6.2 The sky was cobalt-blue.
6.3 The hole was deep.
6.4 It was rimmed by treetops.

7.1 The air smelled sweet.
7.2 The air smelled fiercely green.
7.3 It was a first taste of spring.

Vocabulary

Revising Tip

In cluster 7, try a *first taste of spring* at the beginning, in the middle, and at the end of the sentence. Which position do you think works best?

Extension Move farther into the clearing, describing what you see and sense around you. Link your description to "Throwaway."

Directions   Combine each cluster of numbered items into one or more sentences. Combine clusters if you wish.

1.1 The car lay rusting.
1.2 The car lay abandoned.
1.3 It was at the bottom of a ravine.
1.4 It was near the stream's edge.

2.1 Scabs of paint had lifted off.
2.2 The scabs were black.
2.3 The paint was oxidized.
2.4 This revealed blotches of primer.
2.5 The primer was gray.

3.1 The driver's door hung open.
3.2 It was permanently ajar.
3.3 Bullet holes ventilated the windows.

4.1 Inside was a single shoe.
4.2 It was under the dash.
4.3 Its leather was cracked.
4.4 Its leather was twisted.
4.5 Inside was a *Life* magazine.
4.6 It was from 1948.

5.1 Springs pushed through seats.
5.2 The springs were coiled.
5.3 The seatcovers were worn.
5.4 The seatcovers were fabric.

6.1 The car smelled dead.
6.2 It was now home to mice.
6.3 It was now home to birds.
6.4 It was now home to seasons.
6.5 The seasons changed.

7.1 Once its fenders had been stroked.
7.2 Once its interior had been caressed.
7.3 That day was long gone.

Vocabulary

Drafting Tip

As you begin to combine sentences in each cluster, reread your sentence from the cluster before. How does the language in that sentence relate to the new cluster?

Extension   What thoughts does the old car prompt about forgotten lives—or about recycling? Share the text you create with a writing partner.

8.2 Narration

Exercise A: Solo

Directions Combine each cluster of numbered items into one or more sentences. Combine clusters if you wish.

1.1 The mood was festive.
1.2 The mood was energetic.
1.3 The mood was focused on homecoming weekend.
1.4 This was felt especially on the dance floor.

2.1 A jazz band had played for two hours.
2.2 Their playing was inspired.
2.3 The audience was chanting for more.
2.4 The audience was appreciative.

3.1 The soloist stepped into the lights.
3.2 He mouthed his thanks to the audience.
3.3 He laced his fingers around his trumpet.
3.4 His fingers were long.
3.5 The trumpet was gleaming.

4.1 The applause grew louder.
4.2 The applause grew more enthusiastic.
4.3 He raised the trumpet.
4.4 He grinned at the flashbulbs.
4.5 The flashbulbs were exploding.

5.1 Faces below him shone expectantly.
5.2 The faces were radiant.
5.3 He nodded a cue to the drummer.
5.4 The cue was decisive.
5.5 The drummer was nearby.

6.1 Sound swirled through the room.
6.2 The notes of the solo were crisp and clear.
6.3 The solo was intricate.
6.4 The drum and bass provided a beat.
6.5 The beat was steady and insistent.

7.1 Each player in turn picked up the tune.
7.2 The players were talented.

Grammar
Revising Tip

In cluster 3, try using one or two participial phrases (beginning with *stepping, mouthing,* or *lacing*) as modifiers for the base sentence. For more on participial phrases, see page 489.

Extension Narrate what happens next in the "Solo" scenario. Link this narrative to the accompanying "Good Vibrations" exercise.

Directions Combine each cluster of numbered items into one or more sentences. Combine clusters if you wish.

1.1 Music surged through the room.
1.2 Music vibrated through the room.
1.3 It drew in the listeners.

2.1 Students moved their feet in patterns.
2.2 The patterns were rhythmic.
2.3 Students shuffled on the wax.
2.4 The wax was dusty.

3.1 Students tapped to the sound.
3.2 Students swayed with the sound.
3.3 Their bodies made shadows on the walls.
3.4 The shadows were moving.

4.1 The boys betrayed concentration.
4.2 Their faces were tight-lipped.
4.3 Their heads bobbed.
4.4 Their heads dipped.
4.5 Their arms hung loose.

5.1 The girls danced with ease.
5.2 Their ease was practiced.
5.3 They whirled with the music.
5.4 They turned with the music.
5.5 The music was irresistible.

6.1 On stage the trumpeter closed his eyes.
6.2 He threw himself into the song's windup.
6.3 The windup was a final chorus.
6.4 The chorus was triumphant.

7.1 The musicians took their bows.
7.2 The musicians were exultant.
7.3 The musicians beamed at the dancers.
7.4 The dancers cheered in unison.
7.5 The dancers clapped in unison.

Grammar
Revising Tip

In cluster 6 try an appositive—a phrase that describes the song's windup. For more on appositives, see page 487.

Extension What next? Narrate an effective ending for "Solo" and "Good Vibrations." Share your text with a writing partner.

Directions Combine each cluster of numbered items into one or more sentences. Combine clusters if you wish.

1.1 Mona reached for the travel alarm.
1.2 The travel alarm was palm-sized.
1.3 It was beside her bed.
1.4 She squinted at the numbers.

2.1 A crow screamed on the window sill.
2.2 Its screaming was brazen.
2.3 It welcomed the day's first light.
2.4 The light was a thin skin of gray.
2.5 The skin was on the landscape.

3.1 Each morning the crow did not stay long.
3.2 It stayed only for a few moments.
3.3 The moments were raucous.

4.1 It delivered its message.
4.2 It began a fixed routine.
4.3 It first bounced between the pines.
4.4 It floated to the lawn.
4.5 The lawn was dewy.
4.6 It then fussed over the dumpster.
4.7 The dumpster was next door.

5.1 Its work was finished.
5.2 The crow always spread its feathers.
5.3 The feathers were glossy.
5.4 The feathers were black.
5.5 It always headed east.

6.1 She watched its ritual once again.
6.2 She knew it was time for her work.
6.3 Her work was a run toward town.
6.4 The run was through quiet streets.

7.1 Mona had heard the crow call her name.
7.2 She now needed to get started.

Vocabulary
Revising Tip

Notice the strong, specific nouns, verbs, and adjectives in each cluster. Do your combined sentences make good use of these words? For more information on strong nouns, verbs, and adjectives, see pages 401, 415, and 422.

Extension Narrate Mona's getting out of bed in clear, precise detail. Use your narration to link "The Crow" to "Training Run."

Directions   Combine each cluster of numbered items into one or more sentences. Combine clusters if you wish.

1.1 Outside the air was cool.
1.2 It was still.
1.3 There was no hint of breeze.

2.1 Mona bent down.
2.2 She tightened her shoelaces.
2.3 She began her leg stretches.
2.4 She took time to loosen her calves.
2.5 She took time to loosen her thighs.
2.6 She took time to work out all the kinks.

3.1 Then she set off on her usual course.
3.2 She jogged easily at first.
3.3 She jogged through the damp grass.
3.4 She let her body set its own pace.

4.1 Patches of light filled the sky.
4.2 The light was creamy.
4.3 She picked up the pace.
4.4 She settled into a rhythm.
4.5 The rhythm was loping.

5.1 Sweat blossomed on her forehead.
5.2 Sweat blossomed on her arms.
5.3 Her lungs gulped for oxygen.

6.1 She turned off her usual course.
6.2 She cut through the town cemetery.
6.3 She bounded down a gravel path.
6.4 The gravel was crunchy.
6.5 She bounded past stone markers.
6.6 The markers were faceless.

7.1 Finally Mona slowed to a walk.
7.2 She listened to inner whispers.
7.3 She felt herself being drawn east.

Grammar
Revising Tip

To open cluster 6 with participial phrases, use *turning* and *cutting* as key words. For more on participial phrases, see page 489.

Extension   To complete the story, narrate what happens next. Share your text—"The Crow" plus "Training Run"—with a writing partner.

8.3 Exposition

Directions Combine each cluster of numbered items into one or more sentences. Combine clusters if you wish.

1.1 Cars serve practical ends.
1.2 They get us from place to place.
1.3 They also serve as objects of ornament.
1.4 They are much like clothing.

2.1 Cars make statements.
2.2 The statements are about who we are.
2.3 The statements are about what we value.
2.4 They create a "public identity."

3.1 A sports car projects a lifestyle.
3.2 The lifestyle is carefree.
3.3 The lifestyle is romantic.
3.4 A station wagon projects an image.
3.5 The image is family-oriented.

4.1 An economy runabout suggests thrift.
4.2 An economy runabout suggests efficiency.
4.3 It zips nervously through traffic.
4.4 A luxury sedan makes a different statement.
4.5 It guzzles gas.
4.6 It wallows toward its destination.

5.1 Such images shape our thinking.
5.2 They are reinforced by advertising.
5.3 The advertising is relentless.
5.4 They influence how we see others.
5.5 They influence how we see ourselves.

6.1 We may make snap judgments about people.
6.2 The judgments are based on their automobiles.
6.3 We may choose a car to satisfy our fantasies.
6.4 We may choose a car to impress others.

7.1 Judging books by their covers is dangerous.
7.2 So is judging drivers by their cars.

Grammar
Revising Tip

In clusters 1, 3, and 4, try several connectors—*but, yet, however, while, although*—before settling on one. For information on the correct punctuation, see pages 702 and 705–709.

Extension Write about someone whose personality *differs* from that suggested by the car that he or she drives (as noted by cluster 7). Relate what you write to "Car Culture."

Exercise B: Car Colors

Directions   Combine each cluster of numbered items into one or more sentences. Combine clusters if you wish.

1.1 Early car buyers had one choice of color.
1.2 The color was "basic black."
1.3 Today's consumer has many color options.

2.1 Psychologists contend something.
2.2 Car colors can reveal personality traits.
2.3 These traits are basic.
2.4 Car colors can express "hidden selves."

3.1 Red appeals to attention-seekers.
3.2 Red is a fire color.
3.3 They may be impulsive.
3.4 They may be aggressive.

4.1 Cautious people often choose brown.
4.2 The people are analytical.
4.3 Active types often like yellow.
4.4 These types may have an artistic bent.

5.1 Blue is linked with steadiness.
5.2 Blue is linked with consistency.
5.3 It appeals to many introverts.
5.4 It appeals to some extroverts.

6.1 Drivers often choose white.
6.2 The drivers may be critical.
6.3 The drivers may be compulsively neat.
6.4 The drivers may be safety conscious.

7.1 Green typically appeals to romantics.
7.2 Green typically appeals to intellectuals.

8.1 And black is a "power color."
8.2 It appeals to sophisticates.
8.3 The sophisticates are self-confident.
8.4 They wish to be taken seriously.

Extension   Based on what you know about cars and colors, write about the kind of car—and color—that you might choose for yourself. Relate what you write to "Car Colors."

Directions   Combine each cluster of numbered items into one or more sentences. Combine clusters if you wish.

1.1 Many of us have heard of cholesterol.
1.2 Its dangers have been widely publicized.
1.3 Few of us know much about it.

2.1 Cholesterol is found in the bloodstream.
2.2 Cholesterol is found in all body tissues.
2.3 It is a fatlike substance.
2.4 It is white and waxy.

3.1 It is used in the outer membrane of cells.
3.2 It is used as a sheath around nerve fibers.
3.3 It is used as a building block for hormones.
3.4 It is clearly essential to life.

4.1 Our bodies convert fats into cholesterol.
4.2 Our bodies convert proteins into cholesterol.
4.3 Our bodies convert carbohydrates into cholesterol.
4.4 Our bodies also ingest it directly from various foods.

5.1 The body manufactures its own cholesterol.
5.2 We don't have to consume it to stay healthy.

6.1 Confusion surrounds cholesterol.
6.2 There are two types of the substance.
6.3 One type is called HDL.
6.4 The other type is called LDL.

7.1 HDL is "helpful" cholesterol.
7.2 LDL is "harmful" cholesterol.

8.1 HDL takes cholesterol back to the liver.
8.2 The cholesterol is in the bloodstream.
8.3 The liver reprocesses or excretes the substance.

9.1 But LDL circulates cholesterol through the body.
9.2 It accumulates on arterial walls.

Extension   Develop a character sketch or dramatic incident to introduce "Cholesterol Facts" and "More Cholesterol Facts."

Exercise D: More Cholesterol Facts

Directions   Combine each cluster of numbered items into one or more sentences. Combine clusters if you wish.

1.1 Cholesterol is found primarily in meat.
1.2 Cholesterol is found primarily in dairy products.
1.3 Few Americans know this fact.

2.1 Plant foods contain no harmful cholesterol.
2.2 These foods include vegetables.
2.3 These foods include fruits.
2.4 These foods include grains.
2.5 These foods include nuts.

3.1 One can decrease cholesterol intake.
3.2 This is done by eating more plant foods.
3.3 This is done by cutting back on animal products.
3.4 These include meats and poultry.
3.5 These include dairy goods.
3.6 These include eggs.

4.1 But one must also eat less saturated fat.
4.2 Fat is found in both plant and animal foods.
4.3 Fat stimulates one's cholesterol production.

5.1 Beef is high in saturated fat.
5.2 Some pork is high in saturated fat.
5.3 Poultry skin is high in saturated fat.
5.4 Whole milk is high in saturated fat.
5.5 So is coconut oil.
5.6 So is palm oil.

6.1 Finns and Americans have diets.
6.2 The diets are rich in saturated fat.
6.3 Both groups have very high cholesterol levels.
6.4 This makes them world leaders in heart disease.

7.1 Japanese have the world's lowest level of cholesterol.
7.2 Japanese have the world's lowest level of heart disease.
7.3 Their diets are extremely low in saturated fat.

Vocabulary
Revising Tip

In clusters 4, 5, and 6, try causal connectors such as *because, since, therefore, consequently,* and *so.* For more information on punctuation with causal connectors, see pages 708 and 710.

Extension   Write a concluding paragraph for "Cholesterol Facts" and "More Cholesterol Facts." Then share your text with a writing partner.

8.4 Persuasion

Exercise A: Success Story

Directions Combine each cluster of numbered items into one or more sentences. Combine clusters if you wish.

1.1 A bald eagle spreads its wings.
1.2 The eagle is white-maned.
1.3 Its wings are enormous.
1.4 It soars on the morning wind.
1.5 It scans the terrain below.

2.1 This predator faced extinction in 1963.
2.2 This predator is magnificent.
2.3 It is America's national bird.
2.4 Only four hundred pairs of eagles remained in 1963.
2.5 The eagles were in the lower forty-eight states.

3.1 America had been home to thousands of bald eagles.
3.2 They were decimated by loss of habitat.
3.3 They were decimated by illegal hunting.
3.4 They were decimated by the use of DDT.
3.5 They were decimated by other poisons.

4.1 Eagles were at the top of the food chain.
4.2 They were especially vulnerable to DDT.
4.3 DDT affected their ability to reproduce.

5.1 The ban on DDT gave eagles a chance.
5.2 Breeding programs gave eagles a chance.
5.3 Strict law enforcement gave eagles a chance.
5.4 Their numbers slowly began to build.

6.1 The bald eagle is still endangered.
6.2 About 2,600 nesting pairs now exist.
6.3 This is in the continental United States.
6.4 They are mostly in western states.

7.1 Yet the eagle's future remains uncertain.
7.2 Each year hundreds die from eating meat.
7.3 The meat has been poisoned with pesticides.
7.4 The pesticides are illegal.

Extension What does the eagle's success story suggest about the spirit of the country it symbolizes? Develop a follow-up paragraph.

Directions   Combine each cluster of numbered items into one or more sentences. Combine clusters if you wish.

1.1 Predators are part of the ecosystem.
1.2 The ecosystem is on public rangelands.
1.3 Western ranchers graze their sheep there.

2.1 Ranchers lose about 500,000 sheep annually.
2.2 This is about 5 percent of their flocks.
2.3 The loss is to coyotes.
2.4 The loss is to wild dogs.
2.5 The loss is to other predators.

3.1 These predators include eagles.
3.2 The eagles feed mainly on fish.
3.3 The eagles feed mainly on small game.
3.4 The eagles also dine on spring lamb.

4.1 Some ranchers have fought back.
4.2 They are frustrated by predator attacks.
4.3 They are angered by economic losses.
4.4 They have injected carcasses with poisons.
4.5 The poisons are illegal.

5.1 Their targets have mainly been coyotes.
5.2 Their targets have mainly been dog packs.
5.3 They have also killed hundreds of eagles.
5.4 The eagles have eaten the meat.
5.5 The meat is toxic.

6.1 At issue are questions of land use.
6.2 At issue are questions of public policy.
6.3 Ranchers pay fees for grazing rights.
6.4 Ranchers contribute much to local economies.

7.1 A final point must be underscored.
7.2 Bald eagles are protected by law.
7.3 There are threats to their safety.
7.4 The threats are serious.

Extension   Should taxpayers support the losses of ranchers to keep them from resorting to extreme measures? Develop a follow-up paragraph that presents your point of view.

Exercise C: Ozone Problem

Directions   Combine each cluster of numbered items into one or more sentences. Combine clusters if you wish.

1.1 We have too much ozone at ground level.
1.2 We have too little ozone in the stratosphere.
1.3 The stratosphere is ten to twenty-five miles above us.

2.1 Both types of ozone are chemically alike.
2.2 One is a dangerous component of smog.
2.3 Smog results from burning fossil fuels.
2.4 The other serves as a natural screen.
2.5 It protects us from the sun's radiation.

3.1 Something is unfortunate.
3.2 The ozone in smog cannot reach the stratosphere.
3.3 It might do some good there.
3.4 It might reduce the greenhouse effect.

4.1 The ozone screen is destroyed by compounds.
4.2 The ozone screen is in the upper atmosphere.
4.3 The compounds are synthetic.
4.4 The compounds are called chlorofluorocarbons (CFCs).

5.1 CFCs have a wide range of industrial uses.
5.2 They serve as coolants for refrigerators.
5.3 They serve as coolants for air conditioners.
5.4 They serve as foaming agents for food packages.
5.5 They serve as foaming agents for mattresses.
5.6 They serve as solvents in microchip production.

6.1 CFCs are released during product use.
6.2 CFCs eventually rise into the stratosphere.
6.3 Radiation breaks them down, releasing chlorine.
6.4 Chlorine has an effect on ozone.
6.5 The effect is devastating.

7.1 CFCs take decades to reach the stratosphere.
7.2 We do not know the full extent of their damage.
7.3 The damage is continuous.

Vocabulary
Drafting Tip

To create an adverb in cluster 3, add -ly to *unfortunate.* For sentence variety, try opening cluster 6 with *released.*

Extension   Write a paragraph that introduces "Ozone Problem" by focusing on the problem in an everyday situation.

Exercise D: Ozone Solutions

Directions Combine each cluster of numbered items into one or more sentences. Combine clusters if you wish.

1.1 NASA has found holes in the ozone layer.
1.2 The holes are ominously vast.
1.3 The holes are over Antarctica and the Arctic.

2.1 Scientists have predicted something.
2.2 Increased radiation will lead to more melanoma.
2.3 Melanoma is an especially deadly skin cancer.
2.4 The radiation may also damage crops on earth.
2.5 This damage includes plankton in the oceans.

3.1 Ozone depletion is a worldwide problem.
3.2 Its solution depends on cooperation.
3.3 The cooperation must be international.
3.4 Its solution depends on consumer awareness.

4.1 Governments must agree to timetables.
4.2 The timetables phase out CFC production.
4.3 American consumers must curtail CFC use.

5.1 Air conditioners cause most of our CFC emissions.
5.2 The air conditioners are in automobiles.
5.3 One should go to service stations.
5.4 The stations are equipped to recycle CFCs.

6.1 One should avoid food-packaging products.
6.2 The products are made from plastic foam.
6.3 They are often found in fast-food restaurants.

7.1 One should check labels on aerosol cans.
7.2 This is to ensure the cans are environmentally safe.

8.1 One should also choose a refrigerator.
8.2 The refrigerator should be energy efficient.
8.3 It will release fewer CFCs into the atmosphere.
8.4 It eventually wears out and is discarded.

Extension Link "Ozone Problem" and "Ozone Solutions" and write a conclusion. Then share your text with a writing partner.

8.5 Literature Exercises

Exercise A

Directions   Scan the sentences below, which are adapted from *Blue Highways* by William Least Heat-Moon. Decide which of the numbered sentences belong together, and combine them in your own way. Then compare your sentences with the originals on pages 37–38.

1. It was nearly May.
2. The rain popped.
3. It then stopped.
4. It popped.
5. It stopped.
6. The incline became steeper.
7. Light rain fell steadily.
8. It rolled red dust off the roof.
9. The dust was from the desert.
10. I hadn't hit showers since east Texas.
11. It was good.
12. The pleasant cool turned to cold.
13. I switched on the heater.
14. The headlights glared off snowbanks.
15. The snowbanks were edging closer to the highway.
16. The highway climbed.
17. The rain became sleet.
18. That's when I began thinking something.
19. I might have made a little miscalculation.
20. I looked for a place to turn around.
21. There was only narrow road.
22. The road was twisted.
23. The sleet got heavier.
24. The headlights were cutting only thirty feet into it.
25. Maybe I could drive above and out of the storm.
26. The wind came up at eight thousand feet.
27. It was rough.
28. It was nasty.
29. It bullied me about the road.

Grammar

Prewriting Tip

Read quickly through all sentences to get a sense of the entire piece before you begin combining.

Directions Scan the sentences below. Some are from "My Furthest-Back Person—The African," by Alex Haley. The numbered sentences are adapted from Haley's original. Decide which of the numbered sentences belong together, and combine them in your own way. Then compare your sentences with the originals on pages 109–110.

"About the time the king's soldiers came, the eldest of these four sons, Kunta, when he had about 16 rains, went away from this village, to chop wood to make a drum . . . and he was never seen again . . ."

1. Goose-pimples seemed to pop all over me.
2. They were the size of lemons.
3. My cumulative notebooks were in my knapsack.
4. The first of them included something.
5. In my boyhood my Grandma told of the African *"Kin-tay."*
6. In my boyhood Cousin Georgia told of the African *"Kin-tay."*
7. In my boyhood others told of the African *"Kin-tay."*
8. Kin-tay always said he was kidnapped near his village.
9. He was chopping wood to make a drum.
10. I showed the interpreter.
11. He showed and told the *griot*.
12. The *griot* excitedly told the people.
13. They grew very agitated.
14. They then formed a human ring.
15. This happened abruptly.
16. They were encircling me.
17. They were dancing.
18. They were chanting.
19. Perhaps a dozen of the women rushed in toward me.
20. They were carrying their infant babies.
21. They thrust the infants into my arms.
22. I later learned something.
23. This conveyed "the laying on of hands."
24. "This flesh is part of us."
25. "We are you."
26. "You are us."

The men hurried me into their mosque, their Arabic praying later being translated outside: "Thanks be to Allah for returning the long lost from among us."

Directions   Scan the sentences below. One comes directly from *The Solace of Open Spaces*, by Gretel Ehrlich. The numbered sentences are adapted from Ehrlich's originals. Decide which numbered sentences belong together, and combine them in your own way. Then compare your sentences with the originals on page 154.

1. Conversation goes on.
2. It sounds like a code.
3. The code is private.
4. A few phrases imply a complex of meanings.
5. You ask directions.
6. You get a list of details.
7. The list is curious.
8. I was trailing sheep.
9. I was told something.
10. "Ride up to that kinda upturned rock."
11. "Follow the pink wash."
12. "Turn left at the dump."
13. "Then you'll see the water hole."

One friend told his wife on roundup to "turn at the salt lick and the dead cow," which turned out to be a scattering of bones and no salt lick at all.

14. Sentence structure is shortened.
15. It expresses the skin and bones of a thought.
16. Descriptive words are dropped.
17. Even verbs are dropped.
18. A cowboy will say something to a wrangler.
19. The cowboy is looking over a corral.
20. The corral is full of horses.
21. "Which one needs rode?"
22. People hold back their thoughts.
23. It seems to be a dumbfounded silence.
24. Then they erupt with a remark.
25. The remark is perceptive.
26. The remark is excoriating.
27. Language is compressed.
28. It becomes metaphorical.
29. A rancher ended a relationship with one remark.
30. "You're a bad check."
31. This meant bouncing in and out was intolerable.
32. This meant even coming back would be no good.

Directions   Scan the sentences below. One comes directly from *A Book of Bees*, by Sue Hubbell. The numbered sentences are adapted from Hubbell's original. Decide which numbered sentences belong together, and combine them in your own way. Then compare your sentences with the originals on page 263.

1. Each worker bee is covered with hairs.
2. The hairs are stiff.
3. These hairs catch the granules.
4. The bee brushes against the flower's anthers.
5. The anthers bear pollen.
6. She is soon covered with pollen.
7. She stops to use her two front pairs of legs.
8. She combs the pollen from her body.
9. The pollen is sticky.
10. She packs it into the baskets.
11. The baskets are on her rear pair of legs.
12. Her legs become heavy.
13. The heaviness is wads of pollen.
14. She returns to her hive to unload.
15. House bees arrange the pollen granules.
16. The arrangement is in the honeycomb cells.
17. The cells are around the bee larvae.
18. The larvae are developing.
19. The pollen is available to the nurse bees.
20. The availability is convenient.

In the springtime, a typical frame of brood—as beekeepers call developing bees—contains a large central semicircle of cells containing eggs and larvae in various stages.

21. The eggs and larvae are there to see.
22. The oldest brood have spun themselves cocoons.
23. Their stomachs are full.
24. They pupate [develop] within the cocoons.
25. They are hidden from human eyes.
26. They are sealed in their cells by a covering.
27. The covering is tough and velvety brown.
28. They will emerge as adults from beneath it.
29. The entire semicircle of brood is bordered by a ring.
30. The ring is of cells filled with pollen.
31. The ring in turn is surrounded by honey.
32. It is surrounded by nectar as the season progresses.

> **Vocabulary**
>
> **Revising Tip**
>
> Read your combined sentences to a partner. If he or she cannot easily follow your description, discuss what revision would help make your writing clear.

Directions   Scan the sentences below. One comes directly from "A Plague on Tennis," by Mark Mathabane. The numbered sentences are adapted from Mathabane's original. Decide which numbered sentences belong together, and combine them in your own way. Then compare your sentences with the originals by Mathabane on page 309.

 1. I took up tennis in the early 1970s.
 2. The sport was synonymous with wooden rackets.
 3. The players all relied on wooden rackets.
 4. I idolized the players.
 5. I enjoyed watching them.
 6. I sought to emulate them.
 7. They included Arthur Ashe.
 8. They included Stan Smith.
 9. They included Rod Laver.
10. The rackets enabled them to carve out illustrious careers.
11. The rackets enabled them to win major championships.
12. The championships included Wimbledon.
13. The championships included the U.S. Open.
14. Their talent on the court was unmistakable.
15. Their finesse on the court was unmistakable.
16. They served and volleyed.
17. They hit groundstrokes flat.
18. They hit groundstrokes sliced.
19. They hit groundstrokes with topspin.
20. The occasion made its demands.
21. They played delicate touch strokes.
22. These included angled drop shots.
23. In sum, they possessed all-around games.
24. They were the closest thing to the "complete player."
25. They were a delight for spectators to watch.
26. The demise of wooden rackets changed all that.
27. The nature of tennis today is expressed in a single word.
28. The word is "power."

The new rackets can generate so much power in the hands of just about anyone that players of modest abilities are transformed into giant-killers on the court, capable on any given day, usually in the early rounds, of defeating the game's finest.

Use Troubleshooter to help you correct common errors that you might make in your writing. You can indicate the errors on your paper using the handwritten codes in the left-hand column. Then the Table of Contents below will help you locate solutions to correct errors.

9.1 Sentence Fragment

PROBLEM 1

Fragment that lacks a subject

frag Jamal is very athletic. Plays a great game of tennis.

Solution

Jamal is very athletic. He plays a great game of tennis.
Add a subject to the fragment to make it a complete sentence.

PROBLEM 2

Fragment that lacks a complete verb

frag Sabra saw a bright light in the sky. A meteor with brilliant colors.

frag We can hardly hear ourselves think. Ruth trying out her new set of drums.

Solution A

Sabra saw a bright light in the sky. A meteor with brilliant colors was flashing by.

We can hardly hear ourselves think. Ruth is trying out her new set of drums.
Add a complete verb or a helping verb to make the sentence complete.

Solution B

Sabra saw a bright light in the sky—a meteor with brilliant colors.

With Ruth trying out her new set of drums, we could hardly hear ourselves think.
Combine the fragment with another sentence.

Fragment that is a subordinate clause

frag José often succeeds. Because he is persistent.

frag I am reading a book by Alice Walker. Who is one of my favorite writers.

Solution A

José often succeeds because he is persistent.

I am reading a book by Alice Walker, who is one of my favorite writers.

Combine the fragment with another sentence.

Solution B

José often succeeds. He is persistent.

I am reading a book by Alice Walker. She is one of my favorite writers.

Rewrite the fragment as a complete sentence, eliminating the subordinating conjunction or the relative pronoun and adding a subject or other words necessary to make a complete thought.

PROBLEM 4

Fragment that lacks both a subject and a verb

frag Kate felt ill and left the theater. Before the end of the movie.

Solution

Kate felt ill and left the theater before the end of the movie.

Combine the fragment with another sentence.

Need More Help?

If you need more help in avoiding sentence fragments, turn to Lesson 13.9, pages 519–520.

9.2   Run-on Sentence

PROBLEM 1

Comma splice—two main clauses separated only by a comma

> run-on   Paula told me the answer to the riddle, I have forgotten what she said.

Solution A

Paula told me the answer to the riddle. I have forgotten what she said.

Replace the comma with an end mark of punctuation, such as a period or a question mark, and begin the new sentence with a capital letter.

Solution B

Paula told me the answer to the riddle; I have forgotten what she said.

Place a semicolon between the two main clauses.

Solution C

Paula told me the answer to the riddle, but I have forgotten what she said.

Add a coordinating conjunction after the comma.

PROBLEM 2

Two main clauses with no punctuation between them

> run-on   The lights flickered a few times then they went out.

Solution A

The lights flickered a few times. Then they went out.

Separate the main clauses with an end mark of punctuation, such as a period or a question mark, and begin the second sentence with a capital letter.

PROBLEM 3

Two main clauses with no comma before the coordinating conjunction

run-on

Ilona would like to own a pet but she is allergic to most animals.

run-on

My brother just started playing soccer and he wants me to play as well.

Solution

Ilona would like to own a pet, but she is allergic to most animals.

My brother just started playing soccer, and he wants me to play as well.

Add a comma before the coordinating conjunction to separate the two main clauses.

Need More Help? *If you need more help in avoiding run-on sentences, turn to Lesson 13.10, pages 521–523.*

PROBLEM 1

A subject that is separated from the verb by an intervening prepositional phrase

agr   A complex system of roads (link) the two cities.

agr   The sounds of the traffic (keeps) her awake.

Do not mistake the object of a preposition for the subject of a sentence.

Solution

A complex system of roads links the two cities.

The sounds of the traffic keep her awake.

Make the verb agree with the subject, which is never the object of a preposition.

PROBLEM 2

A predicate nominative that differs in number from the subject

agr   Grapes (is) his favorite snack.

Solution

Grapes are his favorite snack.

Ignore the predicate nominative, and make the verb agree with the subject of the sentence.

PROBLEM 3

A subject that follows the verb

agr   On the wall (hangs) two handsome watercolors.

agr   There (goes) the last two bicyclists.

On the wall hang two handsome watercolors.

There go the last two bicyclists.
In an inverted sentence look for the subject *after* the verb. Then make sure the verb agrees with the subject.

PROBLEM 4

A collective noun as the subject

> *agr*   The soccer (team) have won consistently.
>
> *agr*   The group of men (has) different views.

The soccer team has won consistently.
If the collective noun refers to a group as a whole, use a singular verb.

The group of men have different views.
If the collective noun refers to each member of a group individually, use a plural verb.

PROBLEM 5

A noun of amount as the subject

> *agr*   Five dollars (are) too much for that item.
>
> *agr*   Five pennies (makes) a nickel.

Five dollars is too much for that item.

Five pennies make a nickel.
Determine whether the noun of amount refers to one unit and is therefore singular or whether it refers to a number of individual units and is therefore plural.

PROBLEM 6

A compound subject that is joined by **and**

> *agr* Copper and zinc (makes) brass.
>
> *agr* Rice and beans (are) a healthful main dish.

Solution A
Copper and zinc make brass.
If the parts of the compound subject do not belong to one unit or if they refer to different people or things, use a plural verb.

Solution B
Rice and beans is a healthful main dish.
If the parts of the compound subject belong to one unit or if both parts refer to the same person or thing, use a singular verb.

PROBLEM 7

A compound subject that is joined by **or** *or* **nor**

> *agr* Neither my cousins nor my aunt (resemble) her.

Solution
Neither my cousins nor my aunt resembles her.
Make the verb agree with the subject that is closer to it.

PROBLEM 8

A compound subject that is preceded by **many a, every,** *or* **each**

> *agr* Many a bluejay and robin (have) visited that feeder today.

When *many a*, *every*, or *each* precedes a compound subject, the subject is considered singular.

Many a bluejay and robin has visited that feeder today.
Use a singular verb when *many a*, *each*, or *every* precedes a compound subject.

PROBLEM 9

A subject that is separated from the verb by an intervening expression

> *agr* My karate class, as well as Kazuo's
> swimming class, (take) place on Saturday.

Certain expressions, such as *as well as*, *in addition to*, and *together with*, do not change the number of the subject.

My karate class, as well as Kazuo's swimming class, takes place on Saturday.
Ignore an intervening expression between a subject and its verb. Make the verb agree with the subject.

PROBLEM 10

An indefinite pronoun as the subject

> *agr* Each of the contestants (receive) a gift.

Some indefinite pronouns are singular, some are plural, and some can be either singular or plural, depending upon the noun they refer to. (See page 567 for a list of indefinite pronouns.)

Each of the contestants receives a gift.
Determine whether the indefinite pronoun is singular or plural, and make the verb agree.

If you need more help with subject-verb agreement, turn to Lessons 16.1 through 16.7, pages 575–587.

9.4 Lack of Pronoun-Antecedent Agreement

PROBLEM 1

A singular antecedent that can be either male or female

ant   An attorney must protect (his) clients' interests.

Traditionally a masculine pronoun was used to refer to an antecedent that may be either male or female. This usage ignores or excludes females.

Solution A

An attorney must protect his or her clients' interests.
Reword the sentence to use *he or she, him or her,* and so on.

Solution B

Attorneys must protect their clients' interests.
Reword the sentence so that both the antecedent and the pronoun are plural.

Solution C

An attorney must protect every client's interests.
Reword the sentence to eliminate the pronoun.

PROBLEM 2

A second-person pronoun that refers to a third-person antecedent

Isaiah drinks milk because it supplies
ant (you) with calcium and protein.

Be sure not to refer to an antecedent in the third person using the second-person pronoun *you.*

Solution A

Isaiah drinks milk because it supplies him with calcium and protein.

Use the appropriate third-person pronoun.

Solution B

Isaiah drinks milk because it supplies people with calcium and protein.

Use an appropriate noun instead of a pronoun.

PROBLEM 3

A singular indefinite pronoun as an antecedent

ant Each of the mothers brought (their) own child to the zoo.

ant Neither of the boys at the table finished (their) dinner.

Each, everyone, either, neither, and *one* are singular and therefore require singular personal pronouns.

Solution

Each of the mothers brought her own child to the zoo.

Neither of the boys at the table finished his dinner.

Don't be fooled by a prepositional phrase that contains a plural noun. Determine whether the indefinite pronoun antecedent is singular or plural, and make the noun agree.

If you need more help with pronoun-antecedent agreement, turn to Lesson 16.7, pages 585–587, and Lesson 17.5, pages 606–610.

9.4 Lack of Pronoun-Antecedent Agreement **385**

9.5 Lack of Clear Pronoun Reference

A pronoun reference that is weak or vague

ref The musicians played, (which) we enjoyed.

ref Economists differ about how to improve the economy, and (that) has led to inconsistent economic policies.

ref The author argues at length that there is life on other planets, but (it) is not convincing.

Be sure that *this*, *that*, *which*, and *it* have a clear antecedent.

Solution A
The musicians played several old songs, which we enjoyed.
Rewrite the sentence, adding a clear antecedent for the pronoun.

Solution B
Economists differ about how to improve the economy, and their disagreement has led to inconsistent economic policies.

The author argues at length that there is life on other planets, but his theory is not very convincing.
Rewrite the sentence, substituting a noun for the pronoun.

A pronoun that refers to more than one antecedent

ref When Nelson gave his father the book, (he) beamed with pleasure.

ref The parents met with the teachers, and (they) asked whether the principal could be present.

Solution A

When Nelson gave his father the book, the boy beamed with pleasure.

Rewrite the sentence, substituting a noun for the pronoun.

Solution B

The teachers asked whether the principal could be present at their meeting with the parents.

Rewrite the sentence, making the antecedent of the pronoun clear.

PROBLEM 3

The indefinite use of you *or* they

> *ref* In court (you) are innocent until proved guilty.
>
> *ref* In that store (they) have some excellent bargains.

Solution A

In court defendants are innocent until proved guilty.

Rewrite the sentence, substituting a noun for the pronoun.

Solution B

That store has some excellent bargains.

Rewrite the sentence, eliminating the pronoun entirely.

If you need more help in making clear pronoun references, turn to Lesson 17.6, pages 611–613.

PROBLEM

An incorrect shift in person between two pronouns

> *pro*   Kenji and Jeanne are going on a trip
> to the mountains, where (you) can hike
> and breathe fresh air.
>
> *pro*   I like movies that keep (you) guessing.
>
> *pro*   When one examines the card catalog, (you)
> find a wealth of information.

Incorrect pronoun shifts occur when a writer or speaker uses a pronoun in one person and then illogically shifts to a pronoun in another person.

Solution A

Kenji and Jeanne are going on a trip to the mountains, where they can hike and breathe fresh air.

I like movies that keep me guessing.

When one examines the card catalog, one finds a wealth of information.

Replace the incorrect pronoun with a pronoun that agrees with its antecedent.

Solution B

Kenji and Jeanne are going on a trip to the mountains, where vacationers can hike and breathe fresh air.

I like movies that keep the audience guessing.

Replace the incorrect pronoun with an appropriate noun.

If you need more help in eliminating incorrect pronoun shifts, turn to Lesson 17.5, page 606.

9.7 Shift in Verb Tense

PROBLEM 1

An unnecessary shift in tense

shift t   Jan opens the can and (savored) the aroma.

shift t   Otis left the room just as we (arrive).

When two or more events occur at the same time, be sure to use the same verb tense to describe each event.

Solution

Jan opens the can and savors the aroma.

Otis left the room just as we arrived.

PROBLEM 2

A lack of correct shift in tenses to show that one event precedes or follows another

     By the time the coach sent him in, Julius

shift t   (sat) on the bench for an hour.

When events being described have occurred at different times, shift tenses to show that one event precedes or follows another.

Solution

By the time the coach sent him in, Julius had sat on the bench for an hour.

Shift from the past tense to the past perfect tense to indicate that one action began and ended before another past action began. Use the past perfect tense for the earlier of the two actions.

Need More Help? *If you need more help with shifts in verb tenses, turn to Lesson 15.4, pages 555–557, and Lesson 15.6, pages 560–561.*

9.8   Incorrect Verb Tense or Form

PROBLEM 1

An incorrect or missing verb ending

> *tense*   Last Saturday night I (baby-sit) for my neighbors.
>
> *tense*   Have you ever (want) to study modern dance?

> **Solution**
> **Last Saturday night I baby-sat for my neighbors.**
>
> **Have you ever wanted to study modern dance?**
> Add *-ed* to a regular verb to form the past tense and the past participle.

PROBLEM 2

An improperly formed irregular verb

> *tense*   Emilio (swinged) the bat but missed the ball.
>
> *tense*   That is the third time Claude has (beat) me at chess.

Irregular verbs form their past and past participle in some way other than by adding *-ed*. Memorize these forms, or look them up.

> **Solution**
> **Emilio swung the bat but missed the ball.**
>
> **That is the third time Claude has beaten me at chess.**

PROBLEM 3

Confusion between the past form and the past participle

> *tense*   The committee has (chose) Juana as chairperson.
>
> *tense*   He has (broke) our school's high-jump record.

The committee has chosen Juana as chairperson.

He has broken our school's high-jump record.
Use the past participle form of an irregular verb, not the past form,
when you use the auxiliary verb *have*.

PROBLEM 4

Improper use of the past participle

> *tense* He (swum) across the lake.
>
> *tense* The school choir (sung) beautifully at the
> class assembly.
>
> *tense* The bell (rung.)

The past participle of an irregular verb cannot stand alone as a verb.
It must be used with the auxiliary verb *have*.

He has swum across the lake.

The school choir has sung beautifully at the class assembly.

The bell has rung.
Add the auxiliary verb *have* to the past participle to form a complete
verb.

He swam across the lake.

The school choir sang beautifully at the class assembly.

The bell rang.
Replace the past participle with the past form of the verb.

*If you need more help with correct verb
forms, turn to Lesson 15.1 and Lesson
15.2, pages 547–550.*

9.9 Misplaced or Dangling Modifier

PROBLEM 1

A misplaced modifier

mod The insects fascinated the children (with) (their long antennae.)

mod (Hanging on the wall,) Tamiko saw her painting.

mod The cat hissed at the goldfish (staring at the fishbowl.)

Modifiers that modify the wrong word or seem to modify more than one word in a sentence are called misplaced modifiers.

Solution

With their long antennae, the insects fascinated the children.

Tamiko saw her painting hanging on the wall.

Staring at the fishbowl, the cat hissed at the goldfish.
Move the misplaced phrase as close as possible to the word or words it modifies.

PROBLEM 2

The adverb only *misplaced*

mod Sylvia (only) orders soup as an appetizer.

The meaning of your sentence may be unclear if *only* is misplaced.

Solution

Only Sylvia orders soup as an appetizer.

Sylvia orders only soup as an appetizer.

Sylvia orders soup only as an appetizer.
Place the adverb *only* immediately before the word or group of words it modifies. Note that each time *only* is moved in the sentence, the meaning of the sentence changes.

A dangling modifier

mod (By paying attention to the instructions,) the bookcase was assembled easily.

mod (Concerned about making mistakes,) the driving lesson went surprisingly well.

mod (Standing on the mountaintop,) the view was breathtaking.

Dangling modifiers do not logically seem to modify any word in the sentence.

Solution

By paying attention to the instructions, Rachel easily assembled the bookcase.

Concerned about making mistakes, Duane felt that his driving lesson went surprisingly well.

Standing on the mountaintop, Ted found the view breathtaking.

Rewrite the sentence, adding a noun to which the dangling phrase clearly refers. Often you will have to add other words to complete the meaning of the sentence.

If you need more help with misplaced or dangling modifiers, turn to Lesson 18.7, pages 636–641.

9.10 Missing or Misplaced Possessive Apostrophe

PROBLEM 1

Singular nouns

> *poss* That (artists) painting is (James) favorite.

Solution
That artist's painting is James's favorite.
Use an apostrophe and an -*s* to form the possessive of a singular noun, even one that ends in -*s*.

PROBLEM 2

Plural nouns ending in -s

> *poss* The (officers) quarters are in that building.

Solution
The officers' quarters are in that building.
Use an apostrophe alone to form the possessive of a plural noun that ends in -*s*.

PROBLEM 3

Plural nouns not ending in -s

> *poss* (Womens) shoes are sold on the third floor.

Solution
Women's shoes are sold on the third floor.
Use an apostrophe and an -*s* to form the possessive of a plural noun that does not end in -*s*.

PROBLEM 4

Pronouns

> *poss* (Anyones) guess is as good as mine.
>
> *poss* I see every painting but (your's.)

Solution A
Anyone's guess is as good as mine.
Use an apostrophe and an -*s* to form the possessive of a singular indefinite pronoun.

Solution B
I see every painting but yours.
Do not use an apostrophe with any of the possessive personal pronouns.

PROBLEM 5

Confusion between *its* and *it's*

> *poss* That car has lost (it's) front bumper.
>
> *poss* (Its) always good to try new things.

The possessive of *it* is *its*. *It's* is the contraction of *it is*.

Solution
That car has lost its front bumper.

It's always good to try new things.
Do not use an apostrophe to form the possessive of *it*. Use an apostrophe to form the contraction of *it is*.

Need More Help? *If you need more help with apostrophes and possessives, turn to Lesson 17.1, page 600, and Lesson 21.11, pages 722–724.*

9.11 Missing Commas with Nonessential Element

PROBLEM 1

Missing commas with nonessential participles, infinitives, and their phrases

com The team defeated trudged wearily to the bus.

com The waves gleaming in the sunlight pounded the beach.

com To be sure I have no experience with this kind of problem.

Solution

The team, defeated, trudged wearily to the bus.

The waves, gleaming in the sunlight, pounded the beach.

To be sure, I have no experience with this kind of problem.
Determine whether the participle, infinitive, or phrase is truly not essential to the meaning of the sentence. If so, set off the phrase with commas.

PROBLEM 2

Missing commas with nonessential adjective clauses

com Kai-chi who comes from Shanghai is studying piano.

Solution

Kai-chi, who comes from Shanghai, is studying piano.
Determine whether the clause is truly not essential to the meaning of the sentence. If so, set off the clause with commas.

Missing commas with nonessential appositives

com   Mr. Lomawaima◯our anthropology professor◯
will speak on Hopi customs.

Solution

Mr. Lomawaima, our anthropology professor, will speak on Hopi customs.

Determine whether the appositive is truly not essential to the meaning of the sentence. If so, set off the appositive with commas.

Missing commas with interjections and parenthetical expressions

com   Oh◯I know what you mean.

com   Derrick◯I believe◯offered to help with the
scenery for the play.

Solution

Oh, I know what you mean.

Derrick, I believe, offered to help with the scenery for the play.

Set off the interjection or parenthetical expression with commas.

Need More Help?

If you need more help with commas and nonessential elements, turn to Lesson 21.6, pages 707–709.

PROBLEM

Missing commas in a series of words, phrases, or clauses

↓ com   Birches‿maples‿and hemlocks covered the sides of the mountain.

↓ com   The motor sputtered‿coughed‿whined‿and finally died.

↓ com   The ivy crept up the wall‿around the drainpipe‿and over the roof.

↓ com   Lila sat nervously, biting her lip‿frowning‿and drumming her fingers on the table.

↓ com   The rain stopped‿the clouds rolled away‿and the sun came out.

Solution

Birches, maples, and hemlocks covered the sides of the mountain.

The motor sputtered, coughed, whined, and finally died.

The ivy crept up the wall, around the drainpipe, and over the roof.

Lila sat nervously, biting her lip, frowning, and drumming her fingers on the table.

The rain stopped, the clouds rolled away, and the sun came out.
When there are three or more elements in a series, use a comma after each element, including the element that precedes a conjunction.

Need More Help?

If you need more help with commas in a series, turn to Lesson 21.6, page 705.

Part 2

Grammar, Usage, and Mechanics

10.1 Nouns

A **noun** is a word that names a person, a place, a thing, or an idea.

PERSON	woman, man, Juanita Brown, great-grandfather
PLACE	planet, Texas, farm, high school
THING	dolphin, parrot, ivy, bookmark
IDEA	success, affection, freedom, courage

A **concrete noun** names an object that occupies space or can be recognized by any of the senses. Concrete nouns are things you can see, hear, taste, touch, smell, or feel.

thorn	stars	thunder	gas	milk
child	drum	velvet	headache	dove

An **abstract noun** names an idea, a quality, or a characteristic.

excitement	honesty	innocence	happiness	harmony
truth	bravery	softness	fear	peace

Most nouns can take either a singular or a plural form, depending upon whether they name *one* person, place, thing, or idea or *more than one.*

SINGULAR	desk, bench, sky, wolf, man
PLURAL	desks, benches, skies, wolves, men

The possessive form of a noun can show possession, ownership, or the relationship between two nouns.

SINGULAR POSSESSIVE	PLURAL POSSESSIVE
the **girl's** coat	the **girls'** coats
a **business's** debts	those **business'** debts
a **prince's** crown	the **princes'** crowns
a **man's** voice	the **men's** voices

Exercise 1   Identifying Nouns

Find the 20 nouns that appear in the following paragraph and write them on your paper.

Musical Flair

[1] When Seiji Ozawa, the colorful principal conductor of the orchestra, performs, the auditorium is usually overflowing. [2] He performs with a stylish blend of intelligence, fierce concentration, and theatricality. [3] As the famed director leads the orchestra through fast, loud, and dramatic passages, his baton flashes like a sword, and his thick mop of black hair bobs furiously up and down. [4] There are no sheets of music on the podium as he conducts because he routinely memorizes the entire score of each work.

Supplying Abstract and Concrete Nouns

For each concrete noun in items 1–10, write an abstract noun that names an idea with which the concrete noun can be associated. For each abstract noun in items 11–20, write a concrete noun that has the quality of the abstract noun.

SAMPLE ANSWERS   dancer—grace
redness—tomato

1. quarterback
2. scream
3. perfume
4. pepper
5. bruise
6. dog
7. binoculars
8. teeth
9. lamb
10. book

11. intelligence
12. friendliness
13. darkness
14. aroma
15. stupidity
16. anger
17. hospitality
18. noise
19. celebration
20. luck

Writing Singular and Plural Nouns

On your paper write the plural form of each singular noun below. If you need help, consult a dictionary.

1. lesson
2. cheese
3. tax
4. boy
5. radio
6. brush
7. half
8. country
9. aptitude
10. woman

11. church
12. concern
13. stereo
14. city
15. child
16. calf
17. business
18. moose
19. valley
20. envelope

Writing Possessive Forms of Nouns

On your paper write each of the following phrases, supplying the possessive form of the italicized noun.

1. my three *sisters* bedrooms
2. the *men* tailor
3. a *friend* misfortune
4. the *bus* fumes
5. several *galaxies* stars
6. the *mice* squeals
7. the *wives* trip
8. the *video* stars
9. the *boy* parents
10. the *children* behavior

Adding Nouns to Categories

On your paper, add one more noun to each group of nouns listed below.

SAMPLE   tulips, roses, carnations, _____
ANSWER   tulips, roses, carnations, peonies

1. lion, gorilla, orangutan, _____
2. hatred, hostility, battle, _____
3. aunt, cousin, great-grandmother, _____
4. plateau, mountain, river, _____
5. neighbors, strangers, merchants, _____
6. justice, democracy, fairness, _____
7. library, theater, convention center, _____
8. Jenny's, Kim's, Mariana's, _____
9. potatoes, noodles, bread, _____
10. mathematics, sociology, anthropology, _____
11. sensitivity, kindness, concern, _____
12. Paris, Buenos Aires, Kuala Lumpur, _____
13. container, plate, dish, _____
14. teacher, doctor, private investigator, _____
15. courage, honor, decency, _____
16. planet, space, solar system, _____
17. insect, bird, reptile, _____
18. defendant, witness, prosecutor, _____
19. possibility, prospect, opportunity, _____
20. Thomas, Derek, Anthony, _____

Exercise 6   **Completing Sentences with Nouns**

On your paper complete each sentence by filling in the blanks with nouns. Be sure that your completed sentences make sense.

1. The two _____ bought new _____.
2. The _____ coat was made of _____.
3. The _____ watched a(n) _____.
4. Her _____ seems to be her best _____.
5. Seven _____ sat on the _____.
6. My three _____ moved to a new _____.
7. The _____ shoes were covered with _____.
8. In _____ I enjoy the _____ and the _____.
9. One _____ stood alone on his _____.
10. _____ are at the _____.

Proper and Common Nouns

A **proper noun** is the name of a particular person, place, thing, or idea.

A **common noun** is the general—not the particular—name of a person, place, thing, or idea.

Proper nouns are capitalized, whereas common nouns are not usually capitalized.

TYPE OF NOUN	PROPER NOUNS	COMMON NOUNS
PERSON	Aunt Shirley, Uncle Arnold	relatives
	General Powell, General Lee	generals
PLACE	Atlantic Ocean, Pacific Ocean	oceans
	Mars, Venus, Jupiter	planets
THING	Labor Day, Fourth of July	holidays
	The Lion King, Aladdin	movies
IDEA	Buddhism, Hinduism	religions
	Middle Ages, Great Depression	eras

Exercise 7   Matching Proper Nouns with Common Nouns

On your paper match proper nouns 1–10 on the left with common nouns *a–j* on the right. Then match proper nouns 11–20 with common nouns *k–t*.

1. Santa Fe
2. *National Geographic*
3. Kleenex
4. Shakespeare
5. Denzel Washington
6. Florence Griffith-Joyner
7. Africa
8. the Grand Canyon
9. the Empire State Building
10. Linda Ronstadt
11. Theodore Roosevelt
12. Islam
13. Grammy
14. Canada
15. Chrysler
16. Macintosh
17. Industrial Revolution
18. *Hamlet*
19. David Letterman
20. Mississippi

a. actor
b. continent
c. gorge
d. magazine
e. skyscraper
f. author
g. athlete
h. city
i. tissue
j. singer
k. automobile
l. computer
m. comedian
n. country
o. historical movement
p. play
q. president
r. religion
s. state
t. award

Collective Nouns

A **collective noun** names a group.

army	committee	(the) public
team	choir	(a) pride (of lions)

You can consider collective nouns either singular or plural, depending upon the meaning you wish to convey. If a collective noun refers to a group as a whole, it is considered singular. If a collective noun refers to the individual members of a group, it is considered plural. Note the differences in meaning in the following examples:

SINGULAR   The **committee** wants our attention.
PLURAL   The **committee** have gone their separate ways.
SINGULAR   The **class** likes to read plays.
PLURAL   The **class** take their seats.

Exercise 8   **Identifying Collective Nouns**

On your paper list the five collective nouns in the following paragraph.

Observing the Wonders of Ocean Life

[1]After the crew of the merchant ship finish their chores, they love to watch the sea. [2]Occasionally at night a swarm of plankton makes the ocean glow softly. [3]A young sailor watches in amazement as a pod of feeding whales suddenly breaks the calm surface. [4]Only a few days earlier, along the coast of California, the sailors had spotted a herd of sea lions frolicking in the waves. [5]The varied population of the sea never ceases to delight the young sailor.

Exercise 9   **Using Plural and Singular Collective Nouns**

On your paper complete the sentences in each pair by writing one of the collective nouns listed below. Indicate how the noun is used by writing *plural* or *singular*.

family	jury	audience	club	people	infantry

1. a. The _____ struggle into their coats after the play.
    b. The _____ applauds when the curtain falls.
2. a. The _____ meets every other Thursday.
    b. The _____ vote for a chairperson and treasurer every two years.
3. a. The _____ plans a vacation.
    b. The _____ each have different chores.
4. a. The _____ disagree on a verdict.
    b. Has the _____ reached a decision?
5. a. _____ have different characteristics.
    b. This _____ has created a great civilization.

Exercise 10 — Classifying Common Nouns, Proper Nouns, and Collective Nouns

On your paper classify each of the following nouns by writing *common*, *proper*, or *collective*. Some nouns belong in more than one category.

1. Uncle John
2. assembly
3. uncle
4. juror
5. Cape May
6. troop
7. major
8. crowd
9. flock
10. Niagara Falls
11. scout
12. Hilton Hotel
13. chorus
14. University of California
15. class
16. manager
17. Fifteenth Amendment
18. person
19. committee
20. Renaissance

Exercise 11 — Completing Sentences with Different Kinds of Nouns

On your paper complete each sentence by filling in the 25 blanks with the kinds of nouns specified in *italic* typeface. Be sure that your completed sentences make sense.

1. *Proper* left her *common* in the *concrete*.
2. The practice of *common* has become popular with the *common collective*.
3. The *common collective* proved its *abstract* at the *common*.
4. Near the *common* I saw three *common* run across the *concrete*.
5. *Proper* is a famous *common*.
6. Environmental *abstract* is a serious *abstract* for anyone who cares about humankind.
7. A *common collective* of zebras and a *common collective* of ostriches are only two of the spectacular sights on the plains of East *proper*.
8. I was thrilled to be able to watch *proper* practice *common* before the game.
9. The *common collective* voted for the *common*.
10. His *common* was born in *proper* on *proper* 4, 1932.

Exercise 12 — Creating Sentences with Nouns

Write five sentences about one of your favorite places. Rely especially on concrete nouns to convey a vivid picture of the place.

10.2 Pronouns

A **pronoun** is a word that takes the place of a noun, a group of words acting as a noun, or another pronoun. The word or group of words that a pronoun refers to is called its **antecedent.**

> When Sylvia Plath was still a young girl, **she** decided to become a writer. [The pronoun *she* replaces the noun *Sylvia Plath*.]

> George Orwell wrote *Animal Farm* and *1984* in the 1940s. **Both** remain immensely popular today. [The pronoun *both* takes the place of the nouns *Animal Farm* and *1984*.]

> Phillis Wheatley published **her** first poem at the age of sixteen and soon found **herself** a celebrity. [The pronouns *her* and *herself* take the place of the noun *Phillis Wheatley*.]

There are a limited number of pronouns in English, about seventy-five. They fall into one or more of the following categories: personal and possessive pronouns, reflexive and intensive pronouns, demonstrative pronouns, interrogative pronouns, relative pronouns, and indefinite pronouns.

Exercise 13	**Identifying Pronoun Antecedents**

On your paper write the antecedent of each italicized pronoun.

Emily Dickinson

1. In *her* poems, Emily Dickinson wrote about love, nature, and immortality.
2. "I Never Saw a Moor" and "The Sky is Low, The Clouds are Mean" are *both* about nature.
3. For many years, Emily's father did not support *her* interest in poetry.
4. Emily, her brother Austin, and her sister Vinnie grew up in Amherst, Massachusetts. *They* continued to live there as adults.
5. Emily seldom left Amherst. *She* spent many years as a recluse.
6. Some of Emily's acquaintances urged *their* friend to publish her poems.
7. Emily sent a few poems to a poetry critic at *The Atlantic Monthly* and asked for *his* opinion.
8. *They* corresponded until Emily's death in 1886.
9. Emily found beauty in nature and all *its* variations.
10. Emily once wrote of *herself*: "I am small, like the Wren."

Personal and Possessive Pronouns

A **personal pronoun** refers to a specific person or thing by indicating the person speaking (the first person), the person being spoken to (the second person), or any other person or thing being spoken about (the third person).

Personal pronouns, like nouns, are either singular or plural.

Personal Pronouns		
	Singular	**Plural**
FIRST PERSON	I, me	we, us
SECOND PERSON	you	you
THIRD PERSON	he, him	they, them
	she, her	
	it	

FIRST PERSON	Thomas went with **me** to the game. [*Me* refers to the person speaking.]
SECOND PERSON	Ask Gina to show **you** the article. [*You* refers to the person being addressed.]
THIRD PERSON	**He** gave **them** a poor excuse. [*He* and *them* refer to the persons being discussed.]

Third-person singular pronouns express **genders**. *He* and *him* are masculine; *she* and *her* are feminine; *it* is neuter (neither masculine nor feminine).

The **possessive pronouns** in the following chart take the place of the possessive forms of nouns.

Possessive Pronouns		
	Singular	**Plural**
FIRST PERSON	my, mine	our, ours
SECOND PERSON	your, yours	your, yours
THIRD PERSON	his	their, theirs
	her, hers	
	its	

The first form of each pronoun in the preceding chart can be used before a noun. The second form is used alone, like a noun.

USED BEFORE A NOUN	This is **her** radio.
	Its battery is new.
USED ALONE	This radio is **hers.**

Identifying Personal and Possessive Pronouns

On your paper list the personal or possessive pronoun in each of the following items. Then identify the pronoun as *personal* or *possessive*.

Ancient Rome

1. The Romans built a forum in the center of each city and used it for public activities.
2. Their houses had little furniture and usually only a single door as protection against thieves.
3. The father of a Roman family had total power over all members of his household.
4. Roman parents selected marriage partners for their children.
5. As a student in a school in ancient Rome, you would have used a wax tablet for writing.
6. Your day would have started before dawn.
7. For entertainment, citizens went to races and bet on a chariot and its driver.
8. Some entertainment was bloody. It involved gladiators fighting to the death.
9. Wealthy people had servants and often sent them to do the shopping.
10. Servants were often enemy soldiers captured in battle. They tended gardens, served meals, and taught the children.
11. Men and women wore a gown called a tunic. It hung to the knees or below.
12. Men dressed in white, but women dyed their clothing various colors.
13. Romans made few scientific discoveries, but they did collect scientific information.
14. Pliny the Elder assembled scientific knowledge of his day.
15. Most Romans lived by farming. They used crop rotation to enrich soil.
16. Romans invented concrete, which provided a strong building material for their structures.
17. Many roads crisscrossed the Roman empire. They helped hold the empire together.
18. Augustus was the first emperor of Rome. He built an elaborate arch in the middle of town to celebrate a victory in battle.
19. His uncle was Julius Caesar.
20. A Roman woman of noble birth had an important role. She looked after the house and all the servants.

Using Personal and Possessive Pronouns

Improve the following paragraph by replacing each underlined word or group of words with a personal or possessive pronoun. Write your answers on your paper.

Navajo Chants

[1] Two friends and the writer of this article attended a lecture on Native American history and culture. [2] The writer's two friends especially enjoyed the lecture, since the lecture was presented by the two friends' mother, who is an expert on the subject. [3] The lecturer's comments about the importance of music in Navajo religious ceremonies interested the writer of this article. [4] Navajo religious ceremonies regularly feature a male singer, or medicine man, who is a highly respected member of the singer's community. [5] The music is designed to provide healing for tribe members. [6] The singer has a great responsibility, for the singer's chant (which may take several days to complete) must be performed perfectly. [7] Otherwise the chant will not carry its healing powers. [8] The reader of this passage would have loved to hear the demonstration of the Navajo mountain chant. [9] The demonstration was fascinating.

Reflexive and Intensive Pronouns

You form the reflexive and intensive pronouns by adding *-self* or *-selves* to certain personal and possessive pronouns.

Reflexive and Intensive Pronouns		
	Singular	**Plural**
FIRST PERSON	myself	ourselves
SECOND PERSON	yourself	yourselves
THIRD PERSON	himself, herself, itself	themselves

A **reflexive pronoun** refers to a noun or another pronoun and indicates that the same person or thing is involved.

A **reflexive pronoun** reflects back to a noun or pronoun used earlier in the sentence, indicating that the same person or thing is involved. A reflexive pronoun always adds information.

I almost exhausted **myself** working for her in the campaign.

Today, for the first time in months, she is **herself.**

As a team they have no faith in **themselves.**

An **intensive pronoun** adds emphasis to another noun or pronoun.

An **intensive pronoun** does not add information to the sentence. If it is omitted, the meaning of the sentence will still be the same.

An **intensive pronoun** is often placed directly after its antecedent.

You **yoursel**f told me to stop.

Rita **herself** met us.

However, an **intensive pronoun** may come anywhere in the sentence.

I baked the bread **myself**.

We will bake it **ourselves**.

Exercise 16 — Identifying Antecedents of Reflexive and Intensive Pronouns

On your paper write the antecedent of the italicized pronoun in each of the following sentences.

SAMPLE   John Tyler and his wife, Julia, wrote a poem and set it to music *themselves*.
ANSWER   John Tyler and his wife, Julia

Presidents and Their Families

1. During her college years, Pat Nixon supported *herself* as a bank teller and also worked as a movie extra.
2. Mamie Eisenhower and her friends often amused *themselves* by playing cards.
3. To entertain *himself* at his father's inauguration, Charles Taft read a book.
4. The White House *itself* was the focus of much of Jacqueline Kennedy's reading before she actually moved in.
5. Because Gerald Ford *himself* had laryngitis, he asked his wife to extend his congratulations to President-elect Jimmy Carter.

Exercise 17 — Distinguishing Between Reflexive and Intensive Pronouns

On your paper write the reflexive or intensive pronoun in each of the following sentences. Then identify each pronoun as *reflexive* or *intensive*.

Marie Curie

1. As a child, Marie threw herself into her studies.
2. Learning itself was her passion.
3. By the time she married Pierre Curie, he had already made himself a reputation as a well-known physicist.
4. When working with radioactive compounds, even Marie herself was surprised at how much radioactivity they gave.
5. Recognizing the significance of his wife's work, Pierre convinced himself to abandon his research and help Marie.
6. Marie often had to defend herself from attacks made against her because she was a woman scientist.
7. During World War I, Marie promoted the use of the X-ray machine for medical purposes. The doctors themselves were not immediately convinced of the machine's usefulness.
8. Marie's contribution to science was invaluable, but the work itself may have led to her untimely death.
9. Because so little was known about radioactivity, Marie did not realize that she needed to protect herself from polonium radiation.
10. Did Marie congratulate herself when she was appointed as a delegate to the League of Nations?

Demonstrative Pronouns

This is the hat.

A **demonstrative pronoun** points out specific persons, places, things, or ideas.

Demonstrative Pronouns		
SINGULAR	this	that
PLURAL	these	those

A **demonstrative pronoun** can come before or after its antecedent. An antecedent may also be understood.

BEFORE ANTECEDENT   **This** is the hat I want.

These are the potatoes left over from dinner.

AFTER ANTECEDENT   My old shoes are nicer than **those**.

UNDERSTOOD ANTECEDENT   Show me **that** (thing) again.

Exercise 18   **Completing Sentences with Reflexive, Intensive, and Demonstrative Pronouns**

Supply the appropriate reflexive, intensive, or demonstrative pronoun for each blank. On your paper write the pronoun and identify whether it is *reflexive*, *intensive*, or *demonstrative*.

Recollecting the Harlem Renaissance

1. Actually, I _____ suggested a field trip to New York City to learn more about Countee Cullen and the Harlem Renaissance.
2. Our class polled _____ to determine whether there was sufficient interest in the trip.
3. _____ was the most one-sided vote I had ever seen.
4. We surprised _____ by raising enough money to allow the entire class to spend one day and night in New York.
5. During the 1920s and 1930s, Countee Cullen, Langston Hughes, Zora Neale Hurston, W.E.B. Du Bois, and Jean Toomer all lived and supported _____ in Harlem.
6. _____ are only a few of the hundreds of writers, musicians, and artists who helped make Harlem vibrant.
7. The class set two specific goals: they were to find the site of the historic Cotton Club _____ and to locate the building where Countee Cullen grew up.
8. Our teacher reminded us that Cullen _____ had been a schoolteacher in New York's public schools.
9. After a day of nearly four miles of walking, we treated _____ to a picnic in Riverside Park.
10. Back home again, we all said, "_____ was a trip we shall never forget."

Interrogative and Relative Pronouns

An **interrogative pronoun** is used to form questions.

> who?   whom?   whose?   what?   which?

> **Who** are those strangers?
> **Whom** should I invite?
> **Whose** did you borrow?
> **What** did you say?
> **Which** of these personal computers shall I buy?

The intensive forms of the interrogative pronouns are *whoever, whosoever, whomever, whichever,* and *whatever.*

> **Whoever** told you that?   **Whatever** did you say?

A **relative pronoun** is used to begin a special subject-verb word group called a subordinate clause (see Unit 13).

> who   whose   whomever   that   what
> whom   whoever   which   whichever whatever

> The pilot **who** landed the plane is my cousin. [The relative pronoun *who* begins the subordinate clause *who landed the plane.*]

> The plane, **which** landed late, carried our friends. [The relative pronoun *which* begins the subordinate clause *which landed late.*]

| Exercise 19 | Distinguishing Between Interrogative and Relative Pronouns |

On your paper list the interrogative and relative pronouns that appear in the following sentences, and label each pronoun as *interrogative* or *relative.* (Some sentences have more than one interrogative or relative pronoun.)

Frida Kahlo

[1]On a quiz show I heard the question "Which of the modern Mexican artists had a museum named after her?" [2]It was then that I first heard of Frida Kahlo, whose paintings include *The Broken Column.* [3]Kahlo, who in her youth was in a highway accident that forced her to abandon her dream of becoming a doctor, became an artist instead. [4]Whoever sees her work is enchanted by its bright colors and vibrant forms. [5]It is clear, however, that Kahlo's paintings often contain images of figures in pain. [6]One might ask, What was it that gave her the strength to continue painting after the accident had left her in constant pain? [7]After her death in 1954, her husband, Diego Rivera, who was also a celebrated painter, gave Kahlo's home to the Mexican government for use as a museum.

[8]In recent years much has been written about Frida Kahlo, whose art is now displayed in galleries worldwide. [9]The book that tells the story of her life with Diego Rivera is especially fascinating. [10]Whoever wrote it must have known both artists well.

Indefinite Pronouns

An **indefinite pronoun** refers to persons, places, or things in a more general way than a noun does.

Jacob seems to know **everyone** at school. [The indefinite pronoun *everyone* refers to people in general.]

I'm going to bake **something** special. [The indefinite pronoun *something* does not indicate to what it specifically refers.]

We served the bread, not knowing **some** was stale. [The indefinite pronoun *some* has the specific antecedent *bread*.]

Some Indefinite Pronouns				
all	each	many	nothing	somebody
another	either	most	one	someone
any	enough	much	other	something
anybody	everybody	neither	others	
anyone	everyone	nobody	plenty	
anything	everything	none	several	
both	few	no one	some	

Exercise 20   **Identifying Different Kinds of Pronouns**

(a) On your paper list in order the 25 pronouns that appear in the following paragraph.
(b) Identify each pronoun as *personal, possessive, reflexive, intensive, demonstrative, interrogative, relative,* or *indefinite.*

The Riddle of the Sphinx

[1] The Sphinx was a mythical monster that had the body of a lion and the head of a woman. [2] The people of Thebes were under her control, and anyone who met her had to answer a riddle correctly or die. [3] This was the riddle: what walks on four legs in the morning, on two legs at noon, and on three legs at night? [4] Many tried, but none could solve the riddle. [5] Then Oedipus, himself a Greek hero, confronted her. [6] When he correctly answered the riddle, the enraged Sphinx threw herself from a cliff. [7] The people of Thebes, whose deliverance Oedipus had won, were so grateful they made him king. [8] In our time everyone knows the answer to the riddle. [9] It is you and I and all of humankind. [10] We crawl on hands and knees as babies, travel on two legs in our youth, and use a cane to support ourselves in old age.

Exercise 21   **Creating Sentences with Different Kinds of Pronouns**

Write 10 sentences about a favorite meal that you shared with friends or members of your family. Try to use pronouns from all the categories you have studied in this lesson.

10.3 Verbs

A **verb** is a word that expresses action or a state of being and is necessary to make a statement.

Business people **work.**
The curtain **closed** too soon.
Artists **are** creative.

A verb has the ability to express time—present, past, and future—by means of *tense.*

PRESENT TENSE	We **hear** a car outside.
PAST TENSE	We **heard** a car outside.
FUTURE TENSE	We **will hear** a car outside.

Exercise 22   **Completing Sentences with Verbs**

On your paper write 20 complete sentences by supplying a verb for each blank.

Hawks as Hunters

1. The solitary hawk _____ slowly high above the green valley.
2. It _____ black against the blue sky.
3. Sensing the hawk's presence, the rodents _____ in the grass.
4. Riding rising air currents, the hawk barely _____ its wings.
5. Its flight _____ effortless.
6. With its piercing eyes, the hawk _____ the countryside in search of food.
7. A hawk _____ eight times more acutely than a human being.
8. Some hawks will even _____ at night, catching bats on the wing.
9. Hawks are territorial birds that _____ their nests from other hawks.
10. Most hawks _____ their nests high in trees.
11. Some hawks _____ by themselves or in small flocks.
12. Cooper's Hawks often _____ on telephone poles.
13. The osprey, a type of hawk, _____ fish almost exclusively.
14. Hawks _____ for the slightest movement in the grass below.
15. The red-tailed hawk _____ mainly on small rodents.
16. Many bird watchers _____ at Hawk Mountain in Pennsylvania.
17. Experienced bird watchers _____ hawks flying in the distance.
18. Hawks _____ hooked bills and strong talons.
19. Bird watchers _____ different kinds of hawks by their coloring and silhouette.
20. Hawks _____ larger than most other birds.

Action Verbs

An **action verb** tells what someone or something does.

Action verbs can express either physical or mental action.

PHYSICAL ACTION   The huge linemen **lead** the charge through
the defense.

MENTAL ACTION   The coaches **plan** the team's strategy
before each game.

A **transitive verb** is an action verb that is followed by a word or words that answer the question *what?* or *whom?*

Chipmunks **climb** small trees to get at berries and nuts. [The action verb *climb* is followed by the noun *trees*, which answers the question *climb what?*]

An **intransitive verb** is an action verb that is *not* followed by a word that answers the question *what?* or *whom?*.

Chipmunks also **climb** much of the time simply to escape from their enemies. [The action verb is followed by words that tell *when* and *why*.]

To decide if a verb in a sentence is transitive or intransitive, ask *what?* or *whom?* after the verb. If the answer is given in the sentence, the verb is transitive. If the answer is not given in the sentence, the verb is intransitive.

Many action verbs can be either transitive or intransitive, depending on how they are used in a sentence.

TRANSITIVE   Jill usually **ate** her sandwich in the cafeteria.
[*Sandwich* tells what Jill ate.]

INTRANSITIVE   Jill **ate** right before class today. [*Right before class today* tells when Jill ate.]

Some verbs have only transitive or intransitive uses. A dictionary will indicate how a verb may be used.

Identifying Action Verbs

On your paper write the action verb that appears in each of the following sentences. Indicate how the verb is used by writing *transitive* or *intransitive* .

Hints for Backpackers

1. Backpackers often carry contour maps on a hike.
2. Contour lines on a map identify the elevation of each spot.
3. Numerals on a contour line tell an area's distance above sea level.
4. On steep slopes contour lines run close together.
5. Rivers, creeks, and rills always flow downward across the contour lines of a map.
6. Hills and valleys show vividly on a contour map.
7. The abbreviation *BM* (for bench mark) indicates the location of a tablet with the exact elevation of that spot.
8. Surveys by the United States Geological Survey place at least two bench-mark tablets in each township.
9. Hikers use bench marks for reference.
10. With the help of a contour map, compass, and bench marks, backpackers find the right track.

Exercise 24   **Identifying and Using Transitive and Intransitive Verbs**

On your paper write the verb that appears in each of the following sentences. Label each verb *transitive* or *intransitive*, depending on how it is used in the sentence. Then write five new sentences, using each transitive verb as an intransitive verb and each intransitive verb as a transitive verb.

SAMPLE   I type my poetry assignments for English class.
ANSWER   type, transitive
           I type slowly but accurately.

The Challenge of Haiku

1. Most of my classmates wrote poems that rhyme.
2. Barbara and I, however, each composed a haiku—three lines with 17 syllables of unrhymed verse.
3. The great Japanese poet Bashō lived in the seventeenth century.
4. The simplicity of Bashō's verses awakened in many readers a love of all poetry, especially haiku.
5. What other poet thought as simply and clearly as Bashō?

Exercise 25 ʻ   **Creating Sentences with Action Verbs**

Choose five of the action verbs that you identified in Exercise 23. For each verb write one sentence.

Linking Verbs

A **linking verb** links, or joins, the subject of a sentence (often a noun or pronoun) with a word or expression that identifies or describes the subject. A linking verb does not show action.

The most commonly used linking verb is *be* in all its forms—*am, is, are, was, were, will be, has been, was being*.

I **am** a musician.
That singer **is** an artist.
The days **were** hot.
Those **are** mosquitoes.

Several verbs other than the forms of *be* can also act as linking verbs.

Other Linking Verbs			
appear	grow	seem	stay
become	look	sound	taste
feel	remain	smell	

The cake **tastes** good.
He **grew** taller over the summer.
She **felt** good about the election results.
He **seems** better today.

Exercise 26   **Completing Sentences with Linking Verbs**

On your paper write a linking verb to complete each sentence below. Try to use as many different linking verbs as possible.

Weather in the Great Lakes

1. The weather around the Great Lakes _____ quite cold in the winter.
2. The summers, however, _____ either cool or very hot.
3. The weather _____ most pleasant in the fall.
4. The days _____ warm even though the nights _____ colder.
5. People _____ happiest about the weather when the sun shines.

On your paper write the linking verb that appears in each of the following sentences.

The United States Flag

1. After World War II the flag of the United States became a familiar symbol around the world.
2. Before the American Revolution most colonial flags looked similar to the British flag.
3. The traditional story about Betsy Ross's role in the creation of the first U.S. flag now appears unlikely.
4. Francis Hopkinson, a delegate to the Continental Congress, was probably the designer of the first American flag.
5. The stripes in the flag, an idea from a colonial patriot group's flag, are symbolic of the thirteen original colonies.
6. Though not official, a flag with thirteen stars in a circle is often representative of the nation's early years.
7. The colors red, white, and blue on the flag are traditional.
8. After years of confusion about where to place each new star, the positions of the flag's stars became official by presidential order in 1912.
9. By government regulation an American flag is part of every public building and school.
10. The U.S. flag is always the flag on the right in a parade or display with other flags.
11. No other flags are more prominent than the U.S. flag.
12. The blue field of stars appears uppermost in any display against a wall.
13. Most of these regulations seem helpful for the preparation of official exhibits about the flag's history.
14. A flag with a rattlesnake on it was once a symbol of the American colonies.
15. Many of the state flags are red, white, and blue, like the U.S. flag.

On your paper list 10 verbs that appear in the following paragraph. Identify each verb as either *action* or *linking*.

Jesse Owens, Gold Medalist

[1]Jesse Owens was one of the first superstars in track and field. [2]As a junior high school student in Cleveland, Ohio, in the 1920s, Owens sprinted 100 yards in 10 seconds. [3]A few years later, he captured the entire nation's attention with a 10.3-second 100-yard dash at East Technical High School. [4]His fame increased during his years as an athlete at Ohio State University. [5]Owens's performance in four separate events on May 25, 1935, seemed extraordinary. [6]At the age of 22, he shattered world records for the 220-yard dash, the 220-yard low hurdles, and the broad jump. [7]A new record in a fourth event, the 100-yard dash, was just out of his reach. [8]Jesse Owens's fame peaked the following year at the 1936 Olympics in Berlin, Germany. [9]In the presence of the Nazi dictator, Adolf Hitler, Owens won gold medals in four events. [10]Hitler's lack of acknowledgment of the achievements of this famous African American only heightened the world's appreciation of Owens's success.

Verb Phrases

The verb in a sentence may consist of more than one word. The words that accompany the main verb are called **auxiliary,** or helping, **verbs.**

A **verb phrase** consists of a main verb and all its auxiliary, or helping, verbs.

The forms of *be* and *have* are the most common auxiliary verbs. They help the main verb express the various tenses.

I am walking.   **I have walked.**   **I had been walking.**

Auxiliary Verbs			
FORMS OF *BE*	am, is, are, was, were, being, been		
FORMS OF *HAVE*	has, have, had, having		
OTHER AUXILIARIES	can, could	may, might	shall, should
	do, does, did	must	will, would

In addition to expressing time, the other auxiliary verbs are used to express different shades of meaning.

She **might wait.**   We **would have played.**
He **could win.**   I **must be going.**

Exercise 29   **Identifying Verb Phrases**

On your paper write each verb phrase that appears in the following sentences. (Two of the sentences have more than one verb phrase.) Put parentheses around the auxiliary verbs in each phrase. (Words that interrupt a verb phrase are not considered part of the verb phrase.)

San Antonio's April Fiesta

1. For a long time now, the April fiesta has been the highlight of the year in San Antonio.
2. The fiesta may be the world's most enjoyable party, and it attracts visitors from all over.
3. People can enjoy excellent Spanish and Mexican meals while they are listening to delightful music.
4. They might hear country swing, country rock, or Dixieland.
5. The fiesta must begin in front of the Alamo on a Saturday.
6. It may last ten days.
7. Always the highlight, the Battle of Flowers Parade has attracted people since 1891.
8. During the fiesta all of San Antonio's diverse cultures can display themselves and have done so brilliantly over the years.
9. The pomp and lavishness of the fiesta could humble the royalty of Europe.
10. Tourists will long remember the lights, flowers, and music.

Completing Sentences with Verb Phrases

On your paper complete the following sentences by replacing each blank with a verb phrase. Be sure that your completed sentences make sense.

Florida

1. Florida _____ the "sunshine state."
2. Because of environmental problems, many native animals in Florida, such as the manatee and the Florida panther, _____ in number.
3. Tourists _____ to Florida by the warm climate, beautiful beaches, and many entertainment centers.
4. With the opening of Disney World, central Florida _____ from a quiet rural area to a world-renowned tourist destination.
5. The Apollo 11 moon rocket _____ from the Kennedy Space Center near Titusville.
6. Each night the beautiful sunset _____ by the many people congregated in Key West's Mallory Square.
7. St. Augustine, the oldest city in America, _____ in 1565.
8. Miami became an important city after railroads _____ to link it with cities farther north.
9. Many ships _____ at the port in Jacksonville.
10. High-technology and electronics industries _____ in the Melbourne-Palm Bay area.

Completing Sentences with Different Kinds of Verbs

On your paper complete each sentence in the following paragraph by supplying a verb. The kind of verb to use in each case is indicated in italics. Be sure that your completed sentences make sense.

Hobbies

Because people [1]*action verb* more leisure time than ever before, hobbies [2] *verb phrase* in popularity. Preferences for hobbies [3]*action verb* greatly from person to person. Whereas some people [4]*action verb* sculpture, others [5]*linking verb* most content when they [6]*verb phrase* an old car. Photography [7]*action verb* to many people, some of whom [8]*action verb* darkrooms, where they [9] *verb phrase* their own film. Hobby stores [10]*action verb* model planes that actually [11]*action verb* even though they [12]*verb phrase* very fragile. People who [13]*action verb* for a hobby [14]*linking verb* quite pleased when they [15]*verb phrase* their work at an art show. Anyone [16]*verb phrase* a philatelist, which [17]*linking verb* the term for a person who [18]*action verb* stamps. The more a philatelist's collection [19]*action verb*, the more valuable it [20]*linking verb*.

Creating Sentences with Vivid Verbs

On your paper write five sentences about one of your favorite outdoor activities. Choose very specific action verbs and verb phrases vividly to convey a sense of the activity.

10.4 Adjectives

HOW

THAT

THE TULIP IS

THE FLORIST
CONSIDERED IT

THE TULIPS,

BEAUTIFUL

THE TULIP IS !

TULIP WON
FIRST PRIZE.

.

.

IN THE
SUNLIGHT,
DANCED IN
THE WIND.

An **adjective** is a word that modifies a noun or pronoun by limiting its meaning.

An adjective may describe a noun or pronoun by answering one of these questions: *What kind? Which one? How many? How much?*

QUESTION	ADJECTIVES	
What kind?	**green** sweater	**sunny** Greece
	tall woman	**pure** joy
Which one?	**this** book	**these** islands
	that child	**those** rules
How many?	**four** oceans	**few** farmers
	many rings	**both** principals
How much?	**more** money	**no** time
	enough salad	**little** patience

Adjectives appear in various positions according to the words they modify.

How **beautiful** the tulip is!
That **beautiful** tulip won first prize.
The tulip is **beautiful.**
The florist considered the tulip **beautiful.**
The tulips, **beautiful** in the sunlight, danced in the wind.

The words *a, and,* and *the* are special kinds of adjectives called **articles**. *A* and *an* are called **indefinite articles**. *The* is called the **definite article**.

INDEFINITE	We camped near **a** river.
	Kim ate **an** orange.
DEFINITE	We camped near **the** river.
	Kim ate **the** orange.

Forms of Adjectives

Many adjectives have different forms to indicate their degree of comparison. The **positive degree** is the simple form of the adjective. The **comparative degree** compares two persons, places, things, or ideas. The **superlative degree** compares more than two persons, places, things, or ideas.

POSITIVE	COMPARATIVE	SUPERLATIVE
slow	slower	slowest
healthy	healthier	healthiest
strenuous	more strenuous	most strenuous

Comparative adjectives of two or more syllables are usually formed by placing the words *more* or *most* in front of the positive form.

| **Exercise 33** | Identifying Adjectives and the Nouns They Modify |

In the following sentences, identify the adjectives and the nouns they modify. Do not include definite and indefinite articles. On your paper list the words in two columns, one labeled *adjectives* and the other labeled *nouns they modify*.

SAMPLE   Bells are musical instruments that originated in ancient China.

ANSWER | ADJECTIVES | NOUNS THEY MODIFY |
| --- | --- |
| musical | instruments |
| ancient | China |

A Short History of Bells

1. Some of the earliest bells had rich ornamentation.
2. Such bells were used originally to provide an atmosphere of mystery to religious ceremonies.
3. It was once thought that ringing a bell would drive away deadly diseases.
4. The Chinese and Japanese decorated temples with bells that made a delicate sound in the slightest breeze.
5. The ancient Goths stirred reluctant soldiers to military order with the ringing of bells.
6. Women in Persia once wore little bells as jewelry.
7. Bells have also been used to warn off a nearby enemy or other danger.
8. The practical Greeks used bells to announce the arrival of fish fresh from the sea.
9. If we heard a bell in a busy supermarket today, we would consider the sound bizarre.
10. In Rome no bells advertised merchandise, but many bells tolled the news when an emperor died.
11. In ancient Greece and Rome, bells were hung on the tomb and funeral carriage of a king.
12. In Burma, bells were hung in the pagodas to drive away evil spirits.
13. In Africa, healers hung a bell over the doorway of the house of a sick person.
14. The Celts became more famous than the Romans for making melodic chimes.
15. Since the sixth century, Christians have had a great enthusiasm for bells.
16. Bells were once hung in some churches as a protection against violent storms.
17. In Italy special towers, or *campaniles*, were constructed for particularly immense bells.
18. In England a local officer rang a bell to announce a late curfew, a fire, a meeting, or even a certain deadline.
19. A crier in a town would ring a bell to attract a large crowd and then shout the latest news.
20. Today we hear fewer bells because most of them have been replaced by electronic methods of communications.

Proper Adjectives

A **proper adjective** is formed from a proper noun and begins with a capital letter.

Duke Ellington was an **African American** composer.
The term **Victorian Era** refers to the years 1837 to 1901.

Proper adjectives are often created by using the following suffixes: *-an, -ian, -n, -ese, -ish,* and *-ic.*

PROPER NOUNS	PROPER ADJECTIVES
Queen Elizabeth I	Elizabethan
Indonesia	Indonesian
Japan	Japanese
Spain	Spanish

Some words that began as proper adjectives have been used for so long that their origins have been forgotten or disregarded. Such words have become **common adjectives** that begin with lowercase letters.

PROPER NOUNS	COMMON ADJECTIVES
Italy	italic
Rome	romantic
Puritan	puritanical
Bohemia	bohemian

Exercise 34 — Forming Proper Adjectives from Proper Nouns

Write a proper adjective for each proper noun below. Consult a dictionary if necessary.

1. Asia
2. Sigmund Freud
3. King George
4. Greece
5. Turkey
6. Mars
7. Java
8. Charles Dickens
9. Siberia
10. Brazil
11. China
12. Canada
13. William Shakespeare
14. Malta
15. Ireland
16. Iceland
17. Andrew Jackson
18. Hungary
19. King Edward
20. Europe
21. Britain
22. Boston
23. Nepal
24. Norway
25. Paris

Nouns Used as Adjectives

In some cases nouns are used as adjectives. A noun used as an adjective answers one of these questions: *What kind? Which one?*

NOUNS	NOUNS AS ADJECTIVES
music	**music** critic (What kind of critic?)
city	**city** bus (What kind of bus?)
history	**history** lesson (Which lesson?)
United States	**United States** flag (Which flag?)

Sometimes possessive nouns are used as adjectives.

Kate's parrot   the **river's** source   the **story's** end   **Don's** restaurant

---

Exercise 35	Identifying Adjectives and Nouns Used as Adjectives

On your paper list the adjectives in the following sentences. Do not include definite and indefinite articles. If the adjective is also a noun, write *noun* in parentheses.

SAMPLE   In the early 1900s there were few laws against child labor.
ANSWER   early, few, child (noun)

Chicago's "Newsies"

1. In the first part of this century, the newspaper business was thriving in Chicago.
2. The newspapers' success was due largely to a sensational style of journalism.
3. A small army of children sold these papers to commuters in the downtown section of the city.
4. These so-called "newsies" were not street urchins but ordinary kids who wanted to earn a little money after school.
5. They came from every ethnic group in the city.
6. Before the daily supply of papers arrived, the newsies would often play a baseball game.
7. As soon as rush hour began, they went to work.
8. Industrious little hustlers appeared where carefree children had stood.
9. The eager children stationed themselves along streets with the heaviest pedestrian traffic.
10. Some set up shop outside department stores and subway stations.
11. Those newsies who succeeded had a good business sense and an aggressive sales pitch.
12. On a slow day, some of the newsies made up false news headlines to attract customers.
13. The children lived for the great headlines, the large red type that sold editions.
14. The newsies had to anticipate probable sales before they purchased any newspapers.
15. However, they made more money by begging for tips from big spenders.
16. The excitement of street life provided a break from the stuffy classroom.
17. Social reformers feared that the children's lifestyle would lead them to serious crime later on.
18. Few boys, however, became real criminals in the adult world.
19. These industrious children raised themselves from poverty to prosperity.
20. Most of them ended up as successful business executives because of the work ethic they had developed on Chicago's streets.

Pronouns Used as Adjectives

Some pronouns can also be used as adjectives. **Possessive adjectives** are possessive pronouns that answer the question *Which one?*

There are seven possessive pronouns that can also be used as adjectives: *my, your, her, his, its, our,* and *their.*

Woody wrecked **his** car in the crash.
Roller-blading is **our** idea of fun.
The Millers cultivated **their** garden.
Your photo turned out well.

Demonstrative adjectives are pronouns that answer the questions *Which one? How many?* and *How much?*

She went to **that** concert.   They took **those** classes.

Interrogative adjectives are pronouns that are used to ask questions.

Which concert did she hear?
What grade did he get?
Whose party was best?

| Exercise 36 | Identifying Adjectives and Pronouns Used as Adjectives |

On your paper list the 20 adjectives that appear in the following passage. Count possessive pronouns as well as regular adjectives in this exercise, but do not count the words *a, an,* and *the.*

A Farmer and His Land

[1] There was a bright, full moon in the clear sky, and the sunset was still shining faintly in the west. [2] Dark woods stood all about the old . . . farmhouse, save down the hill, westward, where lay the shadowy fields which John Hilton, and his father before him, had cleared and tilled with much toil—the small fields to which they had given the industry and . . . affection of their honest lives. [3] John Hilton was sitting on the doorstep of his house. [4] As he moved his head in and out of the shadows, . . . one could see his good face, rough and somewhat unkempt, as if he were indeed a creature of the shady woods and brown earth, instead of the noisy town.

From "The Hiltons' Holiday" by Sarah Orne Jewett

Identifying Different Kinds of Adjectives

On your paper write the 25 adjectives, including articles, that appear in the following paragraph.

The Hawaiian Islands

[1]Hawaii is a chain of 132 islands. [2]These beautiful islands extend 1,523 miles. [3]Major islands include Maui; Oahu; and Hawaii, an island that is famous for active volcanoes. [4]Although there are a number of islands, Hawaiian people live only on major ones. [5]Kahoolawe has no inhabitants. [6]It is used only for naval purposes. [7]Minor islands, some only as big as great rocks, are too small and infertile to support human life. [8]Hawaii's population displays a mixture of origins. [9]Diversity is one of its sources of vitality. [10]Much of the population is of Asian descent.

Expanding Sentences with Adjectives

On your paper rewrite each of the following sentences, adding at least two appropriate adjectives to each one. In your 10 sentences include at least one comparative or superlative adjective, one noun used as an adjective, and one pronoun used as an adjective.

SAMPLE   A store is located in the mall.
ANSWER   An electronics store is located in the nearest mall.

An Audio Demonstration

1. Music filled the showroom of the electronics store.
2. A salesman showed a speaker system to my two friends and me.
3. Though we liked the size and appearance of the speakers, we were obviously more interested in the sound.
4. The salesman played tapes to demonstrate the speakers' power, clarity, and versatility.
5. First my friends and I listened to a song by Loretta Lynn.
6. Seconds later I heard the notes of a Mozart piano concerto.
7. When the piano, bass, and drums of an Aretha Franklin song kicked in, I noticed a number of feet beginning to tap.
8. Before long, bodies began to sway and customers started to mouth the words of the song.
9. I almost expected the singer to appear out of nowhere.
10. My friends and I are fans of soul music from the 1960s and 1970s—especially the music of Aretha Franklin.
11. She has a way of making music that touches the hearts and souls of all people.
12. As much as I loved the sound that came through those speakers, I knew that I would never own them, for their price was astronomical.
13. My speakers at home have problems that I guess I will have to endure a bit longer.
14. I wonder whether that store will ever have a sale on speakers.
15. I'll look for advertisements in the weeks ahead.

Creating Sentences with Adjectives

Write five sentences about a favorite food. Use at least two descriptive adjectives in each sentence.

An **adverb** is a word that modifies a verb, an adjective, or another adverb by making its meaning more specific.

Adverbs That Modify Verbs

Adverbs add meaning to verbs and verb phrases by answering the questions *when? where? how?* and *to what degree?*

ADVERBS THAT MODIFY VERBS

QUESTION	VERB	ADVERB
When?	fly	fly **now**
	had arrived	had arrived **early**
Where?	jump	jump **aside**
	was charging	was charging **forward**
How?	argued	argued **effectively**
	will speak	will speak **clearly**
To what degree?	finish	finish **completely**
	would have known	**hardly** would have known

When modifying a verb, an adverb may appear in various positions in relation to the verb.

Eventually the train will arrive at the station.

The train will **eventually** arrive at the station.

The train will arrive at the station **eventually.**

Negative words also function as adverbs modifying verbs.

Adverbs include the word *not* and the contraction *-n't*. Other negative words can also function as adverbs of time, place, and degree.

The cow is **not** in the barn.
The cow is **nowhere** in sight.
I **never** saw a purple cow.
The cow **scarcely** chews her cud.

" Nothing can stop me now,"

Tom said tirelessly.

Identifying Different Kinds of Adverbs

On your paper write each of the 20 adverbs in the paragraph below. Then write the verb that each adverb modifies.

SAMPLE   Hercules performed difficult tasks easily because of his strength.
ANSWER   easily—performed

The Labors of Hercules

[1]People usually equate the word *Hercules* with physical strength, and today I learned the Greek myth behind the name. [2]As a child, Hercules earnestly studied the arts of chariot racing, wrestling, and archery. [3]He grew steadily in physical strength but never improved his self-control. [4]Once he attacked his music teacher in a fit of rage; for this misdeed he was sent off to the countryside by the king of Thebes. [5]There he lived in the fresh air and increased his strength daily . [6]As an adult, he still possessed a hot temper and a violent streak. [7]Then the Greek gods sternly ordered him to perform 12 difficult tasks that had not been completed by anyone else. [8]He slew a savage lion and brought back its skin as his initial task. [9]Next he somehow found the land of the Amazons and took away the precious belt of Hippolyta, the queen of the Amazons. [10]Hercules finally tamed his unruly temper, and afterward he became the national hero of Greece. [11]We often refer to difficult tasks as "the labors of Hercules."

Positioning Adverbs That Modify Verbs

Rewrite each of the following sentences, adding the verb-modifying adverb that appears in parentheses. Then write each sentence again, this time placing the same adverb in a different position.

SAMPLE   At the end of the steep trail, we beheld the ruins of Machu Picchu. (finally)
ANSWER   **a.** At the end of the steep trail, we finally beheld the ruins of Machu Picchu.
           b. Finally, at the end of the steep trail, we beheld the ruins of Machu Picchu.

The Lost City of the Inca

1. The ancient Inca city of Machu Picchu was discovered by an American archeologist in 1911. (surprisingly)
2. Hiram Bingham had searched for the city before finding it. (tirelessly)
3. News of the fabulous discovery began to spread. (soon)
4. Archaeologists had found such a splendid site before. (seldom)
5. The Inca held on to Machu Picchu until the sixteenth century. (tenaciously)
6. The Spanish conquistador Francisco Pizarro conquered the Inca Empire in 1533. (ruthlessly)
7. The sacred city of Machu Picchu was abandoned. (then)
8. It has survived earthquakes and erosion. (fortunately)
9. The world has seen finer stonework than that of Machu Picchu. (never)

Adverbs That Modify Adjectives

Adverbs can give additional meaning to adjectives. An adverb that modifies an adjective answers the question *To what degree?*

QUESTION	ADJECTIVE	ADVERB
To what degree?	beautiful	**very** beautiful
	shy	**rather** shy
	optimistic	**unusually** optimistic
	clean	**thoroughly** clean

Adverbs that modify adjectives generally appear directly before the word they modify.

The train is **extremely** late.   June felt **rather** weak.

Will pitches **incredibly** fast.   My **very** best friend moved.

Exercise 42   **Identifying Adverbs That Modify Adjectives**

On your paper list the adverb in each sentence that modifies an adjective. Then write the adjective the adverb modifies.

Hot-Air Ballooning

1. Hot-air ballooning is a somewhat recent sport craze in the United States.
2. The first flight in history was accomplished by the truly talented Montgolfier brothers at Annonay, France, in 1783.
3. It must have seemed a particularly risky undertaking because this was the first time people had defied gravity.
4. Within a few years, balloonists substituted hydrogen gas for hot air because hydrogen was greatly superior in buoyancy.
5. The world's first air force was an understandably small balloon corps established by the French in 1794.
6. In 1793 Jean Pierre Blanchard made the very first balloon flight in America.
7. As late as the 1930s, balloon flights and races were extremely popular events.
8. In the 1960s, ballooning enjoyed a quite amazing revival.
9. The new generation of enthusiasts returned to hot air because they determined that it was much safer than hydrogen.
10. To the spectator, balloons look simply spectacular as they float silently over a large city.

Adverbs That Modify Adverbs

Sometimes adverbs are used to give extra meaning to other adverbs. An adverb that modifies an adverb answers the question *To what degree?*

QUESTION	ADJECTIVE	ADVERB
To what degree?	walked **slowly**	walked **quite** slowly
	always wins	**almost** always wins
	call **often**	call **too** often

An adverb that modifies another adverb appears directly before the modified word.

They were **only** partially convinced.   Please speak **more** slowly

The play ended **somewhat** abruptly.   I know him **very** well.

Exercise 43	**Identifying Adverbs That Modify Other Adverbs**

On your paper list the adverb in each sentence that modifies another adverb. Then write the adverb that is being modified.

The Bermuda Triangle

1. The tabloid press quite frequently writes about bizarre events in an area known as the Bermuda Triangle.
2. Their stories depict most vividly a long list of strange occurrences that presumably have taken place there.
3. Journalists ask their readers to imagine a line that runs somewhat vaguely from Melbourne, Florida, to Bermuda, to Puerto Rico, and back to Florida.
4. They claim that within this triangle a large number of ships and airplanes have too often disappeared under mysterious circumstances.
5. It is known that storms move into this area very quickly.
6. Violent downward air currents occur there more frequently than in other places.
7. Scientists, however, are almost completely dubious about such tales.
8. They reiterate rather patiently that no such peculiarities exist.
9. They cannot understand why people nearly always accept hearsay over scientific evidence.
10. Nevertheless, readers of these tales remain convinced that we have just barely begun to understand the menace of the Bermuda Triangle.

Forms of Adverbs

Like adjectives, some adverbs have different forms to indicate degree of comparison. The comparative form of an adverb compares two actions. The superlative form of an adverb compares more than two actions.

For adverbs of only one syllable, add -*er* to make the comparative form and -*est* to make the superlative form.

POSITIVE	COMPARATIVE	SUPERLATIVE
plays **hard**	plays **harder**	plays **hardest**
climbed **high**	climbed **higher**	climbed **highest**

When an adverb ends in -*ly* , use the word *more* to form the comparative and *most* to form the superlative.

POSITIVE	COMPARATIVE	SUPERLATIVE
walks **slowly**	walks **more slowly**	walks **most slowly**
smiles **easily**	smiles **more easily**	smiles **most easily**

Some adverbs do not form the comparative and superlative in the regular manner.

POSITIVE	COMPARATIVE	SUPERLATIVE
skates **well**	skates **better**	skates **best**
dances **badly**	dances **worse**	dances **worst**
knows **little**	knows **less**	knows **least**
goes **far**	goes **farther**	goes **farthest**

Exercise 44   Using Comparative and Superlative Forms of Adverbs

On your paper write the comparative and superlative form of each adverb below. Then write a sentence using each of those forms.

SAMPLE hard

ANSWER harder, hardest

    He threw the ball harder than Peter, but I threw it hardest of all.

1. thoroughly
2. eagerly
3. low
4. well
5. near

6. badly
7. close
8. angrily
9. quickly
10. curiously

Distinguishing Between Adverbs and Adjectives

Some words can be either adverbs or adjectives, depending on how they are used in a sentence. To distinguish between these two parts of speech, remember that an adjective modifies a noun or pronoun, and an adverb modifies a verb, an adjective, or another adverb.

I arrived **late.** (adverb)   She ate **early.** (adverb)

The bus was **late.** (adjective)   She had an **early** date. (adjective)

You can sometimes distinguish an adverb from an adjective by remembering that many adverbs are formed by adding -*ly* to an adjective.

| a **rare** | book | a **great** | treat |
| ADJ. | NOUN | ADJ. | NOUN |

| **rarely** | find | **greatly** | appreciate |
| ADV. | VERB | ADV. | VERB |

Not all words that end in -*ly* are adverbs. Some are adjectives that have added -*ly* to the noun.

NOUN	ADJECTIVE ENDING IN -*LY*
brother	**brotherly** love
state	a **stately** home

Exercise 45   Distinguishing Between Adverbs and Adjectives.

On your paper identify each of the italicized words as an *adverb* or an *adjective*.

Nostalgia

1. My mother often speaks *nostalgically* about her childhood.
2. She and her two sisters enjoyed a *leisurely* existence in a small town.
3. Mother says her town was a *neighborly* place in which to live.
4. Most people she knew cared *little* for expensive cars and exotic vacations.
5. As she was the youngest, Mother was always getting *sisterly* advice from the other two.
6. They lived *close* to a park where the girls loved to skip rope and play jacks.
7. They felt *close* to each other because they got along so well.
8. Every night, the three young girls went to bed very *early*.
9. Their father told them, "The *early* bird catches the worm."
10. Now Mother's life is more *worldly*, but she misses those simpler times.

Identifying Different Kinds of Adverbs

On your paper write each of the 20 adverbs that appear in the following paragraph. Then write the word or words that each adverb modifies.

A Great African American Dancer

[1]While still a child, Pearl Primus came to the United States from Trinidad. [2]Later she attended college in New York and apparently planned to be a doctor. [3]She never expected to be a dancer. [4]Her obvious talent very quickly distinguished her. [5]Soon she won a scholarship and was studying dance exclusively. [6]Subsequently, she worked with Martha Graham, Doris Humphrey, and other masters of modern dance. [7]When she performed professionally, she received rave reviews everywhere for her beautiful dancing. [8]Critics justifiably called her the finest new dancer of 1943. [9]Primus was greatly interested in African dance and is widely credited with the introduction of African motifs into American dance. [10]Her quite frequent trips to the Caribbean and Africa helped her substantially, and she translated African dances meaningfully for all audiences. [11]At the age of 60 Primus had hardly slowed her pace. [12]She creatively developed programs for the handicapped and worked persistently on her doctoral degree. [13]In 1978 she finally received it.

Exercise 47   Completing Sentences with Adverbs

A Tom Swifty is a sentence in which an adverb comments in a humorous way on an action or object mentioned in a quotation. Note the relationship between each adverb and quotation in the following examples:

"I cleaned my room," Leroy said **tidily.**
"This picture has no color," complained Andrea **drably.**

Tom Swifties

Write the Tom Swifties in items 1–5 on your paper, completing each with an adverb that comments on the quotation. Then write five Tom Swifties of your own, using the adverbs provided in items 6–10. Consult a dictionary if necessary.

   1. "Don't burn yourself!" Min warned _____.
   2. "Nice job of sanding," said the carpenter _____.
   3. "These flowers were just picked," the florist said _____.
   4. "Is the pond frozen yet?" asked Luis _____.
   5. "That lemon made my mouth pucker!" Robin exclaimed _____.
   6. dully
   7. crisply
   8. softly
   9. blandly
  10. coolly

10.6 Prepositions

A **preposition** is a word that shows the relationship of a noun or pronoun to some other word in a sentence.

The garage is **behind** the house. [*Behind* shows the spatial relationship between the house and the garage.]

The engine purred **after** the adjustment. [*After* tells the time relationship between the purring and the adjustment.]

It started **with** ease. [*With* relates the verb *started* to the noun *ease*.]

Commonly Used Prepositions				
aboard	behind	except	opposite	under
about	below	excepting	out	underneath
above	beneath	for	outside	until
across	beside	from	over	unto
after	besides	in	past	up
against	between	inside	pending	upon
along	beyond	into	regarding	with
amid	but*	like	respecting	within
among	by	near	since	without
around	concerning	of	through	
as	despite	off	throughout	
at	down	on	to	
before	during	onto	toward	

*meaning "except"

A **compound preposition** is a preposition that is made up of more than one word.

Compound Prepositions		
according to	because of	next to
ahead of	by means of	on account of
along with	in addition to	on top of
apart from	in front of	out of
aside from	in spite of	owing to
as to	instead of	

Phrases that begin with a preposition usually end with a noun or pronoun, called the **object of the preposition.**

He gave me a book **of poetry.**
Mei Ying sat **next to me.**
I was talking **with Mei Ying.**

On your paper list the prepositions that appear in each of the following sentences. Remember that some prepositions are made up of more than one word. (The numeral in parentheses at the end of each item indicates the number of prepositions in that sentence.)

A Special-Effects Pioneer

1. Willis O'Brien, a creator of special effects for the early film industry, pioneered the use of rubber and clay models in movies. (4)
2. Shooting the film frame by frame and changing the position of the model slightly between shots, he created illusionary movement. (3)
3. By means of this method, O'Brien shot an experimental film with a clay dinosaur that "roamed" through a miniature set. (3)
4. Since the dinosaur's movements looked too choppy in this first attempt, O'Brien shot a second version, using dinosaurs made from rubber and metal instead of clay and wood. (3)
5. Six years after this film, which was distributed throughout the United States, O'Brien worked on a full-length movie concerning dinosaurs in a South American jungle. (5)
6. During one scene, a brontosaurus is brought across the ocean to London, where it escapes and runs around the city. (4)
7. In addition to his dinosaur models, O'Brien used scenery painted onto glass panes that he positioned in front of the action. (3)
8. Because of O'Brien's skill, models and sets were transformed into believable monsters and jungles on the movie screen. (3)
9. Years later, another movie showed a giant gorilla on top of the Empire State Building, high above the frightened crowds. (2)
10. This giant gorilla, which we now know as King Kong, was created by O'Brien. (2)

Exercise 49   Using Prepositional Phrases

Use each of the following prepositional phrases in an original sentence. Then combine your sentences into a coherent paragraph or two. You may combine your sentences in any order.

1. according to his directions
2. underneath the dining-room table
3. near the back door
4. on top of the map
5. outside the house
6. between you and me
7. beyond belief
8. throughout the evening
9. on the highway outside of town
10. against my better judgment

Some words may be used as either prepositions or adverbs. A word is used as a preposition if it has a noun or pronoun as its object. A word is used as an adverb if it does not have an object.

WORD USED AS PREPOSITION	WORD USED AS ADVERB
He left his friends **behind** the stadium.	He left his friends **behind**.
I finally took my boots **off** the step.	I finally took my boots **off**.
The bike is **outside** the garage.	The bike is **outside**.

| Exercise 50 | Completing Sentences with Prepositions and Adverbs |

On your paper, complete each sentence by writing any preposition or adverb that makes sense. Then write whether you used the word as a *preposition* or an *adverb*. Use the charts on pages 435 to help you choose appropriate words.

SAMPLE   I lost my balance and fell _____.

ANSWER   over—adverb

White-Water Rafting

1. Our first exposure to white-water rafting was _____ the Nantahala River.
2. The Nantahala is a swift-flowing river _____ Great Smoky Mountains National Park.
3. Friends had told us that nothing else compares to the thrill _____ white-water rafting.
4. Our guide warned us not to leave our life jackets _____ .
5. Our equipment was a large rubber raft _____ six long oars.
6. We learned how to direct our raft to the right or left, and even how to turn it completely _____.
7. As we started, it felt very chilly _____ the bright sun.
8. At first we were nervous because we were afraid of tipping the raft _____.
9. Soon we relaxed and began to joke with the people in the other raft _____ us.
10. _____ our successful experience this time, we plan to ride an even wilder river in the future.

| Exercise 51 | Creating Sentences with Prepositions |

Choose five prepositions from the lists on page 435. Use each one in a sentence. Add adjectives and adverbs wherever necessary.

10.7 | Conjunctions

A **conjunction** is a word that joins single words or groups of words.

Coordinating Conjunctions

A **coordinating conjunction** joins words or groups of words that have equal grammatical weight in a sentence.

Coordinating Conjunctions						
and	but	or	nor	for	yet	so

She designs **and** builds.
He writes in French **but** not in English.
Practice writing, **or** you will never improve.
She had no homework, **nor** did she have basketball practice.

Exercise 52   **Identifying Coordinating Conjunctions**

On your paper write the coordinating conjunction(s) that appear in the following sentences.

Baseball, an Integrated Sport

[1]Many people know something about the history of baseball in our country, but the story of African Americans and baseball is often neglected. [2]The history of African Americans and baseball began sometime during the Civil War, for it was then that black soldiers learned to play the game. [3]In 1885 a group of waiters from the Argyle Hotel in Babylon, New York, met and organized a paid baseball team. [4]All of the team's players were African American, yet they called themselves the Cuban Giants. [5]Their choice, they thought, was to pretend that they were Hispanic or face discrimination. [6]By the turn of the century, African Americans were playing on several college teams in the northern and the western sections of the country. [7]The 1920s was an important era for minorities and baseball, for several African American teams were organized during that decade. [8]Among them were the Homestead Grays, the American Giants, the Kansas City Monarchs, and the St. Louis Stars. [9]The great Jackie Robinson could have chosen to play on an African American team, but in 1947 he joined the Brooklyn Dodgers, becoming the first African American to play in the major leagues. [10]Prejudice didn't deter African American baseball heroes such as Jackie Robinson, nor were they discouraged by the low pay that they received during those early years.

Correlative Conjunctions

Correlative conjunctions work in pairs to join words and groups of words of equal weight in a sentence.

Correlative Conjunctions		
both . . . and	just as . . . so	not only . . . but (also)
either . . . or	neither . . . nor	whether . . . or

The relationship between words or groups of words is emphasized by using correlative conjunctions rather than coordinating conjunctions.

COORDINATING CONJUNCTIONS	CORRELATIVE CONJUNCTIONS
You **and** I must go.	**Both** you **and** I must go.
You **or** I must go.	**Either** you **or** I must go.
	Neither you **nor** I must go.
We saw Tokyo **and** Kyoto.	We saw **not only** Tokyo **but also** Kyoto.

Exercise 53　　　**Identifying Correlative Conjunctions**

On your paper write both parts of the correlative conjunctions that appear in the following sentences.

Special-issue Stamps

[1] A great many countries issue special stamps either to honor a famous person or to commemorate an important event. [2] Some countries print specially priced stamps in order to both celebrate an event and generate extra funds. [3] Either original art or reproductions of famous paintings may decorate the special stamps. [4] A special 1893 stamp was not only a tribute to the discovery of America but was also the first commemorative stamp issued by the United States. [5] Other stamps have honored both famous leaders and important occasions. [6] Neither the Apollo space program nor the nation's bicentennial passed without a special stamp. [7] During the International Year of the Child, another significant event, children's art appeared on both postage stamps and holiday seals. [8] Neither the American Lung Association, which used children's art on its holiday seals, nor the design sponsors chose the themes for the seals. [9] Each school chosen to take part decided on its own whether to tell its students exactly what to draw or simply to suggest a holiday theme. [10] Just as these holiday seals celebrated children's art, so the postage stamps from many other countries continue to do so.

Subordinating Conjunctions

A **subordinating conjunction** joins two clauses, or ideas, in such a way as to make one grammatically dependent upon the other.

The idea, or clause, introduced by a subordinating conjunction is considered subordinate, or dependent, because it cannot stand alone as a complete sentence.

We cheered the tall ships **because** they were so glorious.
We cheered the tall ships **when** they arrived.
Whenever the ships sail again, we will want to see them.
We will want to see them **if** they sail again.

Common Subordinating Conjunctions			
after	as though	provided (that)	until
although	because	since	when
as	before	so long as	whenever
as far as	considering (that)	so that	where
as if	if	than	whereas
as long as	inasmuch as	though	wherever
as soon as	in order that	unless	while

Exercise 54 — Identifying Subordinating Conjunctions

Write the subordinating conjunction that appears in each sentence below. Remember that some subordinating conjunctions are made up of more than one word.

Harold Krents, a Success Story

1. Considering that Harold Krents was totally blind by his eighth birthday, his achievements are extraordinary.
2. Life is not easy when your vision is impaired.
3. When he was in high school, Krents's classmates elected him president of his school.
4. Because Krents was brilliant, he was accepted by Harvard.
5. Before he went to college, Krents spent the summer as an arts counselor at camp.
6. Whereas others had difficulty finding their way around the tents in the dark, Krents moved about easily and kept the campers quiet after taps.
7. As soon as he had graduated *cum laude* from Harvard University, Krents was accepted at Harvard Law School.
8. Krents met his future wife while she was reading for visually challenged law students.
9. Krents was very surprised when his draft board mistakenly classified him 1-A.
10. After he heard Krents's story, Leonard Gershe wrote the play *Butterflies Are Free*.

Conjunctive Adverbs

A **conjunctive adverb** is used to clarify the relationship between clauses of equal weight in a sentence.

Conjunctive adverbs tend to be stronger and more precise than coordinating conjunctions.

COORDINATING CONJUNCTION	The ships sailed away, **but** they left us with happy memories.
CONJUNCTIVE ADVERB	The ships sailed away; **nevertheless,** they left us with happy memories.

Conjunctive adverbs have several uses:

TO REPLACE *AND*	also, besides, furthermore, moreover
TO REPLACE *BUT*	however, nevertheless, still
TO STATE A RESULT	consequently, therefore, so, thus
TO STATE EQUALITY	equally, likewise, similarly

Exercise 55   **Completing Sentences with Conjunctive Adverbs**

On your paper write each of the following sentences, replacing the blank with an appropriate conjunctive adverb that makes the sentence meaningful. In most cases there will be more than one correct answer.

The Early Inuit

1. Some people think that the Inuit are native to Alaska; _____ , they actually came from Siberia about 5000 years ago.
2. Some people think the Inuit crossed from Siberia to Alaska by sea; _____ , others say that they walked over a land bridge.
3. The early Inuit hunted caribou; _____ , they moved often to follow the herds.
4. They lived in one of the coldest, darkest, and most desolate regions of the world; _____ , their life was harsh.
5. The Inuit invented many words to describe minute changes in the weather; _____ , they had a rich vocabulary of hunting terms.
6. Some Inuit carvings may have magical or religious associations; _____ , archaeologists are not certain of this.
7. It is hard to imagine the Inuit without sled dogs; _____ , the Inuit learned to train dogs only about 900 years ago.
8. The Inuit thought that nothing should be wasted; _____ , they made dozens of useful objects from the animals they killed.
9. Traditional Inuit clothing, made from caribou hides and sealskins, is light and warm; _____ , it is waterproof.
10. Many people refer to these people as *Eskimos*; _____ , the group itself uses the term *Inuit*.

Identifying Different Kinds of Conjunctions

On your paper write the conjunction in each of the following sentences. Label each conjunction as *coordinating*, *correlative*, or *subordinating*. Some sentences contain more than one conjunction.

SAMPLE   Some constellations are named after mythological figures, and some are named after animals.

ANSWER   and, coordinating

The Constellations

1. Because the earth revolves around the sun, different constellations can be seen at different times of the year.
2. While a star map can be very helpful in locating constellations, you must learn how to use it effectively.
3. Astronomers use both binoculars and telescopes to observe the stars.
4. When you look at a constellation of the zodiac, you may see a planet wandering through it.
5. Although there are 88 constellations, only about two dozen are visible at any time.
6. Since the earth revolves around the sun, some constellations can be seen only during certain seasons.
7. An observer at the North or South Pole can see only one hemisphere of stars.
8. Greeks and Romans named groups of stars after animals and mythological characters.
9. Both Leo and Taurus are constellations named for animals.
10. Not only Orion but also Perseus is a constellation named for a Greek hero.
11. Many people think the Big Dipper is a constellation, but it is actually part of the large constellation called the Great Bear.
12. Although the Little Dipper is small, it contains the most important star in our skies, the North Star.
13. Just as you can use the Big Dipper to find the North Star, so you can use the Big Dipper to find Regulus, the brightest star in the constellation Leo.
14. As soon as you find the Great Square of Pegasus, you can find Andromeda and Cassiopeia.
15. You may be able to find the Andromeda Nebula, the most distant object visible to the unaided eye, if the night is clear.
16. The constellation Cassiopeia is thought to represent either the mythological queen Cassiopeia or her throne.
17. In the constellation Taurus the Bull, the Pleiades look like a tiny cloud, yet they are actually a group of stars.
18. After you find the Pleiades, you can look for the orange star Aldebaran in the bull's head.
19. Night and day are the same length when the sun reaches the bottom of the Pisces constellation.
20. This happens about March 21 and marks the beginning of spring.
21. If you find three bright stars in a straight line, you are looking at Orion.
22. After you spot the belt of three stars, you can look below it and find the Orion Nebula.
23. Orion has not only the reddish star Betelgeuse but also the bluish-white star Rigel.
24. Castor and Pollux are stars in the constellation Gemini.
25. Because Gemini is part of the zodiac, planets wander into the constellation and often put on an impressive show.

Completing Sentences with Different Kinds of Conjunctions

On your paper replace each blank in the following sentences with a conjunction that makes sense. The kind of conjunction to use is stated in parentheses at the end of each sentence.

SAMPLE   The country drained by the Flathead River is _____ a valuable ecological area _____ an important recreation area. (correlative conjunction)

ANSWER   The country drained by the Flathead River is both a valuable ecological area and an important recreation area.

The Flathead River

1. The Flathead River lies mostly in the United States; _____ , its headwaters are in Canada. (conjunctive adverb)
2. The lands drained by the Flathead River are forest, _____ they are populated by about two-thirds of the remaining grizzly bears. (coordinating conjunction)
3. _____ the threatened grizzly bear _____ the Rocky Mountain wolf inhabit the Flathead wilderness. (correlative conjunction)
4. The north fork of the Flathead River is eventually joined by _____ the middle fork _____ the south fork. (correlative conjunction)
5. _____ you visit the North Fork valley, you may meet Mary McFarland, a veterinarian. (subordinating conjunction)
6. From Mary McFarland's window you can see mountains _____ you turn. (subordinating conjunction)
7. _____ a Dolly Varden trout _____ a rare cutthroat trout is a likely catch along the Flathead River. (correlative conjunction)
8. Otters play along the Flathead River, _____ bald eagles soar overhead. (subordinating conjunction)
9. _____ it leaves the wild country, the Flathead River meanders through rich farmlands into Lake Flathead, just west of the Mississippi. (subordinating conjunction)
10. _____ the Flathead emerges from the lake, it turns west to join the mighty Columbia River. (subordinating conjunction)

Exercise 58   **Creating Sentences with Different Kinds of Conjunctions**

Think of a favorite room that you have known or read about, in which there are many interesting articles and pieces of furniture. Write several sentences about that room, using as many conjunctions as possible.

10.8 | Interjections

An **interjection** is a word or phrase that expresses emotion or exclamation.

An interjection has no grammatical connection to the other words in the sentence and is set off from the other words by an exclamation mark or a comma.

Different emotions are expressed by different interjections.

surprise	**Oh,** didn't you know?
delight	**Ah,** your father knows the recipe.
confusion	**What!** I didn't know that.
pain	**Ouch!** That hurts.
joy	**Wow!** This is great.

Interjections are used mostly in speech. They should be used sparingly in writing.

Exercise 59   **Using Interjections**

On your paper fill each blank in the following items with an appropriate interjection from the following list:

wow	hey	gee whiz	help	hi
oh my	golly	good luck	hush	whew

1. _____ , the movie is about to begin.
2. _____ ! The sink is overflowing.
3. _____ ! We hope to see you at the finish line.
4. _____ , we just moved into the house next door.
5. _____ ! How did you manage to catch that pass?
6. _____ ! I'm glad that test is over.
7. _____ ! What an incredible view there is from here!
8. _____ , I wish you'd told me that sooner.
9. _____ ! Where do you think you're going with my bicycle?
10. _____ , what a fantastic picture that would make!

Identifying Parts of Speech

On your paper write the part of speech of the italicized word in each of the following sentences.

Seashells

1. Anyone out for a stroll on a beach may find *wonderful* shells.
2. For even better discoveries, *look* in tidal pools.
3. Seashells are often more *numerous* after a storm.
4. Some seashells are *collectors'* items.
5. Such items are *usually* large, beautiful, and not well known.
6. Seashells, unlike stamps and coins, rarely increase *in* value.
7. *These* are the leading families of collectibles: cones, cowries, volutes, murexes, slit shells, and scallops.
8. Prehistoric people *often* used large univalve shells as pots or ladles.
9. Conch shells were sounded like trumpets, *not only* to call buffalos or warriors *but also* to frighten evil spirits or to accompany a funeral.
10. *Which* Central American people "milked" a particular live seashell for its purple dye?
11. In many ancient cultures cowrie shells were used as money *because* of their small size, beautiful shape, and luster.
12. The Chinese used cowries as *their* money from about 2000 B.C. to 600 B.C.
13. *Ah,* how beautiful are some of the seashells depicted in art!
14. Native Americans made wampum belts from shells of the quahog clam, *and* they used the belts as money or to record important events.
15. Pen shells have a tuft of silky threads with which they anchor *themselves* to the bottom of the sea.
16. Some historians think that Jason's Golden Fleece was material woven from *the* pen shells' silky threads.
17. Shells, especially scallop shells, are often used in the decorative arts; *moreover,* the theme is repeated in architecture.
18. Painted during the *Renaissance,* one of Sandro Botticelli's greatest works depicts Venus being gently blown to shore on the lower half of a fluted shell.
19. *Anyone* can see this painting at the Uffizi Gallery in Florence, Italy.
20. Shells truly *are* one of nature's wonders.

Using Parts of Speech

On your paper write a paragraph about a collection or hobby of your choice. Describe the hobby, using at least one example of each of the eight parts of speech. Use as many types of the parts of speech as possible — for example, proper and abstract nouns, subordinating conjuctions, and conjuctive adverbs.

10

Unit Review

Grammar Review

Parts of Speech

The Sound of Waves, by the prolific Japanese writer Yukio Mishima, tells the story of the love between a young boy and girl who live in a fishing village in Japan. World War II has just ended, and the villagers are slowly rebuilding their lives. This scene describes how the women of the island dive for abalone. The passage has been annotated to show the parts of speech covered in this unit.

Literature Model

from THE SOUND OF WAVES

by Yukio Mishima
translated from the Japanese
by Meredith Weatherby

Common noun

Action verb

Coordinating conjunction

Adverb

Linking verb

Subordinating conjunction

Relative pronoun

The young girls of the island faced the arrival of the diving season with precisely the same heart-strangling feeling city youths have when confronted by final school-term examinations. Their games of scrambling for pebbles on the bottom of the sea close to the beach, begun during the early years of grade school, first introduced them to the art of diving, and they naturally became more skillful as their spirit of rivalry increased. But when they finally began diving for a living and their carefree games turned into real work, without exception the young girls became frightened, and the arrival of spring meant only that the dreaded summer was approaching.

There was the cold, the strangling feeling of running out of breath, the inexpressible agony when water forced its way under the water-goggles, the panic and sudden fear of collapsing that invaded the entire body just when an abalone was almost at the fingertips. There were also all kinds of accidents; and the wounds inflicted on the tips of the toes when kicking off against the sea's bottom, with its carpet of sharp-edged shells, to rise to the surface; and the leaden languor that possessed the body after it had been forced to dive almost beyond endurance. . . . All these things had become sharper and sharper in the remembering; the terror had become all the more intense in the ➡

repeating. And often sudden nightmares would awaken the girls from sleep so deep as seemingly to leave no room for dreams to creep in. Then, in the dead of night, in the darkness surrounding their peaceful, dangerless beds, they would peer at the flood of sweat clenched within their fists.

    It was different with the older divers, with those who had husbands. Coming out of the water from diving, they would sing and laugh and talk in loud voices. It seemed as though work and play had become united in a single whole for them. Watching them enviously, the young girls would tell themselves that they could never become like that, and yet as the years passed they would be surprised to discover that, without their quite realizing it, they themselves had reached the point where they too could be counted among those lighthearted, veteran divers.

— Preposition
— Adjective
— Possessive pronoun
— Personal pronoun
— Reflexive pronoun
— Demonstrative pronoun
— Intensive pronoun

Exercise 1

Identifying Nouns   The following sentences elaborate on ideas or images suggested by the passage from *The Sound of Waves*. On your paper identify the nouns and write in parentheses *common*, *proper*, or *collective*, depending upon how it is used in the sentence.

SAMPLE   Japan is a group of islands in East Asia.

ANSWER   Japan (proper), group (collective), islands (common), Asia (proper)

1. On one side of the country lies the Pacific Ocean.
2. On the other side is the Sea of Japan.
3. Many islanders depend upon the ocean for jobs.
4. On Song Island the women dive for abalone.
5. The young girls play games at the beach.
6. Crowds scramble for stones at the bottom of the ocean.
7. Sometimes teams compete for prizes.
8. The competition often improves the girls' diving skills.
9. Later the lighthearted contests become work.
10. Do the young women still enjoy their dives?
11. The search for a colony of abalone is no longer a game.
12. Suddenly the new crew of divers fears the cold waters of the Pacific Ocean.
13. Cuts from the sharp edges of the shells are very painful.
14. The young workers also fear the feeling of exhaustion after a dive.
15. In spring the girls dread the start of the new diving season.

Exercise 2

Identifying Pronouns   The paragraph below describes the Japanese literary tradition from which Yukio Mishima emerged. On your paper list the twenty-five pronouns used in the paragraph.

[1]The Japanese literary tradition out of which Mishima emerged is itself quite interesting. [2]It reflects many of the characteristics of the Japanese people, such as their love of tradition and sensitivity to nature. [3]These elements occur in the oldest existing manuscripts, which date to the eighth century. [4]During the Heian period (794-1185), most of the people who wrote literature were members of the nobility. [5]Of these, the greatest were women, and the greatest of all was Murasaki Shikibu. [6]In her masterpiece, *The Tale of Genji*, she writes about herself and the court life of which she was a part. [7]Drama and poetry have also played important roles in this literary tradition. [8]The verse form that is known as *haiku* was developed in the 1600s by Matsuo Bashō, who established its strict rules. [9]Whoever reads the best of these is entranced by their ability to stimulate the imagination. [10]In modern Japan, Mishima and others like him have blended their own literary tradition with that of western culture.

Exercise 3

Using Pronouns Effectively   The paragraph below is based on passages from *The Sound of Waves* that are not reprinted in this textbook. On your paper rewrite each sentence in the paragraph, substituting pronouns for nouns when a pronoun would make good sense. Do not substitute a pronoun for a noun if the pronoun makes the sentence unclear.

[1]As the day drew to a close, the young women of Song Island gathered at the harbor, where the young women often helped the returning fishers. [2]The fishers had been out in the fishers' boats all day, hoping to fill the fishers' boats with a good catch. [3]The men still had to transfer the men's fish to the boat owned by the Fishers' Cooperative. [4]Then the men had to pull the men's heavy boats up onto the beach, where the boats were kept on wooden frames. [5]The frames were called abacuses because of the frames' shape. [6]The girls dragged the frames down to the shoreline, and the men slipped the frames under the backs of the men's boats. [7]When the boats were safe for the night, the men and women could go home for the men's and the women's evening meal. [8]Later the men would visit the public baths because the men did not have baths in the men's homes. [9]Once a week the unmarried young men attended a meeting of the Young Men's Association. [10]There the young men argued politics and discussed various projects that the young men thought would be good for civic improvement.

Exercise 4

Identifying Verbs and Verb Phrases The following sentences are adapted from the literary passage. Write on your paper any simple verbs and any verb phrases that appear in the sentences, and label them accordingly.

SAMPLE   By early morning the women and girls had assembled on the beach.
ANSWER   had assembled—verb phrase

1. The older women were laughing about the events of the previous evening.
2. The young girls wore more solemn expressions.
3. Some of them might have been remembering their nightmares.
4. Others were probably recalling the carefree dives of earlier years.
5. The women did not waste a moment.
6. They quickly scrambled onto the boats and sailed offshore.
7. Before long the splash of divers in the water could be heard.
8. Then each diver was alone with her thoughts.
9. At noon they would meet again on the beach and eat lunch.
10. After lunch they would return to their daily search for abalone.

Exercise 5

Identifying Transitive and Intransitive Verbs The following sentences contain verbs that appear in the passage from *The Sound of Waves*. For each item write *transitive* or *intransitive* on your paper, depending upon the way the italicized verb is used in the sentence.

SAMPLE   The divers *faced* a challenge of enormous proportions.
ANSWER   transitive

1. They *confronted* the difficulty of diving in heavy seas.
2. More experienced divers *introduced* the younger ones to advanced safety precautions.
3. The younger women's excitement *increased* in anticipation of a bold adventure.
4. Each diver *approached* the event with extreme caution.
5. Fear *overwhelmed* some of the young women.
6. The older divers *possessed* experience and a healthy respect for nature.
7. Watching the older women *awakened* an unexpected strength in the younger divers.
8. They all *peered* into the dark water.
9. All of them *clenched* their teeth at the start of the dive.
10. After a strenuous but successful venture, the divers *sang* songs of the sea and laughed.

Exercise 6

Identifying Adjectives   The following sentences are about abalone. On your paper write the adjectives that appear in each sentence. Count pronouns and proper adjectives, but do not count the words *a*, *an*, and *the*. After each adjective write a dash and the word that the adjective modifies.

SAMPLE   Abalone is valuable for three reasons.
ANSWER   valuable—abalone; three—reasons

1. The fleshy body, or foot, inside the shell makes a tasty meal.
2. The dishlike shell of the abalone is lined with gray mother-of-pearl.
3. From this lustrous substance fancy buttons are made.
4. Like oysters, abalone can also produce valuable pearls.
5. Handsome pearls develop when foreign objects accidentally lodge inside a shell.
6. The shellfish reacts by coating the object with several layers of mother-of-pearl.
7. The entire process may take three years.
8. Although most pearls are white, other colors are found.
9. Between 1893 and 1919 an artificial method of pearl production was developed by Japanese experimenters.
10. Pearls produced by this method must still grow inside shellfish, but the foreign object is inserted by human hands.

Exercise 7

Expanding Sentences with Adjectives   The following sentences elaborate on ideas suggested by the passage from *The Sound of Waves*. On your paper rewrite each sentence, adding adjectives in the places indicated by carets. Although there are no specific correct answers, you should base your choices on what you have learned from reading the passage.

SAMPLE   In July the days were ∧ and ∧.
ANSWER   In July the days were warm and sunny.

1. At Garden Beach the ∧ divers prepared to enter the ∧ water.
2. ∧ rowboats took the ∧ women from the shore to ∧ water.
3. Away from the ∧ beach the water was ∧.
4. A ∧ woman wearing a ∧ turban was the first to dive.
5. Taking a ∧ gulp of air, she plummeted into the ∧ ocean.
6. On the ocean floor she felt ∧ and ∧.
7. Working quickly, the ∧ diver grabbed ∧ abalone.
8. A ∧ push carried her to the surface, where a basket bobbed on a ∧ rope tied to her waist.
9. A few ∧ strokes brought her to the basket, which was soon full of ∧ abalone.
10. In seconds the ∧ diver was ready for another ∧ descent to the bottom of the ocean.

Exercise 8

Identifying Adverbs   The sentences below are about octopus fishing, another typical industry of the islands off Japan. On your paper write each adverb that appears in these sentences. After each adverb write a dash and the word that the adverb modifies.

SAMPLE   The fishers headed sleepily toward their boat.

ANSWER   sleepily—headed

1. The master of the boat was always cheerful.
2. Because of his good humor, his two assistants willingly worked for him.
3. Soon the three reached the village's fishing grounds.
4. There they found the other boats from the village.
5. A bitterly cold wind chilled the fishers as they worked.
6. Laboriously the boys pulled heavy traps from the ocean.
7. In 20 traps they did not find a single octopus.
8. Eventually a full trap was collected.
9. The master and his assistants then grew optimistic.
10. By afternoon they were quite happy with the day's catch.

Exercise 9

Using Adverbs   The following sentences are based on a passage from *The Sound of Waves* that is not reprinted in this textbook. On your paper rewrite each sentence, substituting an appropriate adverb for the prepositional phrase in italics. The adverb should express the same idea as the prepositional phrase.

SAMPLE   As the fishers left their boats, they laughed and sang *with boisterous energy.*

ANSWER   As the fishers left their boats, they laughed and sang boisterously.

1. A young fisher strolled along the beach *in an unhurried manner.*
2. He was carrying a halibut, which he would *in a short time* deliver to the lighthouse keeper.
3. The boy noticed a girl leaning *in a calm way* against some boat frames.
4. Her manner of dress suggested that she had *at some recent time* been working.
5. The boy regarded her *with curiosity*, for he had never seen her before.
6. The girl stared at the sky *with an intent look.*
7. *In a purposeful way* the boy passed quite near the stranger.
8. He stood before her and stared at her *in a rude manner.*
9. *To a surprising degree* the mysterious young woman remained motionless.
10. Finally the boy turned *in an abrupt manner* and moved on.

Exercise 10

Identifying Prepositions The following sentences are based on passages from *The Sound of Waves* that are not reprinted in this textbook. On your paper list the prepositions that appear in each sentence. Remember that some prepositions are made up of more than one word. (The numeral in parentheses at the end of each item indicates the number of prepositions the sentence contains.)

1. At home the young fisher thought about the girl on the beach. (3)
2. He had never seen her before that day. (1)
3. He was tormented by thoughts of her lovely face. (2)
4. One day, because of high winds, none of the fishing boats left the shore. (2)
5. In his free time the young man was doing chores for his mother. (2)
6. A few days earlier she had gathered firewood and left it inside a concrete tower on the mountain. (2)
7. Her son climbed to the tower and looked for the small bundle with his mother's name on it. (4)
8. After a few minutes in the tower, he heard a sound. (2)
9. He hurried up the stone steps and quickly arrived at the top of the tower. (3)
10. There, above the tower, was the girl. (1)

Exercise 11

Completing Sentences with Prepositions Each of the sentences below elaborates on the passage from *The Sound of Waves*. On your paper rewrite each sentence, replacing the blank with a preposition that completes the word or phrase in italics and makes sense in the sentence. In some cases there may be more than one preposition that makes sense.

SAMPLE The young girls thought fearfully _____ *the diving season.*
ANSWER The young girls thought fearfully about the diving season.

1. As children, they ran joyfully _____ *the rocky island coast.*
2. Grabbing pebbles _____ *the ocean floor* was a favorite pastime.
3. Gradually their childish games had become contests _____ *skill.*
4. When diving turned into their life's work, however, they became frightened _____ *it.*
5. _____ *a dive* they often felt that they were strangling.
6. Broken shells _____ *the ocean floor* rubbed their toes raw.
7. _____ *a dive* the girls were exhausted.
8. Did they tell their friends _____ *their nightmares?*
9. The older divers did their job _____ *such fears.*
10. They usually came up from a dive laughing and talking _____ *themselves.*

Exercise 12

Completing Sentences with Conjunctions   The following sentences describe Japan, where *The Sound of Waves* is set. On your paper replace each blank with an appropriate conjunction according to the directions in parentheses. Choose your conjunctions from the list that precedes the exercise. There are more conjunctions listed than you will need.

SAMPLE   Japan's geography _____ history are closely intertwined.
                 (Add a coordinating conjunction.)

ANSWER   Japan's geography and history are closely intertwined.

CONJUNCTIONS

and   but   or   nor   for
both . . . and   neither . . . nor
although   as long as   as soon as   because   if   so that   until

1. Japan is a nation of islands _____ large _____ small.
   (Add a correlative conjunction.)
2. There are four main islands _____ many hundreds of smaller ones.
   (Add a coordinating conjunction.)
3. Japan's rugged mountains create a beautiful landscape _____ leave farmers little land for cultivation.
   (Add a coordinating conjunction.)
4. Thus, _____ Japan's soil is fertile, only a small percentage of it is farmed.
   (Add a subordinating conjunction.)
5. _____ the island nation has a long coastline, fishing has always been a popular occupation.
   (Add a subordinating conjunction.)
6. In the 1600s Japan almost completely closed its borders to foreigners _____ it could protect itself from outside influence.
   (Add a subordinating conjunction.)
7. Japan's rulers were able to maintain a policy of isolation _____ Japanese ports stayed closed to foreign ships.
   (Add a subordinating conjunction.)
8. _____ the United States sent Commodore Matthew Perry to open trade with Japan in 1853, Japan was secluded from the outside world for 250 years.
   (Add a subordinating conjunction.)
9. The Japanese government had a choice: it could fight Perry's fleet _____ submit peacefully and open its ports.
   (Add a coordinating conjunction.)
10. _____ the Meiji Constitution of 1889 modernized Japanese society, Japan became a major world power.
    (Add a subordinating conjunction.)

Exercise 13

Rewriting Sentences with Conjunctive Adverbs   The sentences below are about the land of Japan. On your paper rewrite each sentence, using a conjunctive adverb. Choose your adverbs from the list on page 441.

1. Many people think Japan is one large island; it is actually hundreds of islands.
2. Much of Japan is steep, mountainous terrain; arable farmland is scarce.
3. Japan has a meager supply of minerals but is one of the world's richest nations.
4. Volcanic eruptions take place frequently; earthquakes are common occurrences.
5. Japanese trees are often cultivated as miniatures; gardens are often designed as smaller versions of the surrounding landscape.
6. The main island, Honshu, is less than 200 miles wide at its greatest width; no part of Japan is more than 100 miles from the sea.
7. Few inlets are found on the east coast north of Tokyo, but south of Tokyo are many of the best harbors.
8. Every valley in Japan has a stream; no long navigable rivers exist in Japan.
9. Some scenic Japanese lakes are located in river valleys; most of the lakes are mountain lakes.
10. In the Japanese mountains there are about 200 volcanoes, and only about 50 are still active.

Review: Exercise 14   Proofreading

The following passage describes the artist Andō Hiroshige, whose work appears on the opposite page. Rewrite the passage, correcting the errors in spelling, capitalization, grammar, and usage. Add any missing punctuation. There are twenty-five errors.

Andō Hiroshige

[1]Andō (or Ichiyū-sai) Hiroshige (1797–1858) was the son of a fire-brigade cheif. [2]Shortly after the death of his mother—she died when her son was twelve—Hiroshige inherited his fathers post. [3]He eventually abandoned the position so that he could consentrate on painting, his real love.

[4]Unlike painter's in Europe and America, japanese artists explored a limited number of themes according to strict rules of representation. [5]Hiroshige experiment with a variety of pictorial themes, including portraits and historical scenes, before settling on Landscapes. [6]He focused on this subject throughout his' long and productive life. →

[7]Hiroshige's landscapes are gentle lyrical, and subdued in tone. [8]In many of his prints, the stark beauty of the Japanese landscape are softened by a human presence. [9]Peasants trudge home in great drifts of snow or villagers hurry, heads bowed, through a rainstorm. [10]Variations in weather and the Seasons is depicted with care and precision.

[11]When he was thirty-five, Hiroshige embarked on the more ambitious project of his career. [12]He begun a series of fifty-five woodblock prints illustrating scenes along the great highway that linked the city of kyoto to Edo (now known as Tokyo). [13]These prints established Hiroshige as one of the master's of his day. [14]His later pictures of birds and flowers seems tentative and sentimental by comparison.

[15]The woodblock prints for which Hiroshige is famous was a technical feat. [16]Each color is printed separately by rubbing paper against the woodblock or by running the block through a press. [17]The first prints, generally the clearest and most subtly colored, becomed the most valuable.

[18]*Imagiri Promontory from Maizaka* is typical of Hiroshiges mature style. [19]It's harmonious composition projects a mood of stillness and calm. [20]Hiroshige was particularly famous for his deep blues and reds which are subtle, yet vivid. [21]One can imagine in such a scene the diver's described in *The Sound of Waves*.

Andō Hiroshige, *Imagiri Promontory from Maizaka*, 1833

Exercise 15

The following brief biography of Yukio Mishima (yoo kē ō′ mish′ē mä) is followed by twenty sentences. On your paper rewrite each sentence, replacing the blank with an appropriate word. Use the directions in parentheses as a guide.

Yukio Mishima

Yukio Mishima is the pen name of Kimitake Hiraoka, one of the most famous writers of modern Japan. Born in 1925, Mishima was weak and sickly as a child. He was highly intelligent, however, and took an interest in literature early in life. His first work was published in 1941, when he was just 16. Because he was so young, he decided to take a pen name. *Confessions of a Mask*, published in 1949, established Mishima's reputation as an author. From that time on he devoted himself to writing. *The Sound of Waves*, published in 1954, was inspired by a vacation in the Greek islands. This romantic story is the happiest of Mishima's 40 novels. Mishima also wrote plays, essays, and short stories. He died in 1970.

1. The _____ writer Yukio Mishima was born in 1925. (Add a proper adjective.)
2. As a child Mishima suffered from poor _____. (Add a common noun.)
3. At the same time he was _____ successful in his schoolwork. (Add an adverb.)
4. At an early age Mishima _____ interested in literature. (Add a linking verb.)
5. _____ he reached his eighteenth birthday, his writing had already been published in a magazine. (Add a subordinating conjunction.)
6. To conceal his youth, he _____ a pen name. (Add an action verb.)
7. _____ 1949 writing became a full-time career for Mishima. (Add a preposition.)
8. Mishima wrote *The Sound of Waves* after a trip to _____. (Add a proper noun.)
9. This unusually cheerful _____ romantic novel was later made into a popular movie. (Add a coordinating conjunction.)
10. Yukio Mishima wrote _____ kinds of works, including short stories, essays, and novels. (Add an adjective.)
11. _____ Yukio Mishima _____ Kimitake Hiraoka are names used by the same person. (Add a pair of correlative conjunctions.)
12. _____ his death Mishima produced forty novels. (Add a preposition.)
13. Mishima enjoyed his vacation in the Greek islands; _____, the story inspired by this trip was his happiest. (Add a conjunctive adverb.)
14. By the age of sixteen, Mishima _____ his first novel. (Add a verb phrase.)
15. A common theme _____ his novels is conflict. (Add a preposition.)
16. The novel _____ established Mishima as a reputable author. (Add an intensive pronoun.)
17. Many consider Mishima one of the greatest writers in Japanese _____. (Add an abstract noun.)
18. His readers will _____ know what he might have written had he lived longer. (Add a negative adverb.)
19. _____ work is admired by readers everywhere. (Add a possessive pronoun.)
20. _____ should read Mishima's books. (Add an indefinite pronoun.)

Writing Application

Adverbs in Writing In this passage from Ralph Ellison's short story "Flying Home," a farmer and his son have come across a pilot who has fallen from a small plane. Notice how Ellison uses adverbs to help convey the pilot's shock and confusion. Examine the passage, focusing especially on the italicized adverbs.

> Sounds come to him *dimly*. . . . He lay rigid, hearing their breathing and trying to weave a meaning between them and his being stretched *painfully* upon the ground. He watched them *warily*, his mind traveling *back* over a painful distance. Jagged scenes, *swiftly* unfolding as in a movie trailer [preview], reeled through his mind, and he saw himself piloting a tailspinning plane and landing and falling from the cockpit and trying to stand. *Then*, as in a great silence, he remembered the sound of crunching bone.

Techniques with Adverbs Try to apply some of Ralph Ellison's writing techniques when you write and revise your own work.

1. Use adverbs to clarify actions or behavior. In Ellison's passage, for example, the adverb *painfully* helps explain why the pilot is confused.

Without Adverb . . . his being stretched upon the ground . . .
Ellison's Version . . . his being stretched *painfully* upon the ground . . .

2. Use adverbs to emphasize a point. Compare the following descriptions of the pilot's memories.

Without Adverb Jagged scenes, unfolding as in a movie trailer, reeled through his mind . . .
Ellison's Version Jagged scenes, *swiftly* unfolding as in a movie trailer, reeled through his mind . . .

3. Try to choose adverbs that contribute to the mood, or atmosphere, that you are trying to convey.

Without Adverbs He watched them, his mind traveling over a painful distance.
Ellison's Version He watched them *warily*, his mind traveling *back* over a painful distance.

Practice Practice these techniques by revising the following passage, using a separate sheet of paper. Add adverbs in the places indicated with carets (^).

Afternoon teas at Mrs. Chan's apartment are ^ to be missed. Mrs. Chan ^ brings out her finest china and ^ sets it on the kitchen table. Her best cloth napkins are ^ folded at each place. She ^ prepares delicate almond cakes and pork dumplings to serve to her guests. Each woman comes to the tea ^ dressed. The women chat ^, and newcomers are ^ welcome. When tea is over, the guests ^ leave. Everyone ^ agrees to come back next week.

11.1 Simple Subjects and Simple Predicates

A **sentence** is a group of words expressing a complete thought.

The two basic parts of every sentence are the *subject* and the *predicate*.

The **subject** is the part of the sentence about which something is being said.

The **predicate** is the part that says something about the subject.

Both the subject and the predicate may consist of more than one word.

The **simple subject** is the key noun or pronoun (or group of words acting as a noun) that tells what a sentence is about.

The **simple predicate** is the verb or verb phrase that tells something about the subject.

A simple predicate that is a verb phrase consists of the verb and any helping verbs.

SIMPLE SUBJECT	SIMPLE PREDICATE
Condors	soar.
Spring	will come.
Coretta Scott King	is speaking.
Nora	sang.
Breakfast	is served.

You find the simple subject by asking *who?* or *what?* about the verb. For example, in the first sentence above, the noun *condors* answers the question *what soar?* In the second sentence, *spring* answers the question *what will come?*

Exercise 1   Identifying Simple Subjects and Simple Predicates

On your paper write the simple subject and simple predicate of each sentence. Underline the simple predicate.

1. American teenagers spent $88 billion in 1993.
2. The amount increased to $99 billion in 1994.
3. The cause for the increase was simply an increase in the number of teenagers in the United States.
4. Money came from jobs, allowances, and gifts.
5. Earnings from jobs rose from $84 billion in 1993 to $96 billion in 1994.

11.2 Complete Subjects and Complete Predicates

In most sentences the addition of other words and phrases expands or modifies the meaning of the simple subject and the simple predicate.

The pieces of the puzzle connect in only one way.

The **complete subject** consists of the simple subject and all the words that modify it.

The **complete predicate** consists of the simple predicate and all the words that modify it or complete its meaning.

COMPLETE SUBJECT	COMPLETE PREDICATE
The condors of California	soar gracefully in the sky.
A welcome spring	will come after a cold winter.
Coretta Scott King	is speaking first.
My sister Nora	sang a lullaby.
A late breakfast	was served at the same time as lunch.

Exercise 2	Identifying Complete Subjects and Complete Predicates

Write the following sentences on your paper. Underline each complete subject once and each complete predicate twice.

Canobie Lake Park

1. Canobie Lake Park in the southeastern section of New Hampshire opened in 1902.
2. Many people consider Canobie Lake Park the most beautiful amusement park in the United States.
3. The pleasant grounds feature tree-lined walkways, flower gardens, and a lake.
4. Guests to the park are especially amused by the authentic Mississippi-style paddle-wheel riverboat.
5. The eighty-acre park is regarded as one of the most popular entertainment centers in New England.
6. The entire family will find something of enjoyment there.
7. Everyone loves the antique carousel with its beautiful hand-carved horses.
8. Young and not-so-young thrill seekers ride the park's four roller coasters again and again.
9. Small children squeal in delight at the costumed characters throughout the park.
10. The park presents high-tech fireworks and musical performances all summer long.

On your paper write each of the following sentences, and draw a vertical line between the complete subject and the complete predicate. Then underline the simple subject once and the simple predicate twice.

SAMPLE ANSWER   <u>One</u> of the most important leaders of the abolitionist movement | <u>was</u> Frederick Douglass.

Frederick Douglass, Champion of Equality

1. Frederick Douglass dedicated his life to the fight for racial equality.
2. He was born enslaved in Tuckahoe, Maryland, around 1817.
3. Douglass escaped from his master in 1838.
4. The brave young man spoke at an antislavery meeting in Massachusetts in 1841.
5. The enthusiastic reaction to his speech led to a series of lecture engagements.
6. Douglass staged protests against racial segregation on trains, in churches, and in schools.
7. His activities included the publication of an antislavery newspaper.
8. President Abraham Lincoln conferred with Douglass during the Civil War.
9. The proud African American served as United States minister to Haiti from 1889 to 1891.
10. The African American community owes a great debt to Douglass and his tireless struggle for civil rights.

Expand each of the following sentences by adding words and phrases to both the simple subject and the simple predicate. Write your sentence. Then underline the simple predicate in each sentence. (There are many ways to expand each sentence.)

SAMPLE   Sky darkened.

ANSWER   The previously clear sky <u>darkened</u> suddenly to a furious yellowish-gray.

1. Wind screeched.
2. Rain began.
3. Leaves flew.
4. Trees bent.
5. Windows rattled.
6. Water dripped.
7. Gutters overflowed.
8. Waves crashed.
9. Clouds raced.
10. Sky lightened.

A sentence may have more than one simple subject or simple predicate.

Compound Subjects

A **compound subject** is made up of two or more simple subjects that are joined by a conjunction and have the same verb.

The conjunctions most commonly used to join the subjects in a compound subject are *and* and *or*.

> Shall **you** and **I** go to the nature preserve tomorrow?
> **Eagles** and **owls** hunt for food.
> A **cardinal** or a **robin** will be frightened by these hunters.

Correlative conjunctions may be used to join compound subjects.

> Neither the two **eagles** nor the lone **owl** is hunting.
> Both the **eagle** and the **owl** are strong fliers.

When more than two words are included in the compound subject, the conjunction is usually used only between the last two words, and the words are separated by commas.

> **Eagles, owls,** and **vultures** are birds of prey.

| **Exercise 5** | **Identifying Compound Subjects** |

On your paper write the compound subject in each sentence.

1. Two peach baskets and a gym set the stage for the world's first basketball game in 1891.
2. Two teams and an old soccer ball put the play into motion.
3. Three forwards, three centers, and three guards made up a team.
4. In 1893 Geneva College and the University of Iowa were the first colleges to play basketball.
5. Yale University and Wesleyan University met in New Haven in 1896 for the first intercollegiate match.

| **Exercise 6** | **Expanding Subjects** |

(a) Write five sentences. In each one, use a simple subject and a simple predicate.
(b) Expand each sentence by making the subject compound.

SAMPLE ANSWER

   a. Toni Morrison wrote several highly successful novels.
   b. Toni Morrison and Alice Walker wrote several highly successful novels.

Compound Predicates

A **compound predicate** (or **compound verb**) is made up of two or more verbs or verb phrases that are joined by a conjunction and have the same subject.

> Eagles **soar** and **plunge.**
> Suki either **is** here already or **will be** here momentarily.

In compound verbs that contain verb phrases, the helping verb may not be repeated before the second verb.

> We **have lost** or at least **misplaced** the map.
> Tyrone **will buy** a stamp, **mail** the letter, and **hurry** home.

Some sentences have both a compound subject and a compound predicate.

>   S   S   P   P
> **Eagles** and **condors soar** and **plunge** in the sky.

>   S   S   P   P
> Either **you** or **I have lost** or **misplaced** the map.

Exercise 7   **Identifying Compound Predicates**

On your paper write the compound predicate in each of the following sentences.

Cats

1. Cats are faithful pets and make friendly companions.
2. Cats seem independent and sometimes resist training.
3. They generally are fed canned food but may prefer fish or meat.
4. Cats have good memories and often imitate human activity.
5. Cats open doors, ring doorbells, and drink from water faucets.
6. Their pride, however, keeps them from foolish behavior and sometimes makes them stubborn.
7. An arched back with puffed-out fur is caused by fear or initiated by anger.
8. These physical changes make the cat's appearance larger, give the impression of ferocity, and intimidate enemies and prey.
9. Cats usually approach their prey very stealthily and then pounce.
10. The tabby is easy-going, does not stray far, and appears very affectionate and even tempered.

Exercise 8   **Expanding Predicates**

(a) Write five sentences. In each one, use a simple subject and a simple predicate.
(b) Expand each sentence by making the predicate compound.

SAMPLE ANSWER   **a.** The horse jumped the fence.
                      b. The horse jumped the fence and trotted away.

Identifying Subjects and Predicates

On your paper write the simple subject and the simple predicate from each sentence. Underline the simple predicates. Note that some subjects and predicates are compound.

The Mound Builders

1. Several North American cultures built large mounds of earth thousands of years ago and used them as burial places for their chiefs.
2. The Adena, the Hopewell, and the Mississippians were the three major groups of mound builders.
3. Much time and much effort were devoted to the construction of each mound.
4. Large quantities of dirt and stone were the primary construction materials of the mound builders.
5. Each mound builder carried loads of dirt on his back and transported them to the burial sites.
6. No horses, oxen, or carts assisted the workers in their difficult task.
7. Jewelry or pipes for the deceased chief were often buried in the mounds.
8. Many large mounds still stand in the midwestern United States and Canada.
9. The Giant Serpent Mound near Hillsboro, Ohio, looks like a huge, sinuous snake and is approximately a quarter of a mile long.
10. Monk's Mound near Cahokia in southern Illinois covers about sixteen acres and is about one hundred feet high.

Exercise 10   **Writing Compound Subjects and Predicates**

On your paper expand each of the following sentences by making both the subject and the predicate compound. (You may need to make other changes, too.)

SAMPLE   Worms crawl.
ANSWER   Worms and insects crawl and hide.

Gardening

1. Carly fertilized the garden.
2. Mulch had covered the ground.
3. A garden rake can break up the soil.
4. Crocuses arrive in early spring.
5. Peonies come in many colors.
6. Lilacs flower in late spring.
7. Cottonwoods spread their seeds widely.
8. Some lilies bloom in late June.
9. Sunlight makes a good garden.
10. Carly starts her garden plans earlier each year.

The subject comes before the verb in most sentences in English. Some exceptions to this normal word order are discussed below.

Commands and Questions

The subject *you* is understood rather than expressed in the case of commands or requests.

[You] **Jump**!　　[You] **Tear** it down.　　[You] **Ask** her, please.

Questions frequently begin with a verb or helping verb.

Is he right?　　　　　**Will** you **visit** your cousin?

Other questions often begin with the words *who, what, when, where, why,* or *how.*

What does she want?　　**Why** did he go to the gym?

In both of these cases, the subject generally follows the verb or helping verb.

To locate the subject of a question, rearrange the words to form a statement.

[You] Jump!

SUBJECT	PREDICATE
He	is right.
You	will visit your cousin.
She	does want what.
He	did go to the gym why.

Exercise 11 | **Identifying Subjects and Predicates in Commands and Questions**

On your paper write the simple subject and the simple predicate of each of the following sentences. (Remember that the simple predicate may contain one or more helping verbs.) If the sentence is a command, write *(You)* as the subject.

1. Can anyone name three main types of musical instruments?
2. Notice the string instruments, the wind instruments, and the percussion instruments.
3. Give me an example of a string instrument.
4. What kind of sound does a woodwind make?
5. Beat a drum for a good idea of percussion sound.
6. In what ways are a drum and a xylophone similar?
7. Is a piano a string instrument or a percussion instrument?
8. Study these parts of a saxophone.
9. Do you see the reed in the mouthpiece slot?
10. Watch it carefully.

Inverted Order

A sentence written in **inverted order,** where the predicate comes before the subject, serves to add emphasis to the subject.

PREDICATE	SUBJECT
Over the mountain **soared**	the two **eagles.**
Beyond the eagles **was**	a **condor.**

Remember that a word in a prepositional phrase can never be the subject.

When the word *there* or *here* begins a sentence and is followed by the verb *to be,* the subject generally comes after the predicate. (The sentence appears in inverted order.) Keep in mind that *there* and *here* are almost never the subject of a sentence.

PREDICATE	SUBJECT
There **are**	three **owls** in the nest.
Here **is**	my **sister.**

Exercise 12   **Reordering Sentences**

On your paper rewrite each of the following sentences so that the complete subject comes before the predicate. Then underline the simple subject once and the simple predicate twice. (Remember that both subjects and predicates may be compound.)

The Invention of Motion Pictures

1. In the late 1800s began the development of motion pictures.
2. From George Eastman, the American inventor, came flexible celluloid film.
3. There were two machines invented by Thomas Edison for use with George Eastman's new film.
4. With Edison's kinetoscope came success.
5. Through a peephole could be seen strips of "moving" pictures.
6. There were several short films made in Edison's studio.
7. In and out of the Kinetoscope Parlor in New York City streamed throngs of satisfied customers.
8. There was a new projection machine invented by Thomas Armat.
9. On Armat's projector were shown Edison's first films, the earliest commercial motion pictures.
10. In one film could be seen very realistic waves.

Copy each of the following sentences, draw a vertical line between the complete subject and the complete predicate, and label each. Then underline the simple subject once and the simple predicate twice. Write *(You)* for an understood subject. Finally, indicate with the letter *C* or *I* those sentences that are either a command *(C)* or written in inverted order *(I)*. (Not all sentences will be labeled *C* or *I*.)

                                   S   P
SAMPLE ANSWER   (You) | <u>Look</u> at that clothing. **C**

                                P   S
                 On the hat rack <u>is</u> | a huge <u>sombrero</u>. **I**

                   P   S
                 There <u>are</u> | many beautiful Mexican <u>costumes</u>. **I**

Traditional Dress in Mexico

1. Some residents of Mexican villages still wear traditional types of clothing.
2. Many of these styles of clothing date back many centuries.
3. Look at the young boy in the cornfield.
4. On his head is a wide-brimmed straw hat, or sombrero.
5. The sombrero serves as excellent protection against both heavy rains and the intense Mexican sun.
6. There are several other types of protective clothing for men and women.
7. A poncho, or blanket with a slit in the center for the head, is popular with men in cold or rainy weather.
8. Notice the rebozos, or fringed cotton shawls, covering the heads of those village women near the fountain in the plaza.
9. There are some special costumes for holidays and other occasions.
10. Look at the handsome suits worn by the cowboys, or *charros*, from Guadalajara.
11. Here is an example of a traditional Mexican outfit.
12. The material for the suit of a *charro* may be doeskin or velvet.
13. There are a short jacket, or bolero, and tight pants with gold buttons down the sides of the legs.
14. A white shirt, boots with spurs, and a large sombrero complete the costume.
15. Among popular women's costumes is the beautiful *china poblana*.
16. It was probably named for a seventeenth-century Chinese princess.
17. The costume includes a full cotton skirt, a colorful blouse, and a wide sash.
18. Some women in the southern part of Mexico wear long polka-dot skirts and giant cotton headdresses.
19. There are many styles of *huaraches*, or leather sandals.
20. Many Mexican city dwellers no longer wear traditional clothing.

A **complement** is a word or group of words that completes the meaning of a verb.

The four kinds of complements are *direct objects, indirect objects, object complements,* and *subject complements.*

Direct Objects

A **direct object** answers the question *what?* or *whom?* after an action verb.

The verb in a sentence usually indicates the action being performed by the subject. That action may be received by or directed toward someone or something: the direct object. Direct objects are nouns, pronouns, or words acting as nouns; and they may be compound. Only transitive verbs have direct objects.

Roberto bought **tomatoes**. [Roberto bought *what?*]

Sandra likes **me** very much. [Sandra likes *whom?*]

Ralph reported his **discovery**. [Ralph reported *what?*]

Roberto bought plum **tomatoes** and red-leaf **lettuce**. [Roberto bought *what?*]

Exercise 14   **Identifying Direct Objects**

On your paper write the action verb that appears in each of the following sentences. Then list any direct objects.

Francisco Pizarro, a Spanish Conqueror

1. Francisco Pizarro, a sixteenth-century Spanish explorer, won much fame and fortune for his country.
2. Around 1520 Pizarro heard rumors of a vast and rich empire in the central highlands of South America.
3. In 1524 Pizarro began an expedition to the west coast of South America.
4. Bad weather hindered him in his first visit to the region.
5. In 1528, however, Pizarro located the Inca and their extensive empire.
6. Signs of gold and other riches in the Inca capital of Cuzco pleased the explorer greatly.
7. In 1532 Pizarro captured Atahualpa, a great Inca chief, in the town of Cajamarca.
8. The Incas gave a vast quantity of gold and silver objects to Pizarro in order to save their chief.
9. In the end Pizarro heartlessly killed the Inca ruler.
10. After the death of Chief Atahualpa, Pizarro easily conquered the Inca and their lands.

Indirect Objects

An **indirect object** answers the question *to whom? for whom? to what?* or *for what?* after an action verb.

In most cases a sentence can have an indirect object only if it has a direct object as well. The indirect object always appears after the verb and before the direct object.

Engineers gave **students** awards. [Engineers gave awards *to whom?*]

Trisha gives **homework** her full attention. [Trisha gives her full attention *to what?*]

Juan bought **me** lunch. [Juan bought lunch *for whom?*]

Angela bought **Soo** and **Gloria** lunch. [Angela bought lunch *for whom?*]

Exercise 15	Identifying Direct and Indirect Objects

On your paper write the direct object in each of the following sentences. Then list and underline any indirect objects. (There may be more than one indirect object in a sentence, or there may be none at all.)

Cheryl Toussaint, Olympic Champion

1. In the 1972 summer Olympics, the women's relay team brought the United States a silver medal.
2. The silver medal also gave a determined African American runner great satisfaction.
3. For years Cheryl Toussaint had prepared herself for the games.
4. In 1972 she finally fulfilled her dream.
5. An unexpected problem gave her a scare in a women's 400-meter relay race.
6. In an accidental brush with another runner, Toussaint lost her left shoe.
7. Nevertheless, she successfully passed her teammate the baton.
8. Toussaint's victory brought her family and country much pride.
9. She broke several world records during her memorable career.
10. Toussaint's triumph gave her a chance for a career in professional sports.

Exercise 16	Using Direct and Indirect Objects

On your paper rewrite the following sentences so that each contains both a direct and an indirect object. Write a *D* above each direct object and an *I* above each indirect object.

1. Book groups offer meetings on a regular basis.
2. Members give information about a wide variety of books.
3. One by one each member tells his or her impressions of the book.
4. Sometimes the members write about the book.
5. Book groups also offer the possibilities of new friendships.

Object Complements

An **object complement** answers the question *what?* after a direct object. That is, it *completes* the meaning of the direct object by identifying or describing it.

You will find object complements only in sentences that contain a direct object *and* include one of the following action verbs or a similar verb that has the general meaning of "make" or "consider":

appoint	consider	make	render
call	elect	name	think
choose	find	prove	vote

An object complement follows a direct object and may be an adjective, a noun, or a pronoun.

Engineers find plans **essential**. [adjective]
Nations often make their bridges **symbols**. [noun]
The citizens call that privilege **theirs**. [pronoun]
Mozelle considers me a **close friend** and **helpful adviser**. [nouns with modifiers]

| Exercise 17 | Identifying Object Complements |

On your paper write the object complements that appear in the following sentences. (Two sentences have two object complements, and one sentence does not have any.)

Japanese Prints

1. Art historians and critics consider Japanese prints masterpieces.
2. Museum curators call seventeenth-century Japanese prints irreplaceable and priceless.
3. Some scholars think the early black-and-white prints particularly delicate and expressive.
4. Moronobu, a master of the black-and-white print, found everyday scenes a worthy subject.
5. Somehow he rendered ordinary life beautiful.
6. An eighteenth-century printmaker, Harunobu, made color prints popular.
7. Some collectors prefer Utamaro's color prints.
8. Many in the art world have named Utamaro a master.
9. Quite often Utamaro made women and Kabuki actors his subjects.
10. Some Japanese consider the art of printmaking exclusively theirs.

| Exercise 18 | Using Object Complements |

On your paper, complete the following sentences with object complements. Then write the letter *A*, *N*, or *P* to identify each object complement as an adjective, noun, or pronoun.

1. The selfish children considered all the toys _____.
2. Drivers found the traffic _____.
3. Sunshine made the meadow _____.
4. The highway patrol called the storm _____.
5. Pilots considered the weather _____.
6. Vacationers thought the fog _____.

Subject Complements

A **subject complement** follows a subject and a linking verb and identifies or describes the subject.

The two kinds of subject complements are *predicate nominatives* and *predicate adjectives*.

A **predicate nominative** is a noun or pronoun that follows a linking verb and points back to the subject to identify it further.

Engineers are **scientists**.

The engineer on this project is **she**.

Although predicate nominatives most often appear in sentences containing forms of the linking verb *be*, a few other linking verbs (for example, *become* and *remain)* can be followed by a predicate nominative.

San Francisco is a **city**.
Monday remains a **holiday** for us.
Tanya became a famous **singer** and **dancer**.

A **predicate adjective** follows a linking verb and points back to the subject and further describes it.

The trail looked suspicious!

Engineers are **inventive**.

Engineers must be highly **responsible**.

Predicate adjectives may follow any linking verb.

The hikers had become very **weary**.
The team looks **ready** for the game.
Lena seems **eager** and **determined**.
I feel quite **chilly**.
These plums taste **sweeter**.

Exercise 19　　Identifying Predicate Nominatives

On your paper write the predicate nominatives that appear in the following sentences. (If a sentence has no predicate nominative, write *none*.)

George Mason

1. George Mason was an American statesman during the Revolutionary War era.
2. Born in Virginia, Mason became a brilliant student of law.
3. Mason was not an admirer of politics.
4. Public officials, however, appreciated Mason's legal genius.
5. Mason's work became the basis for Thomas Jefferson's Bill of Rights.

Exercise 20   Identifying Predicate Adjectives

On your paper write the simple subject and predicate adjective in each of the following sentences. If a sentence has no predicate adjective, write *none*.

Rabies

1. The behavior of an animal with rabies seems strange.
2. A rabid animal grows bold.
3. It ventures fearlessly into contact with people.
4. The sick animal looks normal.
5. Its appearance often does not change.
6. The animal's strange actions, not its appearance, should be watched often.
7. Do not go near a strange-acting animal.
8. An animal with rabies feels overwhelmingly thirsty.
9. A normally friendly animal may become unfriendly.
10. Call an authority about a possibly rabid animal.

Exercise 21   Identifying Subject Complements

On your paper write all the subject complements that appear in the following sentences. Identify each as a *predicate nominative* or a *predicate adjective*. (One sentence has more than one subject complement; other sentences have none.)

The Farmer's Market

1. A farmer's market is a place for the sale of the produce of local farmers.
2. In many communities these markets have become quite popular.
3. With the eager crowds, colorful stands, and shouting vendors, a farmer's market seems festive.
4. Locally grown fruits and vegetables, artfully arranged on open stands, look crisp and fresh.
5. Breads and rolls, often still warm from the oven, smell delicious.
6. The farmers must be early risers.
7. Many of them sell preserves or handicrafts as well as fruits and vegetables.
8. Their loud sales pitches always sound persuasive.
9. Spend a morning at a farmer's market.
10. Soon you will be a regular customer.

Exercise 22   Using Subject Complements

On your paper complete each of the following sentences by adding a noun, a pronoun, or an adjective. (You may also add other words.) Write *PN* or *PA* to identify the complement as a predicate nominative or predicate adjective.

1. The most interesting type of character created by Hollywood is _____.
2. The lives of Hollywood-created characters seem _____.
3. In real life, however, most people remain _____.
4. Many of the situations of Hollywood characters appear _____.
5. Compared to these situations, ordinary people's lives look _____.

Identifying Complements (Part 1)

On your paper write the complements that appear in the following sentences. Next to each complement write the kind of complement it is: *direct object, indirect object, object complement, predicate nominative,* or *predicate adjective.*

Batik and Tie-dyeing

1. Batik is a method of fabric decoration.
2. The batik artist applies wax to parts of the cloth.
3. The artist then gives the cloth a dye bath.
4. The bath dyes the unwaxed part a vivid color.
5. The part of the cloth with wax resists the dye.
6. This method gives the cloth intricate designs.
7. The colors of batik appear rich and often subtle.
8. The process of tie-dyeing is similar but easier.
9. Common to both of these crafts is the resist-dyeing technique.
10. The tie-dye artist knots the cloth in different places.
11. The artist then dyes the fabric a color.
12. The knots give the cloth its design.
13. This design often appears random.
14. Most times the fabric does not resist the dye uniformly.
15. Uneven dyeing makes the final product quite beautiful.

Exercise 24   Identifying Complements (Part 2)

On your paper write the complements that appear in the following paragraph. Next to each complement write the kind of complement it is: *direct object, indirect object, object complement, predicate nominative,* or *predicate adjective.*

The Mystery of Lightning

[1]Lightning was mysterious to the ancient Greeks. [2]In fact, for them lightning was a weapon used by their chief god, Zeus. [3]According to mythology, the Greeks gave Zeus the thunderbolt and scepter. [4]Many persons today still consider lightning scary. [5]Of course, the reasons for this fear seem sound. [6]During a storm lightning strikes the earth about one hundred times a second. [7]Sometimes lightning strikes the tallest tree in a field. [8]Often lightning causes fire. [9]In addition, in the United States alone lightning kills approximately one hundred people every year. [10]Lightning can be both mysterious and dangerous.

Exercise 25   Writing Sentences with Complements

Write four sentences about an environmental concern, such as acid rain, air pollution, noise pollution, deforestation, or oil spills. In each sentence use at least one of the four kinds of complements: *direct object, indirect object, object complement,* and *subject complement.* Label the complements.

Grammar Review

Parts of the Sentence

Cairo is the home of Naguib Mahfouz. His novel *Palace Walk* traces the fortunes of a middle-class Cairo family in the years between the two world wars. In this scene the youngest son of the family, Kamal, is on his way home from school. The passage, which has been translated from the Arabic, has been annotated to show some of the parts of the sentence covered in this unit.

Literature Model

from PALACE WALK

by Naguib Mahfouz
translated from the Arabic by
William Maynard Hutchins and Olive E. Kenny

He reached the pastry shop and stretched out his hand with the small change he had hung on to since morning. He took a piece of pastry with the total delight he experienced only on such a sweet occasion. It made him frequently dream of owning a candy store one day, not to sell the candy but to eat it. He continued on his way down al-Husayn Street, munching on the pastry with pleasure. He hummed and forgot he had been a prisoner all day long, not allowed to move, not to mention play or have fun. . . .

On his way, he passed by the tobacco store of Matoussian. He stopped under its sign, as he did every day at this hour, and raised his small eyes to the colored poster of a woman reclining on a divan with a cigarette between her crimson lips, from which rose a curling plume of smoke. She was leaning her arm on the windowsill. The curtain was drawn back to reveal a scene combining a grove of date palms and a branch of the Nile. He privately called the woman Aisha after his sister, since they both had golden hair and blue eyes. Although he was just going on ten, his admiration for the mistress of the poster was limitless. How often he thought of her enjoying life in its most splendid manifestations. How often he imagined himself sharing his carefree days in that luxurious room with its ➡

Direct object

Compound predicate

Simple subject

Object complement

Subject complement
(predicate adjective)

pristine view that offered her, in fact both of them, its earth, palms, water, and sky. He would swim in the green river valley or cross the water in the skiff that appeared ghostlike far off in the picture. He would shake the palm trees till the dates fell around him or sit near the beautiful woman with his eyes gazing at her dreamy ones.

> — Indirect object

He left the vaulted section of the alley for the other half. At the end he could see Palace Walk and the entrance of Hammam al-Sultan. Then his eyes fell on his home's dark green wooden grilles and the large door with its bronze knocker. His mouth opened in a happy smile at the wide variety of amusements this place harbored for him. Soon the boys from all the neighboring houses would run to join him in his wide courtyard, with its several chambers, surrounding the oven room. There would be fun and games and sweet potatoes.

> — Complete predicate
>
> — Simple predicate
>
> — Complete subject
>
> — Sentence beginning with *there*

At that moment he saw the Suarès omnibus slowly crossing the street heading for Palace Walk. His heart leaped. Pleasure at his own cleverness filled him. At once he tucked his book bag under his left arm and raced to catch it. He jumped on the back steps, but the conductor did not let him enjoy his pleasure for very long. He came and asked the boy for his fare, giving him a suspicious, challenging look. Kamal told him ingratiatingly that he would get off as soon as it stopped but could not while it was moving. The conductor turned from him and yelled to the driver to stop the vehicle. He was angrily scolding Kamal, but when he looked away the boy seized the opportunity to tread on the instep of his foot, take a swing at him, and hop to the ground. He shot off in flight.

Exercise 1

Identifying Simple Subjects and Predicates   For each of the following sentences, write the simple subject and simple predicate. Underline the simple predicate.

1. The young boy bought a pastry at a shop on his way home.
2. The tobacco store of Matoussian had a beautiful woman on its sign.
3. Kamal privately called the woman Aisha after his sister.
4. Dreams of a luxurious life filled his imagination.
5. The entrance to Hammam al-Sultan was nearby.

Exercise 2

Identifying Complete Subjects and Predicates   The following sentences are based on the excerpt from *Palace Walk*. Copy each sentence, and draw a line between the complete subject and complete predicate.

1. The woman on the poster seemed exotic to the small boy.
2. She was reclining on a divan and leaning her arm on a windowsill.
3. A scene with a grove of date palms and a view of the Nile could be seen behind her.
4. Kamal's sister Aisha had blond hair and blue eyes, just like the woman on the poster.
5. The boy privately called the woman Aisha.
6. A life of luxury similar to the view in the picture beckoned to Kamal.
7. The water of the Nile in the poster looked good for a swim or a sail in a skiff.
8. The dates from the palm trees might fall on the ground around him and the beautiful woman.
9. Thoughts of this wondrous life filled his mind for many minutes.
10. The young boy finally continued on his way home.

Exercise 3

Writing Sentences with Complete Subjects and Complete Predicates   Each of the following partial sentences elaborates on an idea suggested by the passage from *Palace Walk*. Write either a complete subject or a complete predicate to complete each sentence. Do not repeat the exact wording from the novel. Your sentence should make sense within the context of the passage.

SAMPLE   The young boy _____.
ANSWER   was walking home from school.

1. The pastry shop _____.
2. _____ took the change from Kamal.
3. His precious purchase _____.
4. The happy young boy _____.
5. _____ was another favorite place.
6. _____ caught his eye.
7. The magnificent room in the poster _____.
8. _____ was located near Palace Walk.
9. _____ would soon be playing in the large courtyard.
10. The oven room _____.
11. The Suarès omnibus _____.
12. _____ filled with pleasure at his cleverness.
13. _____ jumped on the back of the bus.
14. The conductor _____.
15. _____ was the boy's response.

Exercise 4

Writing Sentences with Compound Subjects and Compound Predicates   On your paper write a complete sentence to answer each of the following questions about *Palace Walk*. Do not repeat the exact wording from the novel. Begin your sentence with the subject and follow the instructions in parentheses. Then underline and label the simple or compound subject and the simple or compound predicate. Finally, draw a line separating the complete subject from the complete predicate.

SAMPLE   What foods gave Kamal great pleasure? (Use a compound subject.)

                      COMPOUND SUBJECT   SIMPLE PREDICATE

ANSWER   <u>Pastry</u> and other <u>sweets</u> | <u>gave</u> Kamal great pleasure.

1. Who lived in the city of Cairo?
   (Use a compound subject.)
2. What two shops were special to Kamal?
   (Use a compound subject.)
3. What did the young boy do after leaving the pastry shop?
   (Use a compound predicate.)
4. What two women had the same coloring?
   (Use a compound subject.)
5. What was the woman in the poster doing?
   (Use a compound predicate.)
6. What could be seen outside the woman's window?
   (Use a compound subject with three different nouns.)
7. What did Kamal and his friends do in Kamal's courtyard?
   (Use a compound predicate.)
8. What are three things Kamal did on his way home?
   (Use a compound predicate with three different verbs.)
9. Who had an unpleasant encounter on the back steps of the bus?
   (Use a compound subject.)
10. What gave Kamal particular pleasure on his walk?
    (Use a compound subject with three different nouns.)
11. What three features of Kamal's house promised amusement?
    (Use a compound subject with three different nouns.)
12. Who might have been riding on the bus with Kamal?
    (Use a compound subject with two different nouns.)
13. What did Kamal do to the conductor when the man turned his head?
    (Use a compound predicate with two different verbs.)
14. How might the passengers have reacted to Kamal's antics?
    (Use a compound predicate with two or three different verbs.)
15. Who would probably be having dinner at Kamal's house that night?
    (Use a compound subject with three different nouns.)

Exercise 5

Writing Inverted Sentences   The following sentences develop ideas suggested by the passage from *Palace Walk*. On your paper rewrite each sentence in inverted order, following the instructions in parentheses.

1. Kamal walked through the streets of Cairo.
   (Begin the sentence with *Through the streets of Cairo.*)
2. Fascinating sights, sounds, and smells were all around him.
   (Begin the sentence with *There were.*)
3. Nothing was more wonderful than the excitement and freedom of a stroll through the busy city. (Begin the sentence with *There was.*)
4. The luscious aroma of sweet cakes wafted out of one of the shops.
   (Begin the sentence with *Out of one of the shops.*)
5. The eager boy marched into the shop.
   (Begin the sentence with *Into the shop.*)
6. Kamal proceeded down the busy street.
   (Begin the sentence with *Down the busy street.*)
7. An enchanting poster was above the tobacco store.
   (Begin the sentence with *There was.*)
8. Thoughts of a luxurious life floated into Kamal's head.
   (Begin the sentence with *Into Kamal's head.*)
9. A bus, with its promise of new adventure, moved toward him.
   (Begin the sentence with *Toward him.*)
10. A suspicious conductor was on the bus.
    (Begin the sentence with *There was.*)
11. The angry conductor strode toward the boy.
    (Begin the sentence with *Toward the boy.*)
12. An unpleasant frown was on his face.
    (Begin the sentence with *There was.*)
13. A furious glitter was in his eyes.
    (Begin the sentence with *There was.*)
14. The mischievous young boy smiled into the angry face.
    (Begin the sentence with *Into the angry face.*)
15. Words that were lies fell from his mouth.
    (Begin the sentence with *From his mouth.*)
16. The wrathful conductor turned away from the boy.
    (Begin the sentence with *Away from the boy.*)
17. A curious quiet was throughout the bus.
    (Begin the sentence with *There was.*)
18. The angry man bellowed into the silence.
    (Begin the sentence with *Into the silence.*)
19. The laughing boy hopped from the bus.
    (Begin the sentence with *From the bus.*)
20. A narrow alley, a place to escape, was nearby.
    (Begin the sentence with *There was.*)

Exercise 6

Writing Sentences with Predicate Nominatives and Predicate Adjectives   The pairs of words that follow are derived from the passage from *Palace Walk*. For each pair, write a sentence that uses the first word as the subject and the second word as a predicate adjective or a predicate nominative. Do not use the exact wording from the novel, and be sure to add more than just a verb to the pair of words.

SAMPLE   city, home
ANSWER   The city of Cairo was Kamal's home.

1. Kamal, hungry
2. pastry, delicious
3. boy, happy
4. stop, tobacco store
5. person, woman
6. admiration, endless
7. scene, attractive
8. home, place
9. bus, challenge
10. conductor, angry

Exercise 7

Writing Sentences with Direct and Indirect Objects   Each of the following groups of words describes an incident related to the passage from *Palace Walk*. Each word is labeled *S* (for *subject*), *DO* (for *direct object*), or *IO* (for *indirect object*). On your paper write a sentence using these words, but do not use the exact wording from the novel. Try to add modifiers or prepositional phrases to make your sentences more interesting.

SAMPLE   boy (S), merchant (IO), money (DO)
ANSWER   The young boy gave the merchant some money.

1. baker (S), schoolboy (IO), delicacy (DO)
2. sweets (S), Kamal (IO), pleasure (DO)
3. Kamal (S), candy store (DO)
4. poster (S), boy (IO), delight (DO)
5. Kamal (S), woman (IO), affection (DO)
6. Kamal (S), home (DO)
7. home (S), amusements (DO)
8. mother (S), his friends (IO), sweet potatoes (DO)
9. schoolboy (S), bus (DO)
10. conductor (S), Kamal (IO), question (DO)

Exercise 8

Writing Sentences with Direct Objects and Object Complements Each of the following groups of words could describe an incident related to the passage from *Palace Walk*. Each word is labeled *S* (for *subject*), *DO* (for *direct object*), or *OC* (for *object complement*). On your paper write a sentence using these words. Try to add modifiers such as prepositional phrases to make your sentences more interesting.

SAMPLE   Kamal (S), walk (DO), fun (OC)
ANSWER   Kamal found his walk home from school fun.

1. boy (S), sweets (DO), treat (OC)
2. proprietor (S), boy (DO), funny (OC)
3. Kamal (S), woman (DO), beautiful (OC)
4. passengers (S), Kamal (DO), rude (OC)
5. friend (S), story (DO), funny (OC)

Review: Exercise 9

Proofreading

The following passage describes the artist Henri Matisse, whose painting appears on the opposite page. Rewrite the passage, correcting any errors in spelling, grammar, and usage. Add any missing punctuation. There are twenty-five errors.

Henri Matisse

¹Born in northern France, Henri Matisse (1869-1954), who intended to become an attorney studied law. ²He was recovering from a bout of appendicitis in 1890 and he decided to amuse himself by dabbling with paint. ³He imediately took to painting. ⁴Which became his lifelong passion.

⁵In Paris in 1905, he showed some of his' works to the public at a revolutionary exhibit. ⁶Critics labeled Matisse and the other artists in the exhibit *fauves* a French word meaning "wild beasts." ⁷The name sticked. ⁸Became the movement's unofficial leader.

⁹Matisse and his colleagues worked for years to refine fauvist ideas and technics. ¹⁰His pictures were simple, fluid and colorful. ¹¹For the fauves and their supporters, color and light was the keys to a painting's power. ¹²Sometime during the year of 1908, Matisse says, "What I am after, above all, is expression. . . . I am unable to distinguish between the feeling I have for life and my way of expressing it." ¹³As he entered his later years, he frequently abandoned the use of paint altogether and he chose instead to make collages in brilliant hues.

¹⁴Matisse took the first of several trips to Morocco in 1912. ¹⁵He was inspired by Africas architecture ancient cultures, and strong sunlight. ➡

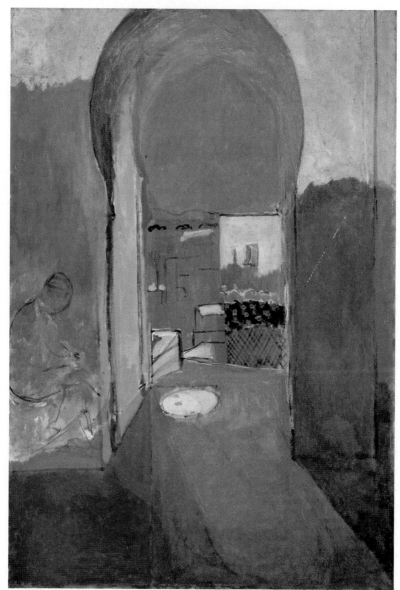

Henri Matisse, *The Casbah Gate*, 1912

[16]Matisse produces many powerful works in Morocco, including *The Casbah Gate*. [17]He painted the picture rapidly, useing loose brush strokes and simple shapes. [18]He wished to produce a mood based on color, light and form, instead of on literal description.

[19]Like the author of *Palace Walk*, Matisse using carefully chosen and rendered details, managed to convey a strong sense of place. [20]The shape of the archway in *The Casbah Gate* suggest the exotic locale. [21]The pictures pale greens pinks, and roses reflects the pure light of the city. [22]Both the passage from *Palace Walk* and the scene in *The Casbah Gate* raises a sense of expectancy, almost as if the viewer were on the edge of a new and glorious adventure.

Mixed Review

Exercise 10

The following sentences describe the life of Naguib Mahfouz [nä gēb´ mä fooz´].
Rewrite each sentence on your paper according to the instructions that appear
after each item. Make sure your answers are complete sentences.

Naguib Mahfouz

1. The Egyptian author Naguib Mahfouz was born *in 1911* in the city of Cairo.
   (Rewrite the sentence so that the phrase in italics, which is part of the complete
   predicate, appears in another position.)
2. Vivid sketches of Cairo are in his books.
   (Rewrite to begin with *There are*.)
3. In Mahfouz's youth, books were his main source of entertainment.
   (Add *and movies* to the complete subject.)
4. Mahfouz describes Egypt's political history.
   (Add *and depicts the desperate lives of the poor* to the complete predicate.)
5. This talented author has written numerous novels.
   (Add *and stories* to create a second direct object.)
6. Because of Mahfouz, the novel and short story have become genres in
   Arabic literature. (Add *popular* as a modifier of the subject complement.)
7. From his novels have come 16 Egyptian movies.
   (Rewrite the sentence so that it begins with the complete subject.)
8. Winner of the Nobel Prize for literature in 1988, Mahfouz gives a realistic
   view of urban Egyptian life.
   (Add *his readers* as an indirect object.)
9. With the translation of his books into English, Mahfouz has become increasingly
   popular in the United States.
   (Add *and respected* to create a second predicate adjective.)
10. Praised as Egypt's finest modern writer, Mahfouz has won honors.
    (Add *high* as a modifier of the direct object.)
11. Mahfouz offers detailed images of the luxury longed for by Cairo's impoverished
    population.
    (Add *his readers* to serve as an indirect object.)
12. These dreams contrast sharply with the reality of their lives.
    (Add another simple subject and a conjunction to form a compound subject.)
13. Mahfouz's words give an accurate picture of Cairo's architecture.
    (Add *the reader* to provide an indirect object.)
14. Readers from other cultures gain an understanding of twentieth-century Egyptian culture.
    (Add *excellent* to modify the direct object.)
15. Through reading Mahfouz's work, students of modern Egyptian culture can enhance
    their understanding of present-day Egyptian life.
    (Rewrite the sentence so that the complete subject comes before the complete predicate.)

Writing Application

Sentence Patterns in Writing   As you read the following passage from "Through the Tunnel" by Doris Lessing, notice how effectively the author varies the length of her sentences and their word order. Pay particular attention to the italicized sentences.

Jerry swam out to the big barrier rock, adjusted the goggles, and dived. . . .

Under him, six or seven feet down, was a floor of perfectly clean, shining white sand, rippled firm and hard by the tides. Two grayish shapes steered there, like long rounded pieces of wood or slate. *They were fish.* He saw them nose toward each other, poise motionless, make a dart forward, swerve off, and come around again. *It was like a water dance.* A few inches above them the water sparkled as if sequins were dropping through it.

Techniques with Sentence Patterns   Try to use Lessing's techniques when you write and revise your work.

1.   Use compound subjects or predicates to tie ideas together.

Choppy sentence   Jerry swam out to the big barrier rock. He adjusted the goggles. He dived.

Lessing's version   Jerry swam out to the big barrier rock, adjusted the goggles, and dived. . . .

2.   Achieve sentence variety by occasionally inverting word order.

General sentence order   A floor of . . . white sand was under him, six or seven feet down. . . .

Lessing's version   Under him, six or seven feet down, was a floor of . . . white sand. . . .

3.   Vary the length of your sentences to maintain the reader's interest. Occasionally use a very short sentence to accent a point.

Monotonous pattern   Two grayish shapes steered there. They were like rounded pieces of wood or slate. The grayish shapes were fish.

Lessing's variation   Two grayish shapes steered there, like long rounded pieces of wood or slate. They were fish.

Practice   Practice these techniques by revising the following passage, adapted from "Through the Tunnel," combining ideas to create a pleasing variety of sentence lengths. Try to write one sentence in inverted order.

He put on his goggles. He fitted them tight. He tested the vacuum. His hands were shaking. Then he chose the biggest stone. He slipped over the edge of the rock. He looked up once at the empty sky. He filled his lungs once, twice. Then he sank fast to the bottom with the stone. He let it go. He began to count. No strain was on his lungs.

UNIT

12

Phrases

| Grammar | Lessons |

A **phrase** is a group of words that acts in a sentence as a single part of speech.

12.1 | Prepositional Phrases

A **prepositional phrase** is a group of words that begins with a preposition and usually ends with a noun or a pronoun, called the **object of the preposition.**

> I voted **against the idea.** [*Idea* is the object of the preposition *against.*]

> The elevator is necessary **for us.** [*Us* is the object of the preposition *for.*]

> The poet Nikki Giovanni was born **in 1943.** [The date *1943* is the object of the preposition *in.*]

For lists of common prepositions, see page 435.

You may find adjectives and other modifiers appearing between the preposition and its object. Note also that a preposition may have more than one object.

> The elevator goes **to the cool, dark basement.** [adjectives added]

> The elevator goes **to the basement and the penthouse.** [two objects]

A prepositional phrase can act as an adjective or an adverb in a sentence. Used as an adjective, a prepositional phrase modifies a noun or a pronoun. Used as an adverb, it modifies a verb, an adjective, or an adverb.

> Take the elevator **on the right.** [adjective phrase modifying the noun *elevator*]

> Which **of these elevators** is working? [adjective phrase modifying the pronoun *which*]

> **After the meeting** you should take this elevator **to the lobby.** [adverb phrases modifying the verb phrase *should take*]

> The elevator is helpful **to us.** [adverb phrase modifying the adjective *helpful*]

> We sometimes work late **at night.** [adverb phrase modifying the adverb *late*]

Identifying Prepositional Phrases

On your paper write each prepositional phrase that appears in the following sentences. (Some sentences have more than one prepositional phrase.)

Art in Nature

1. Great environmental art is alive on the Great Plains.
2. From an airplane the vast cultivated fields resemble monumental works of abstract art.
3. The varied designs are the result of modern farming methods.
4. The plowed fields are basically rectangular or square in shape.
5. Farmers plow along the natural contours of the land.
6. Red, brown, and black patterns with a variety of textures result from the plowing.
7. Modern irrigation equipment pivots around a central water source.
8. This technique produces huge circular areas of bright green.
9. No one on the Great Plains has consciously planned these designs.
10. They are the bonus of an unplanned collaboration between the farmer and nature.

Exercise 2 **Identifying Adjective and Adverb Phrases**

On your paper write the word or words each prepositional phrase in Exercise 1 modifies. Then write whether each phrase is acting as an *adjective* or an *adverb*.

Exercise 3 **Expanding Sentences with Prepositional Phrases**

On your paper copy and expand the following sentences by adding at least one adjective phrase and one adverb phrase to each.

SAMPLE   The loud music blared.
ANSWER   The loud music on the car stero blared through the open windows.

1. The deep blue lake glimmers.
2. No one told me.
3. The two wild horses galloped.
4. The workers piled up the bricks.
5. The dancers rehearsed tirelessly.
6. The engine stopped suddenly.
7. The Dalmatian and the boxer always run.
8. A strong wind is blowing the papers.
9. That old building collapsed.
10. The geese were flying south.

Exercise 4 **Using Prepositional Phrases in Writing**

On your paper write five sentences that include prepositional phrases. Underline each prepositional phrase and write whether it is being used as an *adjective* or an *adverb*.

SAMPLE   The tennis club at school meets on Thursday.
ANSWER   at school, adjective; on Thursday, adverb

12.2 Appositives and Appositive Phrases

An **appositive** is a noun or a pronoun that is placed next to another noun or pronoun to identify or give additional information about it.

> My friend **Myles** sent me a postcard from England. [The appositive *Myles* identifies the noun *friend*.]

An **appositive phrase** is an appositive plus any words that modify the appositive.

> Joanne rode a hydrofoil across the English Channel, **the body of water between England and France.** [The appositive phrase, in bold type, identifies *English Channel*.]

Appositives or appositive phrases that are not essential to the meaning of a sentence should be set off by commas.

> Myles's sister **Jean** lives there. [The appositive *Jean* is essential because Myles has more than one sister.]

> Myles's only brother, **Timothy**, now lives in Ireland. [The appositive *Timothy* is not necessary to identify the brother.]

Usually an appositive or appositive phrase follows the noun or pronoun it identifies or explains. Occasionally an appositive phrase precedes the noun or pronoun.

> **A talented artist**, Myles would like to become an illustrator of children's books.

Exercise 5	Identifying Appositives and Appositive Phrases

On your paper write the appositives and appositive phrases in the following sentences.

1. My cousin Andrea broke her leg.
2. She was visited in the hospital by Dan and Rosalia, two friends from school.
3. During her hospital stay, my mother took Andrea a get-well gift, a very cute toy bear.
4. Andrea stayed in the hospital, Memorial Hospital Center, for two days.
5. On Andrea's cast her sister Camille drew an appropriate cartoon, a rabbit on skis tumbling down a hill.

Identifying Appositives and Appositive Phrases

On your paper write the appositive or appositive phrase that appears in each sentence. Then write the noun or pronoun that is identified or expanded by the appositive or appositive phrase. (Two sentences have more than one appositive or appositive phrase.)

Leaders in Their Fields

1. Sandra Day O'Connor, the first female justice on the United States Supreme Court, was appointed by President Reagan.
2. A familiar figure on the evening news was Connie Chung, a Chinese American.
3. The Native American Maria Tallchief became a highly accomplished ballerina.
4. Ntozake Shange, an African American author and university professor, wrote a wonderful novel, *Betsey Brown*.
5. The United States representative to the United Nations from 1981 to 1985 was Jeane Kirkpatrick, a teacher and scholar.
6. The anthropologist Margaret Mead made her reputation by studying native peoples of the South Pacific.
7. Anna Mary Robertson Moses, a farm wife untrained in art, became the famous painter Grandma Moses.
8. The tennis player Althea Gibson was the first African American to win a national American tennis tournament.
9. Chita Rivera, an American actress, has starred in many movies and musicals.
10. Pearl Buck, who received the Nobel Prize for literature in 1938, is known for *The Good Earth*, her novel about China.

Exercise 7   **Expanding Sentences with Appositive Phrases**

On your paper expand the following sentences by adding an appositive or an appositive phrase to each one. Be sure to use commas where necessary.

SAMPLE   Matthew Henson went on the first expedition to the North Pole.
ANSWER   Matthew Henson, an African American explorer, went on the first expedition to the North Pole.

1. My sister's dog is a champion.
2. My grandfather is my idol.
3. For my birthday my cousin gave me a compact disc.
4. Sasha's friends look almost like twins.
5. On Sundays we always have the same dessert.
6. The film is my favorite.
7. My brother volunteered to read to Elizabeth.
8. Mary preferred to take the old road.
9. My favorite singer is going on tour this summer.
10. Mike will help Mrs. Scott shovel her sidewalk.

12.3 Verbals and Verbal Phrases

A **verbal** is a verb form that functions in a sentence as a noun, an adjective, or an adverb.

A **verbal phrase** is a verbal plus any complements and modifiers.

The three kinds of verbals are *participles*, *gerunds*, and *infinitives*. All of these types can be expanded into phrases.

Participles and Participial Phrases

A **participle** is a verb form that can function as an adjective.

Present participles always end in *-ing*. Although *past participles* often end in *-ed*, they can take other forms as well. Many adjectives commonly used in sentences are actually participles.

The **freezing** rain slowly turned to hail.

The **heated** argument occurred among the **losing** players.

A participle can be used as an adjective or as part of a verb phrase.

PARTICIPLE AS ADJECTIVE   The **married** couple have jobs.

PARTICIPLE IN VERB PHRASE   The judge **has married** the couple.

A **participial phrase** contains a participle plus any complements and modifiers.

Participial phrases can be used in various positions in a sentence. They always act as adjectives.

Pete Sampras **playing tennis** draws large crowds.

Sampras, **disappointed with his first serve,** vowed to improve his game.

Sitting quietly during one of Sampras's games, his fans watch him intently.

Graciously accepting a trophy from the sponsors, he smiled at the crowd.

In general, a participial phrase at the beginning of a sentence is followed by a comma.

Exercise 8   **Identifying Participles and Participial Phrases**

On your paper write the participle or the participial phrase that acts as an adjective in each of the following sentences. Then identify the word or words each one modifies.

Fashions from Other Lands

1. Americans looking for more variety often adopt the fashions of other countries.
2. The demand for goods imported from other lands is often great.
3. Chinese textile mills export silk decorated by hand.
4. A wool scarf woven in Ecuador is warm and colorful.
5. Brides prize lace veils made by French nuns.
6. Fine cotton fabrics used for men's shirts come from Egypt.
7. Batik cloths made in Malaysia make beautiful warm-weather dresses, shirts, and shawls.
8. Freshwater pearls imported from Japan are used for necklaces and earrings.
9. Eastern European garnets glittering in gold rings are prized by American women and men.
10. India exports gold hoops for pierced ears.
11. Embroidered blouses from Mexico contain intricate floral designs.
12. Leather processed in Italy is used in elegant shoes and purses.
13. Aquamarines and topaz mined in Brazil make beautiful jewelry.
14. Sweaters crafted by Irish workers are heavy and durable.
15. Shoppers can find interesting fashions from just about anywhere in the world.

Exercise 9   **Writing Sentences with Participial Phrases**

Use each of the following phrases in a sentence. Be sure to use the phrase as a participle and not as part of a verb phrase. Place your participial phrase as close as possible to the noun or pronoun it modifies. Then underline that noun or pronoun.

SAMPLE   limping down the empty road
ANSWER   Limping down the empty road, the lost <u>dog</u> looked pathetic.

1. panting in the midday heat
2. whining and whimpering with pain
3. frozen in his tracks
4. broken in two places
5. carrying him home on my shoulders
6. reaching our front porch
7. yelling for someone's help
8. hearing my call
9. sprawled helplessly on the porch floor
10. gathering up the dog in her arms
11. grabbing two soft blankets
12. comforted by our tender care
13. arriving at the veterinarian's office
14. known for his skill with animals
15. wagging his tail with glee

Gerunds and Gerund Phrases

A **gerund** is a verb form that ends in *-ing* and is used in the same way a noun is used.

Gerunds

Reading is my favorite pastime. [gerund as subject]

Dana enjoys **running**. [gerund as direct object]

Jin gives **studying** top priority. [gerund as indirect object]

How much time do you devote to **exercising**? [gerund as object of a preposition]

My preference is **dancing**. [gerund as predicate nominative]

Her hobbies, **skiing** and **hiking,** are strenuous and healthful. [gerunds as appositives]

A **gerund** phrase is a gerund plus any complements and modifiers.

Students are responsible for **mastering their subjects.**

Both a present participle and a gerund end in *-ing*. A present participle is used as an adjective, whereas a gerund is used as a noun.

Listening to the radio, Yusuf worked faster. [present participle]
Listening to the radio helps Yusuf work faster. [gerund]

j u m p i n g!

| **Exercise 10** | **Identifying Gerunds and Gerund Phrases** |

On your paper list the gerunds and gerund phrases that appear in the following sentences. (Some of the sentences have more than one gerund or gerund phrase.)

The Yanomamo

1. Surviving is a challenge for the Yanomamo, a Stone Age people from the Amazon Basin of South America.
2. For centuries the Yanomamo have lived by raising crops, gathering fruits and nuts, and hunting.
3. The social activities of the Yanomamo include celebrating feasts and exchanging gifts with people in nearby villages.
4. Living in remote jungle areas has prevented the Yanomamo from having contact with modern civilization.
5. The Yanomamo have found no way of protecting themselves from the outside world.
6. Brazilians who practice mining and ranching have begun to intrude on the ancestral lands of the Yanomamo.
7. Contact with outsiders has endangered the Yanomamo by exposing them to diseases.
8. Contracting unfamiliar illnesses is becoming all too common among the Yanomamo.
9. Coping with culture shock is another challenge for them.
10. Nowadays seeing an airplane or a motorboat is no longer cause for wonderment.

Infinitives and Infinitive Phrases

An **infinitive** is a verb form that is usually preceded by the word *to* and is used as a noun, an adjective, or an adverb.

When the word *to* appears before the base form of a verb, it is part of the infinitive form of the verb and not a preposition.

To sleep is relaxing. [infinitive as subject]
Every baby needs **to crawl**. [infinitive as direct object]
Her wish is **to succeed**. [infinitive as predicate nominative]

I had a tendency **to doze**. [infinitive as adjective]

He was eager **to rest**. [infinitive as adverb]

An **infinitive phrase** contains an infinitive plus any complements and modifiers.

To hike the Appalachian Trail is my sister's dream.
We decided **to dress for the party**.
The committee voted **to appoint Jennifer president**.

Exercise 11   Identifying Infinitives and Infinitive Phrases

On your paper write the infinitive or infinitive phrase that appears in each of the following sentences. (One sentence has two infinitive phrases.)

Mary Harris Jones, Labor Leader

1. One of the most remarkable figures to join the American labor movement was Mary Harris Jones.
2. In 1880, at the age of 50, Jones decided to change her life.
3. After abandoning her work as a teacher and dressmaker, she proceeded to become a union organizer.
4. Her custom was to travel from place to place in a black gown and bonnet.
5. She worked in the cotton mills of the South to gather evidence for her campaign against child labor.
6. Later she moved to New York City to help the garment and streetcar workers.
7. While she was in Pittsburgh to support a steel-mill strike, Jones was asked who had given her the right to speak publicly.
8. Jones, quick to reply, said, "Patrick Henry, Thomas Jefferson, John Adams!"
9. Mary Jones helped to organize the 1919 steel strike.
10. Mother Jones, as she was sometimes called, was able to make a vigorous speech on her hundredth birthday.

Exercise 12   Using Infinitive Phrases

Jot down five action verbs. Then write each one in an infinitive phrase in an original sentence. Underline the infinitive phrases.

On your paper write the verbal phrases that appear in the following sentences. Write whether each phrase is a *participial phrase*, a *gerund phrase*, or an *infinitive phrase*. Some sentences may contain more than one verbal phrase.

The Pueblo

1. For the Pueblo people, kachinas are ancestral spirits connecting the Pueblo nation with divine power.
2. Representing these spirits is the job of the kachina dancers, men with elaborate masks and costumes.
3. The dancers give Pueblo children wooden dolls to remind them of the kachinas' power.
4. Carved and painted with elaborate designs, the dolls also symbolize ancestral spirits.
5. Playing with the dolls teaches children about their religion.
6. Kachina dancers perform their rituals to bring rain.
7. They believe they can heal the sick by dancing outside their homes.
8. By staging beautiful ceremonies, the kachina dancers bring happiness to their people.
9. Their hope is to make the community healthy and whole.
10. The Pueblo also sell the kachina dolls to raise money for their people.
11. By holding ceremonies during the spring and summer, the early Pueblo sought to influence the growth of crops.
12. Religious leaders, respected for their power, were believed to bring rain through their prayers and rituals.
13. To heal the sick was seen as another example of influencing nature's course.
14. To communicate with powerful forces was one goal.
15. Highlighted by colorful dancing, present-day rituals connect the Pueblo with their past.
16. The beating of drums represents rain clouds.
17. Raising money helps the Pueblo directly as much as rainfall helps them indirectly.
18. The Pueblo hope to sell as many dolls as possible and to earn as much money as possible.
19. Learning the traditional ways in which humans interact with nature, the children absorb their Pueblo heritage.
20. Incorporating religious beliefs into everyday life is important to the Pueblo.

On your paper write each of the following verbal phrases in an original sentence. Write whether each phrase is used as a *participial phrase*, a *gerund phrase*, or an *infinitive phrase*.

1. collecting money for a canned food drive
2. to set up a contest between classes
3. asking the community
4. to provide a nutritious meal
5. satisfied with the effort

Grammar Review

Phrases

The Stuff of Heroes is about a young boy named Gervasio, who learns about bravery firsthand during the Spanish civil war. Gervasio's family is divided by the conflict, which began in 1936 and lasted for three bitter years. This excerpt from the novel contains a vivid description of two friends of Gervasio's from school. The excerpt, translated from the Spanish, has been annotated to show the kinds of phrases covered in this unit.

Literature Model

from THE STUFF OF HEROES

by Miguel Delibes
translated from the Spanish by
Frances M. López-Morillas

In those days the gang gained two new members, also leftovers from the Jesuits' departure: Dámaso Valentín and Eduardo Custodio. Dámaso wore his hair in a brush cut; his thin, elastic lips and the open smiling expression of his light brown eyes brought an enormous joie de vivre to the group. The youngest of five brothers, all of whom had left home, he lived with his widowed mother and two old servants in the most aristocratic part of town. Perhaps because life was easy for him and his weekly allowance double that of his friends, Dámaso was always smiling, and when he did so he displayed a notched front tooth (souvenir of a childhood fall) which he daintily caressed with the tip of his active red tongue. An adaptable and generous boy, he accepted enthusiastically any plan suggested by his friends and his prosperity even allowed him to place his small personal properties at the group's disposal. This was the case of the hard rubber ball with which, shortly after they had met him, they began to play after school on the sidewalk that ran alongside the park, defying the zeal of the municipal guards. ➡

Prepositional phrase
(adjective phrase)

Prepositional phrase
(adverb phrase)

Appositive phrase

Participial phrase
(past participle)

Participial phrase
(present participle)

Eduardo Custodio was the other; pale, slow, and roundabout in speech, with a touch of humor, he suffered from a premature aging that showed in his nearsightedness, his heavy eyelids, his limpness, and a certain stiffness of the legs for which he tried to compensate with tenacity and pride when he played soccer, his great passion. He did not use glasses, and usually combated his myopia by pulling at the outside corner of his eye to make images clearer, and when he went to the movies or some other kind of show he used opera glasses that had belonged to his great-grandmother.

— Infinitive phrase

— Gerund phrase

Exercise 1

Expanding Sentences with Prepositional Phrases   The following sentences describe an imaginary street scene. Read through the sentences quickly to get an idea of the scene, and then rewrite each sentence, adding at least one prepositional phrase, used as an adjective or an adverb, to each sentence.

SAMPLE   Today was market day.

ANSWER   Today was market day in the small Spanish town.

1. The town had a spacious plaza.
2. The fountain was a gathering place.
3. Farmers brought fresh potatoes and melons.
4. Farmhands arranged their produce.
5. Storekeepers exhibited their wares.
6. Some merchants displayed bundles.
7. Weary teams pulled heavy wagons.
8. Men carefully unloaded the wagons.
9. Fishmongers arranged their freshest fish.
10. The pearly scales gleamed.
11. Weavers exhibited woolen rugs.
12. Each rug had been carefully woven.
13. The leather merchant sold belts.
14. He also sold gloves.
15. A breeze cooled the air.
16. The hot sun cast shadows.
17. Baskets decorated the greengrocer's stall.
18. Wooden crates overflowed.
19. A noisy group assembled.
20. They splashed their hands and ran off.

Exercise 2

Expanding Sentences with Appositives and Appositive Phrases   The sentences below elaborate on ideas suggested by the passage from *The Stuff of Heroes*. Each sentence is followed by a group of words in parentheses. Rewrite each sentence, incorporating the words in parentheses as an appositive or an appositive phrase. Use a comma or commas to set off the appositive or appositive phrase from the rest of the sentence.

SAMPLE   Dámaso and Eduardo were the two new members of the gang. (leftovers from the Jesuits' departure)

ANSWER   Dámaso and Eduardo, leftovers from the Jesuits' departure, were the two new members of the gang.

1. Dámaso Valentín brought to the group great verve, along with a taste of prosperity. (a high-spirited boy)
2. He lived with his mother. (a widow)
3. Dámaso's family lived in a house in the nicest part of town. (relatively affluent aristocrats)
4. Dámaso's constant smile revealed a notched front tooth. (the result of a fall)
5. The others in the group could usually count on Dámaso's generosity. (less affluent boys)
6. After school the group would play on the sidewalk with a hard rubber ball. (a possession of Dámaso's)
7. Eduardo Custodio's nearsightedness and stiff legs made him seem old before his time. (middle-aged infirmities)
8. Eduardo played soccer with tenacity. (his great passion)
9. At the movies he used opera glasses. (relics of his great-grandmother's day)
10. In many ways Eduardo was the opposite of the lighthearted Dámaso. (a slow and cautious boy)
11. While Dámaso was quick, Eduardo was slow. (a sluggish and arthritic boy)
12. At soccer, Eduardo's self-discipline moved him beyond his limitations. (a game that punishes the slow)
13. He always played for a goal. (proof of his athletic skills)
14. The others admired Eduardo's persistence. (a quality that made him one of the best players)
15. Eduardo's dignity earned him respect. (a trait not often found in one his age)
16. Pride kept Eduardo from wearing glasses. (a symbol of weakness in his opinion)
17. In sharp contrast to Eduardo was Dámaso. (a vibrant and agreeable boy)
18. Dámaso seemed to float through the ups and downs of daily life. (a very different sort of person)
19. His background gave him a favorable view of the world. (a life of comfort)
20. Dámaso was immensely likable. (an easy-going and kindly boy)

Exercise 3

Expanding Sentences with Participial Phrases   The following sentences describe scenes in *The Stuff of Heroes*. Each sentence is followed by another sentence in parentheses. Combine the sentences, changing the sentence in parentheses into a participial phrase. Be sure to place the participial phrase near the word that it modifies.

SAMPLE   Dámaso and Eduardo found their school closed.
          (They were beginning the new school year.)

ANSWER   Beginning the new school year, Dámaso and Eduardo found their school closed.

1. The Jesuits shut their schools. (The Jesuits were expelled from Spain by the government.)
2. Dámaso and Eduardo sought new friends. (Dámaso and Eduardo were feeling self-conscious in their new school.)
3. Gervasio warmly greeted his two new classmates. (Gervasio was seeing new faces.)
4. Gervasio's circle of friends gained two new members. (The circle of friends was welcoming Dámaso and Eduardo.)
5. Dámaso quickly made friends with everyone. (Dámaso was smiling his customary smile.)
6. His smile drew attention to a front tooth. (The front tooth was notched during a fall.)
7. Dámaso looked sleek and contemporary. (Dámaso was wearing his hair in a brush cut.)
8. He had an enormous zest for life. (He was accepting his friends' plans enthusiastically.)
9. Dámaso's mother had two old servants. (His mother had been widowed for some years.)
10. Dámaso's friends often visited his house. (The house was located in an aristocratic part of town.)
11. Dámaso's mother was generous. (She was giving him double the weekly allowance of his friends.)
12. The boy had an easy life. (He was experiencing little hardship.)
13. The municipal guards once caught Gervasio's gang. (The boys were playing ball on the sidewalk alongside the park.)
14. One of Gervasio's relatives used his influence on the boys' behalf. (The relative was conferring with a sergeant of the guards.)
15. The police freed the boys and returned their ball. (The police were dropping the charges.)
16. Eduardo Custodio was pale and slow. (He was suffering from premature aging.)
17. Eduardo competed with tenacity and pride. (Eduardo was never complaining.)
18. Eduardo never made excuses for himself. (He was often vexed by the stiffness in his legs.)
19. He did not wear eyeglasses. (He was hiding his nearsightedness.)
20. The violence of civil war would soon interrupt the boys' sheltered lives. (The violence was provoked by a miners' strike.)

Exercise 4

Writing Sentences with Gerund Phrases   Each of the following items consists of a question followed by a phrase in parentheses that answers the question. For each item write a sentence that answers the question, using the words in parentheses as a gerund phrase.

SAMPLE   What helps us explain Spain's role in Europe today?
(understanding Spanish history)

ANSWER   Understanding Spanish history helps us explain Spain's role in Europe today.

1.   What was Spain's goal at one time? (creating a vast colonial empire)
2.   What set off Spain's decline? (losing its Latin American colonies)
3.   What divided the country before World War II? (fighting a bloody civil war)
4.   By what means did General Francisco Franco unify Spain? (ruling the country as a dictator from 1939 to 1975)
5.   Many people opposed Franco for what action? (accepting military aid from Hitler)
6.   What made Spain an outcast in postwar Europe? (being ruled by the fascist dictator Franco)
7.   Many people in Spain feared what turn of events? (returning to the violence of civil war)
8.   What brought political reforms to Spain? (restoring the monarchy in 1975)
9.   What did King Juan Carlos favor? (liberalizing Franco's harsh policies)
10.   What finally made Spain a full participant in Western European society? (joining the European Economic Community in 1986)
11.   What has begun to improve the standard of living in Spain? (participating in free trade with other countries)
12.   What made Spain attractive to the United States during the cold war? (Franco's opposing the Soviet Union and communism)
13.   How did the United States help Spain during the cold war? (loaning Franco's government millions of dollars)
14.   What did Spain do to help the United States during the cold war? (allowing the United States to set up military bases in Spain)
15.   What was the purpose of the American military bases in Spain? (defending Europe against possible Soviet attack)
16.   What improved Spain's standing with other nations? (joining the United Nations in 1955)
17.   How did the United States help Spain during its time of economic hardship? (donating millions of dollars in aid)
18.   What helped pull Spain out of its economic difficulties in the early 1960s? (undertaking a financial reform program)
19.   What was Spain's reward for undergoing financial reform? (receiving membership in the European Economic Community)
20.   To what can the Spanish people now look forward? (becoming an even more prosperous and respected nation)

Review: Exercise 5

Writing Sentences with Infinitive Phrases   The following sentences are based on passages from *The Stuff of Heroes* that are not reprinted in this textbook. Each item consists of a question followed by a phrase in parentheses that answers the question. For each item write on your paper a sentence that answers the question, using the words in parentheses as an infinitive phrase.

SAMPLE   What was Gervasio's childhood dream? (to be a crusader)
ANSWER   Gervasio's childhood dream was to be a crusader.

1. What was Gervasio's great desire? (to perform deeds of courage)
2. What did he hope to do? (to battle the enemy)
3. What did these ambitions only manage to do? (to give him goose flesh)
4. What did Gervasio's fervor make his classmates want to do? (to laugh at his zeal)
5. When rebels attacked, what was Gervasio's plan? (to shoot stones from his slingshot at the attackers)
6. What did Gervasio have to do to become a hero in his own eyes? (to participate fully in the battle)
7. What was Gervasio able to do because he began his career as a hero? (to feel triumphant)
8. Later, when the civil war broke out, what did Gervasio, Dámaso, and Eduardo volunteer to do? (to join Franco's navy)
9. According to Dámaso, what was the greatest honor? (to die for the cause)
10. What did a torpedo attack force Gervasio to do? (to confront paralyzing fear)
11. What would Gervasio be able to do if he performed courageous deeds? (to fulfill a personal goal)
12. What was Gervasio's personal goal? (to prove to himself that he was brave)
13. What did his thoughts of bravery continue to do? (to show him how frightened he really was)
14. What did Gervasio's classmates continue to do? (to ridicule his enthusiasm)
15. When he used his slingshot, what was Gervasio's hope? (to have accurate aim)
16. What did Gervasio have to do to gain self-respect? (to fight bravely)
17. As a hero, what would Gervasio have to do? (to take on more responsibility)
18. What did Gervasio, Dámaso, and Eduardo want to do during the civil war? (to become sailors)
19. What might be necessary when fighting for a cause? (to sacrifice oneself for one's beliefs)
20. What would Gervasio be able to do by engaging in armed conflict? (to meet his fear and work through it)

Exercise 6

Writing Sentences with Phrases   On your paper write sentences according to the directions that follow. Make your sentences relate to the passage from *The Stuff of Heroes*, but do not copy sentences directly from the passage.

SAMPLE   Write a sentence that includes a prepositional phrase used as an adjective.
ANSWER   The *Stuff of Heroes* is a book about a young boy named Gervasio.

1. Write a sentence using a prepositional phrase that is an adverb.
2. Write a sentence that begins with an appositive phrase.
3. Write a sentence in which a participial phrase modifies the direct object.
4. Make a gerund phrase the subject of a sentence.
5. Write a sentence using an infinitive phrase as a noun.

Proofreading

Review: Exercise 7

The following passage describes Henri Cartier-Bresson, the photographer whose work appears on the opposite page. Rewrite the passage, correcting the errors in spelling, grammar, and usage. Add any missing punctuation. There are twenty-five errors.

Henri Cartier-Bresson

[1] Born in Chanteloup, France, in 1908 the photographer Henri Cartier-Bresson ranks among the worlds great photojournalists. [2] The son of a wealthy thread manufacturer he began drawing and painting when he was very young. [3] Recuperating from an illness at the age of twenty-three he discovered photography.

[4] Cartier-Bresson beleived that a photographer should record life as it is, not as the photographer wants it to be. [5] Disliking the posed pictures common in studio photography he liked to capture the "decisive moment" of a situation the moment in which the essence of a scene is revealed. [6] During the year of 1933, he bought his first Leica camera a small instrument equipped with a quiet shutter. [7] This camera enabled you to take photographs quickly easily, and inconspicuously. [8] Indebted to the great films of the past Cartier-Bresson learned to choose expressive images for his photos. [9] Trained as a painter he always carried a sketch pad along with his camera.

[10] In the decade of the 1930s, Cartier-Bresson documented the lives of people in Mexico worked with the great French film director Jean Renoir, and made his own documentery about Spanish hospitals. [11] Captured by the Germans during World War II he escaped from prison on his third attempt. [12] Later, he helped establish Magnum a photo agency.

[13] *Seville* is typical of Cartier-Bressons documentary style. [14] Taken through a break in a wall the photograph shows a group of children playing in a poor neighborhood in Seville a city in Spain. [15] The composition is extrordinary and seemingly casual. [16] All the elements in the picture hangs in a delicate balance. ➡

Henri Cartier-Bresson, *Seville*, 1933

[17]Writing about the Spanish Civil War in *The Stuff of Heroes* Miguel Delibes describes children who are forced to endure hardships. [18]Each of the boys in Delibes's story manage to survive by creating their own imaginary world. [19]This world mirrors the real worlds conflict, yet it is also full of humor and joy.

Mixed Review

Exercise 8

The biographical sketch of Miguel Delibes [mē gel′ dā lē′ bes] that appears here is followed by 10 numbered sentences. Use the facts in the sketch to revise the 10 items, following the guidelines that appear in parentheses at the end of each sentence. Be sure to place any phrase you add near the word it modifies.

Miguel Delibes

   Miguel Delibes is one of Spain's most admired novelists. He was born in 1920 in Valladolid in the province of Castile, and most of his novels are set in that region. During Delibes's youth Spain was torn by a civil war (1936–1939). General Francisco Franco's Nationalist forces, supported by Nazi Germany and Fascist Italy, battled the leftist Republican forces, which were aided by the Soviet Union. Franco emerged victorious, ruling Spain as a dictator until 1975. During the civil war, Delibes served as a volunteer in Franco's army.

   After the war Delibes earned degrees in law, business, and journalism. His first novel, *The Cypress Casts a Long Shadow*, won the Nadal Prize in 1947. This early success inspired Delibes to become a writer in addition to pursuing an academic career. Six of his many novels and works of nonfiction have been translated into English, including his most popular novel, *El Camino* (1950), published in English as *The Path*. Delibes's novel *The Stuff of Heroes* (1987) is a coming-of-age story based on his experiences as a schoolboy in Valladolid and as a volunteer in the civil war. Through Gervasio, its main character, the novel explores the meaning of heroism, bravery, and loyalty against the backdrop of divided allegiances within a family and a nation.

1. Miguel Delibes is a popular and admired novelist. (Add an adjective prepositional phrase.)
2. Delibes was born in the province of Castile. He sets most of his fiction in that region. (Combine the sentences by turning the first sentence into a participial phrase.)
3. The Spanish civil war began. (Add an adverb prepositional phrase.)
4. Spain was torn by something. It was fighting between fascists and socialists. (Combine the sentences by turning the second sentence into a gerund phrase.)
5. What did Delibes volunteer to do during the civil war? (Respond with a sentence that includes an infinitive phrase.)
6. After the war Delibes devoted himself to something. He was studying law, business, and journalism. (Combine the sentences by turning the second sentence into a gerund phrase.)
7. *The Cypress Casts a Long Shadow* won the 1947 Nadal Prize. (Add an appositive phrase.)
8. Delibes was inspired by this prestigious award. Delibes decided to write more novels. (Combine the sentences by turning the first sentence into a participial phrase.)
9. Six of Delibes's works have been translated. (Add an adverb prepositional phrase.)
10. In *The Stuff of Heroes,* Gervasio is the name. (Add an adjective prepositional phrase.)

Writing Application

Phrases in Writing   William Least Heat-Moon uses many phrases in this passage from *Blue Highways: A Journey Into America* to convey the grandeur of the scenery in the Southwest. Examine the passage, focusing especially on the italicized phrases.

> The highway made an unexpected jog toward Navajo Bridge, *a melding of silvery girders and rock cliffs*. Suddenly, there it was, far below *in the deep and scary canyon of sides so sheer* they might have been cut *with a stone saw*, the naturally silted water turned an unnatural green (*colorado* means "reddish") *by the big settling basin a few miles upriver* called Glen Canyon Dam. Navajo Bridge, *built in 1929 when paved roads began opening the area*, is the only crossing *over the Colorado* between Glen Canyon and Hoover Dam several hundred miles downstream.

Techniques with Phrases   Try to apply some of William Least Heat-Moon's techniques when you write and revise your own work.

1.   Use prepositional phrases to explain location and to add precision to your writing.

General Words Suddenly, there it was, far below . . .
Least Heat-Moon's Version Suddenly, there it was, far below *in the deep and scary canyon of sides so sheer* they might have been cut *with a stone saw* . . .

2.   Consider whether the addition of appositive phrases can help make ideas or images clearer or more vivid. For example, Least Heat-Moon uses an appositive phrase to help readers picture the Navajo Bridge.

General Words The highway made an unexpected jog toward Navajo Bridge. . . .
Least Heat-Moon's Version The highway made an unexpected jog toward Navajo Bridge, *a melding of silvery girders and rock cliffs.*

3.   Consider using verbal phrases to improve the flow of your sentences and to show relationships between ideas.

Repetitive Sentences Navajo Bridge was built in 1929 when paved roads began opening the area. Navajo Bridge is the only crossing . . .
Least Heat-Moon's Version Navajo Bridge, *built in 1929 when paved roads began opening the area*, is the only crossing . . .

Practice   Practice these techniques by expanding the following paragraph. Use prepositional phrases, appositive phrases, and verbal phrases to make ideas more precise and vivid.

> My friends and I stood on the rim of the canyon. The sun was setting. The canyon walls reflected the soft rays. Different shades of red blended into each other. Long shadows crossed the ground. Long shadows hid some of the detail on the canyon's floor. In the distance we could see a small village. An old man rode his horse next to the river. A solitary woman tended a fire. Smoke from the fire rose. A lone eagle soared in and out of the gorge. The only noise I could hear was the slight breeze. It was rustling the leaves on the trees nearby.

13.1 Main Clauses

A **clause** is a group of words that has a subject and a predicate and that is used as a part of a sentence.

Clauses fall into two categories: *main clauses*, which are also called *independent clauses*, and *subordinate clauses*, which are also called *dependent clauses*.

A **main clause** has a subject and a predicate and can stand alone as a sentence.

There must be at least one main clause in every sentence. Both of the clauses in each of the following examples are main clauses because both can stand alone as sentences.

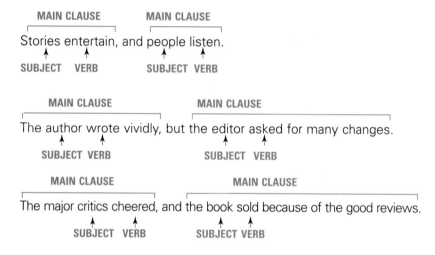

Exercise 1   Identifying Main Clauses

On your paper copy the following sentences and mark each main clause. Then write *S* below each subject and *V* below each verb. Be sure that each clause you mark can stand alone as a sentence.

SAMPLE ANSWER

The book reached the bookstores, and the advertising campaign began.
    S   V   S   V

1. The publishers advertised, and the bookstore owners responded.
2. The book's cover was a striking design, and the author was pleased.
3. The author toured, and television hosts interviewed her.
4. Sometimes she gave readings, but few people attended.
5. Eventually sales increased, and the author celebrated.

13.2 Subordinate Clauses

A **subordinate clause** has a subject and a predicate, but it cannot stand alone as a sentence.

In order for a subordinate clause to make sense, it must be attached to a main clause. Many subordinate clauses begin with subordinating conjunctions or relative pronouns. (Subordinating conjunctions are listed on page 440, and relative pronouns are on page 413.)

In the first example the subordinate clause, *because they are amusing*, is attached to the main clause, *Stories entertain*. The subordinate clause is introduced by the subordinating conjunction *because*, which is placed before *they are amusing*. Note that the subordinate clause does not express a complete thought even though it has a subject and a predicate.

In the second example the subordinate clause comes between the subject and the verb of the main clause. This subordinate clause begins with the relative pronoun *that*, which also serves as the subject of the clause.

Exercise 2   Identifying Clauses

Each of the following sentences has a clause that appears in italics. On your paper indicate whether it is a *main clause* or a *subordinate clause*.

Mahalia Jackson, Gospel Singer

[1]Mahalia Jackson was an African American singer *who became popular worldwide as a performer of gospel music.* [2]*Although she was strongly associated with religious music,* her vocal style was influenced by jazz. [3]*Jackson grew up in New Orleans,* where she sang in a church choir. [4]*When she was 16 years old,* Jackson moved to Chicago. [5]*She worked as a maid and food packager* during the first years that she lived in the city. [6]*Because she possessed a powerful, beautiful voice,* record companies soon offered her contracts. [7]In the 1950s she gave a series of gospel concerts across the United States *that drew huge audiences.* [8]*Jackson performed internationally* after her United States tours proved so successful. [9]*Although she was a popular gospel star,* Jackson was also very much concerned with politics. [10]*Since she viewed song as an inspiration for peace,* she performed at many civil rights rallies and marches.

13.3 Simple and Compound Sentences

A **simple sentence** has only one main clause and no subordinate clauses.

A simple sentence may contain a compound subject or a compound predicate or both. The subject and the predicate can be expanded with adjectives, adverbs, prepositional phrases, appositives, and verbal phrases. As long as the sentence has only one main clause, however, it remains a simple sentence.

Stories entertain. [simple sentence]

Stories and riddles entertain. [simple sentence with compound subject]

Stories entertain and amuse. [simple sentence with compound predicate]

Stories and riddles amuse and entertain. [simple sentence with compound subject and compound predicate]

Stories about the Old West entertain adults and children alike. [simple sentence expanded]

A **compound sentence** has two or more main clauses.

Each main clause of a compound sentence has its own subject and predicate, and these main clauses are usually joined by a comma and a coordinating conjunction (such as *and, but, or, nor, yet,* or *for*).

MAIN CLAUSE 1	MAIN CLAUSE 2
Stories entertain, and	riddles amuse.
S V	S V

MAIN CLAUSE 1	MAIN CLAUSE 2	MAIN CLAUSE 3
Stories entertain, and	riddles amuse, but	poems delight.
S V	S V	S V

Semicolons may also be used to join the main clauses in a compound sentence.

MAIN CLAUSE 1

Few wild animals live in China's densely populated plains;

MAIN CLAUSE 2

in remoter areas wildlife is abundant.

Bob shrieked, and Mary cried, but Dan laughed.

Compound Sentence

Identifying Simple and Compound Sentences

On your paper write *simple sentence* or *compound sentence* to identify each sentence. (Remember that a single main clause can have a compound subject and a compound predicate.)

Currier and Ives

1. Nineteenth-century American scenes and customs were recorded and preserved by the firm of Currier and Ives.
2. Nathaniel Currier was a printer, and James Ives was an executive.
3. The two men produced "prints for the people."
4. Currier favored current events; he produced prints of ships, battles, and news events.
5. Ives had broader interests and generally favored country scenes.
6. Together they published color lithographs depicting every facet of American life.
7. Currier and Ives produced thousands of lithographs, and each print was rich in color and detail.
8. Many prints showed city life, but others depicted life in the country.
9. In the last century most Americans lived in the country, and many events took place outdoors.
10. Currier and Ives's prints show Americans at work and at play in the nineteenth century.

Exercise 4   **Writing Simple Sentences**

On your paper combine each pair of ideas below into a simple sentence. Remember that each sentence must have only one main clause, although the sentence may have a compound subject and/or predicate.

Grandma Moses

1. Grandma Moses was born in 1860.
   She was an American painter.
2. She embroidered all her life.
   She didn't take up painting until the age of 76.
3. Moses had no formal art training.
   She possessed great natural talent.
4. Farm scenes and old-fashioned farm activities are her subjects.
   Her paintings are simple and colorful.
5. Moses's talent flourished.
   She died at the age of 101.

Exercise 5   **Writing Compound Sentences**

Use the information in each item from Exercise 4 to write a compound sentence. Remember that each sentence must have two or more main clauses. The clauses may be joined by a comma and a coordinating conjunction—or by a semicolon.

13.4 Complex and Compound-Complex Sentences

A **complex sentence** has one main clause and one or more subordinate clauses.

MAIN CLAUSE

I like Toni Cade Bambara's stories
S V

SUBORDINATE CLAUSE

because they have real-life characters.
S V

SUBORDINATE CLAUSE   MAIN CLAUSE   SUBORDINATE CLAUSE

When I read her stories, I enjoy them because they are true to life.
S V   S V   S V

A **compound-complex sentence** has two or more main clauses and at least one subordinate clause.

MAIN CLAUSE   SUBORDINATE CLAUSE

I read *Frankenstein,* which was written by Mary Shelley,
S V   S   V

MAIN CLAUSE

and I wrote a report about it.
S   V

Exercise 6   Identifying Subordinate Clauses

On your paper write the subordinate clause from each of the following sentences. If a sentence has no subordinate clause, write *none*.

1. American pioneers built their houses out of the materials that were readily available.
2. Settlers in heavily forested regions erected log cabins, and newcomers on the treeless plains built sod houses.
3. When they journeyed across the continent, the pioneers lived in their covered wagons.
4. Native Americans of the woodlands built wooden houses, but Native Americans of the Great Plains preferred tepees because they were easy to move.
5. Today Americans who live in the Southwest often build their houses of adobe.

Identifying Complex and Compound-Complex Sentences

On your paper write the subordinate clause from each of the following sentences. Indicate whether each sentence is a *complex sentence* or a *compound-complex sentence*.

Adobe Homes

1. When people in Mexico build their homes, they sometimes use adobe.
2. Adobe is the Spanish name for sun-dried bricks, which are made according to an ancient process.
3. Workers who manufacture adobe mix sandy clay with water and a small amount of straw.
4. After the clay, water, and straw are thoroughly mixed together, the adobe is shoveled into wooden forms and molded into rectangular bricks.
5. The blocks bake in the sun for about two weeks, and the result is strong adobe bricks that can be used for construction.
6. Once the bricks are dry, workers remove the forms.
7. Traditional adobe houses are covered with mud, but modern adobe homes are sometimes covered with a plasterlike material that is called stucco.
8. Many people prefer adobe houses, since they remain cool in hot weather.
9. Although adobe is a popular building material in Mexico and the southwestern United States, it is not good for very damp or cold areas.
10. If adobe is exposed to frequent rains, the bricks will eventually crumble.

Exercise 8 **Writing Simple, Compound, Complex, and Compound-Complex Sentences**

Use your own knowledge and the information below to write four original sentences about mobile homes. Write *simple, complex, compound,* or *compound-complex* to identify each sentence you write. (You should write one sentence of each kind.)

Mobile homes are easily moved.
Some people travel in them.
Some people live in them.
They are pulled by cars or trucks.
They became popular during a wartime housing shortage.
They can be connected to utilities.

One quarter of all new single-family dwellings are mobile homes.
Their length varies from 12 to 30 feet.
Communities regulate their placement.
They were once called trailers or caravans.
Sites in trailer parks are usually rented.

Exercise 9 **Creating Sentences with Various Structures**

On your paper write a simple sentence. Then rework it, making it a compound sentence. Rework the simple sentence again, making it part of a complex sentence. Finally, rework your compound sentence into a compound-complex sentence. Label your four sentences.

13.5 Adjective Clauses

An **adjective clause** is a subordinate clause that modifies a noun or a pronoun.

An adjective clause usually follows the word it modifies.

The horror story **that has always been my favorite** is "The Black Cat."

The writer **whom my sister likes best** is Yoshiko Uchida.

I like a writer **who surprises me.**

Adjective clauses may be introduced by the relative pronouns (*who, whom, whose, that,* and *which*) and by the subordinating conjunctions *where* and *when.*

The Elizabethan Age spans the time **when Elizabeth I ruled.**
That is the house **where I was born.**

At times the relative pronoun is dropped at the beginning of an adjective clause.

This is a story **every science enthusiast should read.** [The relative pronoun *that* has been omitted.]

Some adjective clauses are called *essential clauses,* or *restrictive clauses.* Without them the meaning of the sentence would be unclear.

Edgar Allan Poe is the only American writer **who always fascinates me.** [essential clause]

"The Black Cat" is the story **that I like best.** [essential clause]

Some adjective clauses are *not* needed to make the meaning of the sentence clear. Such clauses are called *nonessential clauses,* or *nonrestrictive clauses.* A nonessential clause is always set off with commas.

Edgar Allan Poe, **who is my favorite author,** wrote "The Black Cat." [nonessential clause]

"The Black Cat," **which was written by Edgar Allan Poe,** is my favorite short story. [nonessential clause]

The word *that* usually introduces an essential clause; the word *which* usually introduces a nonessential clause.

"The Black Cat," **which I like best,** is thrilling. [nonessential clause]
I like a story **that thrills me.** [essential clause]

The detective *who works under cover* was unrecognizable.

Identifying Adjective Clauses and the Words They Modify

On your paper write the adjective clause that appears in each of the following sentences. Then write the word that the clause modifies. (In one sentence the relative pronoun has been dropped.)

The Story of O. Henry

1. William Sydney Porter wrote stories under a pseudonym, which is another word for a pen name.
2. Porter, who lived from 1862 to 1910, used the pseudonym O. Henry.
3. Porter contributed a number of articles to a humor magazine, which he had founded in Texas in 1894.
4. He wrote a daily column that was humorous and witty.
5. As O. Henry, Porter published many stories that were sympathetic and touching.
6. He created unusual plots that ended in surprising ways.
7. *The Four Million,* which is a collection of O. Henry's short stories, was published in the year 1906.
8. "The Gift of the Magi" is a story many people enjoy.
9. Another O. Henry work that is very popular is "The Third Ingredient."
10. Readers who enjoy the unusual and the humorous will delight in the short stories of O. Henry.

Identifying Essential and Nonessential Clauses

For each sentence in the pairs below, write the adjective clause, and then identify it as an *essential clause* or a *nonessential clause*.

Sally Ride: First U.S. Woman in Space

1. a. The 1983 U.S. space mission that received the most public attention was the six-day voyage in June of the *Challenger* space shuttle.
   b. The *Challenger* space shuttle, which went on a six-day mission in June 1983, received much public attention.
2. a. Sally Ride, who was flight engineer on the *Challenger,* became the first U.S. woman to enter outer space.
   b. The U.S. woman who first entered outer space was *Challenger* flight engineer Sally Ride.
3. a. The background that Ride had in astrophysics helped her qualify for NASA's space program.
   b. Ride's doctorate in astrophysics, which she earned from Stanford University, helped her qualify for NASA's space program.
4. a. Sally Ride used a remote-control mechanical arm, which she had helped design, to retrieve a satellite in space.
   b. To retrieve a satellite in space, Sally Ride used the remote-control mechanical arm that was 50 feet in length.
5. a. Today's astronauts are people who have training in specific fields.
   b. Today's space program is using mission specialists, who are astronauts with training in specific fields.

13.6 Adverb Clauses

An **adverb clause** is a subordinate clause that modifies a verb, an adjective, or an adverb. It tells *when, where, how, why, to what extent,* or *under what condition.*

I studied hard **before I took the test.** [The adverb clause modifies the verb *studied.* It tells *when.*]

I was happy **because I passed the test.** [The adverb clause modifies the adjective *happy.* It tells *why.*]

I can study better **if there is no noise.** [The adverb clause modifies the adverb *better.* It tells *under what conditions.*]

Adverb clauses are introduced by subordinating conjunctions, such as those listed on page 440. Remember that an adverb clause may either precede or follow the main clause. When the adverb clause comes first, separate it from the main clause with a comma. The first example above might have been written as follows:

Before I took the test, I studied hard.

At times words may be left out of an adverb clause. You can easily supply the omitted words, however, because they are understood, or implied. Adverb clauses in which words have been omitted are called *elliptical adverb clauses.*

She can swim faster **than I [can swim].**
The news made José happier **than [it made] me [happy].**

Exercise 12　　　**Identifying Adverb Clauses**

On your paper write the adverb clause that appears in each of the following sentences.

Squanto, Friend of the Pilgrims

1. Although he led a life of hardship, Squanto, a Pawtuxet from Massachusetts, accomplished a great deal.
2. After he was kidnapped by a group of English fishers in 1614, Squanto was taken to Spain.
3. He was taken to Spain so that he could be sold there as an enslaved person.
4. Once the opportunity arose, Squanto escaped to England and taught himself English.
5. As soon as it was safe, Squanto returned home to Massachusetts.
6. When Squanto met the Pilgrims at Plymouth in 1621, they were hungry and discouraged.
7. The Pawtuxet were angry because the Pilgrims had taken their corn.
8. Since he spoke fluent English, Squanto became a peacemaker for the two groups.
9. As if that were not enough, Squanto also taught the Pilgrims about corn.
10. No one could have worked more tirelessly than he.

Identifying Adverb Clauses

On your paper write the adverb clause that appears in each sentence in the paragraph below. In one of the sentences, the adverb clause is elliptical.

King Philip's War

[1]Metacomet, better known as King Philip, felt threatened when the Puritan settlements began to spread. [2]Like Squanto, in earlier times he had aided the Pilgrims so that they could survive in a harsh new environment. [3]In 1671 the Pilgrims became angry with Metacomet because, in their minds, he seemed disloyal. [4]After he was tried, convicted, and severely punished, Metacomet swore revenge. [5]"King Philip's War," a series of battles, began as Metacomet's troops staged raids along the Massachusetts-Connecticut frontier. [6]Metacomet's soldiers were brave because, in their opinion, they were defending their homelands. [7]Metacomet might have been more successful if his fighting force had been larger. [8]The Native Americans fought as fiercely as the Puritans, but the Puritans were better armed and more numerous. [9] Before he was killed by one of his own men, Metacomet had destroyed several towns. [10] When the surviving Native Americans saw the futility of their efforts, they surrendered and the war ended.

Exercise 14   **Adding Adverb Clauses to Sentences**

On your paper rewrite each of the following sentences, adding an adverb clause either before or after the main clause. Consult the list of subordinating conjunctions on page 440 for ideas.

SAMPLE   I remember the story of one particular Native American.
ANSWER   Whenever I think about colonial America, I remember the story of one
              particular Native American.
              OR
              I remember the story of one particular Native American whenever I think
              about colonial America.

  1. The Pilgrims did not know how to survive in America.
  2. Squanto was able to communicate with the Pilgrims.
  3. Metacomet had been friendly with the Pilgrims.
  4. Metacomet decided to wage war.
  5. The Native American troops were discouraged.
  6. Life was more secure for the Puritans.
  7. New England's population grew steadily.
  8. The New England colonists lived longer, healthier lives.
  9. The Native American population decreased.
  10. The Native Americans might still be the only Americans in New England.

13.7 Noun Clauses

A **noun clause** is a subordinate clause used as a noun.

Like a noun or pronoun, a noun clause can have different functions in a sentence: it can act as a subject, a direct object, an indirect object, an object of a preposition, or a predicate nominative.

NOUN

Farmers often eat home-grown food.
S

NOUN CLAUSE

Whoever lives on a farm often eats home-grown food.
S

NOUN

A drought affects crops.
DO

NOUN CLAUSE

A drought affects whatever grows outdoors.
DO

In the preceding examples, each noun clause forms an inseparable part of the sentence's main clause (the entire sentence).

The following are some of the words that can be used to introduce noun clauses.

how	whatever	which	whoever
that	when	whichever	whose
what	where	who, whom	why

The following are additional examples of noun clauses.

Give **whoever comes to the door** a donation for Farmer's Aid. [indirect object]

This is **how most farmers plant their crops.** [predicate nominative]

Crops are fertilized with **whatever will make them grow fast and strong.** [object of a preposition]

The subordinating conjunction *that* is sometimes dropped at the beginning of a noun clause.

I believe [that] **nobody works harder than farmers.** [The subordinating conjunction *that* is omitted.]

Identifying Noun Clauses

On your paper write the noun clauses that appear in each of the following sentences. (Some of the sentences have two noun clauses each.)

The History of Kites

1. Whoever has flown a kite knows that kite flying can be fun.
2. Few people realize that kites are not only for children.
3. What many may not know is that kites have existed for ages.
4. No one knows for sure where kites were invented, but they probably first appeared in China.
5. Historians tell us that the Chinese military of about two thousand years ago attached bamboo pipes to their kites.
6. The result was that the noise from the wind in the pipes panicked the enemy soldiers on the ground below.
7. In Hamamatsu, Japan, the three-day kite-flying festival in early May brings pleasure to whoever attends.
8. What attracts people to this festival is seeing so many brightly painted kites taller than themselves.
9. That the Hamamatsu festival is popular is proved by what is now a 400-year-old tradition.
10. Do you agree that kite flying is an enjoyable activity?

Exercise 16   **Writing Sentences with Noun Clauses**

On your paper complete the following sentences about baseball by replacing the blanks with noun clauses. Begin each noun clause with the word in parentheses.

SAMPLE   Do you know (why) _____?
ANSWER   Do you know why baseball is America's favorite sport?

Baseball

1. Many people agree (that) _____.
2. (Whoever) _____ can go to first base.
3. (How) _____ is exciting to watch.
4. The umpire decides (who) _____.
5. A fast-paced game with lots of action is (what) _____.
6. Few fans understand (when) _____.
7. The catcher and the pitcher consult about (whose) _____.
8. The batter's biggest worry is (where) _____.
9. His excuse for striking out is (whatever) _____.
10. The coach has decided (which) _____.

Identifying Subordinate Clauses

On your paper write the subordinate clause that appears in each sentence. Then write *adverb clause*, *adjective clause*, or *noun clause* to indicate what kind of clause it is.

A Historic Court Decision

[1]*Brown* v. *Board of Education of Topeka* was a legal case that changed the face of the American school system. [2]What began as a local matter in a Kansas town in 1951 had gained national attention by 1954. [3]Because his daughter could not attend an all-white school near her home, an African American parent sued the Topeka Board of Education. [4]Thurgood Marshall, who later became the first African American justice on the Supreme Court, represented the student's father, Oliver Brown. [5]Marshall was an attorney whom people respected and admired for his legal skills. [6]In 1954 the Court ruled that segregated schools deprived minorities of an equal education. [7]The chief justice of the Supreme Court, Earl Warren, declared that segregation violated a citizen's right to equal protection under the law. [8]After the decision was announced, schools across the country changed their enrollment policies. [9]Many schools adopted a policy of integration, which allowed children from different ethnic backgrounds to learn together. [10]Few Supreme Court cases have had a greater impact on American society than this one.

Adding Adjective, Adverb, and Noun Clauses to Sentences

On your paper combine the following pairs of sentences by turning one of them into a subordinate clause. Write the sentence, and then write *adjective clause*, *adverb clause*, or *noun clause* to identify what kind of clause you created.

SAMPLE   (a) A boomerang is a throwing stick.
          (b) A boomerang was used originally by Australian Aborigines.
ANSWER   A boomerang is a throwing stick that was used originally by Australian Aborigines. (adjective clause)

Boomerangs
1. (a) A boomerang returns to the thrower.
   (b) It rotates horizontally in flight.
2. (a) Early European travelers wrote in their diaries.
   (b) The Aborigines used boomerangs to trap game.
3. (a) The use of boomerangs declined.
   (b) More sophisticated hunting weapons were introduced by the British.
4. (a) Every year the Smithsonian Institution stages a boomerang festival.
   (b) It takes place on the mall in Washington, D.C.
5. (a) The term *boomerang* is sometimes used as a verb.
   (b) It means "to result in harm to the user or doer."

Writing Subordinate Clauses in Sentences

On your paper, write four original sentences. In the first one, use an adverb clause. In the second one, use an adjective clause. In the third one, use a noun clause as a subject. In the fourth one, use a noun clause as a direct object.

13.8 Four Kinds of Sentences

A **declarative sentence** makes a statement.

> A lion is chasing the ostriches.
> The huge birds run fast.

The declarative sentence is the most frequently used type of sentence. It normally ends with a period.

An **imperative sentence** gives a command or makes a request.

> Look at the fleeing ostriches.
> Please take pictures of them.

In an imperative sentence, the subject "you" is understood. An imperative sentence usually ends with a period, but it may end with an exclamation point if it expresses strong emotion.

An **interrogative sentence** asks a question.

> What did the lion chase?
> Is the lion chasing the ostriches?

An interrogative sentence ends with a question mark.

An **exclamatory sentence** expresses strong emotion.

> What a good time we had!
> How ferocious the lion looks!

An exclamatory sentence ends with an exclamation point.

| **Exercise 20** | Identifying and Punctuating Four Kinds of Sentences |

On your paper write *declarative, imperative, interrogative,* or *exclamatory* to identify each sentence below. Then write the correct end mark of punctuation.

1. Have you ever been to an African game park
2. What a wonderful adventure it is
3. Kruger National Park is located in the northeastern part of South Africa, not far from the Limpopo River
4. If you go, you should plan to spend the night in one of the thatch-roofed huts
5. Don't ever get out of your car to take pictures of the elephants

| **Exercise 21** | Creating Four Kinds of Sentences |

On your paper write four sentences about a recent news story. Use one declarative, one imperative, one interrogative, and one exclamatory sentence. Remember to punctuate each sentence correctly.

13.9 Sentence Fragments

In general, avoid sentence fragments in your writing. A **sentence fragment** is an error that occurs when an incomplete sentence is punctuated as though it were a complete sentence.

There are three things you should look for when reviewing your work for sentence fragments. First, look for a group of words without a subject. Next, be alert for a group of words lacking a verb, especially a group that contains a verbal rather than a complete verb. Last, make sure that you have not mistaken a subordinate clause for a complete sentence.

You will often be able to correct a sentence fragment by joining it to a main clause that precedes or follows the fragment. At times you may have to add missing words to make a complete sentence.

FRAGMENT	Woodpeckers ate suet from my bird feeder last winter. **Seemed to be particularly fond of it.** [lacks subject]
COMPLETE SENTENCE	Woodpeckers ate suet from my bird feeder last winter, and they seemed to be particularly fond of it.
FRAGMENT	**A large bird with blue feathers eating from the feeder for weeks.** [lacks complete verb]
COMPLETE SENTENCE	A large bird with blue feathers has been eating from the feeder for weeks.
FRAGMENT	I filled the feeder with sunflower seeds. **Which both the jays and the cardinals seem to like.** [has subordinate clause only]
COMPLETE SENTENCE	I filled the feeder with sunflower seeds, which both the jays and the cardinals seem to like.

Professional writers sometimes use sentence fragments. They do so for special effect—to add emphasis or to convey realistic dialogue. They use sentence fragments *carefully* and *intentionally*. In most of the writing you do, however, including your writing for school, you should avoid sentence fragments.

Exercise 22　Identifying Sentence Fragments

On your paper write whether each numbered item is a *complete sentence* or *sentence fragment*.

Mexico City

[1]Can you guess which city is the largest in the world? [2]Mexico City, with more than 21 million inhabitants. [3]There are few cities with greater problems related to rapid growth. [4]Once the capital of the Aztec Empire, built on an island in the center of a lake. [5]Then the arrival of the Spanish, surprising the Aztecs. [6]The Spaniards conquered the city because of their superior weapons. [7]Also because of their alliances with traditional enemies of the Aztecs. [8]Many residents of modern Mexico City are descendants of the Aztecs and of other groups native to the area. [9]Or else of the Spaniards who came to Mexico in the sixteenth century and intermarried with the native population. [10]Modern Mexico City: a blend of Native American and Spanish, American and European, modern and traditional.

Exercise 23　Correcting Sentence Fragments

Revise the preceding paragraph by correcting each fragment. Wherever possible, combine the fragments with other sentences in the paragraph. You may need to change some words as well.

Exercise 24　Writing Sentences from Sentence Fragments

On your paper rewrite each sentence fragment below to create a complete sentence. You may add or change words as needed. Make sure that your sentences make sense.

The Aztec

1. The Aztec, a native civilization that rose to a position of dominance.
2. A warlike group with an excellent military organization.
3. Settled near the western shore of Lake Texcoco.
4. In the thirteenth century in the valley of central Mexico.
5. When they established a tribute-collecting empire that included most of present-day Mexico and extended south to what is now Guatemala.
6. Which continued to the time of the Spanish conquest.
7. Montezuma I's attempts to find food for the growing population of Tenochtitlán.
8. Conquering war captives and acquiring luxury goods.
9. Before Hernán Cortés arrived in 1519.
10. A civilization that was in full flower.
11. Despite discontent with autocratic policies, the many groups that made up the Aztec civilization.
12. As they grew in political status.
13. Communal land ownership with each farm supporting a few families.
14. Worked at irrigating, terracing, and fertilizing the land.
15. Helped by some native groups, Cortés, who defeated the Aztecs in 1521.

13.10 Run-on Sentences

Avoid run-on sentences in your writing. A **run-on sentence** is two or more complete sentences written as though they were one sentence.

There are three basic kinds of run-on sentences.

1. The most common type of run-on sentence is a **comma splice.** A comma splice occurs when two main clauses are separated by a comma instead of a period or a semicolon. You can correct a comma splice by replacing the comma with an end mark and starting the new sentence with a capital letter. You can also correct a comma splice by adding a coordinating conjunction.

RUN-ON	Tanya and Naoko are both going to work as camp counselors this summer, they are looking forward to the experience.
CORRECT	Tanya and Naoko are both going to work as camp counselors this summer. **T**hey are looking forward to the experience.
CORRECT	Tanya and Naoko are both going to work as camp counselors this summer, **and** they are looking forward to the experience.

2. A second type of run-on sentence occurs when two main clauses are written with *no* punctuation between them. To correct this kind of run-on, separate the main clauses with a mark of end punctuation or with a semicolon. Another way to correct the error is by adding a comma and a coordinating conjunction between the main clauses.

RUN-ON	Tanya and Naoko feel the job has many advantages working with children is one of them.
CORRECT	Tanya and Naoko feel the job has many advantages. **W**orking with children is one of them.
CORRECT	Tanya and Naoko feel the job has many advantages; working with children is one of them.
CORRECT	Tanya and Naoko feel the job has many advantages, **and** working with children is one of them.

3. A third type of run-on occurs when the comma is left out before a coordinating conjunction that joins two main clauses. Correct this error by simply adding a comma before the coordinating conjunction.

RUN-ON	They will enjoy what they will be doing and they will be earning money, too.
CORRECT	They will enjoy what they will be doing**,** and they will be earning money, too.

On your paper write *run-on sentence* or *correct* to identify each of the following items.

Taos: An Artist Colony

1. Taos, a relatively small town in the north-central section of New Mexico, is one of the oldest settlements in the United States.
2. It was founded in 1615 and it became an important trading center on the Santa Fe Trail during the nineteenth century.
3. An ancient Pueblo village lies north of the town, a Spanish farming center, Ranchos de Taos, lies to the south.
4. Since the early 1900s, Taos has been a noted artist colony and has attracted such well-known artists as Georgia O'Keeffe, Peter Hurd, and Henriette Wyeth.
5. In 1949 O'Keeffe established her home in Taos, its atmosphere and its beautiful scenery inspired some of her finest work.

On your paper write each of the following sentences, correcting the run-ons. Watch for the three types of run-on errors shown on page 521. You may choose from among the several ways of correcting run-ons that you have learned.

Georgia O'Keeffe: An American Artist

1. The American artist Georgia O'Keeffe became famous for her paintings of natural objects, her canvases are stunning.
2. The objects she painted appear huge and overwhelming her enlarged flowers and stones seem unique.
3. Her paintings are energetic, strong, and realistic nevertheless, most of them have an abstract quality.
4. O'Keeffe's colors are bold and startling, a patch of blue and green on a field of white looks stark and compelling.
5. Most of her paintings remain popular with art lovers, her work is intense, realistic, and unique.
6. O'Keeffe was greatly influenced by the landscape of the American Southwest and there are many recognizable southwestern images in her paintings.
7. Many people think only of the Southwest when they think of Georgia O'Keeffe yet she also painted cityscapes.
8. O'Keeffe married the American photographer Alfred Stieglitz the wedding took place in 1924.
9. Stieglitz operated two art galleries in New York City and he often displayed his wife's work in them.
10. He also took many photographs of O'Keeffe, these are well-known today.

Review: Correcting Sentence Fragments and Run-on Sentences

On your paper write the following items, correcting all sentence fragments and run-on sentences. Write *correct* for any sentences that do not need revision.

Gemstones

1. Gemstones are minerals in crystal form, they occur naturally as chemical elements or compounds.
2. The value of a gem is based on certain properties beauty, durability, and rarity are three of these.
3. Diamonds being the hardest natural substance in the world. They cannot be scratched by any other substance.
4. Two gemstones come from corundum. Which is harder than any other substance except diamonds.
5. The red variety is called ruby and the blue variety is called sapphire.
6. One of the costliest gemstones of all is emerald, which is a kind of beryl.
7. A good emerald stone has a deep green color and is free of flaws. May cost several thousand dollars per carat.
8. The most common of all minerals is quartz. Which may crystallize into such gemstones as citrine, amethyst, tiger eye, and agate.
9. Some gemstones come from living things, among these are pearls, amber, and coral.
10. Gems have continued to fascinate people for ages. Their beauty and value make them among the most exciting and intriguing of objects.

Review: Correcting Sentence Structure

On your paper write the following paragraphs, correcting all sentence fragments and run-on sentences.

Lasers

[1]The word *laser* from the expression "light amplification by stimulated emission of radiation." [2]Both radio waves and light waves are forms of energy nevertheless, neither weak radio waves nor weak light waves harm us. [3]Producing and transmitting intense light being the basic purpose of a laser. [4]Either a rare metal or a rare gas used for the intensification of light waves. [5]Chromium and helium were used in early lasers, today various kinds of lamps produce the light that lasers intensify. [6]Electrons and light waves interacting to make the light extremely intense.

[7]Lasers have many practical applications, they are used in everything from surveying equipment to high-tech "smart" weapons. [8]Lasers in intricate eye surgery and to clean out blocked arteries. [9]In photography, three-dimensional images called holographs produced with lasers. [10]We can thank lasers for the latest developments in the communications revolution, compact discs, videodiscs, and fiber-optic telephone cables are but three examples of laser technology at work.

Grammar Review

Clauses and Sentence Structure

Set in the mid-nineteenth century, Willa Cather's novel *Death Comes for the Archbishop* tells the story of Bishop Jean Latour, who has left his parish in France and returned to New Mexico, where he had served as a young man. In this scene the bishop awakes in the same small room he had lived in years earlier, and he muses about the past. The passage has been annotated to show some of the clauses and sentence structures covered in this unit.

Literature Model

from DEATH COMES FOR THE ARCHBISHOP

by Willa Cather

He felt a great content at being here, where he had come as a young man and where he had done his work. The room was little changed; the same rugs and skins on the earth floor, the same desk with his candlesticks, the same thick, wavy white walls that muted sound, that shut out the world and gave repose to the spirit.

Adverb clause — As the darkness faded into the gray of a winter morning, he listened for the church bells,—and for another sound, that always amused him here; the whistle of a loco-

Compound sentence — motive. Yes, he had come with the buffalo, and he had lived to see railway trains running into Santa Fé. He had

Simple sentence — accomplished an historic period.

❧

In New Mexico he always awoke a young man; not until he rose and began to shave did he realize that he was

Noun clause — growing older. His first consciousness was a sense of the light dry wind blowing in through the windows, with the fragrance of hot sun and sage-brush and sweet clover; a wind that made one's body feel light and one's heart cry "To-day, to-day," like a child's.

Beautiful surroundings, the society of learned men, the charm of noble women, the graces of art, could not make ➡

up to him for the loss of those light-hearted mornings of the desert, for that wind that made one a boy again. He had noticed that this peculiar quality in the air of new countries vanished after they were tamed by man and made to bear harvests. Parts of Texas and Kansas that he had first known as open range had since been made into rich farming districts, and the air had quite lost that lightness, that dry aromatic odor. The moisture of plowed land, the heaviness of labor and growth and grain-bearing, utterly destroyed it; one could breathe that only on the bright edges of the world, on the great grass plains or the sagebrush desert.

That air would disappear from the whole earth in time, perhaps; but long after his day. He did not know just when it had become so necessary to him, but he had come back to die in exile for the sake of it. Something soft and wild and free, something that whispered to the ear on the pillow, lightened the heart, softly, softly picked the lock, slid the bolts, and released the prisoned spirit of man into the wind, into the blue and gold, into the morning, into the morning!

— Complex sentence

— Adjective clause

— Compound-complex sentence

Exercise 1

Identifying Main and Subordinate Clauses   The following sentences are based on the passage from *Death Comes for the Archbishop*. Each sentence contains a clause that appears in italics. On your paper indicate whether the italicized clause is a *main clause* or a *subordinate clause*.

1. *Because Bishop Jean Marie Latour had once lived in the room*, he felt at home there.
2. *The room had changed remarkably little*, even though many years had passed.
3. The furnishings *that he recalled so well* still stood in the room.
4. The bishop awoke, began to shave, and reflected about the land and *why he felt so content there*.
5. The bishop, *who was now an old man*, felt almost like a boy again in his former surroundings.
6. He experienced a feeling of newness and vigor *whenever he breathed the light, dry morning air of New Mexico*.
7. The source of the invigorating air was the country around him, *which was still untamed*.
8. Other places had once produced this remarkable effect, but *they no longer did*.
9. A sense of newness disappeared *after an area was developed*.
10. Although progress brought with it many civilized comforts and pleasures, *it also carried a high price*.

Exercise 2

Identifying Compound, Complex, and Compound-Complex Sentences
The following sentences provide some background details from the novel *Death Comes for the Archbishop*. On your paper write whether each sentence is *compound, complex,* or *compound-complex*.

1. In the late 1840s, after the Mexican War, the Catholic Church renewed its interest in New Mexico because the territory had just become part of the United States.
2. Missionaries had been working there since 1500, but control over Church activities was limited.
3. A new bishop could renew the Church in the territory if the right man could be found.
4. A few years after the Mexican War a young French priest who had just been elevated to the position of bishop was sent to Santa Fe, New Mexico.
5. Bishop Latour was exhausted when he finally arrived in New Mexico, for the trip had taken nearly a year.
6. There was a railroad out of New York, but it ended in Cincinnati, Ohio.
7. From Ohio Bishop Latour had gone by boat to Galveston on the Texas coast, and then he had traveled across Texas.
8. He needed both strength and flexibility, or he would not succeed in his job.
9. After Bishop Latour had worked effectively in the area for many years, he finally retired.
10. Now he had come back to New Mexico, for he knew that he would soon die.
11. Willa Cather modeled Bishop Latour on two real priests who had lived in New Mexico during the nineteenth century.
12. John B. Lamy went to Santa Fe as bishop in 1846, and the Reverend Joseph P. Machebeuf, who later became bishop of Colorado, accompanied Lamy as his able assistant.
13. Lamy instituted extensive reforms, and religious conditions in New Mexico improved greatly during his time there.
14. A few years after his arrival, Lamy built the Cathedral of Saint Francis of Assisi, which stands today in Santa Fe as an impressive landmark.
15. When Cather first visited New Mexico, she was impressed with the history of the Catholic Church in the region, but she didn't have enough facts to write about it.
16. She went back often, for the subject continued to fascinate her.
17. On one trip she discovered a book about the life of Father Machebeuf; this book inspired her to write her own book.
18. The book also contained detailed information about Lamy because the two men were colleagues and friends.
19. Father Machebeuf's letters gave Cather a sense of the mood in which these two missionaries accepted the hardships of desert life.
20. She titled *Death Comes for the Archbishop*, the writing of which she called "a happy vacation from life," after a painting by Albrecht Dürer.

Exercise 3

Writing Sentences with Adjective Clauses   The sentences that follow elaborate on ideas in the passage from *Death Comes for the Archbishop*. On your paper rewrite each sentence, adding an adjective clause that answers the question in parentheses. Your clause must begin with a relative pronoun (see the list that follows), and it must contain a verb. Your sentence should make sense within the context of the passage but should not use Cather's exact words. There may be more than one correct answer.

RELATIVE PRONOUNS   who   whom   whose   which   that

SAMPLE   He was a bishop. (What had he done?)
ANSWER   He was a bishop who had worked in New Mexico for many years.

1. Bishop Latour was back in New Mexico. (How did he feel about being there?)
2. The old rugs, desk, and candlesticks were still in the room. (From what time did the bishop remember these items?)
3. He took comfort from the solid white walls. (How did the walls make him feel?)
4. He was an aging man. (How did he feel when he came to New Mexico?)
5. The room was cooled by a gentle wind. (What did the wind bring in?)
6. Bishop Latour had almost forgotten his age. (How did his body feel that morning?)
7. He had abandoned many cultural advantages. (How did they compare with the benefits of the desert?)
8. To the bishop the desert had a special wind. (What was special about the desert wind?)
9. The air in places like Texas and Kansas had lost its lightness. (What was happening to those places now?)
10. The bishop could find this special air only in open, undeveloped areas. (What could this air do for the bishop?)
11. When he looked around the room he saw the rugs and skins on the floor. (How did the room look compared to before?)
12. The walls were painted white. (What did the walls do to sound?)
13. He listened to the whistle of the locomotive. (How did the sound of the whistle make him feel?)
14. The sun shone through the window. (How did the sun feel on his skin?)
15. Bishop Latour had once lived in other surroundings. (How did he remember them?)
16. He had enjoyed the society of men. (What sort of men were they?)
17. The special air of the desert floated in on the morning breeze. (What did the air smell of?)
18. The air whispered in his ear. (What qualities did the air have?)
19. His spirit was released. (How had his spirit felt before?)
20. His spirit was caught up in the morning. (What color was the morning?)

Exercise 4

Writing Sentences with Adverb Clauses   The sentences that follow elaborate on ideas suggested by the passage from *Death Comes for the Archbishop*. On your paper rewrite each sentence, adding an adverb clause that answers the question in parentheses. Your clause must begin with one of the subordinating conjunctions listed below, and it must contain a verb. The sentence should make sense within the context of the passage but should not use Cather's exact words. There may be more than one correct answer for each item.

SUBORDINATING CONJUNCTIONS

after	as if	in order to	though	whenever
although	because	since	until	where
as	before	than	when	wherever

SAMPLE   The room was familiar to Latour. (Why?)

ANSWER   The room was familiar to Latour because he had lived there before.

1. Bishop Latour felt quite happy. (Why?)
2. He listened for church bells. (When?)
3. He had first come to New Mexico during an earlier period in the territory's history. (When?)
4. Bishop Latour felt like a young man. (When?)
5. He realized that he was old. (When?)
6. That morning the aging bishop became aware of the fragrant wind from his window. (When?)
7. The light, dry wind made the bishop feel eager and full of life. (To what extent?)
8. The bracing mornings of the desert had been worth his sacrifice of the comforts of civilization. (Why?)
9. Unfortunately, the air in a new, untamed country lost its freshness and lightness. (When?)
10. For example, the dry, fragrant air had changed in parts of Texas and Kansas. (When?)
11. The bishop's room seemed little changed. (Why?)
12. The walls gave repose to the spirit. (How?)
13. He was amused. (Why?)
14. The air had lost that dry aromatic odor. (When?)
15. It was still quite possible, however, for one to breathe the fresh, sweet air. (Where?)
16. The special air would very likely disappear. (When?)
17. He had to come back to die in exile. (Why?)
18. His heart lightened. (Why?)
19. The air whispered in his ear. (When?)
20. His spirit was outdoors. (Where?)

Exercise 5

Identifying Noun Clauses   The following sentences describe the history of New Mexico. On your paper write the noun clauses that appear in the sentences. Two of the sentences have two noun clauses each.

1. Whoever is familiar with the Southwest recognizes that New Mexico's history makes it one of the most intriguing states in the country.
2. Does this reference book tell whether the earliest human settlements in New Mexico date from ten thousand years ago or twenty thousand years ago?
3. Pueblos and cliff dwellings were constructed by whoever originally inhabited the region.
4. How these structures were built can be determined by examining the remaining ruins.
5. What historians also know is that the Navajo and Apache later moved down to New Mexico from the north.
6. The sixteenth century was when the Spanish explorers and Catholic missionaries arrived.
7. The Spanish adventurers believed that they would find huge amounts of gold in the Americas.
8. Have you read about how the Spaniards treated the Native Americans?
9. What had become part of Mexico's territory in 1821 was ceded to the United States in 1848, after the Mexican War.
10. This history of settlement and conquest tells us why three cultures come together in New Mexico today: Native American, Spanish, and Anglo-American.
11. The history of New Mexico in the nineteenth century is the story of how the area became a United States territory.
12. The opening of the Santa Fe Trail meant that more pioneers could travel to New Mexico.
13. The trading post at Santa Fe was an important stopover for whoever journeyed west along the trail.
14. A major turning point in the Civil War was when the Union troops defeated the Confederates at Glorieta Pass.
15. Why do historians think that the battle of Glorieta was important?
16. That the Union victory kept the Southwest from joining the Confederacy is of major significance.
17. The newly built railroads provided transportation to wherever New Mexicans wanted to go.
18. Why so many settlers poured into New Mexico in the 1890s is a question that has many answers.
19. That is why New Mexico was admitted to the Union as the forty-seventh state in 1912.
20. What attracts people to this state today is its climate, its scenery, and its rich mix of peoples and cultures.

Exercise 6

Writing Four Kinds of Sentences   The following sentences develop an idea or image suggested by the passage from *Death Comes for the Archbishop*. On your paper identify each of the following sentences as *declarative, imperative, interrogative,* or *exclamatory*. Then rewrite each sentence in the form noted in parentheses. There may be more than one correct answer.

SAMPLE   He took the train from New York to Cincinnati.
(Rewrite in the imperative form.)

ANSWER   declarative
Take the train from New York to Cincinnati.

1. How fascinating New Mexico's history is! (Rewrite as a declarative sentence.)
2. New Mexico was annexed to the United States in 1848. (Rewrite as an interrogative sentence.)
3. Did New Mexico formerly belong to Mexico? (Rewrite as a declarative sentence.)
4. Did you investigate the earliest human settlements in New Mexico? (Rewrite as an imperative sentence.)
5. Bishop Latour's first trip to New Mexico took much longer than such a journey would today. (Rewrite as an interrogative sentence.)
6. What a long and difficult journey it was! (Rewrite as a declarative sentence.)
7. Take a ship from New Orleans to Galveston. (Rewrite as a declarative sentence.)
8. How many hardships Latour endured on the way! (Rewrite as an interrogative sentence.)
9. Did Latour have to travel through the Rio Grande Valley? (Rewrite as a declarative sentence.)
10. Bishop Latour worked hard at his mission. (Rewrite as an imperative sentence.)
11. Was the landscape wild and beautiful? (Rewrite as an exclamatory sentence.)
12. Savor the air of this untamed country while you still can. (Rewrite as a declarative sentence.)
13. The bishop loved the desert. (Rewrite as an exclamatory sentence.)
14. How familiar and comforting his old room seemed! (Rewrite as an interrogative sentence.)
15. Latour always felt the gentle wind in the morning. (Rewrite as an imperative sentence.)
16. Make your home in the desert, Bishop Latour. (Rewrite as an interrogative sentence.)
17. How light and fragrant the air was! (Rewrite as an interrogative sentence.)
18. The bishop knew that he had come to the desert to die. (Rewrite as an interrogative sentence.)
19. Did the air make the old man feel like a boy again? (Rewrite as an exclamatory sentence.)
20. He traded the comforts of civilization for something better—his freedom. (Rewrite as an imperative sentence.)

Exercise 7

Correcting Sentence Fragments   The following paragraph describes a scene related to the passage from *Death Comes for the Archbishop*. On your paper revise the paragraph, correcting any sentence fragments. The fragments may be corrected by combining sentences, by adding words (such as a subject or a verb), or by changing the form of a verb.

SAMPLE   The man who came to Santa Fe.
ANSWER   The man who came to Santa Fe had lived there before.

[1]Waking in his old room, felt happy. [2]A white-walled room, filled with familiar furnishings, such as his old rugs, desk, and candlesticks. [3]Also familiar sounds floating in from the outside. [4]For example, the locomotive whistle that always amused him. [5]Most important of all, however, was the wondrous fresh wind from the desert. [6]Made him feel young and spirited like a boy. [7]Actually, an elderly man seeking the wild desert. [8]Because he could not do without its magic air. [9]Would that air last forever? [10]Not after the primitive area tamed.

Exercise 8

Correcting Run-on Sentences   The following sentences are about New Mexico. On your paper revise each sentence, correcting any run-ons with any method that you have learned. For the sentences that do not contain run-ons, write *correct*.

SAMPLE   New Mexico's stunning landscapes attract tourists from all over the world its colorful history fascinates scholars from many fields.

ANSWER   New Mexico's stunning landscapes attract tourists from all over the world. Its colorful history fascinates scholars from many fields.

1. New Mexico has been inhabited for at least 10,000 years early rock carvings can still be found near the Sandia Mountains and the present-day town of Folsom.
2. The landscape of New Mexico is varied and spectacular; it includes not only sandy deserts but also snowy mountains, forests, buttes, and mesas.
3. The population has exploded recently yet New Mexico remains one of the least populous states in the country.
4. More than 38 percent of New Mexico's population is of Spanish or Mexican origin, another 9 percent is made up of Navajo, Pueblo, and other Native American groups.
5. New Mexico includes vast open spaces, but nearly three quarters of the total population is concentrated in urban areas such as Albuquerque and Santa Fe.
6. The Spanish first came to New Mexico in search of gold however, missionary work became the main activity in the 1600s.
7. Navajos were treated harshly their relations with the Spanish were often hostile.
8. In 1848 New Mexico was made a U.S. territory, in 1912 it became a state.
9. The railroad reached New Mexico in 1878 and the population began to expand.
10. The architecture, art, and crafts of the area are exceptional, the arts of three cultures have flourished—and often blended—there.

Review: Exercise 9

Correcting Sentence Structure   The following paragraph describes places of interest in New Mexico. On your paper revise the paragraph, correcting sentence fragments and run-on sentences. Some sentences are correct, but you may wish to combine them with other sentences. Try to vary your sentence structure, and use correct punctuation.

[1]New Mexico has dozens of fascinating places to visit, they range from lush forests to steep ski slopes, include art museums and ancient communities. [2]In the southern part of the state, Carlsbad Caverns National Park, which contains the largest cavern yet discovered. [3]Also in the south is White Sands National Monument, it is a rare gypsum desert. [4]White sand into huge dunes. [5]The most spectacular sight in Albuquerque is the hot-air balloon fiesta. [6]Takes place in October. [7]North of Albuquerque is Santa Fe, its many shops, museums, beautiful old mission churches, and stunning opera house. [8]Nearby the ancient cliff dwellings of the Anasazi people, slightly higher up is the village of Los Alamos, where the first atomic bomb was developed. [9]Scattered through the state are pueblos, Native Americans have lived there for centuries. [10]The two most populous Native American groups in New Mexico are the Navajo and the Apache and many of them live on large reservations.

Review: Exercise 10

Proofreading

The following passage describes the artist Georgia O'Keeffe, whose painting appears on the opposite page. Rewrite the passage, correcting the errors in spelling, grammar, and usage. Add any missing punctuation. There are twenty-five errors.

Georgia O'Keeffe

[1]Georgia O'Keeffe (1887–1986) is born in Sun Prairie, Wisconsin. [2]When she was only seventeen, she begun her formal training at the Art Institute of Chicago. [3]Two years later, she went to New York City to continue her study of art and she remained in the city for several years. [4]During the winters from 1912 to 1918, she teached school in Texas. [5]Was drawn to its dramatic landscape and enormous skies.

[6]O'Keeffe lived in New York for a time and she made her first paintings of nature there. [7]These paintings were not realistic they were filled with flat patterns and bold colors. [8]O'Keeffe began spending your summers in New Mexico in 1929. [9]Moved there permanently in 1949. [10]She refined her lush, highly abstract style in New Mexico and it was there that she painted her most memorable works. [11]Her landscapes often present unusual perspectives which make the viewer feel suspended in air. [12]Other paintings focus closely on a single image, such as a flower or the weather-beaten skul of an animal.

[13]Many critics in the art world considers O'Keeffe one of the forerunners of American abstract art. [14]She deliberately exagerated the shape, proportion, size, and color of the objects and scenes that she painted. [15]What huge flowers she painted [16]Her paintings, particularly those made in New Mexico have a spiritual quality. ➡

[17]*Gate of Adobe Church* (1929) is typical of O'Keeffes abstract style. [18]She captures in this picture which has broad sweeps of color and a simple design, the mood and sense of a place. [19]She paints with uncluttered simplicity which evokes a quiet spirituality an energetic clarity, and a radiant warmth. [20]O'Keeffe's strong sense of place is strikingly similar to Willa Cathers. [21]Indeed, *Death Comes for the Archbishop* is filled with concrete, evocative images of the Southwest [22]Some of the most striking images is evoked by the main character of the novel a French bishop who has returned to New Mexico because he misses the dry, warm wind and the hot sun. [23]Can you feel the hot southwestern sun in this picture

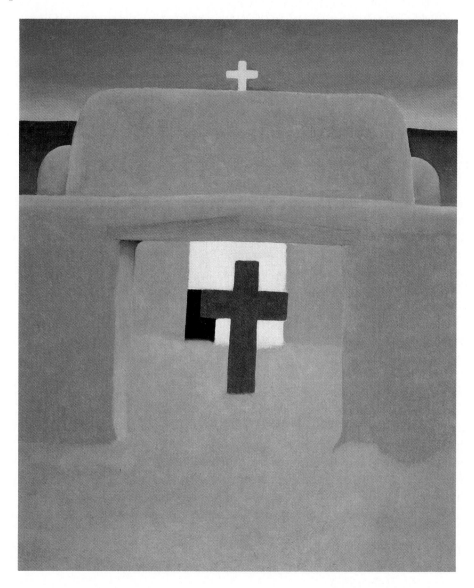

Georgia O'Keeffe, *Gate of Adobe Church,* **1929**

Mixed Review

Exercise 11

The items that follow describe the life of Willa Cather. On your paper revise each item in the manner indicated in parentheses.

SAMPLE Willa Cather often wrote about pioneers. Cather grew up on the Nebraska frontier. (Combine the sentences by turning the second sentence into an adjective clause beginning with *who*.)

ANSWER Willa Cather, who grew up on the Nebraska frontier, often wrote about pioneers.

Willa Cather

1. Willa Cather was born in Virginia in 1873. Her family moved to Nebraska in 1882. (Rewrite as a compound sentence.)
2. In Red Cloud, Nebraska, she lived among European immigrants. They were beginning a new life.
(Combine the sentences by turning the second sentence into an adjective clause beginning with *who*.)
3. Cather attended the University of Nebraska at Lincoln. She began to recognize her talent for writing.
(Combine the sentences by turning the first sentence into an adverb clause beginning with *When*.)
4. She graduated from the university in 1895, and she moved across the continent to Pittsburgh. She began working on the staff of the *Pittsburgh Leader*.
(Rewrite as a compound-complex sentence.)
5. Did Cather work next as principal of a Pittsburgh high school?
(Rewrite as a declarative sentence.)
6. In 1912 Cather decided something. She would become a writer of novels.
(Combine the sentences by turning the second sentence into a noun clause beginning with *that*.)
7. It was then that Cather left her position as managing editor of *McClure's*, the well-known magazine published in New York.
(Rewrite as an interrogative sentence.)
8. Cather was awarded the Pulitzer Prize for her novel *One of Ours* (1922). Deals largely with World War I.
(Eliminate the fragment by creating a complex sentence.)
9. Her early novels were based on her memories of pioneer life. Many of her later works focused on the anguish of creative people trapped in small-town life.
(Combine the sentences by turning the first sentence into an adverb clause beginning with *Although*.)
10. From 1925 to 1931 she produced four great novels. These novels include *The Professor's House* (1925), *My Mortal Enemy* (1926), *Death Comes for the Archbishop* (1927), and *Shadows on the Rock* (1931).
(Combine the sentences by turning the second sentence into an adjective clause beginning with *which*.)

Writing Application

Sentence Structure in Writing   In *Tortuga* Rudolfo A. Anaya uses a variety of sentence types not only to capture the reader's interest but also to develop a pleasing rhythm and an appropriate mood. In the following passage, notice the structure of Anaya's sentences and the kinds of clauses he uses.

> I remembered the rainbows of my childhood, beautifully sculptured arches reaching from north to south, shafts of light so pure their harmony seemed to wed the sky and earth. My mother had taught me to look at rainbows, the mantle of the Blessed Virgin Mary she called them. When a summer thunderstorm passed, she would take me out and we would stand in the thin drops which followed the storm. We would turn our faces up to the sky, and the large, glistening drops of rain would pelt our faces. She would open her mouth and hold out her tongue to receive the large, golden drops. She would stir the muddy ponds and pick up the little frogs which came with the rain.

Techniques with Sentence Structure   Try to apply some of Anaya's writing techniques when you write and revise.

1. Avoid using the same sentence structure repeatedly.

Same Structure   A summer thunderstorm passed. . . She would take me out. . . We would stand. . .

Anaya's Version   When a summer thunderstorm passed, she would take me out and we would stand. . .

2. To emphasize some ideas and downplay others, put some ideas into subordinate clauses.

Equal Attention We would stand in the thin drops [of rain]. The drops of rain followed the storm.

Anaya's Version . . . we would stand in the thin drops which followed the storm.

Practice Practice these techniques by revising the following series of simple sentences and sentence fragments. Decide which ideas you want to stress and which you want to downplay. Try to use a variety of sentences.

I turned my head. I looked out the window of my car. I had stopped my car. By the side of the road. In the distance a bare outline of mountain range. All around me was the white, alkaline desert. Only the hardiest shrubs and grasses could grow on the desert. The cold winter rain continued. It had been only a drizzle at first. It had drizzled when I left home. Then the rain had turned icy. It had become more intense. Quite suddenly the rain stopped, the sun struggling to break through the clouds. The clouds were gray and heavy. Minutes passed. A glorious, glowing rainbow in the east. I sat entranced. The sight reminded me of other rainbows. I had enjoyed rainbows as a child.

14.1 Diagraming Simple Sentences

Diagraming is a method of showing the relationship of various words and parts of a sentence to the sentence as a whole.

You begin to diagram a sentence by finding the simple subject. After you have found the subject, find the action or linking verb that goes with it. Write the subject and the verb on a horizontal or base line. Separate them with a vertical line that bisects the base line. This line indicates the division between the complete subject and the complete predicate.

Senators meet.

Compound Subjects and Verbs

A compound subject or verb is placed on two horizontal lines, with the conjunction on a dotted vertical line connecting the horizontal lines. To diagram a simple sentence with a compound subject and verb, follow the model diagram below. Notice how the compound elements extend from the base line.

Staffers and senators will meet and decide.

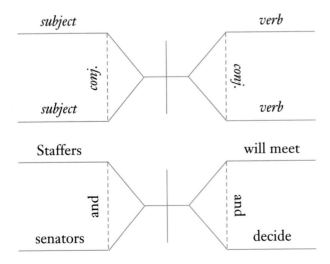

Direct Objects and Indirect Objects

To diagram a simple sentence with an indirect object and a direct object, follow the model diagram below.

Experts have given senators advice.

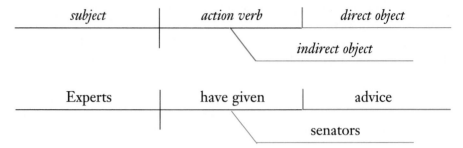

subject	action verb	direct object
	indirect object	

Experts	have given	advice
	senators	

Object Complements

To diagram a simple sentence with an object complement, follow the model diagram below.

Everyone considered her important.

subject	action verb	direct object	object complement

Everyone	considered	her	important

Subject Complements

To diagram a simple sentence with a subject complement (a predicate nominative or a predicate adjective), follow the model diagram below.

Senators are legislators.

subject	linking verb	subject complement

Senators	are	legislators

Senators should be helpful.

| Senators | should be \ helpful |

Adjectives and Adverbs

To diagram a simple sentence with adjectives and adverbs, follow the model diagram below.

The slightly older senators meet periodically.

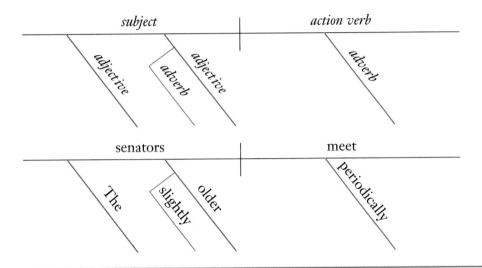

Using the preceding models as a guide, diagram the following sentences.

1. An informed citizen votes thoughtfully.
2. The voters gave the candidate a landslide.
3. Rich and poor elected the senator President.
4. A President is powerful but may seem hesitant.
5. Newspapers called the election an easy victory.
6. Friends and associates sent the winner their congratulations.
7. The elated President-elect spoke happily.
8. The country was now the primary concern.
9. She felt the responsibility keenly.
10. The future would not be easy.

Prepositional Phrases

Place the preposition on a diagonal line that descends from the word the prepositional phrase modifies. Place the object of the preposition on a horizontal line that joins the diagonal. The diagonal line on which the preposition is placed should extend somewhat beyond the horizontal on which the object of the preposition is placed, forming a "tail."

In their work carpenters of today use tools with electric power.

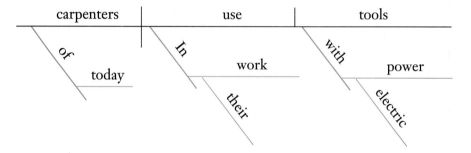

Appositives and Appositive Phrases

Place an appositive in parentheses after the noun or pronoun it identifies. Beneath it add any words that modify the appositive. Any words that modify the noun or pronoun itself, and not the appositive, should be placed directly beneath the noun or pronoun.

Argentina is proud of beautiful Buenos Aires, its cosmopolitan capital.

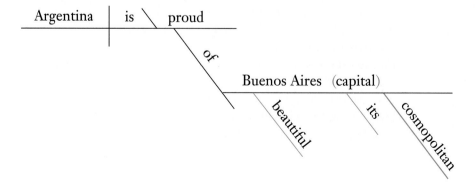

Participles and Participial Phrases

The line on which the participle is placed descends diagonally from the word the participle modifies and then extends to the right horizontally. The participle is written on the curve, as shown below. Add any modifiers, objects, and complements to the horizontal line in the same way that you would show the modifiers, objects, and complements of an action verb.

Whistling, the carpenter completed the work, happily driving the last two nails.

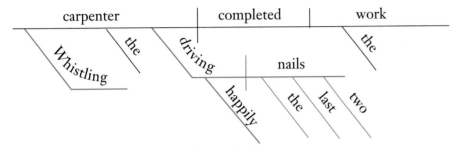

Gerunds and Gerund Phrases

Place a gerund on a "step," and add complements and modifiers in the usual way. Then set the gerund or the gerund phrase on a "stilt," and position the stilt in the diagram according to the role of the gerund in the sentence. (Remember that a gerund can be a subject, a direct object, a complement, an object of a preposition, or an appositive.)

Mitering is a common way of forming corner joints.

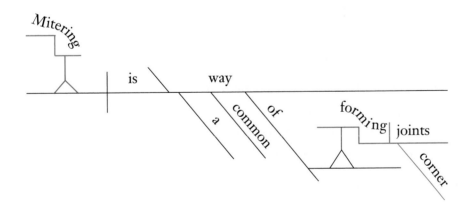

Infinitives and Infinitive Phrases as Adjectives or Adverbs

When an infinitive or an infinitive phrase is used as an adjective or an adverb, it is diagramed like a prepositional phrase.

Carpenters struggled to meet the deadline.

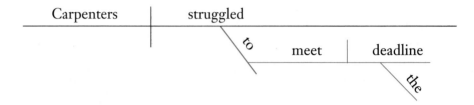

Infinitives and Infinitive Phrases as Nouns

When an infinitive or an infinitive phrase is used as a noun, it is diagramed like a prepositional phrase and then placed on a "stilt" in the subject, object, or complement position.

To work is to know satisfaction.

Exercise 2   **Diagraming Simple Sentences with Phrases**

Using the preceding models as a guide, diagram the following sentences.

1. A plumber from town installed pipes for water.
2. The pipes, copper tubing cylinders, arrived by heavy truck.
3. Several shingles, damaged by the wind, needed repairs.
4. Driving nails can be hard work.
5. To measure accurately is to save work.
6. The trade and craft of carpentry requires working with lumber.
7. To build a house is to know joy.
8. Exhausted, the cabinet maker finished by sanding carefully.
9. Crafting decorative woodwork requires a delicate touch.
10. Roofers, often unappreciated, work carefully to prevent costly leaks.

Compound Sentences

Diagram each main clause separately. If the clauses are connected by a semicolon, use a vertical dotted line to connect the verbs of each main clause. If the main clauses are connected by a conjunction, place the conjunction on a solid horizontal line, and connect it to the verbs of each main clause by vertical dotted lines.

Mechanics like to fix objects, but carpenters must learn to build.

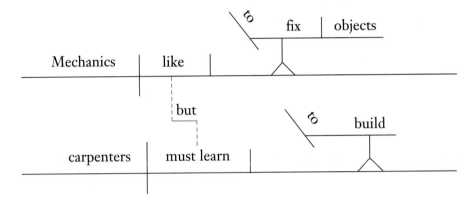

Complex Sentences with Adjective Clauses

Place the main clause in one diagram and the adjective clause beneath it in another diagram. Use a dotted line to connect the relative pronoun or other introductory word in the adjective clause to the modified noun or pronoun in the main clause.

The carpenter whom you hired fixed the shelves that were uneven.

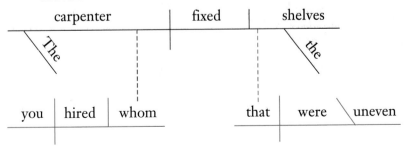

Complex Sentences with Adverb Clauses

Place the main clause in one diagram and the adverb clause beneath it in another diagram. Place the subordinating conjunction on a diagonal dotted line, connecting the verb in the adverb clause to the modified verb, adjective, or adverb in the main clause.

Before they cut the wood, carpenters make a design.

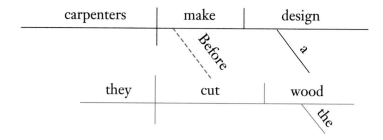

Complex Sentences with Noun Clauses

First decide what role the noun clause plays within the main clause. Is it the subject, direct object, predicate nominative, or object of a preposition? Then diagram the main clause, placing the noun clause on a "stilt" in the appropriate position. Place the introductory word of the clause in the position of the subject, object, or predicate nominative within the noun clause itself. If the introductory word merely begins the noun clause, place it on a line of its own above the verb in the subordinate clause, connecting it to the verb with a dotted vertical line.

NOUN CLAUSE AS SUBJECT

What that carpenter builds is especially sturdy.

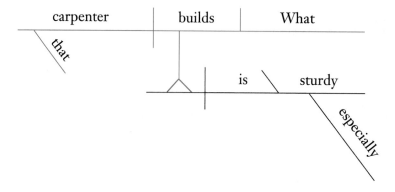

NOUN CLAUSE AS DIRECT OBJECT

We know that the mechanic fixes machines.

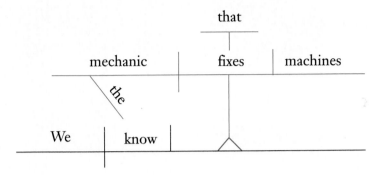

NOUN CLAUSE AS OBJECT OF A PREPOSITION

The carpenter builds cabinets for whoever wants them.

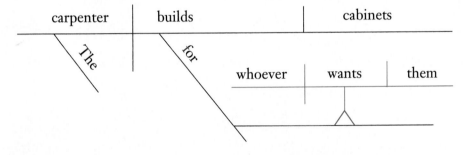

Exercise 3   **Diagraming Sentences with Clauses**

Using the preceding models as a guide, diagram the following sentences.

1. Carpenters work with wood, and masons work with stone.
2. The wood that we use is yellow pine.
3. When you design a house, you think about spaces.
4. An architectural style is what you must choose next.
5. That tastes in style vary is common knowledge.
6. The colonial style is popular with whoever values tradition.
7. Some people like whatever their neighbors like.
8. Before people move, they decide on a style.
9. If you travel in the West, you see more modern houses.
10. The style that I prefer is really a combination.

Verb Tenses and Voice

15.1 Principal Parts of Verbs

All verbs have four **principal parts**—a *base form*, a *present participle*, a *simple past form*, and a *past participle*. All the verb tenses are formed from these principal parts.

Principal Parts of Verbs			
Base Form	**Present Participle**	**Past Form**	**Past Participle**
sail	sailing	sailed	sailed
soar	soaring	soared	soared
work	working	worked	worked
sing	singing	sang	sung
be	being	was, were	been
hit	hitting	hit	hit

You can use the base form (except the base form of *be*) and the past form alone as main verbs. The present participle and the past participle, however, must always be used with one or more auxiliary verbs to function as the simple predicate.

Carpenters **work.** [base or present form]

Carpenters **worked.** [past form]

Carpenters **are working.** [present participle with the auxiliary verb *are*]

Carpenters **have worked.** [past participle with the auxiliary verb *have*]

Exercise 1   Using Principal Parts of Verbs

Copy and complete each of the following sentences with the principal part of the verb that is indicated in parentheses.

1. Most plumbers ____ hot water heaters.
   (base form of *repair*)
2. Our plumber is ____ the kitchen sink.
   (present participle of *repair*)
3. Last month, he ____ the dishwasher.
   (past form of *repair*)
4. He has ____ many appliances in this house.
   (past participle of *repair*)
5. He is ____ his work.
   (present participle of *enjoy*)

15.2 | Regular and Irregular Verbs

A **regular verb** forms its past and past participle by adding *-ed* to the base form.

Regular Verbs		
Base Form	**Past Form**	**Past Participle**
soar	soared	soared
climb	climbed	climbed
ski	skied	skied

When a suffix beginning with a vowel is added to the base form of some regular verbs, the verbs undergo spelling changes.

regulate + **-ed** = regulat**ed**　　try + **-ed** = tri**ed**
stop + **-ed** = stopp**ed**　　　grin + **-ed** = grinn**ed**

An **irregular verb** forms its past and past participle in some way other than by adding *-ed* to the base form.

Irregular Verbs		
Base Form	**Past Form**	**Past Participle**
be	was, were	been
beat	beat	beaten
become	became	become
begin	began	begun
bite	bit	bitten *or* bit
blow	blew	blown
break	broke	broken
bring	brought	brought
burst	burst	burst
buy	bought	bought
catch	caught	caught
choose	chose	chosen
come	came	come
do	did	done
draw	drew	drawn
drink	drank	drunk
drive	drove	driven
eat	ate	eaten
fall	fell	fallen
feel	felt	felt
find	found	found
fly	flew	flown ➡

Base Form	Past Form	Past Participle
freeze	froze	frozen
get	got	got *or* gotten
give	gave	given
go	went	gone
grow	grew	grown
hang	hung *or* hanged	hung *or* hanged
have	had	had
hold	held	held
know	knew	known
lay*	laid	laid
lead	led	led
leave	left	left
lend	lent	lent
lie*	lay	lain
lose	lost	lost
put	put	put
ride	rode	ridden
ring	rang	rung
rise*	rose	risen
run	ran	run
say	said	said
see	saw	seen
set*	set	set
shake	shook	shaken
shrink	shrank *or* shrunk	shrunk *or* shrunken
sing	sang	sung
sink	sank *or* sunk	sunk
sit*	sat	sat
speak	spoke	spoken
spend	spent	spent
spring	sprang *or* sprung	sprung
steal	stole	stolen
swim	swam	swum
swing	swung	swung
take	took	taken
teach	taught	taught
tear	tore	torn
tell	told	told
think	thought	thought
throw	threw	thrown
wear	wore	worn
weave	wove	woven
win	won	won
write	wrote	written

*For more detailed instruction on *lay* versus *lie,* see Unit 19.

*For more detailed instruction on *raise* versus *rise* and *sit* versus *set,* see Unit 19.

On your paper write the principal part of the verb that is indicated in parentheses.

The History of Words

1. The number of words in the English language has _____ over the centuries. (past participle of *grow*)
2. Most words in our language have _____ through changes in spelling or meaning. (past participle of *go*)
3. Etymologists, who study the history of words, have _____ interesting clues to the present meanings of words. (past participle of *find*)
4. Two Latin words meaning "not speaking" _____ the word *infant*. (past form of *become*)
5. An ancient word meaning "blood" has _____ down to us as the word *red*. (past participle of *come*)
6. The word *ketchup* comes from the Malaysian name for a fish sauce that sailors _____ to England in the seventeenth century. (past form of *bring*)
7. Long ago people sometimes _____ their last name on the basis of their profession; it is easy to understand why the names Baker, Carpenter, Miller, Taylor, Wheelwright, and Smith were often selected. (past form of *choose*)
8. Celtic families often _____ their last name with Mac or Fitz, meaning "son of." (past form of *begin*)
9. The name John has _____ various forms in different languages around the world, including Jean, Giovanni, Juan, Hans, and Ivan. (past participle of *take*)
10. The Spanish have _____ us such English words as *brocade, canyon, mosquito, plaza,* and *vanilla*. (past participle of *give*)
11. In the school library, I _____ a dictionary that dealt with the origin of words and phrases. (past form of *see*)
12. My English teacher _____ me his copy of this intriguing reference work. (past form of *lend*)
13. This dictionary _____ to rest many of my misconceptions about language and word usage. (past form of *lay*)
14. The authors of the dictionary have _____ many best-selling references, including the Berlitz language books. (past participle of *write*)
15. One of the authors _____ the advisory editor of a standard dictionary. (past form of *be*)
16. His syndicated newspaper column, "Words, Wit, and Wisdom," has _____ the interest of more than 12 million readers. (past participle of *catch*)
17. The dictionary has _____ my curiosity about the origins of many everyday words and expressions. (past participle of *satisfy*)
18. I never _____ that the abbreviation *COD* stands for "collect on delivery" in the United States and "cash on delivery" in Britain. (past form of *know*)
19. *Hamburger* _____ its name from the city of Hamburg, Germany, and was originally called "Hamburg steak." (past form of *take*)
20. The baseball term *duster* refers to a ball that a pitcher has _____ hard and close to the batter to make the batter step back from the plate. (past participle of *throw*)

15.3 | Tense of Verbs

The **tenses** of a verb are the forms that help to show time.

There are six tenses in English: *present*, *past*, and *future* and *present perfect*, *past perfect*, and *future perfect*.

Present Tense

The present tense of any verb other than *be* is the same as the base form of the verb. To form the third-person singular of these verbs, add *-s* or *-es* to the base form.

	SINGULAR	PLURAL
FIRST PERSON	I **play.**	We **play.**
SECOND PERSON	You **play.**	You **play.**
THIRD PERSON	She, he, or it **plays.**	They **play.**
	Ronnie **plays.**	The children **play.**

	SINGULAR	PLURAL
FIRST PERSON	I **am** happy.	We **are** happy.
SECOND PERSON	You **are** happy.	You **are** happy.
THIRD PERSON	She, he, or it **is** happy.	They **are** happy.
	Ronnie **is** happy.	The children **are** happy.

The **present tense** expresses a constant, repeated, or habitual action or condition. It can also express a general truth.

> The Hudson River **flows** into the Atlantic. [not just now but always: a constant action]

> Jesse **plays** the flute superbly. [now and always: a habitual action]

> Uranium **is** radioactive. [a condition that is generally true]

The **present tense** can also express an action or condition that exists only now.

> Ronnie **feels** sick. [not always but just now]
> I **declare** these games over. [at this very moment]

The present tense is sometimes used in historical writing to express past events and, more often, in poetry, fiction, and reporting (especially in sports) to convey a sense of "being there."

> Above the crowd the *Hindenburg* suddenly **bursts** into flame.

> I **watch** as my sister **runs** after the ducks and **slips** in the mud.

> The pitch **gets** away from the catcher and **bounces** into the fence.

Past Tense

Use the **past tense** to express an action or condition that was started and completed in the past.

The team **defeated** its opponent.
The rivalry **seemed** fierce.
Victory **tasted** sweet.
My friends and I **led** the cheers.

Except for *be*, nearly all verbs—regular and irregular—have just one past-tense form, such as *climbed* or *became*. When you use the past tense of *be*, however, you must choose between the forms *was* and *were*.

	SINGULAR	PLURAL
FIRST PERSON	I **was** happy.	We **were** happy.
SECOND PERSON	You **were** happy.	You **were** happy.
THIRD PERSON	He, she, or it **was** happy.	They **were** happy.

Exercise 3   Using the Present Tense in Sentences

On your paper write a sentence using each of the following verb forms. The content of your sentence should express the kind of present time indicated in parentheses.

SAMPLE   does (now and always)
ANSWER   He does his laundry on Saturdays.

1. works (now and always)
2. sound (just now)
3. is (generally true)
4. says (at this moment)
5. sing (always)
6. finishes (a single sports event)
7. prefer (just now)
8. reads (now and always)
9. changes (generally true)
10. elect (historical present)

Exercise 4   Using the Past Tense in Sentences

On your paper write two paragraphs. In the first use the past tense of verbs 1–5; in the second use the past tense of verbs 6–10. In your paragraphs, use the verbs in any order.

1. give
2. think
3. choose
4. take
5. know
6. beat
7. try
8. run
9. put
10. win

Future Tense

Use the **future tense** to express an action or condition that will occur in the future.

To form the future tense of any verb, use *shall* or *will* with the base form: *I shall talk; you will come.*

> I **shall write** my essay tonight.
> Angela **will mail** the application.
> You **will see** me tomorrow.

There are other ways to express future time besides using the words *shall* or *will*.

1. Use *going to* with the present tense of *be* and the base form of a verb.

> Angela **is *going to* mail** the application.
> You **are *going to* see** me tomorrow.

2. Use *about to* with the present tense of *be* and the base form of the verb.

> I **am *about to* write** my essay.
> Angela **is *about to* mail** the application.

3. Use the present tense with an adverb or an adverb phrase that shows future time.

> Frank **sails *tomorrow.***
> Frank **sails *on the fifteenth of next month.***

Exercise 5	Using Expressions of Future Time

On your paper write the verb in each sentence below in the future tense. Try to use at least two other ways of expressing future time besides adding *shall* or *will* to the base form of the verb.

India's Classical Dances

1. Two classmates and I presented a report about the classical dances of India.
2. First Chandra spoke about *Bharata natyam*, the sacred Hindu dance form.
3. She described its complex movements for the hands, arms, and torso.
4. Chandra demonstrated several of the hand and arm movements.
5. Then Lan described two other highly stylized Indian dance forms: *kathakali*, a dramatic style from southern India, and *kathak*, an ancient dance from northern India.
6. He told us about the *kathakali*'s links to early Hindu mythology.
7. He also presented a videotape of an authentic performance of *kathakali*, showing the dance's strong rhythms and rapid turns.
8. Then it was my turn to describe *manipuri*, a dignified dance from northeastern India.
9. I taught the students a few of the difficult movements typical of *manipuri* dancers.
10. Finally Chandra sang a song and danced a pantomime from the *Bharata natyam* tradition.

Expressing Future Time in Sentences

Write five statements or predictions about the future. Your sentences may be as realistic or as fantastical as you wish. Remember to vary the ways in which you express future time.

SAMPLE ANSWERS   Film companies are going to produce all-day movies.

Rollerblading is about to become the very next craze.

On Friday I fly to Puerto Rico.

Exercise 7   **Changing Verb Tenses**

Change the tense of the italicized verb in each sentence below, following the directions in parentheses. Write the correct tense on your paper.

1. Walt Disney Studio *is* in last place among Hollywood studios during the 1980s. (Change to the past tense.)
2. At that time, Michael Eisner and Jeffrey Katzenberg *take* over the Disney empire. (Change to the past tense.)
3. Frank Wells *left* Warner Brothers and joins Disney as president and chief operating officer. (Change to the present tense.)
4. With the production of animated blockbusters like *Who Killed Roger Rabbit?* and *The Little Mermaid*, profits *soar.* (Change to the future tense.)
5. In the 1990s Disney's triumvirate *won* the triple crown of the entertainment world. (Change to the present tense.)
6. *The Lion King* eventually *becomes* the most profitable movie ever made. (Change to the past tense.)
7. *Home Improvement*, a Disney show, *beats* the competition to become the number-one show on television. (Change to the past tense.)
8. Theatergoers *find* it difficult to buy tickets for Broadway's biggest hit, Disney's *Beauty and the Beast.* (Change to the past tense.)
9. Disney *will release* animated films based on the lives of popular historical and literary figures. (Change to another form showing future time.)
10. A film about the hunchback of Notre Dame *falls* way behind schedule. (Change to the past tense.)
11. Critics *knew* that Disney's dazzling success cannot last forever. (Change to the present tense.)
12. The information superhighway *poses* a threat. (Change to the future tense.)
13. Euro Disney, the theme park located outside of Paris, *lost* money each year. (Change to the present tense.)
14. Attendance *dropped* at theme parks throughout the United States. (Change to the present tense.)
15. Another setback involved the successful partnership that *oversees* the studio's ride to the top. (Change to the past tense.)

15.4 Perfect Tenses

Present Perfect Tense

Use the **present perfect tense** to express an action or condition that occurred at some *indefinite* time in the past.

To form the present perfect tense, use *has* or *have* with the past participle of a verb: *has studied, have chosen.**

> She **has listened** to the recording.
> They **have bought** a new home.

The present perfect tense can refer only to past time that is indefinite. You cannot add adverbs such as *yesterday* to make the time more specific.

> He **has arrived** from Nebraska.

To be specific about completed past time, you usually use the simple past tense.

> He **arrived** from Nebraska yesterday.

You can also use the present perfect tense to show that an action or a condition *began* in the past and *continues* into the present. This use usually involves adverbs of time or adverb phrases.

> He **has spoken daily** from his campaign headquarters.
> Special guards **have remained** at the embassy **around the clock.**
> She **has been** class president **for three months.**

*Do not be confused by the term *present perfect;* this tense expresses past time. Present refers to the tense of the auxiliary verb *has* or *have.*

Exercise 8   Using the Present Perfect Tense

(a) On your paper rewrite each of the following sentences, changing the verb tense from past to present perfect. (b) Add adverbs or adverb phrases to each sentence to show that an action or condition began in the past and continues into the present.

SAMPLE   We looked for a new car.
ANSWER   **a.** We have looked for a new car.
          b. We have looked for a new car for two weeks.

1. He taught swimming classes.
2. Movie critics praised the film.
3. The state highway was under repair.
4. Our art class studied portrait painting.
5. The towering waves cascaded over the craggy shore.
6. The student council met with the principal.
7. The senior class sponsored a schoolwide fundraising project.
8. Several students served meals at the shelter for the homeless.
9. The counselor drove them to their after-school jobs.
10. Many teachers worked on a special exhibit for the library.

Past Perfect Tense

Use the **past perfect tense** to indicate that one past action or condition began *and* ended before another past action started.

April •

May •

June •

She had worked as manager.

On May 15th I took the job.

To form the past perfect tense, use *had* with the past participle of a verb: *had guessed, had driven.*

PAST PERFECT   PAST
She **had worked** as manager before I **took** the job. [She worked; she stopped working; I worked.]

PAST   PAST PERFECT
By the time I **arrived,** several actors **had auditioned.** [They auditioned; they finished auditioning; I arrived.]

PAST   PAST PERFECT
Before I **fell,** I **had noticed** the sticky spots on that section of the floor. [I noticed; I stopped noticing; I fell.]

Exercise 9   **Using the Past Perfect Tense**

Decide which verb in each sentence should be in the past perfect tense. Write the past perfect form of that verb on your paper.

1. She served as mayor of our city for years when she decided to run for Congress.
2. Once she carefully analyzed the pros and cons of entering the race, she called a press conference to announce her decision.
3. Although still young for a politician, she wished she made the decision to enter politics earlier.
4. She told the press she already discussed the decision to run for office with her family.
5. By 6:00 P.M. on election day, she stopped in more than a hundred towns throughout her district.
6. By the week that the election was over, her campaign cost much more than she had calculated.
7. By the time she moved to Washington, D.C., she completed the selection of all members of her staff.
8. When she was sworn in, her chief of staff already accepted job applications from hundreds of job hunters.
9. When her old friends visited her in March, the first-year representative already drafted her first piece of legislation.
10. She organized her entire reelection campaign by the time August arrived.

Future Perfect Tense

Use the **future perfect tense** to express one future action or condition that will begin *and* end before another future event starts.

To form the future perfect tense, use *will have* or *shall have* with the past participle of a verb: *will have talked, shall have talked.*

> By June I **will have worked** here two months. [The two months will be over by the time another future event, the coming of June, occurs.]

| Exercise 10 | Using the Future Perfect Tense |

Use each phrase and verb below to write a sentence in the future perfect tense.

SAMPLE   By early May—plant
ANSWER   By early May I will have planted 100 bulbs.

1. By next Sunday—give
2. Before the beginning of summer—buy
3. By the time I vote for the first time—watch
4. Before Susan's birthday—make
5. By New Year's Day—stop

| Exercise 11 | Writing the Perfect Tenses |

On your paper write the perfect-tense verb indicated in parentheses after each sentence.

African American Folktales

1. Folklorists _____ African American folktales for years. (present perfect of *collect*)
2. African Americans who _____ to this country as enslaved people later adapted West African folktales to suit the circumstances of their new culture. (past perfect of *come*)
3. The folktales about Brer Rabbit, for instance, grew out of trickster tales that African Americans _____ in their native West Africa. (past perfect of *learn*)
4. In the near future some variations of West African folktales _____ in this country for more than 200 years. (future perfect of *survive*)
5. The African American inhabitants of the Georgia Sea Islands _____ variations of West African tales for many generations. (present perfect of *tell*)
6. Once African Americans _____ Western religions, they invented many preacher tales. (past perfect of *adopt*)
7. These religious tales _____ many African American ballads and spirituals. (present perfect of *influence*)
8. Writers such as Zora Neale Hurston found inspiration in folktales that _____ themselves into the fabric of African American culture. (past perfect of *weave*)
9. Many blues singers _____ from folktales themes that describe or allude to the hardships inherent in African American life. (present perfect of *take*)
10. It is likely that all American children _____ some African American folktales by the time they grow up. (future perfect of *hear*)

15.5 Progressive and Emphatic Forms

Each of the six tenses has a **progressive** form that expresses a continuing action.

To make the progressive forms, use the appropriate tense of the verb *be* with the present participle of the main verb.

PRESENT PROGRESSIVE	They *are* listening.
PAST PROGRESSIVE	They *were* listening.
FUTURE PROGRESSIVE	They *will be* listening.
PRESENT PERFECT PROGRESSIVE	They *have been* listening.
PAST PERFECT PROGRESSIVE	They *had been* listening.
FUTURE PERFECT PROGRESSIVE	They *will have been* listening.

The present and past tenses have additional forms, called **emphatic,** that add special force, or emphasis, to the verb.

To make the emphatic forms, use *do, does,* or *did* with the base form.

PRESENT EMPHATIC	I *do* listen.
PAST EMPHATIC	I *did* listen.

Exercise 12	Using the Progressive and Emphatic Forms

For each sentence write the progressive or the emphatic form of the verb in parentheses. Choose the form that makes more sense in the sentence.

Miami's Cuban Community

1. For decades the city of Miami (attract) many visitors from Latin America and the Caribbean.
2. Since the late nineteenth century, when Miami was first developed as a resort, wealthy Cubans, Venezuelans, and Colombians (come) to Miami on vacation.
3. Today many poor Nicaraguans and Mexicans (settle) in Miami, but the largest Spanish-speaking community in the city is Cuban.
4. Before 1959 few people (anticipate) a large influx of Cubans fleeing the new regime of Fidel Castro.
5. Nevertheless, it is clear now that the Cuban revolution of 1959 (have) a major impact on the population of Miami.
6. Today more than half a million people of Cuban descent (live) in Dade County, where Miami is located.
7. By the year 2000, almost as many people (speak) Spanish as English in Miami and the nearby communities.
8. Bilingualism (become) increasingly common and valuable among people who now work in the area.
9. Many Cubans who fled their homeland (hope) at first to return to their country someday.
10. Many Cuban Americans, however, (decide) that Miami is now their permanent home.

On your own paper, complete each of the following sentences by writing the tense or form indicated in parentheses.

Kwanzaa

 1. In 1966 Dr. Maulana Karenga _____ Kwanzaa as a way for African Americans to reflect on and celebrate their rich heritage. (past tense of *create*)
 2. Since its inception this nonreligious and nonpolitical holiday _____ worldwide acceptance. (present perfect progressive form of *gain*)
 3. Dr. Karenga _____ the annual celebration around African cultural and social experiences, particularly the traditional festival of first fruits. (past perfect tense of *develop*)
 4. By the end of the weeklong celebration, African Americans _____ the Nguzo Saba, the Seven Principles of Kwanzaa. (future perfect tense of *observe*)
 5. The Seven Principles _____ a set of values that emphasize accountability, reliability, and concern for one another. (present tense of *be*)
 6. Prior to December 26, the first day of the celebration, millions of African Americans _____ weeks preparing the basic Kwanzaa symbols. (future progressive form of *spend*)
 7. One symbol is the Mkeka, or place mat, which _____ tradition. (present tense of *represent*)
 8. Another symbol is Vibunzi, an ear of corn, which _____ to symbolize each child in the family. (present perfect tense of *come*)
 9. Estimates indicate that 15 to 18 million people _____ this holiday in recent years. (past progressive form of *celebrate*)
10. Many African American and Caribbean American students _____ to celebrate Kwanzaa along with their traditional religious holidays. (present perfect tense of *choose*)

On your paper explain the difference in meaning between the sentences in each of the pairs below. Name the tense(s) used in each sentence.

SAMPLE   **a.** Did she live in Washington long?
           b. Has she lived in Washington long?

ANSWER   In sentence *a* the action occurred in the past and has ended—past.
           In sentence *b* the action occurred in the past and is continuing—present perfect.

 1. **a.** They went to Utah for vacation.
    b. They have gone to Utah for vacation.
 2. **a.** We planned a trip to Virginia to visit friends.
    b. We were planning a trip to Virginia to visit friends.
 3. **a.** Marisa did work in New Mexico.
    b. Marisa has worked in New Mexico.
 4. **a.** She has been visiting them in Texas.
    b. She visited them in Texas.
 5. **a.** Earl is traveling through Colorado.
    b. Earl has been traveling through Colorado.

15.6 | Compatibility of Tenses

Do not shift, or change, tenses when two or more events occur at the same time.

INCORRECT   During the storm the dam **broke,** and the river **reaches** flood level. [The tense shifts from the past to the present.]

CORRECT   During the storm the dam **broke,** and the river **reached** flood level. [Now it is clear that both events happened at nearly the same time in the past.]

Shift tenses only to show that one event precedes or follows another.

INCORRECT   By the time the game **ended,** she **bowled** six strikes. [The two past-tense verbs give the mistaken impression that both events—the ending of the game and the bowling of the strikes—happened at the same time.]

CORRECT   By the time the game **ended,** she **had bowled** six strikes. [The shift from the past tense *(ended)* to the past perfect tense *(had bowled)* clearly indicates that the bowling of six strikes happened before the game ended.]

Keep a statement about a general truth in the present tense even if other verbs are in the past tense.

CORRECT   Then he **remembered** that Christmas **is** on December 25.

Exercise 15   **Choosing Compatible Tenses**

Find the first verb that appears in each sentence below. Then choose and write the correct tense of the second verb in parentheses.

SAMPLE   Jaime had jogged daily after school, but he (has found, found) exercising in the evening difficult.
ANSWER   found

1. Before Jaime began his morning workouts, he (felt, had felt) sluggish and lazy.
2. Then he remembered that exercise (gives, gave) a person more energy.
3. It has been almost a year since he (had bought, bought) a student membership in the gym.
4. If he has time this summer, he (plans, will have planned) to enroll in a diving class.
5. In the summer he works at a hotel and also (teaches, will teach) tennis.

Making Tenses Compatible

First find the two verbs that appear in each of the following sentences. Then rewrite each sentence, making the second verb compatible with the first verb.

Two Opera Stars

1. Victoria de los Angeles was born in Barcelona, Spain, in 1923, where she later had studied music at the Barcelona Conservatory.
2. After she had completed the six-year course at the conservatory in only three years, she makes her concert debut in 1944.
3. Although the public knows her by her stage name, her real name was Victoria Gómez Cima.
4. She took private voice lessons for five years and then wins first prize in an international singing contest in Switzerland.
5. De los Angeles soon discovered that she has offers for concert appearances from all over Europe and America.
6. By the time she made her debut in New York in the fall of 1950, the public already heard many favorable things about her.
7. She had recorded many of her most brilliant roles before she had left the stage in 1969.
8. After she retired from opera, de los Angeles had devoted herself to musical recitals.
9. She began her recitals with operatic arias and was ending them with Spanish flamenco songs.
10. De los Angeles mastered French, Italian, and German and was excelling in each language.
11. Julia Migenes is a popular soprano who gains fame for her memorable performance as Carmen in the film version of the opera.
12. Although she was not nominated for an Oscar, she receives a Grammy for her performance.
13. She appeared in the film with the tenor Placido Domingo, who is performing the role of Don José.
14. The *London Financial Times* called Migenes "mesmerizing" and describes her delivery as "straight and from the heart."
15. Migenes has played many leading roles; two of these will be Jenny in *The Fall of Mahagonny* and the title role in the opera *Lulu.*
16. When the Metropolitan Opera presented *Lulu,* PBS televises it.
17. Migenes will perform at the Kennedy Center where she sang excerpts from her most famous roles.
18. She introduced a program that features popular music, such as French *chansons* and the music of Brecht and Weill.
19. She enjoys performing the music of Leonard Bernstein, who had become one of her favorite composers.
20. Nowadays, Migenes often treats her audiences to several Gershwin songs that will be among her personal favorites.

15.7　Voice of Verbs

An action verb is in the **active voice** when the subject of the sentence performs the action.

> The trainer **teased** the lion.

An action verb is in the **passive voice** when its action is performed on the subject.

> The lion **was teased** by the trainer.

The active voice is generally stronger, but sometimes the passive voice is preferred or even necessary. Use the passive voice if you do not want to call attention to the performer, if you do not know the performer, or if the performer is unimportant.

> The window **was broken.**　[You may not want to identify the culprit.]

> The roses **were sent.**　[You do not know who the sender is.]

> All the cards **were sold.** [It doesn't matter who sold them.]

To form the passive voice, use a form of the auxiliary verb *be* with the past participle of the verb. The tense of the auxiliary verb determines the tense of the passive verb.

> The lion **is teased** by the trainer.　[present tense, passive voice]

> The lion **was being teased.**　[past progressive tense, passive voice]

> The lion **will have been teased** by the trainer.　[future perfect tense, passive voice]

Exercise 17　　**Identifying Active and Passive Voice**

For each sentence write the verb and identify its voice as *passive* or *active*.

1. In 1977 Leslie Marmon Silko published *Ceremony*, a powerful novel.
2. In the book the life of a Native American veteran of World War II is described.
3. Stories about her own Pueblo tribe are often related by Silko.
4. The young Silko was told many stories by her great-aunts and great-grandmother.
5. Silko's writing often depicts the differences between Native American and white cultures.
6. The Bureau of Indian Affairs ran Silko's school in Old Laguna, New Mexico.
7. This school was attended by many children from the nearby Pueblo reservation.
8. The University of New Mexico granted Silko a diploma in 1969.
9. The idea of a career in law initially tempted Silko.
10. Eventually, a career as a writer was chosen by her instead.

On your paper rewrite the sentences below, changing the active voice to the passive or the passive voice to the active. For some passive voice sentences it may not be necessary to include the performer of the action.

SAMPLE   Several popular folk songs were performed by the band.
ANSWER   The band performed several popular folk songs.

Joan Baez, Folksinger

1. A musical career was launched by Joan Baez in 1960.
2. An entire generation was touched by her music and her message.
3. In the late 1950s, a teaching job was offered by the Massachusetts Institute of Technology to Joan's father, Dr. Alberto Vicio Baez.
4. One evening Joan was taken by her father to a coffeehouse in Cambridge's Harvard Square.
5. For the first time, the songs of some popular young folksingers were heard by Joan.
6. From then on, she focused her attention on the guitar and traditional folk ballads.
7. A music promoter saw her performance in a Cambridge coffeehouse.
8. Joan was booked by the promoter into the Gate of Horn, a club in Chicago.
9. There she was invited by singer Bob Gibson to a folk festival in Newport, Rhode Island.
10. As a result of her solo performance, record deals were offered to Joan by several recording companies.
11. A small recording company called Vanguard was chosen by Joan.
12. During the fall of 1960, several weeks were spent by Joan Baez in a recording studio in New York City.
13. Constant touring followed the success of her first album, a major hit nationwide.
14. The Democratic party asked Joan to a gala for President John F. Kennedy.
15. During the 1960s, their country's involvement in the Vietnam War was protested by many young Americans.
16. The anger and frustration of young Americans from all backgrounds was reflected in the music of Joan Baez.
17. Her lyrics revealed deep feelings about peace and war and injustice.
18. Her audiences were moved by such songs as "Blowing in the Wind" and "We Shall Overcome."
19. In 1966 the Reverend Martin Luther King Jr. was joined by Joan Baez in escorting African American children to their newly integrated school.
20. Many young people joined activist and singer Baez in her efforts for political reform.
21. In 1974 an album of Spanish-language songs was released by Joan.
22. The album featured songs of love and death from Central and South America.
23. Joan dedicated the album to her father.
24. Throughout the years, albums of diverse musical styles, including country and western, have been recorded by Joan.
25. Audiences of all ages continue to be thrilled by her voice and her music.

Grammar Review

Verb Tenses and Voice

Set in the imaginary kingdom of Middle Earth, Tolkien's novel recounts the adventures of a group of hobbits, an ancient, peace-loving race. In this episode three hobbits, Frodo, Sam, and Pippin, encounter a mysterious horseman. The meeting so disturbs Frodo that he is tempted to call on the powers of his magical ring. The passage has been annotated to show some of the kinds of verbs covered in this unit.

Literature Model

from THE FELLOWSHIP OF THE RING

by J. R. R. Tolkien

Past progressive →

The sun was beginning to get low and the light of afternoon was on the land as they went down the hill. So far they had not met a soul on the road. This way was not much used, being hardly fit for carts, and there was little traffic to the Woody End. They had been jogging along again for an hour or more when Sam stopped a moment as if listening. They were now on level ground, and the road after much winding lay straight ahead through grassland sprinkled with tall trees, outliers of the approaching woods.

Past perfect →
Passive Voice →
Past perfect progressive →

"I can hear a pony or a horse coming along the road behind," said Sam.

They looked back, but the turn of the road prevented them from seeing far. "I wonder if that is Gandalf coming after us," said Frodo; but even as he said it, he had a feeling that it was not so, and a sudden desire to hide from the view of the rider came over him.

Present tense of a regular verb →

"It may not matter much," he said apologetically, "but I would rather not be seen on the road.... Let's get out of sight!"

The other two ran quickly to the left and down into a little hollow not far from the road. There they lay flat. Frodo hesitated for a second: curiosity or some other feeling was struggling with his desire to hide. The sound of hoofs drew nearer. Just in time he threw himself down in a patch of long grass behind a tree that overshadowed the ➡

Past tense of an irregular verb →

road. Then he lifted his head and peered cautiously above one of the great roots.

Round the corner came a black horse, no hobbit-pony but a full-sized horse; and on it sat a large man, who seemed to crouch in the saddle, wrapped in a great black cloak and hood, so that only his boots in the high stirrups showed below; his face was shadowed and invisible.

When it reached the tree and was level with Frodo the horse stopped. The riding figure sat quite still with its head bowed, as if listening. From inside the hood came a noise as of someone sniffing to catch an elusive scent; the head turned from side to side of the road.

> Past tense of a regular verb

A sudden unreasoning fear of discovery laid hold of Frodo, and he thought of his Ring. He hardly dared to breathe, and yet the desire to get it out of his pocket became so strong that he began slowly to move his hand. . . . At that moment the rider sat up, and shook the reins. The horse stepped forward, walking slowly at first, and then breaking into a quick trot.

> Active voice

Exercise 1

Identifying Principal Parts   The following sentences are based on *The Fellowship of the Ring*. Each sentence contains a verb in one of four forms: (a) the base form, (b) the past form, (c) the present participle, or (d) the past participle. At the end of the sentence is a second verb in parentheses. On your paper write the form of the verb in italics. Then write the verb in parentheses in the same form as the original verb.

SAMPLE   The hobbits *became* fearful. (feel)
ANSWER   past form; felt

1. Their spirits *fall* at the approach of sunset. (sink)
2. The hobbits had *started* their journey too late in the day. (begin)
3. They *locate* a deserted road over the hill. (find)
4. The road *stretched* toward the dark woods ahead of the hobbits. (lead)
5. Few carts had *traveled* on the road in recent years because of its poor condition. (drive)
6. So far they had not *met* a soul along the road. (see)
7. In the fading light, Frodo and the other hobbits nervously *hurried* down the hill. (go)
8. Each hobbit had *carried* a few belongings from home in a pack on his back. (take)
9. Despite the rough road, they were *jogging* steadily toward the Woody End. (run)
10. Sam *heard* the sound of a horse's hoofs. (catch)

Exercise 2

Using the Present, Past, and Future Tenses   Each of the following sentences elaborates on ideas suggested by the passage from *The Fellowship of the Ring*. On your paper write each verb, changing the tense according to the instructions in parentheses. Use only the present, past, and future tenses; with the exception of *will* to express the future tense, do not use any helping verbs.

SAMPLE   The hobbits *remain* in hiding.
          (Change to the future tense.)
ANSWER   will remain

1. Frodo *has* a Ring with magical powers. (Change to the past tense.)
2. Frodo *began* a dangerous journey through the imaginary kingdom of Middle-earth. (Change to the present tense.)
3. Frodo *thinks* admiringly of the powerful wizard Gandalf during his journey. (Change to the past tense.)
4. An unexpected noise *breaks* through the still air. (Change to the past tense.)
5. At the sound of the horseman, a sudden fear *will come* over Frodo. (Change to the past tense.)
6. After a slight hesitation Frodo *told* the other hobbits of his nervousness. (Change to the present tense.)
7. The hobbits *fly* in different directions. (Change to the future tense.)
8. Frodo *sank* swiftly into a patch of tall grass. (Change to the present tense.)
9. His companions *went* to the left side of the road to find a place to hide. (Change to the present tense.)
10. Curiosity about the approaching horseman soon *will arise* in Frodo. (Change to the past tense.)
11. Before long Frodo *saw* a black horse—no mere hobbit-pony—and its rider. (Change to the future tense.)
12. The looming horseman *wore* a long black cloak and hood. (Change to the present tense.)
13. The horseman *speaks* to no one. (Change to the future tense.)
14. The rider's face *draws* back within the folds of his hood. (Change to the past tense.)
15. Frodo *remembers* the magic Ring in his pocket. (Change to the future tense.)
16. Frodo *will think* about the Ring in his pocket. (Change to the present tense.)
17. The horseman *will give* the horse's reins a shake. (Change to the past tense.)
18. The travelers *will take* greater precautions after this incident. (Change to the present tense.)
19. Perhaps Gandalf *comes* to their assistance. (Change to the future tense.)
20. The hobbits *will feel* nervous during the night. (Change to the present tense.)

Exercise 3

Using the Perfect Tenses   Each of the following sentences is based on passages from *The Fellowship of the Ring* that are not reprinted in this textbook. On your paper write the italicized verb in the tense indicated in parentheses, using the past participle of the main verb and the appropriate form of the helping verb *have*.

SAMPLE   Before he started his journey, Frodo ∧his house.
(past perfect tense of *sell*)

ANSWER   had sold

1. Frodo ∧the magical Ring that is in his pocket from his uncle Bilbo. (present perfect tense of *inherit*)
2. Bilbo found the Ring in a cave, where Gollum, a wicked creature, ∧it earlier. (past perfect tense of *lose*)
3. Before Gollum obtained the Ring, it ∧to Sauron the Great, an evil power. (past perfect tense of *belong*)
4. A brave man named Isildur ∧the Ring from Sauron's hand, but Isildur later lost the Ring in a river. (past perfect tense of *cut*)
5. Gollum murdered his friend Deagol, who ∧the Ring from the river bottom. (past perfect tense of *got*)
6. Gandalf, a friendly wizard, ∧Frodo of the Ring's unusual powers. (present perfect tense of *warn*)
7. Over the course of time, the Ring ∧greed in each of its possessors. (present perfect tense of *foster*)
8. Gollum and Sauron's followers ∧for the Ring for many years. (present perfect tense of *search*)
9. By the time the hobbits reach Mount Doom, perhaps some elves ∧them. (future perfect tense of *help*)
10. Soon the Black Riders, Sauron's enthusiastic followers, ∧Frodo. (future perfect tense of *attack*)

Exercise 4

Using Verb Tenses in Writing   Choose a story that you have read recently or one that you have seen in the movies or on television. On your paper write five sentences summarizing the story and describing the main characters. In each sentence use at least two verbs that are compatible in tense. Write the verbs and label the tenses. Use all six verb tenses in your sentences.

SAMPLE ANSWER   Last Saturday I saw a movie that I had heard about for weeks. saw—past tense; had heard—past perfect tense

Exercise 5

Using the Progressive and Emphatic Forms   The following sentences elaborate on ideas suggested by the passage from *The Fellowship of the Ring*. On your paper rewrite the sentence inserting the italicized verb in the form indicated in parentheses. Use the present participle of the main verb with the appropriate tense of the auxiliary verb *be*, or use the base form of the main verb with the appropriate form of *do*.

SAMPLE   The sun∧brightly across the meadow. (past progressive form of *shine*)

ANSWER   The sun was shining brightly across the meadow.

1. The sun has set in the distance, and twilight soon∧. (future progressive form of *come*)
2. An unfamiliar territory∧the group of adventurous hobbits. (present emphatic form of *surround*)
3. For many miles the strange road∧down a steep hill. (past progressive form of *wind*)
4. Sam∧to the thunder of a horse's hoofs. (past progressive form of *listen*)
5. The horse ∧ briskly along the road just behind the travelers. (past progressive form of *gallop*)
6. Unfortunately, the bend in the road∧a view of any approaching rider. (present emphatic form of *obscure*)
7. The hobbits soon∧into hiding places near the edge of the road. (past progressive form of *dash*)
8. Frodo's heart∧fiercely against his chest. (past progressive form of *pound*)
9. Before long Frodo ∧over the roots of a tree at the mysterious rider. (past progressive form of *peer*)
10. The horseman's dark and sinister appearance ∧ threatening. (past emphatic form of *seem*)
11. The rider∧his head. (present progressive form of *bow*)
12. The rider's hooded head∧from one side of the road to the other. (present progressive form of *turn*)
13. The rider∧the air for an elusive scent. (present progressive form of *sniff*)
14. After such a ride, dust∧to the horseman's cloak and saddle. (future progressive form of *cling*)
15. The horse∧heavily when it stops running. (future progressive form of *pant*)
16. In spite of his anxiety, Frodo∧about the identity of the mysterious rider. (present emphatic form of *wonder*)
17. Frodo∧his hand gradually toward the Ring in his pocket. (future progressive form of *move*)
18. Frodo truly∧against his uncontrollable desire for the Ring. (present emphatic form of *struggle*)
19. Frodo indeed∧the motives of the black-cloaked rider. (present emphatic form of *suspect*)
20. Evidently, the horseman ∧ the hobbits on their journey. (present progressive form of *follow*)

Exercise 6

Making Tenses Compatible   The following sentences are based on the passage from *The Fellowship of the Ring* and other passages from the novel that are not reprinted in this textbook. On your paper rewrite the sentence, changing the tense of the italicized verb to a form that makes the tenses of the verbs in the sentence compatible.

SAMPLE   Before the horseman appeared, the hobbits *jumped* into hiding places.
ANSWER   Before the horseman appeared, the hobbits had jumped into hiding places.

1. The mysterious figure sniffed the air as he *pauses* beside Frodo's concealed body.
2. As Frodo longingly *touches* his Ring, he remembered Gandalf's warning.
3. Before he disappeared, Gandalf *explains* the Ring's dangerous powers.
4. To the hobbits' relief, the horse broke into a trot while Frodo *watches*.
5. After the horseman rides away, Frodo *walked* toward his companions.
6. By the time Frodo reached his friends, they *stood* up.
7. The hobbits *discuss* the horseman who had frightened them.
8. Sam's father *saw* a stranger similar to the horseman before the hobbits left on their journey.
9. Frodo knew that the evil creature Gollum *left* his cave months ago in search of the Ring.
10. Frodo wondered whether Sauron *sends* the rider as a spy.

Exercise 7

Changing the Voice of Verbs   The following sentences are based on *The Fellowship of the Ring*. First, identify each sentence as being in the *passive voice* or the *active voice*. Then rewrite each sentence, changing the active voice to the passive or the passive voice to the active.

SAMPLE   The horseman's head was covered by a dark hood.
ANSWER   passive voice; A dark hood covered the horseman's head.

1. The landscape of Middle Earth is described clearly by the novel's author, J. R. R. Tolkien.
2. A gray light bathed the lonely meadow.
3. The grassland around the bumpy road was sprinkled with tall trees.
4. The branches of a large tree overshadowed the road.
5. The curvy road was used by few people.
6. The rapid clatter of the horse's hoofs alarmed Frodo and his friends.
7. Giant tree roots hid the small hobbits from view.
8. A great black cloak concealed most of the horseman's enormous body.
9. Suddenly Frodo was seized by a desire for his Ring.
10. The trembling hobbits were terrified by the horseman.

Exercise 8

Using Verb Tense, Form, and Voice   Using details from the passage or your own ideas, write a sentence about each pair of nouns. Use the verb tense, form, or voice indicated in parentheses.

SAMPLE   hobbits, road (past perfect progressive)
ANSWER   The hobbits had been trudging along the road for an hour.

1. meadow, woods (present tense, passive voice)
2. sun, day (past progressive)
3. horse, rider (present perfect progressive)
4. sounds, fear (past emphatic)
5. hobbits, home (future progressive)

Review: Exercise 9

Proofreading

The following passage describes the artist Samuel Palmer, whose painting appears on the opposite page. Rewrite the passage, correcting the errors in spelling, usage, and grammar. Add any missing punctuation. There are twenty-five errors.

Samuel Palmer

¹Samuel Palmer (1805–1881), the son of a bookseller who lived on the outskirts of London shown an early talent for painting. ²By the time he was fourteen, he has already had works accepted by the Royal Academy in London. ³At the age of seventeen, he meets the artist John Linnell, who encourages him to study European art. ⁴Linnell had a strong personal and professional influence on the young man and Palmer marries Linnell's daughter in 1837. ⁵The relationship between the two men become difficult, however, because of Linnell's bossy and violent personality.

⁶Landscapes were Palmer's chief interest and he painted them with a keen eye. ⁷He fills his notebooks with detailed drawings that expressed a deeply spiritual view of nature. ⁸His view of life was strongly influenced by his friendship with William Blake the visionary English poet and painter. ⁹Unfortunately, when Palmer died, many of his early sketches are destroyed by his son.

¹⁰*Early Morning* was finded among the few early sketches of Palmer's that were not destroyed. ¹¹The gentle lanscape depicted early in the morning. ¹²Palmer has drawed each leaf, stone, and hillock with care and precision. ¹³Rounded shapes predominate, some examples are the oak tree on the left, the cottage roof behind the wheat fields the sloping hills, and even Palmers signature at the bottom of the canvas. ¹⁴In a hollow below the tree sit a group of people. ¹⁵Some critics beleive that the rabbit might symbolize the abundance of nature. ➡

[16]Palmer often drawed his landscapes with a mythological quality, much like the settings in J. R. R. Tolkien's *The Fellowship of the Ring*. [17]He has wove elements of both realism and fantasy into the scene pictured in *Early Morning*. [18]Both Palmer and Tolkien was deeply spiritual men. [19]Both choosed to portray the sanctity of nature and the power of the human spirit.

Samuel Palmer, *Early Morning*, 1825

Mixed Review

Exercise 10

The following sentences describe the life of the author J. R. R. Tolkien [täl'kēn]. Rewrite each sentence, following the instructions in parentheses.

1. As a youth J. R. R. Tolkien learns Greek and Latin and developed his own alphabet. (Change the first verb to make the tenses compatible.)
2. He also studies Finnish, and he invented the imaginary language of Quenya. (Correct the error caused by the use of the present tense.)
3. By the time Tolkien entered college, he already demonstrated an exceptional talent for languages. (Change the second verb to the past perfect.)
4. The gifted young student was awarded a scholarship by Oxford University. (Rewrite the sentence in the active voice.)
5. His studies of *Beowulf*, an early English epic, intensified his interest in Old English literature. (Rewrite the sentence in the passive voice.)
6. While Tolkien was still a student, he already gathered ideas for his future books about a mythological kingdom. (Change the second verb to the past progressive form.)
7. Elves, dwarfs, hobbits, and goblins truly inhabit this kingdom. (Change the verb to the present emphatic form.)
8. *The Hobbit*, the first book that Tolkien wrote about Middle Earth, appears in 1937. (Replace the inappropriate present tense.)
9. The idea of hobbits came to Tolkien as he graded exams at Oxford. (Change the second verb to the past progressive form.)
10. Some scholars think Tolkien's fantasies are reflecting the battle between good and evil in the real world. (Change the second verb from the present progressive to the present.)
11. A reviewer once observed that Tolkien will tap his readers' most common nightmares and fantasies. (Change the second verb to the present tense.)
12. Tolkien is called a "colonizer of dreams." (Change the verb to the active voice.)
13. He presents his readers with a viable alternative to the madness of the real world. (Change the verb to the present emphatic form.)
14. He introduced the word *hobbit*, which find its way into our everyday language. (Change the second verb to make the tenses compatible.)
15. In *The Hobbit* Bilbo Baggins discovered, or perhaps steals, the One Ring of Power. (Change the second verb to make the tense compatible with that of the first.)
16. The last of the trilogy, which Tolkien names *The Return of the King*, was published in 1956. (Change the first verb to make the tenses compatible.)
17. Readers have been awaiting the publication of the final book for years. (Change the present perfect progressive to the past perfect progressive form.)
18. Critics believe that Tolkien's trilogy is one of the great literary achievements of our time. (Change the first verb to the present emphatic form.)
19. Sixty years later the story of the hobbits does remain profoundly relevant. (Change the verb form to the simple present tense.)
20. Tolkien's epic fantasy classic will delight readers for generations. (Change the verb to the future progressive form.)

Writing Application

Verbs in Writing   In this passage from *Roots: The Saga of an American Family*, Alex Haley explains how he began researching the story of his African American ancestors. As you read, note Haley's use of verbs.

The microfilm rolls *were delivered*, and I turned them through the machine with a building sense of intrigue, viewing in different census takers' penmanship an endless parade of names. After about a dozen microfilmed rolls, I *was beginning* to tire, when in utter astonishment I looked upon the names of Grandma's parents: Tom Murray, Irene Murray . . . older sisters of Grandma's as well—every one of them a name that I'd heard countless times on her front porch.

It *wasn't* that I *had*n't *believed* Grandma. You just *didn't* not *believe* my Grandma. It was simply so uncanny actually seeing those names in print and in official U.S. Government records.

Techniques with Verbs   When you write and revise your own work, try to use verbs in some of the ways that Haley uses them.

1. Use the emphatic form for emphasis or make a point. Notice how Haley uses the negative for additional emphasis.

Unemphatic Version   You just believed my Grandma.
Haley's Version   You just *didn't* not *believe* my Grandma.

2. Use a verb form that correctly conveys your exact meaning. Compare the difference in meaning of these two sentences:

Past Tense Version   After about a dozen microfilmed rolls, I *began* to tire.
Haley's Version   After about a dozen microfilmed rolls, I *was beginning* to tire.

Practice   Practice these techniques by revising the following passage on a separate sheet of paper. Choose an appropriate tense, form, and voice for each verb in parentheses. Make other changes to the passage that you think are needed.

When Alex Haley was 17, he enlisted in the U.S. Coast Guard with the permission of his father. During World War II, he (serve) on a warship in the South Pacific. After he (write) adventure stories set on the high seas, he (submit) them to the editors of various magazines. For eight years, Haley (collect) rejection slips. Occasionally one of his stories (purchase) and (publish).

Haley retired from the Coast Guard after serving for 20 years, the last several years as a journalist. Now he (be) ready to begin a full-time career as a writer. He (begin) writing mostly magazine articles. In 1965 Haley (collaborate) on his first book, *The Autobiography of Malcolm X*, which was highly acclaimed. After 12 years of research and travel, Haley (produce) *Roots*, the winner of a special Pulitzer Prize in 1977.

16.1 Intervening Prepositional Phrases

A verb must agree with its subject in person and number.

Number can be singular or plural. Singular words indicate one and take a singular verb. Plural words indicate more than one and take a plural verb.

To show agreement, most verbs change form only in the present tense: when the subject is third-person singular, an -*s* (or -*es*) is added to the base verb.

SINGULAR	PLURAL
She **learns**.	They **learn**.
He **watches**.	They **watch**.
It **runs**.	They **run**.

An exception is the linking verb *be*, which changes form in both the present tense and the past tense.

SINGULAR	PLURAL
The dog **is** happy.	The dogs **are** happy.
The apple **was** sour.	The apples **were** sour.

In order to show agreement with third-person subjects, the auxiliary verbs *be*, *have*, and *do* change form in verb phrases.

SINGULAR	PLURAL
She **is learning**.	They **are learning**.
She **has gone** home.	They **have gone** home.
Does he **live** in Virginia?	**Do** they **live** in Virginia?

Exercise 1 — Making Subjects and Verbs Agree

On your paper write the simple subject from each of the following sentences. Then write the verb form in parentheses that agrees with the subject.

The Class Party

1. Chandra, Bill, and Marco (is planning/are planning) the class party.
2. Carla (offers/offer) her house for the party.
3. The class representatives (votes/vote) to have the party on a Saturday.
4. Three students (visits/visit) the mall for ideas on decorating.
5. A teacher (volunteers/volunteer) to chaperone.
6. All class members (plans/plan) to attend the party.
7. They (knows/know) the food will be good.
8. It (is being/ are being) made by student volunteers.
9. The volunteers (has been/have been) preparing sample dishes.
10. Everybody's favorite so far (was/were) the vegetarian deep-dish pizza.

Do not mistake a word in a prepositional phrase for the subject of a sentence.

The subject of a sentence is never the object of a preposition. The verb must agree with the simple subject of the sentence, not with the object of a preposition.

The **color** of the roses **pleases** us. [The subject, *color*, is singular; *of the roses* is a prepositional phrase; the verb, *pleases*, is singular because it agrees with the singular subject.]

The **flowers** for the bouquet **are** pretty. [The subject, *flowers*, is plural; *for the bouquet* is a prepositional phrase; the verb, *are*, is plural because it agrees with the plural subject.]

| Exercise 2 | Making Subjects and Verbs Agree When Prepositional Phrases Intervene |

On your paper write the simple subject in each of the following sentences. Then write the verb form in parentheses that agrees with the subject.

Elizabeth Keckley

1. A report for one of my history classes (is/are) about Elizabeth Keckley, an African American who became the dressmaker for and confidante of First Lady Mary Todd Lincoln.
2. Keckley in her early years (was/were) enslaved in Virginia.
3. A daughter of her owners (was/were) fond of Keckley and brought her to live with her in St. Louis.
4. Keckley's talents in the art of dressmaking (was/were) so considerable that she was able to help support the family of her owner.
5. In 1855 Keckley, with the help of loans from her customers, (was/were) able to purchase her freedom.
6. To me, Keckley's irrepressible longings for freedom and dignity (seems/seem) extraordinary.
7. Keckley's faith in herself and in her abilities (was/were) rewarded, for she moved to Washington, D.C., and became the dressmaker of President Lincoln's wife.
8. Keckley, as a personal friend of the Lincolns, (was/were) privy to many family matters at the White House.
9. Her opinions about the White House (was/were) published in 1868 in a book entitled *Behind the Scenes.*
10. The success of this determined woman (continues/continue) to inspire people today.

16.2 Agreement with Linking Verbs

Do not be confused by a predicate nominative that is different in number from the subject. Only the subject affects the number of the linking verb.

The last **course was** strawberries with cream. [The singular verb, *was*, agrees with the singular subject, *course*, not with the predicate nominative, *strawberries*.]

The main **courses** for the dinner **were** a selection of fish dishes. [The plural verb, *were*, agrees with the plural subject, *courses*, not with the predicate nominative, *selection*.]

Baskets of flowers **were** the decoration at the banquet. [The plural verb, *were*, agrees with the plural subject, *baskets*, not with the predicate nominative, *decoration*.]

My favorite **part** of musicals **is** the duets.
[The singular verb, *is*, agrees with the singular subject, *part*, not with the predicate nominative, *duets*.]

Exercise 3   Making Linking Verbs Agree with Their Subjects

On your paper write the simple subject or subjects in each of the following sentences. Then write the form of the verb in parentheses that agrees with the subject.

Modern Circuses

1. For many people the joys of the circus (is/are) a pleasure that they never outgrow.
2. Circuses (remains/remain) a popular form of entertainment in many countries.
3. The circuses of ancient Rome (was/were) actually a group of chariot races performed in a ring.
4. Perhaps the first of the modern circuses (was/were) a one-ring show by Philip Astley, an eighteenth-century horse trainer.
5. In the eighteenth and nineteenth centuries, circus performers (was/were) the elite among popular entertainers.
6. The most exotic part of all circuses (is/are) the wild animals.
7. The feats of an acrobat or a trapeze artist (seems/seem) an impossibility to most of us.
8. A clown's acrobatic leaps (appears/appear) an easy trick, but in fact they are quite difficult to perform.
9. The strains of the calliope (is/are) a joyous sound, don't you think?
10. To me, an irresistible temptation (is/are) the aromas of popcorn and roasted peanuts.

In an **inverted sentence**—a sentence in which the subject follows the verb—take care in locating the simple subject, and make sure that the verb agrees with the subject.

Because an inverted sentence often begins with a prepositional phrase, the object of the preposition may easily be mistaken for the subject. In an inverted sentence, however, the subject follows the verb.

V   S

SINGULAR   Near the trees **sleeps** the *camper.*

V   S

PLURAL   Near the trees **sleep** the *campers.*

Inverted sentences may also begin with the word *there* or *here.* *There* or *here* is almost never the subject of a sentence.

V S

SINGULAR   There **is** a *camper* on the mountain.

V   S

Here **comes** the last *runner.*

V S

PLURAL   There **are** *campers* on the mountain.

V   S

Here **come** the last two *runners.*

In interrogative sentences the subject may come after an auxiliary verb. In this case you will find the subject between the auxiliary verb and the main verb.

V   S V

SINGULAR   **Does** that *eagle* **live** in the mountains?

V   S   V

PLURAL   **Do** those *mountains* **contain** eagles?

V S V

SINGULAR   **Is** the *tent* **pitched** in the right place?

V   S V

PLURAL   **Are** the *tents* **pitched** in the right place?

On your paper write the simple subject in each of the following sentences.
Then write the form of the verb in parentheses that agrees with the subject.

Blues from the Delta

1. In many a rock musician (beats/beat) the heart of a blues musician from the region of the United States known as the Mississippi Delta.
2. There (was/were) a dozen or more influential blues musicians born in the Mississippi Delta in the first two decades of this century.
3. In the group work songs of cotton-field workers (lies/lie) the roots of the Delta blues.
4. On the plantations of the Delta (was/were) heard the music of Robert Johnson, Muddy Waters, and John Lee Hooker, among others.
5. (Do/Does) these names seem familiar to you?
6. Unfortunately, there (is/are) few recordings of the very early musical pieces of some of these blues artists.
7. There (was/were) several musicians who carried the blues north, especially to Chicago, in the 1940s and 1950s.
8. (Was/Were) blues singers Howlin' Wolf and Muddy Waters performing in Chicago then?
9. In the blues (lives/live) a sense of hope, strength, and survival.
10. In the debt of Delta blues musicians (is/are) artists as diverse as the Rolling Stones, Robert Cray, and Whitney Houston.

Exercise 5   **Using Subject-Verb Agreement**

On your paper write the simple subject in each of the following sentences.
Then write the form of the verb in parentheses that agrees with the subject.

SAMPLE   There (is/are) much history to be found in Boston and its surroundings.
ANSWER   history is

Bunker Hill

1. One of many famous monuments (stands/stand) above Boston's Charlestown waterfront.
2. Perhaps the most famous one of the Revolutionary War monuments (is/are) this one on Bunker Hill.
3. South of Bunker Hill and the monument (rises/rise) Breed's Hill.
4. Although the battle fought here was named for Bunker Hill, the true site of the first of many Revolutionary War conflicts (was/were) Breed's Hill.
5. Along the base of Breed's Hill (stretches/stretch) the old battle lines.
6. Among the American leaders in that conflict (was/were) Colonel William Prescott.
7. The hastily organized colonial militiamen (was/were) the "irregular" army that faced the better-organized British force.
8. One outcome of the Battle of Bunker Hill (was/were) the colonists' moral triumph.
9. Several patriotic songs and my favorite poem (is/are) based on the story of the Battle of Bunker Hill.
10. There (is/are) always many tourists at the historical site.

16.4 Agreement with Special Subjects

Collective Nouns

A **collective noun** names a group. Consider a collective noun singular when it refers to a group as a whole. Consider a collective noun plural when it refers to each member of a group individually.

SINGULAR   The **squadron** of planes **soars.**
PLURAL   The **squadron land** one at a time.

SINGULAR   The **crowd cheers.**
PLURAL   The **crowd rush** to find their seats.

Special Nouns

Certain nouns that end in -*s*, such as *mumps, measles,* and *mathematics,* take singular verbs.

SINGULAR   **Mathematics interests** many people.

Certain other nouns that end in -*s*, such as *scissors, pants, binoculars,* and *eyeglasses,* take plural verbs.

PLURAL   The **scissors were** defective
                 Your **pants are** too short.

Many nouns that end in -*ics* may be singular or plural, depending upon their meaning.

SINGULAR   **Politics is** often interesting. [one subject of interest]
PLURAL   His **politics are** shameless. [more than one action of a political nature]

Exercise 6   **Making Verbs Agree with Special Subjects**

On your paper write the simple subject of each sentence. Then write the form of the verb in parentheses that agrees with each subject.

1. The team (was/were) victorious in the state finals.
2. The audience (is/are) expressing their opinions about the play.
3. Diabetes (is/are) a disorder of the body's insulin production.
4. The headphones (is/are) on the table.
5. His ethics (was/were) questioned by the local newspaper.

Nouns of Amount

When a noun of amount refers to a total that is considered as one unit, it is singular. When it refers to a number of individual units, it is plural.

SINGULAR	Four **dollars is** a fair price. [one amount]
PLURAL	Four **dollars lie** on the sidewalk. [four individual bills]
SINGULAR	Two **months is** the waiting period. [one unit of time]
PLURAL	Two **months have gone** by. [two individual time periods]

Titles

A title is always singular, even if a noun within the title is plural.

SINGULAR	***Little Women* delights** readers of all ages.
SINGULAR	***Cakes and Bagels* is** my favorite bakery.

Exercise 7	Making Verbs Agree with Special Subjects

On your paper write the simple subject in each sentence Then write the form of the verb in parentheses that agrees with the subject.

Traditional Japanese Sports

1. After two hours the audience at this demonstration of Japanese sports still (wears/wear) expressions of interest on their faces.
2. In traditional Japanese sports, each team (obeys/obey) strict rituals and rules.
3. More than 1,000 years (has/have) passed since Japanese men began to wrestle in the style known as sumo.
4. Statistics (confirms/confirm) that the average weight of a sumo wrestler is 300 pounds.
5. Fifteen feet (is/are) too far for the average person to throw or push a man weighing several hundred pounds, yet sumo wrestlers routinely perform this feat.
6. *Graceful Giants* (is/are) a good title for a sumo-wrestling film.
7. My binoculars (helps/help) me to appreciate the precise movements of the judo wrestlers.
8. While watching the sword game called *kendo*, a crowd of American spectators (is/are) apt to wonder at the significance of the stylized gestures.
9. Now a family of five (presents/present) individual demonstrations of *kyudo*, or Japanese archery.
10. The whole family (has/have) extraordinary poise and skill.

Compound Subjects Joined by *And*

A compound subject that is joined by *and* or *both . . . and* is plural unless its parts belong to one unit or they both refer to the same person or thing.

PLURAL	The ***lawyer*** and the ***client* are** conversing.
	Both the ***book*** and the ***movie* are** enjoyable.

SINGULAR	***Ham*** and ***eggs* costs** two dollars. [The compound subject is a single unit.]
	Her ***husband*** and ***partner* consults** her. [One person is both husband and partner.]

Compound Subjects Joined by *Or* or *Nor*

With compound subjects joined by *or* or *nor* (or by *either . . . or* or *neither . . . nor*), the verb always agrees with the nearer subject.

PLURAL	*Neither* the ***lawyer*** nor the ***clients* are talking.**
	Either the ***lawyer*** or the ***clients* are talking.**

SINGULAR	*Either* the ***lawyer*** or the ***client* is talking.**
	Neither the ***lawyers*** nor the ***client* is talking.**

Many a, *Every*, and *Each* with Compound Subjects

When *many a*, *every*, or *each* precedes a compound subject, the subject is considered singular.

SINGULAR	*Many a* ***man, woman,*** and ***child* knows** hunger.
	Every ***eagle, owl,*** and ***parrot* fascinates** me.
	Each ***eagle*** and ***owl* is soaring.**

Exercise 8   **Making Verbs Agree with Compound Subjects**

On your paper write the correct form of each verb in parentheses.

1. The writer and his researcher (is/are) working together.
2. Neither the editor nor her assistants (has/have) read the manuscript.
3. Both the book and the magazine article (explains/explain) an important historical event.
4. Every history book, article, and biography by that author (interests/interest) me.
5. Either the biographies or the history book (has/have) won a prize.

16.6 | Intervening Expressions

Certain expressions, such as *accompanied by, as well as, in addition to, plus,* and *together with,* have a meaning that is similar to that of *and,* but they do not form a compound subject. These intervening expressions introduce phrases that modify the subject but do not change its number.

The couple, along with a chaperone, is going to the prom.

> **SINGULAR** ***Snow,*** as well as sleet and ice, **makes** driving difficult.

> **PLURAL** ***Sunshine and warm weather,*** in addition to a day off, **lift** the spirit.

If a singular subject is linked to another noun by an intervening expression, such as *accompanied by,* the subject is still considered singular.

> **SINGULAR** ***Water,*** in addition to food, **is** essential on a camping trip.
> The ***father,*** as well as his daughter, **is arriving.**
> ***Rain,*** accompanied by wind and thunder, **is** predicted for tomorrow.
> ***Practice,*** plus talent, **makes** perfect.
> The ***movie,*** together with the book, **tells** a compelling story.

Exercise 9 | Making Subjects and Verbs Agree When Expressions Intervene

On your paper write the simple subject of each sentence, as well as the form of the verb in parentheses that agrees with the subject.

The Cabots

1. John Cabot's life, as well as his voyages, (is/are) somewhat of a mystery to historians.
2. John Cabot, as well as his son Sebastian, (was/were) sent to explore the Americas.
3. Before Columbus's voyage, John Cabot, plus other navigators, (was/were) planning a westward voyage to Asia.
4. John, accompanied by 18 men, (was/were) scheduled to sail from England in 1497.
5. Five ships in the royal fleet, in addition to John's ship, (was/were) prepared to leave on a second voyage in 1498.
6. A crew mutiny, together with a lack of supplies, (appears/appear) to have doomed the voyage.
7. In 1525 Sebastian Cabot, accompanied by three Spanish vessels, (was/were) expected to develop trade with the Orient.
8. However, Cabot, as well as all his men, (was/were) diverted by news of great wealth in South America.
9. Unfortunately, three years, plus tremendous effort, (was/were) wasted, and Cabot was blamed for the failed expedition.
10. Sebastian Cabot, as well as his father, never (seems/seem) to have attained his exploration goals.

Making Verbs Agree with Their Subjects

On your paper write the correct form of each of the verbs in parentheses.

Struggle for Independence

1. Peru, in addition to other regions of South America, (was/were) ruled by Spain from the 1530s until early in the nineteenth century.
2. The famous Venezuelan Simón Bolívar, as well as the leaders José de San Martín and Antonio José de Sucre, (was/were) foremost in the fight for South American independence.
3. Bolívar's imagination and skills as a military tactician (remains/remain) highly regarded by historians today.
4. This statesman and soldier (was/were) also the author of two great political tracts, *El Manifesto de Cartagena (The Manifesto of Cartagena)* and *La Carta de Jamaica (The Letter from Jamaica)*.
5. Napoleon Bonaparte's European victories over Spain, in addition to the unrest in South America, (was/were) crucial in weakening Spain's power around the globe.
6. Between 1808 and 1819, many a devastating battle and dizzying shift of power (was/were) witnessed on the continent of South America.
7. After neither the United States nor Great Britain (was/were) willing to provide military aid, Bolívar successfully appealed to Haiti in 1815 for money and weapons.
8. Neither flooded flatlands nor ice-covered mountains (was/were) able to stop Bolívar's army from ambushing and defeating the Spanish in New Granada in 1819.
9. In later years Colombia and Peru (was/were) ruled by a dictatorship imposed by the Liberator, as Simón Bolívar became known.
10. Unfortunately, neither Bolívar's parents nor his wife (was/were) alive to witness his triumphs.

Writing Sentences with Compound Subjects and Intervening Expressions

On your paper write 10 sentences, using one of the following items as the subject of each sentence. Make each subject agree with a present-tense verb.

1. peanut butter and jelly
2. neither the plaintiff nor the defendants
3. both the *Times* and the *Chronicle*
4. Mother or her cousin
5. many a soldier and sailor
6. every boy and girl
7. each book and article
8. players as well as coaches
9. helmets, together with knee pads,
10. flowers, in addition to crepe paper,

16.7   Indefinite Pronouns as Subjects

A verb must agree in number with an indefinite pronoun subject.

Indefinite pronouns can be singular or plural, as indicated on the following chart.

Indefinite Pronouns			
Always Singular	each anything nothing everything one something	everyone either someone anyone no one	nobody everybody neither somebody anybody
Always Plural	several many	few	both
Singular or Plural	some most	all none	any

Plural indefinite pronouns take plural verbs. Singular indefinite pronouns take singular verbs.

SINGULAR   When we checked, ***everything* was** as it should be.
               Someone at the door **wants** to talk to you.

PLURAL   ***Many*** in my class **are** good in Spanish.
               Several of my friends **were** at the party.

As indicated on the chart, some indefinite pronouns can be singular or plural, depending upon the nouns to which they refer.

SINGULAR   ***All*** of the money **is** gone. [*All* refers to *money*, a singular noun.]
               Most of the cake **was** gone by noon. [*Most* refers to *cake*, a singular noun.]
PLURAL   ***All*** of the children **want** dessert. [*All* refers to *children*, a plural noun.]
               Most of the students **were** in favor of the field trip. [*Most* refers to *students*, a plural noun.]

Making Verbs Agree with Indefinite Pronoun Subjects

On your paper write the simple subject of each sentence and the form of the verb in parentheses that agrees with the subject.

Consumer Regulation

1. Most of us (is/are) consumers.
2. Someone (needs/need) to inform consumers about product safety and quality.
3. Everyone (wants/want) to save money.
4. Some of the people (says/say) we need better standards and more product regulation.
5. No one (expects/expect) poor quality products.
6. Both of these agencies (protects/protect) consumers.
7. Several of today's advertising claims (is/are) credible.
8. Despite all the new products manufactured each year, few (is/are) recalled.
9. Anyone with complaints (has/have) the opportunity to write or call the Better Business Bureau.
10. Do all of the consumers (considers/consider) Ralph Nader the symbol of consumer protection?

Exercise 13 Writing with Indefinite Pronoun Subjects

On your paper write 10 sentences, using one of the following indefinite pronouns as the subject of each sentence. Make each subject agree with a present-tense verb.

SAMPLE   each
ANSWER   Each of the teachers has a master's degree.

1. everyone
2. several
3. few
4. nobody
5. one
6. many
7. anything
8. either
9. both
10. anybody

Exercise 14 Writing with Indefinite Pronoun Subjects

For each indefinite pronoun listed below, write two sentences, using the pronoun as the subject of both sentences. In the first sentence of each pair, use a singular present-tense verb. In the second sentence, use a plural present-tense verb.

SAMPLE   none
ANSWER   (a.) None of the pudding is for me.
           (b.) None of the fans are happy with the call.

1. some
2. all
3. any
4. most
5. none

Writing Sentences with Indefinite Pronoun Subjects

On your paper write a paragraph about something funny or amusing that happened to you or someone else. Use at least five indefinite pronouns as subjects. Make each subject agree with a present-tense verb.

Correcting Errors in Subject-Verb Agreement

The following sentences contain twenty errors in subject-verb agreement. Locate the sentences with errors, and rewrite those sentences using the correct verb form. (Not every sentence has an error.)

The Circus

1. In the center of the field are a large circus tent, as well as cages of animals.
2. The crowd buy their tickets, and soon each of the animals are led from the cages.
3. One little boy, accompanied by his parents, stare in astonishment at a large bear.
4. On the grass is people eating picnic lunches.
5. There is dishes piled with chicken.
6. Bread and butter seems to be a part of everyone's meal.
7. In most cases the dessert course of these lunches are made with fruit.
8. Suddenly someone shouts, "Here comes the performers!" and this nineteenth-century American circus begin.
9. The originator of modern circuses was the Englishman Philip Astley.
10. In eighteenth-century Europe neither traveling troops of acrobats nor the traditional county fair were able to compete with Astley's circus.
11. The diversity of acts were amazing to the audience.
12. Gymnastics was one of Astley's most popular spectacles.
13. Many of Astley's circuses were established during his lifetime.
14. Although much has changed, circuses remain a major event in most towns today.
15. Many a young boy and girl have been delighted by the exotic animals and amazing performers of a circus.
16. All of the circuses today seems to travel from place to place.
17. Most still has animal acts, although some of them have eliminated these shows.
18. For me, animals, together with a good clown, is the heart of the circus.
19. Every trained elephant, dog, and large cat fascinate me.
20. Most of the people in the audience of a circus agree with me.
21. The audience usually cheer loudest for a good animal act.
22. The origin of circuses, according to my encyclopedia, were in ancient Rome.
23. There, a circus was a stadium; today, a circus are both a public entertainment and a circular arena.
24. In the United States, Phineas T. Barnum, one of the greatest promoters, were responsible for opening the first circus, the "Greatest Show on Earth."
25. The most famous circus of all such spectacles were probably the one Barnum formed when he merged with a rival and established Barnum and Bailey.

Grammar Review

Subject-Verb Agreement

In his novel *Elsewhere, Perhaps,* the Israeli author Amos Oz captures the contradictions of contemporary life in his native country. Set on a kibbutz, or collective farm, near the Israeli frontier, the novel describes how a small, close-knit group copes with the threat of enemy fire and with the individuals' own conflicting dreams and desires. The passage, which has been translated from the Hebrew, has been annotated to show some examples of subject-verb agreement covered in this unit.

Literature Model

from ELSEWHERE, PERHAPS

by Amos Oz
translated from the Hebrew by Nicholas de Lange

You see before you the kibbutz of Metsudat Ram: Its buildings are laid out in strict symmetry at one end of the green valley. The tangled foliage of the trees does not break up the settlement's severe lines, but merely softens them, and adds a dimension of weightiness.

The buildings are whitewashed, and most of them are topped with bright red roofs. This color scheme contrasts sharply with that of the mountain range, which completely blocks the view to the east, and at the foot of which the kibbutz lies spread. The mountains are bare and rocky, cut by zigzagging ravines. With the sun's progress their own shadows spill gradually down these folds, as if the mountains are trying to relieve their desolation with this melancholy shadow play.

Along the lower terraces on the slope stretches the border between our land and that of her enemies.

This border, prominently marked on the maps with a thick green line, is not visible to the observer, since it does not correspond to the natural boundary between the lush green valley and the bleak, bare mountains. The soil of Israel overflows the limits of the valley and spreads up the ➡

Agreement between a singular noun subject and the singular verb *does break* with a plural object of a preposition intervening between subject and verb

Agreement between a plural indefinite pronoun subject and the plural form of *be*

An inverted sentence with agreement between a singular noun subject and the singular form of *stretch* lower slopes toward the barren heights. So the eye and the mind —or, more precisely, geology and politics— come to be at odds with one another. The kibbutz itself stands two miles from the international frontier. We cannot define the distance more precisely without entering into the blood-stained controversy over the exact location of this line.

Agreement between a compound noun subject and the plural form of *come*

The landscape, then, is rich in contrasts, contrasts between appearances and reality and also inner contrasts within the appearances. These can be described only by the term "contradiction." There is a kind of enmity between the valley, with its neat, geometrical patchwork of fields and the savage bleakness of the mountains. Even the symmetrical architecture of Kibbutz Metsudat Ram is no more than a negation of the grim natural chaos that looks down on it from above.

An inverted sentence with agreement between a singular noun subject and the singular form of *be*

Exercise 1

Making Subjects and Verbs Agree When Prepositional Phrases Intervene
Each of the following sentences elaborates on the passage from *Elsewhere, Perhaps.* Rewrite each sentence on your paper, following the directions in parentheses. In some cases you will need to change the form of the verb to make the sentence correct; in other cases the verb will remain the same.

SAMPLE   The description of the scene offers many contrasts.
             (Change *description* to *descriptions.*)
ANSWER   The descriptions of the scene offer many contrasts.

1. The fertile soil of the valley supports several kinds of trees. (Change *soil* to *soils.*)
2. The mountains near the building sites are quite barren. (Change *sites* to *site.*)
3. The ravine on the mountainside creates many shadows. (Change *ravine* to *ravines.*)
4. The red of the rooftop shines brightly. (Change *rooftop* to *rooftops.*)
5. The white walls of the structures glisten in the sun. (Change *structures* to *structure.*)
6. The scene to the east offers only mountains. (Change *scene* to *scenes.*)
7. The views in other directions include much farmland. (Change *views* to *view.*)
8. At Metsudat Ram the people farm the land. (Move the prepositional phrase so that it comes directly after the subject.)
9. Fear of the enemy haunts the kibbutz dwellers. (Change *the enemy* to *enemies.*)
10. Near the mountains the border separates the kibbutz from enemy lands. (Move the first prepositional phrase so that it comes directly after the subject.)

Exercise 2

Writing Sentences with Intervening Prepositional Phrases   The following sentences describe a landscape similar to the one in the passage from *Elsewhere, Perhaps*. On your paper rewrite each sentence, adding an appropriate prepositional phrase in the place indicated by the caret and choosing the correct form of the verb in parentheses.

SAMPLE   The valley ∧ (is/are) green and lush.
ANSWER   The valley beyond the mountains is green and lush.

1. A river ∧ (provides/provide) clear, pure water.
2. The foliage ∧ (makes/make) a beautiful sight.
3. Wildflowers ∧ (grows/grow) here and there.
4. People ∧ (farms/farm) the land.
5. The rich soil ∧ (produces/produce) abundant crops.
6. Cows ∧ (grazes/graze) in the valley.
7. The mountain ∧ (is/are) bare and rocky.
8. Ravines ∧ (makes/make) a zigzag design.
9. The colors ∧ (contrasts/contrast) with those of the valley.
10. The landscape ∧ (presents/present) many such contrasts.

Exercise 3

Making Linking Verbs Agree with Their Subjects   Each of the following sentences describes *Elsewhere, Perhaps*. On your paper rewrite each sentence, following the directions in parentheses. If necessary, change the number of the linking verb.

SAMPLE   The work of Amos Oz is a topic of controversy. (Change *work* to *works*.)
ANSWER   The works of Amos Oz are a topic of controversy.

1. The subject of *Elsewhere, Perhaps* is Israeli kibbutz life. (Change *life* to *dwellers*.)
2. The kibbutz's inhabitants are fictional characters. (Change *fictional characters* to *a fictional creation*.)
3. The kibbutz's name is pure invention. (Change *kibbutz's name* to *characters' names*.)
4. The novel's setting is northern Israel. (Change *northern Israel* to *the northern farmlands*.)
5. The kibbutz remains a dangerous place to live. (Change *The kibbutz* to *These communities*.)
6. The kibbutz dwellers' neighbors are often enemies. (Change *enemies* to *the enemy*.)
7. This passage about Metsudat Ram is mostly description. (Change *This passage* to *These details*.)
8. The descriptions become a study in contrast. (Change *descriptions* to *description*.)
9. The contrasts are reflections of the novel's conflicts. (Change *reflections* to *a reflection*.)
10. The book's main conflicts are the private struggles of the characters. (Change *conflicts* to *focus*.)

Exercise 4

Making Subjects and Verbs Agree in Inverted Sentences   Each of the following sentences describes the kibbutz of the passage from *Elsewhere, Perhaps*. First, write each sentence on your paper, choosing the correct form of the verb in parentheses. Then write each sentence in inverted order, making any necessary adjustments to the verb.

SAMPLE   Metsudat Ram (is/are) near the Golan Heights.
ANSWER   Metsudat Ram is near the Golan Heights.
                  Near the Golan Heights is Metsudat Ram.

1. The kibbutz (stands/stand) near the Syrian border.
2. The settlement (sprawls/sprawl) among the trees.
3. The buildings (lies/lie) in a symmetrical pattern.
4. The kibbutz (shines/shine) in white and red.
5. The mountains (is/are) near the kibbutz.
6. The people (lives/live) beside the mountain.
7. Several ravines (cuts/cut) across the mountain.
8. Rich soil (spreads/spread) up the lower slopes.
9. Dark and eerie shadows (looms/loom) on the mountainside.
10. The Syrian frontier (winds/wind) along the terraces.

Exercise 5

Making Verbs Agree with Special Subjects   The following sentences are about a family touring Jerusalem, the capital of Israel. First, on your paper write the subject in each sentence, and then the form of the verb in parentheses that agrees with that subject.

SAMPLE   A family (is/are) on tour in Israel not by itself but with a group.
ANSWER   family is

1. Three weeks (has/have) passed since the family arrived in Israel.
2. Measles (is/are) the reason the youngest child had to stay home.
3. The group (learns/learn) many facts about Jerusalem from the tour guide.
4. Forty-two square miles (is/are) the city's total area.
5. Statistics (shows/show) that the city has benefited from a multitude of pilgrims and tourists.
6. *Interesting Sights in Jerusalem* (is/are) the name of the book the guide recommends to the group.
7. The majority (wants/want) to see the Old City in East Jerusalem before viewing the more modern West Jerusalem.
8. The family (goes/go) off in opposite directions to see different parts of the city.
9. Binoculars (is/are) handy for surveying areas of the Old City.
10. Approximately 40 feet (is/are) the height of the stone walls surrounding the Old City. ➡

11. One hundred sixty feet (is/are) the length of the Wailing Wall, the holiest Jewish shrine in Jerusalem.
12. A congregation of Christian pilgrims (gathers/gather) outside the Church of the Holy Sepulcher.
13. Two hours (flies/fly) by as they tour the Dome of the Rock, an ancient mosque.
14. The group (disagrees/disagree) over what to do the next day.
15. The crowd in the *souks*, or markets, (is/are) definitely another sight worth seeing in the Old City.
16. The throng in the narrow streets (buys/buy) souvenirs in the small, dark shops.
17. Seventeen thousand (is/are) the approximate number of students attending Hebrew University in Jerusalem.
18. Economics (is/are) one of the most important subjects taught there.
19. The tour group also (enjoys/enjoy) viewing the Knesset, the Israeli parliament.
20. "The People of Jerusalem" (is/are) a magazine article that describes the city's three populations—Jewish, Moslem, and Christian.

Exercise 6

Making Verbs Agree with Compound Subjects   Each of the following sentences describes the nation of Israel. On your paper rewrite each sentence, following the directions in parentheses. Make any necessary adjustments to the form of the verb and to any other words.

SAMPLE   Haifa is among Israel's largest cities. (Add *and Tel Aviv* to the complete subject.)
ANSWER   Haifa and Tel Aviv are among Israel's largest cities.

1. The Mediterranean Sea and the Dead Sea lie off Israel's borders. (Delete *and the Dead Sea* from the complete subject.)
2. Jordan and Syria border Israel. (Delete *and Syria* from the complete subject.)
3. Saudi Arabia is also among Israel's neighbors in the Middle East. (Add *and Egypt* to the complete subject.)
4. Tel Aviv has served as the capital of Israel. (Add *and Jerusalem* to the complete subject.)
5. Many a tourist visits Israel each year. (Add *and historian* to the complete subject.)
6. Virtually every Israeli city has a rich history. (Add *and village* to the complete subject.)
7. The Dead Sea and the Rift Valley also attract many visitors. (Delete *and the Rift Valley* from the complete subject.)
8. Hot, dry summer weather and fairly mild winters help to create a pleasant climate. (Delete *and fairly mild winters* from the complete subject.)
9. Desert irrigation and swamp drainage have produced many farmlands. (Delete *and swamp drainage* from the complete subject.)
10. Tourism is vital to Israel's economy. (Add *and agriculture* to the complete subject.)

Exercise 7

Making Subjects and Verbs Agree When Expressions Intervene   The following sentences are about Hebrew, the language in which Amos Oz writes. On your paper rewrite each sentence, correcting any errors in subject-verb agreement. If the sentence contains no errors, write *correct*.

1. Hebrew, together with Arabic, are spoken in Israel.
2. Yiddish, in addition to Hebrew, are the language of some Israeli authors.
3. The German language, plus the Hebrew alphabet and some Slavic words, form the basis of Yiddish.
4. Jewish traditions from Eastern Europe, as well as the Jewish culture of the Mediterranean countries, have influenced the manner in which Hebrew is pronounced.
5. The chief difference between Eastern European (Ashkenazi) and Mediterranean (Sephardic) Hebrew, in addition to the sound of certain vowels, lie in the way some words are pronounced.
6. Hebrew, as well as Arabic, is a Semitic language.
7. This pair of languages, together with Aramaic, have common roots.
8. Ancient Egyptian, plus several modern Ethiopian tongues, is distantly related to the Semitic languages.
9. The Hebrew alphabet, unlike the English alphabet, includes only consonants.
10. The letters of the alphabet, together with symbols used to indicate the vowels, forms words that can be sounded out phonetically.

Exercise 8

Making Verbs Agree with Indefinite Pronoun Subjects   The following sentences describe Israel's collective communities, or *kibbutzim* (the plural of *kibbutz*), as well as its cooperative communities, or *moshavim* (the plural of *moshav*). On your paper rewrite each sentence, replacing the indefinite pronoun in italics with the pronoun in parentheses. If necessary, change the number of the verb.

SAMPLE   *Each* of the kibbutzim engages in agriculture. (All)
ANSWER   All of the kibbutzim engage in agriculture.

1. *Some* of the kibbutz members raise crops or livestock. (Several)
2. *Many* of the other members run small businesses for kibbutz residents. (Some)
3. *All* are welcome to join a kibbutz. (Anyone)
4. *Each* of the kibbutz residents shares in ownership of the collective's property. (All)
5. *Most* of Israel's farmers live in cooperative communities called moshavim. (Many)
6. In a moshav *all* of the families own a separate plot of land. (each)
7. *Both* of these kinds of communities involve group effort. (Either)
8. *Many* in the group are ready and willing to contribute. (Everybody)
9. *None* are allowed to shirk responsibilities. (No one)
10. *Each* of these kinds of communities is important to the Israeli economy. (Both)

Exercise 9

Making Verbs Agree with Indefinite Pronoun Subjects   The following sentences are about Israel's kibbutzim and moshavim. On your paper write the subject and the correct form of the verb in parentheses for each sentence.

1. No one on the kibbutzim (work/works) for personal profit.
2. Everything on a kibbutz, except personal possessions, (is/are) collectively owned.
3. Each of the members (labors/labor) to capacity.
4. Everyone (receives/receive) according to need.
5. Most of the rooms in the kibbutz (is/are) communal.
6. Most of each community (is/are) cooperatively owned.
7. (Is/Are) all of the kibbutzim entirely agricultural?
8. (Has/Have) none established manufacturing industries?
9. (Does/Do) all of the children attend school?
10. (Does/Do) all of this moshav belong to its residents?

Review: Exercise 10

Proofreading

The following passage describes the artist Elias Newman, whose painting is reproduced on the opposite page. On your paper rewrite the passage, correcting the errors in spelling, grammar, and usage. Add any missing punctuation. There are twenty errors.

Elias Newman

[1]Elias Newman was born in 1903 in the Russian-ruled city of Stashow located in Poland. [2]When he is ten, Newman and his family immigrated to the United States. [3]Growing up in New York City, he studied at the National Academy of Design and the Educational Alliance Art School.

[4]Newman traveled too Europe and the Middle East in 1925. [5]He lived for four years in Palestine (now Israel) a country for which he felt a great kinship. [6]During Newman's stay there, Jerusalem and Tel Aviv was the sites of his solo exhibitions.

[7]Newman returned to New York but he also became involved in the art community of Rockport, Massachusetts, where he had a summer studio. [8]In addition, he begun working with the New York Artists' Equity Association, a leading organization of artists in America. [9]One of Newman's great contributions to the arts have been his work to raise funds for artists in financial need.

[10]Newman's other main endeavor, in addition to helping artists, have been his art. [11]His landscapes of Palestine is among his most famous works. [12]Using watercolors and oil pigments, he create simple and forceful paintings. [13]One critic said of Newmans work, "It has an elusive richness and a depth that may well be part of Palestine's experience." [14]Newman's career have included more than a hundred one-person exhibitions, and he has received many awards. ➡

Elias Newman, *Wadi Musserara,* **1926**

[15]*Wadi Musserara* suggest the light and color of a rural landscape in the Middle East. [16]The elements of the landscape conveys movement and design. [17]The green field and plants in the foreground of this painting becomes a directional device to lead the viewer's eyes first to the meandering river and then into the arid hills far in the background.

[18]The pasage from Amos Oz's novel *Elsewhere, Perhaps* have as its setting an Israeli landscape very similar to the one depicted in Newman's painting. [19]Oz's description of the whitewashed buildings bare mountains, and "zigzagging ravines" could very well be a caption for Newman's work.

Mixed Review

Review: Exercise 11

The following sentences describe the life of Amos Oz. For each sentence write on your paper the subject and the appropriate form of the verb in parentheses.

Amos Oz

1. Amos Oz, together with Nobel Prize winner Shmuel Yosef Agnon, (numbers/number) among Israel's best-known writers of fiction.
2. The author of *Elsewhere, Perhaps* (was/were) born in 1939 in Jerusalem, now Israel's capital.
3. Most of Oz's life since his teenage years (has/have) been lived in a kibbutz.
4. He and his wife and children (has/have) recently moved from a kibbutz in northern Israel.
5. Their home (is/are) now in Israel's southern desert lands.
6. Amos Oz's last name, though not his birth name, (means/mean) "strength" in Hebrew.
7. Most of Oz's fiction (takes/take) place in modern Israel.
8. The relationship between Jews and Arabs (is/are) a dominant concern in Oz's work.
9. From his kibbutz experiences (comes/come) his clear understanding of human conflicts and emotions.
10. *Touch the Water,* as well as Oz's earlier novel *Elsewhere, Perhaps,* (depicts/depict) kibbutz life.
11. Each of these books (has/have) won praise from critics.
12. The most successful of Oz's novels (is/are) *My Michael*, which describes the psychological turmoil of an Israeli wife in a troubled marriage.
13. Oz's poetic novels (is/are) a reflection of the struggles of Israeli life.
14. Many of Oz's own experiences on a kibbutz (forms/form) the basis of his literary work.
15. A large part of Oz's literary earnings (has/have) been given to Kibbutz Hulda.
16. There (is/are) an element of religious poetry running through each of Oz's fictional pieces.
17. Oz's favorite writer of all American writers (is/are) Herman Melville.
18. The conflicts in Israel (is/are) the setting for many of Oz's stories.
19. The Jewish community (has/have) been unanimous in praising Oz's novels and short stories.
20. Oz, in addition to several other noted authors, (writes/write) all of his books in Hebrew.
21. Politics (has/have) played an important role in Oz's life.
22. Both Israelis and readers around the world (has/have) learned about life on a kibbutz from Oz.
23. Neither *My Michael* nor *Elsewhere, Perhaps* (has/have) been made into a motion picture.
24. Amos Oz, along with Isaac Bashevis Singer, (has/have) written stories about specifically Jewish topics.
25. The novels of Amos Oz (is/are) the topic for discussion in class today.

Writing Application

Subject-Verb Agreement in Writing In this passage that voices his opinion about the cable channel MTV, Tom Shales demonstrates correct subject-verb agreement. Examine the passage, focusing especially on the italicized subjects and verbs.

> Not for nothing *has MTV earned* the nickname "Empty-V." Instead of denying that emptiness, however, MTV celebrates it. *Members* of the viewing audience *are* frequently *assured* that they are not to be bothered with matters of consequence. "*MTV News*," which is shown frequently every day, *is* "news" about rock stars, pop stars and silly celebrities—puff and fluff spun in the hype mills of Hollywood.

Techniques with Subject-Verb Agreement Try to apply some of Tom Shales's writing techniques when you write and revise your own work.

1. When you check for agreement in inverted sentences, remember that the subject follows the verb.

Non-inverted Sentence MTV has earned the nickname "Empty-V" not for nothing.
Shales's Correct Use Not for nothing has MTV earned the nickname "Empty-V."

2. Be alert to prepositional phrases and other expressions that fall between a subject and its verb. Mentally block out intervening phrases when you check for subject-verb agreement.

Incorrect Use Members of the viewing audience is frequently assured. . . .
Shales's Correct Use Members of the viewing audience are frequently assured. . . .

3. Remember that certain nouns that end in *-s* take singular verbs.

Incorrect Use "MTV News," which is shown frequently each day, are "news". . .
Shales's Correct Use "MTV News," which is shown frequently each day, is "news". . .

Practice Apply these techniques and others you have learned in this unit by revising the following paragraph. On your own paper, rewrite the paragraph, filling each blank with a verb in the present tense. Make other changes, too. Write at least one sentence as an inverted sentence.

> The islands known as the West Indies _____ in the Caribbean Sea. Trinidad and Tobago, the southernmost nation in the island chain, _____ the home of a type of music known as calypso. During the carnival held each February, many of the country's calypso singers _____ before a large crowd. Most of their music _____ improvised lyrics, and many of the lyrics _____ satirical. Each of the calypso singers _____ a distinct style, and all of them _____ how to please an audience. There _____ many recordings of calypso music. Both tourists and residents _____ recordings of the music to enjoy later. Nothing _____ more memorable about the island republic of Trinidad and Tobago than its calypso music.

Using Pronouns Correctly

17.1 Case of Personal Pronouns

Pronouns that are used to refer to persons or things are called **personal** pronouns.

Personal pronouns have three **cases,** or forms, called **nominative, objective,** and **possessive.** The case of a personal pronoun depends upon the pronoun's function in a sentence (whether it is a subject, an object, a complement, or a replacement for a possessive noun).

Study the chart to recall the case forms of the different personal pronouns.

Personal Pronouns			
Case	**Singular Pronouns**	**Plural Pronouns**	**Function in Sentence**
NOMINATIVE	I, you, she, he, it	we, you, they	subject or predicate nominative
OBJECTIVE	me, you, her, him, it	us, you, them	direct object, indirect object, or object of preposition
POSSESSIVE	my, mine, your, yours, her, hers, his, its	our, ours, your, yours, their, theirs	replacement for possessive noun(s)

Exercise 1   Identifying Pronoun Case

On your paper write each personal pronoun in the sentences below. Then tell what case each is, and how it functions in the sentence.

SAMPLE   My father and I took him to a basketball game last Saturday afternoon.
ANSWER   My—possessive, replacement for possessive noun; I—nominative, subject; him—objective, direct object.

1. We arrived early so that he could see the players shoot practice shots.
2. Our seats put Dad, him, and me near the half-court line.
3. One player smiled at us as she stopped to tie her shoes.
4. She knew that they would be playing their biggest game of the season that day.
5. He held up his pennant and waved it excitedly at her.

To use case of personal pronouns correctly, keep the following rules in mind:

1. Use the nominative case for a personal pronoun in a compound subject.

> Ann and **I** play tennis.   **She** and I are equally matched.

2. Use the objective case for a personal pronoun in a compound object.

> Ann challenged Juan and **her**.   She talked to Sue and **me**.

Hint: When choosing the correct pronoun in a sentence with a compound subject or object, it is helpful to say the sentence to yourself without the conjunction and the other subject or object.

3. After a form of the linking verb *be*, use the nominative case of a personal pronoun.

> The winner was **he**.   Ann hoped that it would be **she**.

The ball bounced toward Ann and me.

Today this rule is changing. In informal speech, people often use the objective case after a form of the linking verb *be*; they say *It's me, It was him*. There are some authorities who even advise using the objective case in informal writing to avoid appearing pretentious. In formal writing, however, always use the nominative case after the linking verb *be*.

4. Do not spell possessive pronouns with apostrophes.

> This paddle is **yours**.   The table is **ours**.

Remember that *it's* is a contraction for *it is*. You should not confuse *it's* with the possessive pronoun *its*.

> **It's** my watch that is lying on the dresser.
> **Its** band must be replaced.

5. Use possessive pronouns before gerunds (*-ing* forms used as nouns).

> **Your** singing relaxes the baby.   He is amused by **my** talking.

Exercise 2	Choosing the Correct Case Form

For each sentence, write the correct personal pronoun from each pair in parentheses.

Satchel Paige, a Legendary Pitcher

1. When Marisa offered to help me with my report on a famous athlete, (she/her) and (I/me) chose Satchel Paige, one of the greatest baseball pitchers of all time.
2. It was (he/him) who became one of the first African Americans in the American League.
3. (He/Him) and Jackie Robinson were among the first African American athletes to play for major-league teams.
4. What impressed Marisa and (I/me) is that Paige never gave up.
5. To (she, her) and (I/me), Paige and his fellow African American players are true heroes.

17.2 Pronouns with and as Appositives

Use the nominative case for a pronoun that is in apposition to a subject or a predicate nominative.

> The candidates, **she** and **Mr. Gomez,** will run for that office. [*Candidates* is the subject.]

> The candidates are two people from our district, **Ms. Pierce** and **he.** [*People* is the predicate nominative.]

Use the objective case for a pronoun that is in apposition to a direct object, an indirect object, or an object of a preposition.

> The crowd favored the local pair, **Hilda** and **her.** [*Pair* is a direct object.]

> I gave my friends **Floyd** and **him** a ticket. [*Friends* is an indirect object.]

> The officials talked to both groups of players, **them** and **us.** [*Groups* is the object of the preposition *to.*]

When a pronoun is followed by an appositive, choose the case of the pronoun that would be correct if the appositive were omitted.

> **We athletes** want to win the cash prize. [*We* is the correct form because *we* is the subject of the sentence.]

> It was **we athletes** who practiced for such long hours. [*We* is the correct form because *we* is a predicate nominative.]

> The school awarded **us athletes** a handsome trophy. [*Us* is the correct form because *us* is the indirect object.]

> The prize was divided evenly among **us athletes.** [*Us* is the correct form because *us* is the object of the preposition *among.*]

Hint: When you are confused about which pronoun to use, try saying the sentence aloud without the appositive.

Exercise 3 — Using Pronouns with and as Appositives

For each sentence in the following paragraph, write the correct pronoun from the pair in parentheses.

An Artistic Triumph

[1]In 1959 two New York City theater critics, Brooks Atkinson and (he/him), praised *A Raisin in the Sun*, Lorraine Hansberry's play about the struggles of an African American family. [2]The acting by the stars, Sidney Poitier, Diana Sands, Ruby Dee, and (she/her), was widely applauded. [3]The play was also praised by two famous American playwrights, Tennessee Williams and (he/him). [4]Even today (we/us) young actors are very fortunate to be able to work with such a well-written script. [5]The character of Beneatha, a young girl searching for her identity, had a great impact on one young actor, (I/me).

Exercise 4 — Using Pronouns Correctly with and as Appositives

For each of the following sentences, write the correct personal pronoun from each pair in parentheses.

The Game of Tennis

1. (We / Us) American tennis players would like to claim that tennis, like baseball, was invented in the United States.
2. Our British friends, Jason and (she/her), told us that modern tennis was first played in Britain in the nineteenth century.
3. In preparing a report for our social studies class, the research team, Owen, Marjorie, and (I/me), discovered that the ancestor of tennis was a twelfth-century French handball game.
4. It was two student teachers, Ms. Liu and (she/her), who pointed us to the right sources.
5. It was a surprise to (we/us) hard-working researchers to learn that a version of the French game, called court tennis, is still played in Britain today.
6. Apparently Major Walter Clopton Wingfield, an English gentleman, introduced modern lawn tennis at a party on his estate in 1873—a fact that intrigued (we/us) investigators.
7. We learned from our British friends Claire and (he/him) that the game was brought to America in 1874 by Mary Ewing Outerbridge, who had learned to play tennis during a visit to Bermuda.
8. An article found by two of our school librarians, Ms. Denver and (she/her), said that the tennis court was originally shaped like an hourglass.
9. The chief librarian, Mr. Wolfe, also gave (we/us) researchers several articles that made our report a resounding success.
10. (We/ Us) proud students sent a copy of our report to our advisors Ms. Denver, Ms. Bueno, and (he/him).
11. The librarians and (we, us) students decided to submit the report to a student research contest.
12. Entry forms were filled out by Owen and (I, me) and cosigned by teachers Ms. Bueno and (he, him).
13. A letter came in about six weeks to (we, us) anxious researchers.
14. It was addressed to the two librarians, Mr. Wolfe and (she, her), as well as to (we, us).
15. (We, Us) three—Marjorie, Owen, and (I, me)—had won third prize.

17.3   Pronouns After *Than* and *As*

In elliptical adverb clauses using *than* and *as*, choose the case of the pronoun that you would use if the missing words were fully expressed.

> You finished the puzzle faster than **he.** [The nominative pronoun *he* is the subject of the incomplete adverb clause *than he finished the puzzle.*]

> The movie frightened John as much as **them.** [The objective pronoun *them* is the direct object of the incomplete adverb clause *as much as it frightened them.*]

Some sentences can be completed with either a nominative or an objective pronoun, depending on the meaning intended.

> Tony angered Dana more than **I** [angered her].

> Tony angered Dana more than [he angered] **me.**

In informal speech people often use the objective rather than the nominative form in sentences like *My sister is six years younger than me.* In your writing, however, you should be careful to use the correct case.

Exercise 5   Substituting Pronouns After *Than* and *As*

Each sentence contains an italicized word or group of words. Write on your paper the correct pronoun to substitute for the words in italics.

SAMPLE   Polar bears are more maternal than *other animals.*
ANSWER   they

The Good Mother

1. Mother polar bears seem to take parenting more seriously than *other animals.*
2. Few animals provide as much parental care as *mother polar bears.*
3. Nothing is as important to polar bear cubs as *their mother.*
4. The mother polar bear needs to care for herself as well as *the cubs.*
5. After two-and-a-half years, the cubs will be as independent as *their mother.*
6. In the meantime, they are more dependent on their mother than *most animals.*
7. When the cubs are born, their eyes are not yet open, and the cubs are not as large as *one of their mother's paws.*
8. It will be years before the cubs are as large as *their mother.*
9. A fully grown polar bear may weigh well over 900 pounds—as much as *five large people.*
10. The adult polar bear hunts and eats fish as skillfully as *seals.*

Who will receive
my letter?

To **whom** it
may concern.

Use the nominative pronoun *who* for subjects.

> **Who** called this morning? [*Who* is the subject of the verb *called*.]

> Tell us **who is in charge here**. [*Who* is the subject of the noun clause *who is in charge here*.]

Use the objective pronoun *whom* for the direct or indirect object of a verb or verbal or for the object of a preposition.

> **Whom** are you telling? [*Whom* is the direct object of the verb *are telling*.]

> **Whom** did she want to tell? [*Whom* is the direct object of the verbal *to tell*.]

> **Whom** did you give the report? [*Whom* is the indirect object of the verb *did give*.]

> Jaime asked her **whom** she had seen at the party. [*Whom* is the direct object of the verb *had seen* in the noun clause *whom she had seen at the party*.]

> Bette Bao Lord is a writer about **whom** I know very little. [*Whom* is the object of the preposition *about* in the adjective clause *about whom I know very little*.]

When a question contains an interrupting expression such as *do you think*, it helps to omit the interrupting phrase to determine whether to use *who* or *whom*.

> **Who** do you think gave the best oral report? [Think: *Who* gave the best oral report? *Who* is the subject of the verb *gave*.]

> **Whom** do you think you are asking? [Think: *Whom* are you asking? *Whom* is the direct object of the verb *are asking*.]

When speaking informally, people often use *who* instead of *whom* in sentences like *Who are you calling?* In writing and in formal speech, we should distinguish between *who* and *whom*.

Choosing *Who* or *Whom*

For each sentence in the following paragraphs, write on your paper the correct pronoun from each pair in parentheses.

Stories from Greek Mythology

a. ¹(Who/Whom) do you think the Greeks honored as the goddess of agriculture? ²Hades, (who/whom) ruled the underworld, admired Persephone, the daughter of Demeter, and he kidnapped her. ³Persephone, (who/whom) Hades made queen of the underworld, could not escape. ⁴Demeter, (who/whom) had grown angry at the loss of her daughter, refused to allow any crops to grow. ⁵Hades was persuaded by Zeus, (who/whom) the gods must obey, to let Persephone return for part of each year so that the crops would grow.

b. ¹(Who/Whom) did you say was the supreme architect and inventor of his time, according to Greek mythology? ²King Minos of Crete kept a terrible monster called the Minotaur, for (who/whom) he commanded Daedalus, a skilled craftsman, to build a labyrinth where the monster could safely be kept. ³King Minos was delighted with Daedalus, (who/whom) he would not allow to leave Crete lest Daedalus reveal the secret of the labyrinth he had designed. ⁴Daedalus therefore used feathers and wax to build wings for himself and his son, Icarus, (who/whom) Daedalus warned not to fly too close to the sun. ⁵Icarus, (who/whom) was a vain and foolish boy, ignored his father's warning and did fly too near the sun; consequently, the wax in the wings melted, causing him to fall to his death in the sea.

Using *Who* or *Whom* in Sentences

On your paper write the correct word *who* or *whom*, to complete each sentence.

The Pueblo, a Native American People

1. Reuben and his older sister, Lara, _____ is a college professor, visited several Pueblo villages in Arizona and New Mexico last summer.
2. Reuben, for _____ the trip was a dream fulfilled, had saved several hundred dollars to help pay his way.
3. He had been interested in these Native Americans, _____ many others also admire, for a long time.
4. His sister, _____ he had begged to take him on this trip, is an expert on Native American peoples.
5. The Pueblo, _____ are an ancient people, actually consist of several different groups, each speaking a different language.
6. Besides the Hopi, Acoma, Laguna, Taos, and Tewa nations, there is the Zuñi group, for _____ one of the Pueblo languages is named.
7. According to Reuben's sister, _____ many Native Americans honor for her scholarly work, the Pueblo are best known for their large adobe dwellings.
8. Their conquerors, the Spanish, _____ the Pueblo grudgingly tolerated, named the people after their dwellings (*pueblo* is the Spanish word for "village").
9. _____ do you think is the Pueblo individual Reuben most admires?
10. He admires Popé, the leader _____ drove the Spanish off the Tewa lands in 1680.

An **antecedent** is the word or group of words to which a pronoun refers or that a pronoun replaces. All pronouns must agree with their antecedents in number, gender, and person.

Agreement in Number and Gender

A pronoun must agree with its antecedent in number (singular or plural) and gender (masculine, feminine, or neuter).

The antecedent of a pronoun may be a noun, another pronoun, or a phrase or clause acting as a noun. In the examples that follow, the pronouns appear in bold type and their antecedents appear in bold italic type:

> ***Emily Brontë*** published **her** novel, *Wuthering Heights*, in 1847. [singular feminine pronoun]
>
> ***Emily, Charlotte,*** and ***Anne Brontë*** published **their** collected poems in 1845. [plural pronoun]
>
> ***Langston Hughes*** published **his** first volume of poetry, *The Weary Blues,* in 1926. [singular masculine pronoun]
>
> ***Simon J. Ortiz*** and ***Diana Chang*** have also published poems that reflect **their** backgrounds. [plural pronoun]
>
> The ***spruce,*** because of **its** soft wood, is used to make paper. [singular neuter pronoun]
>
> ***Spruce*** and ***aspen*** are economical to raise because of **their** rapid growth. [plural pronoun]

When the gender of the antecedent is not known or when it may be either masculine or feminine, a masculine pronoun is traditionally used.

> A ***skier*** must keep **his** legs strong and limber.

There is a degree of controversy concerning this rule, however, and some people now prefer to use more gender-neutral wording. If you do not wish to use a masculine pronoun, you can frequently reword the sentence in one of three ways: (1) by using *he or she, his or her,* and so forth, (2) by using a plural pronoun, or (3) by eliminating the pronoun.

> A ***performer*** must understand **his** role.
> A ***performer*** must understand **his or her** role.
> ***Performers*** must understand **their** roles.
> A ***performer*** must understand a role. [no pronoun]

Agreement in Person

A pronoun must agree in person with its antecedent.

Be sure not to refer to an antecedent in the third person by using the second-person pronoun *you*. Use either an appropriate third-person pronoun or a suitable noun.

POOR	Richard and Clara are going to a store where ~~you~~ can buy brand-name clothing at reasonable prices.
BETTER	Richard and Clara are going to a store where **they** can buy brand-name clothing at reasonable prices.
BETTER	Richard and Clara are going to a store where **shoppers** can buy brand-name clothing at reasonable prices.

When a pronoun has another pronoun as its antecedent, the two pronouns should agree in person. Avoid shifting pronouns unnecessarily, as from *they* to *you*, *I* to *you*, or *one* to *you*.

POOR	**They** spent several days in Rome, where ~~you~~ could sense history along every street.
BETTER	**They** spent several days in Rome, where **they** could sense history along every street.
POOR	**I** learned that ~~you~~ cannot see all of Rome in two days.
BETTER	**I** learned that **I** cannot see all of Rome in two days.
POOR	If **one** reads newspapers, ~~you~~ will understand current events.
BETTER	If **one** reads newspapers, **one** will understand current events.
BETTER	If **you** read newspapers, **you** will understand current events.

| Exercise 8 | Making Pronouns and Antecedents Agree |

On your paper complete the following sentences by replacing each blank with an appropriate possessive pronoun. Also write the antecedent of each pronoun that you supply.

Pablo Neruda, Chilean Poet

[1]Like any poet who understands _____ life and times, Pablo Neruda touched deep emotional chords. [2]At the age of 12, he met Gabriela Mistral, a famous Chilean poet, who introduced him to some of _____ favorite authors. [3]Both Neruda and Mistral have been honored for _____ achievements; both poets won the Nobel Prize for literature. [4]When I read Neruda's beautiful verses about the forests and glaciers of southern Chile, I renewed _____ vow to visit Chile someday. [5]My brother and I want to take a trip to Isla Negra; _____ intention is to visit the house in which Pablo Neruda lived for many years.

Making Pronouns and Antecedents Agree

In each of the following sentences, find each personal pronoun and its antecedent. (Some sentences have more than one personal pronoun.) Then revise the sentence in one or more ways to correct the problem or problems in pronoun-antecedent agreement.

The Art of Raku

1. A person who is good at making pottery may like to test their skills by learning to make *raku,* a kind of Japanese earthenware.
2. For centuries a handful of Japanese *raku* artists have been perfecting his craft and passing it down from generation to generation.
3. Students who wish to learn to make *raku* will find that the art tests his patience, for the ceramics often break.
4. The potter throws their *raku* bowls, dries them and paints them with glaze, and then fires them one by one in a kiln until they are red-hot.
5. A *raku* expert may also take their glowing pots from the kiln and throw them into cold water to crack the glaze, but in the process their pots often shatter.

Making Pronouns and Antecedents Agree in Person

On your paper rewrite each of the following items, eliminating the inappropriate use of *you* by substituting a third-person pronoun or a suitable noun or nouns. You may also have to change other words.

Life in Ancient Greece

1. The ancient Greeks ate only two meals a day. You ate in midmorning and then again at sunset.
2. Men and women in Ancient Greece wore tunics. They wore a brown one for work, but you wore a bleached one for special occasions.
3. There were three social classes in Athens, where you might be a citizen, an enslaved person, or a resident alien.
4. The women in Ancient Greece led a more restricted life than the men did. You spent a great deal of your time in the home.
5. Children in the city of Athens attended school, where you learned to wrestle, handle weapons, sing, read, and write.
6. The ancient Greeks were the first to develop the idea of democracy, and they encouraged you to play an active role in government.
7. Only citizens could participate in government. The ancient Greeks usually denied you citizenship unless your father was a citizen.
8. A person could not own land in ancient Greece unless you were a citizen .
9. The people of ancient Greece valued learning. You could hear the world's finest orators, philosophers, and poets there.
10. The Greeks were dominant in the eastern Mediterranean for several centuries. You could hardly travel anywhere without seeing their influence.

Agreement with Indefinite Pronoun Antecedents

In general, use a singular personal pronoun when the antecedent is a singular indefinite pronoun, and use a plural personal pronoun when the antecedent is a plural indefinite pronoun.

Indefinite Pronouns				
Always Singular	each either neither one	everyone everybody everything no one	nobody nothing anyone anybody	anything someone somebody something
Always Plural	several others	few	both	many
Singular or Plural	some none	all	any	most

Neither of the men wants to drive **his** car to work.
Each of the girls rides **her** bicycle to school.
Several of the neighbors make **their** commute by train.

Notice that the number of the personal pronouns is not affected by the plural nouns in the prepositional phrases—*of the men, of the girls.* The personal pronouns *his* and *her* are singular because *neither* and *each*, their antecedents, are singular. When speaking, however, people often use the plural pronoun *their* in such sentences.

INFORMAL   **Neither** of the men drove **their** cars to work.

Writers traditionally make a masculine pronoun agree with an indefinite antecedent when no gender is specified.

Everyone should ride **his** bicycle to school.

Again, this rule is changing, because some people now prefer more gender-neutral wording. If you do not want to use a masculine pronoun when the indefinite pronoun may refer to a female, you can reword your sentence. You might replace the singular indefinite pronoun with a plural one or with an appropriate noun, or you might omit the personal pronoun altogether. (Some people use two pronouns—*his or her*—but many writers consider such wording awkward.)

All should ride **their** bicycles to school.
All students should ride **their** bicycles to school.
Everyone should ride a bicycle to school. [no pronoun]

Making Pronouns Agree with Indefinite Pronoun Antecedents

Write the singular or plural personal pronoun that correctly completes each sentence.

The Reign of Italian Opera

1. Nearly all of the audiences in eighteenth-century Europe selected opera as _____ first choice of contemporary music.
2. Most of the European composers in the 1700s used Italian librettos, or poetic text, in _____ music.
3. In serious opera, each of those librettists, or writers, used the language and melody to give _____ characters depth.
4. In comic opera, one of the playwrights introduced comic situations in _____ operas.
5. Each of Goldini's characters stated _____ point of view at the end of each comic act.
6. Few of the French intellectuals gave _____ approval to Italian opera until the comic opera *La serva padrona* was presented in Paris.
7. One of the French aristocrats wanted _____ government to censor the Italian operas.
8. Almost everyone wanted _____ city to build beautiful new opera theaters in the eighteenth century.
9. Several of the nobility held _____ private parties in the large halls of the Italian opera theaters.
10. One of the most famous composers in the world wrote _____ greatest masterpieces for Italian-style opera.

Making Pronouns Agree with Indefinite Pronoun Antecedents

On your paper write *correct* for each sentence that is correct. Then revise each of the incorrect sentences to make it correct. Most sentences can be revised in more than one way.

African Sculpture

1. Many of the societies in Africa are known for the splendor of its sculptures.
2. Very few of the traditional African sculptors made their figures and masks from stone; most used wood, ivory, clay, and different metals.
3. Practically all of the sculptures in an African society played its own prominent role in the life of the people.
4. For example, each of the households of the Ijo people of Nigeria had a statue of their guardian spirit.
5. All of the children of the Teke people of the Congo River valley would be protected by his own spirit figure.
6. Some of the ancient brass sculptures of the Yoruba people fascinated archaeologists with its naturalistic representations of royal figures and their attendants.
7. Almost all of the traditional societies in Africa created statues to honor their dead.
8. When portrayed in a statue, each of the kings of the Kuba tribe would sit stiffly with their legs crossed.
9. Many of the Central African societies followed a tradition in which its women made pottery while its men created sculptures.
10. Anyone studying African sculpture can discover for themselves the majestic beauty that was part of the daily lives of African people.

Make sure that the antecedent of a pronoun is clearly stated and that a pronoun cannot possibly refer to more than one antecedent.

Vague and Ambiguous Pronoun Reference

Do not use the pronouns *this*, *that*, *which*, and *it* without a clearly stated antecedent.

> Luisa is a fine athlete, and was obvious from her gymnastic feats.

VAGUE	Luisa is a fine athlete, and **this** was obvious from her gymnastic feats. [What was obvious from her gymnastic feats? Her athletic ability was obvious, but the words *athletic ability* have not been specifically mentioned.]
CLEAR	Luisa is a fine athlete, and **her athletic ability** was obvious from her gymnastic feats.
VAGUE	Katrina and Yuki were arguing, **which** started from a misunderstanding. [What started from a misunderstanding? An argument started, but *argument* does not appear in the sentence.]
CLEAR	Katrina and Yuki were having an argument, **which** started from a misunderstanding.
VAGUE	Earl wants to be a doctor because **it** interests him. [What interests him? Medicine does, but *medicine* has not been specifically mentioned.]
CLEAR	Earl wants to be a doctor because **medicine** interests him.

If a pronoun seems to refer to more than one antecedent, either reword the sentence to make the antecedent clear or eliminate the pronoun.

UNCLEAR ANTECEDENT	When the apples fell among the leaves, **they** were hidden. [Which word is the antecedent of *they*? Were the apples or the leaves hidden?]
CLEAR ANTECEDENT	The apples were hidden when **they** fell among the leaves.
NO PRONOUN	When the apples fell among the leaves, **the apples** were hidden.
NO PRONOUN	The fallen apples were hidden among the leaves.

Indefinite Use of Pronouns

Avoid the indefinite use of the pronouns *you* and *they*.

INDEFINITE	In areas that get little rain, **you** must irrigate the crops.
CLEAR	In areas that get little rain, **farmers** must irrigate the crops.
INDEFINITE	In some companies **they** do not work on Fridays during the summer months.
CLEAR	In some companies **employees** do not work on Fridays during the summer months.

Exercise 13   Replacing Unclear Pronoun References

On your paper rewrite each sentence to eliminate the use of the unclear pronoun reference. The pronoun you should replace is indicated in italics.

Gothic Art

1. *You* call medieval Italian art Gothic because the Goths invaded Italy during the Middle Ages.
2. Gothic cathedrals originally had simple lines, but *they* became increasingly ornate.
3. Gothic architects used stained-glass windows, and *they* told religious stories.
4. In Gothic cathedrals *they* used flying buttresses, stone structures against the outside walls, to help support the vaulting.
5. When painters illustrated Gothic manuscripts, *they* sometimes depicted royal families.

Exercise 14   Making Pronoun References Clear

On your paper rewrite the following sentences, making all pronoun references clear. In some cases you may choose to eliminate the pronoun entirely.

Coping with Stress

1. In most industrial societies, they are affected by stress.
2. People can feel anxious about both joyful and sad events, and this affects their health.
3. The Alexanders went on vacation with the Harrises last summer, and they felt anxious about spending so much money.
4. When my brother Richard beat his best friend in a tennis tournament, he suffered a great deal of stress.
5. Richard's spectacular performance at the tournament made him feel guilty, and this surprised everyone.
6. When Mrs. Wong told Carrie that the company they worked for was closing, she became depressed.
7. When a family moves to a new city, it can cause anxiety.
8. In psychology books they often discuss stress.
9. When doctors recommend that patients maintain a good diet and exercise to alleviate stress, they know it will help.
10. Scientists are evaluating the effects of stress on health, and it will have much impact on the medical profession.

Review: Using Pronouns Correctly

On your paper rewrite the following sentences, eliminating any mistakes in the use of pronouns. Each item has one error.

Special Effects

1. My brother Roy and me know much about special effects.
2. Each of us has their own special area of knowledge.
3. Desmond told me that they made the cyclone in *The Wizard of Oz* with a tube of fabric moved by a wind machine.
4. Whom did you say made the shark robots for *Jaws*?
5. One robot was used for side views of the shark, while another was used for the famous close-ups of it's jaws.
6. Actors depend upon special makeup to change their appearance, which most people take for granted.
7. In *Driving Miss Daisy* the stars grow 30 years older; them aging so believably is partly due to great makeup.
8. No one was more surprised than me to discover that the very first movies had special effects.
9. *A Trip to the Moon* was made by the Lumière brothers; it was them who first used special effects to simulate space travel.
10. I guess my favorite special effect occurs during the moment in *Star Wars* when you see the spaceship reach the speed of light.
11. *Star Wars* was made by filmmaker George Lucas, who we all recognize as a trailblazer in the field of special effects.
12. What makes each of his films so remarkable is their use of computer animation.
13. The special-effects breakthroughs in *The Abyss* and *Terminator 2* seemed remarkable to we film buffs, Roy and me.
14. George Lucas is also one of the innovators whom is involved in making computer games of his films.
15. X-Wing is a space-combat simulator. The player pilots his or her Rebel Alliance craft against Darth Vader's Imperial Forces, which is a lot of fun.
16. The game is produced in 3-D, and their sound effects respond to the player, who makes the choices.
17. Do you remember Princess Leia, who had a high-pitched voice? It is her whose whiny commands the game simulates.
18. I, who love computer games, am grateful to George Lucas for him creating this game.
19. Games of the future will let we players move more dramatically and control the actions of their characters more completely.
20. No one could be happier than I to hear that everyone will, in effect, be able to direct the outcome of their own game.

Grammar Review

Using Pronouns Correctly

Written by the West African writer and teacher William Conton, *The African* tells the story of a young man named Kisimi Kamara, who excels in his studies in West Africa and England and launches a successful political career. In this passage, which has been annotated to show some of the kinds of pronouns covered in this unit, Kisimi describes the village where he grew up.

Literature Model

from THE AFRICAN

by William Conton

My name is Kisimi Kamara.

Pronoun in the nominative case used as a subject

I was born at the height of a rainy season, in the village of Lokko in the British West African colony of Songhai. My father cultivated an acre of tired red soil round our hut and fished a near-by muddy stream, wringing from these unimpressive resources a livelihood which most of the other villagers regarded as enviable. I was the second son and the fifth child in a family of eleven, and my childhood was consequently quite unspoilt. . . .

Pronoun in the possessive case

We lived right on the main road; and, it being the first house you came across as you entered the village, now and then a car or lorry would draw up to obtain water for a hissing radiator or for parched throats, or to buy some of my mother's goods. That was always a tremendous event for us children. We grew to tell quite a long way ahead, from the note of the engine, whether or not the driver was looking for somewhere to stop; and we would race out to inspect with solemn awe the wheezing machines we believed to be possessed of some mighty spirit, the conjuring up of which had been done in a distant land called Britain. The supercilious drivers who looked so knowingly under bonnets and chassis during the halt we thought of as a type of high priest, ministering to this spirit; and we would hand them a leaking kerosene tin of muddy well- ➡

The pronoun *us* is followed by the appositive *children.* As the object of a preposition, the pronoun appears in the objective case.

Pronoun *who* in the nominative case used as the subject of *looked* water with almost as much reverence as a server passing the bishop the holy water. The dust-covered passengers, however, we somehow despised rather than envied; for **they** seemed so helpless and unhappy, whether they were in the first-class compartment beside the driver, or in the second-class behind.

> The pronoun *they* in the nominative case is used as a subject. The pronoun agrees in number with its antecedent, *passengers.*

In fact not one of **us** would have allowed himself to be carried a yard away from home in any mechanical contraption of any kind. Our world was then a supremely secure one; and we felt instinctively that those flying lorries, with their cloaks of red dust billowing behind them, came from another world that was not nearly so secure or safe; that they were in some way harbingers of evil. . . .

> Pronoun in the objective case used as the object of a preposition

The village we all loved so well consisted of perhaps twenty mud houses grouped in compounds on either side of the main road. Each compound contained four or five houses arranged in a hollow square. One of these compounds, the biggest by far, was the chief's. **His** was the only house with corrugated iron roofing. Not even his wives' houses in the same compound had this luxury.

> Agreement in number and gender between the possessive pronoun *his* and its antecedent, *chief's*

Exercise 1

Choosing the Correct Pronoun Case   The following sentences elaborate on ideas suggested by the passage from *The African.* Write each sentence on your paper, replacing each italicized word or group of words with an appropriate pronoun. Note that the sentences are written, as the passage is, from Kisimi Kamara's first-person point of view.

SAMPLE   My name is Kisimi Kamara. My family included *Kisimi,* my parents, and my siblings.

ANSWER   My family included me, my parents, and my siblings.

1. Of the children in our household, the second-oldest son was *Kisimi*.
2. Despite our meager resources many of the other villagers envied *Kisimi* and my family.
3. The acre of land that surrounded the family hut was *my family's property*.
4. Similarly, the land around our neighbors' huts was *our neighbors' property*.
5. My father tried to make the soil productive, but *my father's* struggles had little effect.
6. Unfortunately, the tired red soil had lost much of *the soil's* fertility.
7. The best house in the village belonged to the chief, for it was *the chief* who wielded the greatest power.
8. Our neighbors and *my family* lived on the main road that led through the village.
9. Although visitors to our village were rare, it was not really *the visitors* who fascinated us.
10. It was their vehicles that fascinated my brothers and *Kisimi*.

Exercise 2

Using Pronouns Correctly with and as Appositives   The following sentences are based on passages from *The African* that are not reprinted in this textbook. For each sentence determine whether the italicized pronoun appears in the proper form. If it does not, write the pronoun as it should appear. If it is used properly, write *correct*. Note again that the sentences are written from Kisimi Kamara's point of view.

SAMPLE   The villagers, my parents and *them,* worked hard to feed their families.
ANSWER   they

1. My mother devoted much attention to her children, my eight brothers and sisters and *I.*
2. Two members of the family, my elder brother and *her,* ran a small shop in the village.
3. All the men of the village, my father and *them,* fished and cultivated the land.
4. *Us* children were not all able to attend school, for some had to stay home and work.
5. The students, my friends and *me,* enjoyed special status.
6. An American missionary named Miss Schwartz taught the pupils, my friends and *I.*
7. Learning English was important to *us* students, for we knew that it would help us.
8. The two American missionaries, Miss Schwartz and *her,* lived in a bungalow.
9. A Scotsman named Jim Anderson often brought these Americans, Miss Schwartz and *she,* news from district headquarters.
10. I listened to the conversations of these English speakers, the two women and *he.*

Exercise 3

Using Pronouns After *Than* and *As*   The following sentences are based on *The African.* Rewrite each sentence, substituting the correct pronoun for the words in italics. Note that the sentences are written from Kisimi Kamara's point of view.

SAMPLE   The children who could not attend school were less fortunate than *Kisimi.*
ANSWER   The children who could not attend school were less fortunate than I.

1. Because I was able to go to school, I was luckier than *most other village children.*
2. Since all the students were interested in new things, helping out in the teacher's home appealed to me as much as to *the other students.*
3. No volunteers were ever more eager than *the other students and Kisimi.*
4. No one, however, was more anxious to help out than *Kisimi.*
5. The sea of volunteers surprised no one more than *Miss Schwartz.*
6. When Miss Schwartz chose me, no one was happier than *Kisimi.*
7. Few students in the village school did as well as *Kisimi.*
8. The schools in the capital were much larger than *the small village schools.*
9. The prospect of attending secondary school in the capital pleased no one more than *Kisimi and the other students.*
10. When my father left with me for my new school in the capital, no one was more proud than *my father.*

Exercise 4

Choosing *Who* or *Whom*   The following sentences are about Sierra Leone, the West African nation where William Conton has spent most of his life. For each sentence write the correct pronoun from the pair in parentheses.

SAMPLE   William Conton, (who/whom) many critics have praised, lives in Sierra Leone.
ANSWER   whom

1. Sierra Leone was named by Pedro de Sintra, a Portuguese explorer (who/whom) we know lived in the fifteenth century.
2. De Sintra, (who/whom) every schoolchild in Sierra Leone studies, named the country Serra Lyoa, or Lion Mountains.
3. (Who/Whom) did you say are the modern inhabitants of Sierra Leone?
4. There are many people for (who/whom) Sierra Leone is home.
5. The Sierra Leone Creoles, (who/whom) many linguists have studied, are descendants of freed slaves who returned to their native Africa.
6. The Creoles, (who/whom) make up about 2 percent of Sierra Leone's population, developed their own language, Krio.
7. Based on English, Krio also contains African words spoken by the many groups (who/whom) settled in Sierra Leone.
8. Natives of Sierra Leone, each of (who/whom) may speak a different language, often use Krio to communicate when they get together.
9. The many people in the country (who/whom) speak English, the official language of Sierra Leone, also communicate in English.
10. Do you know (who/whom) controlled Sierra Leone during the colonial period?
11. Sierra Leone's people, (who/whom) Britain ruled for more than a century, won their independence in 1961.
12. (Who/Whom) did you tell that the country is bordered on the west by the Atlantic Ocean?
13. I don't know (who/whom) knew that the highest mountain in Sierra Leone is 6,390 feet high.
14. Subsistence farmers (who/whom) produce maize and rice make up a substantial portion of the rural population.
15. Cocoa and coffee are agricultural exports that are profitable for those farmers (who/whom) have larger farms.
16. To (who/whom) do you think go the profits from the export of diamonds and iron?
17. Major population groups include the Mende, Temne, Limba, and Susu, all of (who/whom) are indigenous to the region.
18. Members of the house of representatives, (who/whom) are elected by the people, come from all groups in the country.
19. Did you tell me (who/whom) the first president of the country was?
20. Does anyone in this class know (who/whom) was the most recently elected president of Sierra Leone?

Exercise 5

Making Pronouns and Antecedents Agree   The following sentences elaborate on ideas suggested by *The African*. Each sentence contains an example of pronoun-antecedent agreement. On your paper rewrite the sentences according to the directions given in parentheses, changing the pronouns if necessary. In some cases you will also have to change the form of the verb or another word. Note that the sentences are written from Kisimi Kamara's point of view.

SAMPLE   The village compounds have their huts arranged in a square.
(Change *The village compounds* to *My family's compound*.)

ANSWER   My family's compound has its huts arranged in a square.

1. I spent my youth in a small African village called Lokko in the British West African colony of Songhai.
(Change *I* to *My brothers and I*.)

2. My father farmed his own land and reaped from it a meager harvest.
(Change *My father* to *My father's friends*.)

3. My mother spent her days cooking, sweeping, washing, and caring for her children.
(Change *My mother* to *The women in the village*.)

4. She and my sister also spent many of their waking hours pounding rice.
(Change *She and my sister* to *She*.)

5. At the end of the day, my father slept in his hammock, which hung from the veranda roof.
(Change *my father* to *my parents*.)

6. The babies of the village were carried on their mothers' backs.
(Change *The babies of the village* to *The baby in our family*.)

7. Our mothers hoped that their children would receive a good education.
(Change *Our mothers* to *My mother*.)

8. Our teachers, Miss Schwartz and Miss Costello, did their best to teach us English.
(Change *Our teachers, Miss Schwartz and Miss Costello* to *My teacher, Miss Schwartz*.)

9. English was important to us because it gave us a chance for a better future.
(Change *English* to *Our studies*.)

10. I wanted to go to the capital, where I could study in a big secondary school.
(Change the first *I* to *The students*.)

11. A house in our village had its walls made of mud.
(Change *A house* to *The houses*.)

12. Only the chief had his house covered with corrugated iron roofing.
(Change *Only the chief had* to *Only chiefs could have*.)

13. Drivers along the road might pull their cars into the village for water.
(Change *Drivers* to *An occasional driver*.)

14. A child who spotted a car or truck would quickly tell his friends.
(Change *A child* to *Children*.)

15. We never wanted to put our bodies into those strange vehicles.
(Change *we* to *I*.)

Exercise 6

Making Pronouns Agree with Indefinite Pronoun Antecedents The following sentences are about the storytelling tradition of West Africa. Each sentence contains an example of pronoun-antecedent agreement. Rewrite the sentences according to the directions in parentheses, changing the pronouns if necessary. In some cases you will also have to change the verb. (See page 609 for a list of singular and plural indefinite pronouns. Remember that some pronouns may be either singular or plural, depending upon the context.)

SAMPLE   Each of the storytellers has his favorite stories. (Change *Each* to *All*.)

ANSWER   All of the storytellers have their favorite stories.

1. Most of the folk tales from West Africa have their roots in oral tradition.
   (Change *Most* to *Many*.)
2. All of these stories involve their characters in exciting events.
   (Change *All* to *Each*.)
3. In addition, each of the tales has its educational aspects.
   (Change *each* to *several*.)
4. Much of this body of traditional storytelling also has its historical significance.
   (Change *Much* to *Most*.)
5. Many of West Africa's people call their storytellers *griots*.
   (Change *Many* to *Some*.)
6. People in a rural village give their warmest welcome to a visiting storyteller.
   (Change *People* to *Everyone*.)
7. Most of the children are glad when a griot comes to entertain them.
   (Change *Most* to *Each*.)
8. No one in the village can deny a fascination with the griot's tales.
   (Change *No one* to *Few*.)
9. Each of the storytellers usually asks listeners to join him in his performances.
   (Change *Each* to *All*.)
10. The listeners and the griot enjoy their roles a great deal.
    (Change *The listeners and the griot* to *Both*.)
11. Most of the griots travel from village to village telling their stories.
    (Change *Most* to *Each*.)
12. Some of the tales have their origin in stories told generations ago.
    (Change *Some of the tales* to *Either this tale or that*.)
13. Each one of the griots tells the stories in his own way.
    (Change *Each one* to *All*)
14. A good storyteller incorporates gestures into his storytelling.
    (Change *A good storyteller* to *Many storytellers*.)
15. Have most of this storyteller's tales found their way into print?
    (Change *tales* to *body of work*.)

Exercise 7

Correcting Vague or Ambiguous Pronoun References   The following sentences are based on ideas in the passage from *The African*. Each sentence contains a vague or an ambiguous pronoun reference. On your paper rewrite each sentence to eliminate the unclear pronoun reference. You may have to change only one or two words, or you may find it necessary to revise the entire sentence.

1. Kisimi Kamara was born into a large family in a small African village, which made him an unspoiled child.
2. They had poor land, but other families found the Kamaras's livelihood enviable.
3. Cars stirred up dust as they drove down the dry mud roads, and that must have surprised the children at first.
4. The children watched as the drivers examined their broken-down cars, and they were perplexed by the mechanisms under the hood.
5. Kisimi's father and the village chief both had mud houses, but his roof was made of corrugated iron.

Review: Exercise 8

Proofreading

The following passage describes the artist Clementine Hunter, whose work is reproduced on the opposite page. Rewrite the passage, correcting the errors in spelling, grammar, and usage. Add any missing punctuation. There are twenty-five errors.

Clementine Hunter

[1]The African American artist Clementine Hunter (1887–1988) was borned at the Hidden Hill Plantation near Cloutierville, Louisiana. [2]When she was fifteen, her and her parents moved to nearby Melrose Plantation. [3]She worked in the kitchen and her father and her worked in the cotton fields as well. [4]When Hunter and she family arrived in Melrose, the plantation was being restored. [5]It soon became a monument to a vanishing way of life, attracting writers artists, and tourists.

[6]Hunter made her first paintings on window shades, jars, gourds, skillets and other objects. [7]A French businesman named François Mignon, whom visited Melrose in 1938, grew interested in the place and eventually became the plantations' resident librarian. [8]Mignon noticed one of Hunter's paintings and was astonished at their simple power.

[9]Mignon became Hunters mentor and supporter. [10]Her continued to produce works documenting plantation life—it's harvests, holidays, baptisms and funerals. [11]Her style was abstract and she cared little for proportion or perspective. [12]In the quilt on the opposite page, Hunter stitched together small swatches of fabrik to produce a lively scene of rural life. ➡

Clementine Hunter, patchwork quilt, 1938

¹³Clementine Hunter's skillful use of simple materials and uncluttered dezigns brought she great success. ¹⁴Sold nearly all of her works. ¹⁵Her was presented with an honorary doctorate of fine arts from Northwestern State University in Natchitoches, Louisiana, in 1986.

¹⁶Hunter grew up in poverty in a small, self-contained world and she recorded what she experienced in rich detail. ¹⁷Kisimi Kamara, the narrator of William Conton's *The African* also spent his youth in a poor and confined world, yet he found great beauty in it. ¹⁸Both Hunter and Kisimi Kamara, whom is much like Conton, were keen observers of the world around him.

Exercise 9

Mixed Review

The following sentences describe aspects of William Conton's life and work. For each sentence choose the proper pronoun from the pair in parentheses, and write it on your paper.

William Conton

1. William Conton, (who/whom) we know was born in the tiny West African nation of Gambia, has spent most of his life in Sierra Leone.
2. Readers enjoy Conton's fiction, from which (you/they) can learn a great deal about West African life.
3. Most of Conton's short fiction made (its/their) first appearance in West African journals.
4. Conton's novel *The African* describes the life of an ambitious young man named Kisimi Kamara, (who/whom) Conton resembles in many ways.
5. For example, both Conton and (he/him) went to college in England.
6. Both men, (he/him) and Conton, returned to West Africa in the 1950s, when many independence movements in Africa were growing.
7. Neither of the two West African men was unaffected by (his/their) experiences during those exciting years.
8. All of the people living at that time had (his/their) own vivid stories to tell.
9. Despite the similarities between the author and Kisimi, Conton had a more privileged upbringing than (he/him).
10. Conton was the son of an Anglican minister (who/whom) encouraged him to read at an early age.
11. (His/Him) having such a strong interest in writing no doubt stems from his early love of books.
12. As the child of a rural farm family, Conton's character Kisimi is far less sophisticated than (he/him).
13. Each of the men, Conton and the character Kisimi, nevertheless accomplished many of (his/their) ambitions.
14. Much of Conton's reputation is due to (his/him) holding high office in Sierra Leone.
15. (Who/Whom) do you think serves as Sierra Leone's minister of education?
16. The minister of education is none other than (he/him), William Conton.
17. For that reason Conton has little time to be a prolific author; nevertheless, in Sierra Leone few writers are as famous as (he/him).
18. In 1949 Conton married Bertha Thompson; (she/her) and Conton met when he was teaching in Freetown, the capital of Sierra Leone.
19. In fact, education was the chosen field of both Contons, William and (she/her).
20. The culture of West Africa owes some of (its/it's) richness to the vivid writings of William Conton.

Writing Application

Personal Pronouns in Writing

In the following excerpt from her novel *Song of Solomon*, author Toni Morrison tells about a landlord named Macon Dead and a man named Sonny. As you read, notice the many personal pronouns and focus especially on how the author avoids unclear pronoun references.

> Macon Dead dug in *his* pocket for *his* keys, and curled *his* fingers around *them*, letting *their* bunchy solidity calm *him*. *They* were the keys to all the doors of *his* houses (only four true houses; the rest were really shacks), and *he* fondled *them* from time to time as *he* walked down Not Doctor Street to *his* office. At least *he* thought of it as *his* office, and even painted the word OFFICE on the door. But the plate-glass window contradicted *him*. In peeling gold letters arranged in a semicircle, *his* business establishment was declared to be Sonny's Shop. Scraping the previous owner's name off was hardly worth the trouble since *he* couldn't scrape *it* from anybody's mind.

Techniques with Personal Pronouns

Try to apply some of Toni Morrison's writing techniques when you write and revise.

1. Use pronouns to avoid the awkward, unnecessary repetition of names and words. Compare the following:

Repeated Words . . .dug in his pocket for his *keys*, and curled his fingers around the *keys*, letting the *keys'* bunchy solidity . . .
Morrison's Version . . . dug in his pocket for his *keys*, and curled his fingers around *them*, letting *their* bunchy solidity . . .

2. Make sure each pronoun you use has a clear antecedent.

Unclear Antecedent . . . *his* business establishment was declared to be Sonny's Shop. Scraping *his* name off was hardly worth the trouble . . .
Morrison's Version . . . *his* business establishment was declared to be Sonny's Shop. Scraping *the previous owner's* name off was hardly worth the trouble . . .

Practice Apply the techniques above by revising the following passage on a separate sheet of paper. The passage has been adapted from *Song of Solomon*. Eliminate awkward repetition by using personal pronouns, but also be certain that all your pronoun references are clear.

When Mrs. Bains closed the door, Macon Dead went back to the pages of Macon's accounts book, running Macon's fingertips over the figures and thinking with the unoccupied part of Macon's mind about the first time Macon had called on Ruth Foster's father. Macon had had only two keys in Macon's pocket then, and if Macon had let people like the woman who had just left have such people's way, Macon wouldn't have had any keys at all.

Using Modifiers Correctly

Lessons

18.1 The Three Degrees of Comparison

Most adjectives and adverbs have three degrees of comparison: the positive, or base, form; the comparative form; and the superlative form.

The **positive** form of a modifier cannot be used to make a comparison. (This form appears as the entry word in a dictionary.)

The **comparative** form of a modifier shows two things being compared.

The **superlative** form of a modifier shows three or more things being compared.

POSITIVE	The mechanic's hands are **rough**.
	The canary sang **happily**.
COMPARATIVE	The mechanic's hands are **rougher** than mine.
	My canary sang **more happily** than my neighbor's canary.
SUPERLATIVE	Of the three, his hands are **roughest**.
	The orange canary sang **most happily** of all.

Exercise 1　　　**Identifying Degrees of Comparison**

Write the comparative adjectives and adverbs in the following sentences on your paper. Then indicate the degree of comparison by writing *comparative* or *superlative* after each one.

Early Egyptian Rulers

1. The ancient Egyptians believed that their leaders would rule more wisely than other rulers.
2. One of the most capable rulers was Hatshepsut, the first woman leader in history and a strong leader.
3. Some historians think that she ruled more ably than her father or many later rulers.
4. Hatshepsut's successor, Thutmose III, was more aggressive and set out on a harsh policy of conquest.
5. The pharaoh Amenhotep tried even harder than Thutmose to strengthen the powers of the throne, but he worked hardest at changing religion.

Using The Three Degrees

In general, for one-syllable modifiers add *-er* to form the comparative and *-est* to form the superlative.

> sweet, sweet**er,** sweet**est**
> This is the **sweetest** apple I have ever tasted.

For some words, spelling changes occur when you add *-er* and *-est*.

> sad, sa**dder,** sa**ddest**
> blue, blu**er,** blu**est**
> easy, eas**ier,** eas**iest**

Sometimes it may sound more natural to use *more* and *most* instead of *-er* and *-est* with one-syllable modifiers.

> sour, **more** sour, **most** sour
> That was the **most sour** lemon I have ever tasted.

For most two-syllable adjectives add *-er* to form the comparative and *-est* to form the superlative.

> gentle, gentl**er,** gentl**est**
> The black dog is **gentler** than the brown one.

> happy, happ**ier,** happ**iest**
> My dog is the **happiest** one in the neighborhood.

Use *more* and *most* if *-er* and *-est* sound awkward.

> helpful, **more** helpful, **most** helpful
> No one was **more helpful** than Rita.

For adverbs ending in *-ly,* always use *more* and *most* to form the comparative and superlative degrees.

> quickly, **more** quickly, **most** quickly
> I am able to run **more quickly** in cold weather.

For modifiers of three or more syllables, always use *more* and *most* to form the comparative and superlative degrees.

> delicious, **more** delicious, **most** delicious
> I think pears are **more delicious** than apples.

Less and *least,* the opposite of *more* and *most,* can also be used with most modifiers to show comparison.

> Rosa is **less talkative** than Daryl.
> Bea is the **least talkative** person I know.

Write the word or words that would complete the following sentences with the correct degree of comparison of the modifier in parentheses. (You may need to use the positive degree as well as the comparative and superlative.)

The Early Civilizations of the Middle East

1. Civilizations arose _____ in the Middle East than they did in most parts of the world. (early)
2. More than 5,000 years ago, the _____ civilizations known to historians developed in that region. (old)
3. For the approximately 2,000 years that the Sumerians ruled Mesopotamia, religion played an _____ role. (important)
4. Four Sumerian deities were the _____ of all: the goddess of earth and the gods of water, air, and heaven. (important)
5. To honor their deities, the Sumerians built _____ shrines and temples. (grand)
6. Thousands of workers labored hard for years to build the _____ temple in the empire. (grand)
7. Each story was _____ in area than the one directly beneath it. (small)
8. The top story of the temple, which dominated the entire city, was the _____ of all the stories. (small)
9. The Babylonian empire, which succeeded the Sumerian, was _____ than the Sumerian empire. (strong)
10. Hammurabi, a famous leader, issued a single code of law that centralized the government _____ than it had been centralized under Sumerian rule. (tightly)
11. The code did not grant women equality with men, but it made owning property and borrowing and lending money _____ than before. (easy)
12. In many ways women in Babylonia were able to act _____ than those in any other ancient civilization. (freely)
13. Punishments for violating the laws in the code were harsh, and the _____ penalty of all was death. (harsh)
14. Babylonia fell to the Assyrians, who were the _____ rulers ever to control Mesopotamia. (harsh)
15. The Assyrians were the _____ warriors on horseback. (fast)
16. Within their vast empire, the Assyrians built the _____ system of communication ever seen. (speedy)
17. Encompassing almost all of the Fertile Crescent, the Chaldean empire was the _____ of the Middle Eastern empires. (large)
18. One famous leader, Nebuchadnezzer, constructed _____ fortifications and buildings. (impressive)
19. None was _____ than his own elaborate palace with its lush hanging gardens. (impressive)
20. These gardens, known as one of the seven wonders of the world, were built in Babylon, the _____ city in all of Mesopotamia. (famous)

18.2 Irregular Comparisons

A few modifiers have irregular forms.

Modifiers with Irregular Forms of Comparison		
Positive	Comparative	Superlative
good	better	(the) best
well	better	(the) best
bad	worse	(the) worst
badly	worse	(the) worst
ill	worse	(the) worst
far (distance)	farther	(the) farthest
far (degree, time)	further	(the) furthest
little (amount)	less	(the) least
many	more	(the) most
much	more	(the) most

Exercise 3   Making Correct Comparisons

Complete the following sentences with the correct degree of comparison of the modifier in parentheses. (The positive degree is used in four sentences.)

SAMPLE   Lea's drawings are _____ than mine. (imaginative)

ANSWER   more imaginative

The Art of Drawing

1. Drawing is one of the _____ art forms of all. (old)
2. Even though they drew on some of the _____ surfaces, prehistoric people created colorful images on rock or clay. (bad)
3. During the Middle Ages, parchment was one of the _____ drawing surface available. (good)
4. Partly because silk wore _____ than other materials, Eastern artists often used it as a drawing surface. (well)
5. Since the 1400s artists have preferred using paper, which costs _____ than parchment. (little)
6. Though they worked in _____ conditions than present-day artists, artists of centuries ago produced excellent drawings. (bad)
7. Leonardo da Vinci and Michelangelo were among the _____ of all artists of the High Renaissance. (good)
8. Rembrandt and Goya produced _____ drawings than many of their contemporaries. (much)
9. Many people believe that Pablo Picasso advanced the cause of art _____ than any other artist of this century. (far)
10. Today people will travel _____ than ever to see exhibits of his work. (far)

Writing Correct Comparisons

Write the word or words that could complete the following sentences with the correct degree of comparison of the modifier in parentheses.

SAMPLE   Belinda is the _____ cyclist in our school. (fast)

ANSWER   fastest

Babe Zaharias, All-Around Athlete

1. Many people consider Mildred "Babe" Didrikson Zaharias the _____ all-around athlete of this century. (good)
2. Babe Zaharias excelled in _____ sports than any other athlete, male or female. (many)
3. Of all the sports in which she participated, she was _____ in basketball, track and field, golf, skating, and lacrosse. (outstanding)
4. Zaharias rose to national fame _____ than most other athletes of her generation. (quickly)
5. In high school she held numerous track-and-field records and was the _____ female basketball player in the country. (fine)
6. During the 1932 summer Olympics, held in Los Angeles, Zaharias performed _____ than ever before, breaking three world records that she herself had set earlier in her career. (good)
7. From 1940 to 1950, she achieved the goal of establishing herself as the country's _____ golfer, winning every possible United States and British title. (successful)
8. Zaharias, who won the U.S. Open in 1948, 1950 and 1954 could drive a golf ball _____ than most other golfers. (far)
9. Despite a major operation, Zaharias still played _____ than any other competitor in the 1953 National Women's Open. (skillfully)
10. When Babe Didrikson Zaharias died in 1956, the country lost one of the _____ of all athletes. (talented)

Exercise 5
Writing Sentences That Make Comparisons

Select five of the irregular modifiers from the list on page 628. Write a sentence for each, using the positive and comparative degrees of the modifier.

SAMPLE   far

ANSWER   Chen can throw the ball quite <u>far</u>, but Bernice can throw it <u>farther</u>.

18.3 Double Comparisons

Do not make a double comparison by using both -*er* or -*est* and
more or *most.*

| INCORRECT | Texas is ~~more~~ bigger than Oklahoma. |
| CORRECT | Texas is bigger than Oklahoma. |

| INCORRECT | That is the ~~most~~ funniest joke I have ever heard. |
| CORRECT | That is the funniest joke I have ever heard. |

Exercise 6   **Correcting Double Comparisons**

Write the correct form of the comparison in each of the following sentences.

Winston Churchill, British Statesman

1. Today we recognize Sir Winston Churchill as one of the most ablest statesmen in world history.
2. Churchill's star shone most brightest when he was Great Britain's prime minister during World War II.
3. His courage, eloquence, and faith in victory inspired the British to endure more greater hardships than they had ever before known.
4. One of the most happiest sights during the war was Churchill himself, a cigar in his mouth and two fingers raised in a victory salute.
5. Although he had stuttered as a boy, Churchill gave more clearer speeches than any other leader of his time.
6. Churchill was also one of the most liveliest writers of the day.
7. As a schoolboy, however, he had been the least carefulest student in his class.
8. Physically, Churchill was one of the most fittest leaders of the war.
9. He loved the rough, active life of a soldier, but he also had a more quieter side, which he expressed in some of his excellent paintings.
10. No other British leader of this century is regarded with more higher esteem.
11. The United States was more closer to entering the war than had seemed possible a year before.
12. Churchill and President Roosevelt developed the most strongest friendship of any wartime leaders.
13. Meeting in Yalta in 1945, Churchill and Roosevelt faced one of their most toughest challenges.
14. What was the most fairest way to divide control of postwar Europe?
15. Even more better than his postwar speeches was Churchill's six-volume series, *The Second World War*, which won him a Nobel Prize.

Rewrite the following sentences, correcting the comparisons. If a sentence needs no correction, write *correct*.

Family Dogs

1. Dad had said that bringing two puppies into the house would be the goodest move our family could make.
2. When he brought them home from the animal shelter, the collie weighed littler than the shepherd.
3. Now the collie is more heavier than the shepherd.
4. Dad chose the collie because it had the sadder eyes of all the dogs at the shelter, and he felt sorry for it.
5. The shepherd caught his eye because it had the most prettiest markings.
6. Both dogs have the most sweetest dispositions imaginable.
7. They are more happiest when they are right by our sides.
8. Raising two puppies is hardest than raising just one.
9. When one acts frisky, the other seems to act even friskiest.
10. With two dogs to care for, I have most responsibilities than before.
11. To give them the better care possible, I have had to give up pleasures I once enjoyed.
12. The situation is even badder when one of the dogs is ill.
13. The iller the dog feels, the more time someone must spend with it.
14. The shepherd appears to be in best health than the collie.
15. Since I am the most oldest of three children, it is my responsibility to walk the dogs every morning.
16. Sometimes I wish that the dogs were least playful on their morning walks around our neighborhood.
17. Whenever I am feeling weary, they seem to feel especially adventurous.
18. Then they try to run fastest than ever before, dragging me along with them for blocks at a time.
19. I think that each day both dogs try to run further than the day before.
20. Last week, the shepherd ran off for the gooder part of the morning.
21. No one was happiest than I when he finally returned home.
22. The shepherd, whose sense of smell is more acuter than the collie's, was attracted by picnic leftovers in the park.
23. These leftovers were tastiest treats than his regular canned dog food.
24. In recent months the dogs have become most easiest to train than they were when we first got them.
25. Their training is going the best than before.
26. Now they respond to simple commands most readily than before.
27. Of the two, the collie is gooder behaved than the shepherd.
28. The shepherd is the most stubbornest dog that I have ever known.
29. Sometimes the shepherd is least cooperative than a mule.
30. Raising two young dogs has definitely been entertaining and has brought this family closest together than ever before.

18.4 | Incomplete Comparisons

Do not make an incomplete or unclear comparison by omitting *other* or *else* when you compare one member of a group with the group.

| UNCLEAR | Crayfish are more like lobsters than any animal. |
| CLEAR | Crayfish are more like lobsters than any **other** animal. |

| UNCLEAR | She reads more books than anyone. |
| CLEAR | She reads more books than anyone **else.** |

Make sure that you are comparing like things.

UNCLEAR	The population of Texas is greater than Oklahoma. [One state's population is being compared illogically with everything about another state.]
CLEAR	The population of Texas is greater than **that of Oklahoma.**
CLEAR	The population of Texas is greater than **Oklahoma's.** [The word *population* is understood after *Oklahoma's.*]

UNCLEAR	The duties of a traffic officer are more complex than a game warden. [The duties of a traffic officer are being compared illogically with a person, namely, a game warden.]
CLEAR	The duties of a traffic officer are more complex than **those of a game warden.**
CLEAR	The duties of a traffic officer are more complex than **a game warden's.**

Exercise 8 ◦ Making Complete Comparisons

Rewrite each of the following sentences to correct the incomplete comparison.

The Art of Flamenco

[1]Since discovering flamenco music, I have become more interested in the culture of Spain than in any other country. [2]Flamenco songs and dance are associated more closely with the Gypsies of southern Spain than with anyone. [3]Medieval Arabic music influenced flamenco more than any tradition.[4] After listening to a performance of flamenco music, I am now convinced that flamenco is more dramatic than any music. [5]The rhythmic patterns of flamenco music are more complex and elaborate than American folk music. [6]The tones of a flamenco guitar's nylon strings are softer than a steel-stringed guitar. [7]In a flamenco performance the dancer's role is just as important as the singer. [8]The gestures of a flamenco dancer are more extravagant than a ballerina. [9]As they whirl, strut, and strike dramatic poses, flamenco dancers exude more passion than any performer. [10]If I could, I would rather learn flamenco dancing than anything.

18.5 *Good* or *Well; Bad* or *Badly*

Always use *good* as an adjective. *Well* may be used as an adverb of manner telling how ably something is done or as an adjective meaning "in good health."

Natalie is a **good** speaker. [adjective]
Anita looks **good** in that coat. [adjective after a linking verb]
Daniel speaks **well**. [adverb of manner]

Mr. Chong is not **well** right now. [adjective meaning "in good health"]

Always use *bad* as an adjective. Therefore, *bad* is used after a linking verb. Use *badly* as an adverb. *Badly* almost always follows an action verb.

The machine made a **bad** copy. [adjective]

The air smelled **bad**. [adjective following a linking verb]

I felt **bad** about your losing the race. [adjective following a linking verb]

His cut is bleeding **badly**. [adverb following an action verb]

| **Exercise 9** | **Choosing the Correct Modifier** |

Write *good*, *well*, *bad*, or *badly* to complete each sentence.

Training a Dog

1. Generally it is _____ to begin training a dog when it is about eight weeks old.
2. In order to respond to training, a dog must feel _____ and be in good shape.
3. To train a dog successfully, owners need a great deal of patience and ready access to a _____ training manual.
4. For large or ill-behaved dogs, professional obedience training can result in pets whose temperaments are _____.
5. Some dog owners do not understand that if they communicate _____, their pet will not obey.
6. Communicating _____ means issuing simple, direct commands in a consistent manner.
7. Because repetition only confuses a dog, it is _____ to give a command only once.
8. It is best to speak firmly and clearly—not loudly—when reprimanding a dog that has behaved _____.
9. Both physical and verbal abuse are _____ for a dog; abuse creates fear in an animal but does not make it behave well.
10. Experts agree that nearly all dogs are eager to please their masters and feel _____ when they misbehave.

　　　Using the Correct Modifier

For each sentence write the correct modifier in parentheses. Then write whether the modifier is used as an *adjective* or an *adverb*.

A Dog's Life

1. Elizabeth Marshall Thomas writes (good/well).
2. Her surprise best-seller, *The Hidden Life of Dogs*, speaks (good/well) of dogs.
3. The theme of her book is that dogs do many things as (good/well) as human beings.
4. There are, of course, things that dogs do (bad/badly) or cannot do at all.
5. Some critics of Thomas's book claim that she condones dogs' behavior even when it is (bad, badly).
6. Thomas believes that dogs live (good/well) if their lives are filled with love and intellectual pursuits.
7. According to Thomas, dogs have a "conscience" and feel (bad/badly) about some of the things they do.
8. Thomas's dog Koki skulked around the house for days because Koki knew that she had been (bad/badly).
9. On the other hand, if a dog feels (good, well) about its behavior, it is likely to show this by acting happy.
10. When one of her dogs acts (bad/badly), Thomas usually finds a logical explanation for its behavior.

　　　Correcting Comparisons

Rewrite each of the following sentences, correcting the incomplete or incorrect comparison. If a sentence contains no errors, write *correct*.

Dogs and Cats

1. According to writer Elizabeth Marshall Thomas, dogs are more like human beings than any animal.
2. She believes that the brain of a dog is more complex than a cat.
3. According to Thomas, a cat's brain is not wired as good as a dog's brain.
4. She writes that dogs lead lives that are fuller than cats.
5. Thomas feels that dogs have more stronger emotions than cats do.
6. Cats seldom, if ever, feel bad about things they have done, even when someone is reprimanding them.
7. Dogs' emotional needs may be as great as human beings.
8. What dogs seem to want more than anything is the company of other dogs.
9. According to Thomas, what cats want is good food, preferably mice.
10. When Thomas wrote a book about cats, *The Tribe of Tiger*, her publisher hoped the book would sell even more copies than dogs.

18.6 | Double Negatives

In general, do not use a double negative, two negative words in the same clause. Use only one negative word to express a negative idea.

INCORRECT	I didn't see ~~no~~ accident.
CORRECT	I did**n't** see **any** accident.
INCORRECT	He doesn't know nothing about my plans.
CORRECT	He does**n't** know **anything** about my plans.
CORRECT	He knows **nothing** about my plans.
INCORRECT	She ~~never~~ tells no lies.
CORRECT	She **never** tells **any** lies.
CORRECT	She tells **no** lies.
INCORRECT	We haven't hardly eaten our breakfasts.
CORRECT	We have **hardly** eaten our breakfasts.

Exercise 12   Avoiding Double Negatives

Rewrite the following sentences, eliminating the double negative in each.

Boa Constrictors

1. Boa constrictors do not inject no venom into their prey.
2. Still, I would not want no boa constrictor for a pet.
3. Boa constrictors kill birds and rodents by not allowing them no air.
4. Once captured in the boa constrictor's coils, a bird or rodent cannot do nothing.
5. The boa constrictor is big, but it cannot be compared with no anaconda, or python.
6. Boa constrictors cannot swallow no cows, horses, or people.
7. After a meal these snakes do not eat nothing for a week or more.
8. Often they do not do nothing; they just sleep and digest their food.
9. Like other snakes, boa constrictors can survive for many months without no food at all.
10. Unlike many other snakes, boa constrictors never lay no eggs.
11. Though my friend Jeremy has one, I wouldn't want no boa constrictor for a pet.
12. There aren't scarcely any snakes that appeal to me.
13. Jeremy shouldn't never have brought his boa constrictor to school.
14. He thought it wouldn't never escape from its bag.
15. He didn't have no clue where the snake was after it escaped.
16. First he pretended that he didn't know nothing about all the commotion.
17. He couldn't hardly keep pretending for long, though.
18. There wasn't nobody in the class who didn't know he had the snake with him.
19. Jeremy hadn't hardly expected to become a school celebrity.
20. He won't bring no snakes to school again anytime soon.

Place modifiers as close as possible to the words they modify in order to make the meaning of the sentence clear.

Misplaced Modifiers

Modifiers that modify the wrong word or seem to modify more than one word in a sentence are called **misplaced modifiers.** Moving the modifier as close as possible to the word it modifies or revising the sentence will correct this problem.

MISPLACED	**Proceeding with care,** we stood at the foot of the mountain and watched the determined mountain climbers. [participial phrase incorrectly modifying *we*]
CLEAR	We stood at the foot of the mountain and watched the determined mountain climbers **proceeding with care.** [participial phrase correctly modifying *mountain climbers*]
MISPLACED	The mountains delight many visitors **in their autumn splendor.** [prepositional phrase incorrectly modifying *visitors*]
CLEAR	The mountains **in their autumn splendor** delight many visitors. [prepositional phrase correctly modifying *mountains*]

Exercise 13　Identifying Misplaced Modifiers

Write the misplaced modifier in each sentence. If a sentence is correct, write *correct.*

Winter Storms

1. Dumping more water on an already flooded state, California is hit by still another torrential rainstorm.
2. The winter storm battering northern California for days has worked its way down the coast to the southern counties.
3. Howling through mountain passes, a highway winding through the Sierra Nevada is forced to shut down due to heavy winds.
4. Built in the 1960s, officials estimated that it would take three months to rebuild a bridge.
5. Most meteorologists attributed the storm to a recurring Pacific weather phenomenon known as El Niño.

Dangling Modifiers

Dangling modifiers do not modify any word in the sentence. By supplying a word that the dangling phrase can sensibly modify, you can easily correct this error.

DANGLING	**Digging in the field,** a Native American village was found. [participial phrase logically modifying no word in the sentence]
CLEAR	**Digging in the field,** archaeologists found a Native American village. [participial phrase modifying *archaeologists*]
DANGLING	**After digging for months,** the find was all the more satisfying. [prepositional phrase logically modifying no word in the sentence]
CLEAR	**After digging for months,** the archaeologists deemed the find all the more satisfying. [prepositional phrase modifying *archaeologists*]
DANGLING	**Feeling proud of our find,** our dinner that night was a celebration [phrase cannot modify a possessive form]
CLEAR	**Feeling proud of our find,** we made our dinner a celebration. [rewrite supplies a word for phrase to modify]

Placement of *Only*

Place the adverb *only* immediately before the word or group of words it modifies.

The meaning of your sentence may be unclear if *only* is positioned incorrectly.

UNCLEAR	Bertina **only** has breakfast on Sunday. [Does she have just one meal on Sunday. Does she skip breakfast every day but Sunday? Is Bertina the only person (in a group) who has breakfast on Sunday?]
CLEAR	Bertina has **only** breakfast on Sunday. [She does not have lunch or dinner.]
CLEAR	Bertina has breakfast **only** on Sunday. [She does not have breakfast on any other day.]
CLEAR	**Only** Bertina has breakfast on Sunday. [No one else (in Bertina's house) has breakfast on Sunday.]

Identifying Misplaced and Dangling Modifiers

Write any incorrect modifier in the following sentences. Then write *misplaced* or *dangling* to identify the kind. If a sentence contains no errors, write *correct*.

SAMPLE   Renting huge rafts, rivers become accessible to city people.
ANSWER   Renting huge rafts—misplaced

Outdoor Adventures

1. Looking for adventure, white-water rafting, mountain climbing, and bungee jumping have become popular vacation activities.
2. Adventure travel, now an $8 billion industry, has grown rapidly in recent years.
3. More than 20,000 people a year sign up for rafting trips through the Grand Canyon.
4. Ranging in difficulty from Class I to Class IV, knowledgeable river guides lead inexperienced rafters.
5. Unlike an amusement-park ride, rafters often find their trip down the rapids unpredictable and strenuous.
6. Interested in glaciers and icebergs, the untouched wilderness of the Yukon territory can be very appealing.
7. Some tourists enjoy watching the mountain gorillas with sloping heads and dense black fur that make their home in central Africa.
8. Filled as they are with hidden dangers, some vacationers find ice climbing and rock climbing especially challenging.
9. Climbers in the best physical shape should only climb glaciers.
10. Extremely vigorous outdoor adventures push people to their physical limits.

Correcting Misplaced and Dangling Modifiers

Rewrite the following sentences, correcting the misplaced or dangling modifier in each.

A Day in the Park

1. Driving carefully down the road to the park, the accident was avoided.
2. I saw two squirrels riding my bike in the park.
3. Searching for wildflowers, poison ivy was found instead.
4. We caught a butterfly using a net.
5. Making a nest for their young, Alex and Maria saw two birds in a big tree near the parking lot.
6. Carmen only dreams of being a forest ranger; she knows it is what she wants to be, and no other career interests her.
7. Because of their huge size and strength, many backpackers and campers in the park fear grizzly bears.
8. Myung only knows which trail leads to the waterfall; he won't tell anyone else where it is.
9. Stuck fast on the hook, I had trouble removing the fish that I caught in the lake.
10. After planning for months, the outing was a big success.

Correcting Misplaced and Dangling Modifiers

Rewrite the following sentences, correcting the misplaced or dangling modifiers in each.

Toni Morrison, Novelist

1. During her childhood in Lorain, Ohio, Toni Morrison was surrounded by poor, hardworking people and steel mills with little opportunity to get ahead.
2. Finishing high school with honors, Howard University in Washington, D.C., accepted Morrison as an undergraduate.
3. Constantly on the road during the summer, her acting talent shone in the productions of the university's theater troupe.
4. Attending graduate school at Cornell University, William Faulkner and Virginia Woolf were the subjects of her thesis.
5. Graduating in 1955, jobs in education and publishing followed.
6. Until 1970, when her novel *The Bluest Eye* was published, Morrison had edited only books, not written them.
7. In *The Bluest Eye* a young girl is described by Morrison wishing for blue eyes exactly like Shirley Temple's.
8. With the curious name of Macon Dead, Morrison created a powerful character in her third novel, *Song of Solomon*.
9. Becoming increasingly greedy and cruel, the author convincingly pictures Macon Dead.
10. Some critics liked Morrison's novel *Tar Baby*, but others said that the characters only were stereotypes.
11. Described by some as the last classic American writer, one critic put Morrison in a category with Poe, Twain, and Faulkner.
12. Only *Beloved* was the book written by Morrison to win the Pulitzer Prize.
13. *Song of Solomon* only won the National Book Award for Fiction.
14. Having won such prestigious literary awards, Princeton University offered Morrison a teaching position.
15. Morrison wrote *Jazz*, angry at the injustices experienced by African American women.
16. After many months of writing, it was published.
17. Heartbreaking and powerful, readers were mesmerized by the story woven by Morrison.
18. Writing with passion, the main characters in *Jazz* formed a triangle of jealousy, murder, and redemption.
19. With their daring themes and lyrical passages, readers admire Toni Morrison's novels.
20. Given for distinguished literary work of an idealistic nature, in 1993 Morrison won the Nobel Prize for literature.

Adding Modifiers to Sentences

Revise the following sentences, adding modifiers as indicated in parentheses.

SAMPLE   Martin missed the school bus. (Add *having overslept.*)
ANSWER   Having overslept, Martin missed the school bus.

Summer Programs

1. Many parents have begun their search for the right summer program for their children. (Add *planning ahead.*)
2. Parents collect as much information as possible. (Add *knowing how difficult the decision is.*)
3. Information helps narrow the choices. (Add *though sometimes overwhelming.*)
4. Children need help sorting out the possibilities. (Add *often unsure of their decision-making ability.*)
5. Various programs are available at public libraries and recreational centers throughout the county. (Add *many of them free.*)
6. Some programs have a residency requirement and a small nonresident surcharge. (Add *offered by county agencies.*)
7. College dormitories provide housing for some programs. (Add *empty during summer months.*)
8. Children can find any kind of camp. (Add *suited to their interests.*)
9. There are nature camps, history camps, and even astronomy camps. (Add *designed for aspiring astronauts.*)
10. Students with experience in digital photography can enroll in the animation program at the computer arts camp. (Add *only* to make clear that others cannot enroll.)

Correcting Modifiers

The following paragraphs contain 10 errors in the use of modifiers. Rewrite the paragraphs, correcting the errors.

Apprenticeships

[1]Going to college is a good way to train for some, but not all, kinds of work. [2]Apprenticeship is probably a more better way to train to be a carpenter, for example. [3]Apprentices never gain no practical skill without on-the-job experience. [4]As their training progresses, they learn various job skills good. [5]After about four years—more longer for some trades and not so long for others—they become experts. [6]Then the wages received by these skilled workers are better than the unskilled workers.

[7]The construction industry is more crowded with registered apprentices than any field. [8]There are 450 different occupations that require apprenticeship. [9]Having varying interests, some fields are more attractive than others. [10]Apprenticeship programs have entrance exams and minimum age and education requirements. [11]If you want to become an apprentice, the best thing you can do is find out about your chosen field while you are still in school. [12]Sometimes you will find that the most good thing to do is to finish college first. [13]Not wanting to miss out on a college education, colleges today train a growing number of artists and craftspeople. [14]Nevertheless, many people believe that the close relationship between master and apprentice only can provide suitable training.

Rewrite the following sentences, correcting any errors in the use of modifiers.

Arthurian Sites

1. My summer vacation was more better than any I ever took before.
2. While traveling in England, places associated with King Arthur were my primary destinations.
3. Located on the coast of Cornwall, our tour guide pointed out King Arthur's legendary birthplace at Tintagel.
4. When I learned that no one really knows where King Arthur was born—or even whether he actually lived—I felt badly.
5. I didn't let nothing keep me from seeing Cadbury Castle, which may have been the real Camelot.
6. The Arthurian sites in Glastonbury are more numerous than any other city in England.
7. Standing at King Arthur's legendary grave site, the ruins of Glastonbury Abbey surrounded me.
8. I missed visiting the possible sites of Sir Lancelot's northern castle, because I didn't feel good.
9. Hanging in the hall at Winchester Castle, I gazed intently at what is supposed to be the table top of the Round Table.
10. My tour of Arthurian sites provided me with the most fondest memories of my vacation.

Write 10 sentences, following the directions given in each of the items below.

SAMPLE   Use the comparative of *happy* as an adverb.
ANSWER   I worked *more happiy* after I realized that I was almost finished.

1. Use the comparative form of *tiny* to compare the size of two objects.
2. Use the superlative of *little* (meaning amount) as an adjective.
3. Use the modifiers *good* and *well* following the appropriate kinds of verbs.
4. Use the comparative of *far* to compare distance.
5. Compare two games or activities of your choice, using the superlatives of *good* and *bad*.
6. Write a sentence comparing the population of New York with the population of Oregon.
7. Use the comparative form of the modifier *many*.
8. Express the same idea in two sentences. In one, use the negative *never*; in the other, use *ever*.
9. Use the modifier *only* to explain that you have art class one morning a week.
10. Use the participial phrase *reviewing all the grammar* in a sentence.

Grammar Review

Using Modifiers Correctly

Alessandro Giuliani, the hero of Mark Helprin's epic novel *A Soldier of the Great War*, is a young Italian student whose life is turned upside down by World War I. In this passage, which has been annotated to show some of the kinds of modifiers covered in this unit, Alessandro is returning on foot from Germany to his family estate in Rome.

Literature Model

from A SOLDIER OF THE GREAT WAR

by Mark Helprin

Comparative form of the adjective *high*

He crossed six ridges, each higher than the one preceding it, before he came to the point where he would not see trees until he was in Italy, and when he cleared the forest he was confronted by a world of glaciated mountains. In the dusk, they were a dusty-rose color and the distance to them appeared so vast that he thought it would take a month to reach them, but it was only a trick of light and shadow, and they were neither as far nor as high as they seemed to be.

Positive form of the adjective *far*

Superlative form of the adjective *far*

Here and there in the snow-covered pastures were hay-filled cabins where he could find shelter from the wind. He sought the one farthest from any farmhouse or village and closest to the great glacier upon which he would soon be walking. Several hours after dusk he stopped at the end of the meadows, in a place where the glacier was so close that he could feel the rivers of cold air that flowed from it and carried its sounds—the muffled sound of a locked wheel skidding on a steel rail, thunder-like cracks, a barely perceptible rumble, as if from a giant piece of furniture being pulled slowly across a rough floor. . . .

Correctly placed prepositional phrase modifying *end*

Positive form of the adverb *violently*

He awoke at midnight, shivering so violently that he found it difficult to get to his feet. He buttoned his clothes tight, bloused his pants in his socks, put on every item of wool he could find, and burst out the door, almost falling down the slope that descended to the tongue of the glacier. ➡

The moon was down, his head throbbed, and his fingers were too stiff for him to have opened his food even had he been warm enough to try to eat.

He had to use both axes. The crampons were not necessary, and he would never have been able to strap them on anyway. After struggling up a short fractured ice wall by pulling himself forward with his arms, he was on the glacier. It rose gradually toward a line of mountains that then shot straight into the sky like the spray of a wave exploding through a sinkhole. With luck he would have a moon or a sky clear enough to let the starlight through, and with more than luck he would reach the peaks by daylight.

Correctly placed phrases modifying *he*

Exercise 1

Making Correct Comparisons   The following sentences describe World War I and Alessandro Giuliani's involvement in it. For each sentence write the proper comparative or superlative form of the modifier in parentheses.

SAMPLE   Few men fought _____ than Alessandro Giuliani and his comrades. (bravely)

ANSWER   more bravely

1. World War I was called the Great War because _____ men fought and died in it than in any other war up to that time. (many)
2. The nations that fought in World War I assembled the _____ number of soldiers and armaments ever seen. (great)
3. Before the war Alessandro joined the navy in the belief that wars were fought _____ at sea than on land. (safely)
4. Ironically, he was then sent to fight in the naval infantry and survived some of the _____ battles of all. (dangerous)
5. Alessandro later deserted when German and Austrian forces shattered the Italian front lines; it was Italy's _____ defeat of all in the war. (bad)
6. Desertion was usually punished by the _____ penalty of all: death by firing squad. (severe)
7. The Italian army chose to punish Alessandro's desertion _____ than usual, however; he was simply sent back to fight the Austrians. (harshly)
8. After he was taken prisoner by the Austrians, Alessandro fared _____ than other prisoners did. (good)
9. After Austria's collapse Alessandro slipped cautiously through enemy lines amid the _____ confusion imaginable. (bad)
10. Every step Alessandro took toward the glacier led him _____ from the enemy and closer to his homeland and to freedom. (far)

Exercise 2

Correcting Double Comparisons   Some of the following sentences elaborate on scenes from *A Soldier of the Great War* that are not reprinted in this textbook. Other sentences describe the Alps and glaciers. For each sentence, write the correct comparison. If a sentence contains no errors, write *correct*.

SAMPLE   Mont Blanc, on the border of France and Italy, is the most highest mountain in the Alps.

ANSWER   Mont Blanc, on the border of France and Italy, is the highest mountain in the Alps.

1. The Alps are probably better known than any other mountains in the world.
2. On the lower slopes of the Alps, many varieties of trees flourish, but the most highest slopes are almost bare of vegetation.
3. The more taller peaks attract many competent climbers; among them were the characters Alessandro and his friend Rafi.
4. Making his escape from an Austrian prison, Alessandro chose the most straightest path to Italy and his home.
5. Alessandro climbed until he was more higher than the tree line and within sight of the glaciers.
6. A glacier is a slowly moving river of ice and snow that stays frozen even on the most hottest summer days.
7. There are more than a thousand glaciers in the Alps; the most largest is the 16-mile-long Aletsch Glacier.
8. The most riskiest part of Alessandro's escape from Austria was his crossing a vast glacier at night.
9. Sharp-spiked crampons give climbers a more firmer foothold on the ice than plain climbing boots do.
10. More skillful than most amateur climbers, Alessandro chose not to wear crampons and used only his two ice axes to climb onto the glacier.
11. The glacier on which he climbed was in a more warmer climate than many other glaciers.
12. Glaciers are found both in polar regions and also in more temperate climates.
13. Glaciers become larger when more snow falls and more smaller when snow melts.
14. A glacier moves more slowly when it reaches an area that is less steeply sloped.
15. The steeper the slope, the more faster a glacier generally moves.
16. Many glaciers in the Alps are mountain glaciers that begin on the most highest slopes.
17. As the old snow is compressed into a granular mass by more snow on top, it starts to slide slowly down the slope.
18. The movement causes the mass to become more further compacted into glacier ice.
19. The slowest glacier moves about an inch a day; the most rapidest one, several hundred feet.
20. Climbing on glaciers is often more dangerous than climbing on rock.

Exercise 3

Correcting Incomplete and Unclear Comparisons The following sentences describe World War I and Italy's involvement in it. Rewrite each sentence, correcting any errors of incomplete or unclear comparison. Some of the sentences can be revised in more than one way. If a sentence contains no errors, write *correct*.

SAMPLE World War I shaped Alessandro's life more than any event.

ANSWER World War I shaped Alessandro's life more than any other event.

1. The First World War, which involved all the major powers of Europe as well as the United States, produced carnage greater than any previous war.
2. The use of aircraft, tanks, and machine guns made the Great War more impersonal than any war.
3. Among the Allies, British and French soldiers fought longer than anyone.
4. The Central Powers—Germany, Austria-Hungary, and the Ottoman Empire—were united as much by geography as by anything.
5. When it began fighting in May 1915, Italy's army was less prepared than France or Britain.
6. For two years the Alps, more than any place in Europe, were the site of many battles between the Italian and the Austrian forces.
7. The Isonzo River, in northern Italy, was the site of more battles than any other location on the Italian front.
8. After a devastating battle in 1917, Italy's position was weaker than Austria.
9. The Italian offensive of 1918 forced an Austrian retreat more successfully than had any Italian attacks.
10. By the time World War I ended in 1918, Italy had sustained a million casualties, more than in any war in its history.
11. More civilians were affected by World War I than by war.
12. Technological innovations made survival on the battlefront more difficult than earlier wars.
13. Bigger and better battleships and submarines revolutionized naval warfare.
14. Chemical warfare, more devastating than any form of warfare, was introduced.
15. The cost of rebuilding Europe was higher than the war.
16. Italy's Prime Minister Vittorio Orlando, a delegate to the Paris peace conference, opposed the peace plan more than any delegate.
17. Italy's primary goal was more nationalistic than the other Allies.
18. Italy wanted control of the former Austrian territories more than anything.
19. Orlando took a greater interest in the punishment of Germany than in any other issue discussed at the peace conference.
20. The Italian delegation only walked out of the peace negotiations.

Exercise 4

Choosing the Correct Modifier   The following sentences describe a mountain-climbing expedition that Alessandro and his friend Rafi took before Alessandro enlisted in the Italian navy. For each sentence write the correct form of the modifier in parentheses. Then wrtite whether the modifier is used as an *adjective* or an *adverb*.

SAMPLE   Alessandro had mastered climbing skills (good/well) before becoming a soldier.
ANSWER   well—adverb

1. Leaving the train, Alessandro and Rafi felt (good/well) about the next day's climb.
2. They carried enough equipment to ensure that the expedition would go (good/well).
3. A novice climber, Rafi needed Alessandro's expertise (bad/badly) to keep him safe.
4. Soon, however, Rafi was climbing safely and (well/good).
5. The climbers deftly hammered small spikes, called pitons, into the cliff, for it was essential that the pitons hold (good/well).
6. Once the pitons seemed to have been placed in the rock (good/well), the climbers snapped clips—carabiners—to the pitons.
7. The safety line they slung through the carabiners would not snag (bad/badly) on outcroppings of rock.
8. With Alessandro in the lead, they inched up the face of the cliff, sidestepping any footholds that looked (bad/badly).
9. Their muscles were aching (bad/badly) as they hammered pitons into the cliff.
10. Since they were feeling (good/well) about the day's work, they rested and planned the next day's climb.

Exercise 5

Correcting Double Negatives   Rewrite each sentence, eliminating any double negatives. If a sentence contains no errors, write *correct*.

1. Most novice climbers don't know nothing about the basics of mountaineering.
2. Hiking is the least perilous types of mountaineering; it is not no riskier than walking.
3. Rock climbing and ice climbing should not be undertaken by no beginner without expert supervision.
4. Mixed climbing, a combination of rock climbing and ice climbing, is not meant for novices neither.
5. Climbers not wearing boots with cleated rubber soles should not begin the ascent.
6. It would be unusual for beginning climbers not to feel no jitters when they start.
7. Except when climbing on ice or snow, no more than two climbers should never be tied together on a single rope.
8. Climbing instructors never waste no time before explaining the proper use of pitons and carabiners in securing the rope.
9. Nonclimbers never have any idea of the tight teamwork climbers must develop.
10. Most careful climbers do not have hardly any serious mishaps.

Exercise 6

Correcting Misplaced Modifiers   The following sentences describe the scene from *A Soldier of the Great War* that follows the passage featured in this workshop. Rewrite each sentence, correcting misplaced modifiers. If a sentence has no errors, write *correct*.

SAMPLE   Shining silently in the cold night air, Alessandro gazed at the stars.
ANSWER   Alessandro gazed at the stars shining silently in the cold night air.

1. Alessandro was constantly on the lookout for dangerous crevasses walking across the glacier.
2. Possibly obscuring deep chasms, he avoided any thin patches of snow.
3. The bleak vista lay before this lonely man stretching into miles of darkness.
4. The danger of crevasses recently cut into the glacier haunted the soldier.
5. He ran across the icy surface burning with fierce determination.
6. Perfectly hidden from view by a snowdrift, Alessandro narrowly avoided a pair of crevasses.
7. Alessandro leaped into the air beyond the point of feeling fear.
8. Alessandro completely lost all sense of time falling into a wide canyon.
9. Miraculously, he landed on a soft bed of snow in a kneeling position.
10. When he found that he had only survived by a miracle, he began to laugh.

Exercise 7

Correcting Dangling Modifiers   The following sentences are based on the passage from *A Soldier of the Great War*. Rewrite the sentences, correcting each dangling modifier. In some cases you may need to reword the entire sentence. If a sentence contains no errors, write *correct*.

SAMPLE   After crossing six ridges, trees did not appear again until Alessandro was in Italy.
ANSWER   After crossing six ridges, Alessandro did not see trees again until he was in Italy.

1. Leaving the forest, a world of glaciated mountains stretched toward the horizon.
2. Rising vast in the distance, Alessandro was amazed by the mountains' immensity.
3. Tricked by the play of light and shadow, the mountains seemed distant to him.
4. Surveying the snow-filled pastures, hay-filled cabins dotted the landscape.
5. Offering shelter from the wind, Alessandro chose the cabin farthest from any settlement.
6. After walking for several hours after dusk, Alessandro stopped at the edge of the meadows.
7. Feeling the rivers of cold air, the proximity of the glacier was certain.
8. Rumbling almost imperceptibly, he was awed by its tremendous power.
9. Hoisting his body upward, the ice wall was scaled only with great difficulty.
10. Given a combination of luck and skill and perseverance, the peaks would be reachable by daylight.

Exercise 8

Adding Modifiers to Sentences   The following sentences describe Alessandro and his friend Rafi's mountain-climbing expedition. Rewrite the sentences, adding modifiers as indicated in parentheses. (There will be more than one way to rewrite some sentences.)

1. Alessandro and Rafi began their preparations for their mountain climbing expedition. (Add *making their plans early.*)
2. They packed lightweight, high-energy foods. (Add *wanting to be sure they had nourishment for their journey.*)
3. Rafi was an inexperienced climber, but Alessandro was ready to help him. (Add *who was not used to such heights.*)
4. Novice climbers could easily lose their footing and very possibly their lives. (Add *climbing alone.*)
5. Alessandro reviewed the use of pitons and carabiners with Rafi. (Add *not knowing how much Rafi remembered.*)
6. Alessandro was in the lead, and Rafi followed behind him. (Add *because he was more competent.*)
7. Rafi could watch Alessandro's climbing strategies and copy them. (Add *by letting him go first.*)
8. Alessandro and Rafi inched their way up the face of the first cliff. (Add *checking their footholds carefully.*)
9. The expedition was more of a physical challenge than the two men had first believed. (Add *that they had dreamed about for so long.*)
10. The two men were extremely pleased at the progress they had made in a day. (Add *filled with challenges.*)

Review: Exercise 9

Proofreading

The following passage describes the artist Albert Bierstadt, whose painting appears on the opposite page. Rewrite the passage, correcting the errors in spelling, grammar, and usage. Add any missing punctuation. There are twenty-five errors.

Albert Bierstadt

[1]Born in Germany, Albert Bierstadt (1830-1902) was brought by his parents at the age of two to New Bedford, Massachusetts. [2]When he was twenty-three. [3]He returns to Germany to study painting. [4]He often traveled to Switzerland and Italy and made countless sketches of mountain landscapes becoming intrested in landscape painting.

[5]Bierstadt returned to New Bedford in 1857 and the next year he joined a surveying expedition to the Rocky Mountains. [6]Their size and beauty overwhelmed him, he made many pencil and oil sketches. [7]When he was twenty-nine, moved to New York City and set up a studio there. [8]His huge landscape paintings commanded higher prices than those of anyone. ➡

Albert Bierstadt, *Sunrise on the Matterhorn,* **after 1875**

[9]His training in Europe maked him a master at drawing and oil sketching. [10]Making preliminary sketches from nature, his works were completed in the studio.

[11]Like many of his fellow artists, the unspoiled grandeur of the West was a frequent subject of Bierstadt's paintings. [12]His romantic paintings of the West become a symbol of national pride.

[13]Famous for his unusual technique, Bierstadt's paintings combined enormous scale with the delicatest suggestions of light and shadow. [14]The painting on this page which was based on sketches made during his travels through the Alps, is typical of his' style. [15]The delicately lit peek looks least real than the trees in the foreground.

[16]The hero in Mark Helprin's story crosses the Swiss Alps wanting bad to return home. [17]Here Bierstadt portrays one of the most grand of all the Swiss mountins the Matterhorn. [18]Does the painting remind you of Helprin's description of the "trick of light and shadow" that can make the Alps appear to be more distanter and more unreachable than they really are?

Mixed Review

Exercise 10

Read the following brief biography of Mark Helprin. Then rewrite the sentences that follow it, correcting any errors in the use of modifiers. If you need to obtain information to complete your sentences, consult the biography.

Mark Helprin

Born in 1947 in New York City, Mark Helprin attended Harvard University, earning a bachelor's degree in 1969 and a master's degree in Middle Eastern studies in 1972. He then joined the Israeli armed forces, where he served in the infantry and in an elite unit of the air force. After further study at Princeton and Oxford universities, he moved to Brooklyn and began to write fiction. Helprin submitted a dozen stories to the *New Yorker* magazine before two stories were finally accepted at once. In 1975 he published *A Dove of the East and Other Stories;* two years later his first novel appeared. *Ellis Island and Other Stories* won the National Jewish Book Award in 1982, and Helprin was also awarded the prestigious Prix de Rome by the Institute for Arts and Letters. Helprin published his popular novel *Winter's Tale* in 1983. He now lives in Seattle and last climbed nearby Mount Rainier in 1987. *A Soldier of the Great War* was published in 1991.

1. Helprin performed good as both a scholar and a soldier before turning to a literary career.
2. After settling in Brooklyn, writing became his primary pursuit.
3. The *New Yorker* magazine did not accept none of the first twelve stories that Helprin submitted.
4. The reviews of his third book, *Ellis Island and Other Stories,* were more positive than his first book, *A Dove of the East and Other Stories.*
5. Generally speaking, to Helprin most romantic fantasies are more vivider than most realistic tales.
6. Of all of Helprin's books, *Ellis Island and Other Stories* only received the National Jewish Book Award.
7. Racing over frozen winter landscapes, Helprin's novel *Winter's Tale* describes the exploits of a flying horse.
8. The heroes of Helprin's novels are adventurers who defeat evil beings with great courage and virtue.
9. In *Winter's Tale* the hero is pursued by creatures called Short Tails, who are eviller than anyone.
10. A skilled mountain climber, Helprin's novels often depict courageous mountaineers on treacherous slopes.

Writing Application

Modifiers in Writing Good writers use modifiers correctly and position them carefully to make their meaning clear. Notice, for example, the use of the italicized modifiers in this passage from "Tuesday Siesta," a short story by Gabriel García Márquez that has been translated into English by J. S. Bernstein.

> *Keeping to the protective shade of the almond trees*, the woman and the girl entered the town without disturbing the siesta. They went directly to the parish house. The woman scratched the metal grating *on the door* with her fingernail, waited a moment, and scratched again. An electric fan was humming inside. They did not hear the steps. They *hardly* heard the slight creaking of a door, and immediately a cautious voice, right next to the metal grating. . . .

Techniques with Modifiers Try to apply some of García Márquez's techniques when you write and revise your own work.

1. To avoid confusion, place modifiers as close as possible to the words they modify.

Misplaced Modifier Keeping to the protective shade of the almond trees, *the town* . . .
García Márquez's Version Keeping to the protective shade of the almond trees, *the woman and the girl* . . .

2. Consider whether moving a modifier or other words in the sentence will make your meaning clearer. Compare the two positions of the prepositional phrase *on the door*.

Confusing Placement *On the door* the woman scratched the metal grating with her fingernail . . .
García Márquez's Version The woman scratched the metal grating *on the door* with her fingernail . . .

3. Be careful not to create double negatives, especially with *hardly* and *scarcely*.

Double Negative They *couldn't hardly* hear the slight creaking. . .
García Márquez's Version They *hardly* heard the slight creaking. . .

Practice Practice these techniques by revising the following paragraphs using a separate sheet of paper.

Born in Aracataca, Colombia, many of Gabriel García Márquez's stories and novels are set in small Latin American towns. *One Hundred Years of Solitude* portrays the history of the remote town of Macondo, one of the most popular books ever published in the Spanish-speaking world. Many critics, symbolizing the turbulence of Latin American politics, think Macondo and the people living there eccentric.

Magical and at times surreal, the author has a distinct writing style. After winning the Nobel Prize in literature, many new readers from all over the world were attracted to García Márquez. The author, who doesn't have no patience for human rights abuses, has also won praise worldwide for his humanitarian efforts.

Usage Glossary

Certain usages of English are preferred by most educated speakers and writers. The glossary in this unit presents some aspects of preferred usage that are particularly troublesome. It shows you how to choose between words that are often confused, and it advises you to avoid certain words and expressions when you are speaking or writing for school or business.

a, an   The article *a* is used when the word that follows begins with a consonant sound: *a ticket.* Words that begin with a sounded *h* or the "yew" sound are thus also preceded by *a: a hurricane, a eulogy, a uniform.* The article *an* is used when the word that follows begins with a vowel sound or an unsounded *h: an umbrella, an hour.*

a lot, alot   This expression, which means "a large amount," should always be written as two words. Some authorities advise that you avoid it completely in formal English.

>   **A lot** of television programs show too much violence.

a while, awhile   An article and a noun form the expression *a while.* Often the preposition *in* or *for* precedes *a while,* forming a prepositional phrase. The single word *awhile* is an adverb.

>   She'll speak in **a while.**
>   She'll speak for **a while.**
>   She'll speak **awhile** before showing the filmstrip.

accept, except   *Accept* is a verb meaning "to receive" or "to agree to." *Except* is occasionally used as a verb or a conjunction, but much more frequently it is used as a preposition meaning "but."

>   Miki will **accept** the invitation to lunch.
>   The restaurant is open every day **except** Monday. [preposition]

affect, effect   *Affect* is a verb meaning "to cause a change in" or "to influence." *Effect* as a verb means "to bring about or accomplish." As a noun *effect* means "result" or "that which has been brought about."

>   Daily exercise will **affect** your health.[verb meaning "cause a change in"]
>
>   Daily exercise will **effect** a positive change in your health. [verb meaning "bring about"]
>
>   Daily exercise will have a good **effect** on your health. [noun meaning "result"]

ain't *Ain't* is never used in formal speaking or writing unless you are quoting the exact words of a character or real person. Instead of using *ain't*, say or write, *I am not; she is not;* and so on.

all ready, already *All ready,* written as two words, is an adjective phrase that means "completely ready." *Already,* written as one word, is an adverb that means "before" or "by this time."

> Lloyd was **all ready** to go at seven o'clock, but his friends had **already** left without him.

all right, alright The expression *all right* should be written as two words. Although some dictionaries acknowledge the existence of the single word *alright,* this spelling is not generally accepted as correct.

> I hope the baby is **all right.**

all the farther, all the faster These are informal expressions. It is much better to use *as far as* and *as fast as* in speaking and writing.

> Reno was **as far as** I wanted to go.
> Is this **as fast as** you can walk?

all together, altogether *All together* means "in a group." *Altogether* is an adverb meaning "completely" or "on the whole."

> The actors joined hands and took a bow **all together.**
> **Altogether** it was a very good play.

amount, number *Amount* and *number* both refer to quantity, but *amount* refers to nouns that cannot be counted, and *number* refers to nouns that can be counted.

> A huge **amount** of lava spurted from the erupting volcano.
> A **number** of volcanoes are still active today.

bad, badly See Unit 18.

being as, being that Although these expressions sometimes replace *because* or *since* in informal conversation, you should always avoid them in formal speaking and writing.

> **Because** bears are hibernators, they sleep during the winter.
> **Since** the movie has already started, let's come back later.

beside, besides   *Beside* means "located at the side of." *Besides* is ordinarily used to mean "in addition to."

> The cat sat **beside** the refrigerator.
> **Besides** losing my gloves, I lost two buttons from my coat.

between, among   *Between* should generally be used when comparing one person or thing with another person or thing or with an entire group.

> It was difficult to choose **between** ice cream and pudding for dessert. [Two desserts are compared.]

> What is the difference **between** this opera and others by Verdi? [One opera is compared with the entire group of Verdi's operas.]

Among is generally used to show a relationship in which more than two persons or things are considered as a group.

> Tim's great-grandfather had lived **among** the Iroquois.

Exercise 1   **Making Usage Choices**

On your paper write the correct word or expression from each pair in parentheses.

George Washington, Our First President

1. General George Washington fought with great determination for (a/an) independent United States.
2. As leader of the Continental Army, Washington tried to make sure his troops were (alright/all right), even though a great (number/amount) of them had poor health and low spirits.
3. Washington's courage and determination to win (affected/effected) his soldiers, improving their morale.
4. After his stunning victory, Washington rested (a while/awhile) at home at Mount Vernon on the Potomac River.
5. When delegates from the states met (all together/altogether) to write the Constitution, they chose Washington from (among/between) all the delegates to be their leader.
6. Washington was asked to (accept/except) the office of president after the vote of the first Electoral College.
7. President Washington was (all ready/already) widely known and respected when he took office.
8. As the first president of the United States, Washington did (a lot/alot) to shape the duties of his office and to (affect/effect) a responsive administrative system to lead the nation forward.
9. (Beside/Besides) showing strong leadership, Washington went (all the farther/as far as) he could go to mold the young nation into a strong republic.
10. It (ain't/is not) at all surprising that the capital of the United States was named in honor of Washington.

borrow, lend, loan   *Borrow* is the opposite of *lend*. The verb *borrow* means "to take something with the understanding that it must be returned." The verb *lend* means "to give something with the understanding that it will be returned." *Loan* should be used as a noun. Although *loan* may be used as a verb, *lend* is the preferred usage.

> Mari wants to **borrow** Victor's bicycle. [verb]
> Victor will **lend** her the bicycle if she puts air in the tires. [verb]
> Mari asked her aunt for a **loan** so she could buy a bicycle. [noun]

bring, take   *Bring* means "to carry from a distant place to a closer one." *Take* means "to carry from a nearby place to a more distant one."

> **Bring** the dog when you come to our house on Saturday.
> Don't **take** the dog when you go to the Bradleys'.

can, may   *Can* implies the ability to do something. *May* implies permission to do something or the possibility of doing it.

> You **may** go skiing this weekend if you **can** find a place to rent the necessary equipment.

can't hardly, can't scarcely   These expressions are considered double negatives, since *hardly* and *scarcely* by themselves have a negative meaning. Do not use *hardly* and *scarcely* with *not* or *-n't*.

> Juliana **can hardly** believe that she is taller than both her mother and her brother.

> I **can scarcely** hear my television program when my neighbor plays the drums.

could of, might of, must of, should of, would of   The helping verb *have*, not the preposition *of*, should follow *could, might, must, should,* or *would*.

> I **could have** danced all night.

> I **might have** won the singing award if I had not lost my voice the day before.

different from, different than   The expression *different from* is generally preferred to *different than*.

> Square dancing is **different from** ballroom dancing.

doesn't, don't   *Doesn't* is a contraction, or shortened form, of *does not* and is used with *she, he, it,* and singular nouns. *Don't* is a contraction of *do not* and is used with *I, you, we, they,* and plural nouns.

> My mother is one commuter who **doesn't** mind long bus rides.
> Most subway riders **don't** expect comfort.

emigrate, immigrate   *Emigrate* means "to leave one country to settle in another." *Immigrate* means "to enter a country in order to live there permanently." With *emigrate* use *from,* and with *immigrate* use *to* or *into.*

> Roberto will **emigrate** from Mexico this spring.
> He will **immigrate** to the United States.

farther, further   Use *farther* to refer to physical distance. Use *further* to refer to degree or time.

> Compact cars can go **farther** on a gallon of gasoline than full-sized cars can.

> Argue no **further**—I will do as you suggest!

Exercise 2	Making Usage Choices

On your paper write the correct word or expression from each pair in parentheses.

Abraham Lincoln, a President of the People

1. As a young man, Abraham Lincoln had to (borrow/lend) money in order to open a store.
2. (Because/Being that) Lincoln always dealt fairly with people, he earned the nickname Honest Abe.
3. As president, Lincoln (could of/could have) isolated himself, but his style was (different from/different than) that of his predecessors.
4. If I had to choose (between/among) the Gettysburg Address and Lincoln's second inaugural address, I would choose the second inaugural address as the better speech.
5. Other issues (beside/besides) slavery divided the North and the South.
6. Toward the end of Lincoln's first term, the Civil War was going (badly/bad) for the North.
7. Many people who (emigrate/immigrate) to this country know all about Lincoln.
8. I (can't hardly/can hardly) believe that a great man like Lincoln was assassinated.
9. (Can/May) we borrow this biography of Lincoln? Ted (doesn't/don't) know where ours is.
10. Ann will (bring/take) the biography with her to my house on Sunday.

fewer, less   *Fewer* is generally used to refer to things or qualities that can be counted. *Less* is generally used to refer to things or qualities that cannot be counted. In addition, *less* is sometimes used with figures that are regarded as single amounts or single quantities.

> Why did **fewer** people come to this year's gallery opening than last year's?

> There is **less** space in the new building than there was in the old one.

> The rent in the new gallery is **less** than 400 dollars a month. [The money is treated as a single sum, not as individual dollars.]

good, well   See Unit 18.

had of   The word *of* should not be used between *had* and a past participle.

> I wish I **had known** that you were ill.

hanged, hung   When your meaning is "put to death by hanging," use *hanged*. In all other cases use *hung*.

> Although Benedict Arnold escaped punishment for his treachery in the American Revolution, his messenger, John André, was caught and **hanged** as a spy.

> Clara **hung** her oil painting in a prominent place in the school auditorium.

in, into   Use *in* to indicate location "inside" or "within" a place. Use *into* to indicate movement or direction to a place, generally from the outside to a point within.

> The onions were **in** the stew.
> The chef put the roast **into** the oven.

irregardless, regardless   Both the prefix *ir-* and the suffix *-less* have negative meanings. When they are used together, they produce a double negative, which is incorrect. Therefore, you should use *regardless* rather than *irregardless*.

> **Regardless** of the heat, the workers at the steel mill remained on the job.

this kind, these kinds   Because *kind* is singular, it is modified by the singular form *this* or *that*. *This* and *that* should also be used with the nouns *sort* and *type* (*this type, that type, this sort, that sort*). When the plural *kinds* is used, the plural form *these* or *those* modifies it. *These* and *those* should be used with the plural nouns *sorts* and *types*.

This kind of exercise is challenging.
These kinds of exercises are easy.
That sort of fruit is delicious.
Those sorts of fruits are delicious.

| **Exercise 3** | **Making Usage Choices** |

On your paper write the correct word or expression from each pair in parentheses.

Theodore Roosevelt, a Man of Determination

1. Theodore Roosevelt's ancestors (emigrated/immigrated) from Holland during the 1640s, (bringing/taking) their belongings with them.
2. Roosevelt fought so (good/well) in the Spanish-American War that he gained national attention.
3. Many of President Roosevelt's policies were (different from/ different than) those of his predecessor, William McKinley.
4. Roosevelt's conservation efforts went (farther/further) than those of any previous president; he (could have/could of) been an influence on nature groups.
5. An enthusiastic leader, Roosevelt put a great deal of energy (in/into) his work.
6. (These kind/These kinds) of qualities made Theodore Roosevelt a good president, (regardless/irregardless) of his faults.
7. If I (had/had of) known more about President Roosevelt, I might have seen the merit in much that he did.
8. Even those people who criticize Roosevelt (doesn't/don't) deny his great determination.
9. Theodore Roosevelt wrote no (less/fewer) than forty books.
10. Hunting trophies (hanged/hung) on the walls of his home.
11. Roosevelt was a president who had an unforgettable (effect/affect) on the people of the country.
12. They (could hardly/couldn't hardly) ignore his bravery.
13. Because he kept right on talking after he was shot while making a speech, people (accepted/excepted) him as a hero.
14. Some critics believe that Roosevelt (took/brought) many imperialistic viewpoints to the presidency.
15. Others say those viewpoints were not so (different from/different than) what many politicians of his day believed.

lay, lie   *Lay* means "to place" or "to put" something down. It always takes a direct object. *Lie* means "to recline" or "to be positioned"; it does not take an object.

> **Lay** the bar of soap on the edge of the sink.
> I like to **lie** under a warm blanket in the winter.

Occasionally there is confusion in sorting out the principal parts of these verbs. Notice the similarities and differences between the two.

BASE FORM	lay	lie
PRESENT PARTICIPLE	laying	lying
PAST FORM	laid	lay
PAST PARTICIPLE	laid	lain

He **laid** the bar of soap on the edge of the sink this morning.
Last night I **lay** under my warm blanket and slept soundly.
He had **laid** his toothbrush down beside the soap.
I have **lain** under those wonderful blankets on every chilly night this winter.

learn, teach   *Learn* means "to gain knowledge." *Teach* means "to instruct" or "to give knowledge to."

I **learned** to speak Swahili.
My sister Midori **teaches** organic chemistry at Yale.

leave, let   *Leave* means "to go away" or "to depart." *Let* means "to allow" or "to permit."

Lian had to **leave** the auditorium.
The usher **let** her use the house telephone.

With the word *alone*, however, you may use either *let* or *leave*.

Leave me alone.   **Let** me alone.

like, as   Use *like*, a preposition, to introduce a prepositional phrase. Use *as*, a subordinating conjunction, to introduce a subordinate clause. Many authorities believe that *like* should not be used before a clause in formal English.

Kathleen sings **like** an angel.
Maya thinks **as** I do in this matter.

loose, lose   Use the adjective *loose* when you mean "free," "not firmly attached," or "not fitting tightly." Use the verb *lose* when you mean "to have no longer," "to misplace," or "to fail to win."

That button is so **loose** I'm afraid I will **lose** it.

passed, past   *Passed* is the past and the past participle form of *to pass*. *Past* is used as an adjective, a noun, a preposition, or an adverb.

The challenger in the race **passed** the leader. [verb]
I paid many bills this **past** month. [adjective]
San Antonio is a city with an interesting **past**. [noun]
Make a sharp right turn **past** the bank. [preposition]
When did the bus drive **past**? [adverb]

precede, proceed   Use *precede* when you mean "to go or come before." Use *proceed* when you mean "to continue" or "to move along."

> In a dictionary the entry for *airplane* **precedes** that for *airship*.
> An airplane can **proceed** at a faster speed than an airship.

raise, rise   The verb *raise* means "to cause to move upward" or "to lift up." It always takes an object. The verb *rise* means "to get up" or "to go up." It is an intransitive verb and never takes an object.

> We will **raise** the flag at six o'clock tomorrow morning.
> They will **rise** at seven o'clock for exercise.

reason is, because   *Because* means "for the reason that." Therefore, do not use *because* after *reason is*. Use either *reason is that* or *because* alone.

> The **reason** Leroy entered the marathon **is that** he enjoys long-distance running.
>
> Leroy entered the marathon **because** he enjoys running.

respectfully, respectively   Use *respectfully* to mean "with respect." Use *respectively* to mean "in the order named."

> The basketball champion shook the President's hand **respectfully.**
> Ann and Arlene are my aunt and cousin, **respectively.**

says, said   *Says* is the third-person singular of the verb *say*. *Said* is the past tense of *say*. Do not use *says* when you mean *said*.

> Enrique always **says** that he is just an average pianist.
> Last week my teacher **said** I was ready to perform in public.

sit, set   *Sit* means "to be seated." It rarely takes an object. *Set* means "to put" or "to place," and it generally takes an object. When *set* is used to mean "the sun is going down," it does not take an object.

> Before a show starts, many people find it hard to **sit** quietly.
> The stage manager **set** the flowers on the mantelpiece.
> The lighting designer saw to it that the sun **set** in a blaze of color.

than, then   *Than* is a conjunction. Use it in comparisons and to show exception.

> Winston is more athletic **than** Carl.
> The winner is none other **than** last year's champion, Rashida.

Then is an adverb and is mostly used to refer to time. *Then* is also used to mean "soon afterward," "the time mentioned," "at another time," "for that reason," "in that case," and "besides."

> Sam was an inexperienced cook **then.**
> You bowl first, and **then** it will be my turn.
> By **then** we will be experts.
> If you won't try it, **then** I will.

this here, that there   Do not use *here* and *there* after *this* and *that*.

> I want to look at **this** newspaper.
> Please hand me **that** lantern.

where at   Do not use *at* after *where*.

> **Where** is Salt Lake City?

who, whom   See Unit 17.

Exercise 4	**Making Usage Choices**

On your paper write the correct word or expression from each pair in parentheses.

John F. Kennedy, a Vibrant Leader

1. One reason John F. Kennedy is still admired is (because/that) he showed exceptional leadership qualities.
2. As a young man, Kennedy toured Europe, talking to heads of state to (learn/teach) their political views.
3. (These kind/These kinds) of situations helped prepare Kennedy for the presidency.
4. When Kennedy took office, he (raised/rised) the nation's morale with his inaugural address.
5. Kennedy declared that "the torch has been (passed/past) to a new generation of Americans."
6. Much of his charm (lay/laid) in his fine speaking ability.
7. (Like/As) you would expect from people interested in the arts, the Kennedys invited many performers to the White House.
8. During the missile crisis, Kennedy refused to (leave/let) the Soviet Union keep missiles on the island of Cuba.
9. Kennedy's decision to (precede/proceed) with a naval blockade of Cuba was a difficult one.
10. It was painful for Americans to (loose/lose) such a young and vibrant leader.

Exercise 5   Making Usage Choices

On your paper write the correct word or expression from each pair in parentheses.

Franklin Roosevelt, a President During Hard Times

1. Many people (said/says) that Franklin Roosevelt was one of the greatest of all our presidents.
2. After being stricken with polio in 1921, Roosevelt had to work harder (than/then) ever to maintain an active life.
3. (This/This here) paralysis struck when he was 39.
4. Warm Springs, Georgia, was (where he took treatments/where he took treatments at).
5. Roosevelt did not (set/sit) idly during the Depression.
6. People (who/whom) had lost everything looked to Roosevelt for hope.
7. The Tennessee Valley Authority and the Works Progress Administration were, (respectively/respectfully), a natural resources corporation and an employment program.
8. After Pearl Harbor was attacked, Roosevelt, (then/than) in his third term, led the country into World War II.
9. In February 1945 at Yalta, Roosevelt and Winston Churchill met with Joseph Stalin, with (who/whom) they planned Germany's defeat and its postwar occupation.
10. After Roosevelt's death on April 12, 1945, President Truman (respectively/respectfully) proclaimed a national day of mourning.

Exercise 6   Make Usage Choices

On your paper write the correct word or expression from each pair in parentheses.

Puerto Rico, Past and Future

1. When Christopher Columbus reached Puerto Rico in 1493, the Arawak (already/all ready) inhabited the island.
2. Columbus and the Spanish explorer Ponce de León landed on the island in 1493 and 1508, (respectfully/respectively).
3. (Awhile/A while) after Ponce de León founded the island's first Spanish colony, he became its governor.
4. Spain ceded Puerto Rico to the United States after losing the Spanish-American War in 1898, but 19 years (passed/past) before it was designated a U.S. territory.
5. In 1952 (a/an) effort to establish the Commonwealth of Puerto Rico was approved by the citizens and government leaders of both Puerto Rico and the United States.
6. Since then the debate (between/among) Puerto Ricans has been about whether the island should be a commonwealth, an independent nation, or a state.
7. For decades, more Puerto Ricans have lived in the city of San Juan (then/than) in any other community on the island.
8. (Irregardless/Regardless) of the problems that occurred after World War II, Puerto Rico has one of the highest standards of living among the Caribbean islands.
9. With industrialization came urbanization; (fewer/less) Puerto Ricans than ever before live in rural areas.
10. It seems likely that (farther/further) debate about Puerto Rican statehood is inevitable.

On your paper write the correct word or expression from each pair in parentheses.

Native American Place Names

1. I have found that (a lot/alot) of Americans don't know that many place names are derived from Native American languages.
2. If you (ain't/aren't) sure about the derivation of a place name, see if it is explained in a dictionary or an encyclopedia.
3. The (amount/number) of place names in the United States is currently more than 3.5 million.
4. We (can/may) make a list of Native American place names in our state.
5. Many place names aren't very (different than/different from) their source words.
6. (Beside/Besides) adopting tribal names, such as Dakota and Delaware, as place names, settlers often adopted descriptive Native American words, such as *yaphank*, which means "river bank" in Algonquian.
7. My trip to Meddybemps, Maine, (learned/taught) me two things: that the name comes from an Algonquian word meaning "plenty of alewives" and that an alewife is a type of small fish.
8. A (loose/lose) translation of the Ojibway word *kichi* is "big"; Kichi Lake, in Minnesota, received its name from the Ojibway word.
9. *Nebraska* is a Sioux word that means "a wide, flat river"; the word refers to the Platte River, which (lays/lies) in the southern part of the state.
10. Although the names of Pennawa Creek, Florida, and Penacook, New Hampshire, look similar, their meanings—"turkey" and "sloping place"—are quite (different from/different than) each other.
11. The Mississippi River, whose name means "Father of Waters," is not as long as the Nile River or the Amazon River; the Gulf of Mexico is (all the farther/as far as) it goes.
12. (Because/Being as) so many Cherokee were forced to migrate to Oklahoma during the nineteenth century, Cherokee is a common place name in that state.
13. A well-known Osage chief gave his name to a town in Oklahoma called Pawhuska; (this/this here) word means "white hair."
14. I've learned that the word *ponca* comes from *pa-honga*, meaning "sacred leader," but I don't know how it (could have/could of) become the name of a town.
15. The Native Americans of Acoma, which is located on a mile-high mesa in New Mexico, named their pueblo (good/well); *acoma* means "sky city."
16. (These kind/These kinds) of place names appear to be among the oldest names in North America.
17. The large (amount/number) of lakes in Minnesota may be why the Dakota used the words *minne*, meaning "water," and *sota*, meaning "reflection of sky upon water," to name the region.
18. The banks (beside/besides) the Olentangy River in central Ohio are streaked in red, hence the Algonquian name meaning "place where paint is found."
19. The great hills for which Massachusetts was named (lie/lay) near what is now Massachusetts Bay.
20. May I please (borrow/loan) your book, so that I can find the derivation of the name Nippersink?

On your paper write the correct word or expression from each pair in parentheses.

Spirituals

1. The first time I heard a spiritual, I was surprised by the (affect/effect) the music had on me.
2. I had heard that spirituals were known as sorrow songs, yet I didn't find the music (all together/altogether) sad.
3. In fact, the inspirational lyrics and haunting melody made my spirits (raise/rise).
4. My friends agree that these songs don't make them feel (bad/badly) but, rather, inspired and hopeful.
5. When I decided to do some research on spirituals, the first thing I did was to go (in/into) the library's audio room.
6. I then (preceded/proceeded) to locate such songs as "Go Down, Moses," "Michael, Row the Boat Ashore," and "Steal Away."
7. I decided to (sit/set) all my research books on the table and concentrate on the music.
8. Even now, I (can hardly/can't hardly) believe how inspiring I found these songs of hardship and faith in religious salvation.
9. If you listen closely to a spiritual, you (can/may) hear how the verses alternate with a refrain.
10. The lyrics of some spirituals express the singers' desire to have the cruel world (leave/let) them alone.
11. I listened to a tape of the singers Dock Reed and Vera Hall, (who/whom) researchers recorded in the 1930s and 1940s.
12. The recording was made with primitive equipment, so the sound quality is (alright/all right) but not excellent.
13. Before starting my research, I (had/had of) thought that spirituals originated in America.
14. Some people (doesn't/don't) believe spirituals originated here, since there are African elements in many of them.
15. Spirituals did not achieve international popularity until the Jubilee Singers, an American group from Fisk University, (brought/took) their act to Europe in the 1870s.
16. It (must of/must have) been quite an experience to hear these powerful songs sung by such beautiful voices.
17. By the early twentieth century, the spiritual had begun to be treated (like/as) a true artistic form: songs were published and performed by choral groups and symphony orchestras.
18. African Americans such as Paul Robeson and William Grant Still were (accepted/excepted) around the world as fine performers of spirituals.
19. The reason spirituals are an important part of our musical heritage is (because/that) they have influenced many other types of music, from folk to gospel.
20. Last week my friend Jeanine (says/said) that she would be going to the library to learn more about spirituals.

Grammar Review

Usage Glossary

The following quotations deal with different aspects of our relationship with nature. Conflicts with nature, the need for harmony with nature, and the wonders of nature are all discussed by poets and novelists. The quotations, some of which appear in translation, have been annotated to show usage items covered in this unit.

Literature Model

QUOTATIONS ABOUT NATURE

The articles *a* used before a word beginning with a consonant and *an* used before a word beginning with an unsounded *h*

To see a World in a Grain of Sand
And a Heaven in a Wild Flower,
Hold Infinity in the palm of your hand
And Eternity in an hour.

From "Auguries of Innocence" by William Blake

May used to suggest possibility

It may be that the stars of heaven appear fair and pure simply because they are so far away from us, and we know nothing of their private life.

From *The Romantic School* by Heinrich Heine, translated from the German

The intransitive verb *lie*

The whole secret of the study of nature lies in learning how to use one's eyes.

From *Nouvelles Lettres d'un Voyageur* by George Sand, translated from French

The conjunction *than* used in a comparison

I like trees because they seem more resigned to the way they have to live than other things do.

From *O Pioneers!* by Willa Cather

Doesn't used with a singular pronoun

Something there is that doesn't love a wall,
The sends the frozen-ground-swell under it
And spills the upper boulders in the sun,
And makes gaps even two can pass abreast.

From "Mending Wall" by Robert Frost

Surrounded by the voracity of nature, Aureliano and Amaranta Ursula continued cultivating the oregano and the begonias and defended their world with demarcations of quick lime, building the last trenches in the age-old war between man and ant.

From *One Hundred Years of Solitude* by Gabriel García Márquez, translated from the Spanish by Gregory Rabassa

> The preposition *between* used to show a relationship between two elements

Mankind's true moral test, its fundamental test (which lies deeply buried from view), consists of its attitude towards those who are at its mercy: animals.

From *The Unbearable Lightness of Being* by Milan Kundera, translated from the Czech by Michael Henry Heim

> The relative pronoun *who* in the nominative case because it is the subject of a clause

Exercise 1

Making Usage Choices   The following sentences describe the seasons of the year. On your paper write the correct word or expression from each parentheses.

1. In many areas of this country, each season—spring, summer, autumn, or winter—is (different from/different than) every other season.
2. There is however, (less/fewer) difference in the seasons in the southern United States than in other regions.
3. In the spring the geese fly by the thousands across the prairie sky, (emigrating/immigrating) from their southern winter habitat.
4. Thawing snow fills the streams and rivers with (a lot/alot) of water, sometimes bringing on flooding.
5. The warmth of summer (affects/effects) all plant life, bringing green lawns, buzzing insects, and brightly colored flowers.
6. By June most people have (hanged/hung) their sweaters and jackets back in the closet and are eagerly anticipating the hot summer months.
7. Warm summer weather invites youngsters everywhere to jump (in/into) swimming pools.
8. Summer (proceeds/precedes) the coming of autumn, when the weather usually turns cooler.
9. I wish you (could of/could have) seen the brilliant orange, red, and yellow colors of the autumn leaves in Vermont this year.
10. In the winter all trees (accept/except) the evergreens are bare, brisk winds blow, winter storms leave a white carpet of snow, and streams and rivers freeze solid into thick layers of ice.

Exercise 2

Making Usage Choices   The following sentences describe endangered and extinct animals. On your paper write the correct word or expression from each parentheses.

1. (Because/Being as) dinosaurs are so popular, people flock to museums to see their skeletons.
2. Dinosaurs roamed the Earth for 120 million years (all together/altogether).
3. I wish someone would (learn/teach) me more about dinosaurs.
4. The (number/amount) of dinosaur species that populated the Earth was greater than I had imagined.
5. (Irregardless/Regardless) of how many dinosaurs there once were, they all became extinct.
6. Many animals are (affected/effected) adversely when their habitat is altered.
7. The black rhinoceros and the giant panda, which roam over sub-Saharan Africa and China, (respectively/respectfully), are both endangered.
8. (Where at/Where) do grizzly bears, lynxes, and red wolves live?
9. If people are not careful, they might (loose/lose) these animals permanently.
10. Far too many animals have (already/all ready) become extinct, thus diminishing the world's biological resources and sometimes upsetting the delicate balance of nature.

Exercise 3

Making Usage Choices   The following sentences discuss topics related to astronomy. On your paper write the correct word or expression from each parentheses.

1. (This here/This) machine is a telescope, which is used to view the moon, stars, comets, planets, and other celestial bodies.
2. Scientists will travel (farther/further) than most other people will to get a good view of a total eclipse of the sun.
3. Earth revolves around the sun, just (like/as) the other eight major planets of our solar system do.
4. Our solar system (lies/lays) within one swirling arm of the Milky Way galaxy.
5. The Milky Way acquired its name from our view of it as (a/an) hazy, luminous, milk-like band of stars enveloping the night sky.
6. (Farther/Further) in space, beyond the Milky Way, lie perhaps 100 billion other galaxies.
7. The Milky Way galaxy alone has no (fewer/less) than 200 billion stars.
8. The reason stars appear to twinkle is (that/because) the turbulent motion of the Earth's atmosphere distorts the light that comes from them.
9. The sun and the moon appear to (rise/raise) and set in the sky.
10. Perhaps one day we will be able to travel easily (between/among) the stars.

Exercise 4

Making Usage Choices   The following sentences relate to the study of ocean life. On your paper write the correct word or expression from each parentheses.

1. Some people believe that life (don't/doesn't) exist in the icy depths of the oceans.
2. Oceanographers, however, (can't hardly/can hardly) enumerate the various kinds of life found in the oceans of the world.
3. You must (bring/take) special equipment with you when you explore the ocean depths.
4. (Beside/Besides) being the home of fish and mammals of normal size, the oceans are home for plankton, which are microscopic animals and plants.
5. On a television documentary I saw the other day, an oceanographer (says/said) that *plankton* is a Greek word meaning "wandering."
6. Plankton drifts through the upper levels of the sea rather (than/then) in the depths.
7. (These kind/These kinds) of living organisms become food for other marine life.
8. My cousin, (who/whom) I believe is an expert on ocean life, told me that many deep-sea fish have fantastic shapes.
9. I (should of/ should have) joined my cousin on her last deep-sea adventure.
10. My cousin said that she always thought my idea of a deep-sea adventure was to (sit/set) my fishing line in the water and wait for a fish to bite.

Exercise 5

Making Usage Choices   The following sentences describe rain forests, one of the world's endangered resources. On your paper write the correct word or expression from each parentheses.

1. Many people feel that it is not (alright/all right) to allow the exploitation of the world's rain forests.
2. If care is not taken to preserve these forests, they will be gone after (a while/awhile).
3. Some plants seem to thrive (irregardless/regardless) of where they grow.
4. Plants that grow (well/good) on the forest floor are the same kind as those that thrive in dimly lighted buildings.
5. Far below the forest's green canopy, the ground is interlaced with streams and rivers formed in times (passed/past).
6. No one knows the exact (number/amount) of plants and insects in the rain forest.
7. If you travel to a rain forest, you will want to (bring/take) a camera with you to record on film the beauty of the extraordinary scenery.
8. I was able to capture the exquisite detail of the plants because my friend had (loaned/lent/borrowed) me a special, high-resolution camera.
9. Only after several years of training (can/may) a nature enthusiast identify many of the different forms of wildlife in a rain forest.
10. As I (preceded/proceeded) through the forest on my last visit, I encountered a band of monkeys rapidly making their way through the treetops.

Exercise 6   Writing Sentences with Correct Word Usage

Choose five of the pairs of words below. For each pair, write a sentence using each word.

bring/take   between/among
good/well   in/into
doesn't/don't   bad/badly
who/whom   lay/lie
fewer/less   farther/further

SAMPLE   a.   Our yard has *fewer* weeds this year than our neighbor's yard has.
ANSWER   b.   We have had *less* rainfall this year than we've had in several years.

Review: Exercise 7

Proofreading

Proofreading   The following passage describes the life and work of Louis Comfort Tiffany, whose stained-glass window is reproduced on the opposite page. Rewrite the passage, correcting the errors in spelling, grammar, and usage. Add any missing punctuation. There are twenty-five errors.

Louis Comfort Tiffany

[1]Louis Comfort Tiffany (1848-1933) was the son of Charles Lewis Tiffany a gem merchant and the founder of the famed Tiffany and Company, manufacturers of fine silverware. [2]The younger Tiffany became excepted as a designer of distinctive glass. [3]Louis Tiffanys' designs reflected the Art Nouveau style of the passed, particularly the late nineteenth century. [4]The reason this here art movement came into being was because the handcrafting of objects was being revitalized as a reaction against the intense industrial activity of the late 1800s. [5]The movement toward hand-crafted objects was meant to give naturel beauty and artistic impact to ordinary objects. [6]Art Nouveau was different than other art forms because it characteristically used rounded edges and iridescent colors.

[7]Louis Tiffany began his career making stained-glass windows as the one shown on the opposite page. [8]He used many kinds of colored glass, including opaque glass opalescent glass, and "satin glass," which was developed around 1880. [9]Each piece of glass generally would of contained more then a single color or kind of decoration. [10]The glass pieces were joined together with lead beading and then they were framed in a variety of ways. [11]In the work on the next page, Tiffany sat a natural outdoor scene in a stylized wooden frame.

[12]A increasing amount of artists and writers of this age struggled to "get back to nature." [13]They hoped to counteract the affects of industrialists, who were scavenging the land for raw materials. [14]The literary quotations in this review explores our relationship to nature. [15]We seperate ourselves from nature in our homes and our buildings, and yet you long to act naturally. [16]This conflict among human ways and the ways of nature are reflected in Tiffanys stylized window which celebrates nature in an all together self-conscious, highly crafted way.

Louis Comfort Tiffany, *Autumn Landscape*, 1923

Mixed Review

The following sentences provide information about the authors of the quotations in this review. On your paper write the correct word or expression from each parentheses.

1. Writers often focus on nature, (like/as) many other artists do.
2. Knowing the details of an author's life can help a reader (farther/further) understand that person's writings.
3. In addition to being a poet, the English Romantic author William Blake was also (a/an) artist and illustrator of his own works.
4. The nineteenth-century German composer Robert Schumann had to choose (between/among) many of Heinrich Heine's poems when he was composing the song cycle *Poet's Love*.
5. (Being that/Because) George Sand was troubled by the poor treatment of women in her time, she often wrote about social injustice.
6. Willa Cather frequently wrote about people who had (emigrated/immigrated) to the United States to farm the prairie lands of the Midwest.
7. Robert Frost, (who/whom) many people admire, won four Pulitzer Prizes for his lyrical poetry, most of which describes the people and landscapes of New England.
8. Frost's work, (besides/beside) being highly romantic, also contains much irony.
9. The reading public probably (doesn't/don't) know that Nobel Prize-winning author Gabriel García Márquez founded an organization for human rights.
10. The poet and novelist Milan Kundera agreed to (accept/except) French citizenship in 1980, after his highly political writings cost him his native Czechoslovakian citizenship.
11. As a young man, Blake admired Michelangelo and Dürer, artists of Italy and Germany, (respectfully/respectively).
12. In his later years, Blake created (less/fewer) poems than in his youth.
13. Earning a law degree was (as far as/all the farther) Heine went in his law career.
14. One (couldn't hardly/could hardly) call Sand a conventional woman of her time.
15. Many years (past/passed) before critics recognized Sand's literary stature.
16. The reason Cather wrote about pioneers is (because/that) she lived among them during her childhood in rural Nebraska.
17. Cather's love of the American landscape greatly (effected/affected) her writing.
18. When Robert Frost went to England in 1912, he (took/brought) with him vivid memories of his native land.
19. In *One Hundred Years of Solitude*, García Márquez (sets/sits) the family saga in the fictional town of Macondo, a place much like his own hometown in Aracataca, Colombia.
20. Strains of pessimism keep Kundera's novels from being (all together/altogether) humorous.

Writing Application

Word Usage in Writing The following passage from "The Most Beautiful Place on Earth" by Edward Abbey contains a number of words that writers sometimes use incorrectly. Read the passage, concentrating on the italicized words.

The view is open and perfect *in* all directions *except* to the west where the ground *rises* and the skyline is only a few hundred yards away. Looking toward the mountains I *can* see the dark gorge of the Colorado River five or six miles away, carved through the sandstone mesa, though nothing of the river itself down inside the gorge. Southward, on the far side of the river, lies the Moab valley *between* thousand-foot walls of rock, with the town of Moab somewhere on the valley floor, too small to be seen from here. Beyond the Moab valley is more canyon and tableland stretching away to the Blue Mountains fifty miles south. On the north and northwest I see the Roan Cliffs and the Book Cliffs, the two-level face of the Uinta Plateau. . . .

Techniques with Nouns Try to use these words correctly when you write and revise your own work.

1. *Except* is most frequently used as a preposition meaning "but." It should not be confused with the verb *accept*, meaning "to receive" or "to agree to."

Incorrect use The view is open and perfect in all directions *accept* to the west. . .
Abbey's use The view is open and perfect in all directions *except* to the west. . .

2. The verb *rise*, which means "to get up" or "to go up," never takes an object. It should not be confused with *raise*, which always takes an object.

Incorrect use to the west where the ground *raises*. . .
Abbey's use to the west where the ground *rises*. . .

Practice Practice correct usage by rewriting the following passage, using a separate sheet of paper. Choose the correct word from each pair in parentheses.

The most beautiful place in my city is a large park where I can ride my bike on weekends. Some cities have nothing (accept/except) block after block of high-rise buildings, so I think I'm lucky to live close to a green, wooded area. Every Saturday morning, as soon as the sun (rises/raises), I'm off on my bike along the trail that winds through the park. At one point the path divides, and it's always hard to decide (among/between) the two forks. One leads (in/into) dark, secluded woods. The other goes (passed/past) an area that the city rents out to people who want to (rise/raise) their own vegetables. One of the women (who/whom) gardens there always offers me one of her luscious red tomatoes. I say politely, "No, thanks," but one of these days I just (can/may) (except/accept) her generous gift. The only thing missing on these Saturday outings is someone to talk to. I'm hoping that my classmate Justin will buy a bike. (Among/Between) all my friends, he's the one who would most enjoy Saturday mornings in the park.

20.1 | Capitalization of Sentences

Capitalize the first word of every sentence.

Traditionally a comedy ends with a marriage between the principal characters.

Have you read her latest novel?

Capitalizing Quotations

Capitalize the first word of a direct quotation that is a complete sentence.

Robert E. Lee once wrote, "**D**uty is the sublimest word in our language."

"**H**appiness lies not in the mere possession of money," he observed. "**I**t lies in the joy of achievement."

The first word of a quotation should not be capitalized unless the entire quotation can stand as a complete sentence.

The ecologist reminded the audience to save "**t**he air, the water, the animals, and the trees."

An indirect quotation should not be capitalized. An **indirect quotation,** often introduced by *that*, does not repeat a person's or a document's exact words.

Amendment VI of the U.S. Constitution states that **a**ccused persons have the right to a speedy trial.

| **Exercise 1** | **Capitalizing Sentences and Quotations** |

On your paper rewrite the following sentences, correcting any errors in capitalization.

The Words of Thomas Paine

1. writer and political theorist Thomas Paine wrote, "it is the object only of war that makes it honorable."
2. he pointed out that those who expected to reap the blessings of freedom must "Undergo the fatigue of supporting it."
3. "every spot of the Old World is overrun with oppression," wrote Paine in *Common Sense*. "freedom hath been hunted round the globe."
4. Paine observed that In its best state government was a necessary evil and that In its worst state, government was intolerable.
5. "Suspicion is the companion of mean souls," Paine wrote, "And the bane of all good society."

Capitalizing with Parentheses

Capitalize the first word of a sentence in parentheses that stands by itself. Do not capitalize a sentence within parentheses that is contained within another sentence.

> Webster's first dictionary encouraged a distinctive American spelling of British words. (**F**or instance, the British word *honour* was replaced by the American word *honor*.)

> A major cotton-producing state in the antebellum South (*antebellum* means "before the war") was Georgia.

Exercise 2 | **Capitalizing Sentences and Quotations**

On your paper rewrite any of the following sentences that have errors in capitalization, correcting the errors. Write the word *correct* if a sentence has no errors.

Notable Quotations

1. one line of Langston Hughes's poem "Dream Deferred" asks, "what happens to a dream deferred?"
2. In 1934 Chiang Kai-shek (He was the Chinese Nationalist leader) said that the Chinese people would improve the nation if they could live "Artistically."
3. Helen Keller said that One can never consent to creep when one feels an impulse to soar.
4. Emerson argued, "Nothing is at last sacred but the integrity of your own mind."
5. in his moving speech of surrender, the Nez Percé leader Chief Joseph said, "from where the sun now stands I will fight no more forever."
6. Abraham Lincoln said that Frederick Douglass was "the most meritorious man of the nineteenth century." (He must have been impressed with Douglass's strong leadership.)
7. Golda Meir (She was a prime minister of Israel) said, "to deny oneself various comforts is also easier in talk than in deed."
8. Marian Anderson once said that when there is money, there is fighting. (she meant that greed encourages conflict.)
9. The first line of Gabriela Mistral's poem "Rocking" is "The sea rocks her thousands of waves."
10. Anaïs Nin wrote, "one handles truths like dynamite."

Exercise 3 | **Using Capitalization in Writing**

On your paper write a short paragraph about the philosophy of Benjamin Franklin as expressed in the maxims he published in *Poor Richard's Almanack*. In your paragraph include the quotes below, either as direct or indirect quotations. Make sure that your sentences are capitalized correctly.

1. "But dost thou love life, then do not squander time, for that's the stuff life is made of."
2. "Lost time is never found again."
3. "Early to bed, and early to rise, makes a man healthy, wealthy, and wise."
4. "He that lives upon hope will die fasting."
5. "Laziness travels so slowly, that poverty soon overtakes him."

20.2 Capitalization of Proper Nouns

Capitalize a proper noun.

A common noun should not be capitalized unless it is the first word of a sentence. In proper nouns composed of several words, do not capitalize articles, coordinating conjunctions, and prepositions of fewer than five letters within a proper noun.

1. **Names of individuals**

John **F**. **K**ennedy	**G**randma **M**oses
Kareem **A**bdul-**J**abbar	**S**hirley **C**hisholm
Rita **M**oreno	**S**andra **D**ay **O**'**C**onnor
Uncle **S**am	**T**oshio **M**ori

2. **Titles of individuals**

Capitalize titles used before a proper name and titles used in direct address.

President Lincoln	**G**overnor Pete Wilson
Queen Elizabeth II	**C**ardinal O'Connor
Chief Tecumseh	Yes, **G**eneral. [direct address]

In general, do not capitalize titles that follow a proper name or are used alone. Most writers, however, capitalize *president* when referring to the current president of the United States.

At the White House the **P**resident greeted Alberto Fujimori, the **p**resident of Peru.

In general, capitalize a title that describes a family relationship when it is used with or in place of a proper name.

Dear **C**ousin Yuki,	*but*	My **c**ousin Yuki sews.
Did you see **F**ather?		my husband's **f**ather
Won't you write, **U**ncle?		What did your **u**ncle write?
A few days later **M**other wrote to us.		My **m**other arrived yesterday.

3. **Names of ethnic groups, national groups, and languages**

African **A**mericans
Apaches
Americans
Chinese
Spanish
Russian

4. Names of organizations, institutions, political parties and their members, and firms

Environmental **P**rotection **A**gency
Knights of **C**olumbus
Ohio **S**tate **U**niversity
the **C**ongress
General **M**otors
a **D**emocrat
the **R**epublican party

Do not capitalize the word *party*. Common nouns such as *court* or *university* are also not capitalized unless they are part of a proper noun.

Kim has to appear in **d**istrict **c**ourt today.
Their case is now before the **C**ourt of **A**ppeals for the **F**ederal **C**ircuit.
Teresa visited the **U**niversity of **T**exas.
Teresa enjoyed her visit to the **u**niversity.

Exercise 4   **Capitalizing Names and Titles**

On your paper rewrite the following names, titles, and sentences, adding capital letters as necessary. Write *correct* if the item is already capitalized correctly.

1. governor george pataki
2. senator nancy kassebaum
3. uncle paul and his father
4. the populist party
5. the community college
6. brown university
7. secretary of state thomas jefferson
8. federal trade commission
9. Sign here, admiral.
10. traffic court
11. bell Atlantic corporation
12. nelson mandela, the president of South Africa
13. georgia o'keeffe
14. pope constantine
15. chief justice william rehnquist
16. What did you say, grandma?
17. boy scouts of America
18. first city bank
19. swahili
20. japanese americans

5. Names of monuments, bridges, buildings, and other structures

Tomb of the **U**nknown **S**oldier
Delaware **M**emorial **B**ridge
Empire **S**tate **B**uilding
Sears **T**ower
Grand **C**oulee **D**am
the **T**aj **M**ahal

6. Names of documents, awards, and laws

the **D**eclaration of **I**ndependence	an **O**scar
Treaty of **V**ersailles	**S**herman **A**ntitrust **A**ct
Nobel **P**rize	**C**ivil **R**ights **A**ct of 1968
the **M**agna **C**arta	**F**ourteenth **A**mendment

Do not capitalize short prepositions that appear as part of the name.

7. Trade names

a **F**ord
Gleem toothpaste
Kraft cheese
Sanka

8. Geographical terms

Capitalize the names of continents, countries, states, counties, and cities, as well as the names of specific bodies of water, topographical features, regions, and streets.

Africa	**R**ocky **M**ountains
Brazil	**G**reat **R**ift **V**alley
Kentucky	**M**ojave **D**esert
Essex **C**ounty	**L**ong **I**sland
Denver	**T**ropic of **C**ancer
Pacific **O**cean	**S**outheast **A**sia
Lake **E**rie	**P**ennsylvania **A**venue
Snake **R**iver	**F**orty-second **S**treet
Midwest	**C**entral **A**merica

9. Names of planets and other heavenly bodies

Jupiter	**A**lpha **C**entauri
Venus	the **L**ittle **D**ipper
Polaris	the constellation **P**isces

The words *sun* and *moon* are not capitalized. Capitalize *earth* only when you use it in conjunction with the names of the other planets. Usually you do not capitalize *earth* when it is preceded by the definite article, *the*.

Mercury, **V**enus, and **E**arth are the planets closest to the **s**un.
There will be an eclipse of the **m**oon at midnight.
We looked from the sky above to the **e**arth below.

10. Compass points

Capitalize the words *north*, *east*, *south*, and *west* when they refer to a specific area of the country or the world or when they are part of a proper name. Do not capitalize them when they merely indicate direction.

the **S**outh	*but*	**s**outh Florida
East **G**rand **R**apids		**e**ast of Grand Rapids
North **D**akota		**n**orth Texas

Exercise 5　　　**Capitalizing Proper Nouns**

On your paper rewrite the following sentences, correcting capitalization errors.

Visiting Washington, D.C.

1. Washington, D.C., is located on the potomac river.
2. The capital city was built on land ceded to congress by virginia and maryland.
3. An engineer from france, Pierre Charles L'Enfant, designed and partly laid out the city with the help of Benjamin Banneker, an african american surveyor.
4. D.C. stands for the district of columbia.
5. Its avenues are named after The states; pennsylvania avenue is one of the most famous.
6. The central point of The design of The city was the Capitol.
7. Tourists come from all over the world to visit such famous attractions as the Washington monument, the Vietnam veterans memorial, and the national air and space museum.
8. The senate's working copy of the treaty of Versailles is housed in the national archives.
9. A rough draft of the declaration of independence is on display at the library of Congress.
10. Tourists stand in line for hours to tour the white house and possibly catch a glimpse of the president and his family.
11. They also take time to visit George Washington's home at Mount Vernon, which is located several miles South of the city.
12. In warm weather many tourists spend time boating and fishing on nearby chesapeake bay.
13. Class trips from high schools in the north, south, east, and west visit Washington in the spring.
14. Many people enjoy The cherry blossom festival.
15. Still others drive to the beaches along the atlantic ocean to enjoy the Sun and sand.

11. Names of most historical events, eras, and calendar items

Boston **T**ea **P**arty	the **R**enaissance
Persian **G**ulf **W**ar	**T**hanksgiving **D**ay
Battle of **G**ettysburg	**T**ang **D**ynasty
French **R**evolution	**F**ourth of **J**uly

A historical period referring to a general span of time should not be capitalized.

the **f**ifteenth century	the **s**ixties
the **m**edieval **p**eriod	**t**urn of the **c**entury

Capitalize the days of the week and the months of the year, but do not capitalize the names of the seasons (*spring, summer, autumn, fall, winter*).

They will be here all **s**ummer, beginning the first **S**aturday in **J**uly.

12. Religious terms

Capitalize names of deities, religions and their denominations and adherents, words referring to a supreme deity, and religious books and events.

God	**S**outhern **B**aptist **C**onvention
Allah	**B**uddhists
the **L**ord	**Q**uran
Judaism	**B**ible
Hinduism	**E**aster
Christianity	**Y**om **K**ippur

13. Names of ships, planes, trains, and spacecraft

USS *Independence*	*Silver Meteor*
Air Force One	*Columbia*

14. Names of school courses

Capitalize only those school courses that are the name of a language or the title of a specific course. Do not capitalize the name of a subject.

Japanese	*but*	a **f**oreign **l**anguage
Economics 101		**e**conomics
Advanced **C**alculus		**c**alculus

15. Titles of works

The Pearl [novel]
Washington Post [newspaper]
Grolier Encyclopedia [reference book]
"The Monkey's Paw" [short story]
"Song of Myself" [poem]
"America the Beautiful" [song]
Beauty and the Beast [movie]
Calla Lily with Red Roses [work of art]
Much Ado About Nothing [play]
Out of Africa [memoir]

Always capitalize the first and last word of a title or subtitle. Capitalize all other words except articles, coordinating conjunctions, and prepositions of fewer than five letters.

Capitalize articles (*a*, *an*, and *the*) at the beginning of a title only when they are part of the title itself. It is common practice not to capitalize (or italicize) articles preceding the title of a newspaper or a periodical. Do not capitalize (or italicize) the word *magazine* unless it is part of the title of a periodical.

"The Open Boat"   *but*   the *Post-Dispatch*
"A Christmas Carol"   a *TIME* magazine article

Exercise 6   **Capitalizing Proper Nouns and Explaining Why**

Write the following items, adding capital letters where necessary. For each item, explain why you did or did not add capital letters.

SAMPLE   gulf of mexico
ANSWER   Gulf of Mexico—name of a specific body of water

1. university of texas
2. hillary rodham clinton
3. the golden gate bridge
4. the *new york times*
5. laotians, scots, turks
6. captain McShane
7. aunt marilyn and my uncle jack
8. a republican
9. the atlantic charter
10. the pure food and drug act
11. apple computer, inc.
12. pulitzer prize
13. the first monday in october
14. the northwestern united states
15. first district court
16. appalachian mountains
17. the reformation and renaissance
18. the big dipper
19. world history II and my history class
20. new testament
21. "the star-spangled banner"
22. wheaties cereal
23. Labor Day
24. uss *constitution*
25. Sunset Boulevard in hollywood, california

On your paper rewrite the following sentences, correcting capitalization errors.

The Chippewa People

 1. In my history class I learned about the Chippewas, who were once among the most powerful culture groups of north America.
 2. In canada chippewas are known as ojibways; both names are derived from a word that describes the group's traditional moccasins.
 3. The chippewas, the ottawas, and the potawatomis—all members of a governing body called the Council of Three Tribes—lived peacefully near the shores of lake Superior for several hundred years.
 4. During the Seventeenth Century, the chippewas fought and defeated the sioux to the West, the Kickapoos to the South, and the iroquois to the East.
 5. The Chippewas fought with the french against the british in the 1760s, yet they sided with the british in the american revolution.
 6. By 1871, when the United States congress stopped making treaties with native americans, the Chippewas and the government had signed 42 Treaties.
 7. In the Winter of 1973, the leaders of an organization called the american indian movement seized a piece of federal land in north dakota; it was the site on which the battle of wounded knee had been fought in 1890.
 8. The language of the chippewas is related to several other languages still spoken today, including algonquian, cheyenne, arapaho, shawnee, and cree.
 9. Perhaps the most famous chippewa was not a real person at all; rather, he was the hero of Henry wadsworth longfellow's poem *hiawatha*.
10. Today tens of thousands of chippewas live in cities in the midwest and canada.
11. They also live on Reservations in the provinces of manitoba and ontario in canada.
12. The leech lake reservation is a well-known Chippewa Community in minnesota.
13. For years, a medicine man living in south Dakota has been a spiritual leader for many Chippewas.
14. One of the first questions young people ask him is "what is a native american?"
15. This respected man, whose name is leonard crow dog, points out that Being a native american is to be spiritual. (another well-known modern-day medicine man is Pete Catches.)
16. One of the most prolific Chippewa writers is the Poet Gerald Vizenor, author of the highly acclaimed book *white earth chippewa*.
17. Responding to Native American activism, congress passed a number of laws, including the indian education act of 1972.
18. According to president Richard Nixon, the primary objective of the legislation was "To strengthen the Indian's sense of autonomy without threatening his sense of community."
19. In a poignant poem called "indian," a student at cloquet junior high school reveals what it is like to be a Chippewa today.
20. This poem and other poems and essays written by young Native Americans have been published in a book called *rising voices*.

20.3　Capitalization of Proper Adjectives

Capitalize proper adjectives (adjectives formed from proper nouns).

The following are some of the kinds of proper adjectives that should be capitalized:

1. **Adjectives formed from names of people**

Elizabethan literature	**S**hakespearean actor
Jeffersonian principles	**N**ewtonian physics
Machiavellian character	**A**ristotelian philosophy

2. **Adjectives formed from place names and names of national, ethnic, and religious groups**

Roman candle	**A**frican **A**merican leaders
Chinese checkers	**P**uerto **R**ican heritage
Irish linen	**J**ewish history

Many proper nouns do not change form when used as adjectives.

Senate majority	**O**scar-winning performance
New **Y**ork debut	**R**embrandt exhibit
Vietnam veteran	**W**hite **H**ouse statement

Some proper adjectives that are in common use are no longer capitalized.

venetian blinds	**r**oman numerals

Exercise 8　　**Forming Proper Adjectives**

Form a proper adjective from each of the proper nouns listed below. Consult a dictionary if you need help. On your paper write the adjective plus a noun that the adjective could modify.

SAMPLE　　Israel
ANSWER　　Israeli music

1. Italy
2. Queen Victoria
3. Southwest
4. Sweden
5. Alaska
6. Saturday
7. Buddhism
8. Boston
9. Passover
10. Grammy
11. Karl Marx
12. Charles Dickens
13. Latin America
14. Taiwan
15. Chicago

On your paper rewrite the following sentences, correcting capitalization errors. Write the word *correct* if a sentence has no errors.

Marisol Escobar, Sculptor

1. Marisol Escobar was born into a wealthy venezuelan family living in Paris.
2. The name *Marisol* is a combination of the spanish words *mar y sol*, meaning "sea and sun."
3. Even at a young age, Marisol was fascinated by central and south american art.
4. She was especially drawn to aztec and mayan art.
5. Art critics describe Marisol's work as a cross between modern art and Folk art.
6. Many of her wood and clay figurines are pre-Columbian in style.
7. Her work is displayed in several famous european museums.
8. Some of her more whimsical pieces are in the collections of various american museums.
9. A Marisol Exhibit in Washington, D.C., featured wooden caricatures of well-known public figures, including the british royal family.
10. Today Marisol is a new york city Resident who spends most of her time creating new art.

On your paper rewrite the following sentences, correcting capitalization errors.

Gordon Parks

1. A kansas native, Gordon parks has become one of america's most productive and versatile artists.
2. At the age of 25, Parks decided to move to the chicago area and become a Professional photographer.
3. After holding a successful one-man Photography exhibit, parks served in the military in Europe in the united states office of war information.
4. Returning to the United States after world war II, Parks worked as a filmmaker for a new jersey oil company.
5. Soon afterward *life* magazine hired parks as a Staff Photographer.
6. In the field of photography, parks's awards include magazine photographer of the year (1961) and Syracuse university's newhouse award.
7. Parks has also published such novels as *the learning tree*, an Autobiographical work called *A Choice Of Weapons*, and a book about photography entitled *a Poet And His Camera*.
8. Parks is also a composer, and his musical work entitled *first concerto for piano and orchestra* won favorable reviews.
9. When he directed a movie version of *the Learning Tree* for Warner brothers, parks established himself as the first African american film director at a major hollywood studio.
10. At a white house ceremony in 1988, this distinguished new york resident was honored by president Reagan as one of the 12 recipients of the national medal of arts.

Summary of Capitalization Rules	
Capitalize	**Do Not Capitalize**
He told us to turn to page 506 for the rules of capitalization. (**T**here was no page 506.)	He told us to turn to page 506 (**t**here was no page 506) for the rules of capitalization.
She said, "**H**e liked it very much."	She said that **h**e liked it very much.
Attorney **G**eneral Janet Reno	My **a**ttorney advised me.
Will **G**randmother visit us?	My **g**randmother is 85 years old.
Ohio **S**tate **U**niversity, **J**oslyn **A**rt **M**useum	a **u**niversity in Ohio the **a**rt **m**useum in our city
Dial soap; **C**rest toothpaste	Buy **s**oap and **t**oothpaste.
the **F**irst **A**mendment	The committee added an **a**mendment to the bill.
Atlantic **O**cean; Times **S**quare; **E**ighth **S**treet	the **s**quare at the end of the **s**treet overlooking the **o**cean
Jupiter; **V**enus; **M**ars	the **s**un; the **e**arth; the **m**oon
the **A**merican **C**ivil **W**ar	The country was on the verge of a **c**ivil **w**ar.
Quran; **E**aster **S**unday	**s**acred **b**ook; **h**oliday
German; **A**rt **H**istory II	**f**oreign **l**anguage; **h**istory
Senator Barbara Mikulski	the **s**enator from Maryland
President Jimmy Carter	a former **p**resident
First **D**istrict **C**ourt	**c**riminal **c**ourt
South **P**acific	**s**outh of Honolulu
the **S**tone **A**ge	the **f**ifth **c**entury
"**T**he **B**irthmark"	a **s**hort **s**tory
Friday; **A**pril	**s**ummer; **w**inter

Exercise 11   Using Correct Capitalization in Your Writing

Imagine that you are visiting a friend in another state. On your paper write several sentences of dialogue between you and your friend, discussing the places you would like to visit. Use a variety of proper nouns and proper adjectives. Capitalize all sentences, direct quotations, and proper nouns and adjectives correctly.

On your paper write the letter of the one item that is correctly capitalized in each of the following pairs.

1. **a.** Countee cullen said, "good poetry is a lofty thought beautifully expressed."
   b. Countee Cullen said, "Good poetry is a lofty thought beautifully expressed."

2. **a.** the Supreme court
   b. the Supreme Court

3. **a.** the chair of the Joint Chiefs of Staff, General John Shalikashvili
   b. the chair of the joint chiefs of staff, general John Shalikashvili

4. **a.** In what year did President Lincoln sign the Emancipation Proclamation?
   b. In what year did president Lincoln sign the emancipation proclamation?

5. **a.** Gabriela Mistral was the first latin american writer to win the nobel prize for literature.
   b. Gabriela Mistral was the first Latin American writer to win the Nobel Prize for literature.

6. **a.** Diana Chang wrote the novel *The Only Game in Town*.
   b. Diana Chang wrote the novel *the Only Game in Town*.

7. **a.** I took American History II and a course in mathematics at Stanford University.
   b. I took American History II and a course in Mathematics at Stanford university.

8. **a.** a Hindu shrine
   b. a hindu shrine

9. **a.** Even though the calendar says otherwise, many people consider Memorial Day to be the beginning of the summer season.
   b. Even though the calendar says otherwise, many people consider memorial day to be the beginning of the Summer season.

10. **a.** Explore the southwest.
    b. Explore the Southwest.

11. **a.** I read that article in *The St. Louis Post-Dispatch*.
    b. I read that article in the *St. Louis Post-Dispatch*.

12. **a.** We met Jim Thompson, the former Governor of Illinois.
    b. We met Jim Thompson, the former governor of Illinois.

13. **a.** Hello, Officer.
    b. Hello, officer.

14. **a.** He said that the concert was sold out.
    b. He said that The concert was sold out.

15. **a.** He reminded us that Earth is the third planet from the sun.
    b. He reminded us that Earth is the third planet from the Sun.

Grammar Review

Capitalization

The British writer Bruce Chatwin spent several months walking through southern Chile and Argentina, and *In Patagonia* resulted from that journey. In this passage from his book, Chatwin describes one of Patagonia's more famous residents, the outlaw Butch Cassidy. The passage has been annotated to show some of the rules of capitalization covered in this unit.

Literature Model

from IN PATAGONIA

by Bruce Chatwin

Person's name —

Butch Cassidy, in those years, was drover, horse-wrangler, mavericker, part-time bank-robber, and leader of men; the sheriffs feared him most for the last of these accomplishments. In 1894 they gave him two years in the Wyoming State Penitentiary for stealing a horse he hadn't stolen, valued at five dollars. The sentence soured him to any further dealing with the law. And, from 1896 to 1901, his Train Robbers' Syndicate, better known as The Wild Bunch, performed the string of perfect hold-ups that kept lawmen, Pinkerton detectives and the railroad in perpetual jitters. The stories of his antics are endless; breathless rides along the Outlaw Trail; shooting glass conductors from telegraph poles; or paying a poor widow's rent by robbing the rent man. The homesteaders loved him. Many were Mormons, outlawed themselves for polygamy. They gave him food, shelter, alibis. . . . Today he would be classed as a revolutionary. But he had no sense of political organization.

Butch Cassidy never killed a man. Yet his friends were seasoned killers; their murders drove him to fits of remorse. He hated having to rely on the deadly aim of Harry Longabaugh, the Pennsylvania German with evil blue eyes and a foul temper. He tried to go straight, but there was too much on his Pinkerton card and his pleas for amnesty went unheard. Each new robbery spawned another and added years to his sentence. The costs of operating became unbearable. ➡

Name of an institution —

Name of an organization —

Trade name —

Name of a religious group —

First word of a sentence —

Name of an ethnic group —

In the fall of 1901 Butch met the Sundance Kid and his girl, Etta Place, in New York. She was young, beautiful and intelligent, and she kept her men to heel. Her Pinkerton card says she was a school teacher in Denver; one rumor has it she was the daughter of an English remittance man called George Capel, hence Place. Under the names of James Ryan and Mr. and Mrs. Harry A. Place, the "family of 3" went to operas and theaters. (The Sundance Kid was a keen Wagnerian.) They bought Etta a gold watch at Tiffany's and sailed for Buenos Aires on S.S. *Soldier Prince*. On landing they stayed at the Hotel Europa, called on the Director of the Land Department, and secured 12,000 acres of rough camp in Chubut.

"Are there any bandits?" they asked. They were glad to hear there were none.

Nickname

Place name (city)

Proper adjective

Title preceding a name

First word of a sentence that stands by itself in parentheses

Name of a ship

Title of an individual

Exercise 1

Capitalizing Sentences On your paper rewrite the following sentences about Butch Cassidy, correcting any errors in capitalization. If a sentence has no errors, write *correct*.

1. Robert Leroy Parker (Also known as Butch Cassidy) borrowed his nickname from a friend named Mike Cassidy.
2. the same friend also taught Parker many of his "outlaw" skills. (Mike Cassidy was a hired hand on the Parker ranch.)
3. By the year 1892 Butch Cassidy was well known throughout the West as a notorious Horse Thief.
4. Cassidy's motto was that He would never rob a person with whom he had "Broken bread."
5. When Cassidy asked for a pardon, the Wyoming governor said, "will you give me your word that you'll go straight?"
6. "can't do that," Cassidy said. He did promise, however, that he would never again "molest the state of Wyoming."
7. Years later a friend told the governor that He should have made Cassidy promise to leave Utah alone as well.
8. the Sundance Kid (His real name was Harry Longabaugh) was a dead shot and had a "Foul temper."
9. When asked whether he would ever give himself up to the law, Longabaugh answered, "they'll never take me alive."
10. Interestingly, Cassidy's Pinkerton file described him in this way: "He is a gentlemanly sort of man."

Exercise 2

Capitalizing Proper Nouns and Proper Adjectives   On your paper rewrite the following sentences about Butch Cassidy, correcting any errors in capitalization. If a sentence has no errors, write *correct*.

1. Butch Cassidy grew up on a ranch near Bryce canyon, utah, and spent much of his spare time reading Dime Novels about Jesse James.
2. Cassidy's reputation as the Robin Hood of the West was probably exaggerated but not wholly unjustified.
3. In the Nineteenth Century the Pinkerton Agency did work similar to that done today by the federal bureau of investigation.
4. The Cassidy Gang accidentally blew up thousands of dollars during a holdup of the union Pacific railroad.
5. Trying to escape, they mistakenly stole horses belonging to a republican senator from nevada.
6. Joe lefors, portrayed in paramount's movie *Butch Cassidy and the Sundance kid*, pursued them.
7. For three years the north American outlaws lived quietly on a patagonian Ranch.
8. Cassidy knew that Argentina, Peru, and the Amazonian nations were not Jeffersonian republics: if caught, he would have no assurances of legal rights or due process.
9. Cassidy gave himself away in 1908 when he stole a mule during the theft of a payroll for a bolivian Mine.
10. After dozens of soldiers attacked the outlaws' hut, they found butch and sundance dead, one wearing Etta's tiffany watch.

Exercise 3

Proofreading

The following passage discusses photography in general and the photograph of Butch Cassidy's Wild Bunch shown on the opposite page. On your paper rewrite the passage, correcting the errors in spelling, capitalization, grammar, and usage. Add any missing punctuation. There are twenty-five errors.

Early Photography

[1]the evolution of photography was given a boost in 1837 by Louis-Jacques-Mandé Daguerre of france. [2]Daguerres' process involved the exposure of a polished silver plate to the vapors of iodine (this process formed a sensitive layer of silver iodide). [3]After exposing the plate in the camera, daguerre developed the image with mercury vaper.

[4]The announcement of Daguerre's discovery spurred an english photographer named Henry fox Talbot to develop his own photographic process, which used a paper negative. [5]The photographic process we use today is based on Talbots negative-to-positive principle. [6]not merely a technical expert, Talbot had an eye for beauty and composition as well. [7]According to the Art historian kenneth Clark, "fox Talbot was the first photographer who could properly be called a great artist." ➡

[8]Indeed, the significance of the Photographic camera at first seemed more artistic than practical but it soon had far-reaching effects in many areas. [9]For the first time in history, the World was made visible and accessible. [10]Photography changed our view of ourselves and the World around us. [11]Because there was now a precise means to show what things looked like, science and teknology flourished. [12]Communication was also affected by the advent of Photography: magazine and newspaper reporting became more pictorial.

[13]The photograph shown here of butch Cassidy and his gang was taken in 1901 during the final days of Americas Wild west—a period that began after the Civil war. [14]Butch Cassidy was a charming character with an easy smile but he was an outlaw, nonetheless. [15]Cassidys gang received the name the Wild Bunch because of the uproar they caused while unwinding in town after a hard day of rustling. [16]Do you find it ironic to see the members of the Gang sitting in such a serene and genteel pose?

Photographer unknown, *Butch Cassidy and the Gang,* 1901

Exercise 4

Mixed Review

On your paper rewrite these sentences about Bruce Chatwin, correcting any errors in capitalization. If a sentence has no errors, write *correct*.

Bruce Chatwin

1. In the early Sixties, Bruce Chatwin walked away from a "Brilliant future" at Sotheby's, a fine-arts auction house.
2. At Sotheby's Chatwin attributed his expertise in part to his scant knowledge of chinese porcelain.
3. In time he developed what he termed "A horror of things" and quit his job to write for the *london Sunday times*.
4. he announced his departure with a Telegram stating that he had "gone to Patagonia for six months."
5. Chatwin's strength was writing travel books. (two of the most popular are the semi-fictional *The songlines*, about australia, and *In Patagonia*.)
6. Chatwin's love of travel began during world war II, when his Father was a naval Officer.
7. Even harrowing experiences such as being arrested (In Africa), being harassed, or catching tropical diseases did not dull Chatwin's appetite for travel.
8. Chatwin's himalayan trek convinced him that A person's true home is on the road, not in a house.
9. Chatwin's keen eye made him the pride of his publisher, Viking Press, and the envy of many writers.
10. Chatwin's world was a confusing place full of Legendary tales, Myths, and strange truths.
11. Chatwin described Patagonia as "The uttermost part of the Earth."
12. He was fascinated by this southernmost place in south America, where the darwinian theory of the "survival of the fittest" had been formulated.
13. He owed his interest in Patagonia to a distant cousin, captain Charles Amherst Milward, whose ship sank at the entrance to the strait of Magellan.
14. In a cave in chilean Patagonia, Milward found the frozen remains of a Prehistoric animal, a toothless mammal.
15. The sea captain shipped the skins and bones he recovered from the ice to England, where he sold them to the British Museum.
16. Chatwin returned from Patagonia on a third-class Ship.
17. He acknowledged that he could not have written the book *in Patagonia* without the help of Milward's Daughter Monica Barnett, who lived in lima, Peru.
18. Chatwin won the 1982 whitbread award for his books *the Viceroy Of Ouidah* and *On the Black Hill.*
19. He also received the Hawthornden Prize in Great Britain.
20. "Chatwin's studied style," wrote John Updike in a *New Yorker* Magazine review, "Touches on the epic."

Writing Application

Capitalization in Writing   William Least Heat-Moon, a Native American of Sioux ancestry, chronicled his journey across the less-traveled roads of America in *Blue Highways: A Journey into America*. As you read the passage below, pay special attention to the writer's use of capitalization.

> **W**est of the gorge lay verdant rangeland, much of it given to a buffalo herd maintained by the **A**rizona **G**ame **C**ommission; the great beasts lifted their heads to watch me pass, their dark, wet eyes catching the late sun. To the north rose the thousand-foot butt end of the **V**ermillion **C**liffs; the cliffs weren't truly vermillion, but contrasting with the green valley in the orange afternoon light, they seemed so.

Techniques with Capitalization   Like William Least Heat-Moon, you should apply the rules of capitalization when you write and revise your own work.

1.   Capitalize proper nouns that name specific topographical features, monuments, and other structures. Do not capitalize common nouns or adjectives unless they are part of a proper noun.

Proper Noun Vermillion Cliffs
Common Nouns and Adjectives cliffs, vermillion

2.   Capitalize the names of organizations.

Proper Noun Arizona Game Commission
Common Noun game commission

3.   Do not capitalize *north, south, east, west* when they merely indicate direction, unless the word is the first word in a sentence.

Incorrect Versions west of the gorge lay verdant rangeland . . . To the North rose the thousand-foot butt end . . .

Least Heat-Moon's Correct Versions West of the gorge lay verdant rangeland . . . To the north rose the thousand-foot butt end . . .

Practice   Practice these techniques and other rules of capitalization by revising the following paragraph, using your own paper. (You will need to make 25 changes in capitalization.)

Arizona

As a result of the treaty of Guadalupe Hidalgo in 1848, mexican lands North of the gila river became part of the territory of new Mexico. A southern section of land was added by the so-called Gadsden purchase in 1853. Arizona, which became the forty-eighth state in 1912, is rich in legend and american folklore. Tombstone was the site of the west's most famous gunfight (This battle took place at the O.K. Corral), and it was in Arizona that chief Geronimo surrendered after 25 years of fighting. today, the State is home to 14 native American groups living on 20 Reservations. (the largest reservations are the navajo, hopi, Fort Apache, and Papago reservations.) Throughout the year, especially in the Spring, tourists come to experience firsthand the scenic beauty of Arizona and to visit such natural wonders as the grand canyon, the Petrified Forest, and the painted desert. The Hoover dam and the reconstructed london Bridge are also popular attractions.

21.1 The Period

Use a period at the end of a declarative sentence and at the end of a polite command.

DECLARATIVE SENTENCE	My father came to America when he was not yet twenty-one. —Yoshiko Uchida
POLITE COMMAND	Look in the story for five quotations from Uchida. Please read them aloud.

Exercise 1	**Identifying Use of the Period**

Identify each of the following sentences that should end with a period by writing *declarative* or *command* on your paper. If a sentence is neither a declarative sentence nor a polite command, write *no period*.

Japan's Natural Features

1. Read the following sentences carefully
2. You will learn many fascinating facts about Japan
3. Did you know Japan is an island country in the Pacific
4. Locate Japan on the world map
5. Japan is made up of four large islands and many smaller ones
6. Mountains and hills cover most of the country
7. These beautiful landforms have long been a source of inspiration to poets and painters throughout the world
8. Please open your books to the section about Japan's highest and most famous mountain peak, Mount Fuji, or Fujiyama
9. Mount Fuji is on Honshu, Japan's largest and most heavily populated island
10. Can you find Mount Fuji on your map
11. An inactive volcano, Mount Fuji last erupted in 1707
12. The volcano rises 12,388 feet above sea level
13. In winter, snow covers the mountain's rugged peak
14. In summer thousands of tourists climb the mountain for a view of the crater
15. Consider now how Japan's breathtaking mountains are both an asset and a problem
16. The Japanese Alps attract tourists to the country, thus aiding the economy
17. However, the mountain range covers so much land area that the coastal regions are overcrowded
18. Only one-seventh of Japan's land is suitable for farming
19. How have the Japanese compensated for this scarcity of farmland
20. They farm efficiently and cultivate high-yielding crops, such as rice

21.2 The Exclamation Point

Use an exclamation point to show strong feeling and indicate a forceful command.

> What a colorful garden!
> How exciting the game is!
> Pay attention!

Use an exclamation point after an interjection expressing a strong feeling.

> Wow!   Ouch!

Exercise 2   **Identifying Use of the Exclamation Point**

The following items are declarative sentences, polite and forceful commands, interjections, or exclamatory phrases. Identify the correct type of punctuation for each item by writing *period* or *exclamation point* on your paper.

Japanese Arts

1. How noisy this class is
2. Please pay attention to the presentation on Japanese arts
3. Many Japanese paintings portray the beauty of life in Japan
4. What rich colors the artists used
5. Color printing from wood blocks is very popular
6. Look out
7. We'll pass around this modern wood-block print by Umetaro Azechi
8. Wow
9. What a gorgeous screen painting
10. Japanese sculpture is also outstanding
11. The sculptors worked mostly with wood
12. Please note that some sculptors also used bronze and clay
13. Such fascinating music
14. Traditional Japanese music is made with gongs, drums, flutes, and *samisens* (a banjo-like instrument)
15. Oh my goodness
16. How beautiful Japanese architecture is
17. Most of the houses are small, simple, and unpainted
18. Everyone please listen now
19. Japanese drama is also worth mentioning
20. How very lively *kabuki* drama is
21. By comparison, the *No* drama is slow-moving
22. The actors in a *No* play often wear special masks to represent emotions
23. *Kabuki* dance-dramas are more popular than *No* because they are easier to understand
24. What a surprise
25. Japanese men have traditionally played women's roles in the *kabuki* drama

21.3 The Question Mark

Use a question mark to indicate a direct question.

Was W. E. B. Du Bois born in 1868 or 1869**?**

Should I ask my history teacher**?**

Who knows the answer**?**

Do not place a question mark after a declarative sentence that contains an indirect question.

My friend asked whether W. E. B. Du Bois was born in 1868 or 1869.

I wondered whether I should ask my history teacher.

He asked if anybody knew the answer.

Exercise 3   Identifying Use of the Question Mark

The following items are either direct questions or declarative sentences that contain an indirect question. Identify the correct type of punctuation for each item by writing *period* or *question mark* on your paper.

World Languages

1. How many languages are spoken in the world today
2. My friend asked our Spanish teacher if she knew how many languages exist today
3. Señora Lopez wondered how anyone could know the answer to that question
4. Do you know that estimates have varied from 3,000 to 10,000 languages
5. How can we possibly count all the languages, not to mention the dialects within each language
6. More importantly, what actually counts as a language
7. Our teacher asked if we realized how difficult it is to complete a linguistic survey throughout the world
8. How can linguists stay current when languages are constantly "dying" or being "discovered"
9. A linguist would want to know what factors were considered in the survey
10. The question of how many languages are spoken worldwide does not have a simple answer
11. Have you heard the theory that most of the languages spoken today are descended from one ancient language
12. Linguists hotly dispute whether the theory is valid
13. Some scholars ask how there can be so many similar words without a shared ancestral language
14. Is it ever possible to verify or disprove such a theory
15. Did you know that baby words such as *papa* and *mama* are common across almost all languages in the world

Using End Punctuation (Part 1)

Rewrite the following sentences, adding periods, exclamation points, and question marks where they are needed.

Major-League Baseball

1. Major-league baseball has often been called the national game of the United States
2. What an exciting sport it is
3. I asked how many fans crowd into baseball parks each year
4. How many more Americans, do you suppose, watch the games on television
5. How did such a popular sport get its start
6. Children in colonial Boston were probably the first to use bases with bat-and-ball games
7. Note that these colonial games probably developed from the English sport of cricket, a bat-and-ball game in which each team defends its wicket
8. Should we credit Abner Doubleday for founding the game
9. In 1839 in Cooperstown, New York, Doubleday developed a diamond-shaped field with four bases and named the game *baseball*
10. Did you know that the National Baseball Hall of Fame and Museum opened in Cooperstown one hundred years later

Using End Punctuation (Part 2)

Rewrite the following sentences, adding periods, exclamation points, and question marks where they are needed.

Willie Mays, a Great Baseball Player

1. Baseball fans are forever arguing about who the greatest baseball player was. Which player would you choose
2. Many people would name Willie Mays as an all-time great player
3. In 1951 Mays entered major-league baseball as a center fielder for the New York Giants and quickly became a hero to the fans
4. For years there was a spirited rivalry in New York involving Mays, the Yankees' Mickey Mantle, and the Dodgers' Duke Snider
5. When the Giants moved to San Francisco, Mays electrified the fans there as well
6. He will always be remembered as a fearless base runner and an exceptionally gifted fielder. What a fantastic catch he made in the 1954 World Series
7. Many people wonder whether there will ever be another outfielder as spectacular as Mays
8. Mays's hitting statistics were also impressive. Do you know that he hit 660 home runs and had a career batting average of 0.302
9. How many players have hit more homers than Mays did Only Babe Ruth and Hank Aaron have.
10. In 1979 Mays was elected to the National Baseball Hall of Fame. Some still wonder why the vote was not unanimous

Colons to Introduce

1. Lists

Use a colon to introduce a list, especially after a statement that uses such words as *these*, *the following*, or *as follows*.

> My grandparents' garden contains **these** flowers: camellias, pansies, peonies, tulips, marigolds, and chrysanthemums.

> Perform **the following** operations to start a car with a stick shift: (1) step on the clutch, (2) put the car into first gear, and (3) turn the ignition key.

> Maria's class schedule is **as follows:** English, history, and math.

If a list immediately follows a verb or a preposition, do not use a colon to introduce it.

> The author Alice Walker **writes** poetry, articles, essays, and fiction. [The list follows the verb *writes*.]

> Do not leave for your trip **without** your toothbrush, toothpaste, comb, and brush. [The list follows the preposition *without*.]

2. Illustrations or restatements

Use a colon to introduce material that illustrates, explains, or restates the preceding material.

> You can see how bitterly cold the winters are in Alaska: on a windy morning your breath freezes into ice crystals in front of you.

A complete sentence following a colon is generally lowercased.

3. Quotations

Use a colon to introduce a long or formal quotation. A formal quotation is often preceded by words like *these*, *the following*, or *as follows*.

> Lincoln began the Gettysburg Address with **these** famous words: "Fourscore and seven years ago our fathers brought forth on this continent a new nation . . ."

When poetry quotations take up more than one line and prose quotations take up more than several lines, they generally appear below the introductory statement and are indented.

> Stephen Crane makes this admission in his poem "Truth":

> > For truth was to me
> > A breath, a wind, . . .

On your paper rewrite each of the following sentences, adding colons where they are needed. If a sentence has no errors, write *correct*.

Famous Words

1. In our literature class we memorized famous lines by these writers T. S. Eliot, Emily Dickinson, Edgar Allan Poe, and Federico Garcia Lorca.
2. Noted architect Frank Lloyd Wright once made the following observation "What is needed most in architecture today is the very thing that is most needed in life—integrity."
3. Physicist Albert Einstein placed great value on imagination: he believed imagination was more important than knowledge.
4. According to the Italian poet Petrarch, five great enemies to peace are avarice, ambition, envy, anger, and pride.
5. In "The Still Voice of Harlem," Conrad Kent Rivers writes the following "I am the hope of your unborn."
6. This famous sentence is from a book by Stephen Crane "He wishes that he, too, had a wound, a red badge of courage."
7. An old Native American saying goes something like this "When you were born, you cried and the world rejoiced. Live your life in such a manner that when you die, the world cries and you rejoice."
8. Abolitionist Theodore Parker defined the American ideal as a government of *all* the people, by *all* the people, for *all* the people.
9. Poet Walt Whitman was referring to the death of Abraham Lincoln when he wrote the following lines

   > O powerful western fallen star!
   > O shades of night—O moody, tearful night!
   > O great star disappeared—O the black murk that hides the star!
   > O cruel hands that hold me powerless—O helpless soul of me!
   > O harsh surrounding cloud that will not free my soul.

10. Consider the following observation by Mother Teresa "If you judge people, you have no time to love them."
11. Robert Frost once compared poets and baseball pitchers "Both have their moments. The intervals are the tough things."
12. Addressing a Wellesley College commencement, Barbara Bush, wife of then-president George Bush, made this remark: "Somewhere out in this audience may even be someone who will one day follow in my footsteps and preside over the White House as the President's spouse. I wish him well!"
13. The Declaration of Independence lists these unalienable rights life, liberty, and the pursuit of happiness.
14. The artist Georgia O'Keeffe explained her purpose in these words "I had to create an equivalent for what I felt about what I was looking at—not copy it."
15. Emily Dickinson, one of the most quoted of all poets, was little known before her death only six poems were published in her lifetime.

Other Uses of Colons

Use a colon between the hour and the minute of the precise time, between the chapter and the verse in biblical references, and after the salutation of a business letter.

5:45 P.M.	1 Kings 11:1–13
8:30 A.M.	Madam:
Proverbs 8:22–31	Dear Sir:

Exercise 7   **Using the Colon**

Rewrite the following sentences, adding colons where they are needed. Two items will need two colons.

Quotations

1. "There are two times in a man's life when he should not speculate when he can't afford it and when he can."
   —Mark Twain

2. The Chinese philosopher Lao-Tse described his "three treasures" as follows
   The first is deep love,
   The second is frugality,
   And the third is not to dare to be ahead of the world.

3. Dear Company Officers
   Please send me the following a prospectus, a copy of your annual report, and an application form.

4. Toni Morrison says the following about her work "I always know the ending; that's where I start."

5. Dorothy Parker asked to have this epitaph engraved on her tombstone "Excuse my dust."

6. A haiku by Ezra Pound follows
   The petals fall in the fountain
   the orange-colored rose-leaves,
   their ochre clings to the stone.

7. These famous words are engraved on the Statue of Liberty "Give me your tired, your poor. . . ."

8. The following quotation appeared in Eleanor Roosevelt's autobiography, *This Is My Story* "No one can make you feel inferior without your consent."

9. After he stepped onto the moon on July 20, 1969, astronaut Neil Armstrong spoke these words at 4 17 P.M. "That's one small step for a man, one giant leap for mankind."

10. In reading Genesis 21 1–21, keep in mind that *Sarah* means "princess" and *Isaac* means "laughter."

21.5 The Semicolon

Semicolons to Separate Main Clauses

Use a semicolon to separate main clauses that are not joined by a coordinating conjunction (*and, but, or, nor, yet,* or *for*).

> The acting and directing ability of Orson Welles is considered phenomenal, **and** his film *Citizen Kane* is still studied and appreciated.

> The acting and directing ability of Orson Welles is considered phenomenal**;** his film *Citizen Kane* is still studied and appreciated.

Use a semicolon to separate main clauses joined by a conjunctive adverb (such as *however, therefore, nevertheless, moreover, furthermore,* and *consequently*) or by an expression such as *for example* or *that is.*

A conjunctive adverb or an expression such as *for example* is usually followed by a comma.

> In her youth Mary Cassatt was strongly discouraged from any artistic endeavors**;** nevertheless**,** she later became one of America's foremost painters.

> Many of her associates were world-famous artists**;** for instance**,** she was strongly influenced by the great French painters Edgar Degas and Edouard Manet.

Exercise 8 — Using Semicolons with Main Clauses

On your paper, write each of the following sentences correctly, adding semicolons where necessary.

Mary Cassatt, American Artist

1. Mary Cassatt was born in 1844 to a wealthy Pittsburgh family she later studied at the Pennsylvania Academy of Art.
2. Cassatt's father wanted her to remain in the United States nevertheless, she moved to Paris, France.
3. Edgar Degas became her close friend she relied on him for guidance and counseling.
4. Cassatt's paintings are Impressionist in color however, her delicacy of line resembles that of Japanese prints.
5. Cassatt became famous for her paintings of mothers and children in everyday situations for example, she depicted mothers holding, hugging, and bathing their children.

Semicolons and Commas

Use a semicolon to separate the items in a series when these items contain commas.

> Notable abolitionists were Harriet Beecher Stowe, who wrote *Uncle Tom's Cabin*; Frederick Douglass, who spoke out against slavery; and Harriet Tubman, who led many slaves to freedom through the Underground Railroad.

Use a semicolon to separate two main clauses joined by a coordinating conjunction when such clauses already contain several commas.

> Leonardo da Vinci pursued a wide range of subjects, including mathematics, music, astronomy, and engineering; but he always returned to his primary interest, which was, of course, art.

Exercise 9 **Using Semicolons in Sentences with Commas**

On your paper rewrite the following sentences, adding semicolons where they are needed.

The Arts in Renaissance Italy

1. The Medici family, especially "Lorenzo the Magnificent," became the most famous patrons of the arts in Renaissance Italy, and they summoned poets, philosophers, and artists to the city of Florence.
2. Artists such as Leonardo da Vinci, Michelangelo, and Sandro Botticelli reflected the spirit of the Medici court, for they tried to portray a world of beauty, grace, and nobility.
3. Botticelli's *La Primavera* depicts Venus, who is the goddess of love, Zephyr, who portrays the warm wind of spring, Flora, who is transformed into Spring, Mercury, who holds the symbol of medicine, and the three Graces, who symbolize Poetry, Art, and Music.
4. The famous painter Leonardo da Vinci is also considered a great sculptor, architect, and scientist, yet no existing sculptures and buildings, as well as no specific inventions, can be attributed to him.
5. Michelangelo's most famous achievements include *The Last Judgment*, a fresco that covers the altar wall of the Sistine Chapel, the dome for St. Peter's Church in Rome, which he designed, and his sculptures *Evening* and *Dawn* on the tomb of Lorenzo de Medici.

On your paper rewrite the following sentences, adding semicolons where they are needed.

The Purpose of Art: To Instruct or Delight?

1. "Persons attempting to find a motive in this narrative will be prosecuted persons attempting to find a moral in it will be banished persons attempting to find a plot will be shot."
2. Mark Twain attached the preceding notice to *Huckleberry Finn* he felt that too much analysis made art less enjoyable.
3. "The trouble with music appreciation in general is that people are taught to have too much respect for music they should be taught to love it instead."
   —Igor Stravinsky
4. Among Stravinsky's numerous compositions are the operas *Oedipus Rex*, *The Rake's Progress*, and *Mavra* the ballets *Petrouchka*, *The Firebird*, and *Pulcinella* and three symphonies.
5. Stravinsky lived in Saint Petersburg, Russia Paris, France and the United States.
6. Oscar Wilde agreed with Twain and Stravinsky he said that art should be pleasurable rather than instructive.
7. On the other hand, some writers and artists try to combine pleasure with instruction they seek to teach and delight simultaneously.
8. Simon Ortiz, who is of Acoma Pueblo descent, does not write simply to entertain his readers rather, he wants to impart knowledge about his heritage.
9. In his art Diego Rivera portrays the hard life experienced by some Mexicans he also shows the arrogance of their oppressors.
10. To capture the imagination of their public is enough for most painters, writers, and musicians but other creative people, wanting to raise consciousness, use art to instruct as well.
11. Leo Tolstoy once observed that art was neither a pleasure nor an amusement instead, art was a great matter.
12. By contrast Pablo Picasso was unconcerned with art's role in instruction his only concern was that his paintings evoke emotion.
13. French painter Georges Braque also placed great emphasis on art's emotional role for example, he felt that art was created to disturb.
14. Still other creative people believe art has purposes beyond instructing or delighting in fact, they regard art as revolutionary.
15. Many artistic people have agreed that art inspires revolution, including Paul Gauguin, a painter of South Seas scenes, Jean-Louis Barrault, the French actor, and Mihajlo Mihajlov, a Russian writer.
16. Gauguin said art was either a revolutionist or a plagiarist it could not be otherwise.
17. Barrault went a step further he regarded art as a permanent revolution
18. Mihajlov stated that art was a direct challenge to communist totalitarianism consequently, one true artist was more dangerous than any political adversary.
19. Walter Savage Landor agreed that art creates change he regarded every great writer as a great reformer.
20. British writer John Ruskin provided one of the most eloquent definitions of art he defined good art as that in which the hand, the head, and the heart of the artist go together.

As you study the rules for comma usage, remember that "separating" elements means placing a comma between two equal elements. "Setting off" an element means putting commas *before* and *after* it.

Commas in a Series and with Coordinate Adjectives

Use commas to separate three or more words, phrases, or clauses in a series.

> Alaska, Texas, and California are our three largest states.
> The movie was long, dull, and humorless.
> They have traveled on land, by sea, and in the air.
> I enjoy reading stories, writing articles, and listening to poetry.
> Preheat the oven, beat the eggs, and sift the flour.

When the items are separated by conjunctions, commas are unnecessary.

> The movie was long and dull and humorless.

Nouns used in pairs (*eggs and bacon, salt and pepper*) are considered single units and are not separated by commas. The paired nouns are set off from the other nouns or groups of nouns in a series.

> The storm brought thunder and lightning, high winds, and heavy rain.

Place a comma between coordinate adjectives that precede a noun.

Adjectives that are **coordinate** modify the same noun to an equal degree. You can tell whether adjectives in a sentence are coordinate by reversing their order or putting the word *and* between them. If the sentence sounds right, then the adjectives are coordinate.

> It was a warm, starry, fragrant evening.

Avoid placing a comma between adjectives that precede a noun if they sound strange with their order reversed or with *and* between them. In general, do not use a comma between adjectives that describe size, shape, age, color, and material.

> The big old oak desk stood in one corner of the room.

Some, but not all, of the adjectives in a series may require commas between them.

> A noisy, dusty Japanese truck roared down the street.

Commas and Compound Sentences

Use commas between the main clauses in a compound sentence.

A comma should be placed before a coordinating conjunction (*and, but, or, nor, yet,* or *for*) that joins two main clauses.

I told Eartha what he said, and she advised me to forget it.

I picked up the clay jar carefully, yet it crashed to the floor.

When two very short main clauses are connected by a coordinating conjunction, you may omit the comma between them unless it is needed to avoid confusion.

Alicia opened the door and Manuel came in. [clear]

Alicia opened the door for the dog and the cat ran out. [confusing]

Alicia opened the door for the dog, and the cat ran out. [clear]

Exercise 11   Using the Comma (Part 1)

Rewrite the following sentences, adding commas where they are needed. For the sentence that needs no comma, write *correct*.

Hispanic Culture

1. Hispanic culture is complex diverse and rich in many historical traditions.
2. It has been a vibrant vital part of American life ever since Spanish friars settled in the Southwest in the sixteenth century.
3. People may think Hispanic culture is Spanish but it has also been influenced by Latin American and Caribbean cultures.
4. The influence of Aztec culture can be seen in the popular striking paintings of Carlos Almaraz, a Mexican American.
5. Almaraz's paintings combine beauty oddness power and tranquillity—qualities found in Aztec art.
6. Music from the Spanish-speaking Caribbean islands—Cuba the Dominican Republic and Puerto Rico—sparkles with rhythms brought to the Americas by enslaved people.
7. The lively, syncopated rhythms have been borrowed by such popular American rock groups as the Talking Heads.
8. Hispanic literature is also popular and English translations of Hispanic books are eagerly sought.
9. The works of the Mexican poet and essayist Octavio Paz the Colombian novelist Gabriel García Márquez and the Argentine novelist Julio Cortázar have influenced many American writers.
10. There is no doubt that Hispanic culture will continue to influence enrich and enliven American life.

Commas and Nonessential Elements

1. Participles, infinitives, and their phrases

Use commas to set off participles, infinitives, and their phrases if they are not essential to the meaning of the sentence.

> He read, engrossed, until the doorbell broke his concentration.
> I am not very thirsty, to tell the truth.

If participles, infinitives, and their phrases are essential to the meaning of a sentence, do not set them off with commas.

> The girl watching us is my sister. [The participial phrase tells which girl.]

> To study my notes would not help you much. [The infinitive phrase is used as the subject of the sentence.]

2. Adjective clauses

Use commas to set off a nonessential adjective clause.

A nonessential (nonrestrictive) clause provides additional information about a noun. Considered an extra clause, it does not change the meaning of a sentence but adds to it. It is therefore set off with commas.

> Jackson Pollock, who was an American painter, was born in 1912. [*Who was an American painter* is a nonessential clause.]

Do not use commas with an essential adjective clause. An essential (restrictive) clause gives necessary information about a noun and is thus needed to convey the exact meaning of the sentence.

> One of the few American writers whom she read was Langston Hughes. [*Whom she read* is an essential clause.]

3. Appositives

Use commas to set off an appositive if it is not essential to the meaning of a sentence.

A nonessential (nonrestrictive) appositive provides additional information and is therefore set off with commas.

> Lucha Corpi, teacher and author, has published many poems.

> A historic city, New Orleans was originally settled by the French. [The appositive, *A historic city*, precedes the subject.]

An essential (restrictive) appositive is not set off with commas because it gives necessary information about a noun.

> Both the *Iliad* and the *Odyssey* are traditionally attributed to the poet Homer. [The appositive, *Homer*, identifies the poet.]

Commas with Interjections, Parenthetical Expressions, and Conjunctive Adverbs

Use commas to set off interjections (such as *oh* and *well*), parenthetical expressions (such as *on the contrary, on the other hand, in fact, by the way, to be exact,* and *after all*), and conjunctive adverbs (such as *however, moreover,* and *consequently*).

Yes, I hope to build my own home one day.

The beautiful and historic city of Philadelphia, in fact, is three centuries old.

After all, we did the best we possibly could under extraordinarily difficult circumstances.

We drank two bottles of orange juice last night; consequently, we did not have enough left to make the punch today.

She intended to use the money to buy an expensive stereo, nonetheless.

Exercise 12   **Using the Comma (Part 2)**

Rewrite the following sentences, adding commas where they are needed. For the two sentences that need no commas, write *correct.*

Chinese Pioneers

[1]Thousands of pioneers from China lured by reports of riches rushed to California after gold was discovered there in 1848. [2]Gold Mountain the name these Chinese immigrants gave California tells more about their expectations than it tells about the reality they found. [3]The 7,000-mile journey across the Pacific Ocean which often took more than 3 months drained the pioneers both physically and financially. [4]Chinese men who had arranged passage on credit found themselves in debt to the steamship company for several years. [5]Chinese miners did receive wages; nevertheless the amount they received was usually less than that paid to non-Asian miners.

[6]On the bright side the Chinese miners tireless laborers often succeeded where others had failed. [7]They often worked in abandoned mines hoping to find what previous miners had overlooked. [8]There they sifted through gravel heaps to extract the last traces of gold dust that the others had failed to notice. [9]These Chinese miners determined to succeed persisted despite the severe hardships they faced. [10]To succeed in the United States was to tell the truth far more difficult than they had imagined.

Commas with Introductory and Antithetical Phrases

1. Prepositional phrases

A comma after a short introductory prepositional phrase is not incorrect, but the only time it is necessary is if the sentence would be misread without the comma.

> Among those running, women were well represented. [The comma is needed to prevent misreading.]

> Before the election the candidates will participate in two debates. [A comma would not be wrong but is not needed.]

Use a comma after a long prepositional phrase or after the final phrase in a succession of phrases.

> During the coldest part of winter, she caught a bad cold.

> On the first Wednesday after the first Monday of each month, our book group meets.

If the prepositional phrase is immediately followed by a verb, do not use a comma.

> Among the candidates in the race for mayor were three women from our part of the city.

2. Participles and participial phrases

Use commas to set off introductory participles and participial phrases.

> Gesturing forcefully, the speaker held her audience spellbound.

> Running after my cats, I sprained my ankle.

3. Antithetical Phrases

Use commas to set off an antithetical phrase.

In an **antithetical phrase** a word such as *not* or *unlike* qualifies what comes before it.

> Alaska, not Texas, is the largest state in the United States of America.

> Australia, unlike New Zealand, is an island that is considered a continent.

Commas and Adverb Clauses

Use commas to set off all introductory adverb clauses.

Because it was a beautiful day, we decided to have a picnic.

Use commas to set off internal adverb clauses that interrupt the flow of a sentence.

Our outing, although it was well planned, did not run smoothly.

In general, do not set off an adverb clause at the end of a sentence. (If the clause is parenthetical or the sentence would be misread without the comma, however, the clause should be set off.)

We went home early even though we weren't tired.

Exercise 13	**Using the Comma (Part 3)**

Rewrite the following sentences, adding commas where they are needed. If a sentence is correct, write *correct*.

Jasper Johns and Robert Rauschenberg

1. Throughout the long history of art only a few artists can be said to have changed the course of painting.
2. One candidate might be Jasper Johns because many critics consider him to be the most influential of modern artists.
3. Because Jasper Johns and Robert Rauschenberg have influenced each other it is interesting to compare their work.
4. Putting aside their traditional training both artists preferred to work with abstract images.
5. Their finished works although they were carefully planned and executed sometimes look haphazard.
6. In the middle of a splash of paint and beside a scrap of newspaper Rauschenberg placed a light bulb.
7. Confused by such unusual combinations art critics have held differing opinions ever since they first attempted to interpret Rauschenberg's work.
8. Although the critics were puzzled at first they eventually realized that the everyday objects Rauschenberg used took on new meanings in his work.
9. The use of everyday objects by both artists was meant to be symbolic not absurd.
10. Everyday articles like light bulbs and brooms became mysterious and beautiful things unlike ordinary light bulbs and brooms.

Additional Uses of Commas

1. Titles of people

Use commas to set off titles when they follow a person's name.

Maria Lopez, Ph.D.   George Allen, governor of Virginia

Alberta Jones, D.D.S., will address us.

2. Addresses, geographical terms, and dates

Use commas to separate the various parts of an address, a geographical term, or a date.

Lancaster County, Pennsylvania, is known for its farms.

Please forward my mail to 6390 West Nassau Circle, Englewood, CO 80110, until Thursday, June 20, 1996.

Tuesday, April 1, 1996, was the day I won the scholarship.

Use the following forms for letter writing:

6390 West Nassau Circle
Englewood, CO 80110
April 1, 1995

If only the month and the day or the month and the year are given, do not use commas.

July 4   July 1776

3. References

Use commas to set off the parts of a reference that direct the reader to the exact source.

Refer to John Steinbeck's *The Pearl,* pages 37–47.

We rehearsed Act 2, Scene iii, of Lorraine Hansberry's *A Raisin in the Sun.*

4. Direct address

Use commas to set off words or names used in direct address.

Carlo, are you sure that you can get tickets for the game?

Remain in your seats, students, until the lecture is over.

Please don't forget to call me tomorrow, Anna.

5. Tag questions

Use commas to set off a tag question.

A tag question—such as *shouldn't I?* or *have you?*—suggests the answer to the statement that comes before it.

You checked your baggage, didn't you?
You haven't read that book, have you?
I should return the book to the library, shouldn't I?

6. Letter writing

Place a comma after the salutation of an informal letter and after the closing of all letters.

Dear Juan,   Dear Aunt Miriam,
Sincerely,   Love,

Exercise 14   **Using the Comma**

Rewrite the following letter, adding commas where they are needed. (Twenty corrections are needed altogether.)

714 Williams Road
Charlottesville VA 22901
September 12 1997

Dear Greta

How have you been? I hope that you and your family are in good health. Did I write last time that we are moving? Our new address is 62 Channing Way Cranbury NJ 08512. I hope we will be all moved in by the first of next month.

I am enclosing a copy of the famous speech you requested. You haven't already found a copy of it have you Greta? The original speech was published in the September 9 1963 edition of *Newsweek* page 21. You can use it for your English assignment can't you?

On August 23 1963 there was an important civil rights march in Washington D.C. The march was led by Dr. Martin Luther King Jr. who was a church leader and a political activist. Dr. King believed in nonviolent protest and put his beliefs into practice. He organized a boycott of the segregated bus system of Montgomery Alabama in December 1955.

I hope the speech and this information will be helpful to you Greta.

Your friend
Tamara

Misuse of Commas

Do not use a comma before a conjunction that connects a compound predicate or compound subject.

INCORRECT	The quarterback threw the ball, and then slipped.
CORRECT	The quarterback threw the ball and then slipped.
INCORRECT	The quarterback, and the running back are good athletes.
CORRECT	The quarterback and the running back are good athletes.

If two main clauses are not part of a series, do not use a comma alone to join them. Remember to add a coordinating conjunction, or use a semicolon.

INCORRECT	The North Carolina state flag is red, white, blue, and gold, the state flower is flowering dogwood.
CORRECT	The North Carolina state flag is red, white, blue, and gold, and the state flower is flowering dogwood.
CORRECT	The North Carolina state flag is red, white, blue, and gold; the state flower is flowering dogwood.

A comma should not be used between a subject and its verb or between a verb and its complement.

INCORRECT	What she thought fit to do, was beyond me.
CORRECT	What she thought fit to do was beyond me.
INCORRECT	On our vacation we will bring, our tent, snack food, and beach clothes.
CORRECT	On our vacation we will bring our tent, snack food, and beach clothes.

Exercise 15	Using Commas Correctly

Each item contains one or more examples of incorrect comma usage. On your paper rewrite each sentence to make it correct. You may need to delete commas, use a semicolon in place of a comma, or add a coordinating conjunction with the comma.

The Fascinating World of Seashells

1. The enormous diversity among seashells, makes them one of nature's most delightful creations.
2. Seashells come in all different sizes, and have spectacular patterns.
3. Some shells are fragile and easily broken, others are solid and sturdy.
4. What some people do not know, is that a shell is the outer skeleton of a soft-bodied animal known as a mollusk.
5. The five main classes of shells are, Gastropods, Bivalves, Tusk Shells, Chitons, and Cephalopods.

On a typewriter, indicate a dash with two hyphens (--). On a computer, you may be able to make an actual dash. Refer to the manual of your word-processing program for instructions.

A comma, semicolon, colon, or period should not be placed either before or after a dash.

1. Dashes to signal change

Use a dash to indicate an abrupt break or change in thought within a sentence.

> What was it—I paused to think—what was it that so unnerved me in the contemplation of the House of Usher?
>
> —Edgar Allan Poe

2. Dashes to emphasize

Use a dash to set off and emphasize supplemental information or parenthetical comments.

> The crowd marveled as fifty pounds were lifted by the circus performer—using one finger.
>
> The circus performer—using one finger—lifted fifty pounds.

Exercise 16   **Using the Dash**

On your paper rewrite the following sentences, adding dashes where needed.

Forging Steel at Valley Forge

1. On July 3, 1775, George Washington he had served as commander-in-chief of the Virginia militia assumed command of the Continental Army.
2. One winter the army camped at Valley Forge, an easily defensible site so many people thought located 15 miles from Philadelphia.
3. Few soldiers if indeed they could be called that had ever heard of Valley Forge.
4. Washington himself designed the huts simple log cabins for his troops.
5. That winter was long snow fell early and bitterly cold.
6. The soldiers already exhausted, freezing, and hungry soon found themselves barefoot.
7. Life in Valley Forge an unbearable nightmare for everyone dragged on.
8. Yet Valley Forge a place where boys became men and men became soldiers played a crucial role in the war.
9. The unwavering commitment shown by General Washington he worked alongside his men and earned their devotion also inspired the troops.
10. Washington he developed his military skill by trial and error emerged from his defeat at Valley Forge with a well-trained and loyal army.

21.8 Parentheses

Use parentheses to set off supplemental material.

Parentheses, like commas and dashes, are used to set off supplemental material. Commas set off material that is closely related to the rest of the sentence. Dashes are used not only to set off—but also to emphasize—material that abruptly interrupts the sentence. Parentheses are used to set off material that is not intended to be part of the main statement but is nevertheless important enough to include.

> Minnesota (named after the Dakota Sioux word meaning "cloudy water") was explored by French scouts.

1. With complete sentences

If a complete sentence within parentheses is contained within another sentence, it is not capitalized and requires no period. If a complete sentence stands by itself within parentheses, both a capital letter and a period are required.

> As gold and silver mining waned (**m**ining declined in the 1870s), cattle became Nevada's principal source of revenue.

> Nebraska contains two of the widest and flattest rivers in the country: the Missouri River and the Platte River. (**T**he name *Nebraska* comes from the Native American word *nibrathka,* meaning "flat water**.**")

2. With a comma, semicolon, or colon

Always place a comma, semicolon, or colon *after* the closing parenthesis.

> Although Death Valley may appear barren (it is often called a desert)**,** many plants and animals flourish there.

> Pioneer towns had few women (more than half the population of Seattle were bachelors)**;** in 1864, however, a settler brought a group of widows and orphans to Seattle.

> Washington State is the site of these fur-trapping posts (all built before 1833)**:** Spokane, Walla Walla, and Nisqually.

3. With a question mark or exclamation point

Place a question mark or an exclamation point *inside* the parentheses if it is part of the parenthetical expression.

> There is a city named Clinton (named after American statesman De Witt Clinton**?)** in almost every state.

> Many names have been suggested for the Black Hills of South Dakota (surprisingly, they were almost named the Purple Mountains**!)**.

Place a question mark or an exclamation point *outside* the parentheses if it is part of the entire sentence.

> Did you visit the famous cowpoke capitals of the Old West (Dodge City, Cimarron, Wichita, and Abilene**)?**

> How surprised I was to find out that the Alamo was originally a Franciscan mission (the Mission of San Antonio de Valero**)!**

Exercise 17	**Using the Dash and Parentheses**

Rewrite the following sentences, adding dashes and parentheses where they are needed. Use the marks of punctuation indicated in parentheses at the end of each sentence.

The Story of Anne Frank

1. Anne Frank wrote a remarkable diary about her life in Amsterdam during World War II. She and her family were born in Germany but had moved to Holland before the war. (parentheses)
2. The diary addressed to an imaginary friend named Kitty has been published in over thirty languages. (dashes)
3. Anne, her parents, an older sister, and four friends eight persons in all went into hiding during the Nazi occupation of the Netherlands. (dashes)
4. Their hiding place was an unused section of an office building. In Dutch their secret apartment was called *het achterhuis,* which means "the house in the back." (parentheses)
5. The eight persons hidden in the apartment had to avoid making any noise. How could they have remained so quiet for so long? (parentheses)
6. The diary begun in June 1942 and ended in August 1944 covers Anne's life from the age of thirteen to that of fifteen a significant period in a girl's life. (parentheses, dash)
7. One entry tells how pleased she was who wouldn't be? to find out that a boy she liked also liked her. (parentheses)
8. Another entry reveals that she felt that her hopes could not compete with "the ever approaching thunder" the misery and destruction sweeping through Europe. (dash)
9. When Anne and the others were eventually discovered and taken prisoner, the diary was left behind. The diary was later found along with some short stories and sketches and was published in 1947. (dashes)
10. Anne Frank died in the concentration camp at Bergen-Belsen, Germany, in March 1945. She was not even sixteen. (parentheses)

Quotation Marks for Direct Quotations

Use quotation marks to enclose a direct quotation.

Place quotation marks only around the quoted material.

Introductory or explanatory remarks may be set off from the actual quotation with a comma.

> The Mexican American poet Marina de Bellagente wrote, "You cannot put a fence around the planet earth."

> "I celebrate myself, and sing myself," wrote Walt Whitman.

(For the use of colons to introduce quotations, see page 699.)

When a quotation is interrupted by explanatory words such as *he said* or *she wrote*, use two sets of quotation marks.

Each part of the quotation should be separated from the interrupting phrase with two marks of punctuation, such as two commas or a comma and a period. The second part of the quotation should begin with a capital letter if it is a complete sentence.

> "Luis Tiant," Reggie Jackson once declared, "is the Fred Astaire of baseball."

> "I never think of the future," wrote Albert Einstein. "It comes soon enough."

Quotation marks should not be used in an indirect quotation.

ORIGINAL QUOTATION "I never intended to become a run-of-the-mill person," said Barbara Jordan.

INDIRECT QUOTATION Barbara Jordan said that she never intended to become a run-of-the-mill person.

Use single quotation marks around a quotation within a quotation.

> My instructor smiled and replied, "It was Sarah Bernhardt who said, 'An artiste with short arms can never, never make a fine gesture.'"

In writing dialogue, begin a new paragraph and use a new set of quotation marks every time the speaker changes.

> "What grade you in now, Raymond?"
> "You got anything to say to my brother, you say it to me, Mary Louise Williams of Raggedy Town, Baltimore."
> "What are you, his mother?" sasses Rosie.
>
> —Toni Cade Bambara

> "I never intended to become a run-of-the-mill person."

Barbara Jordan said that she never intended to become a run-of-the mill person.

Quotation Marks with Other Marks of Punctuation

1. With a comma or a period

Always place a comma or a period *inside* closing quotation marks.

> "Everything had its wonders, even darkness and silence**,"** wrote Helen Keller, who was blind and deaf from a young age.

> Gwendolyn Brooks has said, "Poetry is life distilled**."**

2. With a semicolon or a colon

Always place a semicolon or a colon *outside* closing quotation marks.

> Lorraine Hansberry wrote "On Summer**";** this essay tells how her feelings about the season changed over the course of her life.

> There are two Spanish verbs that mean "to be**":** *ser* and *estar.*

3. With a question mark or an exclamation point

Place the question mark or exclamation point *inside* the closing quotation marks when it is part of the quotation.

> My friend asked, "How did you persuade your mother**?"**
> My father kept saying, "That's incredible**!"**

Place the question mark or exclamation point *outside* the closing quotation marks when it is part of the entire sentence.

> Why did he say, "This is only the beginning"**?**
> How wonderful that she will print your story "Winter"**!**

If both your sentence and the quotation at the end of your sentence need a question mark (or an exclamation point), use only one question mark (or exclamation point) placed *inside* the quotation marks.

> When did she ask, "Will the car be fixed in time**?"**
> I ran when he yelled, "Come quickly**!"**

Do not use a comma after a quotation that ends with a question mark or exclamation point.

> "That's incredible**!"** my father said yet again.

Quotation Marks with Titles and Unusual Expressions

1. With titles of short works

Use quotation marks to enclose titles of short works, such as short stories, short poems, essays, newspaper and magazine articles, book chapters, songs, and single episodes of a television series.

"Chee's Daughter" [short story]
"The Road Not Taken" [poem]
"On Summer" [essay]
"Welform Reform Debated" [newspaper article]
"Climates of the Earth" [chapter]
"America the Beautiful" [song]
"A Stranger Comes to Town" [episode in a television series]

2. With unusual expressions

Use quotation marks to enclose unfamiliar slang and other unusual or original expressions.

My roommate calls clumps of dust "dust bunnies."

Exercise 18   Using Quotation Marks

Rewrite the following sentences, adding quotation marks where they are needed. For the sentences that need no changes, write *correct*.

Albert Einstein

1. Albert Einstein's uncle taught him algebra. It is a merry science, he told the boy. When the animal that we are hunting cannot be caught, we call it *x*.
2. The young Einstein was often called oddball.
3. One of Einstein's teachers is supposed to have said to him, Your presence in this class destroys the respect of the students; and someone else apparently told him, You will never amount to anything, Einstein.
4. I am a horse for a single harness, Einstein later said, not cut out for tandem or teamwork.
5. Einstein published a paper called The Influence of Gravity on the Propagation of Light.
6. If Einstein's theory should prove correct, said physicist Max Planck, he will be considered the Copernicus of the twentieth century.
7. Was it in 1916 that Einstein published his paper General Theory of Relativity?
8. Einstein believed—amazingly so at the time—that time and space could disappear!
9. In the 1950s Einstein said he was ready to introduce his unified field theory, in which gravitation, electromagnetism, and subatomic phenomena are explained in one set of laws.
10. The most incomprehensible thing about the world is that it is comprehensible, said Einstein.

21.10 | Italics (Underlining)

Italic type slants upward and to the right. (*This is printed in italics.*) On a typewriter or in handwriting, indicate italics by underlining. (<u>This is underlined</u>.) On a computer you can actually use italic type. Refer to your software manual for help.

Italics for Titles and Foreign Words

1. With titles

Italicize (underline) titles of books, lengthy poems, plays, films and television series, paintings and sculptures, and long musical compositions. Also italicize the names of newspapers and magazines, ships, trains, airplanes, and spacecraft.

The Color Purple [book]	*Appalachian Spring* [ballet]
The People, Yes [long poem]	the *Baltimore Sun* [newspaper]
Macbeth [play]	*Newsweek* [magazine]
On the Waterfront [film]	U.S.S. *Constitution* [ship]*
The Civil War [television series]	*Yankee Clipper* [train]
American Gothic [painting]	*Air Force One* [airplane]
Venus de Milo [sculpture]	*Sputnik I* [spacecraft]

* Do not italicize abbreviations such as U.S.S. in the name of a ship.

Italicize (underline) and capitalize articles (*a, an, the*) written at the beginning of a title only when they are part of the title itself. It is common practice not to italicize (underline) the article preceding the title of a newspaper or a magazine. Do not italicize the word *magazine* unless it is part of the title of a periodical.

The Red Desert	but	the *Boston Globe*
A Farewell to Arms		a *Reader's Digest* magazine

2. With foreign words

Italicize (underline) foreign words and expressions that are not used frequently in English.

> Because Einstein was unconventional as a child, he was considered an ***enfant terrible.***

Do not italicize such words if they are commonly used in English.

> Apple pie **à la mode** is my favorite dessert.

Italics with Words and Other Items Used to Represent Themselves

Italicize (underline) words, letters, and numerals used to represent themselves.

> Why does the author of that poem use the word **essence** instead of **life**?
>
> While I was carefully proofreading my essay, I noticed that the **i** and the **t** were reversed in the title.
>
> In order to complete the mathematical equation, I needed to find the values of **x** and **y**.

Exercise 19   Using Italics

Rewrite the following sentences, underlining the parts that should be italicized.

Noteworthy Americans

1. Lorene Cary's book Black Ice is a memoir of the author's experiences as one of the first African American students at St. Paul's, a boarding school in New Hampshire.
2. When Will I See You Again, painted by Martin Wong, realistically depicts an image from the artist's neighborhood.
3. Américo Paredes, a professor who has also served as editor of the Journal of American Folklore, has written about Mexican proverbs, or dichos.
4. Paredes points out that although the formal word for proverb in Spanish is refrán, many Mexican Americans use the word dichos, meaning "sayings."
5. Mary Tyler Moore has been successful on television in her highly popular comedy series The Mary Tyler Moore Show and later in movies as the star of such films as Ordinary People.
6. A short-lived magazine of the late 1980s was Lear's, created by Frances Lear for women age forty and older.
7. Novelist N. Scott Momaday won a Pulitzer Prize for his book House Made of Dawn in 1969, but he is perhaps best known for The Way to Rainy Mountain, a collection of stories and legends of the Kiowa people.
8. The well-known American composer Aaron Copland was awarded the Pulitzer Prize for his ballet score Appalachian Spring and later received an Academy Award for his film score for The Heiress.
9. Mark Harris once wrote an entire comic novel that consisted of correspondence supposedly composed on a defective typewriter; the work lacked the letter f throughout.
10. The Puerto Rican artist Arnaldo Roche Rabell's emotional and expressionistic style is evident in such paintings as Blind Dreams and You Tell Me If This Is Not an Omen.

21.11 | The Apostrophe

Apostrophes with Possessives

1. Pronouns

Use an apostrophe and -*s* for the possessive of a singular indefinite pronoun.

An apostrophe should not be used with any other possessive pronouns.

one**'s** time	*but*	**his** duty
somebody else**'s** clothes		**its** paws

2. Singular nouns

Use an apostrophe and -*s* to form the possessive of a singular noun, even one that ends in -*s*.

the man**'s** collar	Mexico**'s** landscape
the dress**'s** hem	George Burns**'s** humor
The heiress**'s** instructions	Dickens**'s** novels
the fox**'s** lair	Max**'s** father

Some exceptions to this rule do exist, however. When forming the possessive of ancient proper nouns that end in -*es* or -*is*, the name *Jesus*, and expressions with words such as *appearance* and *conscience*, add an apostrophe only.

Aristophanes**'** plays	Jesus**'** followers
Isis**'** temple	Xerxes**'** army

3. Plural nouns ending in -*s*

Use an apostrophe alone to form the possessive of a plural noun that ends in -*s*.

purple mountains**'** majesty	the Hawaiian Islands**'** charm
the gloves**'** size	the *Ladies' Home Journal*

4. Plural nouns not ending in -s

Use an apostrophe and -*s* to form the possessive of a plural noun that does not end in -*s*.

the men**'s** department	Women**'s** Medical Center
the deer**'s** antlers	the geese**'s** eggs

5. Compound nouns

Put only the last word of a compound noun in the possessive form.

> my mother-in-law**'s** camera
> the district attorney**'s** victory
> the heir apparent**'s** throne
> the surgeon general**'s** warning

6. Phrases

In a phrase or combination of names, add an apostrophe and *-s* to the last word only.

> the President of the United States**'s** inauguration
> the director from Hollywood**'s** last movie
> Chief Medicine Crow of Montana**'s** delegation

7. Joint possession versus individual possession

If two or more persons (or partners in a company) possess something jointly, use the possessive form for the last person named.

> Shiro and Suki**'s** home
> Barnum and Bailey**'s** Circus
> Gilbert and Sullivan**'s** operettas

If two or more persons (or companies) possess an item (or items) individually, put each one's name in the possessive form.

> Jorge Amado**'s** and Jorge Luis Borges**'s** novels
> Mozart**'s** and Beethoven**'s** music

8. Expressions of time and money

Use a possessive form to express amounts of money or time that modify a noun.

It is also correct to express the modifier as a hyphenated adjective. When that is done, the possessive form is not used.

> five dollar**s'** worth   *but*   a five-dollar contribution
> one minute**'s** pause   a one-minute pause
> a day**'s** journey   a one-day journey
> six day**s'** rest   a six-day rest

Apostrophes with Contractions and Special Plurals

1. With contractions

Use an apostrophe in place of letters omitted in contractions.

A **contraction** is a word formed from two words that have been combined by omitting one or more letters. Contractions are generally formed from a subject and a verb or a verb and an adverb.

I'm	*formed from*	I am
you're		you are
it's		it is, it has
doesn't, don't		does not, do not

Use an apostrophe in place of the omitted numerals of a year.

the World Series of '83   the fall television season of '97

2. With special plurals

Use an apostrophe and *-s* to form the plural of letters, numerals, symbols, and words used to represent themselves.

Only the letter, numeral, symbol, or word should be italicized (underlined), not the apostrophe or the *-s*.

Your *a*'s are indistinguishable from your *o*'s.
All of the *8*'s had been typed as *3*'s.

Exercise 20   **Using the Apostrophe**

Rewrite the following sentences, adding apostrophes where they are needed and *-s* wherever necessary.

American Performers

[1]Lets imagine that we are compiling a list of actors and actresses names for a biographical dictionary of American performers. [2]Under the *c*s wed include Kevin Costner, a popular contemporary actor, and Claudette Colbert, a brilliant actress of the thirties and forties. [3]We mustnt forget to include Bill Cosbys name, because hes essential. [4]He and Whoopi Goldberg would probably appear on everybodys list of excellent performers. [5]We would also include Graham Greene, the Native American performer who received critical acclaim for his performance in *Dances with Wolves*. [6]Under the *m*s Id expect to see a good many names. [7]My friend Maxs choice is Pat Morita, whose performance in *The Karate Kid* movies entertained audiences everywhere. [8]Then theres Rita Moreno, whose role as Anita in United Artists *West Side Story* earned her wide praise. [9]After an hours time we would have a much longer list, including Julia Roberts and Susan Sarandons names. [10]My friend James first choice is Tom and Dick Smothers, one of show business best comedy teams from the past.

21.12 The Hyphen

Hyphens with Prefixes

Hyphens are not usually used to join a prefix to a word. The following are some exceptions:

Use a hyphen after any prefix joined to a proper noun or a proper adjective. Use a hyphen after the prefixes *all-*, *ex-* (meaning "former"), and *self-* joined to any noun or adjective.

pre-Columbian	all-encompassing
un-American	ex-governor
mid-August	self-addressed
post-World War I	self-employed

Use a hyphen after the prefix *anti-* when it joins a word beginning with *i-*. Also use a hyphen after the prefix *vice-*, except in *vice president*.

anti-inflationary	vice-principal
anti-inflammatory	vice-chancellor

Use a hyphen to avoid confusion between words beginning with *re-* that look alike but are different in meaning and pronunciation.

re-count the ballots	*but*	recount a story
re-lay the tiles		relay the message
re-mark the papers		remark on her condition

Exercise 21	**Using Hyphens with Prefixes**

On your paper rewrite the following sentences, adding hyphens where they are needed.

The American Revolution

1. The desire for selfgovernment among British colonists grew steadily during the preRevolutionary War period.
2. Antimonarchy and antiimperialist forces prevailed, and the Continental Congress prepared for allout war with Britain.
3. Not only was the British army considered the best allaround fighting force, but it also had the support of the proBritish Iroquois Confederacy.
4. At first British leaders remarked disdainfully that most American soldiers were selftaught.
5. After carefully recreating their government, the exBritish colonies became the United States of America.

Hyphens with Compounds

1. Compound adjectives

Use a hyphen in a compound adjective that precedes a noun.

When a compound adjective follows a noun, it is usually not hyphenated.

up-to-the-minute news	*but*	The news was up to the minute.
a nine-year-old boy		The boy was nine years old.
a well-educated girl		The girl is well educated.

An expression is not hyphenated when it is made up of an adverb ending in -*ly* and an adjective.

a happily married couple	the beautifully prepared dinner
a mainly green interior	the amazingly bright child
a nicely decorated house	the perfectly grand day

2. Compound numbers

Hyphenate any spelled-out cardinal or ordinal compound number up to ninety-nine or ninety-ninth.

forty-five	eighty-eighth
twenty-first	sixty-seventh

3. Fractions used as adjectives

Hyphenate a fraction used as an adjective (but not one used as a noun).

two-thirds majority	*but*	two thirds of the members
one-half liter		one half of a liter
one-eighth mile		one eighth of a mile

4. Connected numerals

Hyphenate two numerals to indicate a span.

pages 354-392	1884-1903
April 1-6	15th-16th centuries

Hyphens to Divide Words at the End of a Line

When a word must be divided at the end of a line, it should be divided between syllables or pronounceable parts. If you are unsure of the correct place to divide a word, check your dictionary.

In general, if a word contains two consonants occurring between two vowels or if it contains a double consonant, divide the word between the two consonants.

rep-resentative	skip-per
fluc-tuate	insig-nificant
impor-tant	big-gest

If a suffix has been added to a complete word that ends in two consonants, divide the word after the two consonants.

track-ing	black-est
roll-ing	full-est

Exercise 22　　**Using Hyphens**

Hyphens must be added to seven of the following sentences. On your paper rewrite those sentences, adding the hyphens where they are needed. If a sentence needs no hyphens, write *correct*. Then make a list of all the italicized words, showing where each would be divided if it had to be broken at the end of a line.

Looking at Statistics

1. Statistics can tell us an extraordinarily broad *spectrum* of things about the American people.
2. In 1830, for instance, nearly three fourths of the U.S. population lived on family farms; today one in *fifty* Americans lives on a farm.
3. There is a clear cut trend toward *urban* living.
4. A look at the *almanac* reveals the wide ranging salaries of United States governors—going from just under $56,000 to well over $100,000 a year.
5. During a period of fifty years (1935 1985), the average annual income of a person *working* in the United States jumped from less than $500 to nearly $14,000.
6. American women, however, continue to earn less than men; on average, for every *dollar* that a man earns, a woman earns sixty nine cents.
7. By the year 2000, the number of Asian Americans and Native Americans in the work force is *expected* to experience a two thirds increase.
8. Whereas most Americans work for others, a significant *number* of adults are self employed.
9. The fast growing Hispanic population is having a great impact on American *culture* and society.
10. One widely known statistic is that more and more African Americans are *holding* public office.

21.13 | Abbreviations

Abbreviations are shortened forms of words. They are used to save space and time and to avoid wordiness. For example, it is more concise and easier to write 800 B.C. than to write *800 years before the birth of Christ*. Periods follow most abbreviations. For guidance on how to write a particular abbreviation, check a dictionary.

Use only one period if an abbreviation occurs at the end of a sentence that would ordinarily take a period of its own.

> I am going to Washington, **D.C.**

If an abbreviation occurs at the end of a sentence that ends with a question mark or an exclamation point, use the period *and* the second mark of punctuation.

> Have you been to Washington, **D.C.?**
> I can't wait to go to Washington, **D.C.!**

Capitalization of Abbreviations

Capitalize abbreviations of proper nouns.

> Dwight **D.** Eisenhower
> 135 Claremont **Ave.**
> **U.S.** Department of Labor

The names of many organizations and agencies, whether pronounced letter by letter or as words, are abbreviated by using the initial letters of the complete name without periods.

> NAACP   YMCA   CIA   FCC   UN   NATO

Capitalize these abbreviations related to historical dates:

A.D. (*anno Domini*), "in the year of the Lord" (since the birth of Christ); place before the date: **A.D.** 66

B.C. (before Christ); place after the date: 336 **B.C.**

B.C.E. (before the common era; equivalent to *B.C.*); place after the date: 1000 **B.C.E.**

C.E. (common era; equivalent to *A.D.*); place after the date: 60 **C.E.**

A.M. (*ante meridiem*), "before noon"; place after exact times: 2:45 **A.M.**

P.M. (*post meridiem*), "after noon"; place after exact times: 10:30 **P.M.**

State Abbreviations

In ordinary prose spell out state names. When addressing mail, however, use the abbreviations of state names that appear in the list below.

Alabama	**AL**	Montana	**MT**
Alaska	**AK**	Nebraska	**NB**
Arizona	**AZ**	Nevada	**NV**
Arkansas	**AR**	New Hampshire	**NH**
California	**CA**	New Jersey	**NJ**
Colorado	**CO**	New Mexico	**NM**
Connecticut	**CT**	New York	**NY**
Delaware	**DE**	North Carolina	**NC**
Florida	**FL**	North Dakota	**ND**
Georgia	**GA**	Ohio	**OH**
Hawaii	**HI**	Oklahoma	**OK**
Idaho	**ID**	Oregon	**OR**
Illinois	**IL**	Pennsylvania	**PA**
Indiana	**IN**	Rhode Island	**RI**
Iowa	**IA**	South Carolina	**SC**
Kansas	**KS**	South Dakota	**SD**
Kentucky	**KY**	Tennessee	**TN**
Louisiana	**LA**	Texas	**TX**
Maine	**ME**	Utah	**UT**
Maryland	**MD**	Vermont	**VT**
Massachusetts	**MA**	Virginia	**VA**
Michigan	**MI**	Washington	**WA**
Minnesota	**MN**	West Virginia	**WV**
Mississippi	**MS**	Wisconsin	**WI**
Missouri	**MO**	Wyoming	**WY**

The ZIP code form for the District of Columbia, for use on envelopes only, is **DC**.

Exercise 23   **Using Abbreviations**

On your paper write the abbreviations for the italicized words or phrases in the following sentences. If an abbreviation should not be used, write *correct*.

1. The *Young Men's Christian Association* has been promoting family and recreational activities since *anno Domini* 1881.
2. The *United States* Capitol is located in Washington, D.C.
3. One ZIP code for Fargo, *North Dakota*, is 58103.
4. The *Federal Aviation Administration* establishes regulations for airline companies.
5. Many Americans begin work at 9:00 *ante meridiem* and end at 5:00 *post meridiem*.

Abbreviations of Titles and Units of Measure

1. Personal titles

Use abbreviations for some personal titles.

Certain titles, including *Mrs.*, *Mr.*, *Ms.*, *Sr.*, and *Jr.*, are almost always abbreviated. Professional and academic titles, such as *Dr.*, *M.D.*, and *B.A.*, are also usually abbreviated. When they are used before a full name, the titles of government and military officials and members of the clergy are frequently abbreviated.

Mrs. Elizabeth Dole	**Gov.** Tommy Thompson
Ms. Amy Tan	**Sen.** Carol Mosely-Braun
Dr. Joseph Fernandez	**Rev.** Jesse Jackson

2. Units of measure

Abbreviate units of measure used with numerals in technical or scientific writing but not in ordinary prose.

In the list below, the abbreviations stand for plural as well as singular units:

ENGLISH SYSTEM		METRIC SYSTEM	
ft.	foot	**cg**	centigram
gal.	gallon	**cl**	centiliter
in.	inch	**cm**	centimeter
lb.	pound	**g**	gram
mi.	mile	**kg**	kilogram
oz.	ounce	**km**	kilometer
pt.	pint	**l**	liter
qt.	quart	**m**	meter
tbsp.	tablespoon	**mg**	milligram
tsp.	teaspoon	**ml**	milliliter
yd.	yard	**mm**	millimeter

Exercise 24   **Using Abbreviations (Part 2)**

Write the abbreviations for the italicized words or phrases in the following sentences. If no abbreviation should be used, write *correct*.

1. *Governor* Nellie Tayloe Ross of Wyoming, elected in 1924, was the first woman to hold that office in any state.
2. Among the guests were *Mister* Diaz and his daughters.
3. *Doctor* C. Everett Koop was the surgeon general during George Bush's administration.
4. The pitcher stood 60 *feet* 6 *inches* from the batter and glanced at first base.
5. Add 20 *milliliters* of water to the formula.

In ordinary prose some numbers are written out in words, and some are expressed in figures. Numbers that are expressed in figures are known as *numerals*.

Numbers Spelled Out

In general, spell out cardinal and ordinal numbers that can be written in one or two words.

The Senate consists of **one hundred** members—**two** senators from each of the **fifty** states.

The building is **sixty-eight** feet tall.

Juanita was the **thirty-sixth** person waiting in line for concert tickets.

Spell out any number that occurs at the beginning of a sentence.

Two thousand twenty-eight people were at the concert.

Twenty-nine students are in our class.

Exercise 25 | Using Numbers

On your paper rewrite the following sentences, spelling out numbers where necessary.

The Inca Empire

1. The Inca Empire dominated the Andes region of South America for more than 1/3 of a century.
2. 2,200 miles of Pacific coastline were controlled by the Incas.
3. The 8th Inca ruler was the first to be called *Sapa Inca*, meaning "emperor."
4. 150 miles a day was not an uncommon distance for a team of Inca runners carrying messages throughout the empire.
5. The mighty Inca Empire was destroyed in only 3 years by the Spanish explorer Francisco Pizarro.
6. In 1531 Pizarro made his 3rd expedition to Peru, determined to conquer the rich and powerful Inca Empire.
7. 180 men went with Pizarro when he sailed from Panama to Peru.
8. At the start of his expedition, Pizarro had only 27 horses and 2 pieces of artillery.
9. Pizarro and his men were the 1st Europeans to reach the interior of Peru and confront the Inca ruler.
10. Within 50 years of the Spanish conquest, there was little trace of the once-glorious Inca civilization.

Numerals

In general, use numerals to express numbers that would be written in more than two words.

> The Homestead Act allowed each farmer to claim **160** acres.
> The speed of light is **186,000** miles per second.

When a large number can be written as a mixed number followed by the word *million* or *billion*, the numeral should appear in decimal form.

> The television station was purchased for $**86.5 million.**

If some numbers can be written out while other related numbers should appear as numerals, use all numerals.

> Of the **435** members of the House of Representatives, **50** were newly elected.

1. Money, decimals, and percentages

Use numerals to express amounts of money, decimals, and percentages.

> **$19.50**   **2.5** pounds
> **$6.25** million   **57** percent

If an amount of money can be expressed in one or two words, however, it should be spelled out.

> **seventy-six** cents   **sixty-five thousand** dollars

2. Dates and time

Use numerals to express the year and day in a date and to express the precise time with the abbreviations A.M. and P.M.

> The First Continental Congress met on September **5, 1774.**
> The President was to meet the ambassador at **3:15 P.M.**

Spell out expressions of time that do not use A.M. or P.M.

> The ambassador's meeting was scheduled for **three** o'clock.

To express a century when the word *century* is used, spell out the number. Likewise, to express a decade when the century is clear from the context, spell out the number.

> The greatest decade of the **twentieth** century was the **twenties.**

When a century and a decade are expressed as a single unit, use numerals followed by *-s*.

> The **1920s** were known as the Jazz Age.

3. Addresses

Use numerals for streets and avenues numbered above ten and for all house, apartment, and room numbers. Spell out numbered streets and avenues with numbers of ten or under.

526 West **111th** Street   **52** South **Ninth** Street
Apartment **6D**   Room **8**
18 East **12th** Avenue   **866 Third** Avenue

4. References

Use numerals to express page, line, act, and scene numbers and the like.

Look on pages **9** and **24** for references to Arthur Ashe.
Read paragraphs **3** and **4** on page **360** of my Chinese cookbook.
We danced in Scenes **i** and **ii** of the community ballet.

Exercise 26	Using Numbers and Numerals

Write out the following sentences, making any necessary changes in the use of numbers and numerals.

Wilma Rudolph, Sprinter

1. One of the fastest female runners of the 20th century, Wilma Rudolph won 3 gold medals at the 1960 Olympic games.
2. Besides placing 1st in the women's one-hundred-meter and two-hundred-meter dashes, she pushed her team to victory in the women's four-hundred-meter relay.
3. Rudolph's feat is all the more astonishing because she was not able to walk until she was 8.
4. Her birth weight was low, well under 5 pounds, and she suffered from a series of illnesses that left her, at the age of 4, without the use of her left leg.
5. By the time Rudolph entered high school, she had recovered so well that she excelled in basketball; in 1 year she scored eight hundred three points in 25 games.
6. At the Millrose Games in nineteen hundred sixty-one, she ran the 60-yard dash in six and nine-tenths seconds; she broke that world record 2 weeks later.
7. 11.3 seconds was her time in the one-hundred-meter dash at the 1960 Olympics— a time she bettered by one tenth of a second on July nineteen, 1961, when she set the women's world record.
8. At 5 feet 11 inches and one hundred thirty pounds, Rudolph was tall yet extraordinarily graceful.
9. After her Olympic victory she toured Europe, greeting 1,000s of people and traveling more than two thousand miles.
10. During the nineteen sixties Rudolph retired from running while still in her 20s; she then devoted herself to developing track-and-field teams for girls.

Grammar Review

Punctuation

Eudora Welty has spent most of her long and productive life in Jackson, Mississippi, where she was born in 1909. This seemingly sheltered life has not been without risk, for "all serious daring starts from within," as she says in her memoir, *One Writer's Beginnings.* In this excerpt from that book, she reminisces about her father's family and alludes to her mother's, the Andrewses. The passage has been annotated to show some of the rules of punctuation covered in this unit.

Semicolon to separate main clauses

Dash to indicate a change in thought

Period at the end of a declarative sentence

Colon to introduce a restatement

Apostrophe to indicate a contraction

Question mark to indicate a question

Commas to separate elements in a series

Apostrophe and *-s* to indicate the possessive form of *father*

Comma to separate two main clauses that are joined by a coordinating conjunction

Literature Model

from ONE WRITER'S BEGINNINGS

by Eudora Welty

The Weltys were originally GermanSwiss; the first ones to come to this country, back before the Revolutionary War here, were three brothers, and the whole family is descended from them, I understand—it seems to hark back to German fairy-tale tradition.

My father is not the one who told me this: he never happened to tell us a single family story; could it have been because he'd heard so many of the Andrews stories? I think it was rather because, as he said, he had no interest in ancient history—only the future, he said, should count. At the same time, he was exceedingly devoted to his father, went to see him whenever he could, and wrote to him regularly from his desk at home; I grew up familiar with seeing the long envelopes being addressed in my father's clear, careful hand: Jefferson Welty, Esquire. It was the only use my father made of the word; he saved it for his father. I took "Esquire" for a term of reverence, and I think it stood for that with him; we were always aware that Daddy loved him.

An English Welti, who spelled his name thus with an *i,* wrote to me once from Kent, in curiosity, after an early book of mine had appeared over there; he asked me about ➡

my name. My father, who had never told us anything, had
died, and this was before my mother set herself as she did
later to looking into records. Mr. Welti knew about the
whole throng of them, from medieval times on, and the
three brothers who set forth to the New World from German Switzerland and settled from Virginia westward over
Pennsylvania, Ohio, and Indiana before the Revolutionary
War. "I expect you know," wrote the British Mr. Welti, "that
one unfortunate Welty fell at Saratoga."

The only part of his letter that would have interested
my father is that about the St. Gotthard Tunnel and the
Welty who pushed it through. The fact that this same Welty
had been President of Switzerland seven times running
would have caused him to say "Pshaw!", his strongest
expletive. (That my mother's strongest exclamation was
"Pshaw!" too rather took away some of its force for both
of them.)

Comma to set off a nonessential adjective clause

Quotation marks to enclose a direct quotation

Exclamation point to indicate strong feeling

Parentheses to set off supplemental material

Exercise 1

Using End Punctuation   The following sentences describe some of Eudora Welty's
early teachers. On your paper rewrite each item, correcting any errors in
end punctuation. If an item contains no errors, write *correct*.

1. Don't most people vividly remember at least one teacher from their childhood.
   One of Eudora Welty's most memorable teachers was Miss Duling.
2. Can you imagine a prim woman, wearing a black-and-white checked dress, a long red
   sweater, black stockings, and black high-top shoes. Wow.
3. What a perfectionist Miss Duling seemed to Eudora?
4. Miss Duling was intolerant of excuses and pretensions. The governor's daughter,
   named Lady Rachel, was just plain Rachel to Miss Duling
5. Miss Duling asked the Mississippi legislature to compete in a spelling match with her
   fourth-grade class?
6. Who won the spelling match. Welty hints that the class did.
7. Miss Eyrich, Welty's physical-education teacher, was also memorable.
8. How her booming commands terrorized reluctant runners?
9. Mrs. McWillie, a stern fourth-grade teacher, once overheard Welty and a friend using
   improper grammar.
10. The furious Mrs. McWillie asked which of the girls had used an incorrect verb form?
    Why, she even threatened to report them to the principal.

Exercise 2

Using Colons and Semicolons   The following sentences tell about Eudora Welty's love of reading. On your paper rewrite each sentence, correcting any errors in the use of colons and semicolons. If a sentence contains no errors, write *correct*.

1. Eudora Welty's parents valued reading: therefore, they purchased books that would delight as well as instruct.
2. Books in the Welty library included those by the following authors; Mark Twain, Ring Lardner, and Charles Dickens.
3. Welty was exposed to books at an early age: in fact, books were a favorite gift in the Welty household.
4. *Our Wonder World,* one of Welty's favorite sets of books, contained: legends about Robin Hood and King Arthur, fairy tales by H. C. Anderson, and fables by Aesop.
5. One critic describes Welty's *One Writer's Beginnings* as follows, "This splendid little book will itself be remembered and used and loved."

Exercise 3

Using the Comma (Part 1)   The following sentences describe Southern writers. Rewrite each sentence, adding the material in parentheses in the place indicated by the caret. If the material is *not* essential to the meaning of the sentence, add commas. If it is essential, do not add commas.

SAMPLE   Writers ∧ have contributed greatly to the body of memorable American literature. (who are from the South)

ANSWER   Writers who are from the South have contributed greatly to the body of memorable American literature.

1. The Mississippi writer ∧ is considered to be among the greatest authors of the twentieth century. (William Faulkner)
2. Faulkner ∧ wrote a saga about life in Yoknapatawpha County. (who won a Nobel Prize in 1949)
3. ∧ He depicts in these books a changing South. (that feature the Snopes family as protagonists)
4. The Southern author ∧ is Alice Walker. (whom I enjoy most)
5. Alice Walker ∧ writes about African Americans. (whose most famous book is *The Color Purple*)
6. ∧ Flannery O'Connor did grow up in Georgia. (Yes)
7. O'Connor ∧ depicts eccentrics and outcasts. (by the way)
8. She writes about a character ∧. (who is called The Misfit)
9. Carson McCullers ∧ depicts an isolated café owner and a hearing-impaired person in one of her novels. (another Georgian)
10. ∧ *The Member of the Wedding* focuses on a lonely Southern girl. (one of the most famous of McCullers's works)

Exercise 4

Using the Comma The following sentences describe the Southern settings used by some American writers. On your paper rewrite each sentence, adding or deleting commas where necessary.

1. The South is often the setting in works written by Eudora Welty Harper Lee and Walker Percy.
2. Lee grew up in Alabama and she used a small, Southern town as the setting for her only novel *To Kill a Mockingbird.*
3. *To Kill a Mockingbird* won a Pulitzer Prize in 1961; subsequently it was made into a movie.
4. By the way the main characters in *To Kill a Mockingbird* seem much like the young Eudora Welty and her father.
5. Walker Percy grew up in Birmingham, Alabama but his novels are set in various locales throughout the South.
6. Although Percy called his view of the world "cold-eyed" and "despairing" his books are popular.
7. Percy's first novel, *The Moviegoer,* is about a young affluent New Orleans stockbroker searching for a new direction in his life.
8. His settings create a mood that is at once grotesque, and humorous, and disturbing.
9. Writers such as Zora Neale Hurston, Alice Walker and Truman Capote left the South but the region remained a presence in their writing.
10. For example Capote's "A Christmas Memory" is a nostalgic story set in Monroeville Alabama.

Exercise 5

Using the Dash and Parentheses The following sentences are about the Saint Gotthard Tunnel, which one of Welty's ancestors helped build. Rewrite each sentence, adding dashes or parentheses where needed. Use the marks of punctuation indicated in parentheses at the end of each sentence.

1. The masonry-lined tunnel it is over nine miles long connects Andermatt to Airolo in the Swiss Alps. (dashes)
2. Did you know that the tunnel, at its highest point of elevation, is 3,786 feet 1,154 meters above sea level? (parentheses)
3. The project after a decade of construction was finally completed in 1882; it was part of the Saint Gotthard Railway. This line connects Lucerne, Switzerland, to Milan, Italy. (dashes, parentheses)
4. The tunnel was costly in human terms hundreds lost their lives during its construction; it was also a financial burden the company almost went bankrupt several times. (two sets of parentheses)
5. This tunnel a massive undertaking cut the traveling time between Milan and Lucerne to ten hours. (dashes)

Exercise 6

Using Quotation Marks and Italics   These sentences are based on other parts of Welty's memoir. On your paper rewrite each one, adding quotation marks or italics (underlining) when necessary.

1. Welty loved listening to music: first, lullabies like Rock-a-Bye Baby and, later, selections from the opera Carmen.
2. Using today's slang, someone might call Eudora's mother's avid reading totally awesome; she read everything from novels such as Jane Eyre to scientific works.
3. Eudora is going to be a writer, we can imagine one of her teachers saying, because she loves fine literature.
4. Welty learned the meaning of words such as somnambulist by watching The Cabinet of Dr. Caligari and other films.
5. Welty relates that the first book she ever bought was In April Once by William Alexander Percy, a Mississippi poet. The first poem in the volume was entitled Home.

Exercise 7

Using the Apostrophe   Rewrite each of the following sentences, adding or deleting apostrophes where necessary. If a sentence has no errors, write *correct*.

1. *One Writers' Beginnings* is about Eudora Welty's early life.
2. Both parent's love for her was steady but unindulgent; its apparent in the book.
3. Their children's success in life was partially due to the Weltys high regard for education.
4. Welty also describes the trip to her Grandma Andrews's house in West Virginia.
5. Grandma Andrews (Mrs. Weltys' mother) must have been pleased with her son-in-law's adoration of her daughter.

Exercise 8

Proofreading

The following passage describes the artist Winslow Homer, whose painting appears on the opposite page. Rewrite the passage, correcting the errors in spelling, usage, and grammar. Add any missing punctuation. There are twenty-five errors.

Winslow Homer

[1]American artist Winslow Homer (1836–1910) was born in Boston Massachusetts. [2]When he was 6 his family moved to the nearby town of Cambridge. [3]Where Homer first developed a love for the outdoors. [4]By the time he was 19 Homer had apprenticed himself to a Boston lithographer. [5] Uninspired by the work there he became a free-lance illustrater for *Ballou's Pictorial*, a Boston periodical and for *Harper's Weekly*, a New York magazine. ➡

Winslow Homer, *Girl on a Garden Seat*, 1878

[6]He moved to New York in 1859 and he continues to make illustrations for *Harper's Weekly*.

[7]When the Civil War began *Harper's Weekly* sent Homer to Virginia to document the fighting along the front lines. [8]His well drawn illustrations of the war were accurate and lacked heroic exageration.

[9]After the war ended Homer turned to painting scenes of contemporary country life. [10]The painting above is typical of Homers work after the war. [11]Like many of his paintings, it was executed in watercolors a medium in which he excelled. [12]Using only a few brush strokes he was able to convey an entire world of light, shadow and color. [13]Homer's paintings always reflected his love of nature recording life acurately without being sentimental. [14]His nature scenes, where the land and sea predominate are very popular. [15]Powerful examples of Homer's trust in nature.

[16]It is easy to imagine that either Eudora Welty or one of Weltys' relatives is depicted in the painting above. [17]The portrait shows a young woman who is prosperous she symbolizes all the young women of her time and class.

Mixed Review

Exercise 9

The following sentences are about Eudora Welty and her family. Rewrite each sentence, correcting all errors in punctuation.

Eudora Welty

1. The author, Eudora Welty, was born in 1909 in Jackson, Mississippi (the state's capital.
2. Her parents who valued reading purchased books that would stimulate their children's imagination.
3. Welty first attended a womens' college in Mississippi: but she graduated from the University of Wisconsin.
4. In 1936 Welty published her first short story "Death of a Traveling Salesman:" moreover she followed it quickly with two collections of stories.
5. "Place", Welty once said, "has the most delicate control over character; she then discussed the role of setting in the fiction of William Faulkner, Emily Brontë and Thomas Mann.
6. Welty's characters sometimes labeled with the word grotesque evoke the atmosphere of the small-town South.
7. Among the memorable characters in Welty's stories are these; Phoenix Jackson, in "A Worn Path," Leota, in "Petrified Man," and Marian, in "A Visit of Charity".
8. After reading the story *A Worn Path*, some readers have asked, "Is Phoenix' grandson really dead"?
9. Another character the narrator of "Why I Live at the P.O.", vividly describes her eccentric relatives.
10. Welty's novel "The Optimist's Daughter" won a Pulitzer Prize in 1973. (It's main characters resemble her parents)
11. Her ancestors on her fathers side who were of German Swiss background) arrived in America before the Revolutionary War.
12. Weltys' father said that "he was not interested in ancient history" and never spoke about his ancestors.
13. However her father did keep in touch with his own father, Jefferson Welty Esquire, for whom he had a deeply felt regard.
14. "It was the only use my father made of the word he saved it for his father," wrote Welty in her memoir *One Writer's Beginnings*.
15. As a result Welty always held the term Esquire in great respect.
16. After her father died an English Welti, who spelled his name with an i told Welty about her ancestors.
17. Three Welty brothers left German Switzerland for the Americas, and settled in Virginia Pennsylvania Ohio and Indiana before the Revolutionary War.
18. Welty said her father would have been interested in the following information one Welty helped push through construction of the St. Gotthard Tunnel.
19. Whenever her mother, and her father, became excited, they would exclaim "Pshaw"
20. Welty wrote of both her fathers family, and her mothers.

Writing Application

Colons and Commas in Writing In the following passage from *Blue Highways*: *A Journey into America*, William Least Heat-Moon describes the fear of being stranded in a snowstorm while attempting to drive across rural America. His careful use of colons and commas enlivens the experience. Examine the passage, focusing on the punctuation in the italicized items.

> I wondered how long I might have to stay in the Breaks before I could drive down. *The cold didn't worry me much: I had insulated the rig myself* and slept in it once when the windchill was thirty-six below. I figured to survive if I didn't have to stay on top too long. Why hadn't I listened to friends who advised carrying a CB? *The headline showed darkly:* FROZEN MAN FOUND IN AVALANCHE. The whole night *I slept and woke, slept and woke, while the hail fell like iron shot, and thunder slammed around, and lightning seared the ice.*

Techniques with Colons and Commas Try to apply some of William Least Heat-Moon's techniques when you write and revise your own work.

1. When introducing information that explains the preceding material, use a colon for greater emphasis and economy of style.

Without colon: The cold didn't worry me much because I had insulated the rig myself . . .

Least Heat-Moon's style: The cold didn't worry me much: I had insulated the rig myself . . .

2. Use commas to vary sentence length and to set off ideas. Notice how Least Heat-Moon's sentence is less choppy but still emphasizes each separate occurrence.

Without commas: I slept and woke. I slept and woke. The hail fell like iron shot. The thunder slammed around. Lightning seared the ice.

Least Heat-Moon's style: I slept and woke, slept and woke, while the hail fell like iron shot, and thunder slammed around, and lightning seared the ice.

Practice On your paper practice using commas and colons by revising the following passage. Correct all improper punctuation as well.

Called a pine snake east of the Mississippi the bullsnake puts on quite a show when it feels threatened. The snake swells up. It hisses loudly. It vibrates its tail. It lunges toward the enemy. Be on your guard The snake is not merely bluffing. It bites. Fortunately, it's bite is not poisonous and a person will recover physically, if not emotionally. Bullsnakes are sometimes referred to as a farmer's best friend. They eat large numbers of mice, rats, and gophers that consume crops. These snakes live primarily in these dry habitats open pinewoods and sandhills and brushlands and deserts. They are also found on grass covered prairies.

Inside Resources

The lessons in this unit give you the skills necessary to prepare and deliver a speech, take a test, use a dictionary, and find books in the library. Each lesson is complete, concise, and easy to use.

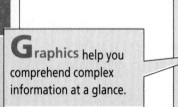

Graphics help you comprehend complex information at a glance.

Wordworks pages like this one provide a humorous look at how we use and misuse our language. These features appear in the first unit in Resources, which puts you in command of basic facts about the English language.

Part 3
Resources and Skills

Part 3 Resources and Skills

22.1 How Language Began

Walk along a busy street in any major metropolitan area—New York, London, Mexico City, Tokyo—and look at the signs in the storefronts you pass. Chances are you'll see signs in a variety of languages from many different parts of the world. Where did all these languages come from? How did language itself originate? No one knows for sure, but linguists, people who study the history and development of languages, have proposed some interesting theories.

Bow-Wow's and Yo-he-ho's

According to the bow-wow theory, language may have begun when people imitated the sounds they heard in the natural world. Imagine some early hunter returning to his family group after discovering a pond alive with ducks. The hunter communicates his discovery by making a quacking sound. The other hunters in the group nod excitedly and grab their weapons. Was this the first sign of the ability to form words having meanings?

Theories of Language Origin			
The Gesture Theory argues that gestures were accompanied by sounds that eventually came to mean what the gesture meant.	**The Ding-Dong Theory** states that primitive people instinctively reacted to every sensory experience with a specific vocal expression.	**The Pooh-Pooh Theory** suggests that language arose from instinctive emotional cries expressing pain, joy, disappointment, anger, and so on.	**The Musical Theory** proposes that language arose from song or that speech and music developed together.

A second attempt to account for the origin of language is referred to as the yo-he-ho theory. A fourteenth-century French scholar named Noiré observed that when people engage in hard physical labor—moving a heavy rock, for example—part of the effort involves trapping air in the lungs by closing the vocal cords. During brief moments of relaxation, the vocal chords open, and involuntary grunting and groaning noises are made. Noiré suggested that these sounds may have evolved into words that meant "heave" or "lift."

Other theories of language origin have been proposed, such as the four listed and described in the chart above. None of these theories accounts for the complexity and richness of human languages. Still, each theory suggests a possible explanation for how people learned to talk to one another.

A Mother Tongue?

Since the late 1700s, linguists have known that certain languages are closely related to other languages, indicating these differing languages developed from a common source. Did all languages originate from one common language—a "mother tongue"? Is it possible that the earliest humans in one part of the African continent created a language that, through contact with other groups of people elsewhere, slowly spread throughout the world? Or did different varieties of human speech begin in different places on the earth with different people? Again, we don't know. What we do know is that a very long time ago, human communication became human language.

Exercise 1

For some years, scientists have attempted to teach chimpanzees to "speak" human language through typing, sign language, and other methods. Other scientists have tried to decode the "language" of dolphins, whales, and other creatures. Investigate one of these attempts at human-animal communication, and write a brief report.

Acronyms

From *A* to Z

In this fast-paced society of ours, it seems everything has speeded up. We have "bullet" trains, supersonic airliners, 150-mph sports cars, and instant satellite communications. We even have a speeded-up language, thanks to acronyms. Acronyms are words formed from the initial letters of other words that make up a phrase. Acronyms can make communicating quicker, easier, and more creative.

Acronyms can take two forms. One type of acronym is a word that is pronounced as a sequence of letters. Examples include *LA* (*L*os *A*ngeles), *CB* (*c*itizen's *b*and radio), *RV* (*r*ecreational *v*ehicle), and *DJ* (*d*isc *j*ockey).

A second type of acronym is pronounced not as a sequence of letters but as a word. These acronyms are usually formed by using the first letter of each word in a phrase: *swat* (*s*pecial *w*eapons *a*nd *t*actics). Other acronyms you're probably familiar with include *scuba* (*s*elf-*c*ontained *u*nderwater *b*reathing *a*pparatus), *radar* (*ra*dio *d*etection *a*nd *r*anging), and *laser* (*l*ight *a*mplification by *s*timulated *e*mission of *r*adiation).

Genuine acronyms develop as a natural process of abbreviation. Reverse acronyms, however, are deliberately created. For example, during World War II, the U.S. Navy created a special force of women to perform volunteer work. The navy called the women *WAVES* and said the acronym stood for *w*omen *a*ccepted for *v*olunteer *e*mergency *s*ervice. It is thought, however, that the navy first came up with the clever name and then created a phrase to support it. That's how reverse acronyms work.

The French "bullet" train, or *train à grande vitesse* (TGV)

Game (*Great Acronym-Making Endeavor*)

Try your hand at creating reverse acronyms. First choose a word; this will be your acronym. Then work out a phrase that supports the acronym. Here are two examples from *The Oxford Guide to Word Games,* by Tony Augarde: **shovel** (*s*harp *h*and-*o*perated *v*ertical *e*arth *l*ifter) and **brain** (*b*ox *r*etaining *a*ssorted *i*nteresting *n*otions). You might want to use the title of a film: **Jaws** (*j*ust *a* *w*hite *s*hark). Share your reverse acronyms with your classmates.

22.2 From Speaking to Writing

Browse through an international bookstore and you'll see books written in many languages using different writing systems. Choose one book written in Chinese, another in Japanese, and a third in Greek, and what will you find? Each of these languages uses a different type of writing system.

Chinese is written using a logographic writing system: each character (there are about 50,000 of them) represents an entire word. Japanese uses a writing system called a syllabary: each of the approximately 50 characters represents a syllable, or a group of sounds. Greek, like English, uses an alphabet: each of the 24 characters in the Greek alphabet represents a sound. All of these writing systems enable people to write what they say and read what they've written. Although these systems have vastly different numbers of characters, each system is capable of expressing a world of ideas.

Three Writing Systems		
Chinese Logography	**Japanese Syllabary**	**Greek Alphabet**
文	こ と ば	λόγος
	ko to ba	l o g o s
wén, "character"	*kotoba*, "language"	*logos,* "word"

Picture Writing

Did people always have writing systems? No. In fact, although spoken language probably originated several hundred thousand years ago, language scholars think that the first fully developed writing system got its start much later—about 5,500 years ago—with hieroglyphs, or picture writing.

Hieroglyphs were pictures that represented objects or ideas rather than words or sounds. This type of writing emerged in many parts of the world at about the same time. You may have seen illustrations of the Egyptian hieroglyphs of northern Africa, in photographs of Egyptian tombs. However, the Hittites, the earliest inhabitants of what is now the country of Turkey, also used hieroglyphs. And half a world away, in Central America, the Maya used hieroglyphic writing to record important information about science, religion, and other aspects of their culture.

Sounds and Symbols

Picture writing, however, proved cumbersome and limiting. Over time, the pictures became streamlined, enabling complex information to be conveyed more efficiently. In Sumer, an ancient region in what is now southeastern Iraq, cuneiform symbols underwent this kind of streamlining.

Cuneiform consisted of about 600 wedge-shaped symbols. At first, these symbols represented objects and ideas. At some point, however, some of the symbols came to be associated with specific sounds as well. For example, the cuneiform arrow symbol represented the object "arrow." The word for "arrow" was pronounced *tē*, so the arrow symbol came to represent the syllable *tē* in all the words in which that syllable occurred, regardless of their meaning. Cuneiform was changing from a logography to a syllabary.

We Get Letters

Another milestone in the development of writing systems took place along the coasts of what are now Syria, Lebanon, and Israel. By 1000 B.C. the Phoenicians, the people who inhabited the coastal region, had developed a great trading and manufacturing civilization. Their society demanded a written language that was easy to use and learn. So the Phoenicians slowly adapted their existing writing system, finally arriving at one that included just 22 characters. Each character in the system represented a single consonant sound. By 900 B.C. the Phoenicians had created an alphabet.

The Greeks further refined the Phoenician alphabet by adding characters that represented vowel sounds. This Greek alphabet proved so useful for expressing and communicating ideas that it has remained virtually unchanged for nearly 3,000 years. All of the alphabets in use in Europe today have their origins in the Greek alphabet.

Cuneiform, 1800 B.C.

Exercise 2

Collect a variety of books, newspapers, or magazines that use different writing systems for a class display. You may find examples from reading materials in your home, or you may be able to photocopy examples at your community library. Try to find examples of Cyrillic, Hebrew, Japanese, Latin, Chinese, Arabic, and Greek writing.

Malapropisms

Plutonic Love

Have you ever unintentionally mis-used a word with humorous results, as in the following bloopers?

Rich? He's a malted [multi] millionaire!

The ancient city of Pompeii was buried in moldy [molten] lava.

These humorous mistaken uses of words are known as malapropisms, from the French expression *mal à propos,* meaning "not appropriate."

In 1775 playwright Richard Sheridan popularized the notion of malapropisms in *The Rivals* through the character of Mrs. Malaprop, who humorously bungled the English language with such utterances as "She's as headstrong as an allegory [alligator] on the banks of the Nile."

Today, malapropisms are also called Pullet Surprises, after a statement in a student essay from Miss Amsel Greene's high school writing class: "In 1957, Eugene O'Neill won a Pullet Surprise [Pulitzer Prize]." Pullet Surprises, according to Miss Greene, are "marvels of ingenuity and logic," like these:

"The doctor prescribed milk of amnesia [magnesia]."

"The flood damage was so bad they had to evaporate [evacuate] four cities."

"So, until next week — Adios, amoebas."

Excuse Me?

See if you can figure out and correct these malapropisms.

1. They put her in an exhilarated class.
2. We couldn't understand his Scottish derelict.
3. The cotton crop was ruined by bold weasels.
4. He plays both guitar and mandarin.
5. She gave him a diamond that sparkled at every faucet.
6. He sent the package by partial post.

22.3　Indo-European Language Family

Have you ever investigated your family tree to discover who your ancestors were? If so, what did you find? Some people have been surprised to discover a famous—perhaps infamous—relative perched on one of the tree's branches. Family trees are sometimes literally drawn as trees, with family groups as branches and individuals as leaves. This enables the diagram to show relationships clearly.

It may surprise you to discover that languages have family trees, too—not in the sense that one language gives birth to another, but rather that languages are related to one another, perhaps with a common source. English, for example, is a member of the Indo-European language family, which is shown on the next page. This is a vast language family that includes most of the languages of Europe as well as those of Iran and India.

As the language tree shows, English belongs to a branch of Indo-European known as Germanic. English shares its linguistic history with the other Germanic tongues. These include Yiddish, which was derived from medieval High German and is spoken today by eastern European Jews and their descendants in many parts of the world. Another Germanic language is Afrikaans, a language spoken by some white South Africans. Afrikaans was derived from Dutch, which was the language of the first white Europeans to settle in South Africa.

The Indo-European languages are believed to have a single "parent" language, although no such parent has yet been found. Language scholars think it is unlikely that direct evidence of this language will ever be found.

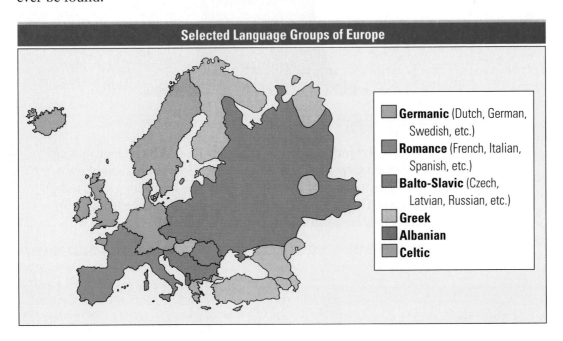

Selected Language Groups of Europe

- **Germanic** (Dutch, German, Swedish, etc.)
- **Romance** (French, Italian, Spanish, etc.)
- **Balto-Slavic** (Czech, Latvian, Russian, etc.)
- **Greek**
- **Albanian**
- **Celtic**

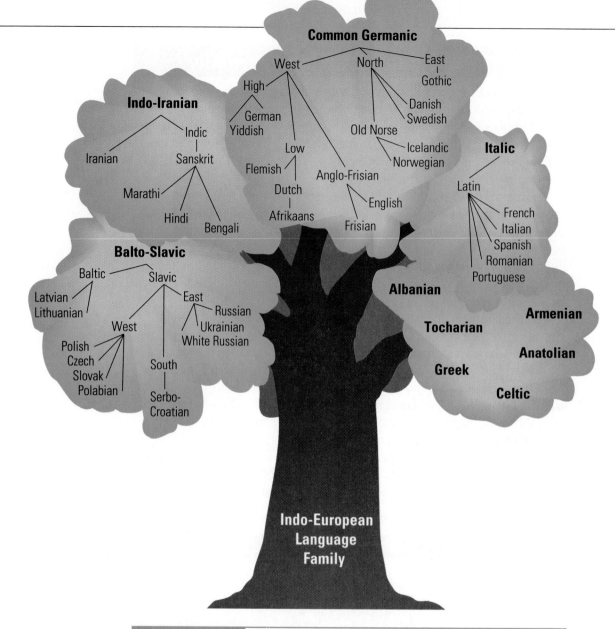

Common Germanic

West — North — East
Gothic

High
German
Yiddish

Danish
Swedish

Low
Flemish

Old Norse
Icelandic
Norwegian

Dutch
Afrikaans

Anglo-Frisian
English
Frisian

Indo-Iranian

Indic
Iranian
Sanskrit

Marathi
Hindi
Bengali

Italic

Latin
French
Italian
Spanish
Romanian
Portuguese

Balto-Slavic

Baltic — Slavic
Latvian
Lithuanian

West
Polish
Czech
Slovak
Polabian

East
Russian
Ukrainian
White Russian

South
Serbo-
Croatian

Albanian

Tocharian

Armenian

Anatolian

Greek

Celtic

Indo-European
Language
Family

Exercise 3

Study the Indo-European language tree. Which languages are descended from Latin? Eastern Slavic? To what branch of the Indo-European language family does Sanskrit belong? Icelandic? Latvian? To what branch does your native language belong? To what other languages is it most closely related?

Idioms

Don't Have a Cow, Man!

Time flies!

You're walking to algebra class one day, and a friend introduces you to Michel, a newly arrived French foreign exchange student.

He speaks some English, but he still has a lot to learn. As you're talking, you suddenly realize you're going to be late for class. "Yikes! Michel, I gotta go. If I'm late for algebra again, Mr. Kim will have a cow!" You expect a laugh from your new friend, but instead Michel gives you a puzzled look. Why?

Well, you used an idiom, a phrase whose real meaning cannot be understood by putting together the meanings of the individual words that make up the phrase.

Some of our most colorful idioms have fascinating histories. *Eat humble pie* means "to be forced to admit a mistake or to accept insult or shame." In medieval England, the master of the manor was the only one allowed to hunt game. When he shot a deer, he kept the meat and gave the innards, or "umbles," to his servants, who would make pies from them. *Eat humble pie* meant being forced to accept the least desirable food.

Buy a pig in a poke means "to buy something sight unseen." Centuries ago in England, a farmer would carry a piglet to market in a sack, or *poke*. Dishonest farmers might substitute a stray cat for the valuable piglet and then sell it to some trusting person who did not bother to check out what he was buying.

Test Your Idiom IQ

See if you can match each of the idioms in the left column with its correct definition in the right column.

1. Sow wild oats
2. Put your shoulder to the wheel
3. Off-the-cuff
4. Pull up stakes
5. Throw in the towel
6. Johnny-come-lately
7. Put on the dog
8. According to Hoyle
9. Lose face
10. Raise Cain

A. To work very hard
B. To do foolish or bad things as a young person
C. Move to another city or area
D. By the rules
E. Be humiliated
F. Become angry and cause a scene
G. To give up
H. A newcomer
I. Unplanned or unprepared
J. Make a flashy display

22.4 Old and Middle English

Can you read these three lines of poetry? They're from *Beowulf*, one of the most famous poems in the English language.

Hafa nū ond geheald hūsa sēlest
gemyne mærþo, mægen-ellen cȳõ,
waca wiõ wrāþum!

Yes, *Beowulf* is written in English—Old English, the earliest form of a language that is spoken today by people in many areas of the world.

Old English was the language of the inhabitants of Britain from about A.D. 449 to 1100. The Celts had been living in Britain under Roman rule for several centuries when Rome withdrew its legions to battle invading barbarians back home. The Celts were left defenseless against a series of invasions by the Picts and Scots from the north and west; Germanic-speaking Saxons, Angles, and Jutes from western Europe; and the Scandinavians. Britain soon became Engla Land, "land of the Angles," and the principal language was largely West Germanic with Scandinavian and Latin influences. This language was Old English.

Old English had three important characteristics. First, it was an inflected language. That means Old English nouns, pronouns, and adjectives had case endings to indicate their function in a sentence—for example, subject or object.

Second, nouns as well as pronouns had grammatical gender. A noun was masculine, feminine, or neuter. Adjectives and certain other modifiers had three sets of endings, and each was used with a noun of a specific gender.

Finally, Old English was characterized by irregular word formation. There were many ways to form the plurals of nouns and the past tense of verbs.

From Old to Middle English

597 Pope Gregory I orders Christian missionaries to Britain to convert the heathens. Monks open schools and teach Latin. Latin words relating to learning and religion enter English: *master (magister), candle (candela), temple (templum).*

| 100 B.C. | A.D. 400 | 500 | 600 | 700 |

55 B.C. Julius Caesar invades Britain and claims it for the Roman Empire. Latin vocabulary is introduced into Celtic.

A.D. 449 At the Celts' request, Germanic Saxons, Angles, and Jutes arrive to defeat the Picts and Scots. The conquerors then turn on the Celts, subjugating them. Celtic is gradually replaced by the Germanic languages of the invaders.

Middle English

By about 1100, enough cumulative changes had occurred to signal the beginning of a great transitional period for English. This period, Middle English, lasted until 1450.

How did Middle English differ from Old English? Read these lines from Geoffrey Chaucer's "The Nun's Priest's Tale," written in Middle English.

We alle desiren, if it might bee,
To han housbondes hardy, wise, and free.

This text is much easier to understand than the Old English of *Beowulf*. The changes were more than just cosmetic, however. Compared with Old English, Middle English was grammatically simpler. Grammatical gender began to disappear, as did inflected case endings. Irregular verb forms gave way to regular forms, and the addition of *-s* to a noun became the standard for forming plurals. Unfortunately, these changes were not applied to all words. That's why we still have irregular verbs and plurals today. *Oxen*, the irregular plural for *ox*, dates back to Old English and is still in use today!

Exercise 4

Look up each of the following words in a dictionary. Write the word as it was formed in Old or Middle English and the language from which English borrowed the word. Look in the front of your dictionary for an explanation of abbreviations.

1. city (Middle English)
2. priest (Old English)
3. adjourn (Middle English)
4. ugly (Middle English)
5. school (Old English)
6. altar (Old English)

1066 William the Conqueror (right) defeats King Harold II at the Battle of Hastings, ushering in a period of French domination over the affairs of England. Many French words relating to government enter English: *authority (auctorité), liberty (liberté), pardon (pardoner),* and *verdict (verdit).*

| | 800 | 900 | 1000 | 1100 | 1500 |

865 A large Viking army invades England. Decades of raids follow, and Vikings conquer half the country. Vikings contribute many words to English, including *law (log), skin (skinn), sky (sky),* and *die (deyja).*

1100 The Old English period ends and Middle English begins. English grammar begins to undergo simplification.

Weasel Words

New, Different, and Improved!

Have you ever purchased a skin cream that you thought promised a clear complexion after a few applications? Have you ever used a new toothpaste, expecting it to give you a dazzling smile? Chances are the ads for these products used phrases like "new and improved formula," "helps give you a brighter smile," or "fights oily skin." Such phrases are full of weasel words—*new, improved, helps, fights*—words that seem to say one thing but that turn out to mean something quite different.

ACTS FAST!

Cleans most surfaces!!!

Spring Fresh Scent

The term *weasel word* is derived from the habits of the weasel, which robs eggs from other species' nests. The weasel makes a small hole in the eggshell and then sucks out the yolk and the white, leaving just an empty shell. The emptied egg *looks* whole, but it is actually hollow. Weasel words are just like that egg—not what they appear to be.

Weasel words work because most people don't pay very close attention to the words they read and hear. Look at that toothpaste claim, "helps give you a brighter smile." What does the word *help* really mean? *Help* simply means "to give assistance or aid." *Help* is a weasel word. To get that dazzling smile you still have to brush after every meal, have your teeth professionally cleaned twice a year, and floss regularly.

Think about the claim "fights oily skin." Does this slogan say the shine will disappear from your face? Does it claim your troubled skin will magically clear up? No, of course not. The promise, like the remnants of the weasel's meal, is not what it appears to be.

Weasel Watch

While watching television or skimming magazines, list the weasel words you find in advertisements or hear in political speeches. Besides the ones mentioned above, other important weasel words to watch for are *works* (not the same as *performs*); *virtually*, as in "leaves glasses virtually spotless" (*virtually* means "almost," not "entirely"); *like*, as in "gives you skin like peaches and cream" (what qualities does skin have in common with peaches and cream?). Share your collection of weasel words with your classmates.

22.5 Modern English

By the 1590s, when William Shakespeare asked the famous question that begins his "Sonnet 18," the transition from Middle English to Modern English had taken place.

> SHall I compare thee to a Summers day?
> Thou art more louely and more temperate:
> Rough windes do fhake the darling buds of Maie,
> And Sommers leafe hath all too fhort a date:

With the exception of some words such as *thee*, *thou*, and *hath*, Shakespeare's vocabulary could easily be mistaken for contemporary English. In fact, aside from some spelling, vocabulary, and pronunciation changes that would take place over the next century or two, the language spoken in Shakespeare's time was essentially the English we speak today.

Modern English, as the English spoken after 1450 is called, continued the trends of Middle English. English was no longer an inflected language—word order, not case endings, determined the function of words in sentences. Grammatical gender was gone—modifiers no longer needed gender endings to match the gender of the nouns they modified. And thanks to a marvelous new invention, standardization was beginning to take hold of the language.

Prior to the mid-1400s all written English was handwritten. Then around 1440 Johannes Gutenberg and some associates began using movable raised type on a printing press. In 1476 William Caxton built and began operating the first printing press in England, and English hasn't been the same since.

Printed matter was now available to a much wider audience than ever before. Because London was the center of England's printing industry, the Londoners' ways of speaking and writing soon spread throughout the country. Pronunciation became more standardized; spelling, too. There were still inconsistencies in written English, but printers were doing their best to bring order to the language.

Contemporary English

None of the changes that transformed Old English into Modern English happened overnight. The evolution of a language is a slow process, and often changes aren't even noticed until decades or centuries later.

Even now, the English you speak continues to evolve. New words have entered the vocabulary from foreign sources: *apartheid* from Afrikaans, *contra* from Spanish, *ayatollah* from Persian, *perestroika* from Russian. New technology, new ideas, and other innovations demand the

Middle English
"Whan that Aprille with
     hise shoures soote
The droghte of March
     hath perced to the roote . . ."

Modern English
"O Gertrude, come away!
The sun no sooner shall the mountains touch
But we will ship him hence."

Contemporary English
"Roger, Houston. I copy. Over."

creation of new words: *CAT scan, modem, yuppie*. Some existing words have taken on new meanings: *mouse, rap, network*.

Grammatical shifts are also taking place. The verb *read*, for example, is sometimes used as a noun today: *Joan Didion's new book is a good read*. The noun *audible* (which originally meant "able to be heard" but took on a new meaning for football as "a new play called at the line of scrimmage") has now been transformed into a verb: *Montana audibilized his way out of a potential loss of yardage*.

One fact about the English language is certain. English is a living language, always changing, always growing. Perhaps several hundred years from now, language scholars will look back at the 1990s and conclude that important changes were taking place in English during this time.

Exercise 5

You can keep track of some of the changes taking place in the English language. Create several pages called "Language Watch" in your journal or another notebook. Label individual pages "New Words," "Existing Words with New Meanings," "Current Slang," "New Acronyms," and "Grammar Shifts." Whenever you run across a word that fits one of these categories—in your reading, in talking with friends, as you listen to radio or television, and so on—add it to your Language Watch files, and date the entry.

Jargon

Clips and Red Dogs

The exasperated supervisor hands a sheaf of papers to her young assistant and says, "Try a new slug, and a new cutline, too. And see if you can come up with a new head." What is this person talking about? Fishing with a cutline and slugs? Or maybe one boxer slugging another? Or is it science fiction? "We're ready for the head transplant, doctor."

In this case, *slug* doesn't have anything to do with slimy sea creatures or with punching somebody out. *Slug, cutline,* and *head* are newspaper jargon, the specialized language used by newspaper people. A *slug* is a story name, a *cutline* is a caption, and a *head* is a headline.

Most trades and professions have their own kind of jargon, or specialized language. Doctors use it. Lawyers use it. Auto mechanics, educators, and engineers use it. Even football players use jargon, such as the words you may have recognized in the title above and in the cartoon.

Jargon often sounds like gibberish to people outside the profession. But jargon can enable people within a specialized group to communicate quickly and clearly. Take, for example, this exchange between two medical professionals:

"Her vitals are failing. BP is low. Start an IV and order an MRI. Call Code Blue!"

Confusing? Maybe to you. But when a patient's life is hanging in the balance, it's much quicker than saying:

"This patient is in danger. We're having trouble detecting a pulse and respiration. Her blood pressure rate is falling. Let's inject her arm with an intravenous tube and then order a magnetic resonance image. Call immediately for an emergency team and a cart with resuscitator and other equipment."

Name That Profession!

How many kinds of jargon can you recognize? For each of the following examples of jargon, name the field or profession in which it is used. Then explain what the jargon means.

1. RBI
2. differential
3. tort
4. hacker
5. cross-check
6. stet

23 Library Resources

23.1 Arrangement of a Library

Learning about the organization of a library will enable you to use its many resources efficiently. Most school and public libraries are organized into the same general sections. The map below shows these sections.

Stacks The stacks, or shelves, hold fiction and nonfiction books. Fiction books are works of the imagination, such as novels and short-story collections. Nonfiction books, which are fact based rather than imaginative, include books about such subjects as history, science, and religion.

Young Adult and Children's Section Fiction and nonfiction books for younger readers are often grouped together in a separate section of the library.

The Librarian Librarians are trained to know the library's resources and can assist you in finding the book or information you need.

Reference Reference materials include encyclopedias, dictionaries, almanacs, and atlases. In some libraries a reference librarian can help in locating reference materials. Most reference materials can be used only in the library.

Audio-Visual Materials Audio-cassette tapes, compact discs, record albums, and videos can be found in the audio-visual section. Ask a librarian which items can be checked out.

Newspapers and Periodicals Periodicals, which include magazines and journals, are publications issued on a regular schedule. Some magazines are issued weekly and others monthly. Current issues of newspapers and periodicals are kept in a general reading area. The *Readers' Guide to Periodical Literature,* a reference index for magazines, is kept in either the reference area or the periodical area.

Catalogs Both the card catalog and computer catalog contain information about books in the library and give their locations.

Exercise 1

In which section of the library might you find these items?

1. *Sports Illustrated*
2. *Dictionary of American Biography*
3. *A History of Southeast Asia*
4. Beethoven's Fifth Symphony (a compact disc)
5. *To Kill a Mockingbird* (a novel)

How do you find a book once you're in the library? To determine whether the library has a particular book you want, first check the card catalog or the computer catalog.

Card Catalog

The card catalog, a cabinet of deep, narrow drawers, contains alphabetically arranged cards for every book in the library. Look at the diagram below to familiarize yourself with the different kinds of catalog cards. A call number is printed in the upper left-hand corner of each card. This number matches the number printed on the spine of the book. Because library books are arranged on the shelves by call numbers, knowing the exact call number allows you to locate a book easily.

Most fiction books have an author card and a title card. Nonfiction books usually have an author card, a title card, and a subject card. Cross-reference cards direct you to different subject headings or other related subjects. Some libraries file subject cards separately in a subject index and author and title cards in an author/title index.

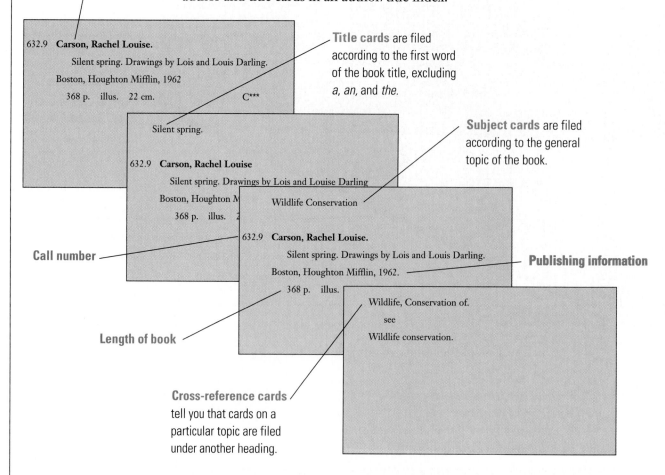

Author cards are filed according to the author's last name.

Title cards are filed according to the first word of the book title, excluding *a, an,* and *the.*

Subject cards are filed according to the general topic of the book.

Call number

Length of book

Publishing information

Cross-reference cards tell you that cards on a particular topic are filed under another heading.

632.9 **Carson, Rachel Louise.**
    Silent spring. Drawings by Lois and Louis Darling.
  Boston, Houghton Mifflin, 1962
    368 p. illus. 22 cm.   C***

Silent spring.

632.9 **Carson, Rachel Louise**
    Silent spring. Drawings by Lois and Louise Darling
  Boston, Houghton M
    368 p. illus.

Wildlife Conservation

632.9 **Carson, Rachel Louise.**
    Silent spring. Drawings by Lois and Louis Darling.
  Boston, Houghton Mifflin, 1962.
    368 p. illus.

Wildlife, Conservation of.
    see
Wildlife conservation.

Computer Catalog

Some libraries have a computer catalog that contains the same information as a card catalog. Computer catalogs have separate search categories for authors, titles, and subjects. For example, if you were looking for a book by Flannery O'Connor, you would enter *O'Connor, Flannery* under the author search. You would then see a list of all the books by Flannery O'Connor that the library owns. A number appears before each book title. For more detailed information, such as a call number or publication date, you would enter the item number for that book. Computer catalogs often provide circulation information, which tells if a book has been checked out or is on reserve.

Some computer catalogs contain information only on relatively new books in the library's collection. If you can't find catalog information in the computer, the book you're looking for may be older. Therefore, you may need to look in the card catalog. If you can't find a book in either catalog, ask a librarian for assistance.

Classification Systems

Once you have found the information you need, you can look for the book. Libraries organize books on the shelves according to call numbers, which are based on classification systems. Although a few libraries create and use their own classifications, almost all libraries use either the Dewey Decimal System or the Library of Congress Classification.

Dewey Decimal System   In 1876 U.S. librarian Melvil Dewey created a 10-category system that grouped books into areas of thought and study. In a library that uses the Dewey Decimal System, books are shelved and organized numerically according to the categories listed below.

Dewey Decimal System		
Category Numbers	**Major Category**	**Examples of Subcategories**
000–099	General works	Encyclopedias, bibliographies
100–199	Philosophy	Ethics, psychology
200–299	Religion	Theology, mythology
300–399	Social sciences	Law, political science, education
400–499	Language	Dictionaries, foreign languages
500–599	Sciences	Chemistry, astronomy, mathematics
600–699	Technology	Medicine, engineering, agriculture
700–799	Arts	Painting, music, theater, sports
800–899	Literature	Poetry, plays, essays
900–999	History and geography	Ancient history, biography, travel

These general categories also contain subcategories—the more specific the topic, the more specific the classification number. For example, look at the Dewey Decimal number below for the book entitled *The Story of Spanish Painting*.

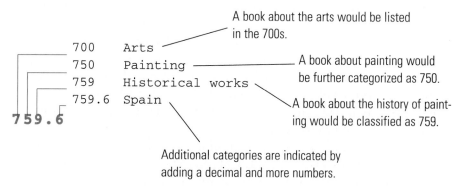

Books are shelved numerically by Dewey Decimal number and then alphabetically by author. For instance, two books about the American Revolution would both be filed in the 973.3 section, but a book by Robert Middlekauff would appear before a book by Barbara Tuchman.

Most libraries that use the Dewey Decimal System do not assign classification numbers to fiction. Instead, the first line of the call number is either an *F* or *Fic* for fiction, and the second line contains the first three letters of the author's last name. Fiction works are organized alphabetically on the shelves by authors' last names. If a library has more than one book by the same author, those books are also alphabetized by title.

Library of Congress Classification Another system is the Library of Congress Classification, or LC, used mostly by larger libraries. The LC was created in 1904 when the collection of the Library of Congress, the national library in Washington, D.C., was reorganized. Rather than categorize books into general areas of study, as Dewey had done, the Library of Congress staff created a system according to the books already in the collection. Books are divided into 21 categories, and each category is assigned a letter, as shown in the chart on the next page.

Like the Dewey Decimal System, the LC also has subcategories, which are identified by letters. Compare the Dewey Decimal number above to the following LC call number for *The Story of Spanish Painting*.

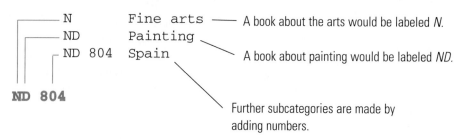

Library of Congress Classification System			
Category Letter	Major Category	Category Letter	Major Category
A	General works	N	Fine arts
B	Philosophy, psychology, religion	P	Language and literature
		Q	Science
C–F	History	R	Medicine
G	Geography, anthropology, recreation	S	Agriculture
		T	Technology
H	Social sciences	U	Military science
J	Political sciences	V	Naval science
K	Law	Z	Bibliography and library science
L	Education		
M	Music		

Special Sections Many libraries group special categories of books, such as reference, biographical, and oversize, in separate areas. Letters above the call number indicate that a book is shelved in a special section. The catalog call number matches the number on the book's spine.

An *R* or *Ref* identifies a reference book. You would look for this book in the reference area.

Guinness book of world records

Ref **McWhirter, Norris,** comp.
031 Guinness book of world records [1st ed.] New York,

Exercise 2

Use the card or computer catalog to find a book about each of the following topics. List the author, title, call number, and publication date of the book you find.

1. Chinese military history
2. Space exploration
3. Architecture in New York City
4. Celtic mythology
5. African American painters
6. Aztec culture
7. Rock music in the 1950s
8. Life of Chinua Achebe
9. Triathlons
10. Greenhouse effect

23.3 Newspapers and Periodicals

Do you want information on current events? Periodicals, such as magazines and journals, and newspapers offer the best source of up-to-date information. Recent issues of these resources are often kept on open shelves in a reading area.

Older issues of newspapers and magazines are often kept separately from the current issues. Back issues of newspapers are usually stored on microforms, which are small photographs of printed pages. Reproduced on either microfilm (filmstrips) or microfiche (film cards), microforms can be viewed on a special machine that enlarges the tiny photographs so they can be read. Back issues of magazines are either bound in hardback volumes (grouped by months or years) or stored on microforms. Several useful indexes can help you locate information on specific topics.

Readers' Guide to Periodical Literature

The best source for finding magazine articles on almost any subject is the *Readers' Guide to Periodical Literature*. Articles from over 175 magazines are indexed by author and subject. New paperback indexes are published every two weeks, larger paperback indexes covering a three-month period are published quarterly, and hardbound volumes of all the year's entries are issued at year's end. The following annotated excerpt from the *Readers' Guide* shows you how to read the information you will find in the index.

WHITEWATER BOATING *See* Running rapids

WHITNEY MUSEUM OF AMERICAN ART
Ross tagged as Whitney director [D. Ross] por *Art in America* 79:37 F '91 — Title of article

WHITTINGHAM-BARNES, DONNA
Blueprints for success. il *Black Enterprise* 21:80-1+ F '91 — Subject entry

WHOOPING COUGH — Name of periodical
The costs of apathy [epidemic in Canada] A. Walmsley. *Maclean's* 104:60 F 4 '91

WIDE AREA NETWORKS — Volume number
Wider area networks [Banyan Systems Inc.] D. Churbuck. il por *Forbes* 147:106 F 18 '91

WIDE SCREEN TELEVISION — Page number
A little off the top (and bottom) [Expand-A-Scope system invented by B. Bergfeldt] B. Butterworth. il *Video* 14:13 Ja '91
New TV breaks the wide-screen barrier [Wide-MAC set introduced by Thomson Consumer Electronics] D. Lachenbruch. il *Video* 14:14+ Ja '91 — Date of periodical

WILD ANIMALS *See* Wildlife

WILD RICE
Gene flow from the jungle to farmers. D. A. Vaughan and L. A. Sitch. bibl f il *BioScience* 41:22-8 Ja '91 — *See* cross-reference

WILDAVSKY, AARON B.
(jt. auth) *See* Mullins, Kerry, and Wildavsky, Aaron B. — Author entry

WILDERNESS AREAS

Alaska

See also
Arctic National Wildlife Refuge (Alaska)
The fight to save Alaska [passage of the Alaska National Interest Lands Conservation Act; cover story] D. W. Scott. il maps *Sierra* 76:38-44+ Ja/F '91

WILDERNESS CONSERVATION *See* Wilderness areas

WILDLIFE

Africa — *See also* cross-reference

See also
American Museum of Natural History. Akeley Hall of African Mammals

Alaska — Subheading

See also
Arctic National Wildlife Refuge (Alaska)
Wolves don't live by the rules [Alaskan gray wolves; reprint from March 1968 issue]; ed. by Jim Rearden. F. Glaser. il *Outdoor Life* 187:54-5+ Ja '91

Brazil
Diet for a small primate [Brazilian buffy-headed marmosets] S. F. Ferrari. il *Natural History* p38-43 Ja '91 — Author of article
The face of discovery [black-faced lion tamarins] C. Zimmer. il map *Discover* 12:57-8 Ja '91 — Topic of article

(Illustrated article)

Other Indexes

The *New York Times* newspaper is a good source for information on current events. The *New York Times Index* lists articles published in the newspaper by title, subject, and author.

Some indexes contain listings for specific topics. For instance, the *Humanities Index* lists articles covering topics such as the arts and philosophy. The *Social Sciences Index* contains listings for articles about economics and political science. Some magazines, such as *National Geographic* and *American Heritage*, have their own indexes.

Many libraries also have periodical and newspaper indexes on computer. Like printed indexes, computerized indexes often list articles by title, subject, and author.

Exercise 4

Use the excerpt from the *Readers' Guide* on the previous page to answer the following questions.

1. Which magazine contains an article about whooping cough?
2. What two animals are featured in articles about wildlife in Brazil?
3. Where in the *Readers' Guide* would articles about whitewater boating be listed?
4. What is the publication date of the *BioScience* article on wild rice?
5. What are the subheadings for "Wildlife"?
6. On which page in *Video* does D. Lachenbruch's article on wide-screen television appear?
7. What is the name of the article written by Donna Whittingham-Barnes?
8. Under what heading are additional articles about wilderness areas listed?
9. Who is featured in an article on the Whitney Museum of American Art?
10. Under what entry would you find an article by Aaron B. Wildavsky?

23.4 Sources of Information

The library contains many information resources. Knowing how to use these materials can help you find information for class assignments and research papers. The following chart shows some widely used reference works.

Using General Reference Works to Answer Questions		
Question	**Where to Look for an Answer**	**Examples of Sources to Check**
When did Mexico win independence?	**Encyclopedias** include general information on a variety of topics.	• *Grolier Encyclopedia* • *World Book Encyclopedia* • *Encyclopaedia Britannica*
Who won the Nobel Peace Prize last year?	**Almanacs and yearbooks** provide statistics, lists, and detailed information on recent issues.	• *Information Please Almanac* • *Guinness Book of World Records*
What is the average temperature in Bangkok, Thailand, in June?	**Atlases** are collections of maps. They often include special maps on climate, land use, history, and other features.	• *Hammond Contemporary World Atlas* • Times *Atlas of World History* • *Cambridge Atlas of Astronomy*
Where was Barbara Jordan born?	**Biographical reference works** include short life histories of noteworthy individuals, both living and deceased.	• *Webster's New Biographical Dictionary* • *Current Biography* • *Dictionary of American Biography*

Other Reference Sources

In addition to general reference works, libraries often contain more specialized sources of information.

Government Documents   Pamphlets, journals, and reports published by the United States government provide statistical information on topics such as agriculture, population, and economics.

Vertical File   If you are researching a current topic that may not be covered completely in magazines or newspapers, you should refer to the vertical file, the library's collection of pamphlets and brochures on current topics. These materials, which also include clippings and photographs, are arranged alphabetically by subject and stored in file cabinets in or near the reference area.

Computer Databases   Some reference works, such as the *New Grolier Electronic Encyclopedia*, are stored on computer. Libraries are sometimes connected to computer networks that provide a variety of reference services, such as interlibrary information searches. Ask a librarian whether your library has these computer services.

Parts of a Book

Using all parts of a book, not just the main text, can help you find information quickly or determine whether or not a book has the information you need. The pages shown below are found in the front of a book, before the main text.

On the **title page,** you can find the complete book title and edition number.

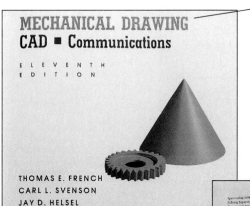

From the **table of contents,** you can identify the main topics covered in the book.

On the **copyright page**, you can find out when the book was first published and how recently it was updated.

By reading the **preface, foreword,** or **introduction,** you can learn about the author's purpose in writing the book.

The following pages, found in the back of the book, after the main text, can also provide valuable information about the main subject of the book or the book itself:

- An **appendix** contains additional information such as maps, charts, tables, illustrations, or graphs.
- The **glossary** is an alphabetical list of special or unfamiliar terms used in the book.
- The **bibliography** lists information sources for material covered in the book.
- The **index** is an alphabetical listing of all people, places, events, and significant topics covered in the book.

Exercise 5

Using the reference works in your school library, answer the following questions, and write down which reference work you used to find your answer.

1. On what river was the ancient city of Mohenjo-Daro located?
2. Who won the Best Actor Oscar in 1980?
3. What are the three leading coal-mining states?
4. Who was Golda Meir?
5. Niamey is the capital of what country?
6. What was the total value of U.S. exports three years ago?
7. When it is 2:00 P.M. in Los Angeles, what time is it in Buenos Aires, Argentina?
8. What is the difference between an alligator and a crocodile?
9. How many moons does Jupiter have?
10. Who holds the world record for women in the marathon?

Exercise 6

Use the pages in the front of this book to answer the following questions.

1. What are the publisher's name and location?
2. What was the first publication date?
3. How many units are in this book?
4. On what page does the index begin?
5. List the names of three consultants who worked on this textbook.

Using Dictionaries

24.1 General Dictionaries

A dictionary is an alphabetical listing of words with their definitions, called entries. Most dictionaries of the English language fall into one of three categories—unabridged, college, school—based on their size and comprehensiveness. The characteristics of each type of dictionary are shown at the bottom of this page.

The Main Entries

Look at the sample dictionary page opposite to familiarize yourself with the organization of entries in a dictionary. Two features of the page, the guide words and the pronunciation key, help you find and understand dictionary entries.

Types of Dictionaries

Unabridged Dictionaries   250,000 or More Entries

Characteristics
- Extensive word histories
- Detailed definitions
- May be in several volumes
- Found mostly in libraries

Examples
- *Random House Dictionary of the English Language*
- *Webster's Third New International Dictionary*
- *Oxford English Dictionary*

College Dictionaries   About 150,000 Entries

Characteristics
- Detailed enough to answer most questions on spelling or definitions
- Widely used in schools, homes, and businesses

Examples
- *Random House Webster's College Dictionary*
- *American Heritage Dictionary of the English Language*
- *Webster's New World Dictionary*

School Dictionaries   90,000 or Fewer Entries

Characteristics
- Definitions based on students' backgrounds
- Emphasizes common words

Examples
- *Macmillan Dictionary*
- *Webster's School Dictionary*

ka·o·lin (kā'ə lin) *also,* **ka·o·line.** *n.* fine white clay used chiefly to fill and coat paper and to make pottery and other ceramics. [French *kaolin,* from Chinese *Kao-ling* name of a mountain (literally, high hill) in China where it was first obtained.]
ka·on (kā'on) *n. Physics.* subatomic particle of the meson group. See **subatomic particle** for table. [*Ka* the letter *k* + (MES)ON.]
ka·pok (kā'pok) *n.* light, fluffy fiber obtained from the seedpods of the silk-cotton tree; used as a stuffing for life preservers, pillows, and mattresses, and as an insulating material. Also, **silk cotton.** [Malay *kāpoq* cotton tree.]
kap·pa (kap'ə) *n.* tenth letter of the Greek alphabet (K, κ), corresponding to English *K. k* and sometimes *C; c.*
kappa meson, kaon.
ka·put (kə poot', kä-) *adj. Informal.* defeated, destroyed, or ruined. [German *Kaputt,* from French *capot* without tricks (in the game of piquet); literally, hoodwinked, from *capot* hooded cloak, going back to Late Latin *cappa.* See CAPE¹.]
Ka·ra·chi (kə rä'chē) *n.* largest city and former capital of Pakistan, a port in the southern part of the country, on the Arabian Sea. Pop. (1975 est.), 2,800,000.
kar·a·kul (kar'ə kəl) *n.* **1.** sheep of a breed originally native to central Asia, having a narrow body and a broad tail. The young karakul has a coat of curled, gray or glossy black fur which becomes long, coarse, and gray or brown when the lamb matures. Height: to 3 feet at the shoulder. **2.** caracul. [From *Kara Kul,* lake in Turkestan, where it was first raised.]
kar·at (kar'ət) *also,* **car·at.** *n.* unit of measure used to express the fineness of gold, 24 karats equaling pure gold. Fourteen-karat gold is 14 parts gold and 10 parts alloy.
ka·ra·te (kə rä'tē) *n.* Japanese system of unarmed self-defense in which the hands, elbows, knees, and feet are used to strike an opponent at various vulnerable points of the body. [Japanese *karate* literally, empty hand (in the sense of weaponless).]
Karl-Marx-Stadt (kärl'märks'shtät') *n.* city in southern East Germany, formerly known as Chemnitz. Pop. (1977 est.), 310,770.
Kar·lo·vy Va·ry (kär'lō vē vär'ē) town in northwestern Czechoslovakia, a famous health resort. Pop. (1977), 61,000. Also, **Carls'bad;** German, **Karls'bad.**
Karls·bad (kärlz'bad', -bät) German. Karlovy Vary.
Karls·ruh·e (kärlz'roo'ə) *also,* **Carls·ruh·e,** *n.* city in southwestern West Germany. Pop. (1977 est.), 275,828.
kar·ma (kär'mə) *n.* **1.** Hindu and Buddhist doctrine that the morality of a person's actions determines the status of the person's future incarnations. **2.** fate; destiny. [Sanskrit *karma* action, fate.]
Kar·nak (kär'nak) *n.* village in Egypt, on the Nile, site of a large group of ancient temples. Karnak is located on part of the site of ancient Thebes.
kar·roo (kə roo') *pl.* **-roos,** *also,* **ka·roo.** *n.* **1.** dry tableland of southern Africa. **2. Karroo,** vast plateau region in the southern part of the Republic of South Africa, in Cape of Good Hope province. [Afrikaans *karo,* probably from Hottentot *garo* desert.]
karyo- *combining form* nucleus of a cell: *karyokinesis.* [Greek *karyon* kernel, nut.]
kar·yo·ki·ne·sis (kar'ē ō ki nē'sis, -kī-) *n.* mitosis. [KARYO- + Greek *kinēsis* movement, motion.]
Kash·mir (kash'mēr, kash mēr') *also,* **Cash·mere.** *n.* area in the extreme northern part of the Indian subcontinent, disputed by India and Pakistan, each of which occupies part of the territory. Area, 86,024 sq. mi. Pop. (1971, excluding Pakistan-occupied area), 4,617,000. Also, **Jammu and Kashmir, Kash·mir·i** (kash mēr'ē), *adj., n.*
Kashmir goat, goat native to India, Tibet, and other regions of Asia, raised esp. for its fine, soft undercoat, which is used to make cashmere wool. Also, **Cashmere goat.**
Ka·tan·ga (kə täng'gə, -tang'-) *n.* former province in the southern part of Zaire, now known as Shaba.
Kat·man·du (kät'män doo') *also,* **Kath·man·du.** *n.* capital of Nepal, in the central part of the country. Pop. (1971), 150,402.
Kat·te·gat (kat'ə gat') *also,* **Cat·te·gat.** *n.* broad arm of the North Sea between Denmark and Sweden.
ka·ty·did (kā'tē did') *n.* any of a group of large green grasshoppers, family Tettigoniidae, having long threadlike antennae. The male produces a shrill, rasping noise by rubbing its wings together. [Imitative of this sound.]

Katydid

Kau·ai (kou'ī) *n.* northernmost island of Hawaii. Area, 551 sq. mi. Pop. (1970), 29,761.
kau·ri (kour'ē) *pl.* **-ris.** *n.* **1.** tall evergreen tree, *Agathis australis,*

found in Australia, New Zealand, and California, having broad flat leaves. Also, **kauri pine. 2.** fine, ever-grained wood of this tree, used in shipbuilding. **3.** resin obtained from this tree, used esp. in making varnish and linoleum. [Of Maori origin.]
kau·ry (kour'ē) *pl.,* **-ries.** *n.* kauri.
Kay, Sir (kā) rude and boastful knight of the Round Table who was the foster brother and steward of King Arthur.
kay·ak (kī'ak) *also,* **kai·ak.** *n.* **1.** Eskimo canoe made of animal skins stretched over a light framework of wood or whalebone, having a small opening in the center for a paddler. **2.** light, highly maneuverable canoe resembling this, used esp. in sports and usually covered with canvas. [Of Eskimo origin.]

Kayak (def. 2)

kay·o (kā'ō') *n.* knockout in boxing. —*v.t.* **kay·oed, kay·o·ing.** to knock out in boxing.
Ka·zakh·stan (kä'zäk stän') *n.* republic of the Soviet Union, in the Asian part of the country. Official name: **Kazakh Soviet Socialist Republic.** Area, approx. 1,048,300 sq. mi. Pop. (1965 est.), 11,853,000.
Ka·zan (kə zän') *n.* city in the European part of the Soviet Union, near the Volga River. Pop. (1970 est.), 869,000.
ka·zoo (kə zoo') *pl.* **-zoos.** *n.* toy musical instrument consisting of a tube containing a strip of catgut or a piece of paper that vibrates and produces a harsh buzzing sound when the player hums into the tube. [Probably imitative.]
kc., kilocycle.
K.C., Knights of Columbus.
ke·a (kē'ə) *n.* New Zealand parrot, *Nestor notabilis,* having a sharp, hooked bill and predominantly olive-green plumage. It feeds on fruit and insects in the summer, but in the winter may feed on carrion or attack and kill sheep by tearing their backs to eat the kidney fat. [Of Maori origin.]
Keats, John (kēts) 1795–1821, English poet.
ke·bab (kə bob') *also,* **ke·bob,** shish kebob.
kedge (kej) **kedged, kedg·ing.** *v.t.* to move (a boat or ship) by pulling on a rope attached to a small anchor that has been dropped at some distance. —*v.i.* (of a boat or ship) to move by kedging. —*n.* small anchor used esp. in kedging. Also, **kedge anchor.** [Of uncertain origin.]
keel (kēl) *n.* **1.** main timber or steel piece extending lengthwise along the center of the bottom of a ship or boat and supporting the entire frame. **2.** part in an aircraft, esp. an airship, corresponding to a ship's keel. **3.** any structure or part resembling a ship's keel. **4.** *Archaic.* ship. **5. on an even keel.** in a state of stability; steady; balanced: *His clear-headedness helped keep everyone on an even keel.* —*v.i., v.t.*

Keel

1. to capsize or nearly capsize; turn over: *The boat keeled when the wind came up.* **2. to keel over, a.** to turn bottom up; capsize. **b.** to fall over suddenly; topple; collapse: *to keel over in a faint.* [Old Norse *kjölr* lowest timber along the bottom of a ship.]
keel·boat (kēl'bōt') *n.* flat-bottomed river boat having a keel but no sails, propelled by being rowed, towed, or poled, formerly used to carry freight in the western United States.
keel·haul (kēl'hôl') *v.t.* **1.** to drag (a person) under the keel of a ship from one side or end to the other as a form of punishment. **2.** to rebuke or punish severely. [Dutch *kielhalen,* from *kiel* keel + *halen* to haul.]
keel·son (kel'sən, kēl'-) *also,* **kel·son.** *n.* long beam running parallel with and fastened to the main keel of a ship in order to strengthen it. [Of Germanic origin.]
keen¹ (kēn) *adj.* **1.** having a fine cutting edge or point; able to cut or pierce easily; sharp: *a keen sword.* **2.** having or showing great mental sharpness; clever; perceptive: *a keen mind, a keen understanding of a subject.* **3.** highly sensitive or acute, as a sense or sense organ: *keen eyes, a keen sense of smell.* **4.** vividly felt or experienced; intense; strong: *a keen sense of loss; The hounds followed the keen scent.* **5.** of a piercing, penetrating, or cutting nature: *A cold, keen wind blows in from the ocean.* **6.** enthusiastic; eager: *Kate is keen about traveling.* [Old English *cēne* wise, brave.] —**keen'ly,** *adv.* —**keen'ness,** *n.* —**Syn. 6.** see **eager.**
keen² (kēn) *Irish. n.* wailing lament for the dead. —*v.i.* to wail loudly for the dead. [Irish *caoinīm* ī wail.] —**keen'er,** *n.*
keep (kēp) **kept, keep·ing.** *v.t.* **1.** to retain in one's possession, power, or control: *I told Joan she could borrow my sweater but not keep it.* **2.a.** to cause to continue in some specified place, condition, relation, or position: *to keep things in order, to keep the door open, to keep a child*

at; āpe; cär; end; mē; it; īce; hot; ōld; fôrk; wood; fōōl; out; up; ūse; turn; sing; thin; this; zh in treasure; ə in ago, taken, pencil, lemon, circus. 561

Guide words indicate the first and last entry on the page **kaolin/keep**.

The first entry on the page is **kaolin**.

The last entry on the page is **keep**.

Pronunciation key uses well-known words to indicate how to interpret the pronunciation symbols **a**t; **ā**pe; c**är**; **e**nd; m**ē** . . .

Homographs   Two or more words that are spelled the same but have different meanings and histories are listed as separate entries. Such words are called homographs. For example, *sole* could mean "the bottom of a foot," "acting alone," or "a type of fish." Since these three meanings are so distinct from each other, *sole* is listed as a main entry three times. Each is labeled with a small, raised number. Notice the different meanings and histories of *real¹* and *real²* shown on the next page.

Entry Information   Most often you probably look up a word to find a definition. However, entries also provide other information, such as

- correct hyphenation of words with more than one syllable
- pronunciations
- preferred spellings when alternate forms of words are acceptable
- inflected forms of the main entry word, such as plurals, adverbs, or adjectives
- part or parts of speech
- cross-references to synonyms, words with the same or similar meanings, and to antonyms, words with opposite meanings

Etymology   Many entries also include an etymology, which is the history of a word. For example, the word *telephone* comes from two Greek words—*tele* ("far off, afar") and *phone* ("voice, sound"). From etymologies you can also learn when a word is derived from another, such as *atomic* from *atom*.

Look at the following dictionary entry for *real* to review the elements of an entry.

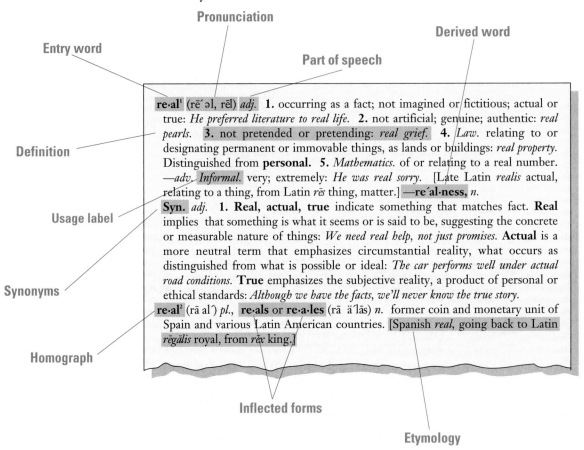

Pronunciation

Derived word

Entry word

Part of speech

Definition

Usage label

Synonyms

Homograph

re·al¹ (rē′əl, rēl) *adj.* **1.** occurring as a fact; not imagined or fictitious; actual or true: *He preferred literature to real life.* **2.** not artificial; genuine; authentic: *real pearls.* **3.** not pretended or pretending: *real grief.* **4.** *Law.* relating to or designating permanent or immovable things, as lands or buildings: *real property.* Distinguished from **personal. 5.** *Mathematics.* of or relating to a real number. —*adv. Informal.* very; extremely: *He was real sorry.* [Late Latin *realis* actual, relating to a thing, from Latin *rē* thing, matter.] —**re′al·ness,** *n.*
Syn. *adj.* **1. Real, actual, true** indicate something that matches fact. **Real** implies that something is what it seems or is said to be, suggesting the concrete or measurable nature of things: *We need real help, not just promises.* **Actual** is a more neutral term that emphasizes circumstantial reality, what occurs as distinguished from what is possible or ideal: *The car performs well under actual road conditions.* **True** emphasizes the subjective reality, a product of personal or ethical standards: *Although we have the facts, we'll never know the true story.*
re·al² (rā al′) *pl.,* **re·als** or **re·a·les** (rā ä′lās) *n.* former coin and monetary unit of Spain and various Latin American countries. [Spanish *real,* going back to Latin *rēgālis* royal, from *rēx* king.]

Inflected forms

Etymology

Usage Guidelines   A dictionary entry also provides you with guidelines on usage, meaning the way words are used in different contexts. Labels identify situations in which the word can be used appropriately. For example, the definition of the word *dig* that means "to understand" is labeled "slang." This usage label tells you that this meaning of *dig* does not belong to standard English.

Many dictionaries include a phrase or a sentence illustrating the use of a particular definition of a word. In some dictionaries these phrases and sentences are quotations from actual pieces of writing, in which case the dictionary may also identify the writer and the date of the piece.

Common usage labels are described in the table located at the top of the next page.

Usage Information in Dictionary Entries		
Type of Information	**Description**	**Example**
Capitalization	Indicates when a particular meaning of a word needs to be capitalized	**confederate** . . . **2. Confeder-ate.** citizen or supporter of the Confederate States of America.
Special field usage	Identifies a definition used only in a particular activity or area of study	**travel** . . . **7.** *Basketball.* To walk or run illegally while holding the ball.
Regional usage	Indicates words with special meanings in certain geographical areas	**submarine** . . . **3.** *Chiefly Northeastern and North Midland U.S.* a hero sandwich.
Usage note	Provides guidelines for using (or not using) words in particular situations	**oyez** . . . ▲ used to announce that court is in session and to ask for silence.
Out-of-date usage	Labels words as archaic, used only in special contexts, or obsolete, no longer used	**transport** . . . **4.** *Archaic.* to kill.

Information in Dictionaries

Many dictionaries also include special sections, such as a biography section listing famous people and a geography section describing cities, countries, and other places. These additional sections make dictionaries even more useful.

Exercise 1

Use a school or college dictionary to answer the following questions.

1. Who was Haile Selassie?
2. Hyphenate the word *edema*.
3. What is the plural of the noun *echo*?
4. What are the past and past participle of *tread*?
5. Does *forte* have one or two syllables? Explain.
6. Is *theater* or *theatre* the preferred American spelling?
7. Is *Levantine* always capitalized?
8. Which syllable in *hiatus* is accented?
9. What are the origins of the homographs spelled *bow*?
10. What synonyms or antonyms are given for *spectator*?

24.2 Using a Thesaurus

One special type of dictionary is a book of synonyms, also known as a thesaurus. Such a book can help a writer find colorful, precise words about any given subject. The best-known thesaurus is *Roget's,* first developed by a British doctor, Peter Mark Roget, in 1852. Roget grouped together words related to the same basic concept, such as *improvement,* into categories. He then developed an index to the categories. Thesauruses exist today both in this original form and an updated, dictionary form.

Original Form

Using Roget's original thesaurus is a simple two-step process. First, you look up a word in the index to find the category under which it is listed. Then you look up the category to find synonyms for the word. For example, look at the following thesaurus entries for the word *change.*

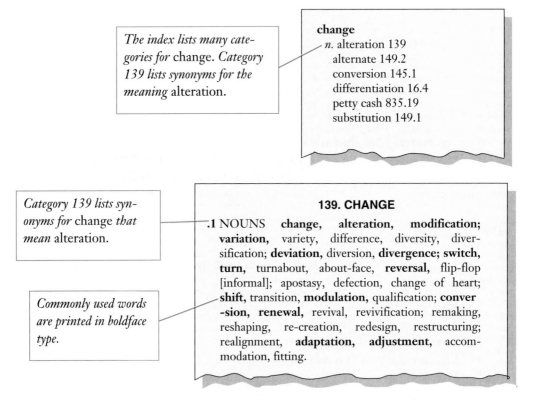

The index lists many categories for change. *Category 139 lists synonyms for the meaning* alteration.

change
n. alteration 139
alternate 149.2
conversion 145.1
differentiation 16.4
petty cash 835.19
substitution 149.1

Category 139 lists synonyms for change *that mean* alteration.

Commonly used words are printed in boldface type.

139. CHANGE

.1 NOUNS **change, alteration, modification; variation,** variety, difference, diversity, diversification; **deviation,** diversion, **divergence; switch, turn,** turnabout, about-face, **reversal,** flip-flop [informal]; apostasy, defection, change of heart; **shift,** transition, **modulation,** qualification; **conver -sion, renewal,** revival, revivification; remaking, reshaping, re-creation, redesign, restructuring; realignment, **adaptation, adjustment,** accommodation, fitting.

Dictionary Form

A variation of Roget's original system is even simpler to use. A thesaurus in dictionary form presents words in alphabetical order. A regular word entry is followed by a few synonyms and cross-references to one or more related major categories, as in the entry for *grow* on the next page.

> **grow,** *v.* raise, plant, sow (FARMING);
> vegetate, germinate, sprout (PLANT LIFE);
> fill out, wax, accumulate (INCREASE).

If you can't find an appropriate synonym under the regular entry, try one of the major categories, which are in parentheses. Under a major category entry you will find nouns, verbs, adjectives, and adverbs all related to one main idea. Major categories include cross-references to antonyms. The following excerpt shows the entry for *increase*.

Major category

INCREASE—*N.* **increase,** raise, rise, boost, step-up; addition, increment, accrual, access.

growth, surge, swell, rise, accretion; accumulation, overgrowth, spread.

[*abnormal bodily enlargement*] giantism, gigantism, elephantiasis, acromegaly.

V. **increase,** enhance, aggrandize, augment, add to, heighten, aggravate, intensify, step up, raise, lift, boost, up; multiply, propagate, redouble, magnify, exaggerate, maximize, lengthen.

grow, surge, swell, fill out, inflate; wax, accumulate, rise, skyrocket; overgrow, overrun, spread.

expand, distend, dilate, inflate, swell, develop, extend, spread, stretch, widen; enlarge, pad, amplify, bulk.

enlarge on (*a subject, etc.*), amplify, develop, dilate on, elaborate on, expand, expatiate on, extend.

Adj. **increasing,** etc. (see *Verbs*); accretive, crescent, crescive, incremental, increscent, addititious, cumulative, accumulative.

See also ADDITION, EXAGGERATION, SPREAD, SWELLING.

Antonyms—See DECREASE, DEDUCTION.

Synonyms for increase

Subcategories

Cross-references to other major categories

Cross-references to antonyms

Exercise 2

Use a thesaurus to find two synonyms for each word below. Then write an original sentence to illustrate the meaning of each synonym. You may wish to check the exact meaning of each word in a dictionary before you use it in a sentence.

1. want (verb)
2. angry (adjective)
3. hold (verb)
4. like (verb)
5. near (adverb)
6. deny (verb)
7. throw (verb)
8. good (adjective)
9. condemn (verb)
10. place (noun)

Unit 25 | Vocabulary

25.1 | Building Vocabulary

Most words that you know you learned through listening and reading. One way to learn new words is by analyzing the passage in which they appear.

Analyzing Specific Context Clues

You can often figure out the meaning of a word from its context—the words surrounding the word. The following chart describes five different context clues and the clue words that help you interpret them. In the "Example" column, clue words are in bold type. Unfamiliar words and words that indicate a definition are in italics.

Interpreting Clue Words		
Type of Context Clue	**Clue Words**	**Example**
Definition: The meaning of the unfamiliar word is stated in the sentence.	which means also known as in other words or	The course emphasized *demography,* **which means** *the study of changes in human population.*
Example: The meaning of the unfamiliar word is explained through other illustrations.	for instance such as for example like	He was the president's *amanuensis;* **for instance,** he *took dictation and copied manuscripts.*
Comparison: The unfamiliar word is similar to a familiar word or phrase.	likewise also similarly as	Consuela had a height *phobia;* **likewise,** she *feared* caves.
Contrast: The unfamiliar word is the opposite of a familiar word or phrase.	however but on the contrary unlike	We were *pertinacious* about the topics; **however,** we were *flexible* about the time of the meeting.
Cause and Effect: The unfamiliar word describes a cause in a sentence in which the effects are understood.	therefore since because when as a result	Otis was typically *loquacious;* **therefore,** the rest of us were unusually *quiet.*

Analyzing the General Context

What if there are no specific context clues to help you figure out an unfamiliar word? Often you can deduce a meaning of a word because you know other words that appear with it, as in the following sentence: The bowl contained apples, oranges, plantains, cherries, and plums. You may not know that plantains are a fruit similar to bananas. However, because the other items in the list are fruits, you might assume that plantains are a type of fruit.

Sometimes you can begin to figure out the meaning of a word by determining its part of speech. You can use this approach even if practically no words are familiar. For instance, Lewis Carroll began his poem "Jabberwocky" with these two lines: " 'Twas brillig, and the slithy toves / Did gyre and gimble in the wabe." Even though Carroll made up most of the words, you can still begin to figure out their meanings.

Start with the word *toves*. You know that *toves* is the subject of the sentence because it is performing some kind of action—"the slithy toves did gyre and gimble in the wabe." The article *the* provides another clue; *the* appears only before nouns. From these two clues, you can figure that *toves* is a noun. In fact, given the plural *-s* ending, *toves* probably means "more than one tove."

Another way to figure out an unfamiliar word's part of speech is to compare the sentence in which it appears to similar sentence constructions. Look at the sentence " 'Twas brillig," which means "It was brillig." *Brillig* follows a verb of being, *was*, and could therefore be a noun or an adjective. Think of other times when you have used or read a similar sentence construction. *Brillig* might describe the weather—"It was chilly"— or indicate the time of year—"It was spring."

Remembering Words You've Learned

Increasing your vocabulary improves your reading and writing skills and your chances of scoring well on standardized tests. The following tips will help you remember new words you encounter.

Tips on Learning New Words
1. Write down new words in a notebook. Just writing the word will help you remember it.
2. Check the meaning and pronunciation of the new word in a dictionary. Looking up a word helps you learn its meaning.
3. Relate the new word to words you already know. Associating its spelling or meaning with a familiar word makes a new word easier to remember.
4. Practice using the word in your writing and conversation. Using the word repeatedly is the best way to remember it.

Each of the following passages contains an italicized word that may be unfamiliar. Determine the meaning by examining the context. Look for the context clues described in the chart on page 746. Write the italicized word and its meaning. Then indicate the strategy used in each case by writing *definition, example, comparison, contrast,* or *cause and effect.*

1. Television in the 1950s portrayed a *homogeneous* national population; however, the United States actually included a number of different ethnic groups.
2. Our biology teacher told us to rely only on *empirical* evidence, that is, our careful observations and experiments.
3. The beginning of Beethoven's Sonata Pathétique is to be played in *grave* tempo—like a funeral march, only slower.
4. Early tribes were usually *nomadic,* but because of the development of agriculture, some tribes stayed in one place.
5. The defenders of the western bridge were undefeatable, and since the defense of the eastern bridge was also *insurmountable,* the attacking forces gave up.
6. The woman was a true *miser;* for instance, she never donated to charities and spent very little money on presents.
7. At the fall of Berlin, *anarchy,* or complete disorder, prevailed until Allied forces took control.
8. Our creative writing teacher instructed us to use a *pseudonym* to hide our real identities. I chose "Lian Chen" as my pen name.
9. Do not keep *volatile* substances in places where they will be exposed to extremely high temperatures, because they may explode.
10. The World Trade Center and the Empire State Building are among New York City's tallest *edifices.*

25.2 Word Parts

Another way to figure out the meaning of a word is by analyzing its parts. The main part of a word is its root. When the root is a complete word, it is sometimes called a base word. The root or base word is often combined with a prefix (a word part attached to the beginning of a word), a suffix (a word part attached to the end of a word), or another root to form a different word.

Consider a word you already know—*unbreakable*—and look at its parts. Added to the base word *break* are the prefix *un-* and the suffix *-able.*

The prefix *un-* means "not." The suffix *-able* means "capable of." Therefore, *unbreakable* means "not capable of being broken."

Word Roots

While prefixes and suffixes can give hints about a word's meaning, the most important clue is the root. The following diagram shows several words that have been formed from the Latin root *spec.* From what you know about the words given, what do you think *spec* means?

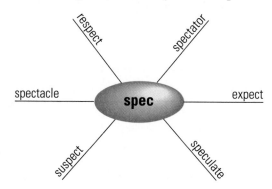

As you might have figured out, *spec* means "to look at." The next diagram shows several words. See if you can figure out which root the following words share and the meaning of the root.

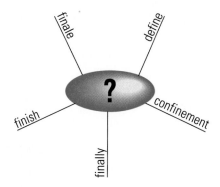

The root of each of these words is *fin.* What do you think *fin* means? All the words relate to some kind of ending, like *finish, finale,* and *finally,* or limitation, like *define* and *confinement.* Therefore, you can deduce that *fin* means "end" or "limit." The root *fin* comes from Latin; more than 50 percent of the English vocabulary originates directly or indirectly from Latin. Many other roots come from Greek or Anglo-Saxon.

When you are trying to determine the meaning of a new word, think of words that might share a root with it. The meanings of these other words might give you clues to the meaning of the unfamiliar word. The chart on the following page lists some common roots and some words that share them.

Analyzing Word Roots		
Words	**Meanings**	**Roots**
aqueduct aquarium	means of moving water tank of water	*aqu* means "water"
astronaut astronomy	traveler among stars study of stars	*astro* means "stars"
biology autobiography	study of living things story of a person's life written by that person	*bio* means "life"
century centimeter	a hundred years measurement equal to one hundredth of a meter	*cent* means "hundred"
chronological synchronize	arranged in time order cause to happen at the same time	*chron* means "time"
democracy epidemic	rule by the people rapidly spreading among many people	*dem* or *demo* means "people"
geology geocentric	study of the earth measured from center of the earth	*geo* means "earth"
anonymous pseudonym	with no name known or acknowledged pen name	*nym* means "name"
agoraphobia monophobia	fear of open spaces fear of being alone	*phobia* means "fear"
portable transport	capable of being carried to carry across	*port* means "carry"
inscribe scribble	to write or mark on to write messily	*scrib* means "write"
constrict stringent	draw together; bind strict; severe	*string* or *strict* means "bind"
unique unified	one-of-a-kind joined into one	*uni* means "one"
revive vivisection	bring back to life operation on a living animal for science	*viv* means "live" or "alive"

Prefixes

Prefixes are important tools for building, and learning, new words. Prefixes change the meaning of words, sometimes drastically. Certain prefixes, such as *un-* and *in-*, can even reverse the meaning of a root.

The following chart lists other prefixes and their meanings. You will see that some prefixes can have more than one meaning. Notice how some prefixes can change the meaning of a word.

Analyzing Prefixes		
Words	Meanings	Prefixes
amoral atypical	without morals not typical	*a-* means "without" or "not"
coauthor colead	write together lead together	*co-* means "together"
contradict contrary	to act in opposition opposed	*contra-* means "opposed"
demote deduction	move down in rank conclusion drawn from reasoning	*de-* means "from" or "down"
dishonest distrust	not honest lack of trust	*dis-* means "lack of" or "not"
emit expel	send out drive out	*e-* and *ex-* mean "out"
illegal immoral insignificant irregular	not legal not moral not significant not regular	*il-, im-, in-,* and *ir-* mean "not"
international interject	among nations to throw between	*inter-* means "among" or "between"
microscopic microwave	invisible to the naked eye very short electromagnetic wave	*micro-* means "small"
misplace mistreat	put in wrong place treat badly	*mis-* means "wrong" or "bad"
monochromatic monogamy	of one color marriage with one mate	*mono-* means "one"
prearrange preliminary	to arrange beforehand coming before the main action	*pre-* means "before"
replay recall	to play again to call back	*re-* means "again" or "back"
submerge subzero	to place under water below zero	*sub-* means "under" or "below"

Suffixes

In English, suffixes are more common than prefixes. Suffixes, added to the ends of words, create new words with new meanings. Many suffixes also change the original word's part of speech. Remember the example of *unbreakable* at the beginning of this lesson? When added to the verb *break*, the suffix *-able* forms a new word with a new part of speech, the adjective *breakable*. With certain words, the spelling of the original word may change slightly when a suffix is added, as with *forgivable* (*forgive* + *-able*).

The following chart lists other suffixes, their meanings, and the parts of speech they form. See if you can figure out the meaning of the suffix by looking only at the first two columns in the table.

Analyzing Suffixes			
Words	**Meanings**	**Suffixes**	**Part of Speech Formed**
occupant dependent commandant	one who occupies one who depends one who commands	*-ant* and *-ent* mean "one who does an action"	Concrete noun
boredom freedom	state of being bored condition of being free	*-dom* means "state" or "condition"	Abstract noun
shorten quicken enliven	to become short to become quick to become lively	*-en* means "to become"	Verb
fearful hopeful	full of fear full of hope	*-ful* means "full of"	Adjective
crystallize minimize	to become a crystal to make minimal, or smaller	*-ize* means "to become" or "to make"	Verb
hopeless treeless effortless	without hope without trees without effort	*-less* means "without"	Adjective
quickly slowly	in a quick manner in a slow manner	*-ly* means "in the manner or way mentioned"	Adverb
kindness fondness darkness	state of being kind state of being fond quality of being dark	*-ness* means "quality" or "state"	Abstract noun
furious joyous	full of fury full of joy	*-ous* means "full of"	Adjective

Exercise 2

Divide into groups of three, and have each member in a group write down the meaning of one word from each of the following groups of words. Use a dictionary, if necessary. After you share your definitions, decide as a group what root the words share and what the root means.

1. philosophy, bibliophile, philanthropy
2. autocratic, technocrat, bureaucratic
3. photophobia, photography, photosynthesis
4. beneficial, benevolent, benefactor
5. mortician, immortality, mortuary

Exercise 3

Rewrite each of the following sentences, replacing the underlined words with a single word that uses a prefix. You may want to change the word order in some cases.

1. Cooperating with <u>workers with whom you are employed</u> makes work more enjoyable.
2. Many countries have experienced recessions <u>after a war</u>.
3. The journalist <u>spelled incorrectly</u> the senator's name.
4. Students can improve their grades by changing study habits that are <u>not efficient</u>.
5. When a doctor recommends surgery, many patients decide to be <u>examined again</u> by another doctor.

Exercise 4

Rewrite each of the following sentences, replacing the underlined words with a word that uses a suffix. You may want to change the word order in some cases.

1. Jon noticed that when he runs, his heartbeat <u>is made quick</u>.
2. The hero of the tale, Beowulf, is <u>without fear</u>.
3. Mel Allen and Red Barber both helped <u>to make popular</u> radio broadcasting of baseball.
4. As she left the garage, Joan gave her car keys to the <u>one who attended to</u> parking.
5. The eyewitness showed <u>a state of being willing</u> to cooperate with the police investigators.

Spelling

26.1 | Improving Your Spelling

As a writer, you want your readers to understand your ideas. Using correct spelling in your writing will enable your readers to focus on what you have to say and understand your ideas more easily.

You can improve your spelling—and in turn help make your writing understood—in several ways. First, you can learn some basic rules that will help you spell correctly. Second, you can pay attention to the new words you encounter and learn to spell them.

Basic Spelling Rules

The following rules, examples, and exceptions will help you master the spellings of many words.

Spelling *ie* and *ei* Many writers find the rules for certain combinations of letters, like *ie* and *ei*, difficult to remember. One helpful learning strategy is to develop a rhyme to remember a rule. Look at the following rhyme for the *ie* and *ei* rule.

Rule		Examples
Put *i* before *e*,	→	achieve, chief, lien
except after *c*,	→	conceit, receive, ceiling
or when sounded like *a*, as in *neighbor* and *weigh*.	→	eighth, reign, sleigh, freight, veil, neigh

Exceptions
seize, leisure, weird, height, either, forfeit, protein

Spelling *-cede*, *-ceed*, and *-sede* Because various letters in the English spelling system are sometimes pronounced the same way, it is often easy to make slight spelling errors between two different letters. The similarity of pronunciation between *c* and *s* accounts for the confusion in spelling words ending in *-cede*, *-ceed*, and *-sede*. Because there are only four exceptions, however, you should be able to memorize them.

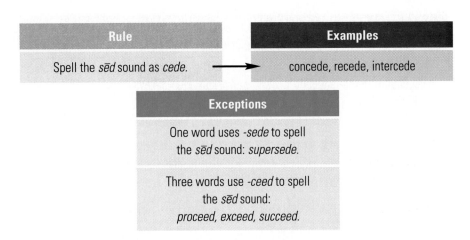

Rule	Examples
Spell the *sēd* sound as *cede*. ⟶	concede, recede, intercede

Exceptions
One word uses *-sede* to spell the *sēd* sound: *supersede*.
Three words use *-ceed* to spell the *sēd* sound: *proceed, exceed, succeed*.

Spelling Unstressed Vowels   Notice the vowel sound in the second syllable of the word *or-i-gin*. This is the unstressed vowel sound, and it can be spelled several ways. Dictionary respellings use the schwa symbol (ə) to indicate it. To help spell words with unstressed vowels correctly, try thinking of a related word in which the syllable containing the vowel sound is stressed. The chart below shows examples of this process.

Spelling Unstressed Vowels		
Unknown Spelling	**Related Word**	**Word Spelled Correctly**
leg_l	le**gal**ity	legal
fant_sy	fan**tas**tic	fantasy
host_le	hos**til**ity	hostile
opp_site	op**pose**	opposite

Adding Prefixes   When adding a prefix to a word, keep the original spelling of the word. If the prefix forms a double letter, keep both letters.

dis- + appear = disappear   ir- + regular = irregular
mis- + direct = misdirect   co- + operate = cooperate

Suffixes and the Silent e   Many English words end in a silent letter *e*. Sometimes the *e* is dropped when a suffix is added. The following chart shows when to keep and when to drop the *e*.

Adding Suffixes to Words with Silent *e*	
Rule	**Examples**
When adding a suffix that begins with a consonant to a word that ends in silent *e*, keep the *e*. **Common exceptions**	place + -ment = placement rare + -ly = rarely *awe + -ful = awful* *judge + -ment = judgment* ⟹

Adding Suffixes to Words with Silent *e* (continued)	
Rule	**Examples**
When adding a suffix that begins with a vowel or *y* to a word that ends in silent *e*, usually drop the *e*.	excite + -able = excitable
	shine + -y = shiny
Common exceptions	*mile + -age = mileage*
When adding a suffix that begins with *a* or *o* to a word that ends in *ce* or *ge*, keep the *e* so the word will retain the soft *c* or *g* sound.	change + -able = changeable
	trace + -able = traceable
When adding a suffix that begins with a vowel to a word that ends in *ee* or *oe*, keep the *e*.	agree + -able = agreeable
	see + -ing = seeing
	canoe + -ing = canoeing

Suffixes and the Final *y* When adding a suffix to a word that ends in a consonant + *y*, change the *y* to *i*. Do not change the *y* to *i* when the suffix begins with *i*.

try + -ed = tried   copy + -ing = copying

When adding a suffix to a word that ends in a vowel + *y*, keep the *y*.

joy + -ous = joyous   convey + -ed = conveyed
boy + -ish = boyish   play + -ing = playing

Doubling the Final Consonant When adding a suffix to a word, you sometimes need to double the final consonant before adding the suffix. You double the consonant when adding a suffix that begins with a vowel to a word that ends in a single consonant preceded by a single vowel, if the original word

- is a one-syllable word
  dip + -ing = dipping   stop + -age = stoppage

- has an accent on the last syllable and the accent remains there after the suffix is added
  occur + -ence = occurrence   repel + -ing = repelling

- is a prefixed word based on a one-syllable word
  reset + -ing = resetting

Based on the preceding rule, you would not double the final consonant when

- the accent is not on the last syllable
  develop + -ing = developing

- the accent shifts when the suffix is added
  refer + -ence = reference

- the final consonant is preceded by two vowels
  train + -ing = training

- the final consonant is preceded by another consonant
  remind + -er = reminder

- the word ends in a consonant and the suffix begins with a consonant
  reck + -less = reckless

Adding -ly   When adding *-ly* to a word that ends in a single *l*, keep the *l*. When the word ends in a double *l*, drop one *l*. When the word ends in a consonant + *le*, drop the *le*.

real + -ly = really   dull + -ly = dully   terrible + -ly = terribly

Adding -ness   When adding *-ness* to a word that ends in *n*, keep the *n*.

sullen + -ness = sullenness   keen + -ness = keenness

Forming Compound Words   When joining a word that ends in a consonant to a word that begins with a consonant, keep both consonants.

after + noon = afternoon   key + board = keyboard

Forming Plurals   English nouns form plurals in many ways. Most nouns simply add *s*. The following chart shows other ways of forming plural nouns and some common exceptions to the patterns.

General Rules for Plurals		
If the Noun Ends In	**Then Generally**	**Examples**
ch, s, sh, x, or *z*	add *-es*	wish ➤ wishes crutch ➤ crutches
a consonant + *y*	change *y* to *i* and add *-es*	cannery ➤ canneries baby ➤ babies
a vowel + *y*	add *-s*	day ➤ days key ➤ keys
a vowel + *o*	add *-s*	studio ➤ studios stereo ➤ stereos
a consonant + *o* **Common exceptions**	generally add *-es* but sometimes add *-s*	potato ➤ potatoes cargo ➤ cargoes *silo* ➤ *silos halo* ➤ *halos*
f or *ff* **Common exceptions**	add *-s* change *f* to *v* and add *-es*	reef ➤ reefs *leaf* ➤ *leaves*
lf	change *f* to *v* and add *-es*	half ➤ halves wolf ➤ wolves
fe	change *f* to v and add *-s*	life ➤ lives knife ➤ knives

A few plurals are exceptions to the rules listed on the previous page or present some other special problem, but they are easy to remember. The following chart lists these plurals and some examples.

Special Rules for Plurals	
Special Case	**Examples**
To form the plural of proper names, add either -s or -es.	D'Amico → D'Amicos Sanchez → Sanchezes
To form the plural of one-word compound nouns, follow the general rules for plurals.	penknife → penknives blackberry → blackberries
To form the plural of hyphenated compound nouns or compound nouns of more than one word, generally make the most important word plural.	father-in-law → fathers-in-law attorney general → attorneys general
Some nouns have irregular forms. These nouns do not follow any rules.	man → men ox → oxen
Some nouns have the same singular and plural form.	series → series deer → deer

Learning to Spell New Words

As you read, note unfamiliar words that you meet as well as words that you recognize but that look hard to spell. As you write, pay attention to any words that you have difficulty spelling. Then try the simple process shown below to learn to spell those words.

Say It
Look at the printed word, and say it aloud. Then say it again, pronouncing each syllable correctly.

Visualize It
Picture the word in your mind. Avoid looking at it printed or written on the page. This will help you memorize what the word looks like.

Write It
Look at the printed word, and write it. Then write it again, without looking at the printed word.

Check It
Check what you have written against the printed word. Did you spell the word correctly? If not, try the process again.

Remember that the dictionary is a source for finding the correct spelling of words. You might ask, How can I look up a word if I don't know how to spell it? Typically you will be able to spell enough of a word to find it in the dictionary. If you don't find a word in the first place you look, think of other probable spellings. Once you have located the correct spelling of a word, use the process described above to learn the word.

Exercise 1

In each group of words, find the one word that is misspelled. Write the word correctly. Cite the rule that applies to the spelling of the word. If the word is an exception to a rule, note that as well.

1. yield, freight, concieve
2. exceed, supercede, accede
3. sincerely, responsiveness, engagment
4. sheriffes, scarves, thieves
5. headdresses, stone crabs, commander in chiefs

26.2 Spelling Difficult Words

Clearly, some words are more difficult to spell than others. As you have learned, not all words follow basic spelling rules. But you can learn to spell even the most difficult words.

One very useful strategy for learning difficult words is to develop a personal word list. What words are especially difficult for you? What words do you frequently misspell? Include those words in your personal word list. Study the words, using the four-step process you learned in Lesson 26.1, page 790.

Developing memory devices is another helpful strategy for learning to spell difficult words. Imagine, for example, that you have trouble remembering if the word *tomorrow* has one *m* or two. You might think of the sentence "Tom will arrive tomorrow" to help you remember that *tomorrow* begins with the letters *tom*.

Frequently Misspelled Words

Following is a list of words that many people often misspell. Which words on the list do you have difficulty spelling?

Words Often Misspelled			
abdomen	arctic	cafeteria	commercial
accidentally	attendant	canceled	complexion
accommodate	ballet	canoe	conscience
advertisement	beautiful	catastrophe	conscientious
alcohol	benefited	cemetery	conscious
allot	buffet	changeable	definite
all right	bureau	choir	descent
answer	business	colonel	develop ➡

26.2   Spelling Difficult Words   **791**

Words Often Misspelled (continued)			
discipline	hippopotamus	occasion	rhythm
disease	humorous	original	schedule
elementary	hypocrite	pageant	separate
eligible	immediate	pamphlet	sincerely
embarrass	incidentally	parallel	succeed
environment	jewelry	pastime	sufficient
essential	laboratory	permanent	supersede
exceed	leisure	pharmacy	technique
familiarize	library	physical	technology
fascinating	license	physician	theory
February	maintenance	picnic	traffic
foreign	mischievous	precede	truly
forty	misspell	prevalent	unanimous
fulfill	mosquitoes	proceed	usually
genius	muscle	receipt	vacuum
government	necessary	recognize	variety
guarantee	neighborhood	recommend	villain
height	niece	restaurant	Wednesday

Easily Confused Words

Some words are easily confused because they contain similar sounds. Other confusing words are homophones, words that have the same pronunciation but different meanings and spellings. Study the following list of easily confused words. Are there any words on the list that you confuse?

Words Often Confused	
accept	to agree to take; to assume; to approve We accept your plan for the next meeting.
except	but; to omit I remembered everything except my ticket!
affect	to influence; to act upon I'm sure that sad movie will affect her mood.
effect	a result What effect did the punishment have on him?
capital	a city that is the seat of government On our trip we stopped in Jefferson City, the capital of Missouri.
capital	wealth The company invested its capital.
capitol	a building in which a legislature meets In the capitol we observed the Senate in session. ➡

formally	politely; officially; according to custom or rule
	Because our visitor was so important, we addressed him formally.
formerly	previously
	The principal was formerly a teacher.
holy	sacred
	Religious travelers make pilgrimages to holy places.
holey	having holes
	You should probably stop wearing that holey jacket.
wholly	completely; fully
	I am wholly satisfied with your story.
lose	to misplace; to drop
	Did you lose your assignment on the way to school?
loose	free; not confined; not tight
	My clothes are loose since I lost 10 pounds.
passed	moved through or by; elapsed; completed satisfactorily
	I passed you in the hall several times today.
past	the time before the present; gone by; ended; over
	You can't change the past.
principal	the head of a school; greatest; first; main
	My principal concern is for the victims of the disaster.
principle	a basic truth; a rule of conduct
	The principle of fair play is important in sports.
stationary	fixed; unmoving
	For a moment the plane appeared stationary in the sky.
stationery	writing paper and envelopes
	Rhonda wrote me a letter on hot pink stationery.
than	in comparison with
	You studied harder today than I have ever seen you study.
then	at that time; next
	He did his chores, and then he played a computer game.

Exercise 2

For each sentence below, determine which word in parentheses correctly completes the sentence.

1. Is Mexico City or Acapulco the (capital/capitol) of Mexico?
2. That store sells (stationery/stationary) of every color.
3. What were the (affects/effects) of the tornado?
4. Put your money away, or you may (loose/lose) it.
5. Will you (accept/except) this gift?

27.1 Studying Effectively

Some students learn more than others who spend as much time studying. Why? Part of the answer lies in how different students study.

Taking Notes in Class

Taking notes during class discussions and lectures can help you remember what you hear. While taking notes, you think about and rephrase the information.

Outlining Your Notes One common and very useful way of organizing notes is the modified outline form. Like the outline you might write for a research paper (see Lesson 7.2 in Composition, pages 320–323), notes in outline form summarize the main ideas and supporting details of a lecture. However, unlike formal outlines that you write, your notes need not follow precise guidelines about parallel structure or number of entries. By highlighting the main ideas and the relationships among them, an outline makes reviewing the material easy.

Recognizing Signals Signal words, such as *first, most importantly, on the other hand,* and *finally,* indicate important information or point out relationships among ideas. Such words help you know what to write down.

The speaker's voice and gestures also provide clues. By suddenly speaking more loudly or quickly or punctuating a point with an emphatic sweep of the hand, the speaker may be signaling an important point.

> *Identify the main idea first; indent supporting information underneath it.*

> *To write down information quickly, use phrases, symbols, and abbreviations.*

> *Write down each key term and its definition.*

Plate Tectonics
    the study of the formation & movement of plates
Plates
    rigid sections of the earth's crust
Boundaries of plates
    earthquakes & volcanoes
    3 types of plate boundaries
        converging — plates coming together
        diverging — plates separating
        transform fault — plates sliding past each other

Using Study Time Wisely

Most studying occurs outside of class. Whether in study hall, in a library, or at home, you want to make the most of your study time.

Recognizing Your Learning Style You can improve your studying by identifying your best learning style. People learn in a variety of ways—by reading, discussing, writing, drawing diagrams, and so on. However, each individual probably has one best mode of learning. If you learn best by discussion, meet with a friend to talk about your schoolwork. If you learn best by writing, try rewriting the lesson you are studying.

Preparing to Study Planning your study time wisely lets you make the most effective use of each minute. Here are some tips to help.

Tips on Planning Your Study Time

1. Study at the same time and place each day. Doing so makes studying a habit; your mind will be prepared when the time comes.

2. Update your list of assignments and due dates weekly. This will help you stay aware of what you need to accomplish.

3. Break down long assignments into stages. Many assignments include researching, reading, and writing stages.

4. Estimate the amount of time each stage of each assignment will require.

5. Don't plan to study one subject for too long. Many students find that changing subjects every thirty to forty-five minutes keeps their mind fresh.

Studying Effectively When you actually sit down to study, you can increase your efficiency by following the guidelines listed below.

Tips on Studying

1. Set objectives for each study session. Identifying what you want to read, write, or learn helps you focus your efforts.

2. Take notes while reading. The act of writing down information helps you remember it.

3. Create tables, charts, or diagrams. Seeing information in a different form can help you understand and remember it better.

4. Begin your study session with the hardest assignment. This way you can tackle the toughest work while you are freshest.

5. Summarize what you've learned at the end of each study session. (See Lesson 1.2 in Composition, pages 14–16, for information on keeping a learning log.)

Reading and Remembering

Reading is probably your most-used study skill—and your most important. Like any skill, reading can be used in various ways to accomplish different learning objectives.

Three Ways to Read   Before you begin to read, think about what information you want to learn from the material. Do you want a general idea of the topics covered? Are you looking for a specific fact or definition? Or do you want to learn everything in the passage? The highlighted text that follows shows the information you would learn from reading a passage in three different ways: skimming, scanning, and in-depth reading.

Skimming is glancing over the text to identify main ideas by reading chapter and lesson titles, words in bold or italic type, and topic sentences.

Scanning is glancing over the text in search of specific information by looking for key words.

In-depth reading is reading over the text carefully to absorb new ideas and facts.

Family and Government Promoting order was Confucius's principal concern. He believed that everyone had a proper role in society. If each person would accept that role and perform the related duties, social and political disorder would end.

Individuals, Confucius taught, should live according to principles of **ethics** — good conduct and moral judgment. Ethics began with respect for family, especially elders, and reverence for the past and its traditions. Ethics should govern each person's behavior in these five primary relationships: ruler and subject, parent and child, husband and wife, old and young, friend and friend.

Each reading style is useful at times. Here are a few suggestions of when each style might be appropriate:

- Skimming is useful when you're previewing material before a study session, reviewing before a test, or deciding whether a book covers a subject you're interested in.
- Scanning is useful when you're reviewing key terms, looking for a detail to support an opinion, or searching for a book that covers certain narrow topics.
- In-depth reading is useful when you're learning the material for the first time, evaluating the information presented, or preparing to explain the information to someone else.

The SQ3R Method   An effective method for learning and remembering written information is known as SQ3R. The name comes from the steps in the process: survey, question, read, record, review. Applying this method can help you remember what you read. Look at the chart at the top of the next page to find out how to use this method in your studying.

Survey	Question	Read	Record	Review
Preview the material by skimming. Read heads, highlighted terms, and the first sentence of each paragraph. Look at all pictures and graphs.	Ask questions about the material. Your questions might begin with *who, what, when, where, why,* and *how.*	Read the selection carefully. Identify the main idea of each section. Take notes and add questions to your list.	Write answers to your questions without looking at the text. Make brief notes about additional main ideas or facts.	Check your answers in the text. Continue to study the text until you can answer all questions

Mnemonic Devices   Rhymes, sayings, or words that help you recall basic information, called mnemonic devices, can also help you remember what you study. The list below gives some examples. By looking for patterns in what you study, you can develop your own mnemonic devices.

Common Mnemonic Devices	
Purpose	**Word or Phrase**
To remember that the order of scientific classification of living things is *k*ingdom, *p*hylum, *c*lass, *o*rder, *f*amily, *g*enus, and *s*pecies	*K*ing *P*hilip *c*ame *o*ver *f*rom *G*ermany *S*aturday.
To remember that the person who runs a school is a principal, not a principle	A principal is a pal.
To remember that the lines of the treble clef are the notes *E, G, B, D,* and *F*	*E*very *g*ood *b*oy *d*eserves *f*udge.
To help you interpret centigrade temperatures	30° is hot, 20° is nice; 10° is cool, 0° is ice.
To remember that the order of the planets from the sun is *M*ercury, *V*enus, *E*arth, *M*ars, *J*upiter, *S*aturn, *U*ranus, *N*eptune, and *P*luto	*M*y *v*ery *e*xcellent *m*other *j*ust *s*erved *u*s *n*ine pickles.
To remember that the order of colors in the spectrum is *r*ed, *o*range, *y*ellow, *g*reen, *b*lue, *i*ndigo, and *v*iolet	Roy G. Biv
To remember that the five Great Lakes are *H*uron, *O*ntario, *M*ichigan, *E*rie, and *S*uperior	homes

Evaluating What You Read

Another study tool is critical reading. In critical reading, you might ask yourself questions such as the following: Is this statement true? Are these connections logical? Do I agree with the values underlying this writer's viewpoint? Remember that even well-researched and carefully considered writing can contain mistakes or reflect an author's bias.

Identifying Facts and Opinions   One step in evaluating writing is recognizing the difference between facts and opinions. A fact is a statement that can be verified or proved true. The proof of a statement might come from direct experience—something you saw or experienced yourself—from an authoritative source, such as a reference book or a quotation from an expert on the subject.

An opinion is a personal judgment. Since opinions are expressions of someone's beliefs or feelings, they cannot be proved either true or false. Opinions can provide useful information, but they should be supported by evidence.

The following chart shows examples of facts and opinions and how to separate them from each other.

Distinguishing Facts from Opinions	
Statement	**Fact or Opinion**
1. George Bush was elected president in 1988.	1. Fact: Reference books, public documents, and experts would all agree that Bush won the 1988 election.
2. George Bush was the greatest president of the twentieth century.	2. Opinion: While facts might be used to support or oppose this idea, it is a matter of one's personal political views. It cannot be proved true.
3. The scientists who launched the Hubble Space Telescope hoped it would provide the sharpest images ever of many planets and their moons.	3. Fact: This goal was clearly stated by those advocating the development of the Hubble Space Telescope. Their statements in congressional hearings appeared in newspapers and magazines.
4. Manufacturers' carelessness caused severe flaws in the Hubble Telescope mirror.	4. Opinion: Although experts have presented evidence to support this point, other experts remain unconvinced of the connection.

Interpreting Figurative Language   Writers sometimes express ideas using figurative language, a word or phrase used in an imaginative, rather than literal, sense. You will often see examples of figurative language in literature, newspaper and magazine articles, and textbooks. For example, in a U.S. history textbook, you might read Theodore Roosevelt's advice on United States foreign policy: "Walk softly and carry a big stick." He meant that the United States should be cautious in foreign affairs but willing and able to use a powerful military. Be attuned to figurative language so that you can pick up on the subtleties of the materials you read and study.

Exercise 1

Reorganize the following notes into a modified outline. Use abbreviations and symbols when possible.

```
Types of reptiles: about six thousand
species of reptiles are alive today; most of
these are classified into one of three orders
  Squamata includes lizards, such as iguanas
and Gila monsters, and snakes, including
pythons, rattlesnakes, and garter snakes
  Chelonia includes reptiles with shells, such
as turtles and tortoises; some live on land,
others in fresh water, others in salt water;
all members of this order lay their eggs on
land
  Crocodilia includes reptiles such as croco-
diles and alligators, also caimans and
gavials; crocodiles have more pointed snouts
and more teeth visible when their mouth is
closed than do alligators
```

Exercise 2

Prepare for your next assignment in this class by using the SQ3R method to study either the following lesson or one that your teacher assigns. Then write a paragraph analyzing whether or not the SQ3R method helped you.

Exercise 3

Identify at least two facts and two opinions in the following paragraph.

The slider is a major-league baseball pitcher's best friend. To the batter the pitch looks like a fast ball. Even the pitcher's motion is the same as the motion for throwing the fast ball, so there's no hint about what's coming up. The ball will start out in a straight, easy-to-hit line toward the center of the plate. Then, suddenly and unexpectedly, the ball changes direction. It doesn't change much, mind you, just enough to turn solid hits into foul balls, pop-ups, and easy grounders. It's no wonder every hitter hates the slider and every pitcher can't wait to serve one up.

27.2 Reading Graphs and Diagrams

Writers often use charts, diagrams, tables, and other graphics to present information. By using a graphic, writers can make relationships between ideas easy to see. A clear graphic usually has the following components:

- title—a phrase that summarizes the main topic of the graphic
- labels—words or phrases that show the organization of the information in the graphic
- data—words or numbers that provide the actual information in the graphic

Tables

Tables present large amounts of information. They are often used to compare one or more characteristics of a list of similar items. For example, a box score for a baseball game lists each player's name and the number of hits, at bats, and runs batted in for each. At a glance you can see who had the most hits, who had none, and so forth.

The table below shows how the African-American population of five cities changed between 1920 and 1930. Notice how easily you can compare the changes in these cities.

Urban Black Population, 1920–1930			
City	**1920**	**1930**	**Increase**
New York	152,467	327,706	114.9%
Chicago	109,458	233,903	113.7%
Philadelphia	134,229	219,599	63.6%
Detroit	40,838	120,066	194.0%
Los Angeles	15,579	38,894	149.7%

You can read most tables horizontally (across) or vertically (down). By looking across the row labeled "New York," you can see how the African-American population of that one city changed in a 10-year period. By looking down the column labeled "1920," you can compare the African-American population of five cities in one year.

Pie Charts

Tables can show characteristics of several items, but pie charts, sometimes called circle graphs, focus on the parts that make up one item. In a pie chart each slice of the pie represents one part of the whole. A pie chart easily and quickly shows you how big the slices are in relation to each other.

Because they are mathematical parts of a whole, percentages are often shown in pie charts. In the pie chart shown here, the circle represents the entire world population in 1988. Each slice shows a specific region's population as a percentage of the world's total population.

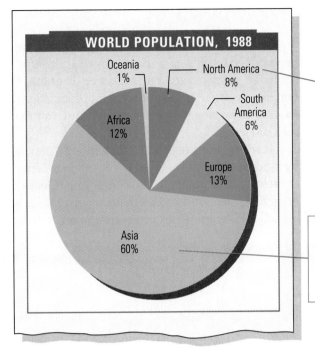

North America is represented by a slice that is 8 percent of the whole pie chart, the same as its portion of the world's population.

Asia is 60 percent of the whole pie chart—and 60 percent of the world's total population.

Line Graphs

Line graphs show changes over a period of time. You will often see them in history books showing trends such as population growth in the 1800s. Newspapers use line graphs to show changes in temperature during a year, variations in interest rates, and other constantly shifting trends.

To read a line graph, first look at the labels on the axes. The axes are the main vertical line and main horizontal line that make up the graph. The labels tell you what is being compared and the time interval over which the data is being reported.

On the following graph, the vertical axis shows the number of immigrants entering the United States. The horizontal axis shows the year.

The line's highest point indicates that immigration was highest in 1990.

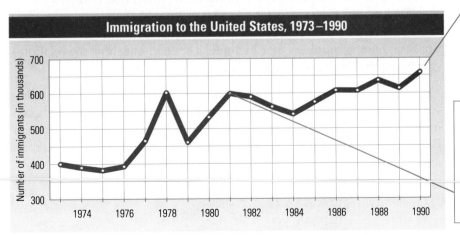

In 1981 the line intersects at 600. Because the data is given in thousands, this means that about six hundred thousand immigrants arrived in 1981.

Tree Diagrams

Unlike the previously discussed graphics, tree diagrams rarely show numerical data. Instead, they show relationships between things or ideas. Sentence diagrams are a form of tree diagram. They show how words in a sentence relate to one another. An organizational chart for a company is another example of a tree diagram. To see an example of a tree diagram, turn to Lesson 22.3, page 752.

Tree diagrams usually begin with one main idea. In this example the main idea is literature. Closely related ideas are linked to the main idea by branches that connect to the center line. Ideas related directly to the branching ideas and indirectly to the main idea are connected to the branches. The branches can continue on, with each idea leading to others.

Nonfiction is a type of literature, so it branches off the main idea.

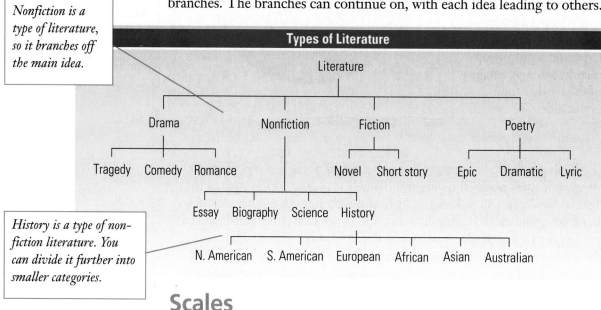

History is a type of nonfiction literature. You can divide it further into smaller categories.

Scales

A scale is a line segment, divided into categories, that represents a specific distance, time, or quantity in the real world. A thermometer is a scale that measures temperature. In mathematics, scales demonstrate relationships among numbers. For example, a scale might show the relationship between positive and negative integers on a number line.

Map Scales   Scales are commonly used on maps. A map scale tells you that so many inches or centimeters on the map represents a certain number of miles or kilometers. By finding the number of inches between Boston and Denver on a map of the United States, for example, you could determine the number of miles or kilometers between the two cities.

One inch on the map equals 250 miles.

The top line of the scale indicates miles. The bottom line indicates kilometers.

Time line   A time line shows events during a given period of time by representing time as a line. The space between the events on the time line is proportional to the amount of time that passed between the events. For example, a line segment 3 inches long could represent a period of 300 years, with one inch equaling 100 years.

Time lines are often used to show key events leading up to a major event. The time line below shows developments in space exploration.

Early Landmarks in Space Exploration, 1957–1963						
The Soviet Union launches *Sputnik I*, the artificial satellite.		*Luna 2* becomes the first space probe to reach the moon.		Valentina Tereshkova becomes the first woman to fly in space.		
1957	**1958**	**1959**	**1960**	**1961**	**1962**	**1963**
	The United States launches its first satellite, *Explorer I*.			Yuri Gagarin becomes the first human in space.		

The title indicates the subject and time period covered.

Each mark on the time line indicates one year.

The space between two events reflects the time that passed between them.

Exercise 4

Answer each of the following questions about graphs and diagrams studied in this lesson.

1. Which graph or diagram would best show changes in the cost of a college education over the last 30 years? Why?
2. Which graph or diagram would best show what portion of a 24-hour day you spend sleeping, going to school, eating meals, and doing any other daily activities? Why?
3. Which graph or diagram would best compare the average high temperature, average low temperature, and average precipitation in 10 U.S. cities? Why?
4. Which graph or diagram would you use to show the relationships among different types of foods? Why?
5. Which graph or diagram would you use to show the order in which various forms of music, such as classical, jazz, blues, and rock-and-roll, developed? Why?

Exercise 5

Collect copies of five different graphs used in newspapers or magazines. Write a short statement identifying the source of each graph and explaining the main point of each.

Taking Tests

28.1 Preparing for Classroom Tests

On exam day you walk into class at the appointed hour. How do you feel? Overwhelmed and panicky? Or confident and relaxed? How you feel and how you perform have a lot to do with how well prepared you are for the test. The following time line suggests steps you can take in prepar-ing for a test.

How to Prepare for a Test	
10 **9**	**Ten days or more before the test** Find out about the test. By writing down any information your teacher provides about the test—when it will be given, what it will cover, and so on—you can plan your study time effectively.
8 **7**	**Eight days before the test** Gather your information. Review your textbook, quizzes, homework assignments, class notes, and handouts. By keeping all of your papers in one folder, you'll save time gathering study materials.
6 **5**	**Six days before the test** Test yourself. Develop your own study questions about main ideas and important details, and practice answering them. Writing down your answers allows you to check what you have learned.
4 **3**	**Four days before the test** Form study groups. Meet with members of your class to review material. Try to answer one another's study questions. Explaining information to a peer is one of the best ways to learn the material.
2 **1**	**Day before the test** Sleep well the night before a test. Spreading your study time over several days will give you enough confidence to go to bed at your regular time the night before a test.
TEST	**Day of the test** Eat a good breakfast. Students who eat a full meal the morning of a test usually score higher than those who don't. Eating well helps you remain alert during the test.

Taking Objective Tests

Many of the tests you take during high school will be objective tests. These tests ask for very specific information about the material you've studied.

The most common type of objective test item is multiple choice. Each item includes a specific question or an incomplete sentence, and four or five responses. You are to pick the response that best answers the question or completes the sentence. When selecting the best response, consider the following tips.

Tips for Answering Multiple-Choice Items

1. Read the item carefully. You need to know what information you are looking for.

2. Read all the responses provided. Even if the first response seems almost correct, a later response may be better.

3. Eliminate any responses that are clearly incorrect. This helps you focus your attention on the responses that might be correct.

4. Be cautious about choosing responses that contain absolute words—*always, never, all,* or *none.* Since most statements have exceptions, absolute statements are often incorrect.

The following item might appear on an earth science test. As you read it, focus on what information is being asked for and how you would select the correct answer.

```
What were the first clues that led scientists
to believe that the continents of the earth
were once connected as a single landmass?
  a. Alfred Wegener, a German meteorologist,
     proposed the theory of continental drift.
  b. Scientists found that all continents could
     be fitted together perfectly like a puzzle.
  c. Similarities in ancient climates, fossils,
     and rock structures seemed to link separate
     landmasses.
  d. Scientists discovered ancient historical
     records describing a giant landmass called
     Pangaea.
  e. all of the above
```

Note that the item calls for "first clues." Choice a is accurate, but since it does not list "first clues" it is incorrect.

Since this statement includes the words all and perfectly, you should select it only if you are sure it is correct.

This statement is incorrect because it is factually wrong. The answer is c.

The chart below describes other types of objective test items and provides some suggestions for answering them.

Tips for Answering Objective Test Items		
Type of Item	**Example**	**Tips**
True-False	_____ Soil erosion on the earth's surface is a natural process unaffected by human activities.	If any part of the item is false, the correct answer is "false." Since the last phrase of this item is wrong, the answer is "false."
Short Answer	Why is the planet Venus known as Earth's twin?_____	Use complete sentences to help you write a clear response. "Venus is almost exactly the same size as Earth."
Fill-in	The most important prophet of the _____ faith was Muhammad.	After completing the sentence, read it again to check that your answer is grammatically correct. In the example, "Islamic," not "Islam," would be the correct answer.
Matching	_____ an Indian leader who emphasized nonviolence _____ a German leader who led the Nazi party _____ a Chinese leader who led a communist revolution _____ an American leader who started the New Deal a. Mao Zedong b. Mohandas Gandhi c. Franklin Roosevelt d. Adolf Hitler	Note in the directions whether some responses can be used more than once or are not used at all. Quickly read each list to become familiar with the choices. Do easy items first to limit the number of choices for the difficult ones.

Using Time Wisely

Because test time is usually limited, you will need to use your time efficiently. First, read the directions carefully. If any are unclear, ask questions. Respond to each item on the test, answering the easier ones first. Skip difficult items rather than dwelling on them. When you have answered the easier items, go back and answer hard items that you skipped earlier. Save some time to review your test before handing it in.

Exercise 1

Read the paragraph below, and use your test-taking strategies to help you answer the questions that follow.

The Arabian Peninsula is a wedge of land of about one million square miles between the Red Sea and the Persian Gulf. The peninsula is made up of two distinct regions. The southwestern area, across from the northeast coast of Africa, has well-watered valleys nestled between mountains. The rest of the peninsula, however, consists of arid plains and deserts. Mountains block moist air from reaching the interior, which is hot and dry. Drifting sand dunes cover most of the southeastern part of the peninsula. This area, about the size of Texas, is so barren that it is called the Empty Quarter.

1. Why is part of the Arabian Peninsula called the Empty Quarter?
   a. It is completely uninhabited.
   b. The landscape is barren.
   c. Drifting sand dunes make travel dangerous.
   d. none of the above

2. To reach Africa from the Arabian Peninsula, one would travel
   a. northeast.
   b. northwest.
   c. southeast.
   d. southwest.

3. True or false: The Arabian Peninsula is about the size of Texas.

4. Explain why the interior of the peninsula is dry.

   _____

   _____

5. The Arabian Peninsula is located between the _____ _____ and the _____ _____.

28.2 Preparing for Standardized Tests

Along with the exams that you take in each class, you will often take standardized tests—tests designed to measure your general knowledge, abilities, and interests. They are called standardized because the results are compared with those of other students around the country who have taken the test. The performance of a large group of students provides a standard by which to measure individuals who take the test.

The Purpose of Standardized Tests

You might take a standardized test for one of several reasons. The chart below lists and describes the basic types of standardized tests.

Three Types of Standardized Tests		
Type	**Purpose**	**Examples**
Ability	Ability tests use questions about different subject areas to evaluate your general learning skills and to predict how well you will do in college.	Stanford-Binet tests Preliminary Scholastic Aptitude Test (PSAT)
Achievement	Achievement tests measure your knowledge in specific content areas, such as American history or algebra.	Test of Achievement and Progress
Aptitude	Aptitude tests discover your individual talents and interests. They can help you choose an educational program and a career suited to your needs.	Differential Aptitude Test

Types of Items

You can prepare for standardized tests by reviewing general areas of knowledge, such as English usage and grammar, math, science, and social studies, that the tests usually cover. In addition, you can prepare for tests by learning about the types of questions presented. The following pages show examples of commonly used question formats and hints for answering each.

Reading Comprehension   The objective of reading comprehension items is to measure your ability to understand what you read. You will be presented with a passage and asked a series of questions—usually multiple-choice—about it. All of the information you need to respond to each question should be in the passage. Skimming the questions before you read the passage will help you know what to look for. However, you should read the passage completely before answering any question. Read the passage below, and answer the questions that follow.

According to Muslim tradition, the Abbasid caliph Ma'mun (mah MOON) founded the House of Wisdom at Baghdad in A.D. 830. This research center specialized in the translation into Arabic of Greek, Persian, and Indian scientific texts. Ma'mun staffed the center with salaried Christian, Jewish, and Muslim scholars who used Arabic to share ideas from different intellectual traditions. They performed scientific experiments and mathematical calculations and studied and built upon the ideas of the ancients. The House of Wisdom, therefore, served as a catalyst for many mathematical and scientific achievements in the Islamic world.

1. Which of the following would be the best title for this passage?
   a. Islamic Translation
   b. Islamic Scholars
   c. Abbasid caliph Ma'mun
   d. The House of Wisdom
   e. none of the above

To answer this question, you need to pick out the main idea of the passage. Since d summarizes the entire passage, it is the correct answer.

2. The House of Wisdom scholars
   a. were paid for their efforts
   b. translated scientific texts into Arabic
   c. had different backgrounds
   d. based their work on the ideas of previous scholars
   e. all of the above

Answer a seems correct, but never answer a question until you have read all the choices. Since b, c, and d seem correct also, the correct answer is e.

3. The point of view shows that the author
   a. doubts the existence of the House of Wisdom
   b. is objective about the subject
   c. has contempt for the ancient sciences
   d. is biased in favor of Islamic achievements
   e. believes that science is the most important area of study

Since the author avoids praising or condemning the information, b is the correct answer.

Synonyms   Tests that ask you to identify synonyms usually give you a word and ask you to choose the word from a list that has the closest meaning. Look for the best choice; no two words have exactly the same meanings. Study the example below.

> _All of the choices describe space in some way. Only d describes the distance around, so it is the correct response._

```
_____ perimeter
a. circle
b. middle
c. direction
d. circumference
```

Sentence Completion   This type of question is designed to test your ability to complete sentences with logical and grammatically correct words. You generally need to choose one or more missing words from a list to complete a sentence. Consider the following example.

> _Identify the relationship between the first and the last parts of the sentence._

> _The words "rather than" and "actually" suggest that the two parts express opposite ideas. The words in a are the only pair that are opposites._

```
The paralysis of his leg, rather than _____ his
expectations, actually _____ his drive to
succeed.
a. lowering/heightened
b. redefining/acknowledging
c. limiting/lessened
d. clouding/confused
```

Items Testing English Skills

Standardized tests often include sections that test your knowledge of written English. Items might ask you to identify usage problems, grammatical errors, and incorrect sentence constructions.

English Usage   Tests of English usage often ask you to identify a variety of mistakes in the following areas:

- grammar
- spelling
- capitalization
- subject-verb agreement
- pronoun references
- improper word choice

Often English usage items include a sentence in which several words or phrases are underlined. Each underlined part is lettered. You are to identify the part of the sentence that includes an error and mark the corresponding letter on your answer sheet. Many items include a choice _e_, which states that the sentence contains no error. The following example is typical of English usage items.

> The fall of the Berlin Wall has had a positive
>   a   b
> affect on the human struggles around the world
>   c   d
> for freedom and peace. no error
>   e

The word "affect" is incorrect; the correct word would be "effect."

Sentence Correction   In these items you will be given a sentence with one section underlined and choices for replacing the section. Choice *a* usually is identical to the section in the sentence; choose it if the sentence is without error. The other choices suggest other ways to word the section. Tests often include common errors such as wordiness, lack of parallel construction, and awkward wording. Try the following example.

> Ms. Sanchez's plan for redesigning the
> city's public transportation system is
> financially feasible and has a sound
> structure.
>
> a. is financially feasible and has a sound
>   structure
> b. has good financial feasibility and has a
>   good structure
> c. is financially feasible and sound in
>   structure
> d. is financially feasible and structurally
>   sound

Identify the problem in the underlined section. In this example the two parts in the section are not parallel.

Find the choice that corrects the problem you identified. Choice d is correct because its structure is parallel.

Analogies   While vocabulary items test your knowledge of word meanings, analogies test your ability to see the relationships between word meanings. An analogy item may contain a pair of words separated by a colon, and four or five other pairs of words. You are to choose the pair with the same relationship as the first. Here is an example.

> praise : insult ::
> a. admire : like
> b. wasteful : slow
> c. chide : encourage
> d. shoe : leather
> e. lion : cat

Identify the relationship: praise is the opposite of insult.

Identify the pair showing the same relationship: chide is the opposite of encourage. Therefore, c is the correct answer.

To improve your scores on analogies tests, develop your vocabulary. See Unit 25, pages 778–785, for tips on building your vocabulary. In addition, practice identifying the relationship between two items. Following are some of the common relationships used on analogies tests.

Analogy Relationships	
Type	**Examples**
Cause and effect—one word causes or is the result of the other word	tornadoes : damage boredom : yawn
Opposites—one word is the opposite of the other word	happy : sad poor : rich
Users—one word uses or is used by the other word	doctor : stethoscope mechanic : wrench
Synonyms—the two words share a general meaning	elated : happy ready : prepared
Time sequence—one word comes before or after the other word	lunch : dinner sunset : sunrise
Characteristic—one word is a characteristic of the other word	leopard : carnivorous steel : hard
Category—one word is a specific item in the general category of the other word	broccoli : vegetable jazz : music

Standardized tests are sometimes given outside of regular class time. You may need to register to take some tests, such as college entrance exams. If so, register early to ensure that you can take the test on the day you need. In addition, follow the tips in the chart below.

Tips for Taking Standardized Tests

1. Show up ready for the test. Try to arrive early so you can relax before beginning.

2. Sleep and eat well before the test. Get enough sleep the night before the test so that you are well rested. Eat a good breakfast so you don't get hungry during the test.

3. Pace yourself during the test. You usually have a limited amount of time to take the test, so don't get stalled on hard items. Skip them and move on.

4. Repeatedly compare the item numbers in your test booklet and answer sheet. Be careful to put your answers on the proper lines.

5. If time permits, check your answers. If you are not penalized for guessing, fill in answers for any items you might have skipped.

Use the test-taking strategies described in this lesson to help you complete the following items. Write your answers on a separate piece of paper.

1. Which of the following is the best synonym for *analogous*?
   a. different
   b. representative
   c. incongruous
   d. alike
   e. agreeable

2. Choose the word that best completes the sentence below.

   _____ his many hours of hard work at the computer, he realized that his progress was insignificant.
   a. Despite
   b. Because of
   c. Through
   d. Besides
   e. By

3. Examine the sentence below, and decide if it contains an error in standard English usage. Mark the correct letter.

   All the students <u>who attended</u> the assembly <u>were instructed</u>
                   a   **b**
   to leave <u>his or her</u> books <u>in the cafeteria.</u> <u>no error</u>
            c   **d**   **e**

4. Decide whether the underlined portion of the sentence below needs correcting. Pick the best correction from the choices that follow.

   As public outrage over contaminated foods becomes stronger, <u>people who will demand</u> more organically grown vegetables and fruits.
   a. people who will demand
   b. people that will demand
   c. people will demand
   d. people demanding
   e. people who have demanded

5. Choose the pair of words whose relationship is most similar to the following pair.

   paintings : frame : :
   a. photographs : margin
   b. brooms : handle
   c. spectacles : rim
   d. faces : hair
   e. globe : universe

Listening and Speaking

29.1 | Listening with a Purpose

With a little attention you can probably improve how well you listen—to your teachers, your parents, and your friends.

Listening in Class

To improve your listening skills, particularly in school, consider the following suggestions.

Listening Skills Checklist

1. Put yourself in a listening mode. Clear your mind of other concerns, and concentrate on what you are hearing.

2. Listen with an open mind. This allows you to hear what the speaker is saying rather than what you expect him or her to say.

3. Identify the main ideas. These are the most important points to remember.

4. Identify supporting details and connect each detail to the main idea the detail supports. You will remember both main ideas and details better.

5. Note verbal clues from the speaker. Phrases such as *the main reason* tip you off to what the speaker considers important.

6. Evaluate information as you listen. The more you try to analyze information, the better you will retain it.

Interpreting Nonverbal Clues

Speakers communicate ideas not only by what they say but also by how they say it. As you listen, note these clues:

- **Facial expressions,** such as widening the eyes or raising an eyebrow, often indicate a point the speaker wants to emphasize.
- **Gestures,** such as rapid hand movements or shrugging the shoulders, can convey excitement or uncertainty.
- **Tone of voice** conveys a speaker's opinion and also signals the audience to examine what is being said. For instance, a sarcastic tone of voice indicates doubt about what is being said and signals the audience to examine it.

Listening to Television and Radio

In addition to listening to class lectures and discussions, you probably listen to television and radio. Here again, good listening skills will help you understand, interpret, and remember what you hear.

Paying attention to commercials provides excellent practice in careful listening. Commercials often make claims with little or no supporting evidence, or they appeal to the listener's emotions. For example, testimonials—comments praising a product—often feature famous people. If you listen carefully, you may realize that the basketball star or the singer knows little more about the product than you do. The advertiser wants you to associate the product with the star and buy the product on that basis.

Exercise 1

Listen to an in-depth news program, a panel discussion, an interview, or a documentary. Prepare an oral report based on what you heard. In your report summarize the main ideas discussed in the program, give examples of important details, and evaluate how well organized each speaker was. Make special note of any gesture, voice change, or other nonverbal clue that you thought was effective.

Exercise 2

Prepare a written analysis of a commercial that you like. Examine why the commercial is effective, how it appeals to your emotions, and whether it is truthful.

29.2 Speaking Effectively

Effective speaking can have great impact on people's thinking and action. However, effective speaking takes skill and practice.

Informal Speeches

You make informal speeches all the time. Whether telling your friends about a trip you took, explaining some of the causes of the Civil War when called on in class, or giving directions to the video store, you use some kind of informal speech. You usually don't plan what you are going to say, and others might do as much talking, or informal speech-making, as you do. The chart below describes some typical informal speech situations.

Tips on Making Informal Speeches		
Type	**Description**	**Hint**
Conversations	Conversations are the most common and least formal speaking situation. Subjects are usually spontaneous and varied, and each party both listens and speaks.	Letting others speak without interruption helps encourage participation by all members of the group.
Discussions	Discussions usually focus on one topic, which is often predecided. You often encounter discussions in your classes. One person, perhaps a teacher or another student, directs the discussion.	Taking turns speaking and listening respectfully to others should make a discussion more interesting and informative.
Announcements	Announcements provide brief, important information about events, meetings, or projects. They should be clear and give all necessary details.	Asking if anyone has questions about the announcement is a way to be sure you've communicated clearly the necessary information.
Demonstrations	Demonstrations usually involve an explanation of a procedure or process. They often take place in the classroom, such as an explanation of a solution to an algebra equation.	Using transitions, such as *then* and *next*, or numbering steps helps listeners follow your demonstration.
Telling Stories	Most stories are personal narratives or anecdotes. They usually entertain or convey a particular idea or point.	Changing your voice to portray different characters and using facial expressions to communicate different emotions enliven your storytelling.

Formal Speeches

Giving a speech can make anyone, even professional lecturers, nervous. But certain techniques will help you prepare and deliver formal speeches in the classroom and other group situations.

A speech usually contains an introduction, a thesis statement, supporting facts and details, and a conclusion. As in the writing process, following certain preliminary steps helps you create a speech before you actually deliver it. The following chart outlines the steps in preparing and delivering a speech. The rest of this lesson will explain these steps.

Prewriting	Drafting	Revising	Practicing	Presenting
• Choose and narrow a topic. • Determine purpose and audience. • Do research.	• Organize notes. • Write a thesis statement. • Create an outline. • Put outline on note cards.	• Check organization of ideas. • Make organizational changes and word changes. • Add transitions.	• Read the speech aloud. • Time the presentation of the speech.	• Be organized. • Speak clearly. • Use nervous energy.

Prewriting   In the prewriting stage find a topic that is appropriate for the situation. A topic such as ancient China is too broad to cover in a short classroom speech. Consequently, you might narrow your topic to one aspect of ancient China, such as a particular ruler. You also need to decide on the purpose of your speech. Are you trying to inform your audience? Persuade them of something? Entertain them?

Consider what your audience may already know. Your speech will be more successful if you include unusual or intriguing details not known to the rest of the class.

Drafting   Next, create a preliminary draft of your ideas, just as if you were preparing a written piece. Organize your notes. Decide what main ideas your speech will cover, and choose details, examples, and statistics to support your ideas. Write a thesis statement that expresses the focus of the speech, and make an outline using your notes.

You may want to write down only a few notes on note cards, instead of writing out all you want to say. Many people find that giving a speech from note cards helps them sound natural and expressive. Number your note cards so you can easily keep them in order. Write out your thesis statement and any words and phrases that will help you remember the order of your speech.

Revising   To revise your speech, read through your note cards. Check that your main points support your thesis statement, and make any necessary organizational changes. Jot down transitional phrases at appropriate points so that you remember to keep your audience on track.

Practicing   Take time to practice your speech. Because most formal speeches are timed, you might want to time your presentation to find out how long your speech is. If you write out your speech word for word, take care to say your speech, not read it. You can record your speech on an audiocassette or videocassette, practice in front of a mirror, or ask a willing friend to give you suggestions for improving the speech.

Presenting   When it comes time to deliver your speech, you can remain calm by using simple techniques such as taking a few deep breaths, reviewing your note cards or text, and keeping in mind what you want to tell your listeners. Remember that some nervousness is good, because you can use nervous energy to keep your delivery lively. Have your note cards in order so that you're organized and prepared.

Speaking Style

How a speaker sounds and looks influences how well the audience receives the message of the speech. The following chart lists some tips on speaking style.

Tips on Speaking Effectively
1. Speak at a normal pace, and try to pronounce words clearly.
2. Vary the volume and pitch of your voice according to what you are saying.
3. Pause after making an important point or after giving your audience a lot of information. Give them a moment to take in what you've just said.
4. Visually emphasize your main points. Hand gestures and visual aids will help convey your message.
5. Maintain eye contact with people in the audience. If a person in the audience smiles, smile back.

Responding to audience needs is also an important part of presenting your speech. Pay attention to your audience's actions and body language for clues on how they are responding to you. The following chart will help you recognize audience signals that require immediate attention.

Reacting to Your Audience	
Audience Signals	**Speaker Response**
1. If people are yawning or fidgeting in their chairs, you can assume at least some of them are bored.	Vary the tone and volume of your voice. Consider speaking more quickly.
2. If people are frowning as you explain or describe some point in your speech, it probably means they're confused.	Go back and repeat important points. Clarify complex ideas with an example. Ask if anyone is confused.
3. If people are leaning forward in their seats or asking each other questions, they may not be able to hear you clearly.	Speak up. Ask if there's a sound problem and whether you should repeat any of the points you've made.
4. If people are listening, smiling, nodding in agreement, and laughing when appropriate, you have their attention.	Keep going. You're doing a great job.

Practice your delivery techniques. Each member of the class should choose a poem, or a short passage from a story or essay, to use for a dramatic reading. Then, as a class, create a critique form. After each class member gives his or her reading, fill out the form. Follow up with a class discussion.

Each member of the class should prepare a three- to five-minute speech, using the steps described in this lesson. Everyone should have an opportunity to present his or her speech, and then the class should discuss the speech's strengths and weaknesses.

29.3 | Working in Groups

In academic and social activities and later, in your career, you'll often work closely with other people. For groups to be successful and fulfill their purpose, group members need to follow certain rules and procedures.

Roles in Groups

Suppose you are serving on the homecoming dance committee, and the group needs to raise money for the dance which is scheduled next month. When the committee meets, members should organize as a group. The following diagram shows the roles and responsibilities of group members.

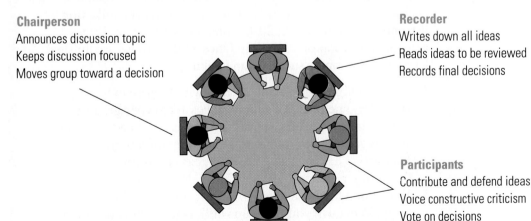

Chairperson
Announces discussion topic
Keeps discussion focused
Moves group toward a decision

Recorder
Writes down all ideas
Reads ideas to be reviewed
Records final decisions

Participants
Contribute and defend ideas
Voice constructive criticism
Vote on decisions

Group Procedures

After the chairperson announces the topic at hand, the participants contribute ideas on raising money. One member suggests selling candy. Another suggests holding a raffle. You suggest a bake sale. Someone criticizes your idea, saying that a bake sale won't make enough money. Criticizing ideas is an essential task of the participants in a discussion, and it's important to remember that the criticism is not meant personally.

Discussing Ideas   You can respond to criticism by agreeing with the other person or by defending all or part of your idea. Let's say you point out that the dance is next month, and ordering candy to sell may take too much time. Holding a raffle means you have something to raffle off. Criticizing politely and constructively will help the discussion move along smoothly. Offering specific reasons for your disagreement, not personal attacks or unsupported opinions, is also helpful.

Making Decisions   Suppose that suddenly all the members are involved in a heated discussion. The chairperson makes sure the discussion stays on track. After the participants have discussed several ideas thoroughly, the chairperson may have the recorder read off the suggestions. The chairperson then moves the group toward a decision by giving each member a last chance to present his or her ideas. Then the chairperson calls for a vote. The participants vote, the chairperson announces the decision, and the recorder writes the decision down. The meeting has been a success.

Sometimes more time is required to generate and think about ideas. In this case, the meeting might end without a decision but with everyone clearly understanding their responsibilities for the next meeting.

Exercise 5

Form discussion groups of six to eight members. Appoint a chairperson and a recorder. Choose a topic from the following list, and hold an informal, 20-minute discussion on it. Try to arrive at a decision or a solution. Once all the groups are finished, let each report on its successes and failures.

1. How can high school students deal with the rise in teenage violence? The board of education has asked your group to suggest guest speakers, specific problems that need attention, and suggestions for solutions. What will you report?
2. Your group has been asked to organize a fund-raiser to benefit the local arts council. What will you do and how?
3. Your group has been asked to choose this year's theme for the prom. What will you come up with? What factors do you need to consider?

Index

A

A, an, 653
Abbreviations, 728–730
  capitalization of, 728
  defined, 728
  punctuation of, 728
  of states, 729
  of titles of people, 730
  of units of measure, 730
Ability tests, 808
Abstract noun, 401–402
Accept, except, 653, 792
Achievement tests, 808
Acronyms, 747
Action verbs, 416–417
Active voice, of verbs, 562–563
Ad campaign
  audience for, 293
  Case Study in, 270–274
  creation of, 292–295
  drafting, 273
  prewriting, 272
  word choice in, 294
Addresses
  commas in, 711
  numerals in, 733
Adjective clauses, 511–512
  commas to set off, 396, 707
  diagraming, 534
Adjectives
  articles as, 422
  commas in a series, 705
  common, 424
  comparative form of, 422–423,
    625–627
  comparisons, 628–632
  compound, 726
  coordinate, 705
  definition of, 422
  demonstrative, 426
  diagraming, 539
  effective use of, 427
  fractions used as, 726
  infinitives and infinitive phrases
    as, 492, 542
  interrogative, 426
  nouns as, 425
  as object complement, 470
  participial phrases as, 489

participles as, 489
positive form of, 423, 625–627
possessive, 426
predicate, 471–472
prepositional phrases as,
  485–486
pronouns as, 426
proper, 424
superlative form of, 423,
  625–627
Adverb clauses, 513–514
  commas to set off, 710
  diagraming, 544
  elliptical, 513, 603
Adverbs
  comparative form of, 432,
    625–627
  comparisons, 628–632
  conjunctive, 441, 708
  definition of, 428
  diagraming, 539
  different kinds of, 429–431, 434
  infinitives and infinitive
    phrases as, 492, 542
  position in sentence, 429
  positive form of, 432, 625–627
  prepositional phrases as,
    485–486
  superlative form of, 432,
    625–627
Advertising, 270–275, 292–295
Affect, effect, 653, 792
Agreement. *See* Pronoun-
  antecedent agreement;
  Subject-verb agreement
Ain't, 654
Airplanes, capitalizing names of,
  681
All ready, already, 654
All right, alright, 654
All the farther, all the faster, 654
All together, altogether, 654
A lot, alot, 653
Alphabetical order
  in a card catalog, 762
  in a thesaurus, 776
American Heritage, 772
Among, between, 655
Amount, nouns of, 381
Amount, number, 654

Analogies, on standardized tests,
  811–812
And, and subject-verb agreement,
  384
Anecdotes, 182–185
  literature model for, 182–183
  in narrative writing, 184–185
Annotations, writing, 21
Antecedent. *See also*
  Pronoun-antecedent
  agreement
  definition of, 407
Antithetical phrases, commas to
  set off, 709
Antonyms, in thesaurus, 777
Apostrophes
  in contractions, 724
  correcting missing or mis-
    placed, 394–395
  with possessives, 394–395,
    401–402, 722–723
  with special plurals, 724
Appendix, 771
Appositive phrases, 487
  commas with, 677
  diagraming, 540
  essential, 397, 487
  nonessential, 397, 487
Appositives,
  commas to set off, 707
  diagraming, 540
  pronouns with and as, 601–602
Aptitude tests, 808
Arguments
  formal, 282, 816–818
  in persuasive writing, 282
Art, list of works herein. *See* xxiii
Art, writing topics in, 21, 29,
  225, 233, 291
Articles, 422
As, like, 660
As, personal pronouns following,
  603
Audience
  analysis of, for advertising, 293
  for book review, 301
  in expository writing, 221
  identifying, 61
  importance of, 91
  in persuasive writing, 279, 285

Audio-visual materials, in library, 761
Author card, in card catalog, 762
Auxiliary verbs, 420–421
Awards, capitalizing names of, 679
A while, awhile, 653

B

Bad, badly, 633
Bar graphs, 239–241
Base words, 780
Be
    conjugation of, 551
    as helping verb, 420, 547, 558
    as linking verb, 418
    passive voice, 562
    principal parts, 547
    and progressive form of verbs, 558
Because, reason is, 661
Being as, being that, 654
Beside, besides, 655
Between, among, 655
Bias, 281
Bible, references to, 701
Bibliography
    in book, 771
    in research paper, 317
Biography section, in dictionary, 775
Biology, writing topics in, 167, 193, 283
Body, of business letter, 298
Books, parts of, 770–771
Borrow, lend, loan, 656
Borrowed words, 757–758
Brainstorming, 56–59, 63, 166, 181, 237, 251, 281
Bridges, capitalizing names of, 679
Bring, take, 656
Buildings, capitalizing names of, 679
Business letters, 298, 701

C

Calendar items, capitalizing names of, 681
Call number, 762

Can, may, 656
Can't hardly, can't scarcely, 656
Capital, capitol, 792
Capitalization
    of abbreviations, 728
    of compass points, 680
    of proper adjectives, 684–687
    of proper nouns, 677–683
    of sentences, 675–676
Capitol, capital, 792
Card catalog, 761, 762
Cases of pronouns
    defined, 599
    nominative, 599
    objective, 599
    possessive, 408, 599
Cause-and-effect
    as context clue, 778
    order, 77, 79, 229
    testing for, 227
    transitions showing, 78, 228
Cause-and-effect writing
    definition of, 215
    exploring relationships in, 228
    guidelines for, 228
    literature model for, 226
    organization of, 227
Character, 169, 253
Charting, 165, 167
Chronological order, 77, 79, 137, 166, 172, 225
Classification
    compare and contrast, 215, 230–232
    defined, 215
    drafting, 211, 232
    in logical order, 223
    prewriting, 210
    presenting 212, 244
    revising, 224
    as strategy for writing, 215
Classification systems, in library, 763–765
Clauses
    adjective, 511–512, 543
    adverb, 513–514, 544
    dependent, 506
    diagraming, 543–545
    essential, 511
    main, 505
    nonessential, 396, 511
    noun, 515–516, 544
    semicolons to separate main, 672–673

subordinate, 506
Climax, in story, 174–175, 188, 244
Closing, of business letter, 298
Clustering, 57–59, 249, 281
Coherence, revising for, 80–84
Collaborative learning. *See* Cooperative Learning
Collective nouns, 405
    and subject-verb agreement, 381, 580
Colons
    in biblical references, 670
    to introduce illustrations or restatements, 699
    to introduce lists, 699
    parentheses with, 715
    quotation marks with, 699
    before quotations, 699
    after salutation of business letter, 701
    in time expressions, 701
Combining sentences. *See* Sentence combining
Comma fault, 521, 682
Commas
    in addresses, 711
    with adjective clauses, 707
    with adverb clauses, 710
    with antithetical phrases, 709
    with appositives, 707
    and compound sentences, 507, 706
    with conjunctive adverbs, 708
    and coordinate adjectives, 705
    in dates, 711
    and direct address, 711
    in geographical terms, 711
    with infinitives, 707
    with interjections, 397, 708
    in letter writing, 712
    missing, with nonessential adjective clause, 396
    missing in a series, 398
    misuse of, 713
    with nonessential appositives, 397, 707
    with nonessential clauses, 396
    with nonessential elements, 707
    with nonessential phrases, 396, 707, 709
    with parentheses, 715
    with parenthetical expressions, 397, 708

Italics
    with foreign words, 720
    with titles of trains, ships,
        aircraft, spacecraft, 720
    for titles of works, 720
    with words, letters, or numbers
        used to represent themselves,
        721
It's, its, 395, 600

J

Jargon, 759
Journalism, writing topics in, 25,
    133
Journal Writing, 4–8, 9, 10–12,
    13, 15, 19, 23, 27, 41, 42, 51,
    55, 57, 61, 65, 69, 73, 77, 81,
    83, 87, 91, 95, 121, 123, 127,
    131, 135, 139, 143, 165, 169,
    171, 175, 179, 183, 187, 191,
    197, 215, 219, 223, 227, 231,
    235, 239, 243, 247, 249, 253,
    259, 277, 281, 285, 289, 293,
    297, 301, 307
    commonplace books in, 18–21,
        42
    experimenting in, 12
    format for, 11
    learning log in, 14–17, 41, 42
    reader-response journals in,
        22–25, 29, 42
    types of entries in, 11

L

Language. *See also* English
    language
    acronyms in, 747
    alphabet development, 749
    bow-wow theory of, 745–746
    capitalizing name of, 677
    idioms, 753
    Indo-European families, 751
    jargon, 759
    malapropisms, 750
    mother tongue in, 746
    picture writing, 748–749
    weasel words, 756
    yo-he-ho theory of, 745–746

Laws, capitalizing names of, 679
Lay, lie, 659
Lead, in an investigative report,
    49
Learning log, 14–17, 41, 42
Learn, teach, 660
Leave, let, 660
Lend, loan, borrow, 656
Less, fewer, 658
Letters
    forming plural of, 724
    italics with, 721
Letter writing
    business, 298, 701
    commas in, 712
Library
    arrangement of a, 760–761
    call number, 762–763
    card catalog in, 762
    classification systems, 763–765
    computer catalog, 763
    Dewey decimal system,
        763–764
    locating book in, 762–765
    sources of information in,
        768–771
    special sections in, 765
Library of Congress
    classification, 764
Like, as, 660
Line graphs, 240, 801
Linking verbs, 418–419
    personal pronoun after, 600
    subject-verb agreement with,
        577
Listening
    in class, 814
    interpreting nonverbal clues,
        814
    to television and radio, 815
Listing, 9, 31, 64–65, 67, 79,
    97, 129, 133, 171, 175,
    210, 257
Lists, colons to introduce,
    699–700
Literary analysis. *See* Writing
    about literature
Literary, comparing and
    contrasting, 252–254
    guidelines for writing, 254
    literature for, 252–253
    making point in, 254

selecting focus for, 253
Literature. For a complete list of
    works herein, see p. xxii
Literature, types of
    compare-and-contrast, 252–254
    evaluation, 253–254
    strategies for responding to,
        182–184, 186–188, 252–254
Literature, responding to, 41,
    111, 155, 205, 267, 311
    See also Writing about literature

M

Magazine articles
    capitalization of titles, 682
    in list of works cited, 331
    punctuation of titles, 720
Magazines, as reference source,
    766–768
Main clauses, 505
Main idea
    in paragraph, 73, 83
    and unity, 80, 83
    See also Thesis statement;
        Topic sentence
Malapropisms, 750
Many a, and subject-verb agree-
    ment, 382–383
Mapping, 12, 165, 167, 298
Map scales, 802
Matching tests, 806
Mathematics, writing topics in, 17
May, can, 656
Measure, abbreviations of units
    of, 730
Mechanics
    capitalization, 675–687
    punctuation, abbreviations,
        and numbers, 695–733
    Troubleshooter, 375–398
    See also Capitalization;
        Punctuation
*Might of, must of, should of, would
    of, could of,* 656
Misplaced modifiers, 392,
    637–641
Mixed imagery, 139–140
Mnemonic devices, 797
Modified (semi) block form, for
    business letters, 298

Modifiers
  dangling, 395, 637–641
  diagraming, 539
  Grammar Review on, 642–650
  irregular, 628
  misplaced, 392, 637–641
  See also Adjectives; Adverbs
Money, numerals to express, 700
Monuments, capitalizing names
  of, 679
Mood, and setting, 142–144
Multiple-choice tests, 805
Music, writing topics in, 11
*Must of, might of, should of, would
  of, could of,* 656

N

Names, personal, 677
Narrative writing
  analyzing conflict in, 193
  anecdotes in, 182–185
  conflict analysis, 190–193
  dialogue in, 178–181
  drafting, 160, 195–196
  editing, 161, 197
  fictional narratives, 168–176
  finding a story, 159–160
  fine-tuning a story, 161
  literature models in, 164,
    168–169, 176, 178–179,
    182–183, 195, 198–204
  organizing a fictional narrative,
    174–175
  performing a story, 162
  personal experience, 164–167
  plot summary, 186–189
  portfolio in, 206
  presenting, 162, 197
  prewriting, 159, 195
  revising, 161, 196
  sentence combining in,
    358–361
National groups, capitalizing
  names of, 677
Negatives, double, 635
Negative words, as adverbs, 428
News articles, 242–244
  adding details, 244
  adding quotations to, 244
  five *w*'s and *h* in, 243
  getting facts for, 243
  guidelines for writing, 244

  writing effective leads for, 243
Newspapers
  in library, 761
  as reference source, 766–768
New York Times Index, 768
Nominative case for personal
  pronoun, 599–600
Nominatives, predicate, 380, 471
Nonessential appositives,
  commas with, 397, 487
Nonessential clauses, 511
  commas with, 396, 707
Nonessential elements, commas
  with, 707
Nonessential phrases, commas
  with, 396, 707
Nonfiction, anecdotes in,
  182–183
Nonfiction book review, 300–303
  editing, 302
Nonrestrictive clauses, 511
Nonverbal clues, interpreting,
  814–815
Nor, and subject-verb
  agreement, 382
Note cards, for research paper,
  317–318
Note taking, 127
  in class, 794
  for descriptive writing, 128
  in interview, 69–70
  for research paper, 318
  as study skill, 794
Noun clauses, 515–516
  defined, 515
  diagraming, 544
  introductory words for, 515
  special, 515
Nouns, 401
  abstract, 401–402
  collective, 405–406
  common, 404–406
  compound, 790
  concrete, 401–402
  definition of, 401
  effective use of specific, 406
  gerunds as, 491
  infinitives and infinitive
    phrases as, 492
  as object complement, 470
  possessive form of, 401–402
  proper, 404, 406, 677
  singular or plural, 401–402, 405
Nouns of amount, 381

  and subject-verb agreement,
    381, 581
Number, amount, 654
Numbers, 731
  forming plural of, 724
  hyphens in, 726
  pronoun-antecedent agreement
    in, 606
  spelled out, 731
Numbers as numbers, italics
  with, 690
Numerals, 732–733

O

Object complements, 470
  diagraming, 538
Objective case for personal
  pronouns, 600–601
Object of preposition, 485–486
  noun clause as, 515
  whom as, 604
Observation, in descriptive
  writing, 127
Omniscient point of view, 95, 97
Opinions
  distinguishing, from facts, 798
  evaluating audience, 285
  finding a topic, 285
  guidelines for presenting, 286
  literature models, 280, 281,
    282, 284
  in persuasive writing, 281, 287
  prewriting, 285
Or, and subject-verb agreement,
  382
Order of ideas
  cause-and-effect, 77, 79, 229
  chronological, 77, 79, 137, 166,
    172, 225
  compare-and-contrast, 77
  by importance, 77, 79, 122
  methods of, 322
  spatial, 77, 79
Order of importance
  cause-and-effect explanation,
    226–228
  description, 122
  evaluation, 290
  literary analysis, 143, 303
  personal essay, 16
  persuasive essay, 286
  and writing process, 77

Organizations, capitalizing
names of, 678
Outline, 25
correct form for, 321
developing, 320–322
for fictional narrative, 174–175
notes, 794
use of a computer in, 229
in writing a research paper, 325

P

Paragraphs
cause-and-effect order in, 77
chronological order in, 77
coherence of, 84
compare-and-contrast order
in, 77
definition of, 72
drafting, 72–75
geography writing topics in, 79
linking ideas in, 78
literature models for, 72, 74, 78
main idea, 83
order of importance in, 77
organizing, 76–78
revising, 224
spatial order in, 77
topic sentence in, 73
transitions for, 78
types of supporting details for,
74
Paraphrasing, in note taking,
318
Parentheses
capitalization of sentence in,
676
with other marks of punctuation, 715
to set off supplemental material, 715
Parenthetical documentation,
329–330
Parenthetical expressions,
commas with, 397, 708
Participles and Participial
phrases
as adjectives, 489
commas to set off, 707, 709
diagraming, 541
past, 390–391, 547
present, 547
Parts of speech

adjectives, 422–426
adverbs, 428, 430–434
conjunctions, 438–441
Grammar Review on, 446–457
interjections, 444
nouns, 401, 404–405
prepositions, 435, 437
pronouns, 407–408, 410,
412–414
verbs, 415–416, 418, 420
Passed, past, 660, 793
Past participles, 390–391, 547
distinguishing between past
form and, 390–391
improper use of, 391
Past perfect tense, 556
Past tense, 552
Peer editing, 32, 81–83, 181,
224, 237, 285
Percentages, numerals to express,
732
Periodical indexes, 768
Periodicals, in library, 761
Periods
in abbreviations, 728
to end declarative sentences,
518, 695
to end imperative sentences,
518
quotation marks with, 717
Person, pronoun-antecedent
agreement in, 606
Personal experience narrative,
164–167
Personal pronouns, 408
nominative case for, 599–600
objective case for, 599–600
possessive case for, 599
after *than* and *as*, 603
Personal writing
in commonplace book, 18–21,
42
drafting, 7, 31–32
editing, 33
journal writing, 10–13, 42
learning log, 14–16, 42
literature models, 10, 26, 34–40
portfolio for, 42
prewriting, 6, 31
in a reader-response journal,
22–25, 42
responding to a short story,
26–29
revising, 32

for self-discovery, 13
Persuasive appeals
distinguishing fact from
opinion, 281
recognizing bias, 281
Persuasive writing
ad campaigns as, 270–274,
292–295
audience, 279, 285
complaint letters as, 296–
299
definition of, 277
details, 278
drafting, 273, 286, 305–306
editing, 307
effective definitions, 237
elements of, 278
evidence, 280–283
facts, 281
guidelines for, 286
literature models, 276, 280,
281, 282, 284, 288, 308–310
opinion, 281
portfolio, 312
preparing arguments for, 282
presenting, 274, 307
presenting an opinion, 279,
284–287
prewriting, 272, 281, 285, 305
product evaluation, 288–291
review of nonfiction book as,
303
revising, 278, 306
sentence combining in,
366–369
stating a case in, 286
taking a stand in, 285
Photo-realism, 237
Phrases
adjective, 485
adverb, 485
appositive, 487, 540
gerund, 491, 541
infinitive, 492, 542
participial, 489–490, 541, 707,
709
verb, 420–421
verbal, 489–490
Pie charts, 240, 800–801
Plagiarism, avoiding, 319
Planets, capitalizing names of,
679
Plot, 169, 253
Plot diagram, 175

Prewriting *(continued)*
    in Writing Process in Action
      lessons, 31, 99, 147, 195,
      257, 305
Principal parts of verbs, 547
Principal, principle, 793
Principle, principal, 793
Proceed, precede, 661
Process explanation, 222–225
    checklist for, 223
    literature model of, 222
    prewriting, 224
    writing, 222–224
Product evaluation, 288–290
    literature model of, 288
    prewriting, 289
    writing a, 291
Progressive forms of verbs, 558
Prompts. *See* Writing prompts
Pronoun-antecedent agreement
    correcting problems with,
      384–385, 606–608
    with indefinite pronoun
      antecedents, 609–610
    in number and gender, 606
    in person, 607
Pronoun reference, 386–387,
      606–612
Pronouns
    ambiguous reference with, 611
    antecedent for, 407, 606–612
    as appositives, 601–602
    case of, 599–600
    definition of, 407
    demonstrative, 412
    Grammar Review on, 614–622
    indefinite, 414, 609, 612–613
    indefinite use of, 612–613
    intensive, 410–411
    interrogative, 413
    lack of clear reference with,
      386–387, 611
    as object complement, 470
    person of, 607
    personal, 408, 599–600
    possessive, 394–395, 408, 599
    reflexive, 410–411
    relative, 413
    shift in, 388
    as subjects, 599, 604
    use of, before gerunds, 582
    with and as appositives, 601
    See also Pronoun-antecedent
      agreement

Proofreading
    essay question answer, 250
    symbols for, 88
    See also Editing; Revising
Proper adjectives, 424
    capitalization of, 684–685
Proper nouns, 404, 406
    abbreviation of, 728
    capitalization of, 677
    commas with, 711
    forming plurals of, 790
    forming possessive of ancient,
      ending in *-es* or *-is,* 691
Publishing. *See* Presenting
Punctuation
    apostrophe, 722–724
    colon, 699–701
    comma, 705–713
    dash, 714
    exclamation point, 696
    hyphen, 725–727
    italics, 720–721
    parentheses, 715–716
    period, 695
    question mark, 697
    quotation marks, 717–719
    semicolon, 702–703
Purpose for writing
    to analyze, 22–25
    to describe, 120–125
    to express yourself, 10–13
    identifying, 60
    to inform, 222–225
    to persuade, 278
    to tell a story, 164–167

Q

Question mark, 697–698
    to end interrogative sentences,
      578
    parentheses with, 716
    quotation marks with, 719
Questions
    asking, in interview, 69–70
    asking, in topic exploration, 65
    tag, 712
    who versus *whom* in, 604
    See also Interrogative sentences
Quotation marks
    and commas, 717
    with dialogue, 717

for direct quotations, 717
    with indirect quotations, 717
    with other marks of punctua-
      tion, 718
    quotation within a quotation,
      717
    with titles of short works, 719
    with unusual expressions, 719
Quotations
    capitalization of first word of,
      675
    colons to introduce, 699
    direct, 180
    indirect, 180

R

Raise, rise, 661
Reader-response journal, writing
    in, 22–25, 29, 42
*Readers' Guide to Periodical
    Literature,* 766–767
Reading comprehension, on
    standardized tests, 808–809
Reading styles, 796
Reason is, because, 661
Reference materials, in library,
    761
References
    commas to set off, 711
    numerals in, 733
Reference works
    almanacs, yearbooks, atlases,
      769
    bibliographies, 768
    computer data bases, 769
    dictionaries, 772–775
    encyclopedias, 769
    government documents, 769
    in libraries, 761, 768–769
    magazines as, 761, 768–769
    periodical indexes, 768
    periodicals as, 761, 766–767
    *Readers' Guide to Periodical
      Literature* as, 766–767
    thesaurus as, 131, 776–777
    vertical file, 769
    See also Library
Reflecting, 33, 101, 149, 197,
    259, 307
Reflexive pronoun, 410–411
Regardless, irregardless, 658
Regular verbs, 548

Relative clauses. *See* Subordinate clauses
Relative pronoun, 413
  to introduce adjective clause, 511
  to introduce noun clause, 505
Religious terms, capitalizing, 681
Research paper
  avoiding plagiarism in, 319
  bibliography cards, 317
  citing sources in, 328–333
  conclusion in, 326
  drafting, 324–327
  editing, 338
  endnotes in, 331
  final copy of, 338
  footnotes in, 330
  introduction in, 322, 326
  locating information for, 316
  organization for, 322
  outlining, 320–323
  parenthetical documentation in, 329–330
  portfolio in, 348
  presenting, 338–339
  prewriting, 314–323
  quotations in, 318
  research process in, 315–316
  revising, 334–337
  selecting topic for, 315
  source materials for, 316, 319
  student model of, 340–347
  taking notes for, 318, 320
  thesis statement in, 322–323
  types of, 314
  working bibliography for, 317
  Works Cited list, 331–333
Resolution, in fictional narrative, 170
Respectfully, respectively, 661
Responding to literature. *See* Literature, responding to
Responding to the Case Study, 9, 49, 119, 163, 213, 275
Response from readers, 41, 111, 155, 205, 267, 311
Restatements, colons to introduce, 699
Restrictive clauses, 498
Revising, 51, 53, 100, 112
  anecdotes, 184, 185
  for common errors, 396–398
  descriptive writing, 120, 148
  dialogue, 179

for exact verbs, 131
expository writing, 211, 258
formal speech, 817
for misplaced or dangling modifier, 392–393
narrative writing, 161, 196
paragraphs, 83–85
personal writing, 32–33
persuasive writing, 278, 306
plot summary, 188
for pronoun-antecedent agreement, 384–385
for pronoun reference, 386–387
research papers, 334–337
for run-on sentences, 378–379
for sentence fragments, 376–377
for sentence variety, 325
for shift in pronoun, 388
for subject-verb agreement, 380–383, 575–587
for unity and coherence, 80–85
for verb tense or form, 389–391
in writing process, 53, 100–101
in Writing Process in Action lessons, 32, 100, 148, 196, 258, 306
  See also Editing; Proofreading
Rise, raise, 661
Roget's, 776
Role playing, 13
Root words, 780–782
Run-on sentences, 521–523
  correcting, 378–379

S

Said, says, 661
Salutation, colon after, 701
Says, said, 661
Scales, reading, 802–803
Scanning, 796
School courses, capitalizing names of, 681
Science, writing topics in, 167
Script, formatting interview as, 71
Semicolons
  and commas, 703
  to join main clauses in compound sentence, 507
  parentheses with, 715
  quotation marks with, 718
  to separate main clauses, 702

Sensory images, in descriptive writing, 125
Sentence combining, 350–374
  in descriptive writing, 354–357
  in expository writing, 362–365
  literature-based activities and, 370–374
  in narrative writing, 358–361
  in persuasive writing, 366–369
Sentence fragments, 519–520, 523
  correcting, 376–377
Sentences
  capitalization of, 675–676
  complex, 509–510, 526, 543–545
  compound, 507–508, 526, 543
  compound-complex, 509–510
  correcting errors in, 87
  declarative, 518, 695, 697
  diagraming, 536–545
  effective use of, 325
  exclamatory, 518, 696
  imperative, 518
  interrogative, 518, 697
  position of adverb in, 422
  position of subject and verb in, 465–467
  run-on, 378–379, 521–523
  simple, 507–508
  subjects of, 459
  topic, 123
  Troubleshooter for, 376–379
  variety in, 325
Sentence writing exercises, 404, 411, 414, 417, 421, 427, 434, 452–454, 457, 461, 474–475, 476, 479, 480, 497, 505, 539, 542, 545, 566, 567–568, 610
Series, commas in, 400, 675
Set, sit, 661
Setting, 169, 253
  analyzing, in a short story, 142–145
  uses of, 142
Sexist language, correcting, 384, 606
Ships, capitalizing names of, 681
Short-answer tests, 806
Short story
  analyzing setting in, 142–145
  character in, 27
  plot in, 27
  responding to, 26–29

Short story *(continued)*
  setting in, 27
  theme in, 27
Should of, might of, must of, would of, could of, 656
Signal words, recognizing, 794
Simile, 220
Simple predicates, 459
Simple sentences, 507–508
Simple subjects, 459
Sit, set, 661
Skimming, 796
Slang, 237
Social studies paper, revising, 336–337
Source cards, for research paper, 317
Spacecraft, capitalizing names of, 681
Spatial order, 77, 79
Speaking, 815–819
  style, 818
  in writing conference, 32, 100, 148, 196, 258, 306
Speeches
  formal, 816–818
  informal, 815–816
Spelling
  basic rules for, 786–790
  difficult words, 790–793
  in editing process, 88
  learning, of new words, 790
  list of frequently misspelled words, 791–792
SQ3R study method, 796–797
Standardized tests
  analogies in, 811–812
  English skills items in, 810–813
  purpose of, 808
  reading comprehension in, 808–809
  sentence completion in, 810
  synonyms in, 810
  tips for taking, 812
  types of items in, 808–812
States, abbreviations of, 729
Stationary, stationery, 793
Story writing. *See* Narrative writing
Student models, 16, 20, 22, 24, 28, 50–52, 55, 73, 77, 96, 124, 128, 166, 172, 175, 184, 188, 192, 244, 296, 340–347

Study skills
  evaluating what you read, 797–798
  mnemonic devices, 797
  note taking in class, 794
  outlining, 794
  reading graphs and diagrams, 800–803
  reading and remembering, 796–797
  SQ3R method, 796–797
  time management, 795
Style, 350–353
Subject
  complete, 460
  compound, 382, 462–464
  diagraming, 537
  noun clause as, 515–517
  position in sentence, 380–381, 465–467
  problems of agreement of, with verbs, 380–383
  simple, 459
  who as, 604–605
Subject card, in card catalog, 762
Subject complements, 471
  diagraming, 538
Subjective pronoun, as subject, 599
Subject-verb agreement
  checking for, 575
  with collective nouns, 381, 580
  with compound subjects, 382–383, 582
  correcting problems with, 380–383
  and indefinite pronouns, 383, 585–587
  with intervening expressions, 583–584
  and intervening prepositional phrases, 380, 576
  and intervening words, 380, 383
  in inverted sentences, 380–381, 578–579
  with linking verbs, 577
  with nouns of amount, 381, 581
  with number and person, 575
  with predicate nominatives, 380
  with special nouns, 580
  with special subjects, 580–581

with titles of works, 581
Subordinate clauses, 431–432, 506
  adjective, 511
  adverb, 513
  noun, 515
  and sentence combining, 366
  who versus *whom* in, 604–605
Subordinating conjunctions, 440, 506
  to introduce adjective clauses, 511
  to introduce adverb clauses, 513
Suffixes, 784–785, 787–789
Summarizing, 189
  in note taking, 318
Superlative form, of modifiers, 422–423, 432, 625–627
Supplemental material, parentheses to set off, 715
Supporting details, 121, 122, 220. *See also* Details
Symbols, forming plural of, 724
Synonyms, 131
  on standardized tests, 810
  See also Thesaurus

T

Tables, reading, 800
Tag lines, in dialogue, 180
Tag questions, and commas, 712
Take, bring, 656
Teach, learn, 660
Tenses, of verbs, 551–560
Tests
  essay, 246–251
  fill-in, 806
  matching, 806
  multiple-choice, 805
  short answer, 806
  standardized, 808–813
  time management in, 807
  true-false, 806
  See also Study skills
Than, personal pronouns following, 603
Than, then, 661, 793
Theater arts, writing topics in, 89
Then, than, 661, 793
Thesaurus, 131

Acknowledgments

(continued from page v)

Text

8 *The Last of the Menu Girls* courtesy of Arte Publico Press. **10** From *The Journals of Sylvia Plath* by Sylvia Plath. Copyright © 1982 by Ted Hughes as the Executor of the Estate of Sylvia Plath. Published by The Dial Press. **16** From *Biology: The Dynamics of Life.* Copyright © 1991 by Merrill Publishing Company. **22** From *Appreciating Literature.* Copyright © 1991, 1989 by Glencoe/McGraw-Hill Educational Division. **26** From *Nine Stories* by J. D. Salinger. Copyright 1948, 1949, 1950, 1951, 1953, by J. D. Salinger. Published as a Signet Book by arrangement with Little, Brown & Company, Inc. (b); From *Picked-Up Pieces* by John Updike. Copyright © 1966, 1967, 1968, 1969, 1970, 1971, 1972, 1973, 1974, 1975 by John Updike. Published by Alfred A. Knopf (t). **32, 34** From *Blue Highways: A Journey Into America* by William Least Heat-Moon. Copyright © 1982 by William Least Heat-Moon. By permission of Little, Brown and Company. **48** Mark Trahant, courtesy of *The Arizona Republic.* **61** From *Technics and Civilization.* Copyright © 1934 by Lewis Mumford. Published by Harcourt, Brace, & World (t); From *About Three Bricks Shy of a Load: A Highly Irregular Lowdown on the Year the Pittsburgh Steelers Were Super but Missed the Bowl* by Roy Blount Jr. Copyright © 1974 by Roy Blount Jr. Published by Little, Brown and Company (b). **72** From "Nuestra Señora de la Concepción" by William M. Mathers. Copyright © National Geographic. Published September 1990. **74** From *Legacies: A Chinese Mosaic* by Bette Bao Lord. Copyright © 1990 by Bette Bao Lord Enterprises, Inc. Published by Alfred A. Knopf. **78** From "The *Bismarck* Found" by Robert D. Ballard. Copyright © National Geographic. Published November 1989. **100, 102** Copyright © 1972 by Alex Haley. Reprinted by permission of John Hawkins & Associates, Inc. **118** Thurston Clarke, courtesy of William Morrow and Co., Inc. **120** From *The Tommyknockers* by Stephen King. Copyright © 1987 by Stephen King, Tabitha King, and Arthur B. Greene, Trustee. Used by permission of New American Library, a division of Penguin Books USA Inc. **121** From *Learning to Dance and Other Stories* by Sharon Oard Warner. Copyright © 1992 by New Rivers Press. **122** Reprinted by permission of *Negro Digest* Magazine and Eugenia Collier, © 1969 Johnson Publishing Company, Inc. **123** Excerpted from the short story "Boys and Girls," from the story collection *Dance of the Happy Shades* by Alice Munro. Copyright © 1968 by Alice Munro. Reprinted by arrangement with Virginia Barber Literary Agency. All rights reserved. **126** Excerpt from "The Only Living Boy in New York" by Ameena Meer. Copyright © 1991 by Ameena Meer. Excerpt reprinted from *The Portable Lower East Side.* **131** From *To the Lighthouse* by Virginia Woolf. Copyright © 1989 by Harcourt Brace. **135** Reprinted by permission of Don Congdon Associates, Inc. Copyright © 1968 by Edward Abbey. **136** Reprinted by permission of Don Congdon Associates, Inc. Copyright © 1968 by Edward Abbey. **138** The lines from "Corsons Inlet" are reprinted from *Collected Poems, 1951–1971,* by A. R. Ammons, by permission of W. W. Norton & Company, Inc. Copyright © 1972 by A. R. Ammons. **147, 150** "The Solace of Open Spaces," from *The Solace of Open Spaces* by Gretel Ehrlich. Copyright © 1985 by Gretel Ehrlich. Used by permission of Viking Penguin, a division of Penguin Books USA Inc. **166** From *Merlyn's Pen: The National Magazine of Student Writing,* January/February 1986, Vol. 1, No. 2. Reprinted by permission of *Merlyn's Pen.* **167** From *My Life and Hard Times* by James Thurber. Copyright © 1933 by American Biography Series. **168** Reprinted by permission of the Putnam Publishing Group from "Wine on the Desert" by Max Brand. Copyright © 1940 by Max Brand. **172** From *Merlyn's Pen: The National Magazine of Student Writing,* October/November 1988, Vol. 4, No. 1. Reprinted by permission of *Merlyn's Pen.* **175** From *Merlyn's Pen: The National Magazine of Student Writing,* October/November 1989, Vol. 5, No. 1. Reprinted by permission of *Merlyn's Pen.* **176** "User Friendly" by

T. Ernesto Bethancourt, copyright © 1989 by T. Ernesto Bethancourt. From *Connections: Short Stories by Outstanding Writers for Young Adults* by Donald R. Gallo, Editor. Used by permission of Delacorte Press, a division of Bantam Doubleday Dell Publishing Group, Inc. **178** From "The Story of the Widow's Son" by Mary Lavin. Copyright © 1992 by Creative Ed. **182** From "Six Across Antarctica" by Will Steger. Reprinted with permission of National Geographic Society. Published November 1990. **184** From *Merlyn's Pen: The National Magazine of Student Writing,* February/March 1990, Vol. 5, No. 3. Reprinted by permission of *Merlyn's Pen.* **195, 198** From *Tortuga* by Rudolfo A. Anaya. Published by University of New Mexico Press, 1720 Lomas Blvd. NE, Albuquerque, New Mexico 87131. Copyright © 1979 by Rudolfo A. Anaya. **209** "America's Sleep Debt" cover courtesy of Wang Associates Health Communications. **212** Anastasia Toufexis, courtesy of *TIME* magazine. **216** From *The Avalanche Book* by Betsy Armstrong and Knox Williams. Copyright © 1986. Published by Fulcrum Publishing. **218** "The Solace of Open Spaces," from *The Solace of Open Spaces* by Gretel Ehrlich. Copyright © 1985 by Gretel Ehrlich. Used by permission of Viking Penguin, a division of Penguin Books USA Inc. **220** From *The Africans* by David Lamb. Copyright © 1982. Reprinted with permission of Random House, Inc. **222** Excerpt from *Hangin' Out: City Kids, City Games* by James Wagenvoord. Copyright © 1974 by James Wagenvoord. Reprinted by permission of HarperCollins Publishers. **226** Copyright 1979 Time Warner Inc. Reprinted by permission. **229** From *The Poetry of Robert Frost* edited by Edward Connery Lathem. Copyright 1923, © 1969 by Holt, Rinehart and Winston. Copyright 1951 by Robert Frost. Reprinted by permission of Henry Holt and Company, Inc. **230** From *Scholastic Update.* Copyright © 1989 by Scholastic, Inc. Reprinted by permission. **242** From "2 Condors to Fly Free Late in '91" by Gina Lubrano. Reprinted with permission of the *San Diego Union.* Published August 3, 1991. **251** From *A Sand County Almanac, with Other Essays on Conservation from Round River* by Aldo Leopold. Copyright 1949, 1953, 1966, renewed 1977, 1981 by Oxford University Press, Inc. Reprinted by permission. **252** *Silent Spring* by Rachel Carson. Copyright © 1962 by Rachel L. Carson. Reprinted by permission of Houghton Mifflin Company. All rights reserved. **255** William Carlos Williams: *The Collected Poems of William Carlos Williams, 1909–1939, Vol. I.* Copyright 1938 by New Directions Publishing Corporation. Reprinted by permission of New Directions Publishing Corporation. **257, 260** From *A Book of Bees . . . and How to Keep Them* by Sue Hubbell. Copyright © 1988 by Sue Hubbell. Reprinted by permission of Random House, Inc. **272, 274** Mitchiner, Ross and Kahn, courtesy of The Museum of Contemporary Art, Chicago. **280** © 1991, Washington Post Writers Group. Reprinted with permission. **281** From "Is It MTV, or Is It 'Empty-V'?" by George Varga. Copyright © The San Diego Union. Published July 28, 1991. Reprinted by permission from *The San Diego Union.* **282** Courtesy of Anderson & Lembke, Inc. **284** From May/June 1989 *NEA Today* article by Betty Berry and Jennifer March.**288** Copyright 1991 by Consumers Union of United States, Inc., Yonkers, NY 10703. Excerpted by permission from *Consumer Reports,* August 1991. **302** By David Fricke. From *Rolling Stone,* June 13, 1991. By Straight Arrow Publishers, Inc. 1991. All Rights Reserved. Reprinted by Permission. **306, 308** From *Kaffir Boy in America* by Mark Mathabane. Copyright © 1990 by The New York Times Company. Reprinted by permission. **340** From *The Concord Review,* Fall 1990, Volume Three, Number One. Copyright © 1991 by *The Concord Review,* P.O. Box 661, Concord, Massachusetts 01742. Reprinted by permission. **446** Excerpt from *The Sound of Waves* by Yukio Mishima. Reprinted by permission of Random House, Inc. **457** Excerpt from "Flying Home" by Ralph Ellison from *Cross Section.* Copyright © 1944 by Ralph Ellison. Reprinted by permission of the author. **474** Excerpt from *Palace Walk* by Naguib Mahfouz. Copyright © 1990 by American University in Cairo Press. Used by permission of Doubleday, a division of Bantam Doubleday Dell Publishing Group, Inc. **494** Excerpts from *The Stuff of Heroes* by Miguel Delibes, translated by Frances M. Lopez-Morillas. English translation copyright © 1990 by

Random House, Inc. **524** Excerpts from *Death Comes for the Archbishop*. Copyright © 1927 by Willa Cather and renewed by the Executors of the Estate of Willa Cather. Reprinted by permission of Alfred A. Knopf, Inc. **564** Excerpt from *The Fellowship of the Ring* by J. R. R. Tolkien. Copyright © 1954, 1965 by J. R. R. Tolkien. Copyright © 1982 by Christopher R. Tolkien, Michael H. R. Tolkien, John F. R. Tolkien and Priscilla M. A. R. Tolkien. Reprinted by permission of Houghton Mifflin Company. All rights reserved. **588** From *Elsewhere, Perhaps* by Amos Oz. Copyright © 1985 by Harcourt Brace. **614** Excerpts from *The African* by William Conton. Copyright © 1960 by William Conton. **623** Two excerpts from *Song of Solomon* by Toni Morrison. Reprinted by permission of ICM. **642** Excerpt from *A Soldier of the Great War* by Mark Helprin. Reprinted by permission of Harcourt Brace Jovanovich, Inc. Copyright © 1991 by Mark Helprin. **666** "Auguries of Innocence" by William Blake from *Common Ground: An Anthology*. Copyright © 1989. Published by Carcanet Press; From *The Romantic School* by Heinerich Heine. Copyright © 1985. Published by Continuum; From *Nouvelles Lettres d'un Voyageur* by George Sand. Copyright © 1979. Published by Editions D'Aujourd'hui; From *O Pioneers!* by Willa Cather. Copyright © 1989. Published by NAL-Dutton; "The Mending Wall" by Robert Frost from *Anthology of Poetry*. Copyright © 1983. Published by Azenel Books. **667** From *One Hundred Years of Solitude* by Gabriel García Márquez. Copyright © 1976. Published by Avon; From *The Unbearable Lightness of Being* by Milan Kundera. Copyright © 1988. Published by Harper Collins. **688** Excerpt from *In Patagonia* by Bruce Chatwin. Copyright © 1977 by Bruce Chatwin. Reprinted by permission of Summit Books, a division of Simon & Schuster, Inc. **695** From "Of Dry Goods and Black Bow Ties" by Yoshiko Uchida. Copyright © by Yoshiko Uchida. **734** Excerpt from *One Writer's Beginnings* by Eudora Welty. Reprinted by permission of Harvard University Press Cambridge, Mass. Copyright © 1983, 1984 by Eudora Welty.

Photos

AR=Art Resource, New York; EF=Eric Futran; RJB=Ralph J. Brunke; SB=Stock Boston, Inc.; SK=Stephen Kennedy; TIB=The Image Bank, Chicago.

Front Cover Keith Gunnar/FPG International. **iii** Edward Hopper, American, 1882–1967, *Nighthawks*, oil on canvas, 1942, 76.2 x 144 cm, Friends of American Art Collection, 1942.51 © 1991 the Art Institute of Chicago. All rights reserved. **1** Francis Picabia, *Edtaonisl*, 1913, oil on canvas, 301.6 x 300.4 cm, Anonymous Gift, © 1992 The Art Institute of Chicago. Photo by RJB. **4** Chel Beeson. **5** Chel Beeson. **6** Chel Beeson. **7** Chel Beeson. **8** Chel Beeson (l); RJB (r). **9** RJB. **10** SCALA/AR. **13** © Carmen Lomas Garza. **14** SK. **18** SK. **19** RJB. **21** Photo courtesy of the artist and the American Craft Museum. **22** © John G. Herron/SB. **23** EF (l, r). **26** Courtesy Mrs. Mary Weatherall. **29** Rousseau, Henri. *The Sleeping Gypsy*. 1897. Oil on canvas, 51" x 6'7" Collection, Museum of Modern Art, New York. Gift of Mrs. Simon Guggenheim. **35** The Oakland Museum, Bequest of Abilio Reis. **37** Courtesy Bernice Steinbaum Gallery, New York. **39** © Field Museum of Natural History, Chicago, Neg. # A 109069c. **41** EF (l); RJB (r). **44** Monty Roessel. **45** EF. **47** Monty Roessel. **48** RJB. **49** RJB (tl, bl, bc); EF (br). **53** Edward Hopper, American, 1882–1967, *Nighthawks*, oil on canvas, 1942, 76.2 x 144 cm, Friends of American Art Collection, 1942.51 © 1991 The Art Institute of Chicago. All Rights Reserved. **56** SK. **59** © Edna Davis Jackson. **60** EF. **64** © Gregg Mancuso/SB. **67** AR. **68** Reprinted by permission: Tribune Media Services. **72** © Sisse Brimberg. **75** Courtesy of Richard and Nancy Bloch. **76** *Paul Explaining Pictures to Mie Kakigahara, Tokyo, Feb. 1983*. Photographic Collage 30 3/4 x 42 1/2". © David Hockney. **80** © The Estate of E. B. White. Courtesy of the Olin Library Department of Rare Books at Cornell University. **81** EF (l, c, r). **86** *The Far Side* cartoon by Gary Larson is reprinted by permission of

Chronicle Features, San Francisco. **90** EF. **91** SK (l, cl, c, cr, r). **94** *The Far Side* cartoon by Gary Larson is reprinted by permission of Chronicle Features, San Francisco. **97** Courtesy Muzeum Narodwe w Poznaniu, Poznan, Poland. **105** Wadsworth Atheneum, Hartford. Ella Gallup Sumner and Mary Catlin Sumner Collection. **111** EF (r); RJB (l). **114** © Jerry Bauer, Courtesy Julian Bach Agency. **116** © Suzanne L. Murphy/FPG International (l); © Graphic House/ FPG International (r). **117** © M. Scheler/TIB. **118** EF. **119** EF. **120** © J.W. Meyers/SB. **122** Courtesy Bernice Steinbaum Gallery, New York. **125** Blackbear Bosin, Courtesy The Philbrook Museum of Art, Tulsa, Oklahoma. **128** SK. **129** The Cleveland Museum of Art, Anonymous Gift (l); John Marin, American, 1870–1953, *Movement, Fifth Avenue*, watercolor, 1912, 43.3x35cm, Alfred Stieglitz Collection, 1949.554. Photograph by Kathleen Culbert-Aguilar, photograph © 1991, The Art Institute of Chicago. All rights reserved (r). **130** Reprinted from *Green Lantern #15* Copyright 1991 DC Comics, Inc. All rights reserved. Reprinted by permission. Art by M. D. Bright, Romeo Tanghal, Anthony Tollin. **134** © Robert Bishop, 1988. **139** Milwaukee Art Museum, Gift of Mrs. Edward R. Wehr. **140** Giraudon/AR. **145** National Museum of American Art, Washington, D.C./AR. **151** Frederic Remington. *The Fall of the Cowboy*, 1895. Oil on canvas. (1961.230) Amon Carter Museum, Fort Worth, Texas. **153** © Ann Taylor. **155** EF (l); RJB (r). **158** SK. **160** © Michael Holford. **161** EF (b); SK (l, c, r). **162** © Chattanooga Free Press. **163** SK. **164** RJB. **168** from *THE CIVIL WAR: Confederate Ordeal*. Photograph by Larry Sherer © Time-Life Books, Inc. **170** © Robert Tringali Jr./Sportschrome, Inc. (t); © Sportschrome, Inc. (b). **173** Courtesy Donald Morris Gallery, Inc. **174** © 1989 Donald Dietz/SB. **177** Des Moines Art Center, Purchased with funds provided by the AVA Program, 1982.7. **181** © Gilberto Ruiz/Courtesy of the Barbara Gillman Gallery. **182** RJB. **190** Nasjonalgalleriet, Oslo, Norway. **193** Private Collection, Courtesy of the Texas Gallery, Houston. Photo by Bill Kennedy. **203** Fundación Rufino Tamayo/AR . **205** EF (l, r). **208** © Ellen Denuto 1991. **209** EF. **211** © Billy E. Barnes/SB. **212** RJB. **213** © Peter Southwick/SB. **214** © Eric Haase. **217** Russian Museum, St. Petersburg, Russia. **218** © Wyoming Division of Tourism. **221** The Howard University Gallery of Art, Washington, D.C. Permanent Collection. **222** RJB. **225** © 1938 M.C. Escher/Cordon Art-Baarn-Holland/AR. **226** The Bettman Archive. **233** Alma Thoma (American, 1891–1978). *Iris, Tulips, Jonquils and Crocuses*, 1969. Acrylic on canvas, 60 x 50 in. The National Museum of Women in the Arts. Gift of Wallace and Wilhelmina Holladay. **234** © Billy E. Barnes/TSW-Click/Chicago Ltd. **237** Collection of the Chase Manhattan Bank, N.A. **238** © 1986 Kent Knudsen/SB. **242** © Dave Clendenen. **246** Reprinted by permission: Tribune Media Services. **252** © 1961 by Erich Hartmann. **262** Giraudon/AR. **265** AR. **266** Ernest Lawson 1873–1939 *Garden Landscape* 50.8 x 61.0. The Brooklyn Museum. Bequest of Laura L. Barnes. **267** EF (l); RJB (r). **270** EF. **271** RJB. **272** EF (l); Steven Wohlwender (r). **273** RJB. **274** EF (l, r). **275** EF. **276** © James Porto. **278** © Rainforest Action Network. **279** © Jonathan Franklin/Courtesy of the Collection of Wendy Spatz. **280** RJB (l, c, r). **283** Courtesy Roslyn Oxley9 Gallery, Paddington, Australia. **286** Courtesy of the National Wildlife Federation, photo by RJB. **288** © Larry Pierce/TIB. **290** Copyright 1991 by Consumers Union of United States, Inc., Yonkers, New York 10703. Reprinted by permission from *Consumer Reports*, August 1991 (l, r). **292** © American Association of Advertising Agencies. **294** Courtesy of Elgin Syferd/Drake and the Idaho Travel Council. **295** SCALA/AR. **296** *Herman* © 1976 Jim Unger. Reprinted with permission of Universal Press Syndicate. **300** RJB. **309** The Bridgeman Art Library Ltd. **311** EF (l, r). **314** RJB. **320** EF. **328** The Granger Collection. **334** Courtesy of Historical Pictures Service, Inc. **338** Courtesy of Historical Pictures Service, Inc. **455** Andō Hiroshige, Japanese, 1797–1858, *Imagiri Promentory from Maizaka from the Hoeido Tokaido*, 1833 color wood-block print 266 x 351 mm Elvehjem Museum of Art, University of Wisconsin—Madison Gift of Edward Burr Van Vleck, 1980.816. **465** © Andy Keech/Photo Trends.

481 SCALA/AR. **491** © Zao-Grimberg/TIB. **501**© Magnum Photos, Inc. **507** © Roger Tully/TSW-Click. **533** The Carnegie Museum of Art, Pittsburgh; Museum Purchase: gift in memory of Elizabeth Mellon Sellers from her friends. 74.17. **571** Courtesy Ashmolean Museum, Oxford. **583** © P. Markow/FPG International. **595** © Stanley I. Batkin. **604** © HMS Images 1990. **621** Courtesy of the Collection of Mildred Hart Bailey. **649** The Metropolitan Museum of Art, Gift of Mrs. Earl W. Koeniger, 1966 (66.114). **671** The Metropolitan Museum of Art, Gift of Robert W. de Forest, 1925. (25.173). **691** The Bettman Archive. **717** © AP/Wide World. **739** The Mary and Sylvan Lang Collection, Marion Koogler McNay Art Museum, San Antonio, Texas. **743** © 1986 Courtesy of Collier, Macmillan Publishers, London. Photo by RJB. **745** © Susan Anderson (tl, tr, bl, br). **747** © John Elk III/SB. **749** SCALA/AR. **750** *The Far Side* © 1987 Universal Press Syndicate. Reprinted with permission. **754** Courtesy Ashmolean Museum, Oxford (t); SCALA/AR (b). **755** The Bettman Archive. **757** By permission of the Art Collection of the Folger Shakespeare Library. **758** The Bridgeman Art Library Ltd./AR. (l); © Martha Swope (c); NASA (r). **759** By permission of Johnny Hart and Creators Syndicate, Inc. **760** SK. **770** EF (t, c, b). **Back Cover** Aaron Haupt.

Picture Research by Ligature, Inc.